YOU'RE READING THE WRONG WAY!

This book reads *from right to left*. Turn over to the other side of the book to get started.

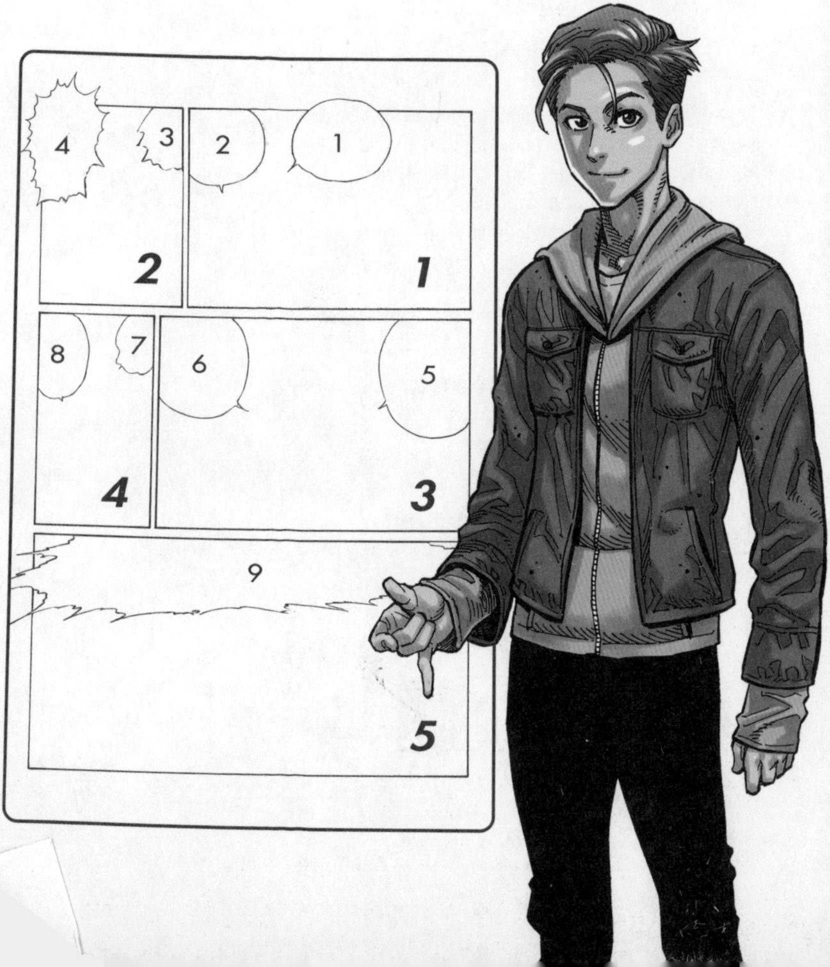
1
2
3
4
1
2
5
6
7
8
3
4
9
5

SPIDER-MAN: FAKE RED

VIZ MEDIA EDITION

Story & Art by: **YUSUKE OSAWA**

Original Cover Design: **TADASHI HISAMOCHI, HIVE&CO., LTD**

Translation: **CALEB COOK**
English Adaptation: **MOLLY TANZER**
Touch-up Art & Lettering: **EVAN WALDINGER**
Design: **FRANCESCA TRUMAN**
Editor: **JOEL ENOS**

Special Thanks to: **C.B. CEBULSKI**

FOR MARVEL PUBLISHING:

JEFF YOUNGQUIST, VP, Production and Special Projects

SARAH SINGER, Associate Editor, Special Projects

JEREMY WEST, Manager, Licensed Publishing

SVEN LARSEN, VP, Licensed Publishing

DAVID GABRIEL, SVP Print, Sales & Marketing

C.B. CEBULSKI, Editor in Chief

The stories, characters, and incidents mentioned in this publication are entirely fictional.

Printed in Canada

PUBLISHED BY VIZ MEDIA, LLC
P.O. Box 77010 | San Francisco, CA 94107

10 9 8 7 6 5 4 3 2 1
First printing, June 2023

viz.com

PARENTAL ADVISORY
SPIDER-MAN: FAKE RED is rated T for Teen and is recommended for ages 13 and up. This volume contains realistic and fantasy violence.

Yusuke Osawa began his professional manga career with the publication of the one-shot "Majo to Megane to Mahojin" (A Witch, Her Glasses, and a Magic Circle) in the July 2009 issue of *Magazine Special,* and won honorable mention in the 82nd *Weekly Shonen Magazine* New Manga Artist Awards. *Spider-Man: Fake Red* ran in *Magazine Pocket* from July 2019 to March 2020. In 2022, Osawa turned his attention to creating a manga adaptation of the *Star Wars* series *The Mandalorian* for *Big Gangan.*

▶Page 209

Emma has a Spider-Man alarm clock at her bedside.

▶Page 303

The metrics on this social media video form the numbers "1962, 8, 15."

Spider-Man made his debut in August of 1962, in issue 15 of *Amazing Fantasy*.

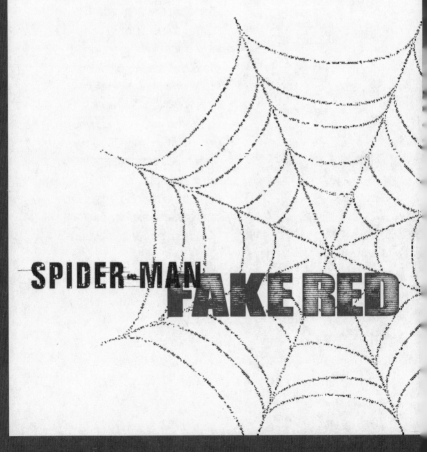

SPIDER-MAN FAKE RED

▶Page 135

The design on Emma's tank top features Iron Man's arc reactor.

▶Page 160

The Oscorp building appears in the background.

Norman Osborn—founder of Oscorp—moonlights as Green Goblin, one of Spider-Man's foes. He's also father to Harry Osborn, one of Peter Parker's friends.

▶Page 164

The billboard atop the building Screwball is perching on is an ad for Horizon Labs—a cutting-edge R&D company. J. Jonah Jameson's wife, Marla, once helped Peter Parker get a job at Horizon Labs, and it's there that Peter developed some of his Spider-Man tech.

▶Page 196

The wall art here is inspired by perhaps the most iconic piece of Spider-Man art—the cover of *Amazing Fantasy* issue 15, drawn by comics legend Jack Kirby for Spider-Man's debut.

In the years since, any number of artists have paid homage to that original composition, and the poster in Yu's room is just one more example.

▶Page 197

The website shown on the tablet screen is that of Alias Investigations—the private detective agency started by the hero Jessica Jones. Jessica went to high school with Peter Parker (before he became Spider-Man) and had a major, unrequited crush on him.

▶Page 86

The wall Emma is staring over features some writing in an unfamiliar language. This is in fact the language used by Doop—an *X-Men* character shrouded in mystery—and the graffiti is a message from the author to readers.

It says, "You're the best!"

▶Page 87

The book cover on the wall over Yu's bed is *The Adventures of Huckleberry Finn*. This is the book that Uncle Ben used to read to Peter Parker when he was sick in bed.

▶Page 88

Yu has Spider-Man and Deadpool stickers inside his locker.

▶Page 89

The logo on Emma's shirt is that of the Punisher, an antihero. In his mission to bring down the forces of evil, the Punisher is willing to become judge, jury, and executioner.

▶Page 103

With phone in hand, Spider-Man is whizzing past the *Daily Bugle* building.

▶Page 110

The billboard Spider-Man uses in his battle against Scorpion says "Stark Unlimited." This is the company headed by Tony Stark, better known as Iron Man.

▶Page 60

One of the headlines on Yu's phone says, "Break-In at Life Foundation, Research Stolen."

The Life Foundation is the organization that researches parasitic, extraterrestrial symbiotes, including Venom. This is how Quentin Beck got his hands on Venom.

▶Page 70

Big Al's Motorcycle Shop appears in the background. It's there that Peter Parker bought the motorcycle that he used to ride around with Gwen Stacy.

▶Page 73

The cabbie who gives Yu a ride is Aaron Davis, and the nephew he mentions is Miles Morales—the hero who inherits the mantle from Peter Parker in a parallel universe (on Earth 1610).

▶Page 83

Look closely at the criminal being hauled out of the water. He's got underpants with a Spider-Man print.

▶Page 84

The graffiti on this page includes the logos of both Daredevil and Doctor Strange.

▶Page 24

Yu has plenty of hero merchandise in his room. In this scene, you can spot a Captain America wall clock and an Iron Man toy.

▶Page 28

The Coffee Bean is the cafe where Peter Parker often hangs out with his friends. Speaking of coffee, did you know that spiders forced to drink coffee sort of become "drunk" and are unable to spin their webs properly? Does coffee have the same effect on our friendly neighborhood Spider-Man...?

▶Page 29

Note the "Asm 13 St" sign above the crosswalk signal. *The Amazing Spider-Man* issue 13 marked the debut of Quentin Beck (Mysterio). On the same page, the blind man with a cane who's crossing the street is none other than the hero, Daredevil. By day, he helps people as a lawyer, and by night, he fights the dark forces that slip through the cracks of the justice system.

Finally, Yu's bag has pins of Spider-Man as well as the wild-card hero, Deadpool.

▶Page 51

The little boy Yu saved is wearing a shirt with the Avengers logo.

▶Page 58

The man lambasting Spider-Man on TV is J. Jonah Jameson.

MARVEL

SPIDER-MAN FAKE RED

EASTER EGG BREAKDOWN

Shrewd readers may have noticed some of the Easter eggs spread throughout the story!

Here's a full breakdown of all those little references.

▶Page 5

A *Daily Bugle* truck appears in the background. *The Daily Bugle* being, of course, the newspaper headed by editor in chief J. Jonah Jameson, whose hatred for Spider-Man once led him to provide funding for Scorpion's bodily enhancement experiments.

▶Page 10

Up on the building's roof is graffiti of Iron Man—the hero who does battle in a power suit of his own creation.

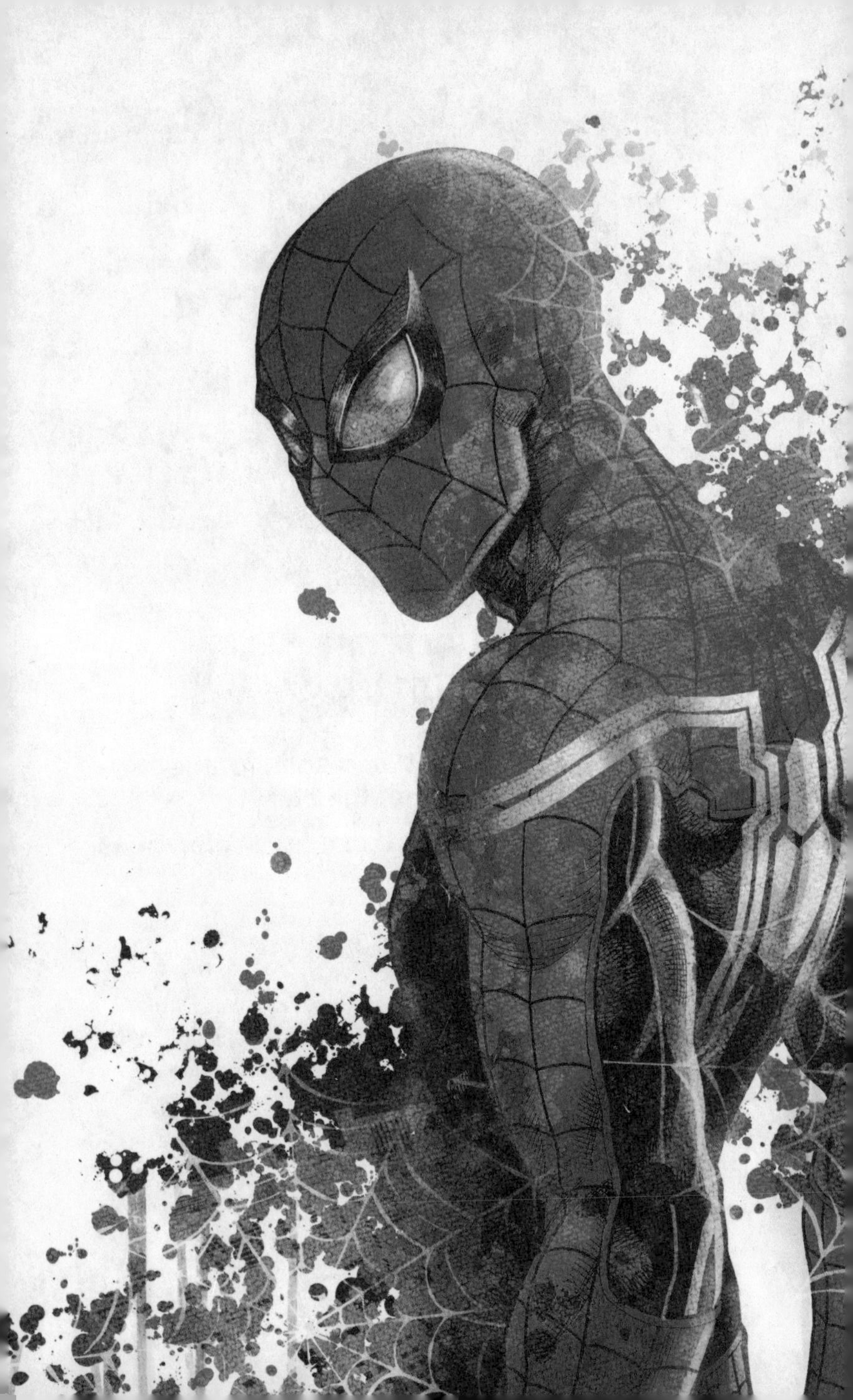

AFTERWORD

First and foremost, I want to thank the editorial department for giving me this chance to create a story with these heroes.

In 2002, I saw Sam Raimi's *Spider-Man* in theaters, back before I ever dreamed of becoming a manga artist. I remember coming away with this powerful feeling: **I hope I get to create a work of art this fantastic someday.**

Who could have imagined that I would one day be given the opportunity to draw Spider-Man himself!

Fake Red is a product of one die-hard fan's love. It's basically my love letter to super heroes, where the theme is exploring what the "super" in "super heroes" actually means.

There are still so many stories I could tell in this world, so my greatest hope is that this book sells well enough for the series to continue.

— **Yusuke Osawa**

STAFF

Akifumi Haba
Katakei
Wah
Koya Ashitaka
Morimoto

Takishita
Hidemasa Idemitsu
Nakamura
Hara
Kosuke Tezuka

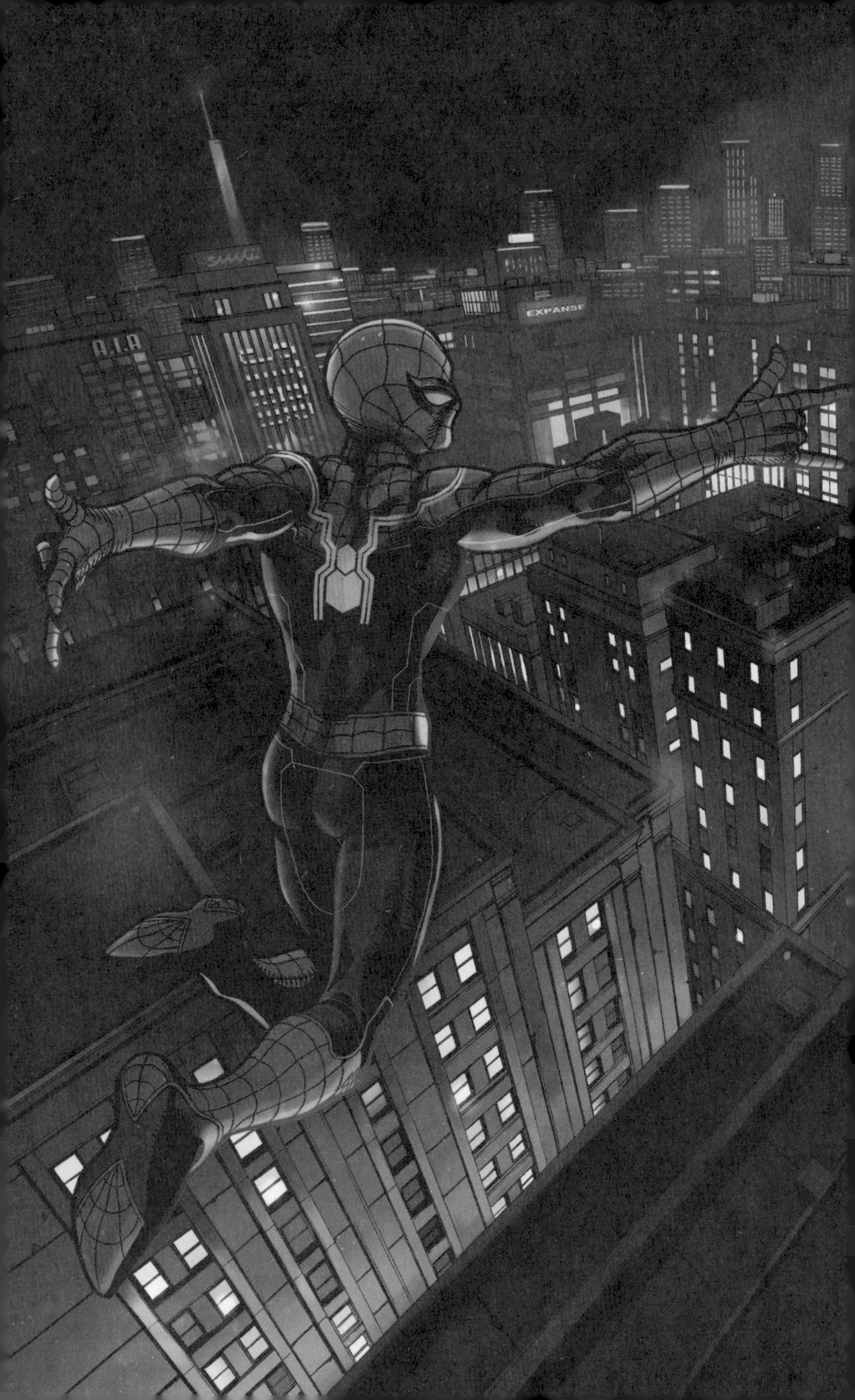
A.I.A
EXPANSE

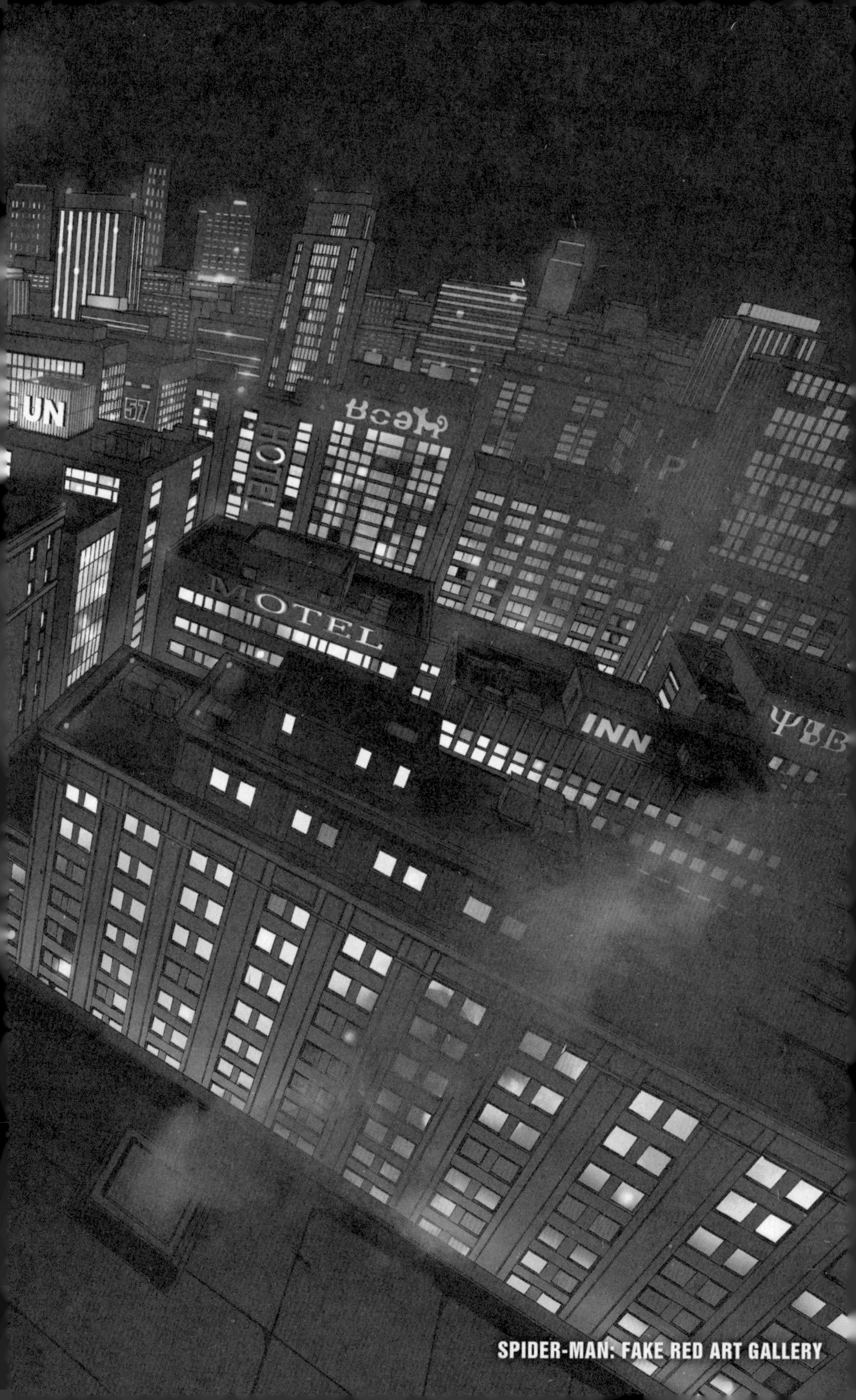
UN
57
MOTEL
INN

SPIDER-MAN: FAKE RED ART GALLERY

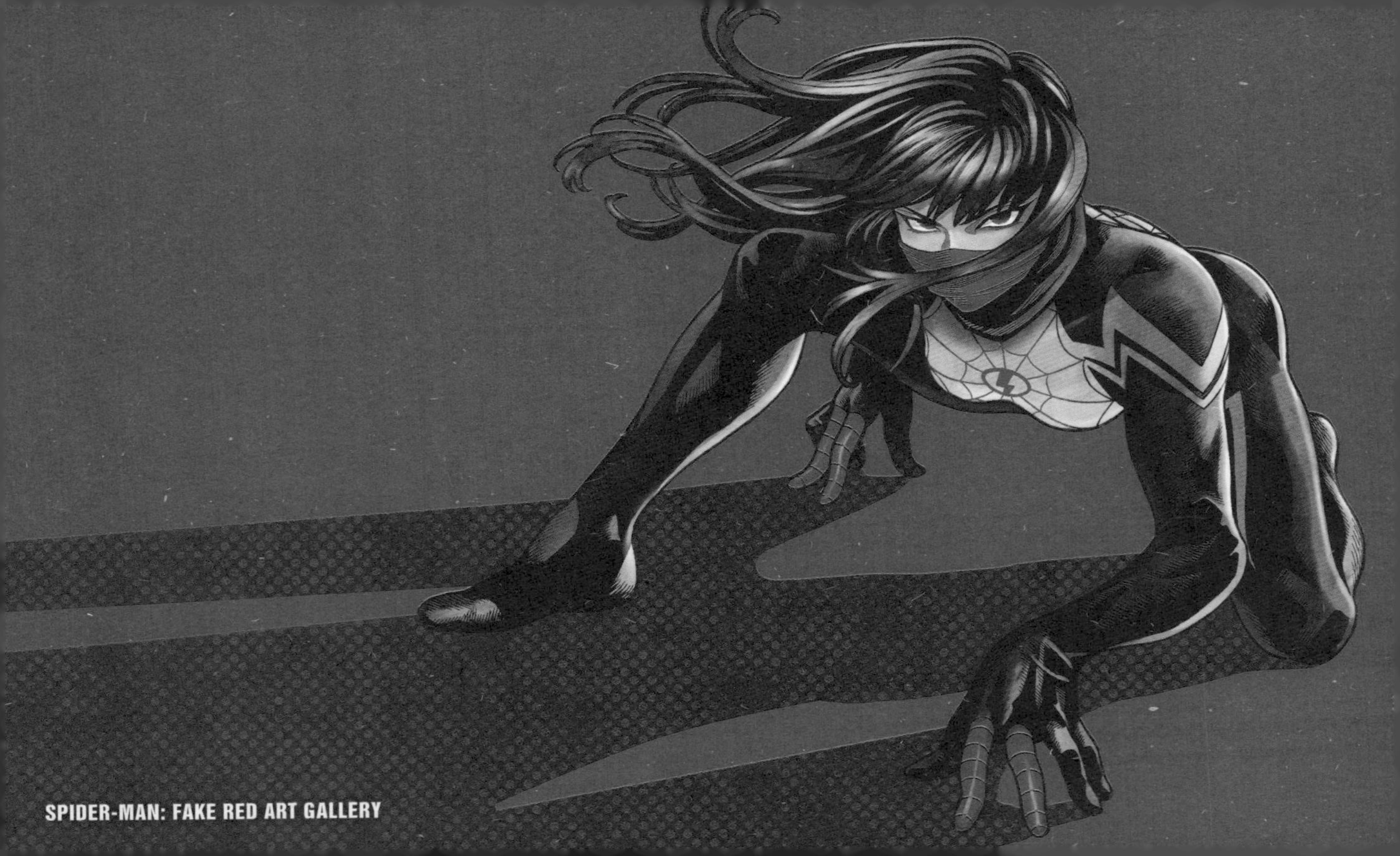

SPIDER-MAN: FAKE RED ART GALLERY

SPIDER-MAN: FAKE RED ART GALLERY

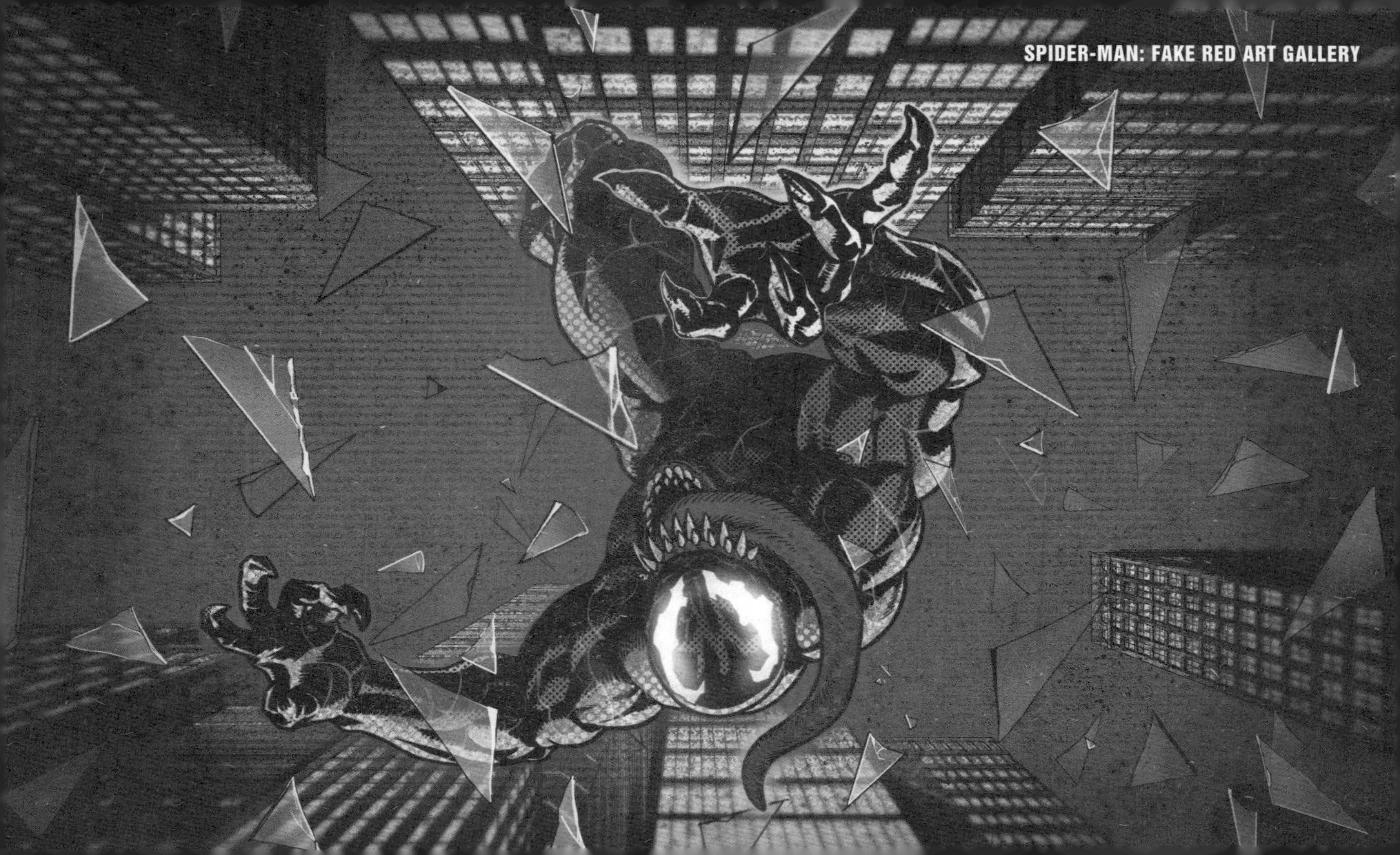

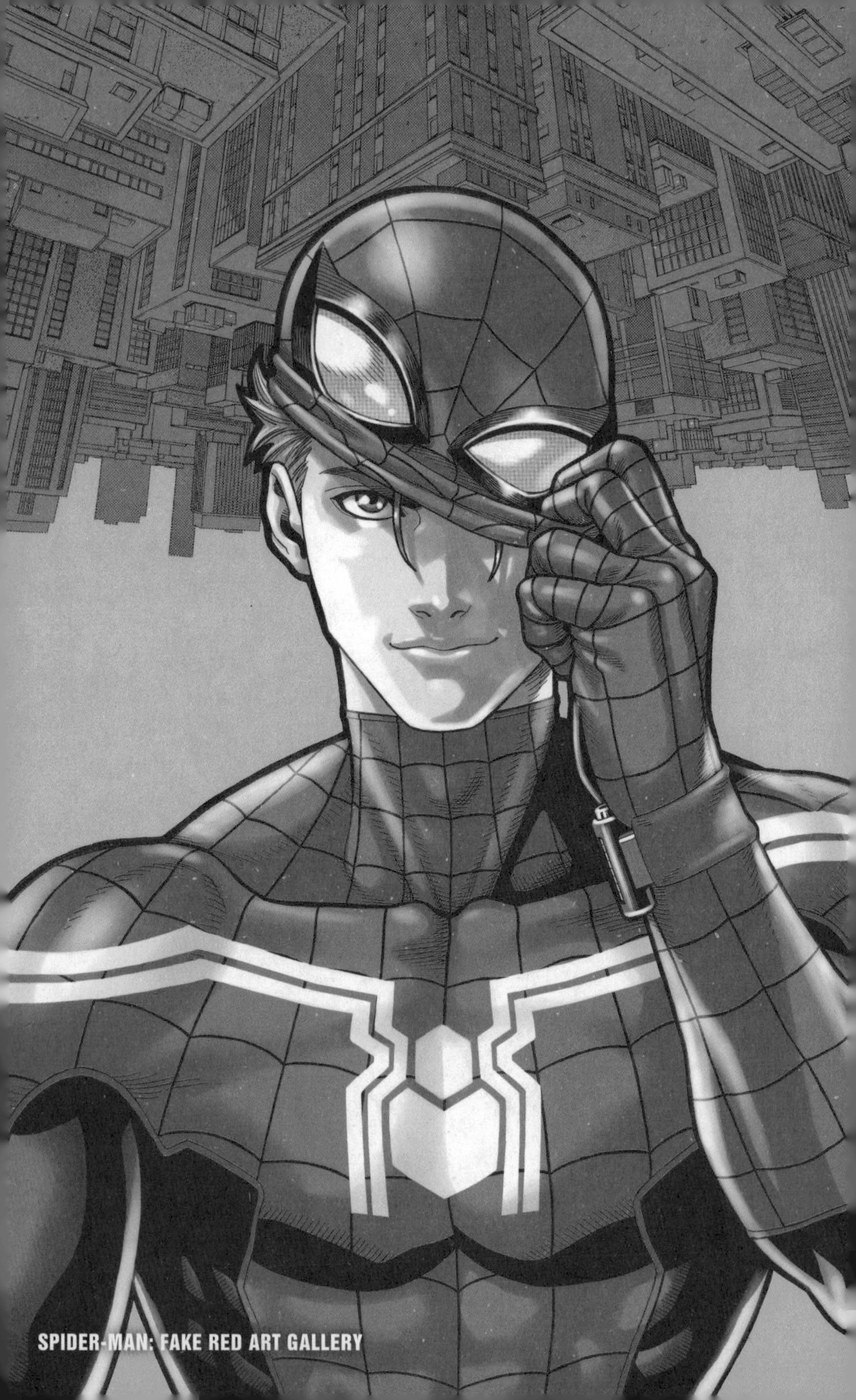
SPIDER-MAN: FAKE RED ART GALLERY

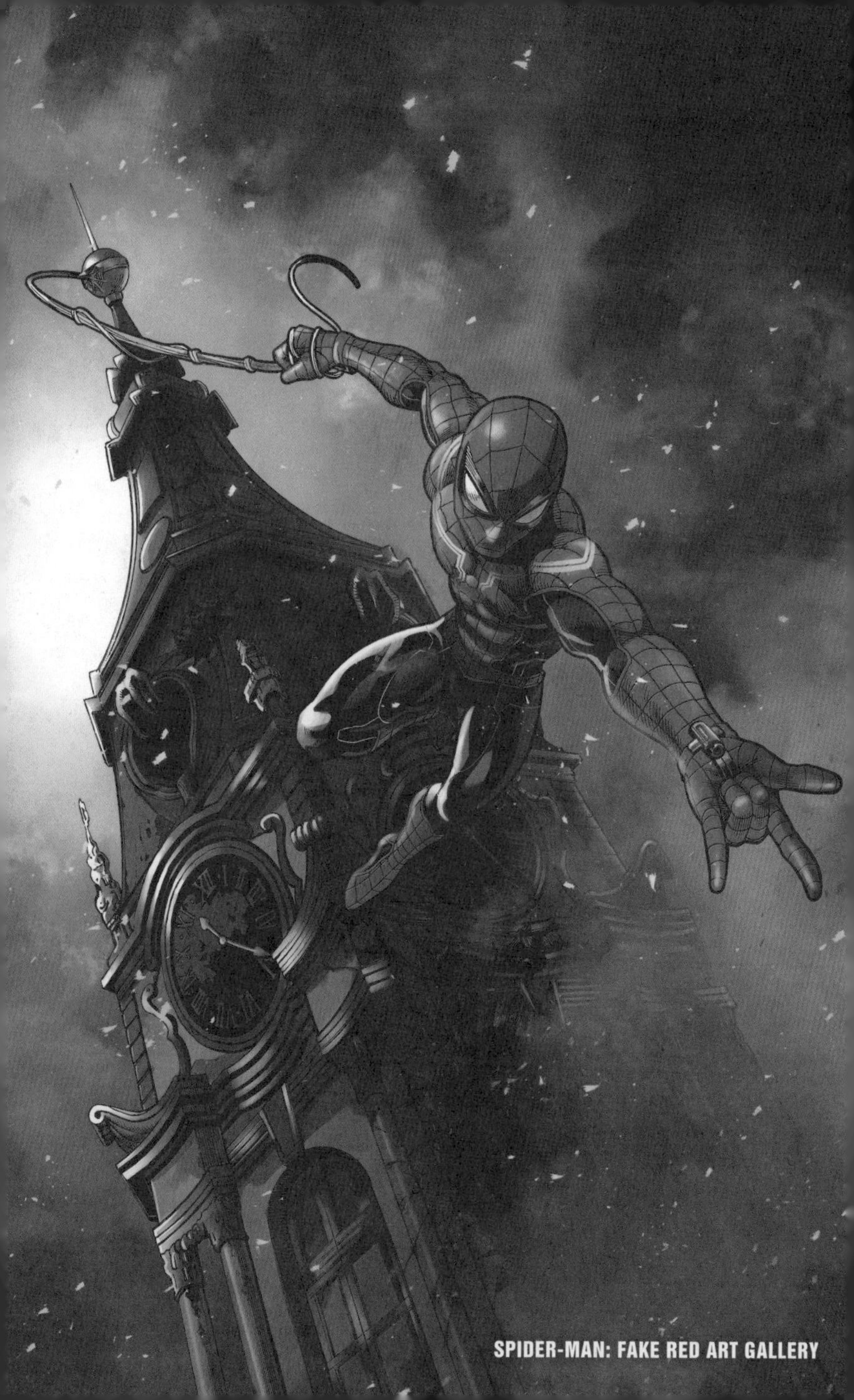

SPIDER-MAN: FAKE RED ART GALLERY

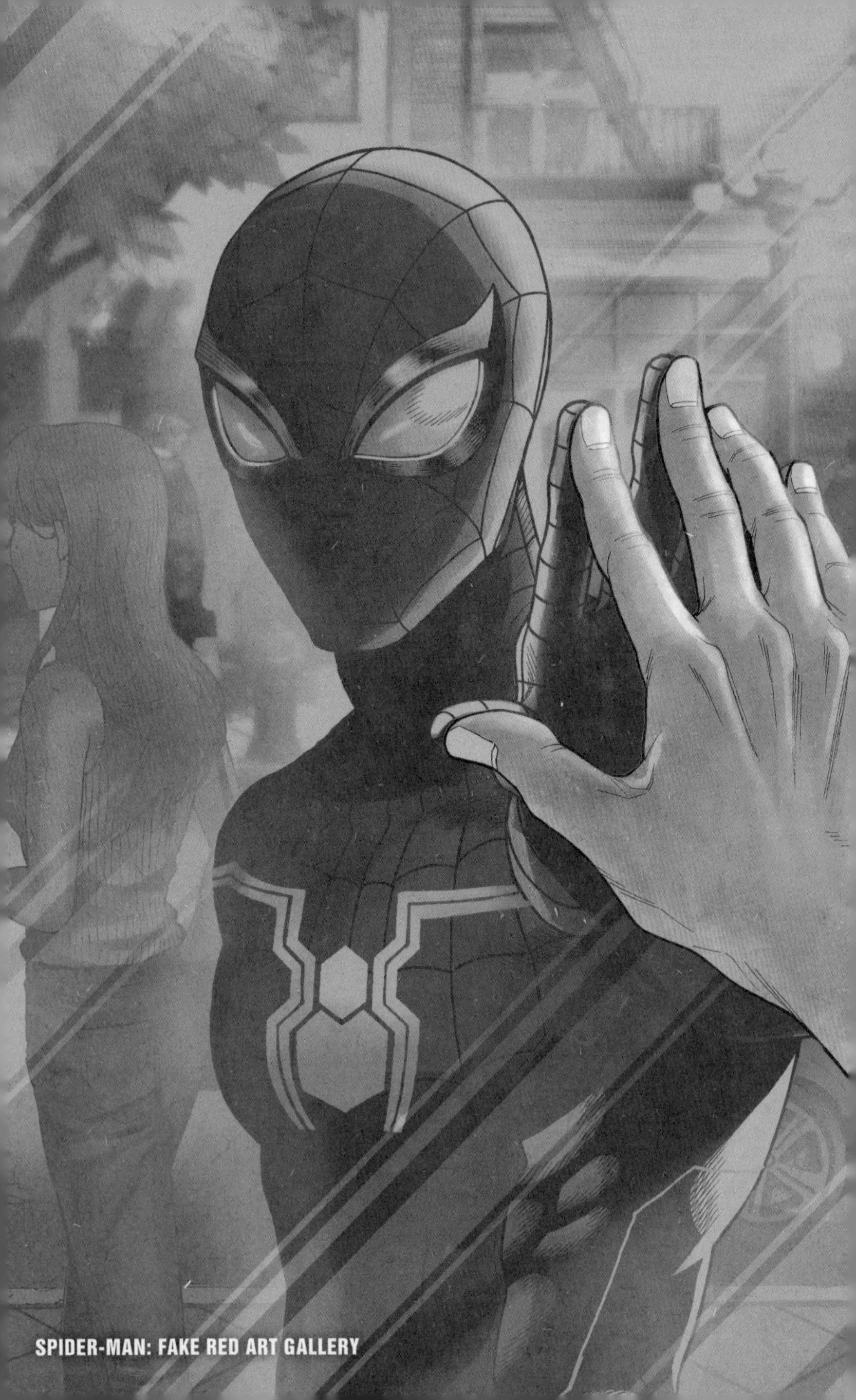

SPIDER-MAN: FAKE RED ART GALLERY

SPIDER-MAN FAKE RED

ART GALLERY

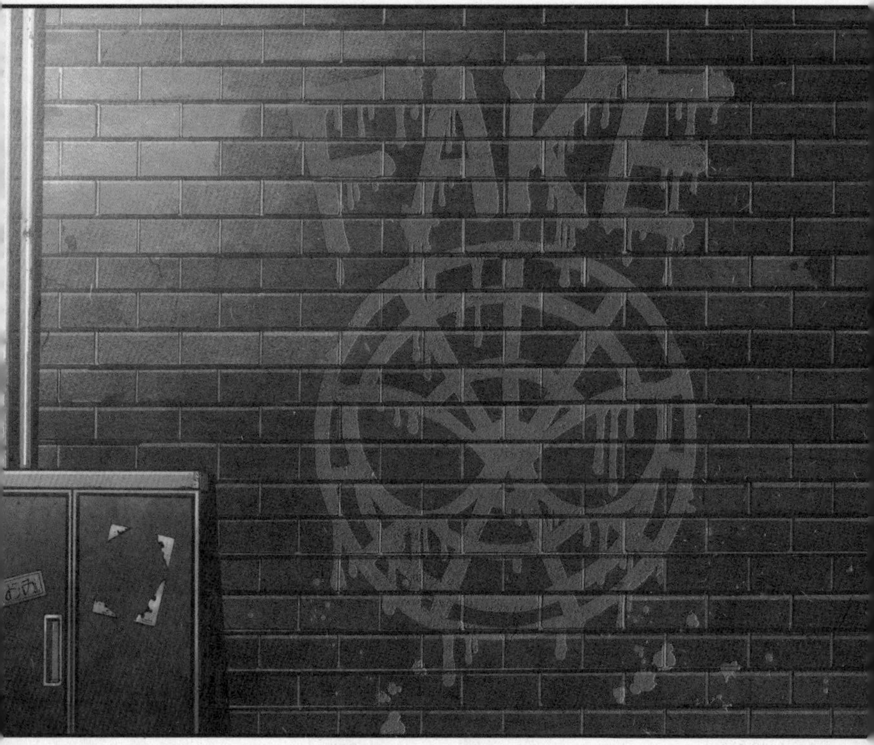

ART BY

YUSUKE OSAWA

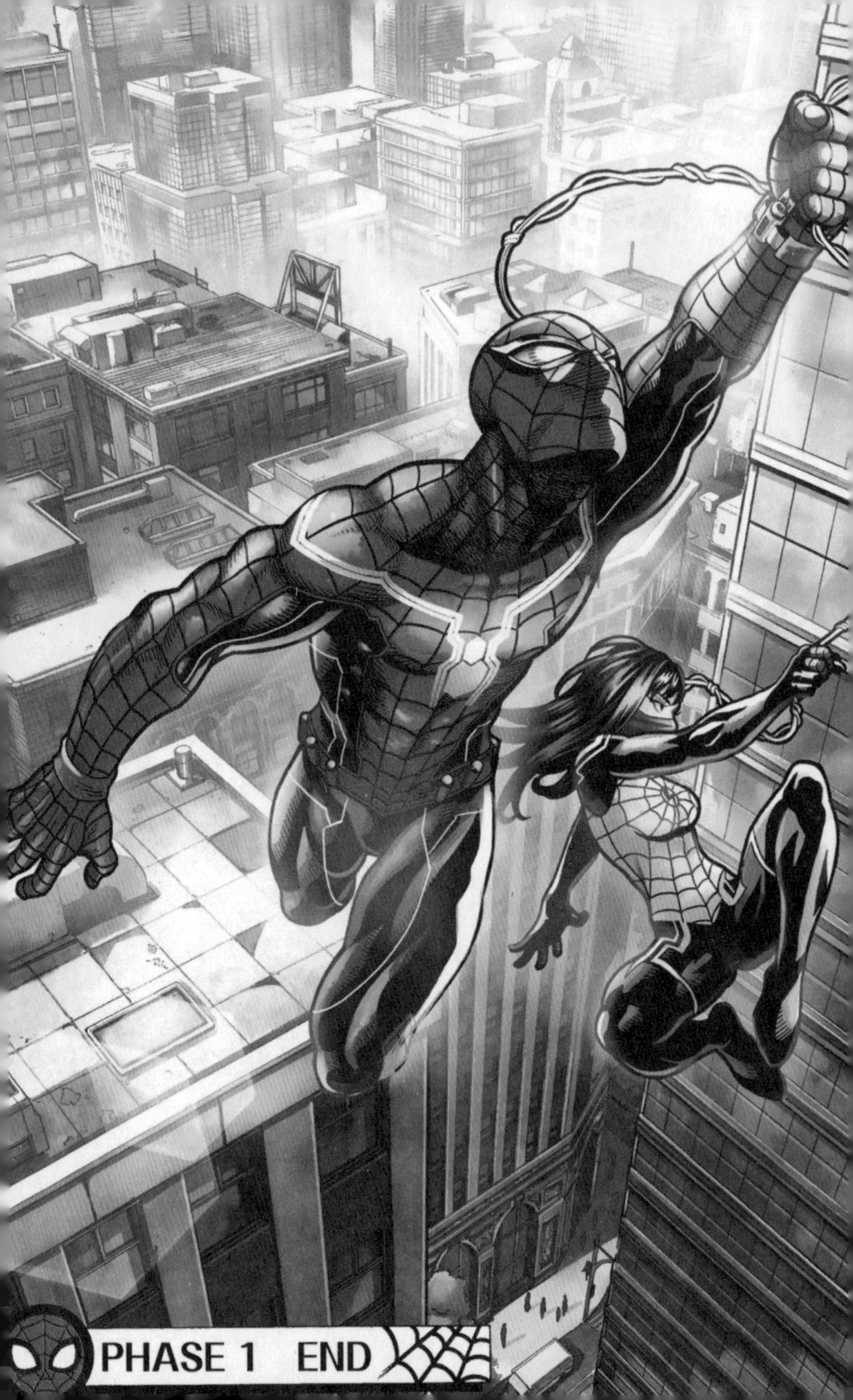
PHASE 1 END

MARVEL

SPIDER-MAN

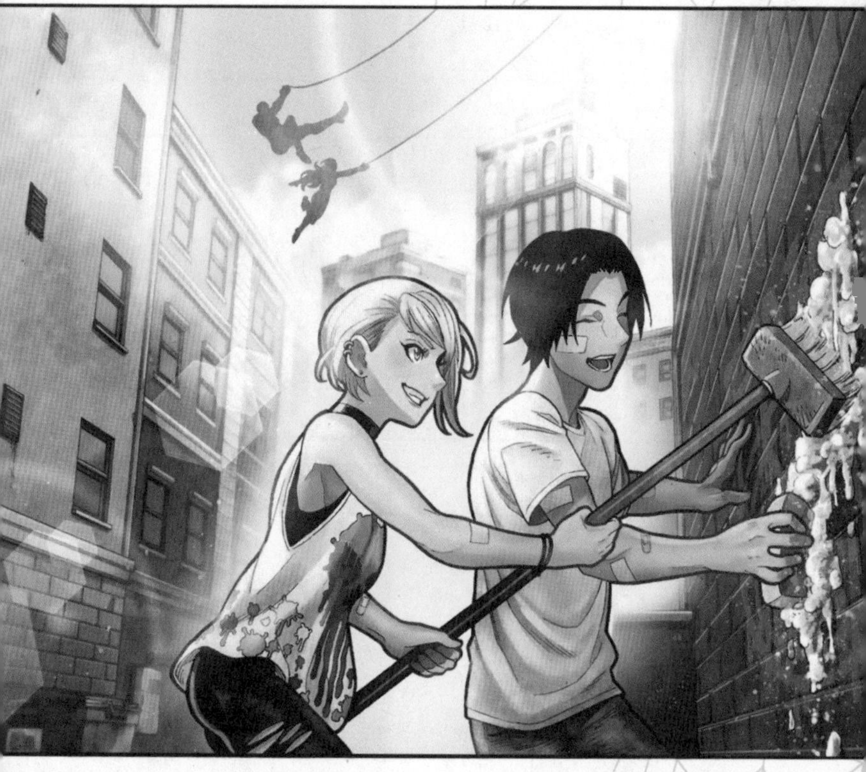

FAKE RED

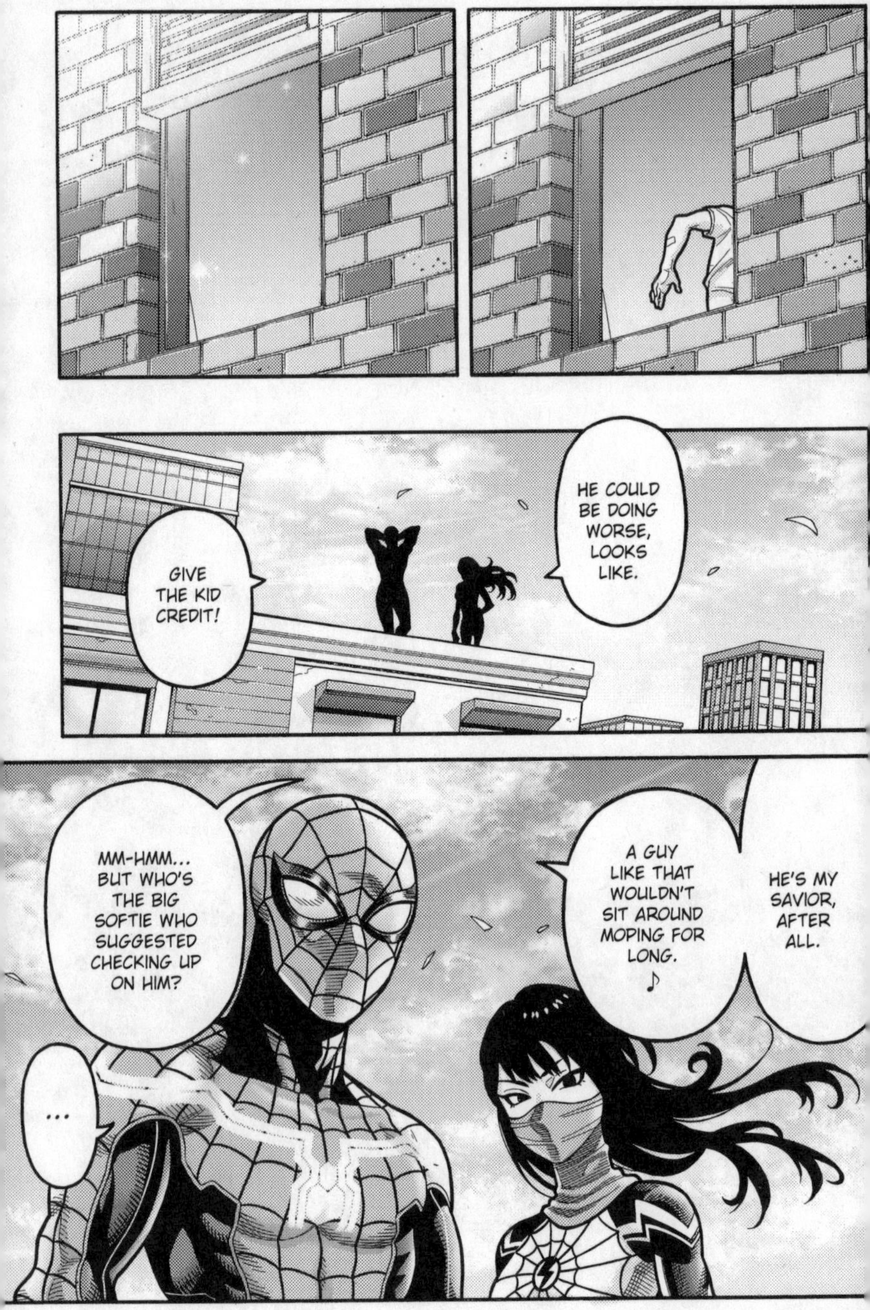
HE COULD BE DOING WORSE, LOOKS LIKE.
GIVE THE KID CREDIT!
HE'S MY SAVIOR, AFTER ALL.
A GUY LIKE THAT WOULDN'T SIT AROUND MOPING FOR LONG. ♪
MM-HMM... BUT WHO'S THE BIG SOFTIE WHO SUGGESTED CHECKING UP ON HIM?
...

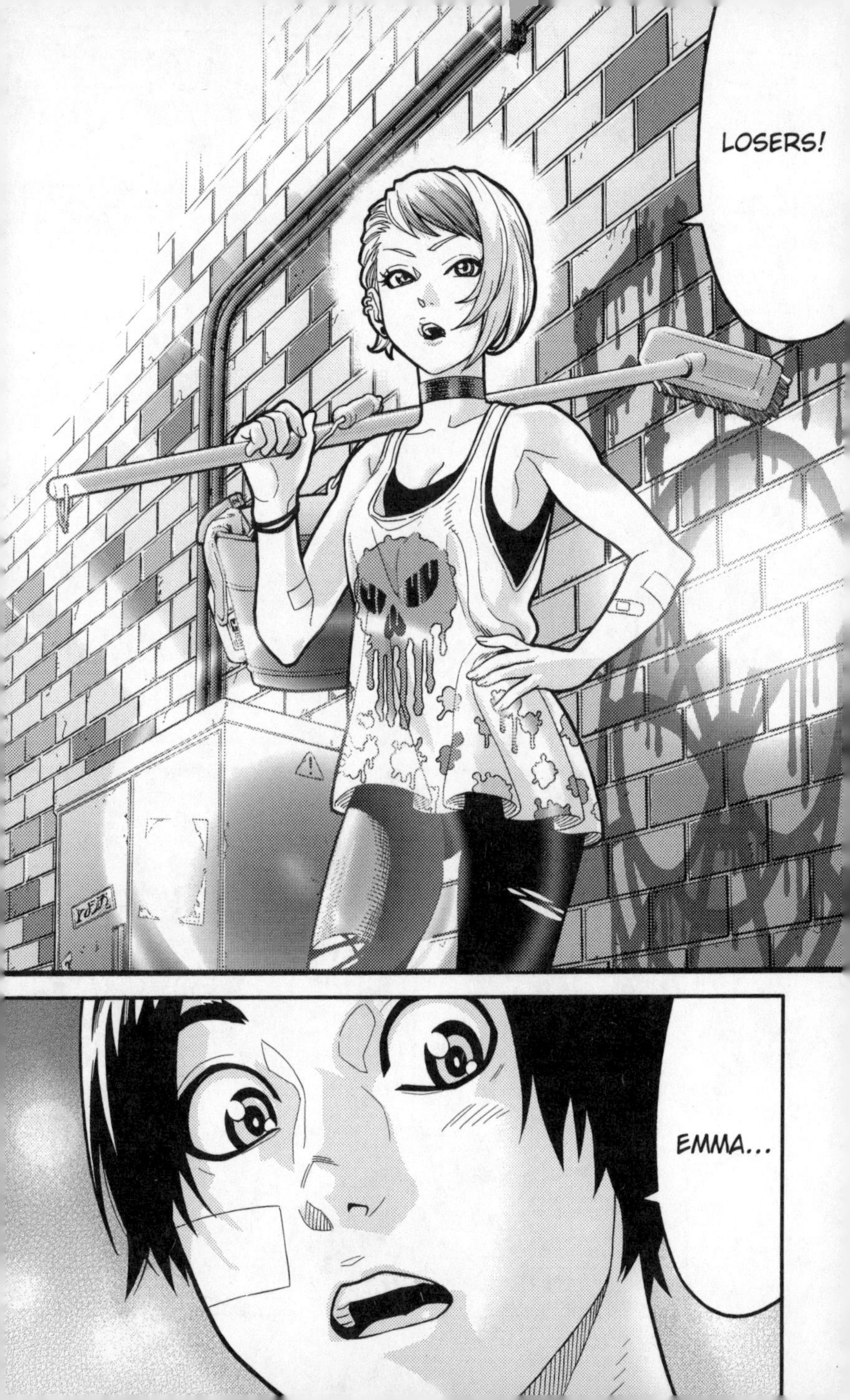
LOSERS!
EMMA...

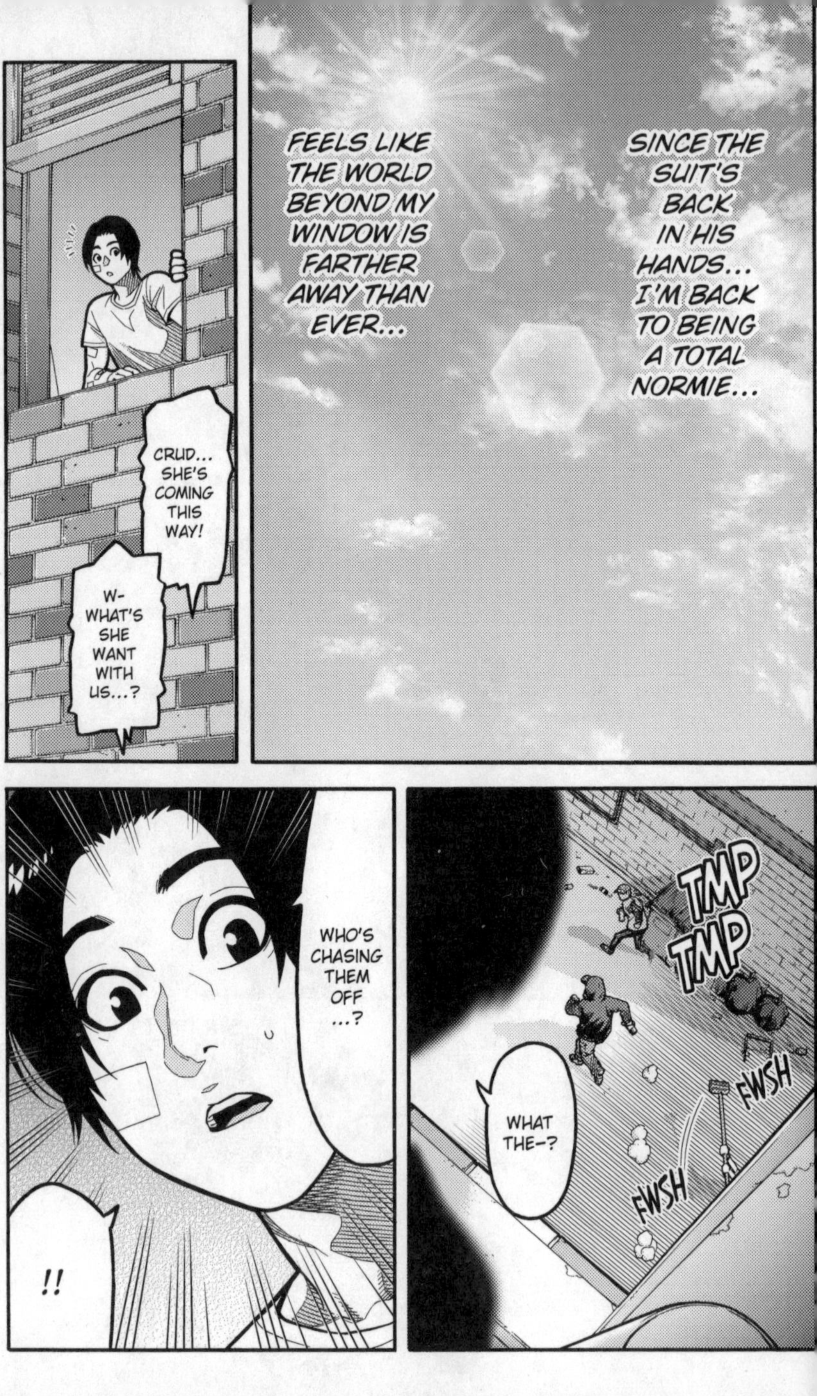
SINCE THE SUIT'S BACK IN HIS HANDS... I'M BACK TO BEING A TOTAL NORMIE...
FEELS LIKE THE WORLD BEYOND MY WINDOW IS FARTHER AWAY THAN EVER...
CRUD... SHE'S COMING THIS WAY!
W-WHAT'S SHE WANT WITH US...?
TMP TMP
FWSH
FWSH
WHAT THE-?
WHO'S CHASING THEM OFF ...?
!!

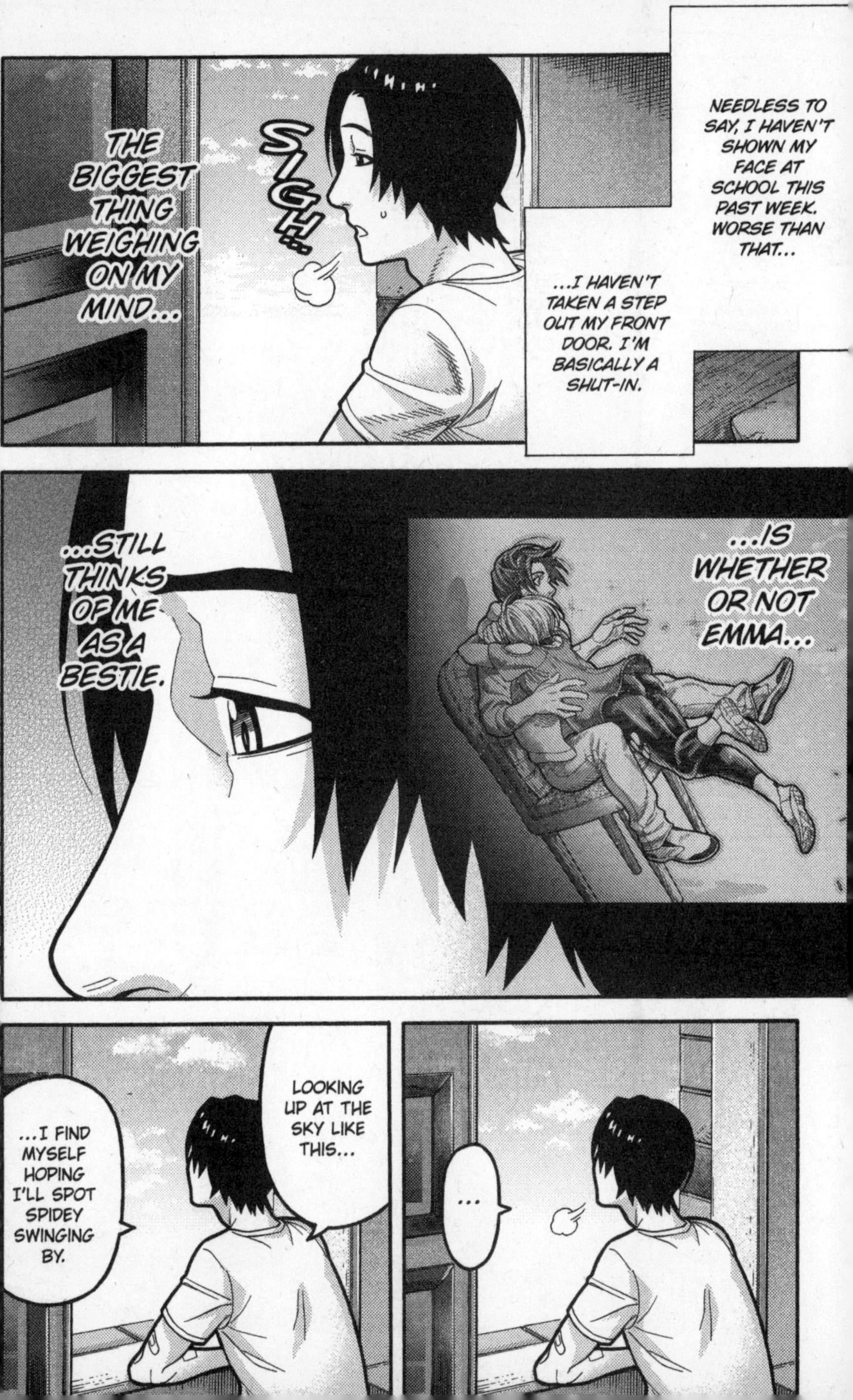
NEEDLESS TO SAY, I HAVEN'T SHOWN MY FACE AT SCHOOL THIS PAST WEEK. WORSE THAN THAT...
...I HAVEN'T TAKEN A STEP OUT MY FRONT DOOR. I'M BASICALLY A SHUT-IN.
SIGH...
THE BIGGEST THING WEIGHING ON MY MIND...
...IS WHETHER OR NOT EMMA...
...STILL THINKS OF ME AS A BESTIE.
...
LOOKING UP AT THE SKY LIKE THIS...
...I FIND MYSELF HOPING I'LL SPOT SPIDEY SWINGING BY.

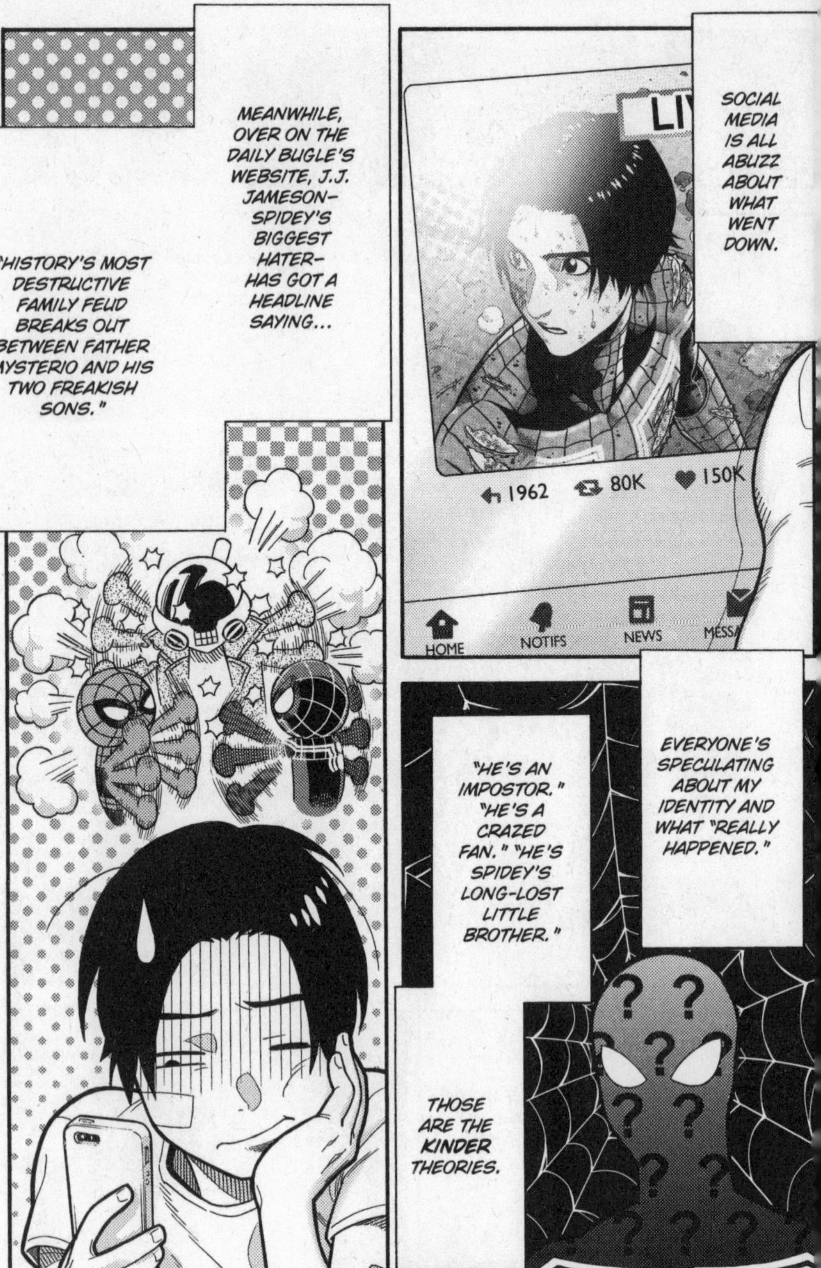
LI
1962
80K
150K
HOME
NOTIFS
NEWS
MESSA
SOCIAL MEDIA IS ALL ABUZZ ABOUT WHAT WENT DOWN.
MEANWHILE, OVER ON THE DAILY BUGLE'S WEBSITE, J.J. JAMESON—SPIDEY'S BIGGEST HATER—HAS GOT A HEADLINE SAYING...
"HISTORY'S MOST DESTRUCTIVE FAMILY FEUD BREAKS OUT BETWEEN FATHER MYSTERIO AND HIS TWO FREAKISH SONS."
EVERYONE'S SPECULATING ABOUT MY IDENTITY AND WHAT "REALLY HAPPENED."
"HE'S AN IMPOSTOR." "HE'S A CRAZED FAN." "HE'S SPIDEY'S LONG-LOST LITTLE BROTHER."
THOSE ARE THE KINDER THEORIES.

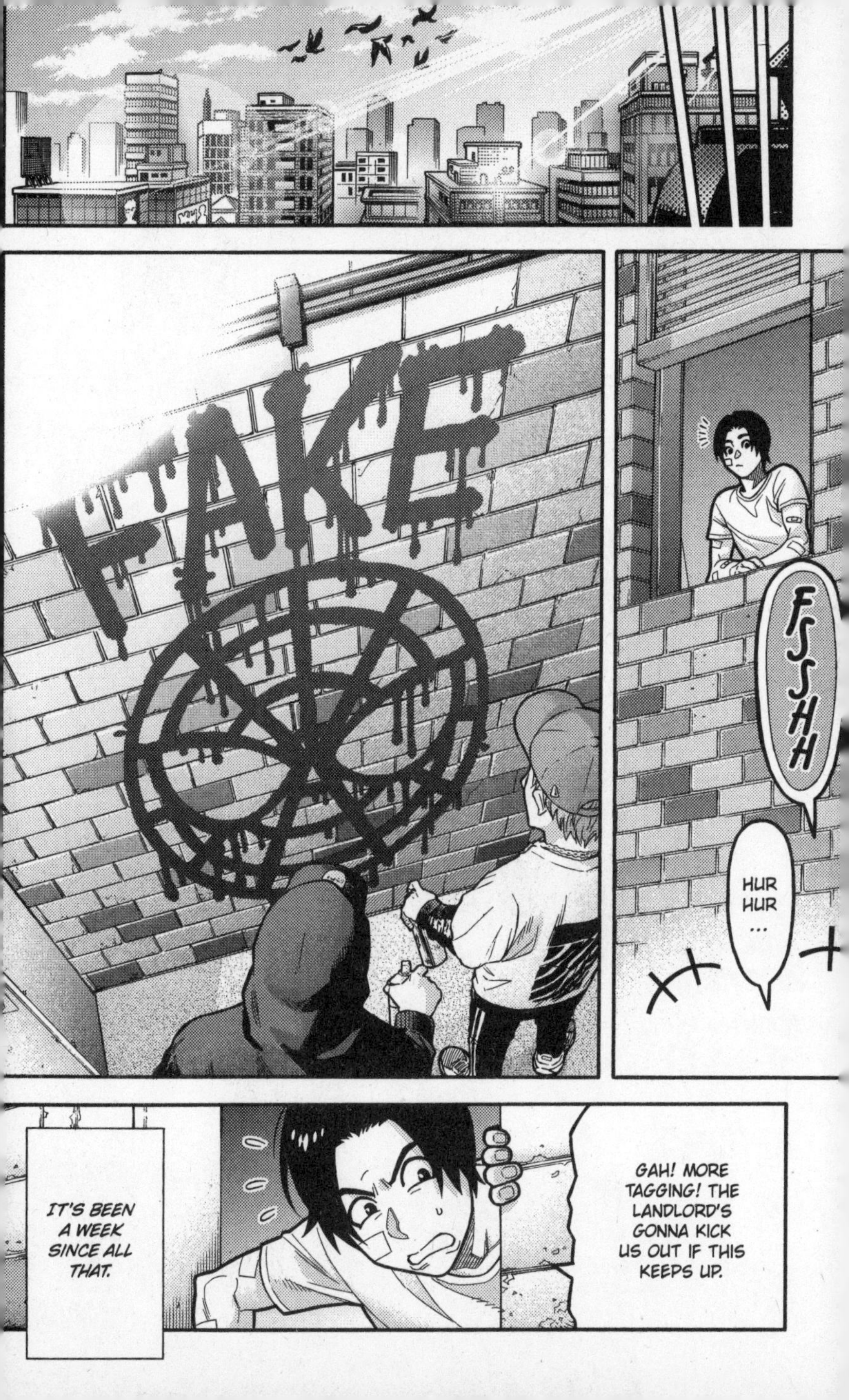
FSSHH
HUR HUR ...
FAKE
GAH! MORE TAGGING! THE LANDLORD'S GONNA KICK US OUT IF THIS KEEPS UP.
IT'S BEEN A WEEK SINCE ALL THAT.

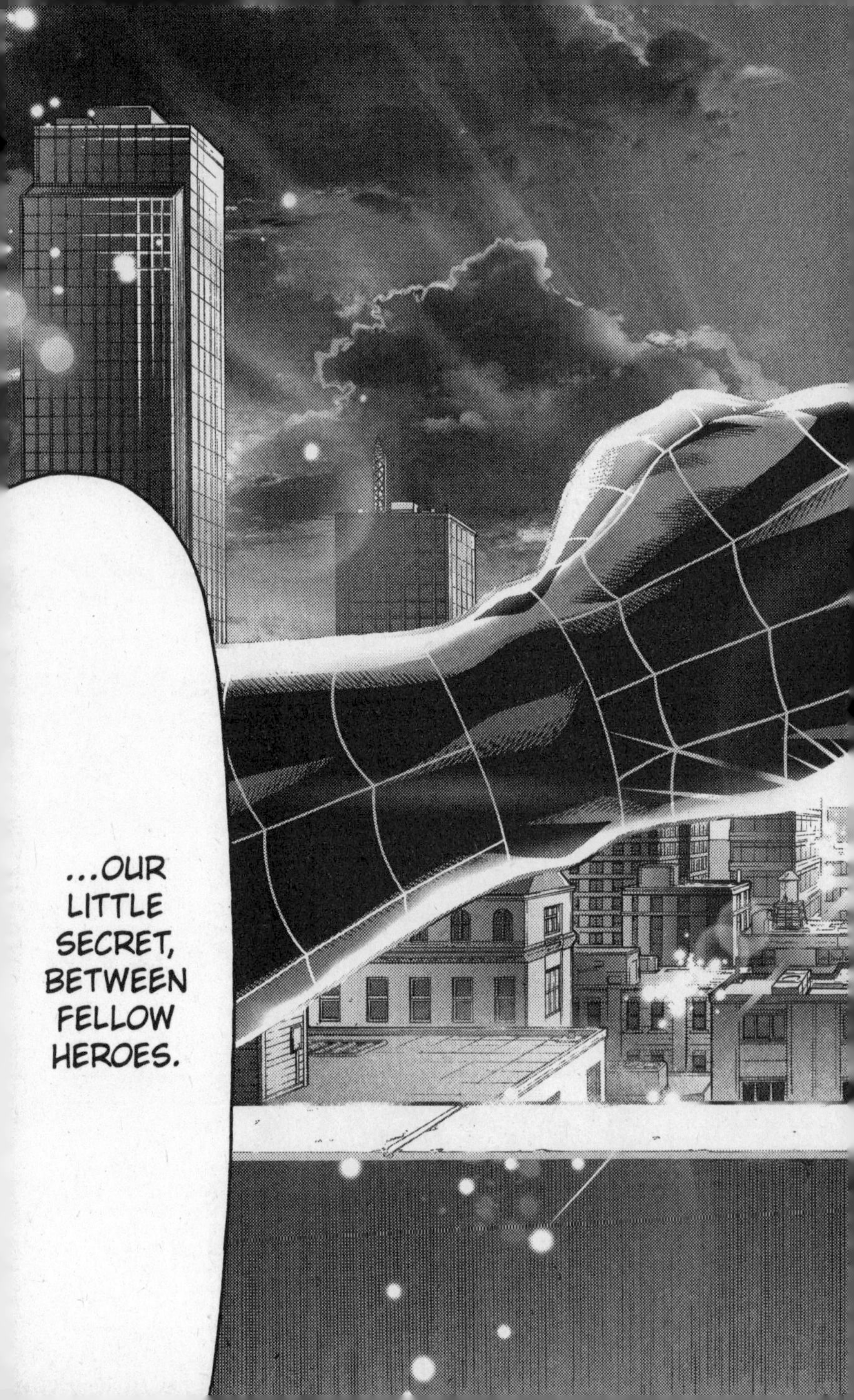
...OUR LITTLE SECRET, BETWEEN FELLOW HEROES.

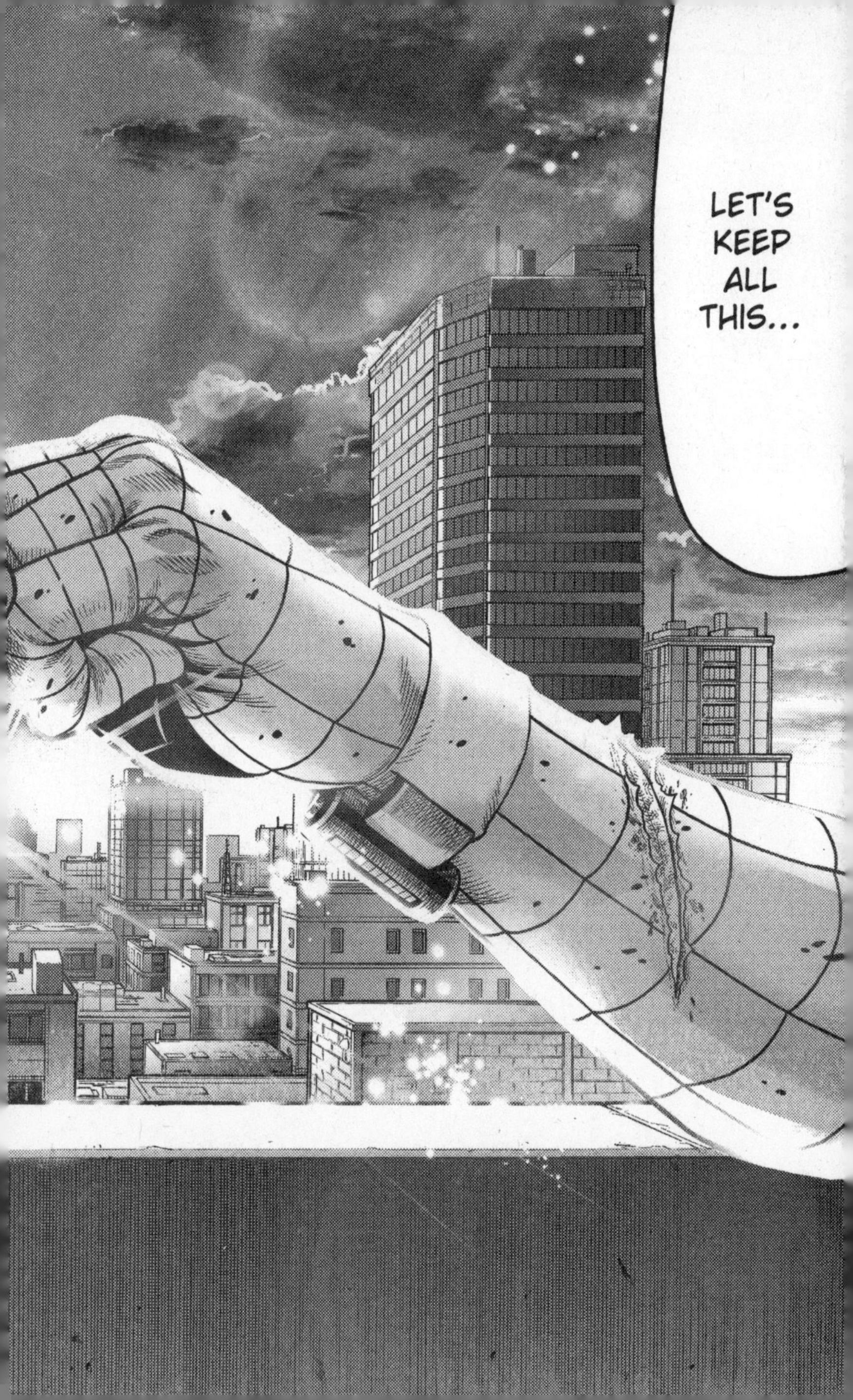
LET'S KEEP ALL THIS...

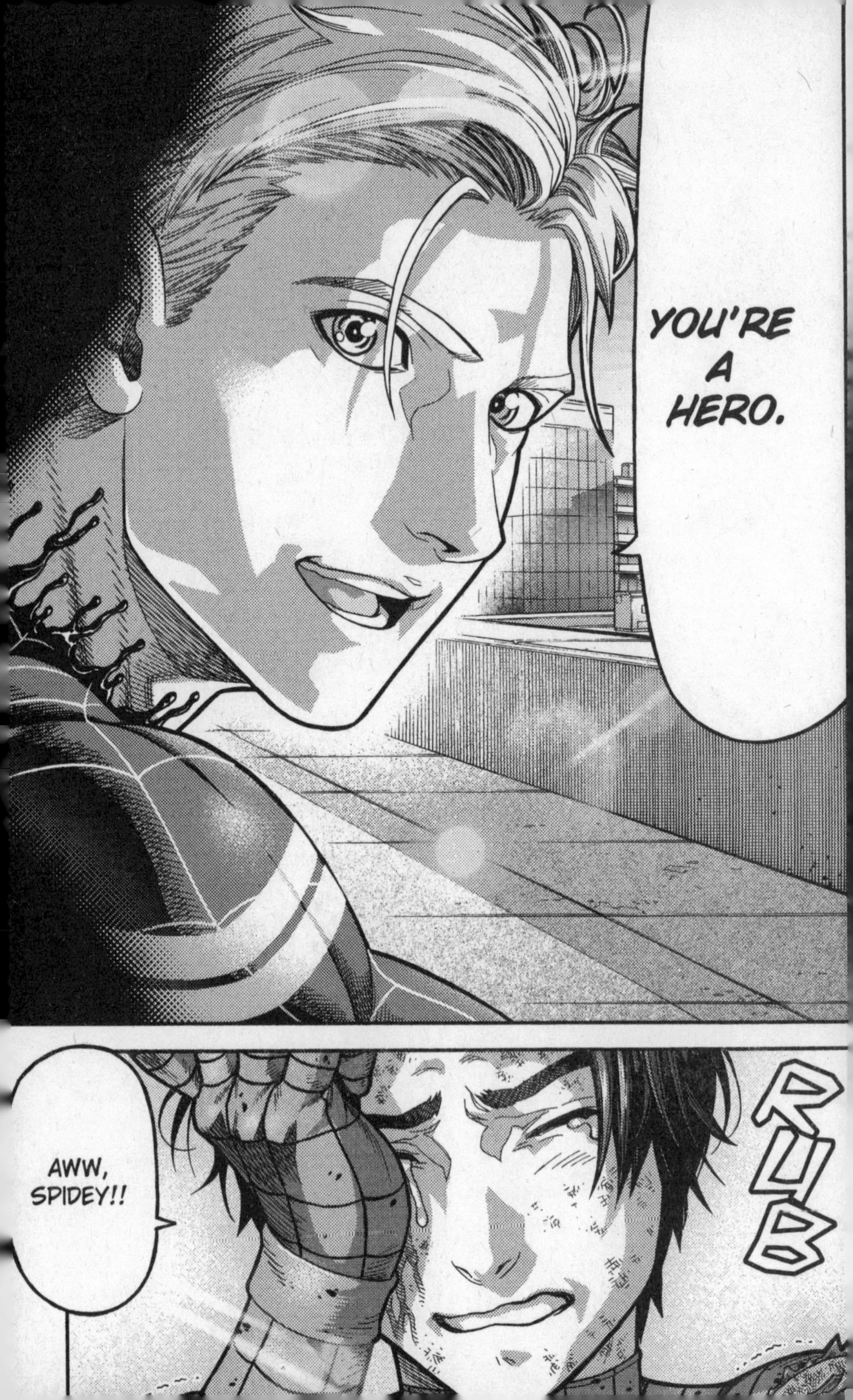
YOU'RE A HERO.
RUB
AWW, SPIDEY!!

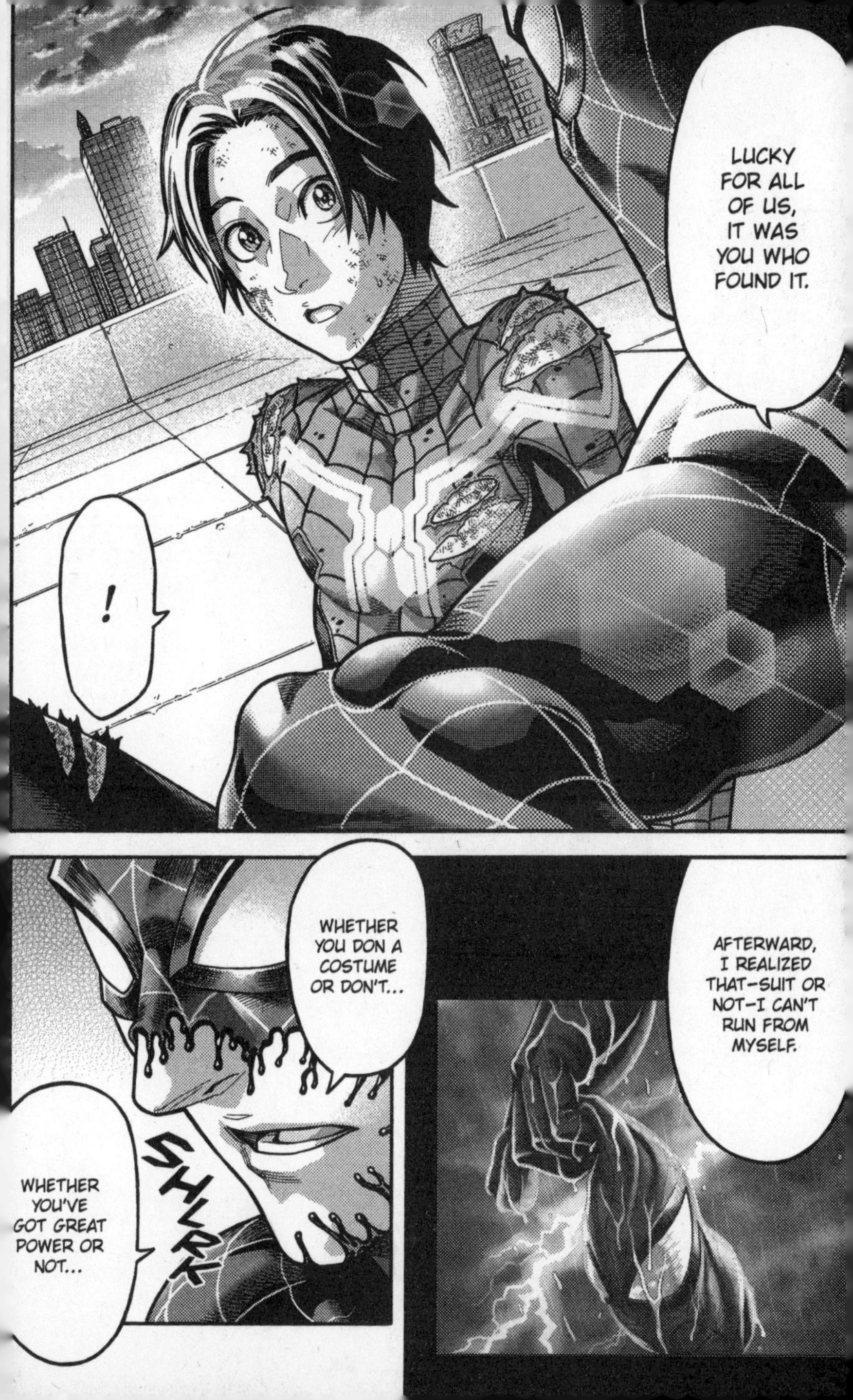
LUCKY FOR ALL OF US, IT WAS YOU WHO FOUND IT.
!
AFTERWARD, I REALIZED THAT—SUIT OR NOT—I CAN'T RUN FROM MYSELF.
WHETHER YOU DON A COSTUME OR DON'T...
SHLRK
WHETHER YOU'VE GOT GREAT POWER OR NOT...

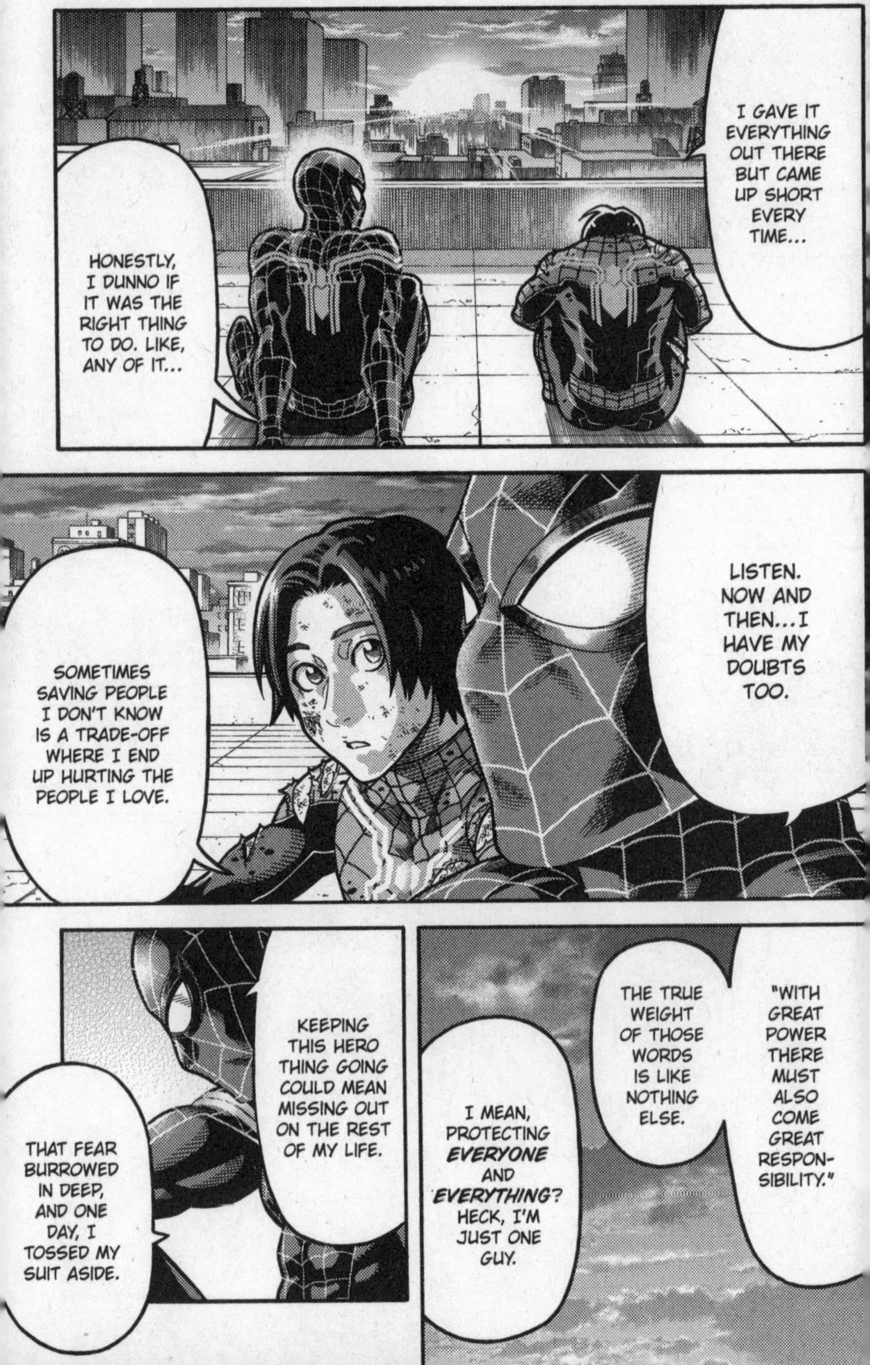
I GAVE IT EVERYTHING OUT THERE BUT CAME UP SHORT EVERY TIME...
HONESTLY, I DUNNO IF IT WAS THE RIGHT THING TO DO. LIKE, ANY OF IT...
LISTEN. NOW AND THEN...I HAVE MY DOUBTS TOO.
SOMETIMES SAVING PEOPLE I DON'T KNOW IS A TRADE-OFF WHERE I END UP HURTING THE PEOPLE I LOVE.
"WITH GREAT POWER THERE MUST ALSO COME GREAT RESPONSIBILITY."
THE TRUE WEIGHT OF THOSE WORDS IS LIKE NOTHING ELSE.
I MEAN, PROTECTING *EVERYONE* AND *EVERYTHING*? HECK, I'M JUST ONE GUY.
KEEPING THIS HERO THING GOING COULD MEAN MISSING OUT ON THE REST OF MY LIFE.
THAT FEAR BURROWED IN DEEP, AND ONE DAY, I TOSSED MY SUIT ASIDE.

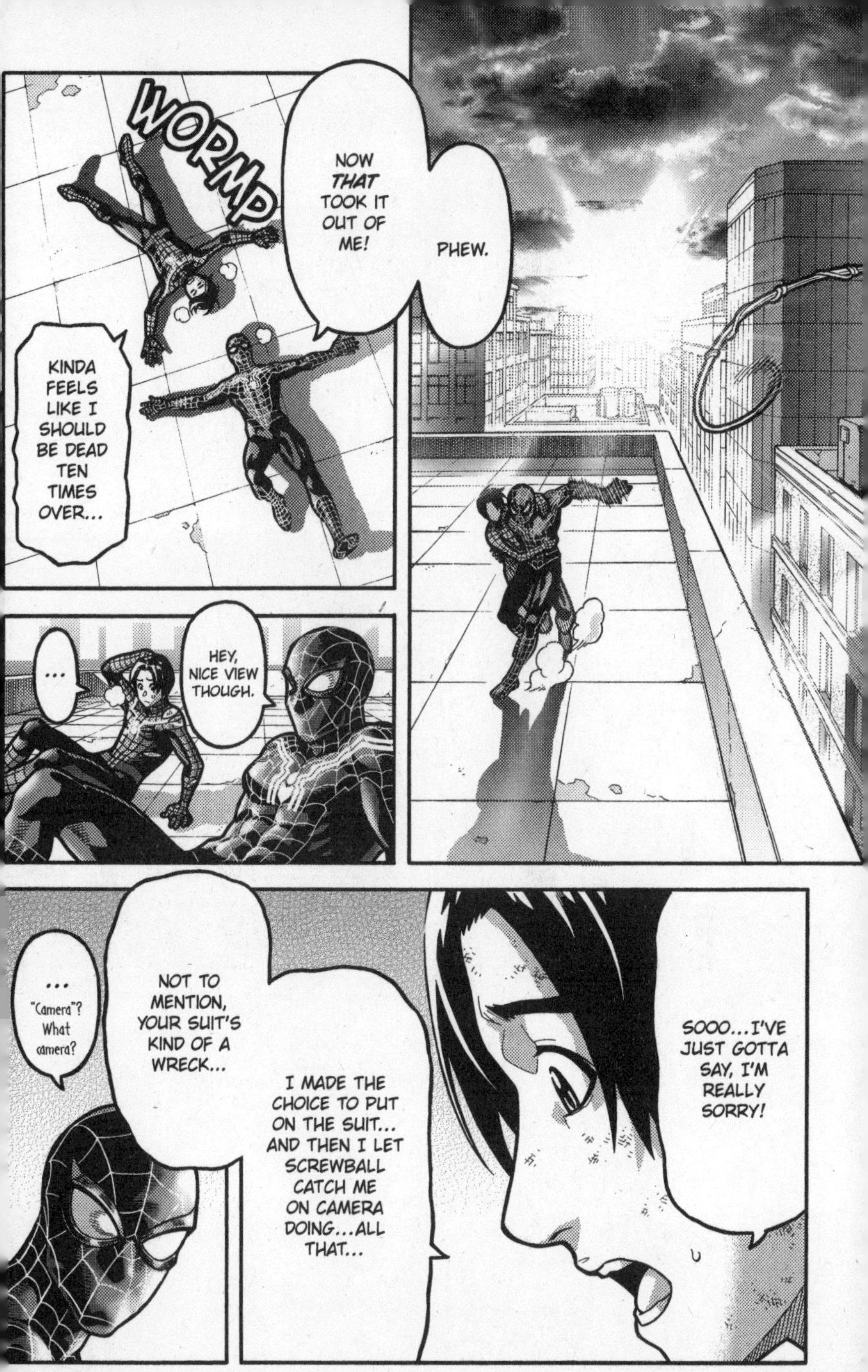
WORMP
NOW THAT TOOK IT OUT OF ME! PHEW.
KINDA FEELS LIKE I SHOULD BE DEAD TEN TIMES OVER...
HEY, NICE VIEW THOUGH.
...
SOOO...I'VE JUST GOTTA SAY, I'M REALLY SORRY!
I MADE THE CHOICE TO PUT ON THE SUIT... AND THEN I LET SCREWBALL CATCH ME ON CAMERA DOING...ALL THAT...
NOT TO MENTION, YOUR SUIT'S KIND OF A WRECK...
... "Camera"? What camera?

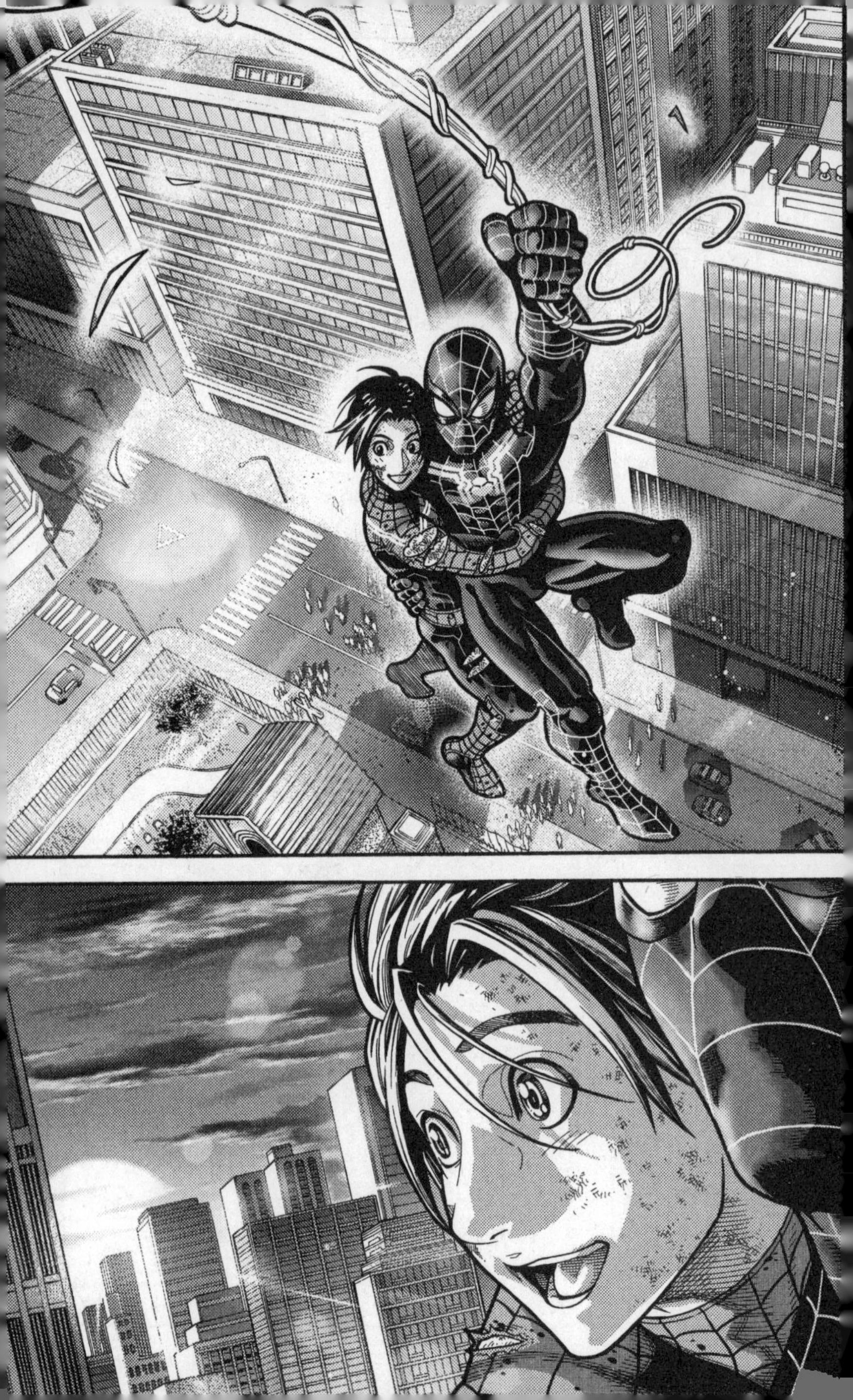

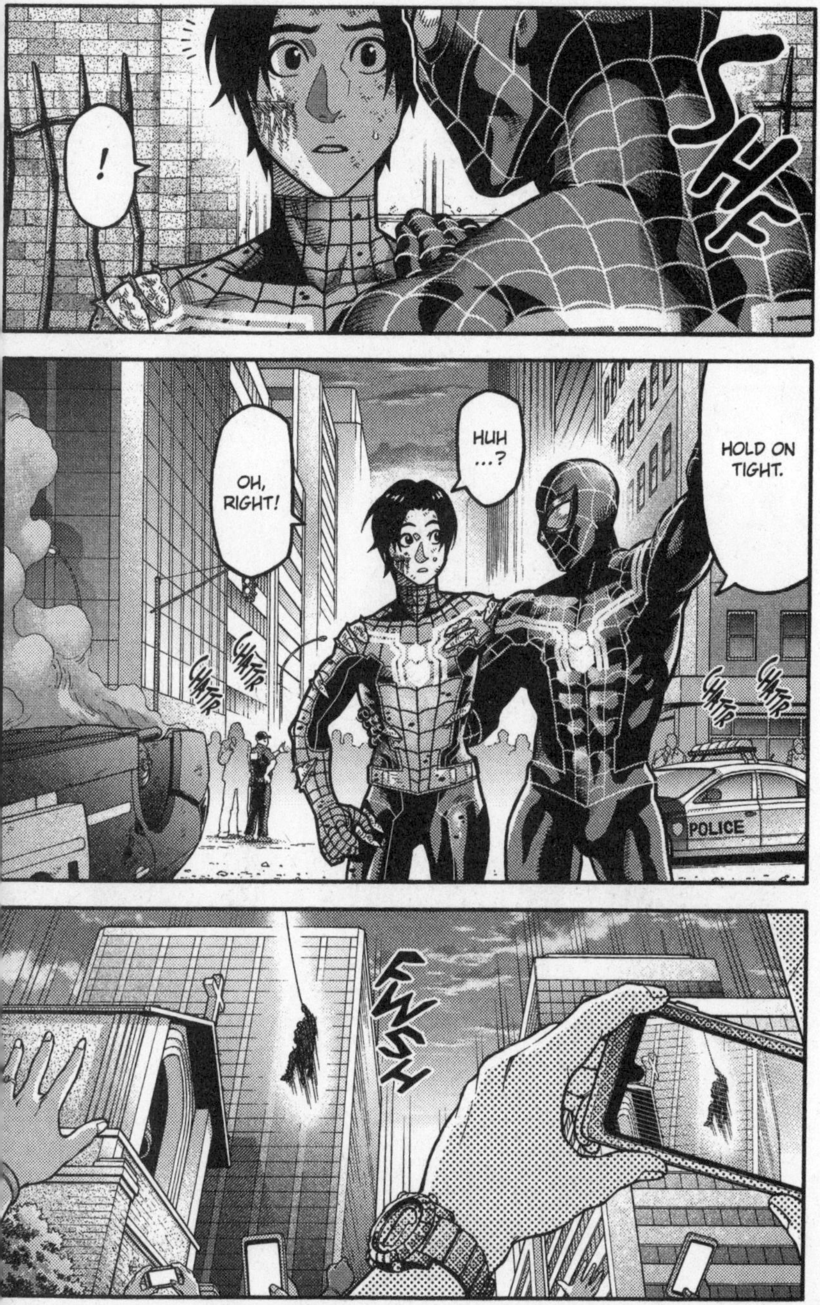
SHK
!
HOLD ON TIGHT.
HUH ...?
OH, RIGHT!
CHATTR CHATTR
POLICE
CHATTR CHATTR
KWSH

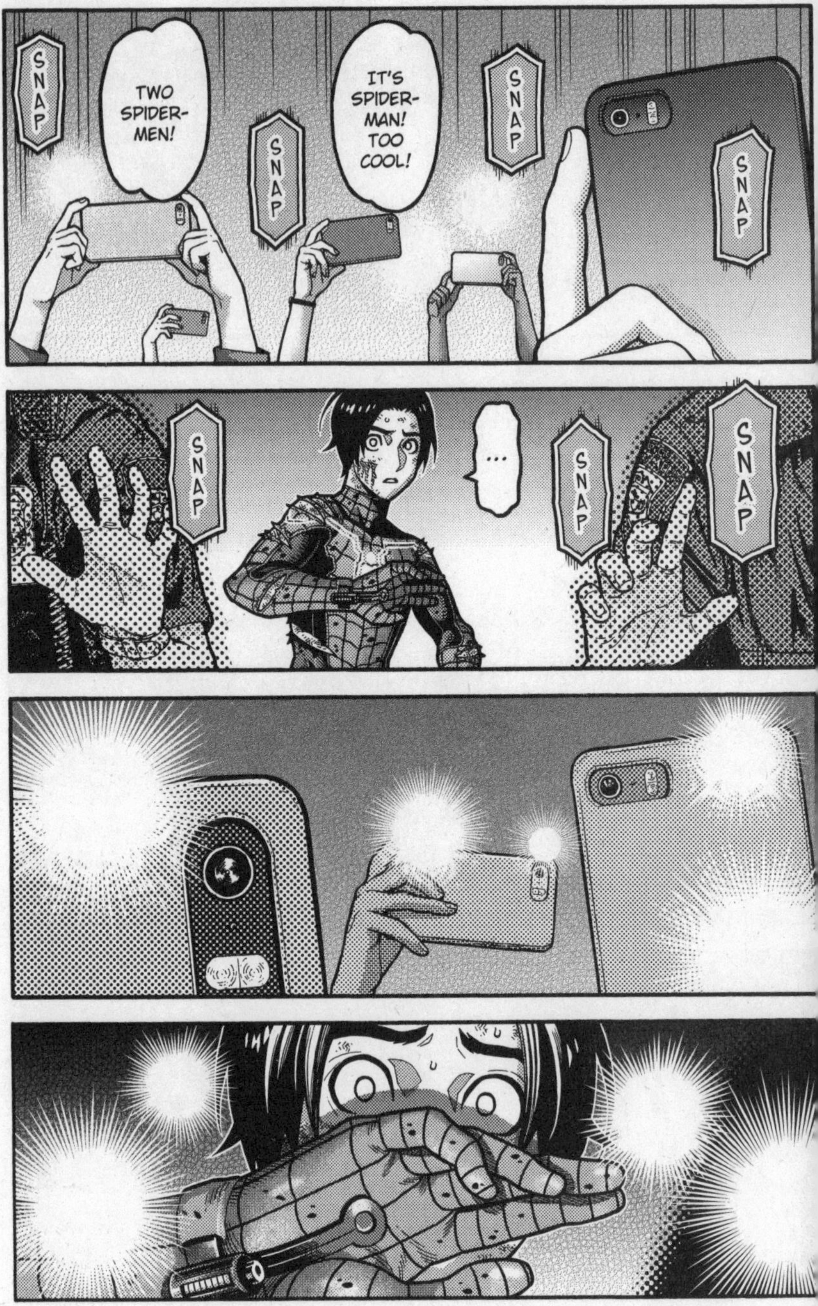
SNAP
SNAP
IT'S SPIDER-MAN! TOO COOL!
SNAP
TWO SPIDER-MEN!
SNAP
SNAP
SNAP
...
SNAP

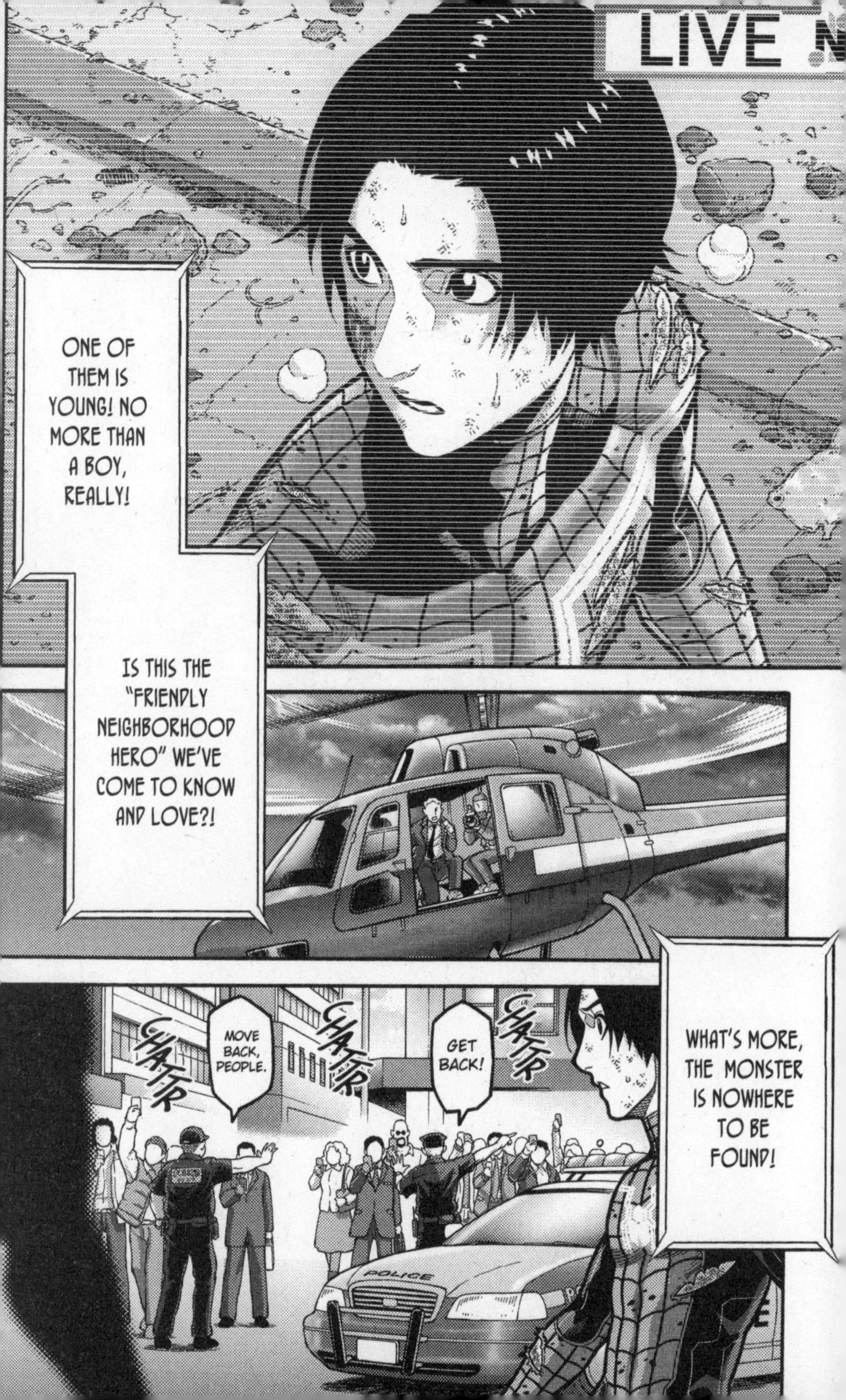
LIVE
ONE OF THEM IS YOUNG! NO MORE THAN A BOY, REALLY!
IS THIS THE "FRIENDLY NEIGHBORHOOD HERO" WE'VE COME TO KNOW AND LOVE?!
WHAT'S MORE, THE MONSTER IS NOWHERE TO BE FOUND!
CHATTR
GET BACK!
CHATTR
MOVE BACK, PEOPLE.
CHATTR
POLICE

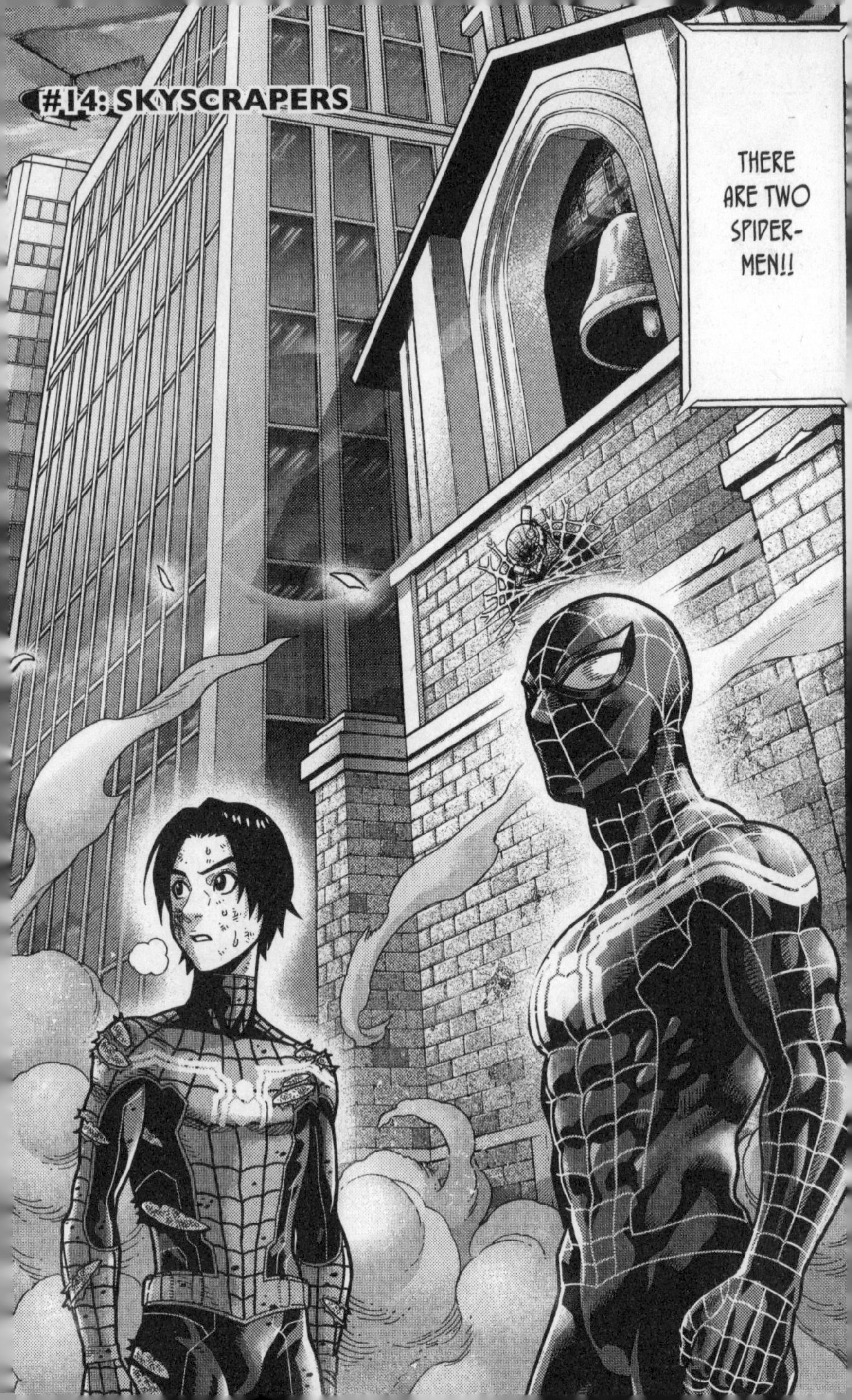
#14: SKYSCRAPERS
THERE ARE TWO SPIDER-MEN!!

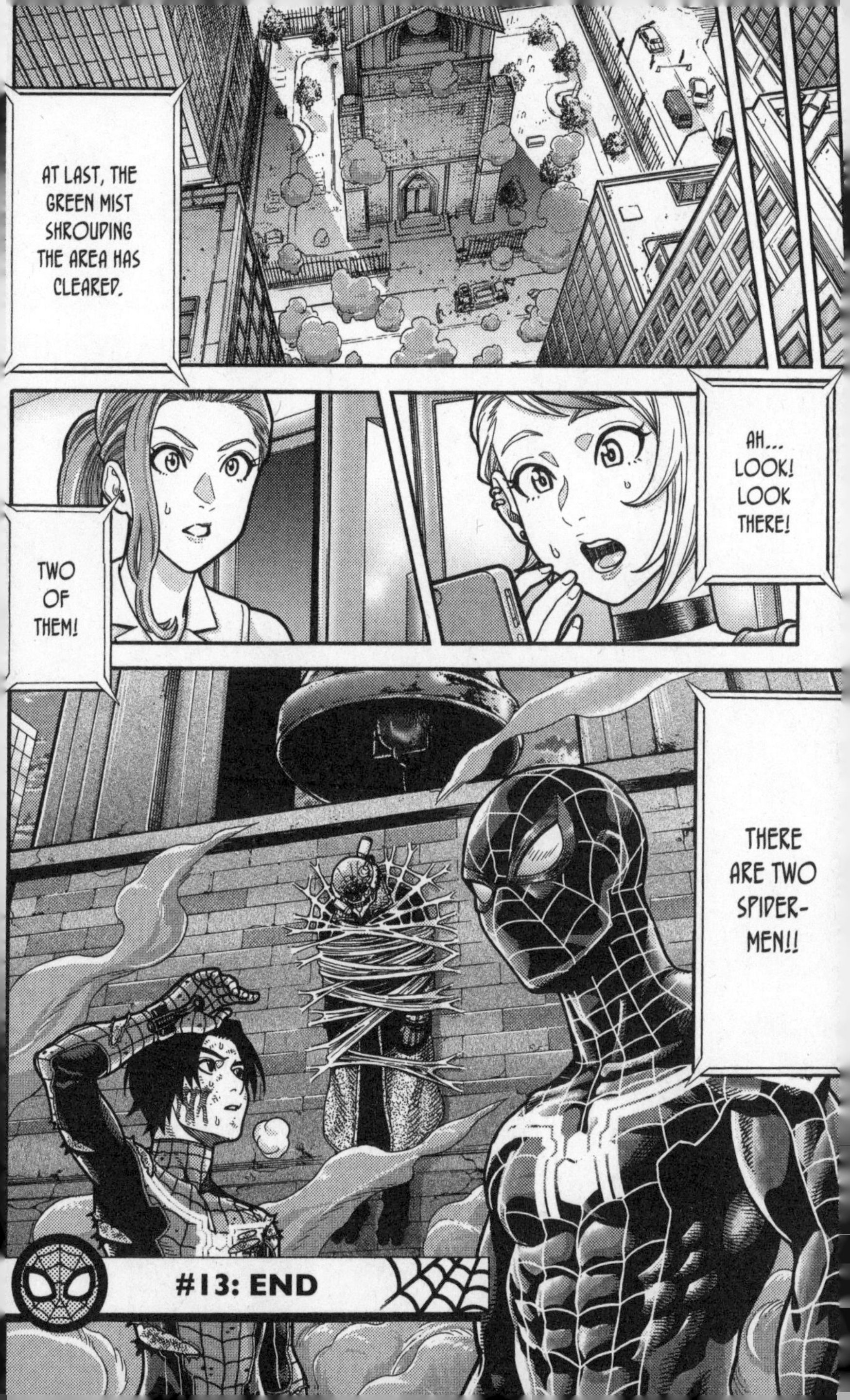

AT LAST, THE GREEN MIST SHROUDING THE AREA HAS CLEARED.
AH... LOOK! LOOK THERE!
TWO OF THEM!
THERE ARE TWO SPIDER-MEN!!
#13: END

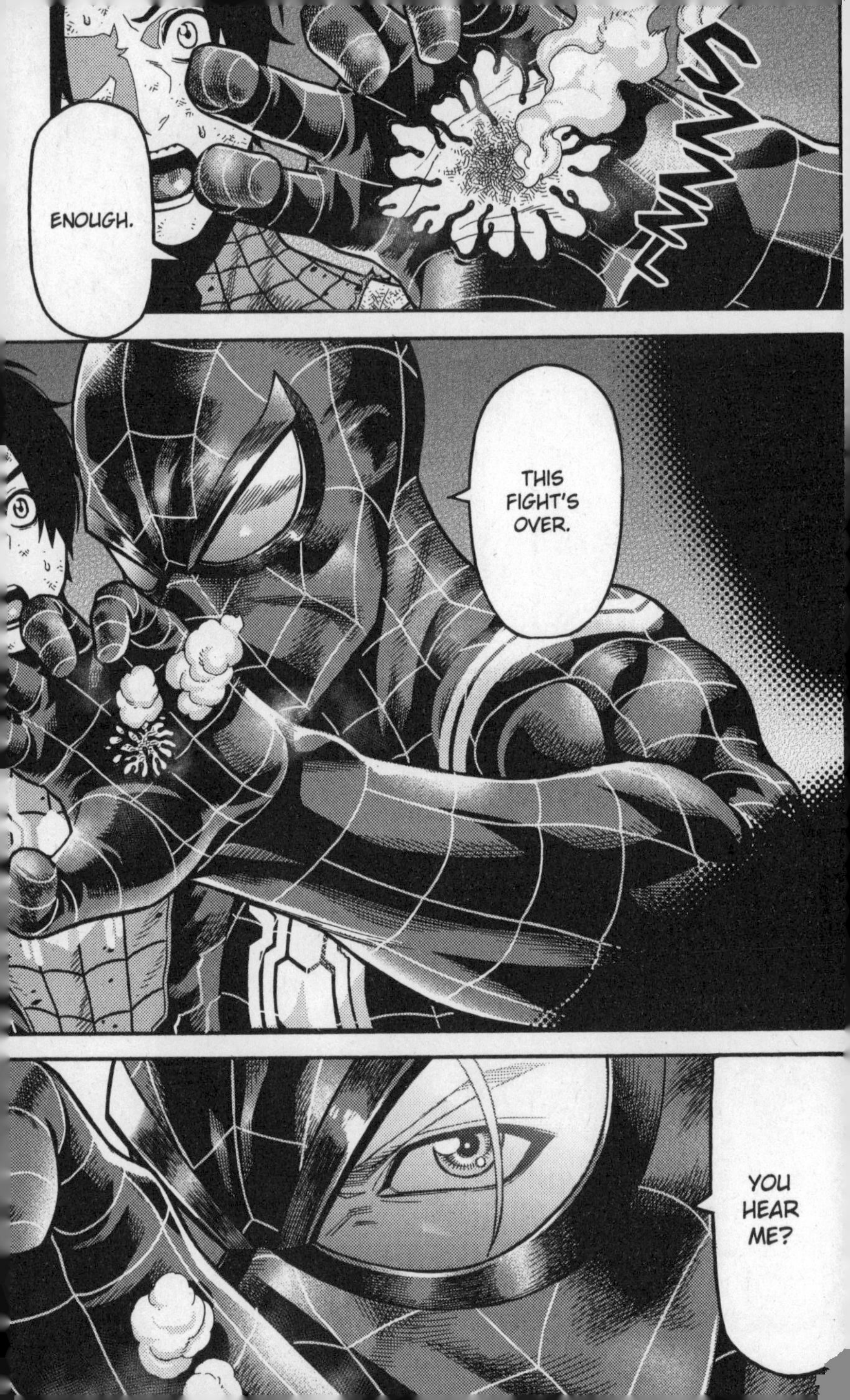
ENOUGH.
THIS FIGHT'S OVER.
YOU HEAR ME?

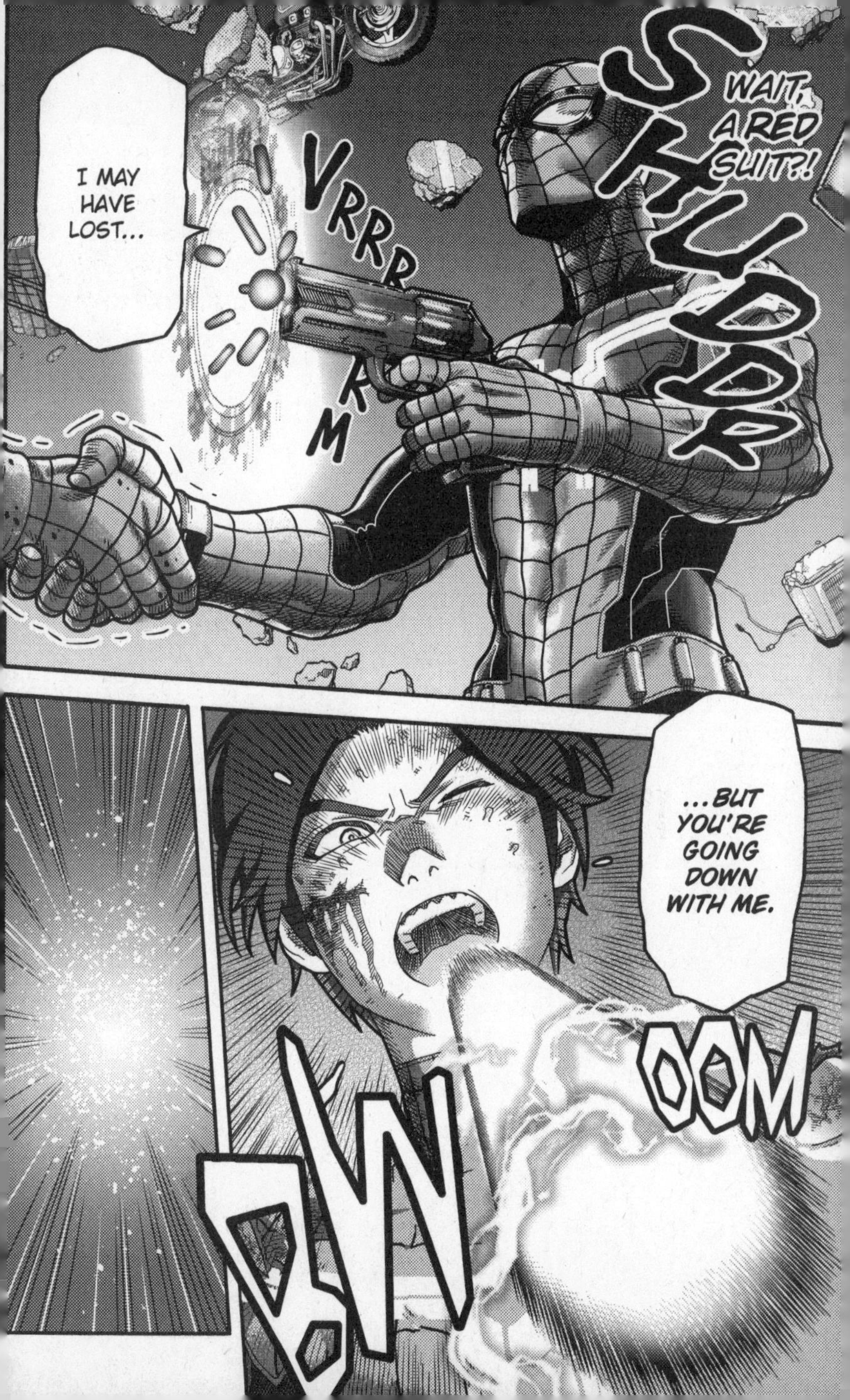
WAIT, A RED SUIT?!
SHUDDR
VRRRRRM
I MAY HAVE LOST...
...BUT YOU'RE GOING DOWN WITH ME.
WOOM

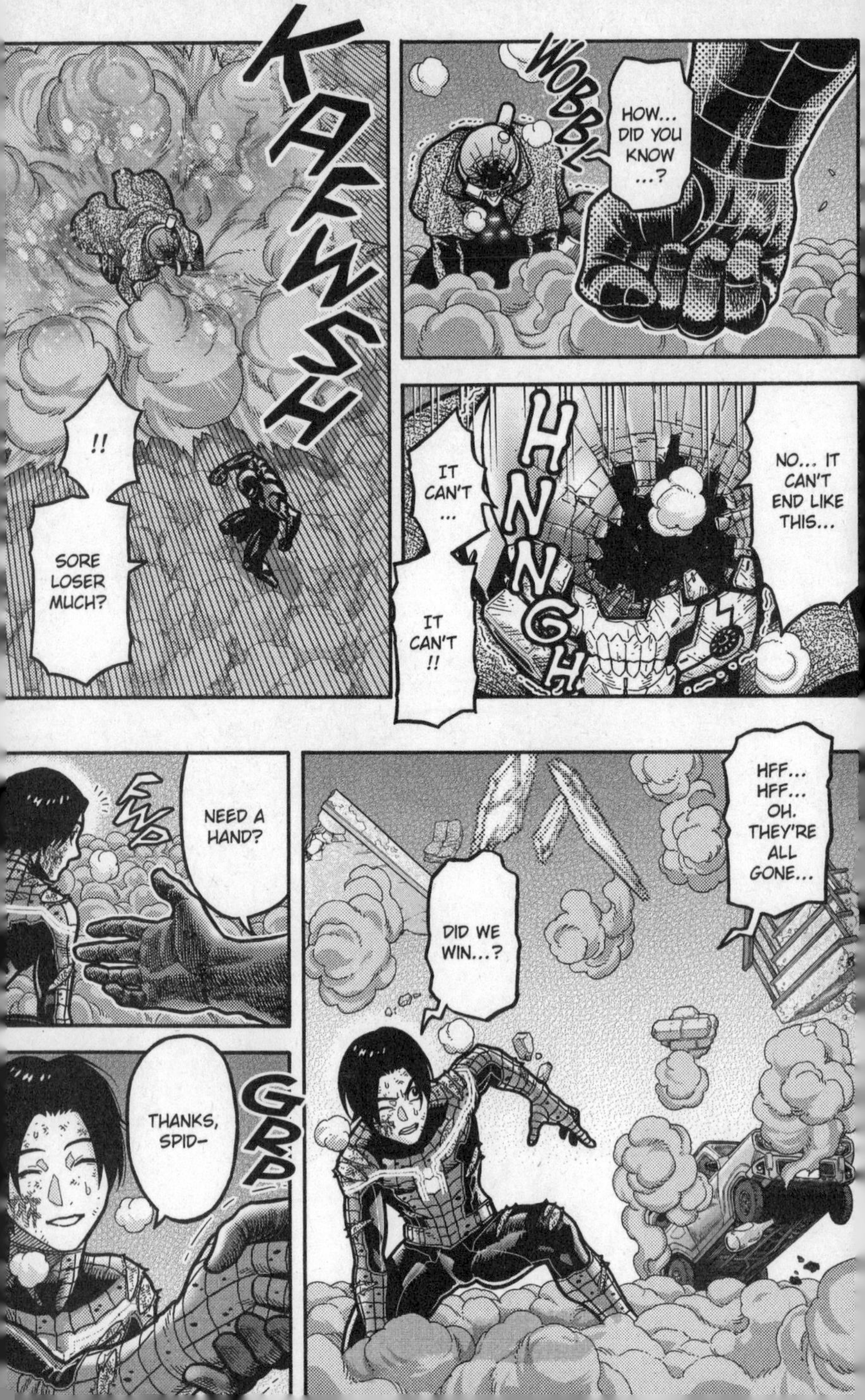
WOBBBL
HOW... DID YOU KNOW ...?
NO... IT CAN'T END LIKE THIS...
HNNGH
IT CAN'T ...
IT CAN'T !!
KAKWSH
!!
SORE LOSER MUCH?
HFF... HFF... OH. THEY'RE ALL GONE...
DID WE WIN...?
NEED A HAND?
FWP
THANKS, SPID-
GRP

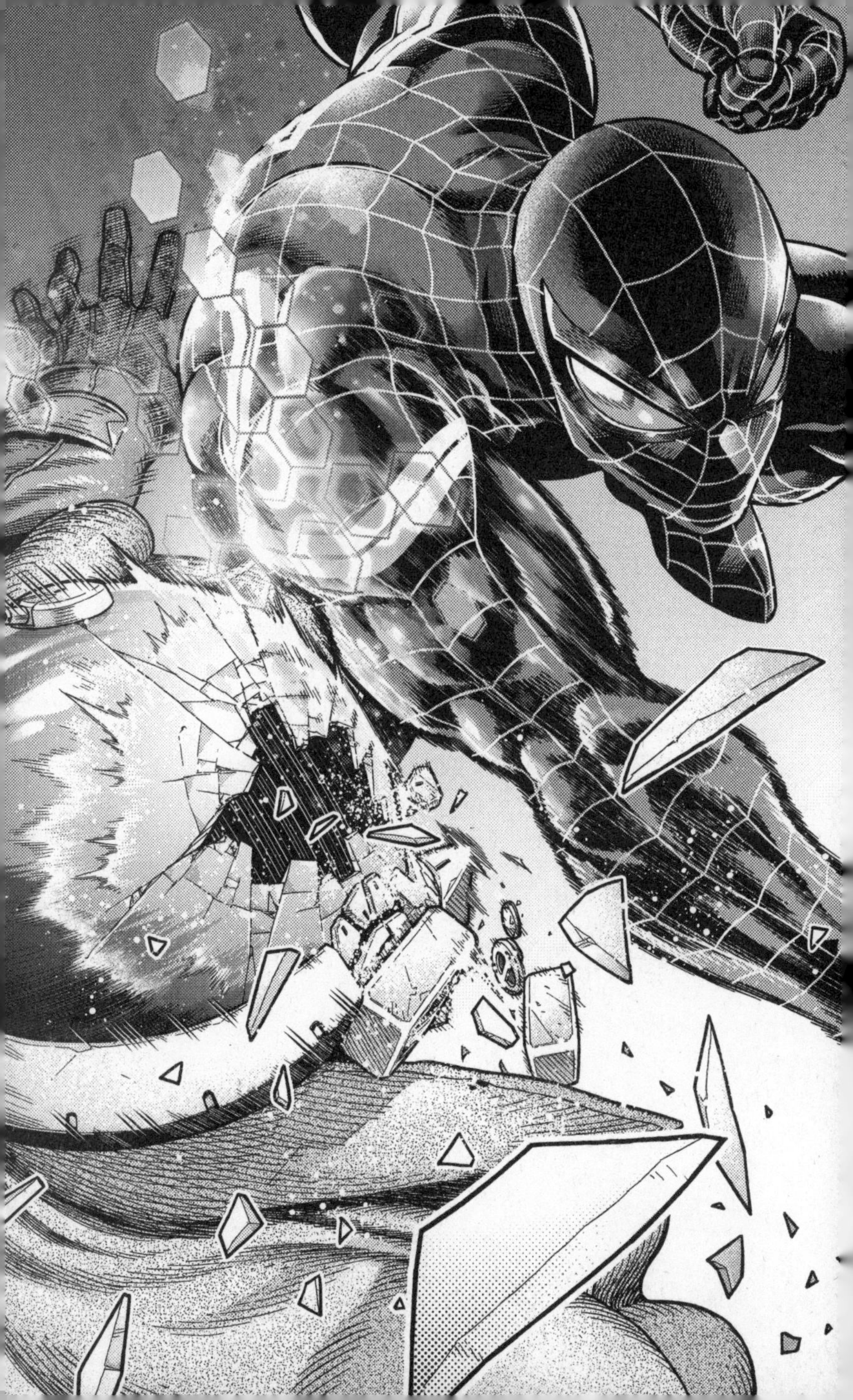

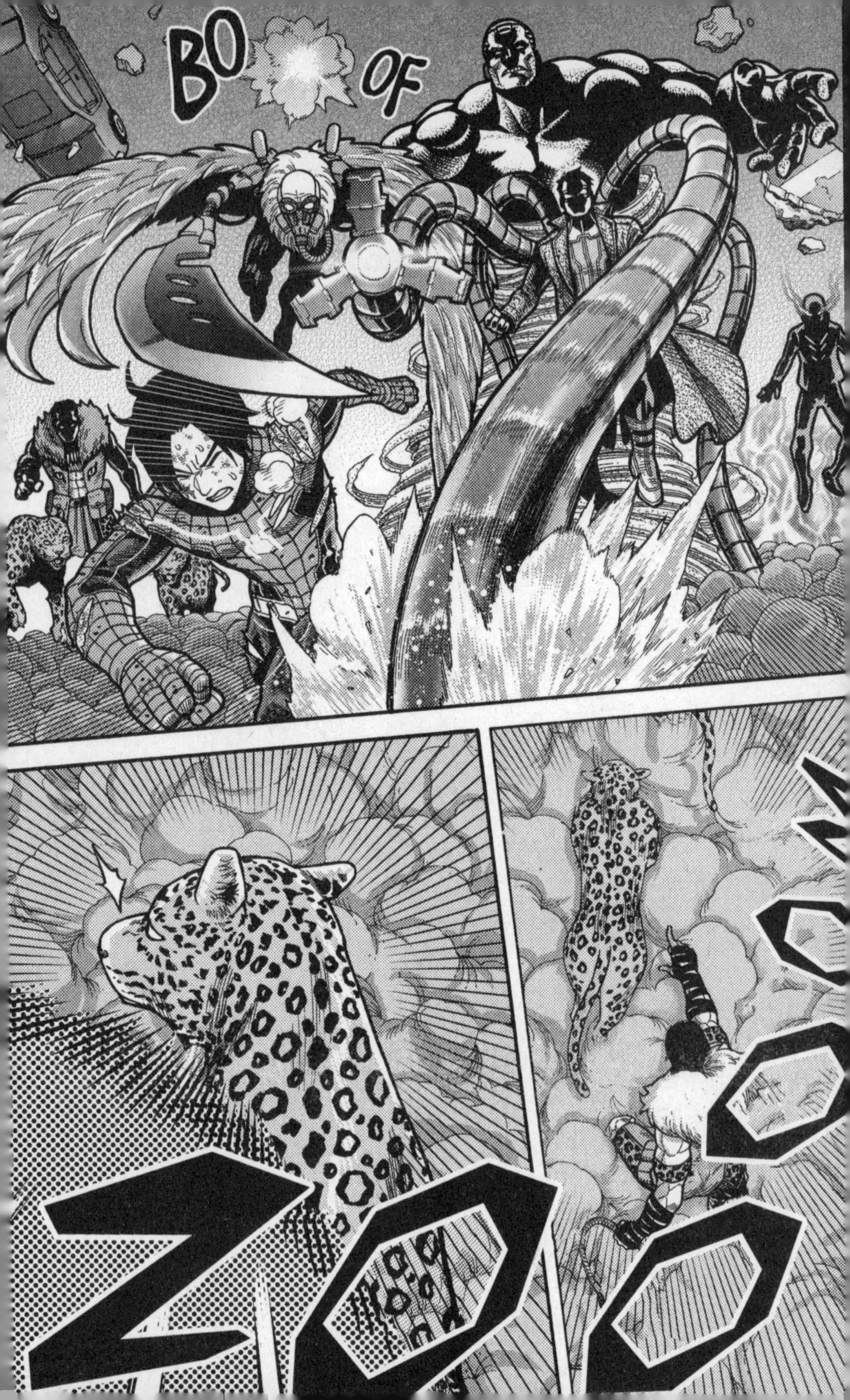
BOOF
ZOOOOM

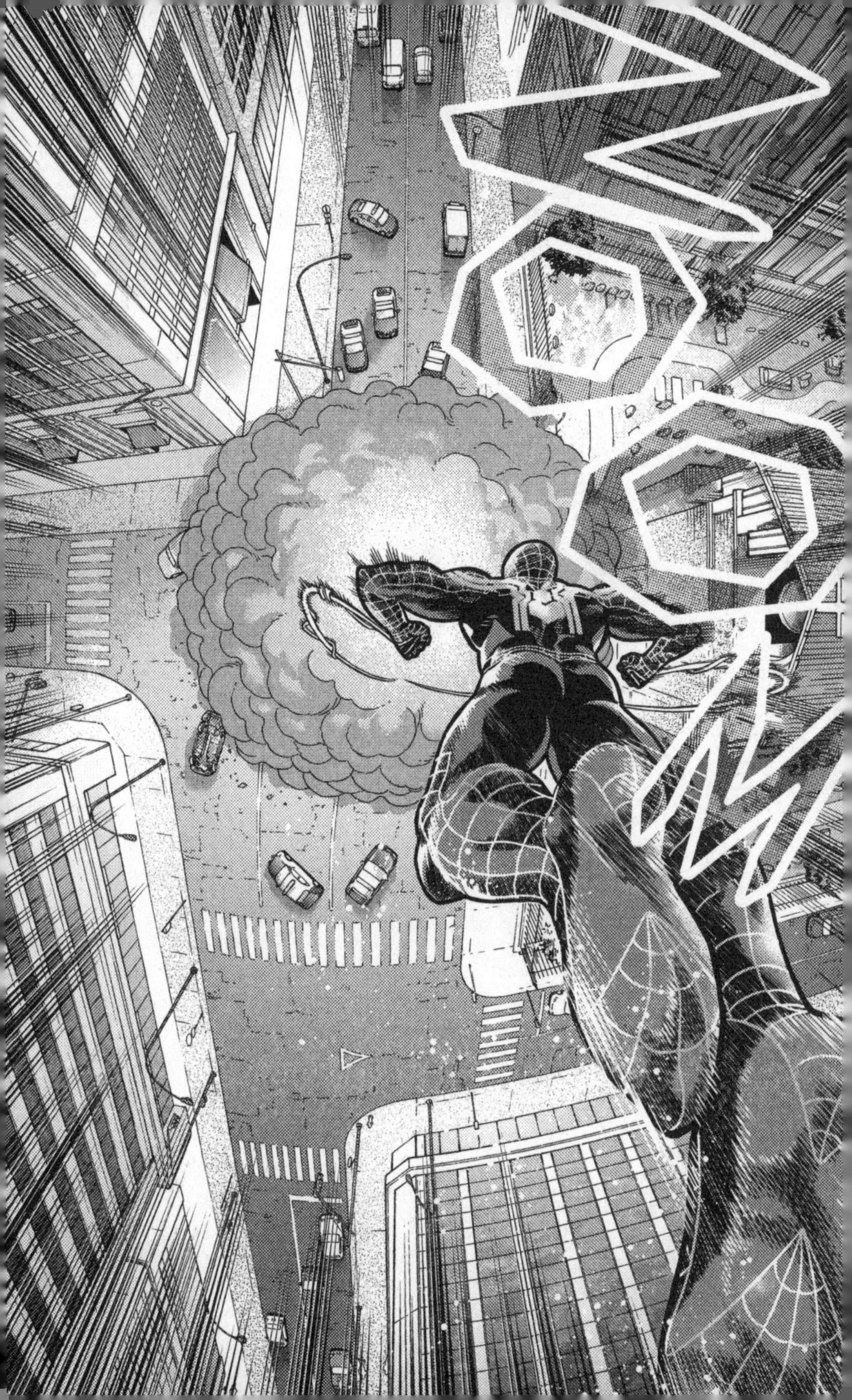
ZOOM

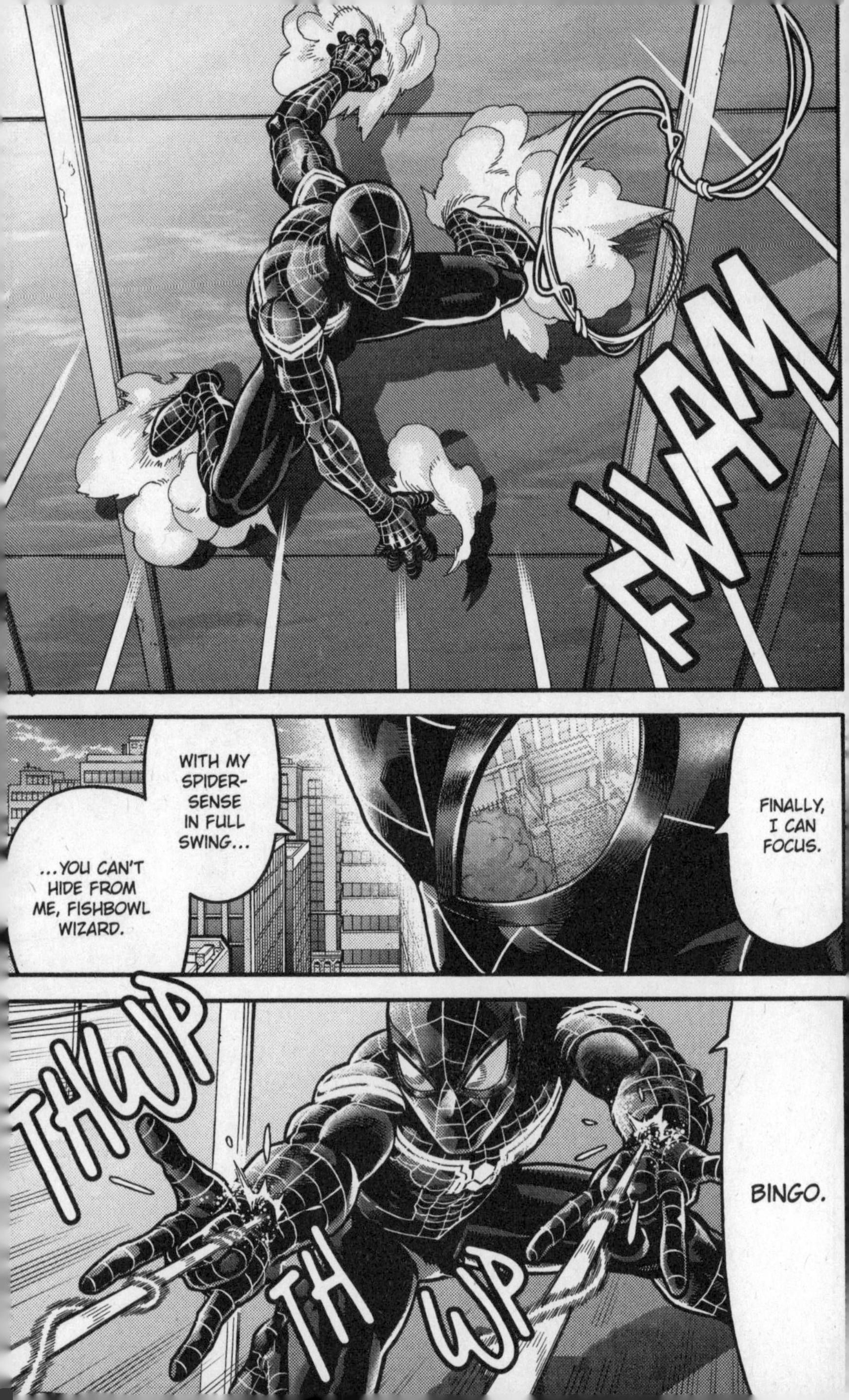
FWAM
FINALLY, I CAN FOCUS.
WITH MY SPIDER-SENSE IN FULL SWING...
...YOU CAN'T HIDE FROM ME, FISHBOWL WIZARD.
BINGO.
THWIP
TH WIP

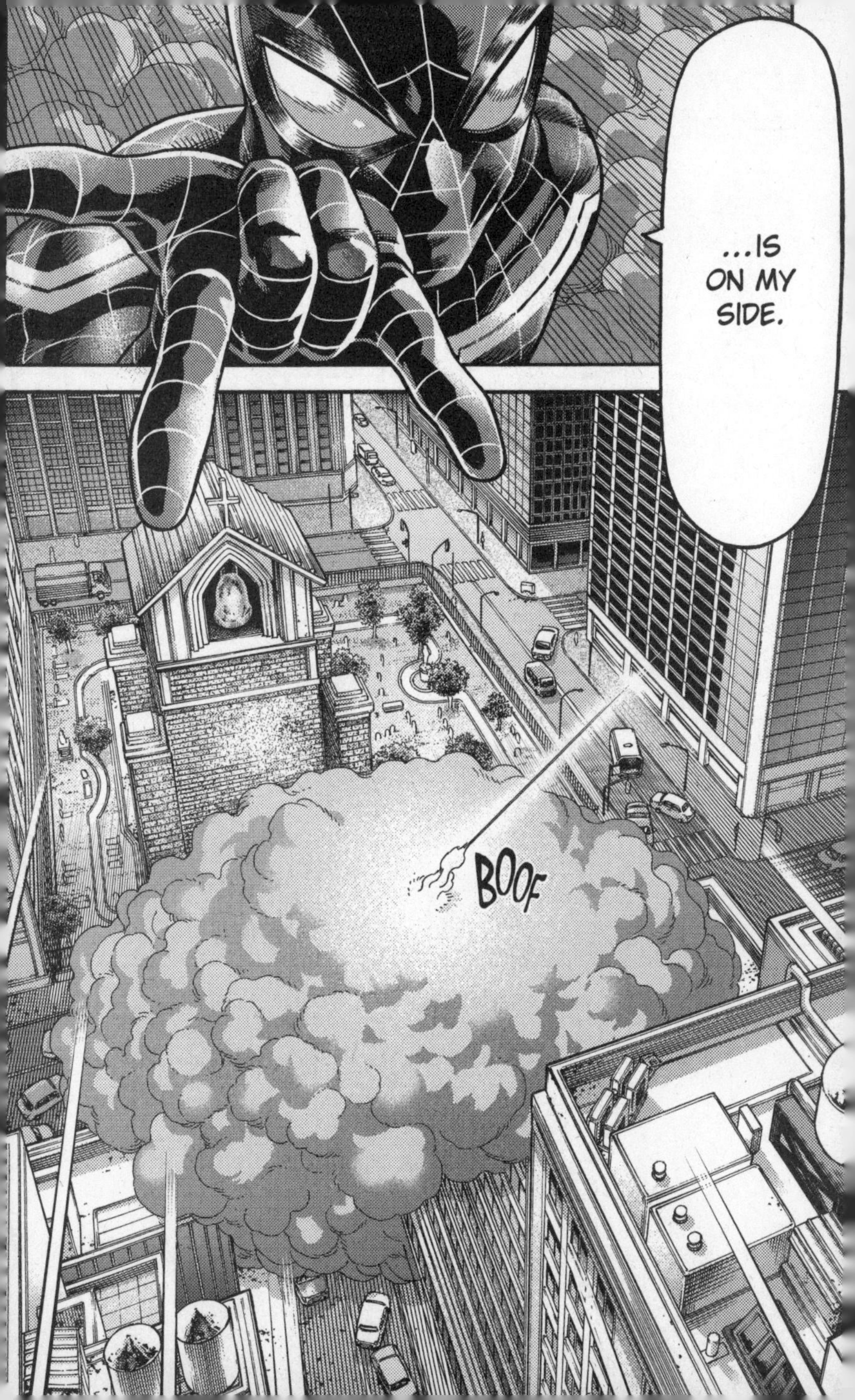
...IS ON MY SIDE.
BOOF

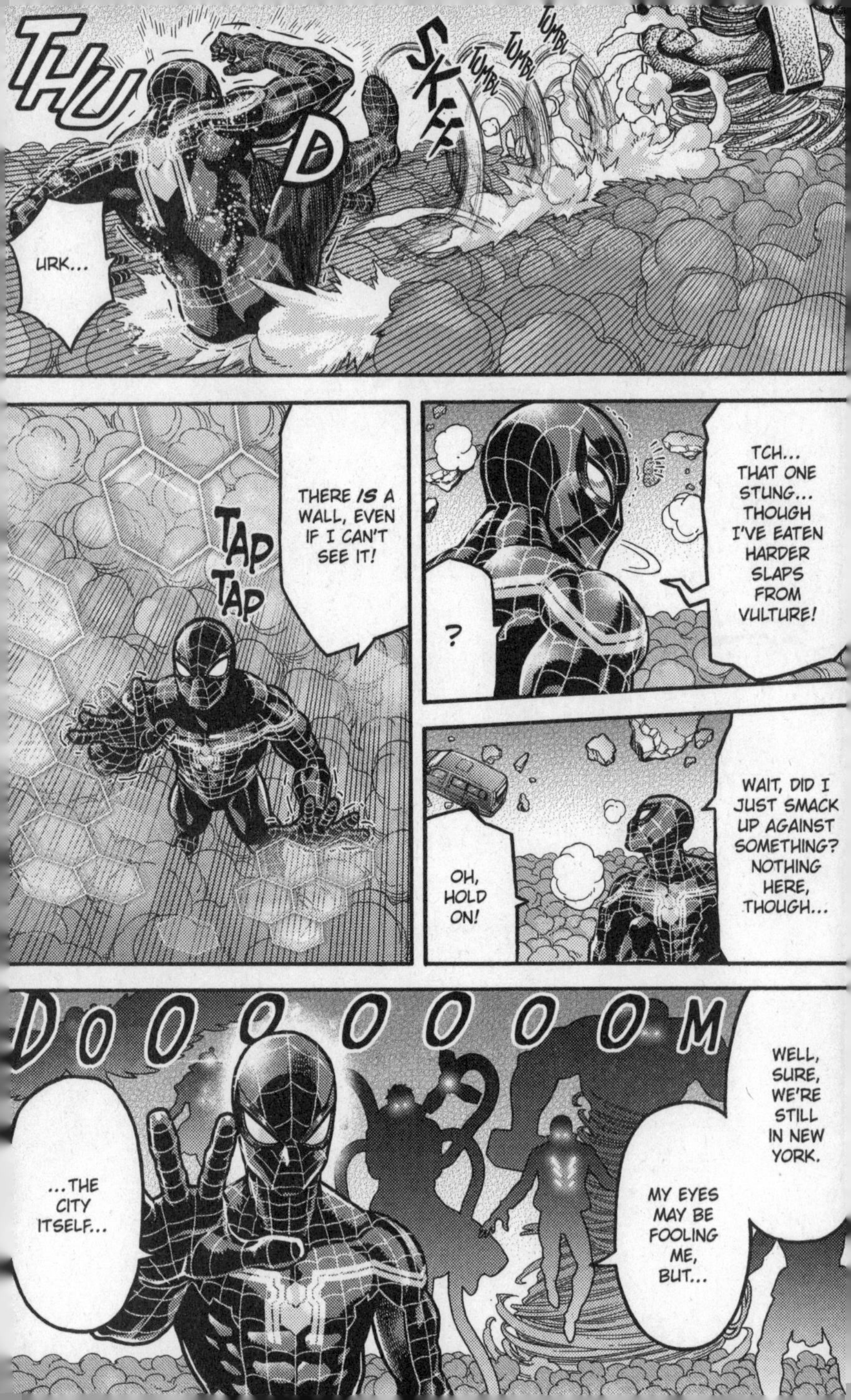
TUMBL TUMBL TUMBL
SKFF
THUD
URK...
TCH... THAT ONE STUNG... THOUGH I'VE EATEN HARDER SLAPS FROM VULTURE!
?
WAIT, DID I JUST SMACK UP AGAINST SOMETHING? NOTHING HERE, THOUGH...
OH, HOLD ON!
THERE *IS* A WALL, EVEN IF I CAN'T SEE IT!
TAP TAP
DOOOOOOOM
WELL, SURE, WE'RE STILL IN NEW YORK.
MY EYES MAY BE FOOLING ME, BUT...
...THE CITY ITSELF...

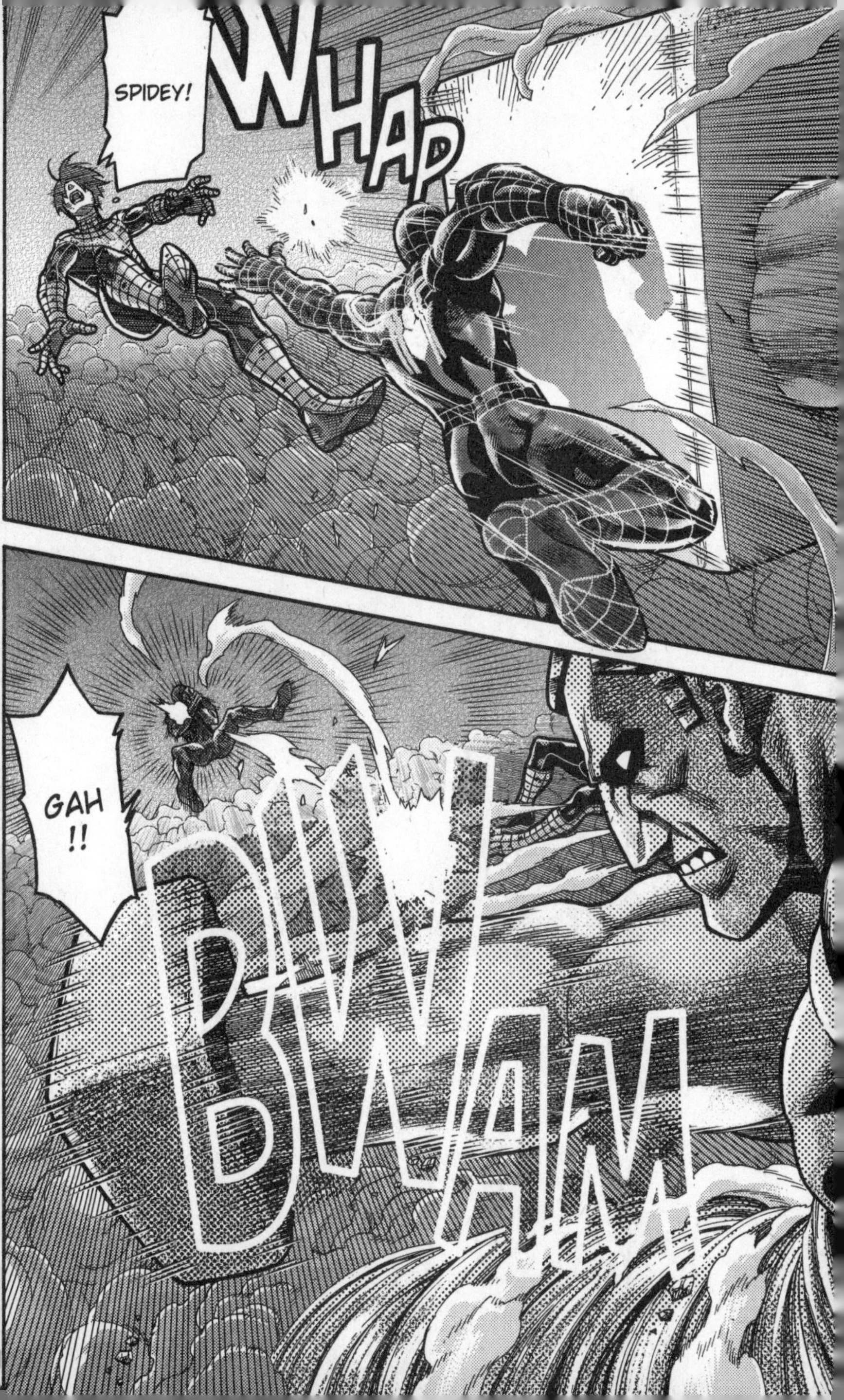
WHAP
SPIDEY!
BWAM
GAH !!

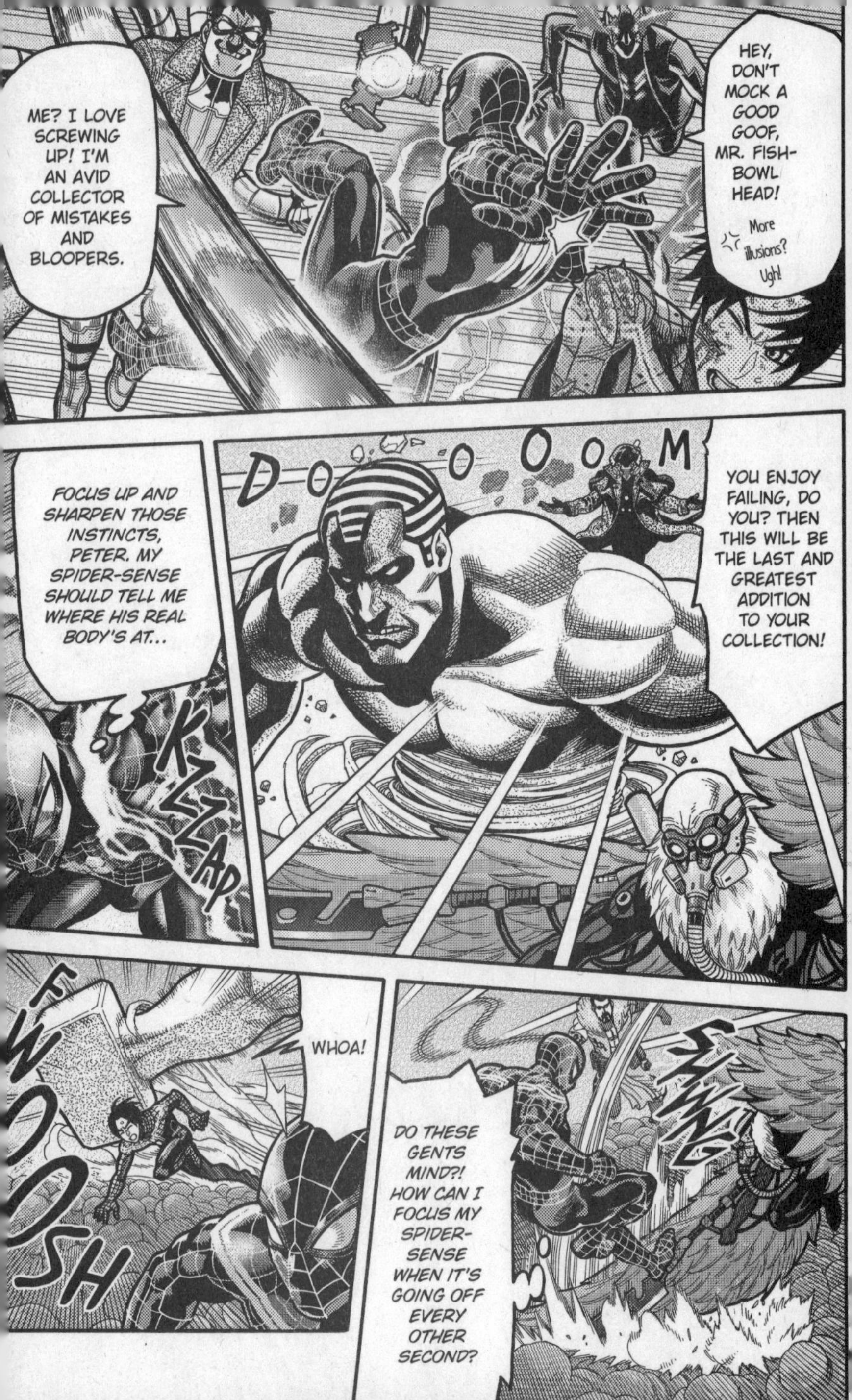
HEY, DON'T MOCK A GOOD GOOF, MR. FISH-BOWL HEAD!
More illusions? Ugh!
ME? I LOVE SCREWING UP! I'M AN AVID COLLECTOR OF MISTAKES AND BLOOPERS.
DOOOOOM
YOU ENJOY FAILING, DO YOU? THEN THIS WILL BE THE LAST AND GREATEST ADDITION TO YOUR COLLECTION!
FOCUS UP AND SHARPEN THOSE INSTINCTS, PETER. MY SPIDER-SENSE SHOULD TELL ME WHERE HIS REAL BODY'S AT...
KZZZAP
SHWING
DO THESE GENTS MIND?! HOW CAN I FOCUS MY SPIDER-SENSE WHEN IT'S GOING OFF EVERY OTHER SECOND?
FWOOSH
WHOA!

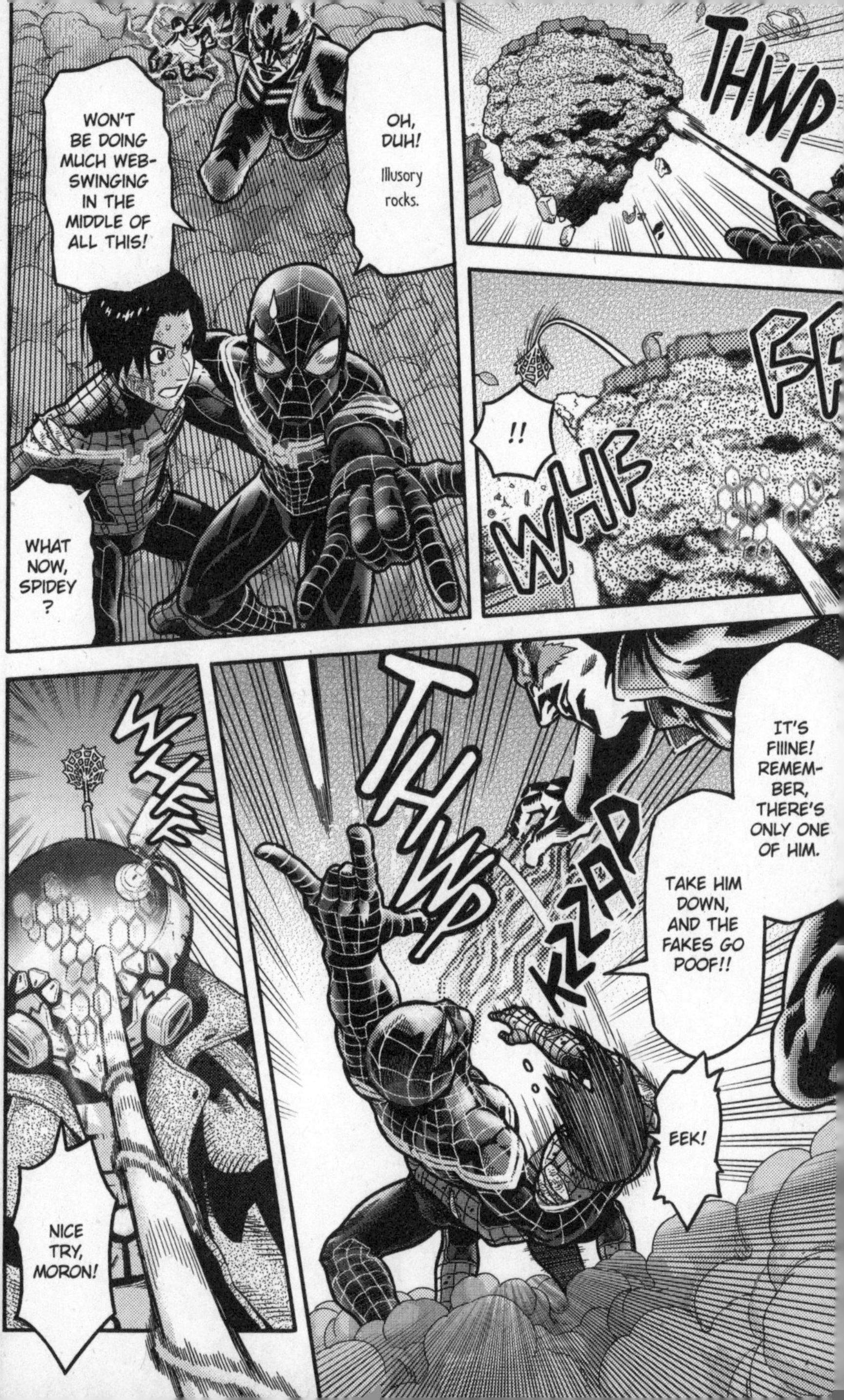
THWP
!!
WHF
FF
OH, DUH!
Illusory rocks.
WON'T BE DOING MUCH WEB-SWINGING IN THE MIDDLE OF ALL THIS!
WHAT NOW, SPIDEY?
IT'S FIIINE! REMEM-BER, THERE'S ONLY ONE OF HIM.
TAKE HIM DOWN, AND THE FAKES GO POOF!!
THWP
KZZAP
EEK!
WHF
NICE TRY, MORON!

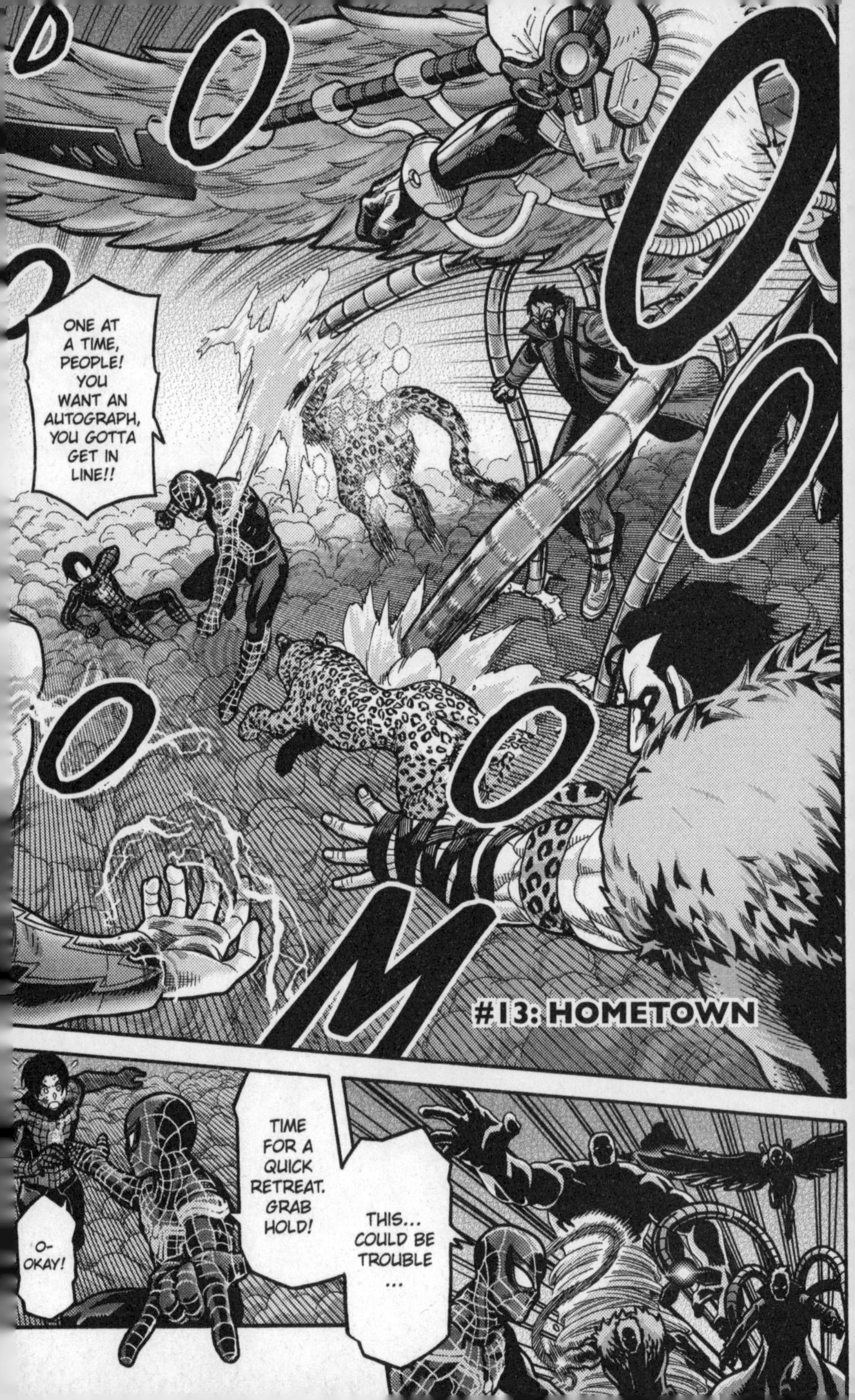
DOOOOOOOM
ONE AT A TIME, PEOPLE! YOU WANT AN AUTOGRAPH, YOU GOTTA GET IN LINE!!
#13: HOMETOWN
THIS... COULD BE TROUBLE ...
TIME FOR A QUICK RETREAT. GRAB HOLD!
O-OKAY!

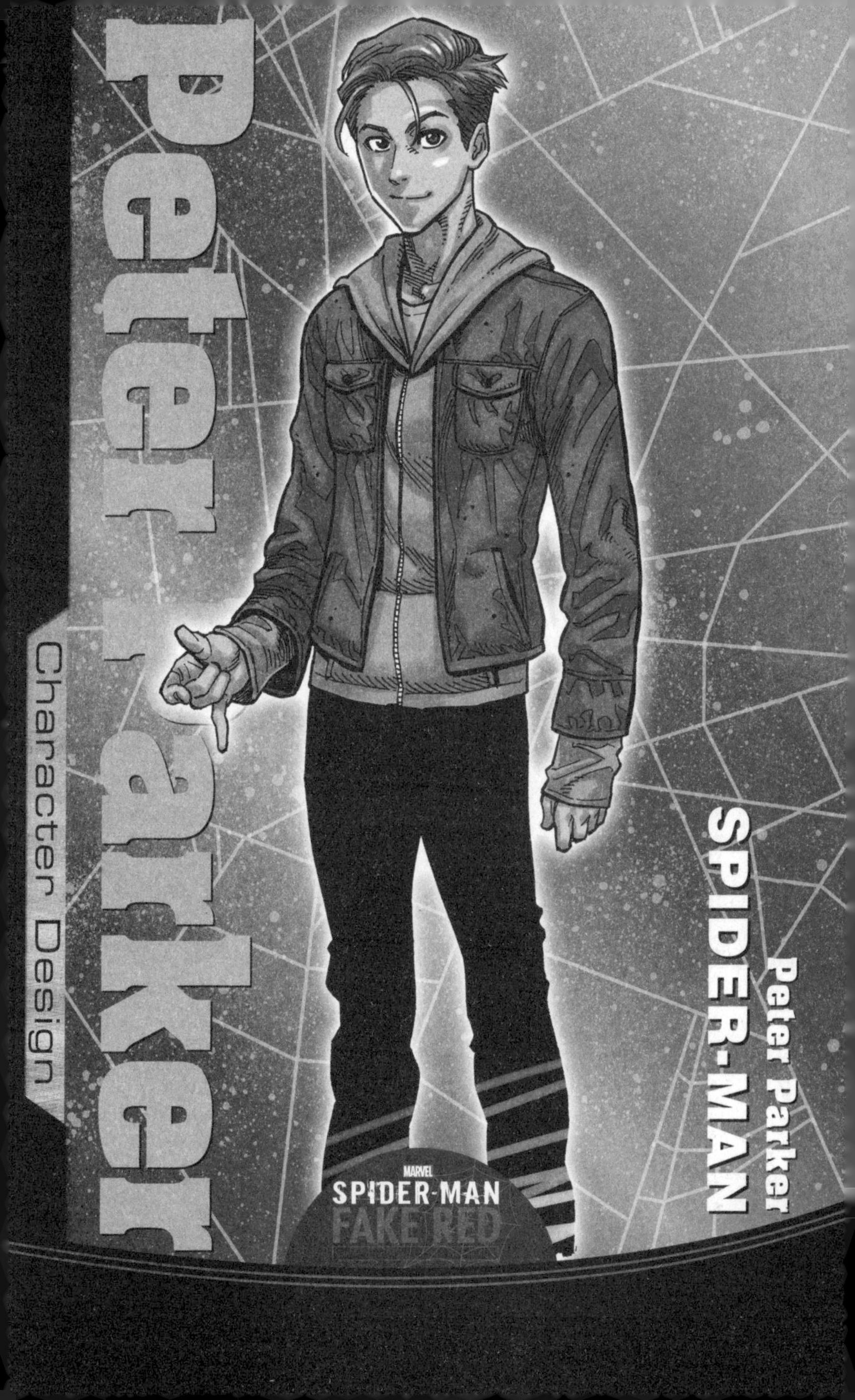
Peter Parker
Character Design
SPIDER-MAN
Peter Parker
MARVEL
SPIDER-MAN
FAKE RED

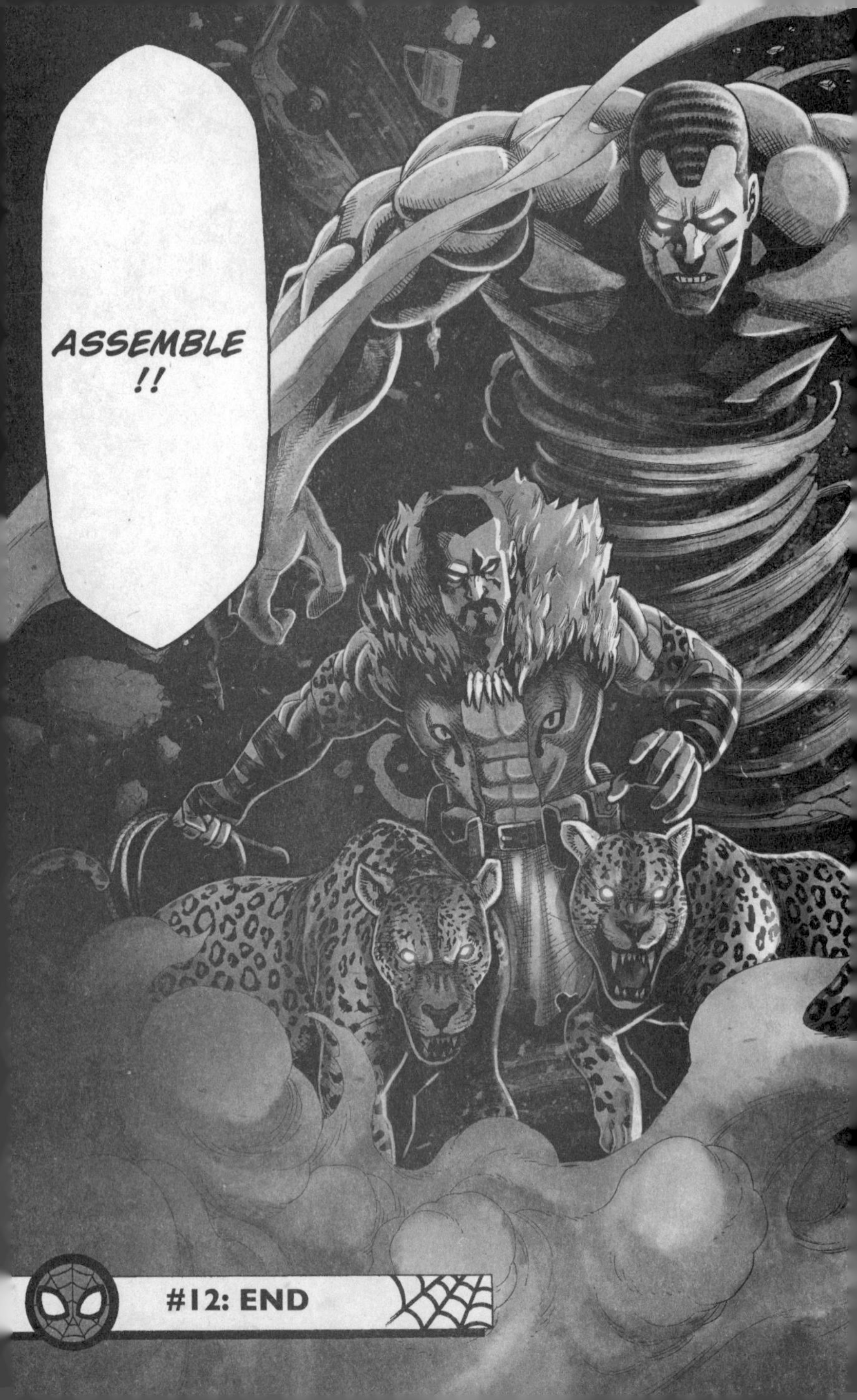
ASSEMBLE !!
#12: END

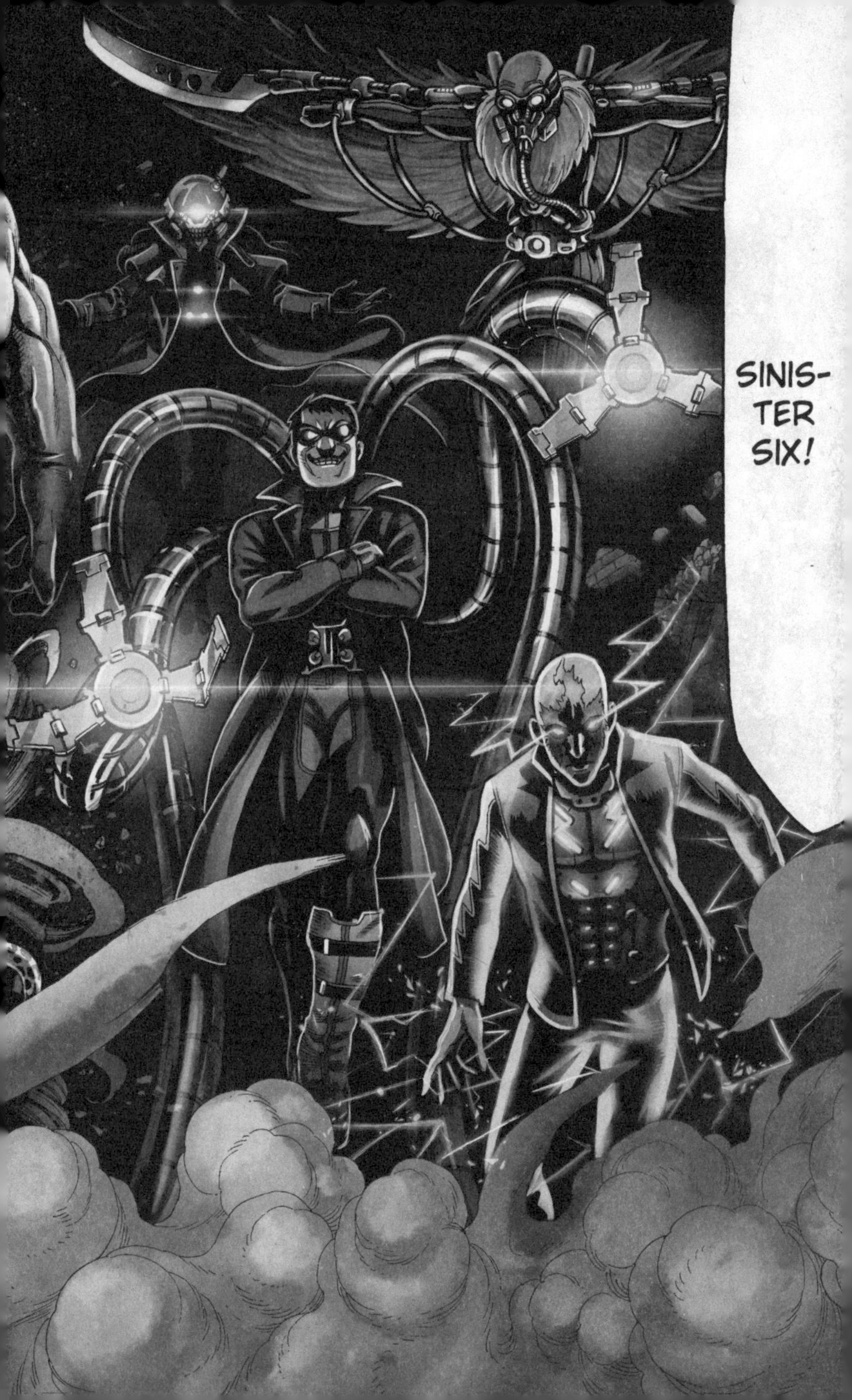
SINIS-
TER
SIX!

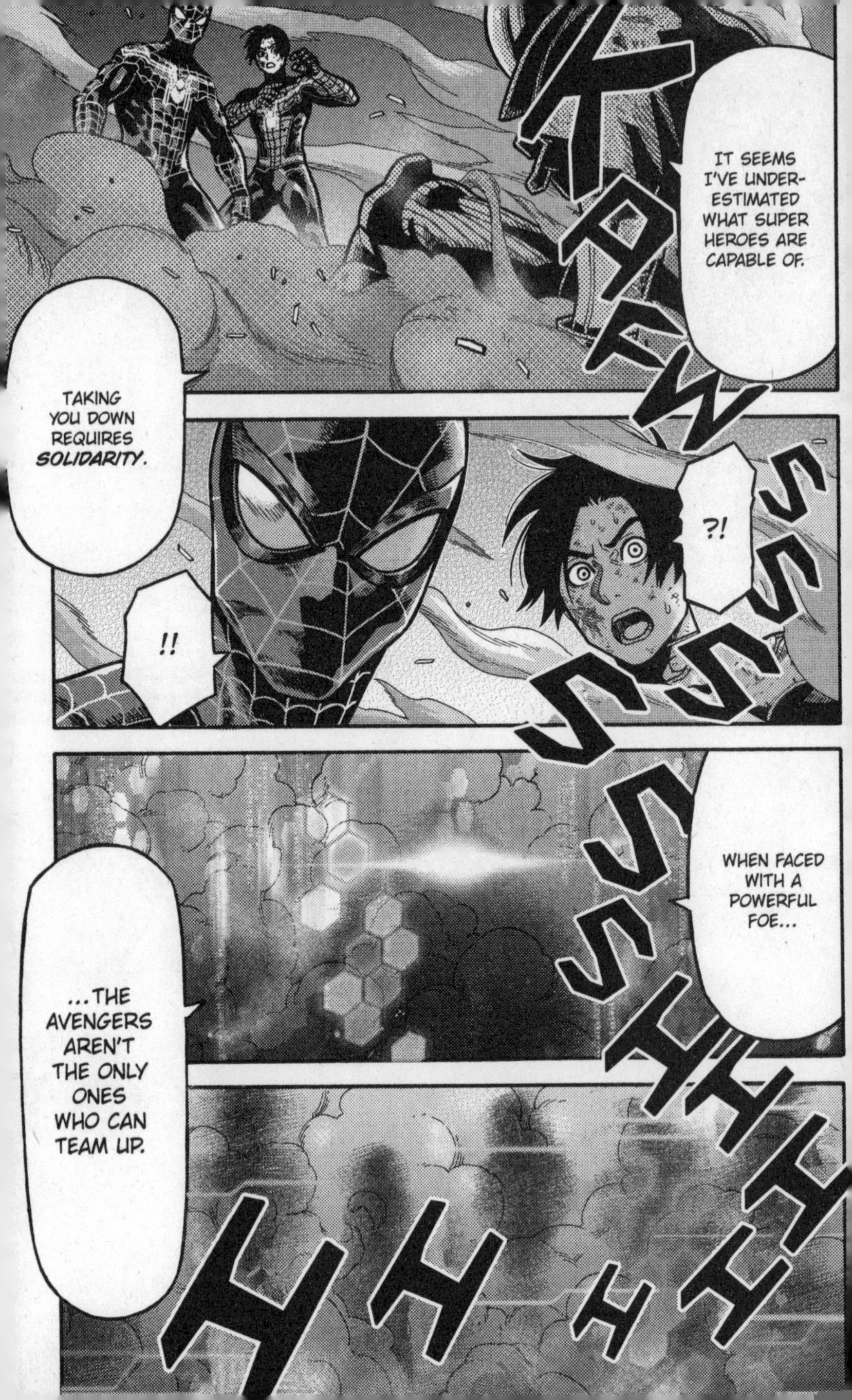
IT SEEMS I'VE UNDER-ESTIMATED WHAT SUPER HEROES ARE CAPABLE OF.
TAKING YOU DOWN REQUIRES *SOLIDARITY*.
?!
!!
WHEN FACED WITH A POWERFUL FOE...
...THE AVENGERS AREN'T THE ONLY ONES WHO CAN TEAM UP.

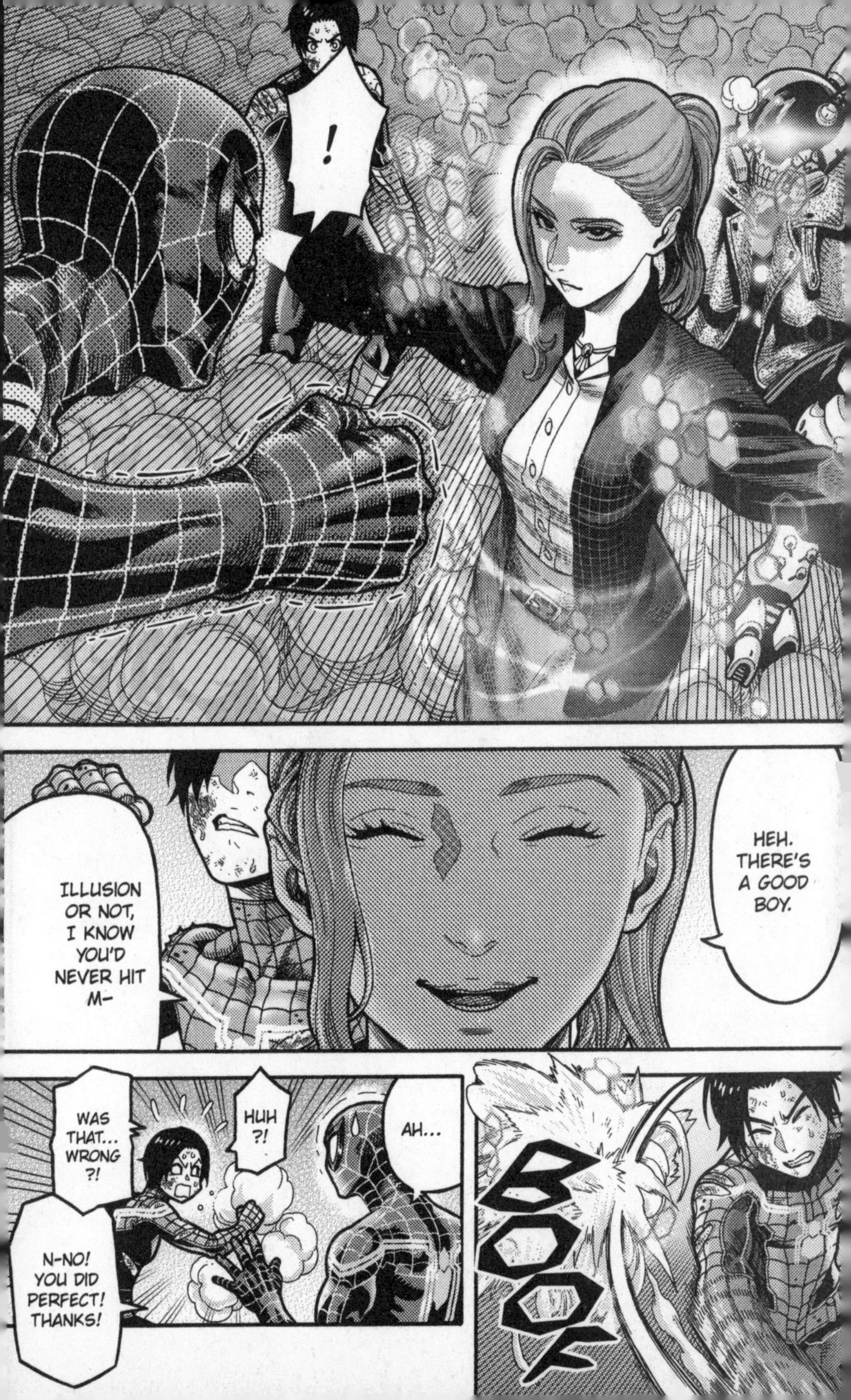
!
HEH. THERE'S A GOOD BOY.
ILLUSION OR NOT, I KNOW YOU'D NEVER HIT M-
BOOF
AH...
HUH ?!
WAS THAT... WRONG ?!
N-NO! YOU DID PERFECT! THANKS!

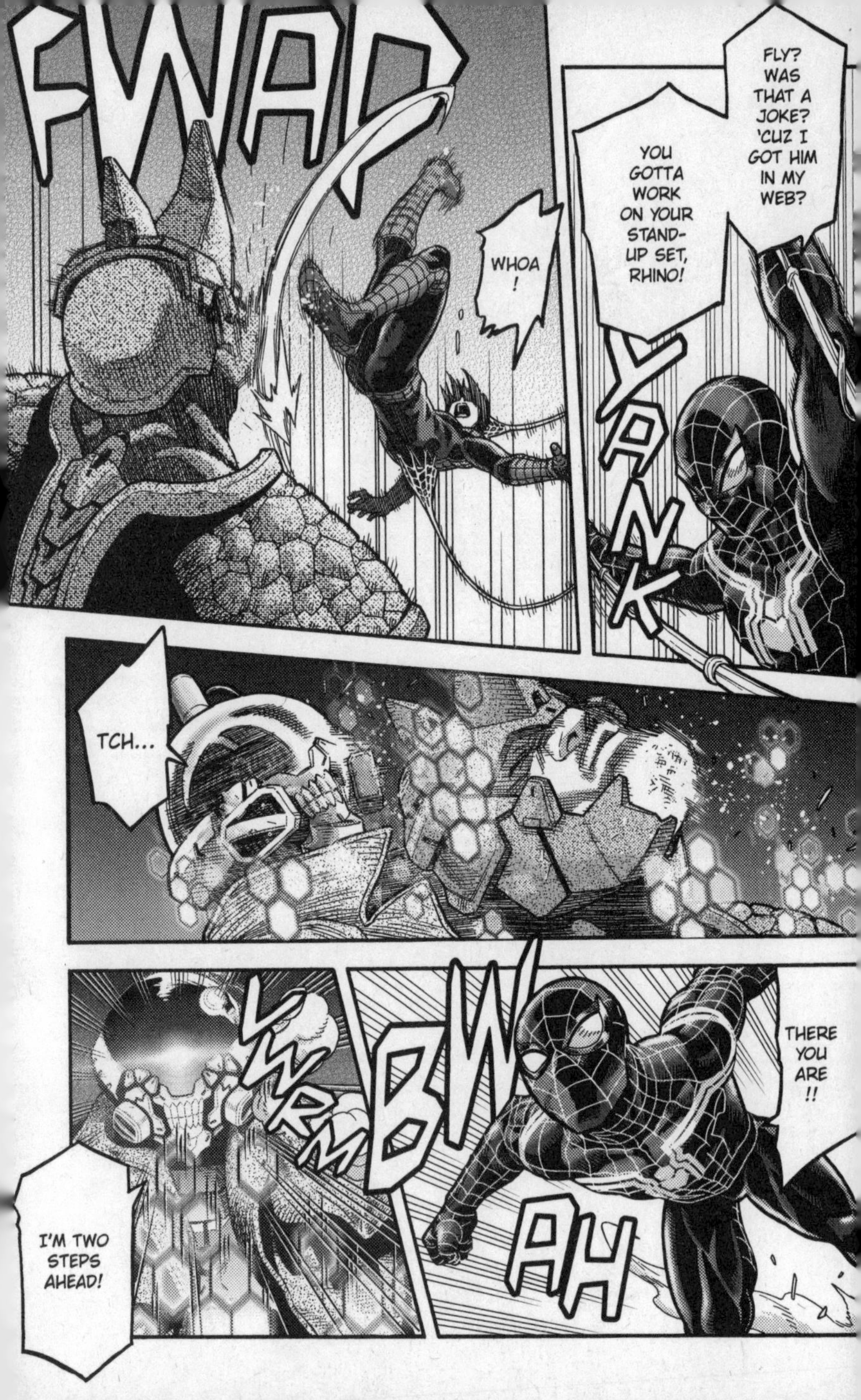
FLY? WAS THAT A JOKE? 'CUZ I GOT HIM IN MY WEB?
YOU GOTTA WORK ON YOUR STAND-UP SET, RHINO!
YANK
FWAP
WHOA!
TCH...
THERE YOU ARE!!
BWAH
VWRM
I'M TWO STEPS AHEAD!

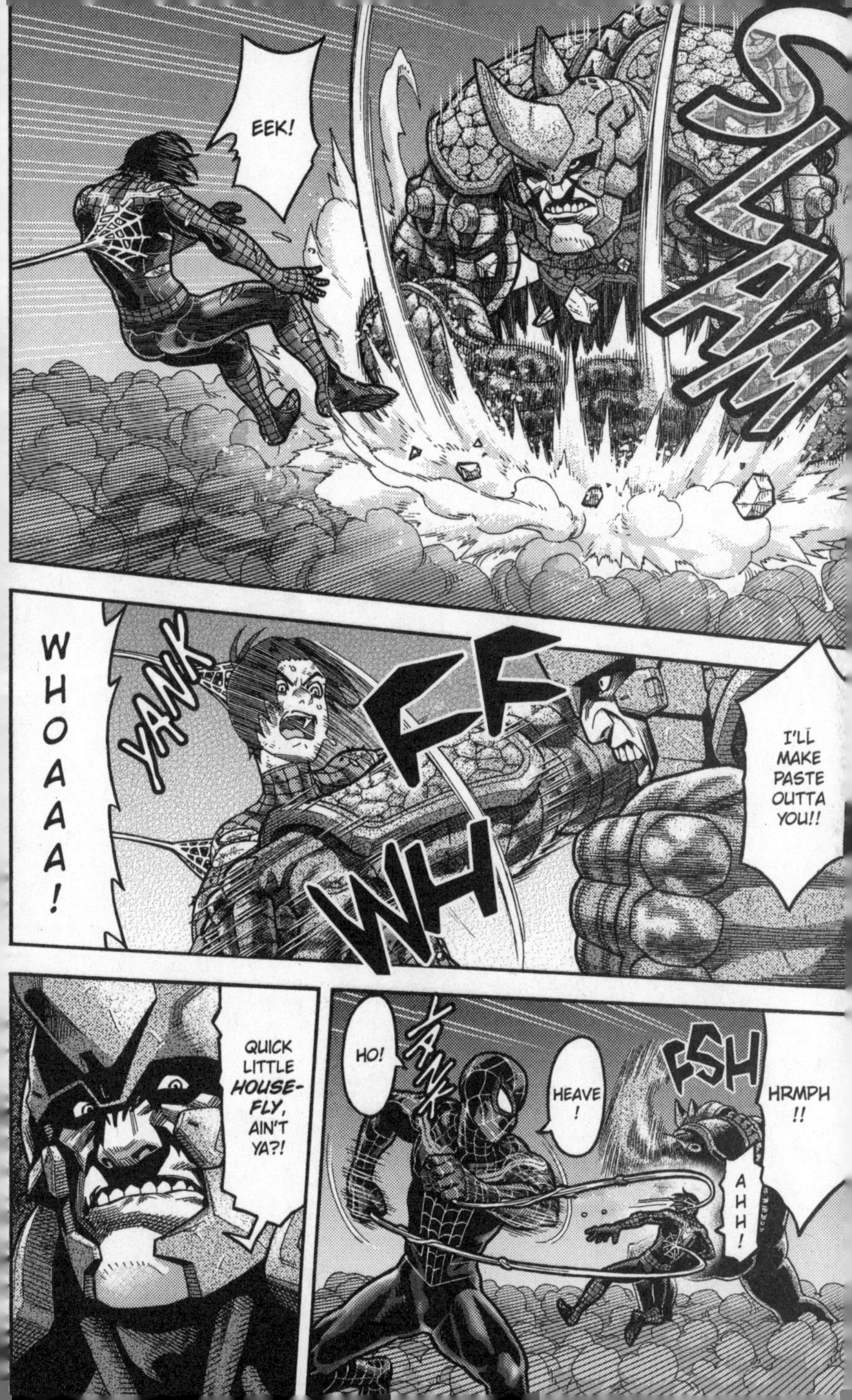
SLAM
EEK!
I'LL MAKE PASTE OUTTA YOU!!
WHFF
YANK
WHOAAAA!
HRMPH!!
FSH
HEAVE!
YANK
HO!
AHH!
QUICK LITTLE **HOUSE-FLY**, AIN'T YA?!

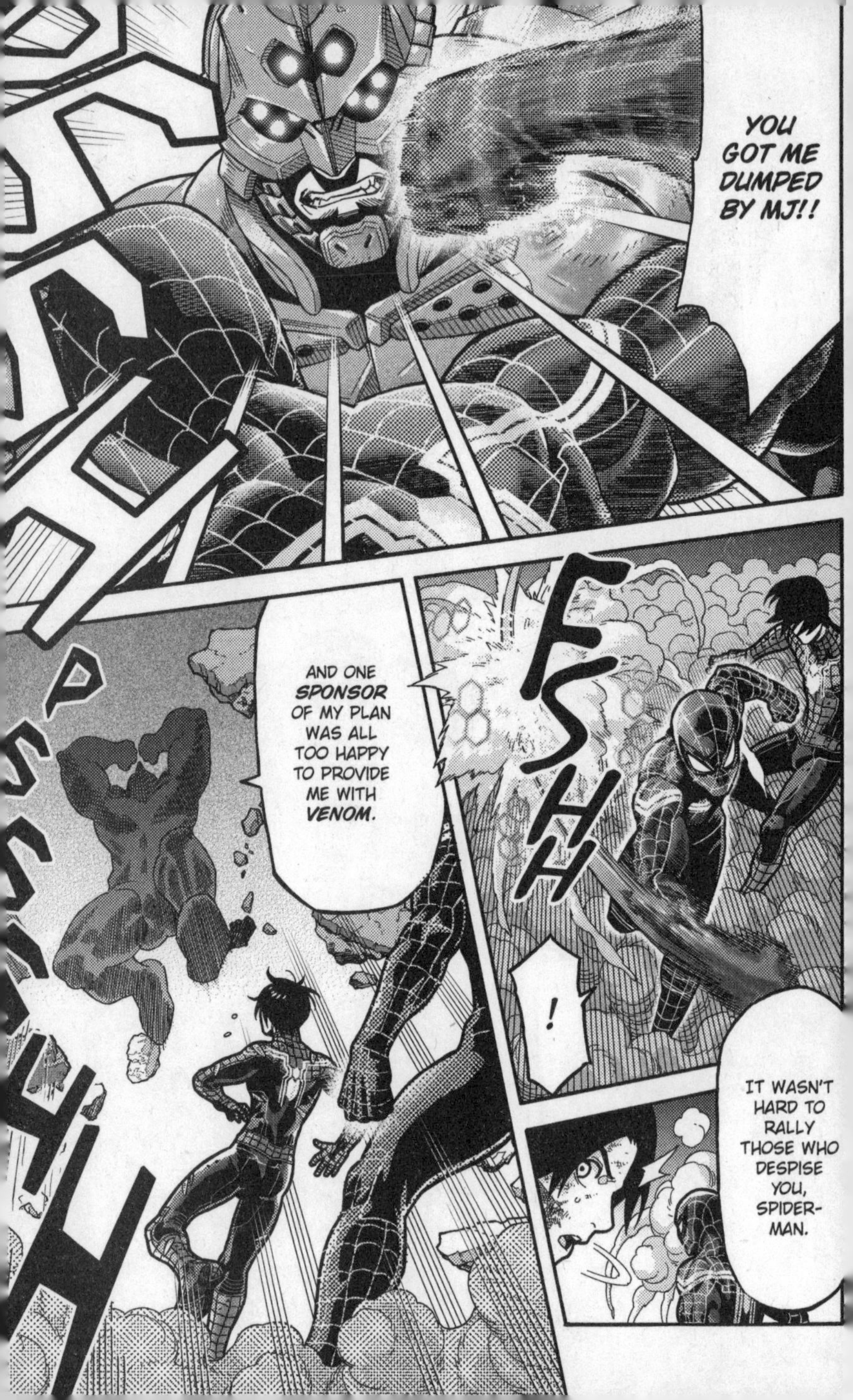
YOU GOT ME DUMPED BY MJ!!
FSHH
!
IT WASN'T HARD TO RALLY THOSE WHO DESPISE YOU, SPIDER-MAN.
AND ONE *SPONSOR* OF MY PLAN WAS ALL TOO HAPPY TO PROVIDE ME WITH *VENOM*.

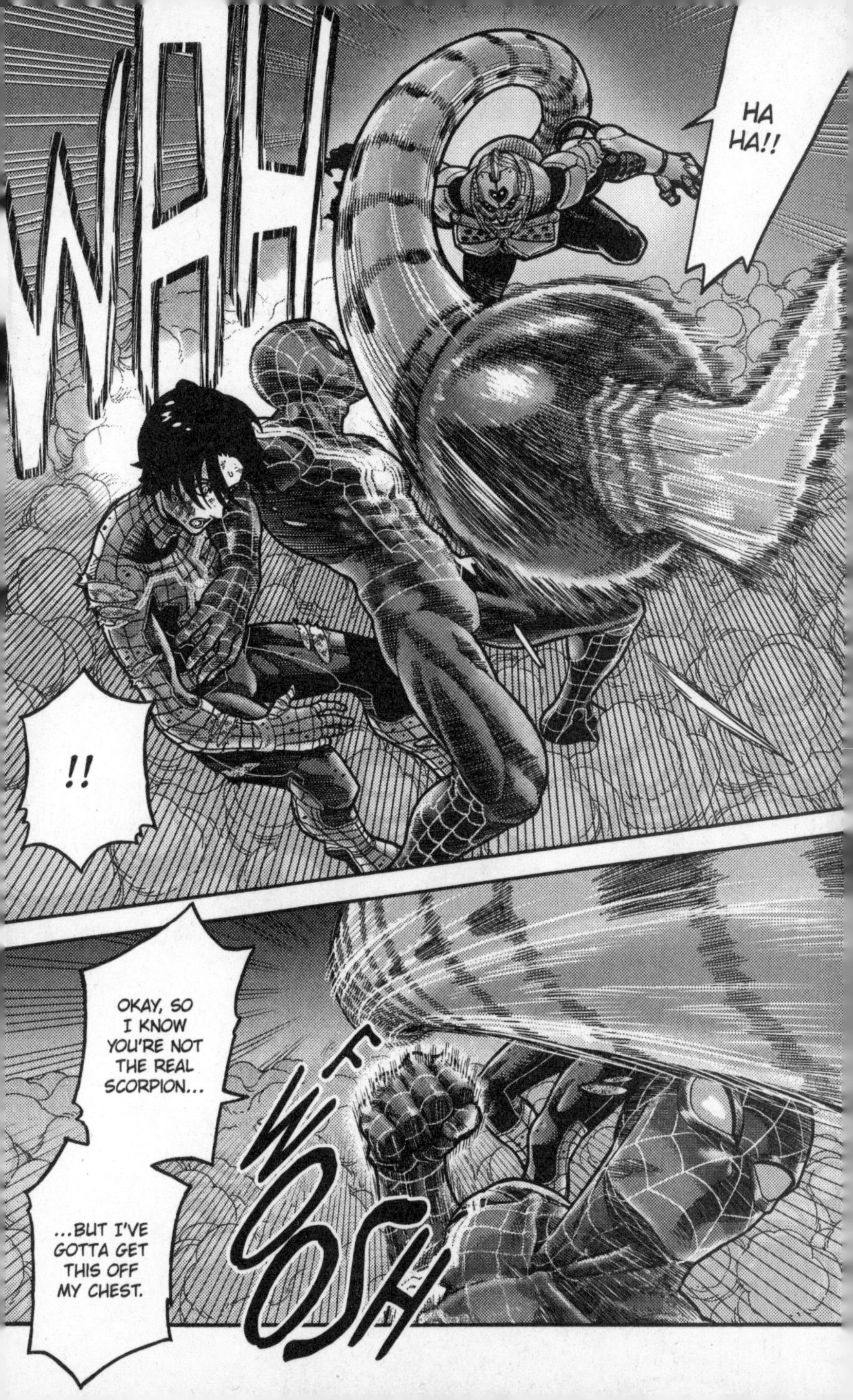
HA HA!!
!!
OKAY, SO I KNOW YOU'RE NOT THE REAL SCORPION...
FWOOSH
...BUT I'VE GOTTA GET THIS OFF MY CHEST.

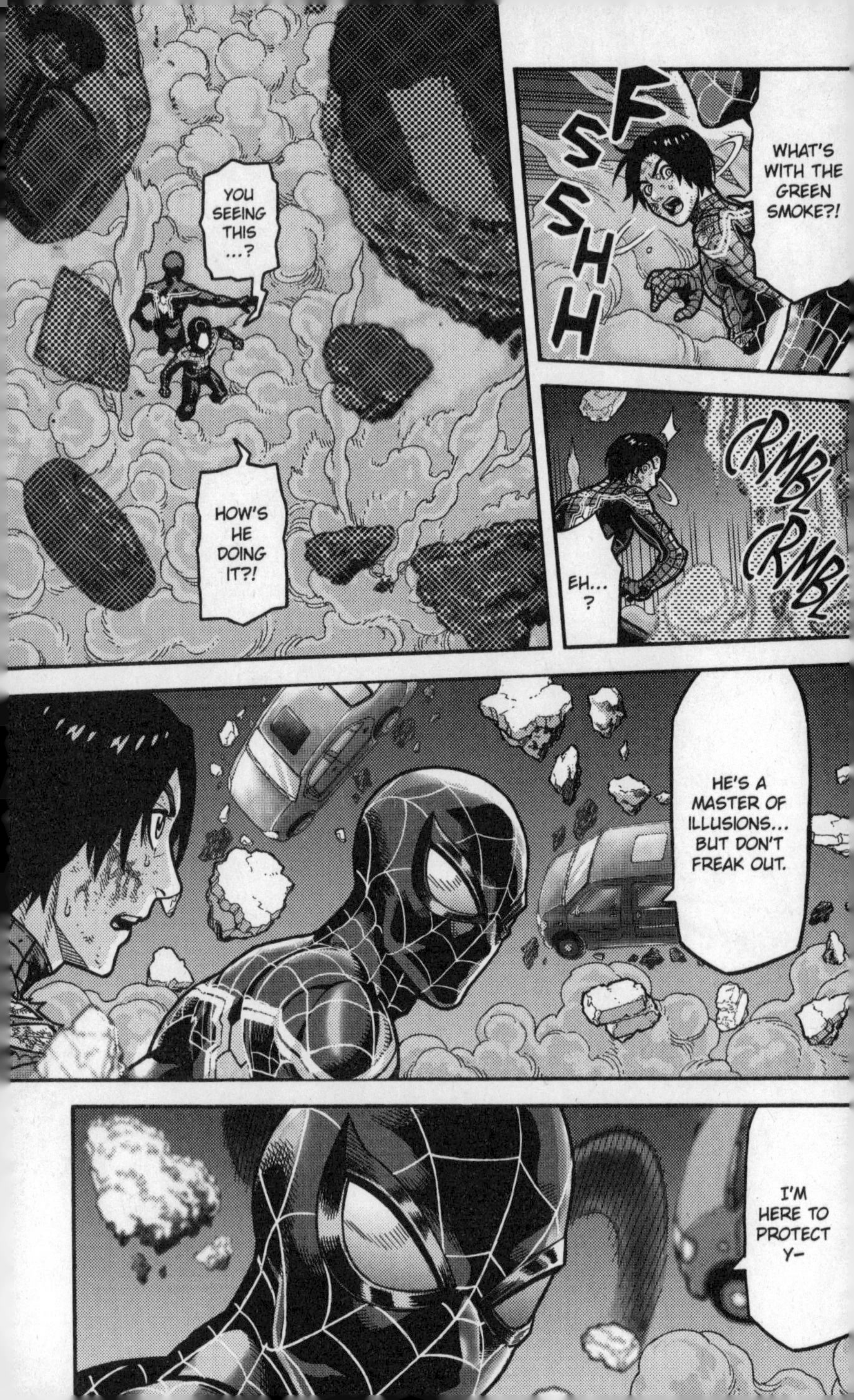
FSSHH
WHAT'S WITH THE GREEN SMOKE?!
CRMBL CRMBL
EH... ?
YOU SEEING THIS ...?
HOW'S HE DOING IT?!
HE'S A MASTER OF ILLUSIONS... BUT DON'T FREAK OUT.
I'M HERE TO PROTECT Y-

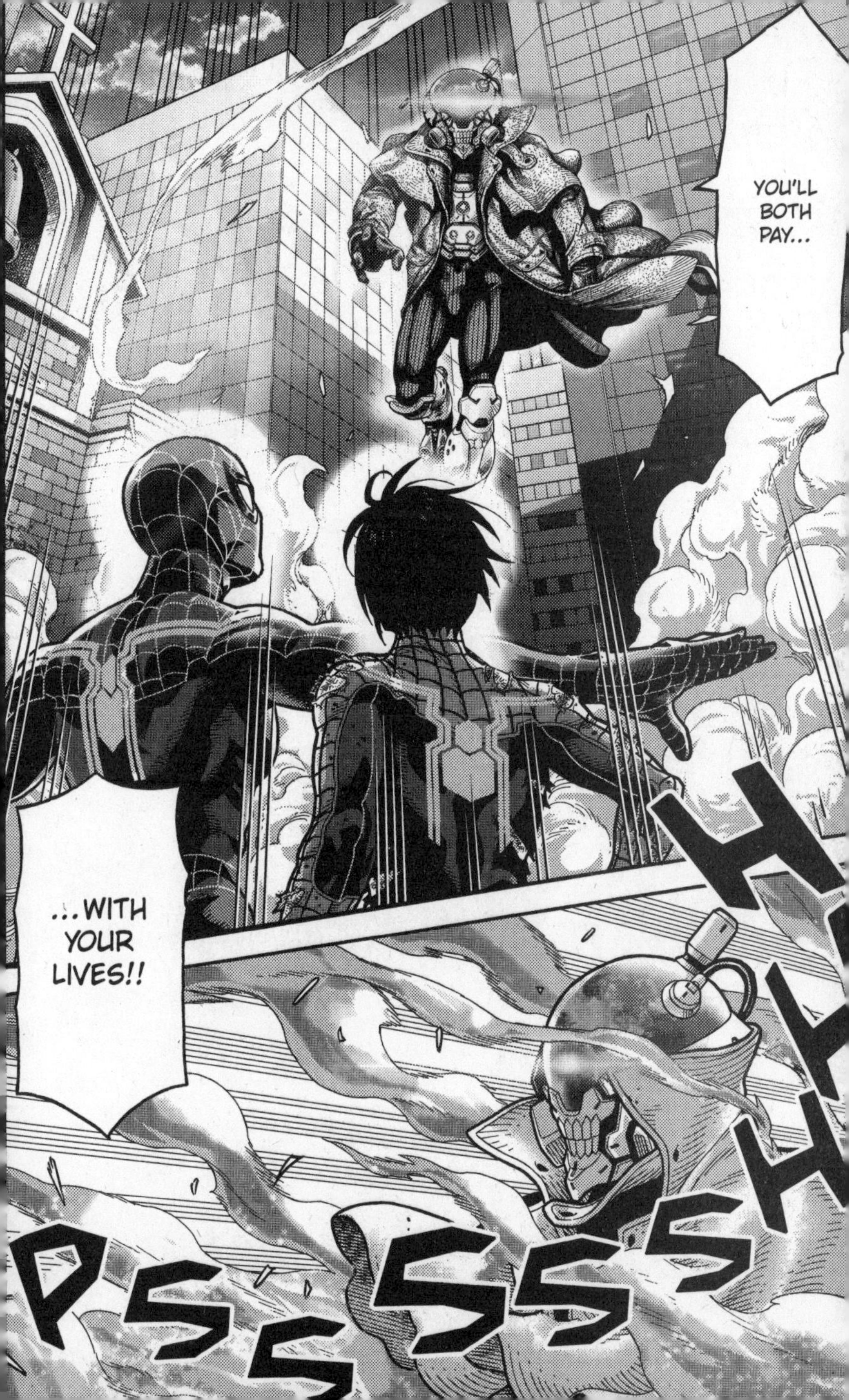
YOU'LL BOTH PAY...
...WITH YOUR LIVES!!
PSSSSSHH

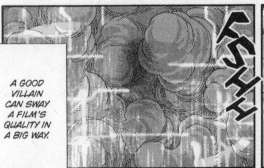

A GOOD VILLAIN CAN SWAY A FILM'S QUALITY IN A BIG WAY.

SO YOU'RE GOING TO PLAY THAT PART, PETER PARKER...

...WHETHER YOU LIKE IT OR NOT.

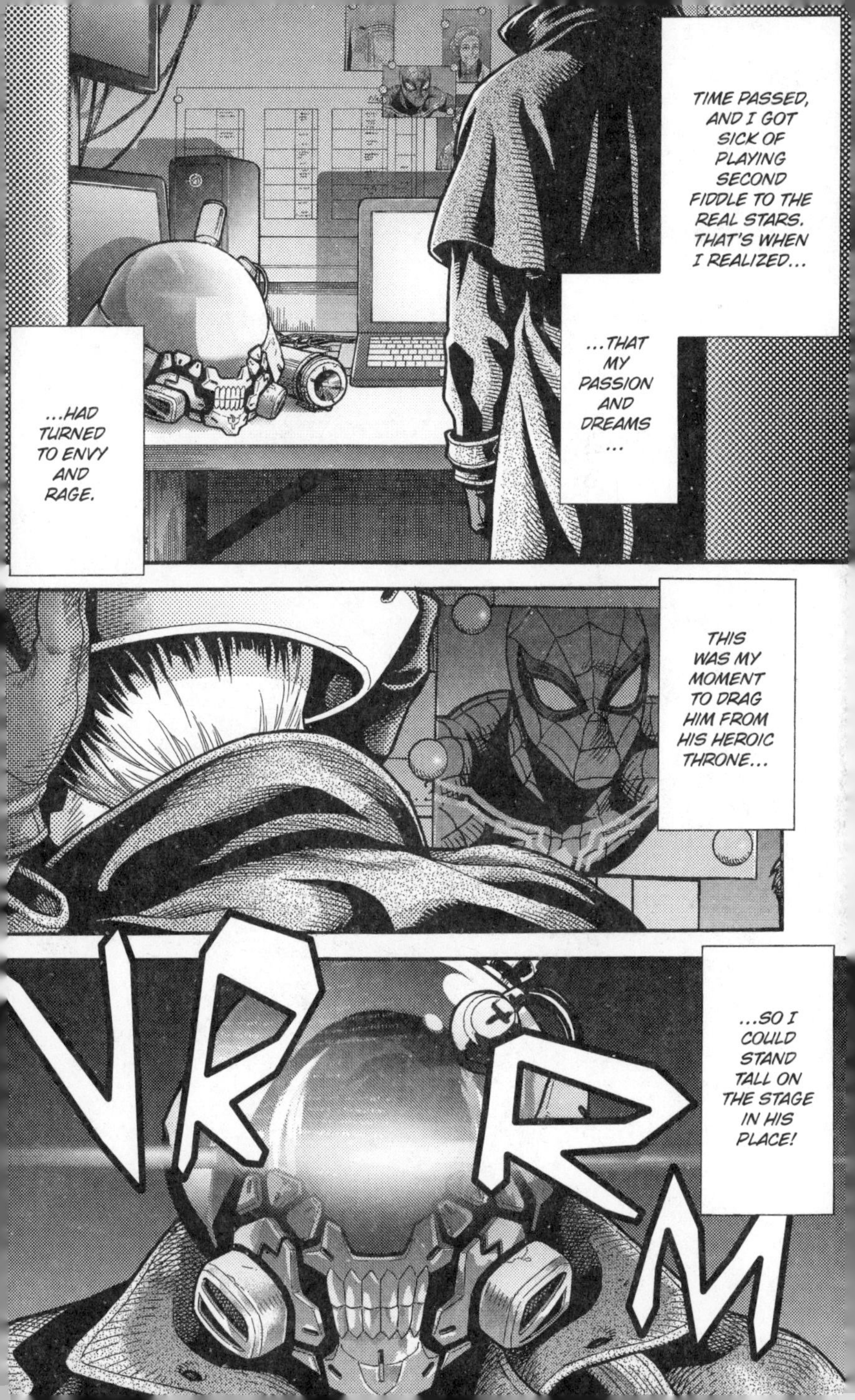
TIME PASSED, AND I GOT SICK OF PLAYING SECOND FIDDLE TO THE REAL STARS. THAT'S WHEN I REALIZED...
...THAT MY PASSION AND DREAMS ...
...HAD TURNED TO ENVY AND RAGE.
THIS WAS MY MOMENT TO DRAG HIM FROM HIS HEROIC THRONE...
...SO I COULD STAND TALL ON THE STAGE IN HIS PLACE!
VRRM

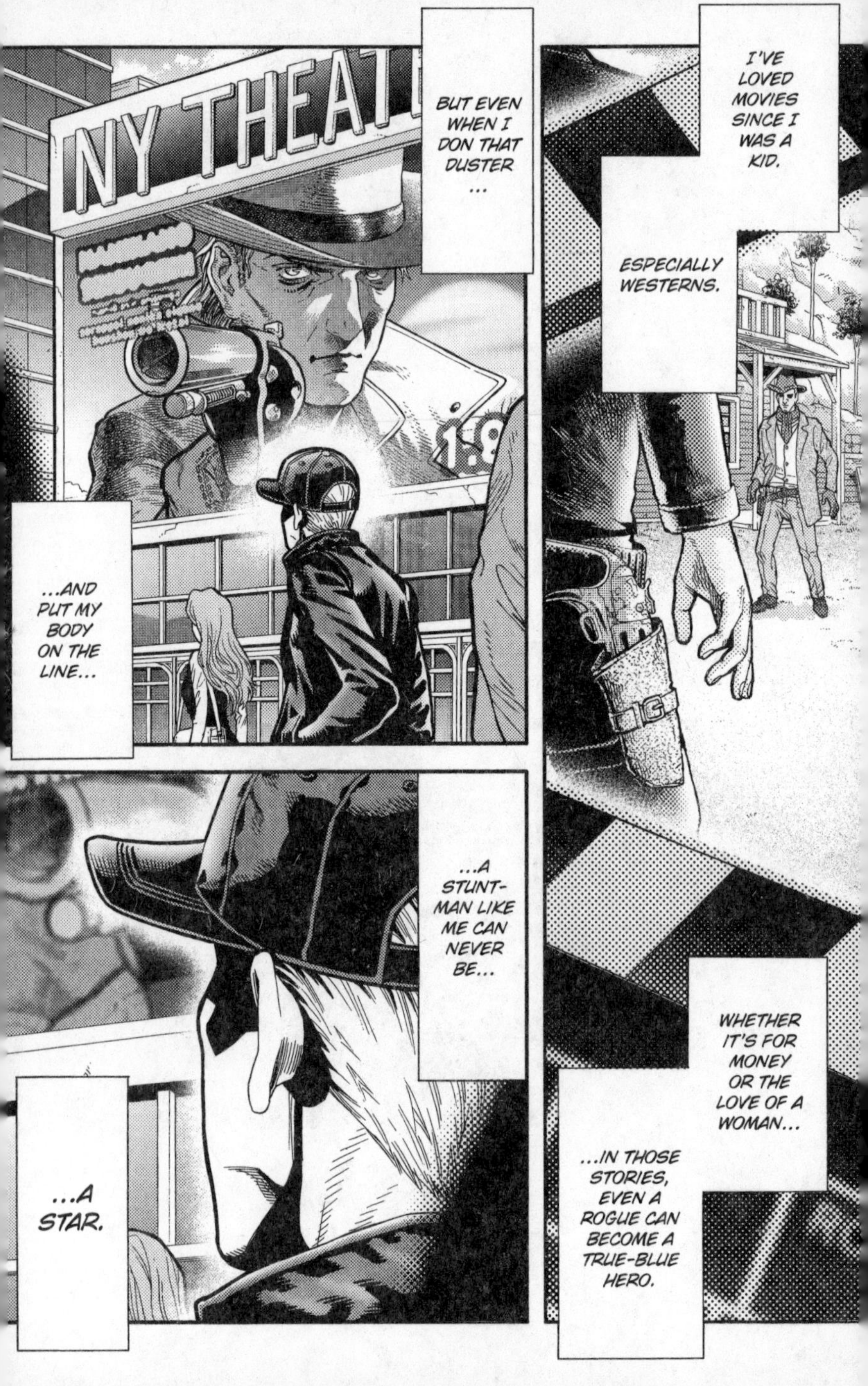
I'VE LOVED MOVIES SINCE I WAS A KID.
ESPECIALLY WESTERNS.
WHETHER IT'S FOR MONEY OR THE LOVE OF A WOMAN...
...IN THOSE STORIES, EVEN A ROGUE CAN BECOME A TRUE-BLUE HERO.
NY THEAT
BUT EVEN WHEN I DON THAT DUSTER ...
...AND PUT MY BODY ON THE LINE...
...A STUNT-MAN LIKE ME CAN NEVER BE...
...A STAR.

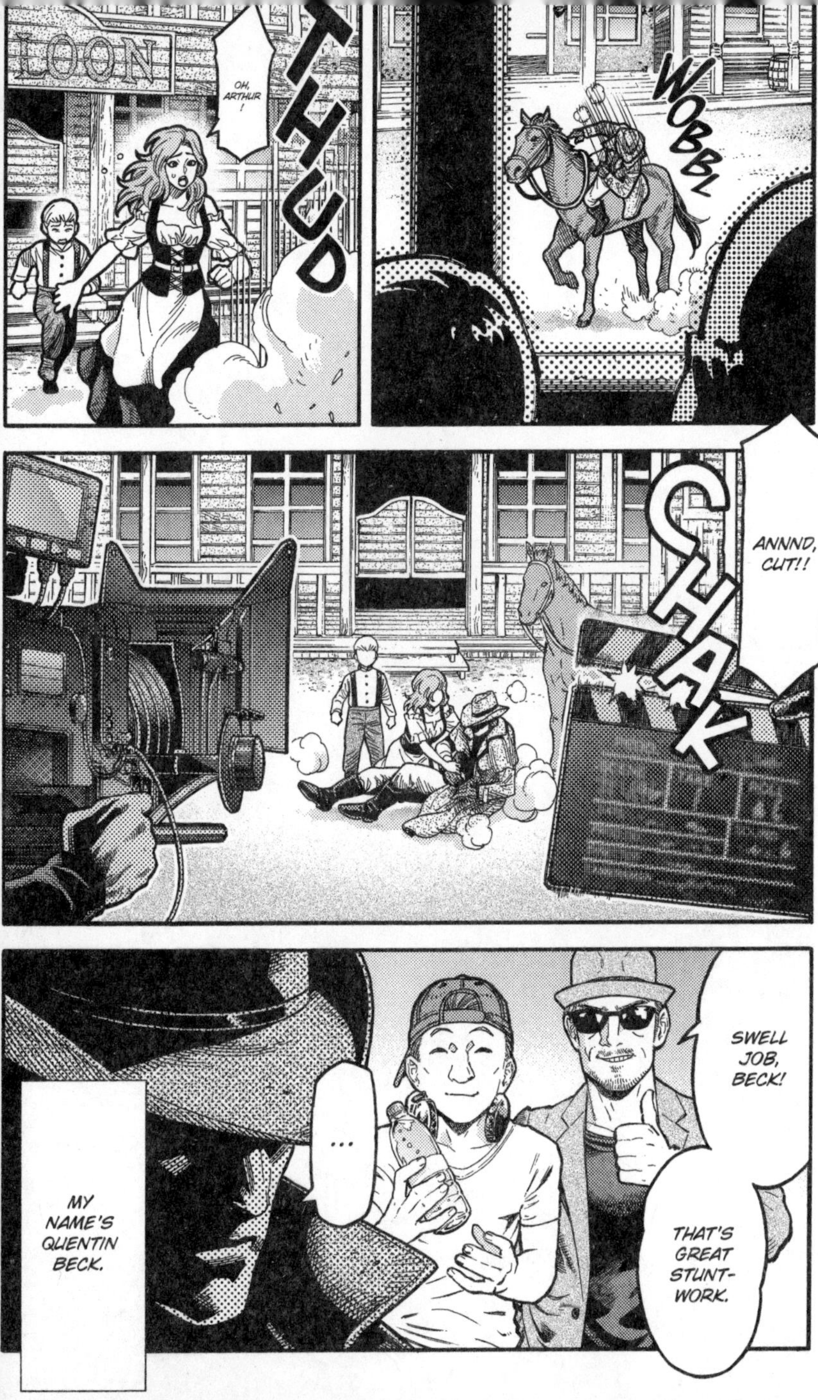
WOBBBL
THUD
OH, ARTHUR!
LOON
ANNND, CUT!!
CHAK
SWELL JOB, BECK!
THAT'S GREAT STUNT-WORK.
...
MY NAME'S QUENTIN BECK.

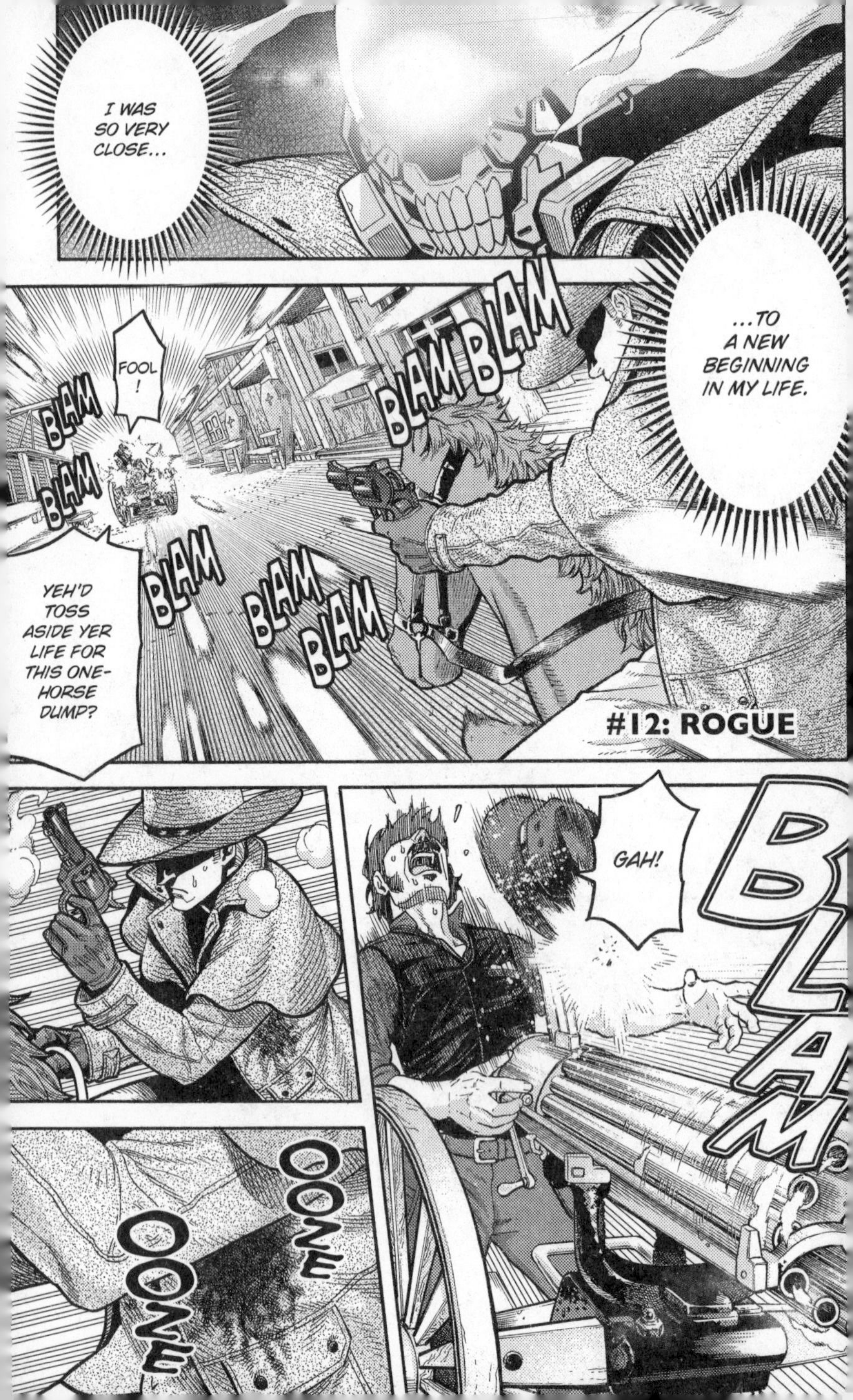
I WAS SO VERY CLOSE...
...TO A NEW BEGINNING IN MY LIFE.
BLAM BLAM
FOOL!
BLAM BLAM
YEH'D TOSS ASIDE YER LIFE FOR THIS ONE-HORSE DUMP?
BLAM
BLAM BLAM
#12: ROGUE
BLAM
GAH!
OOZE
OOZE

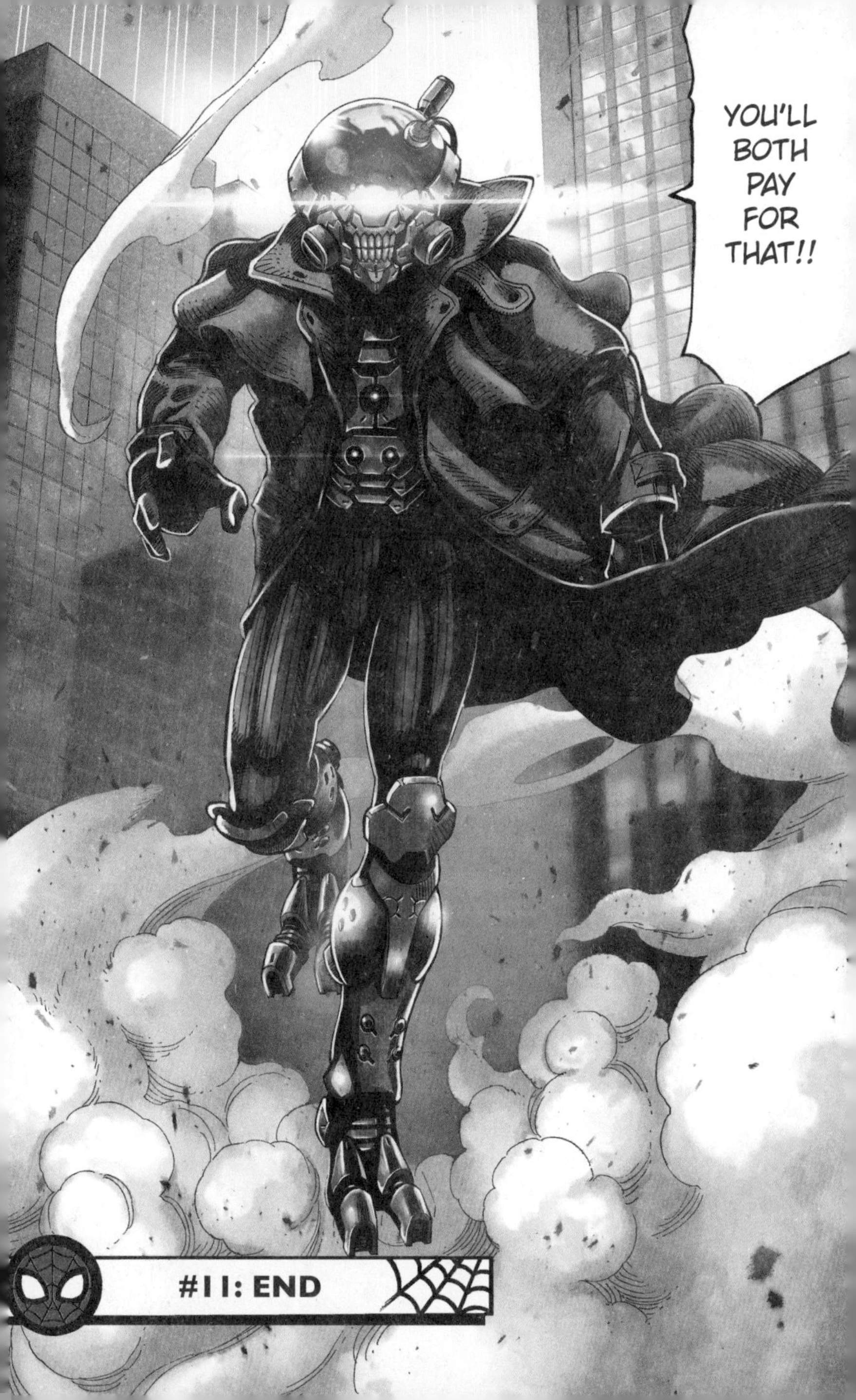
YOU'LL BOTH PAY FOR THAT!!
#11: END

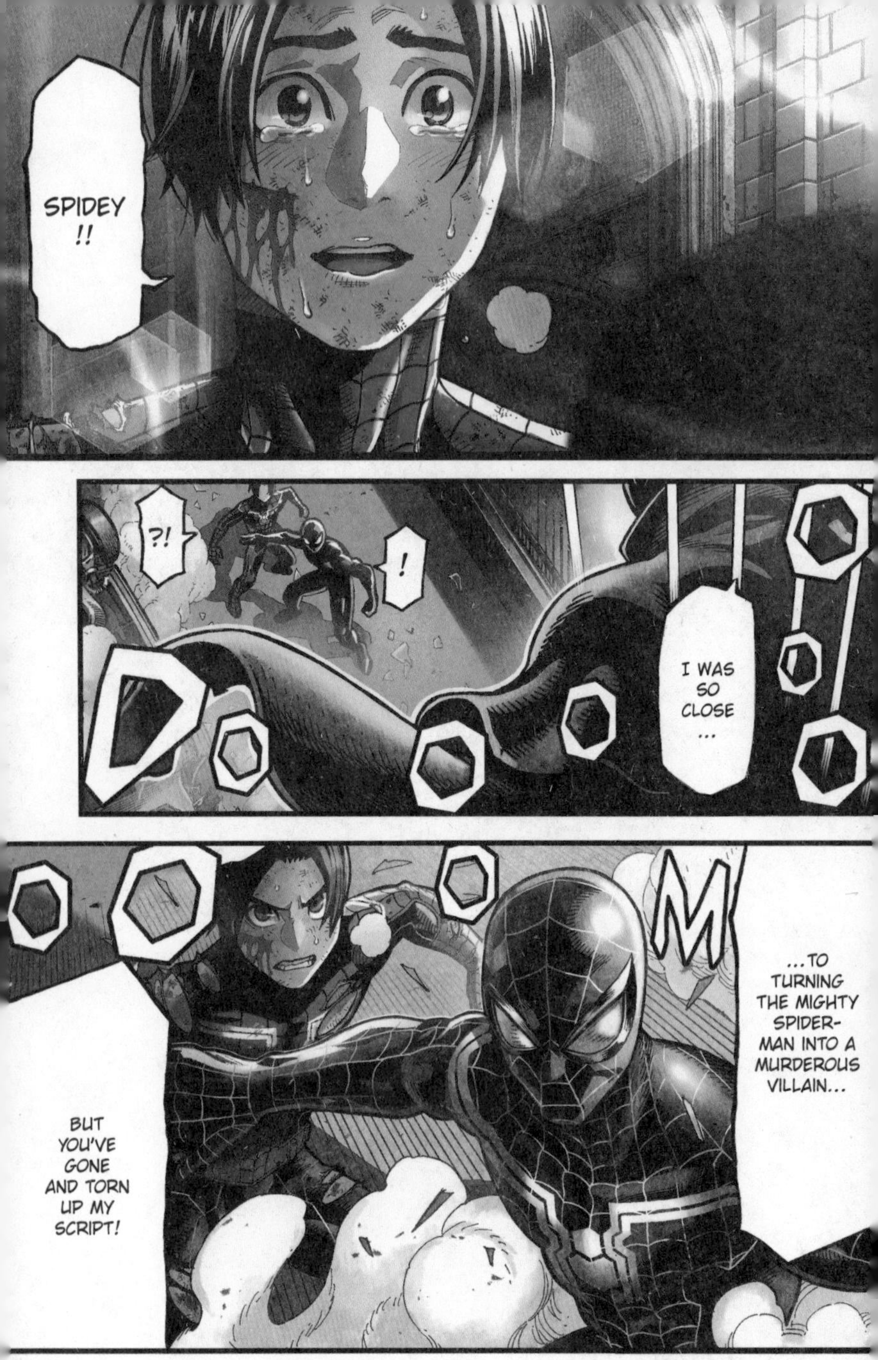
SPIDEY !!
I WAS SO CLOSE ...
!
?!
DOOOOOO
OOOM
...TO TURNING THE MIGHTY SPIDER-MAN INTO A MURDEROUS VILLAIN...
BUT YOU'VE GONE AND TORN UP MY SCRIPT!

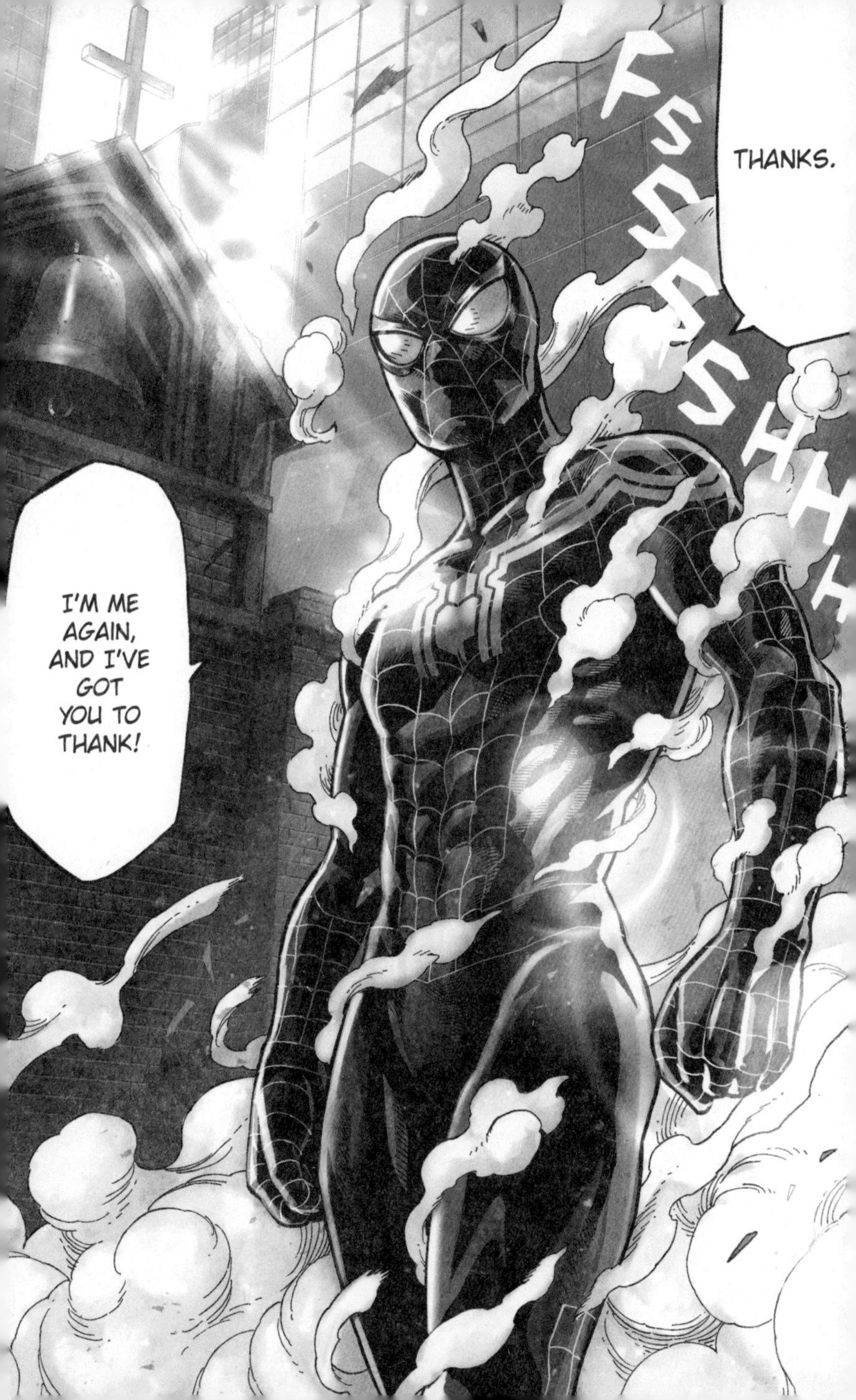
THANKS.
KSSSSHHHH
I'M ME AGAIN, AND I'VE GOT YOU TO THANK!

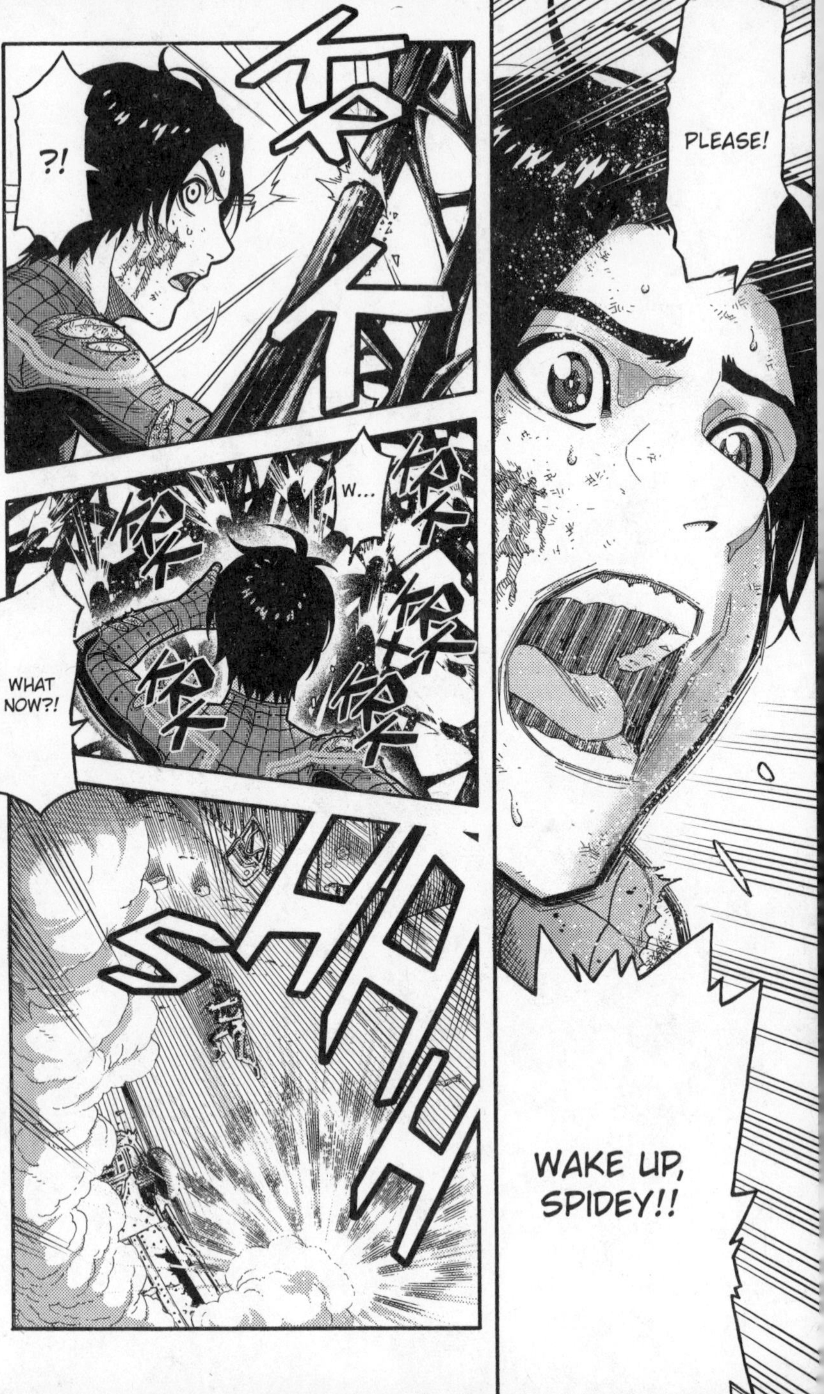
PLEASE!
WAKE UP, SPIDEY!!
?!
W...
WHAT NOW?!

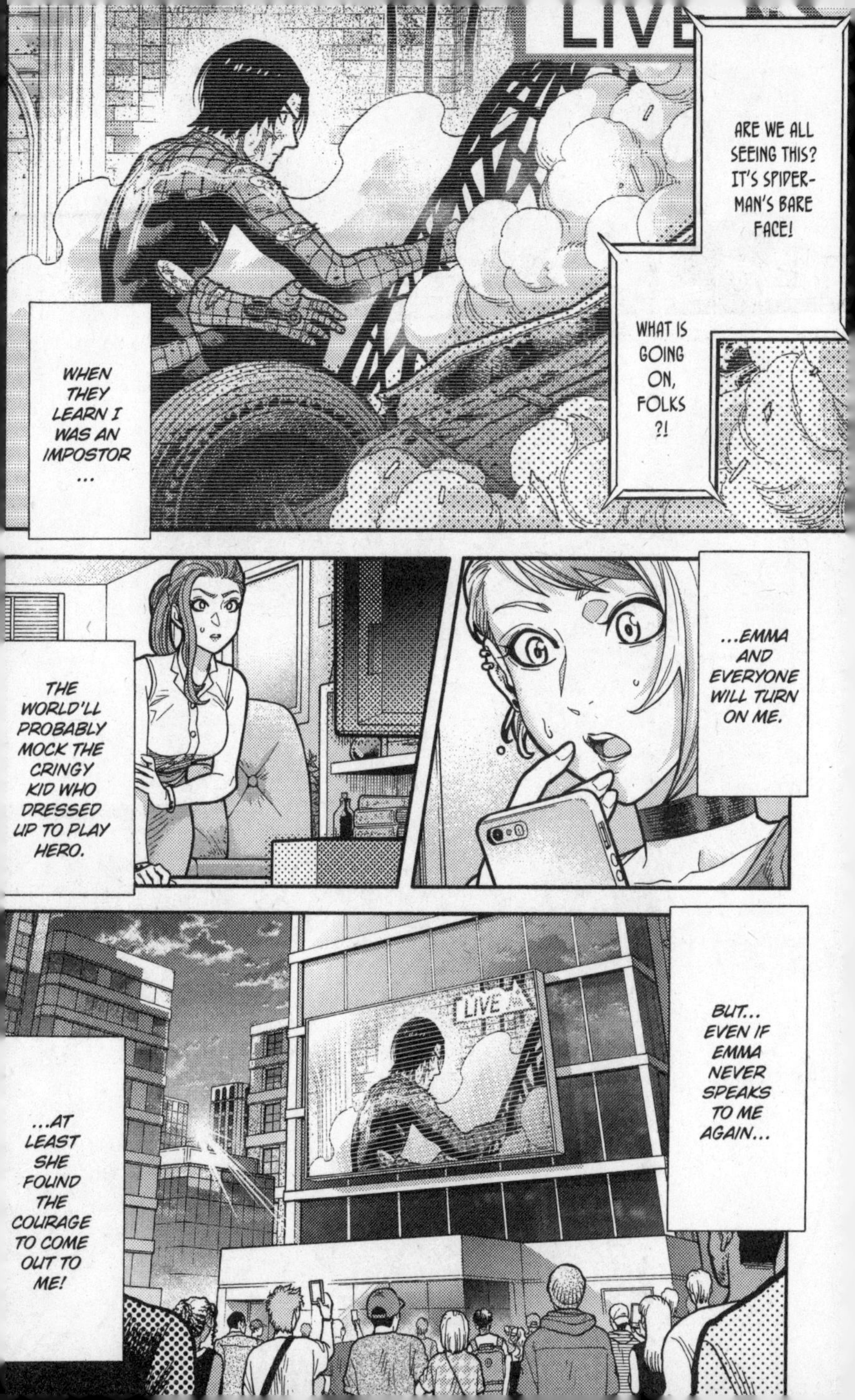
LIVE
ARE WE ALL SEEING THIS? IT'S SPIDER-MAN'S BARE FACE!
WHAT IS GOING ON, FOLKS?!
WHEN THEY LEARN I WAS AN IMPOSTOR...
...EMMA AND EVERYONE WILL TURN ON ME.
THE WORLD'LL PROBABLY MOCK THE CRINGY KID WHO DRESSED UP TO PLAY HERO.
BUT... EVEN IF EMMA NEVER SPEAKS TO ME AGAIN...
LIVE
...AT LEAST SHE FOUND THE COURAGE TO COME OUT TO ME!

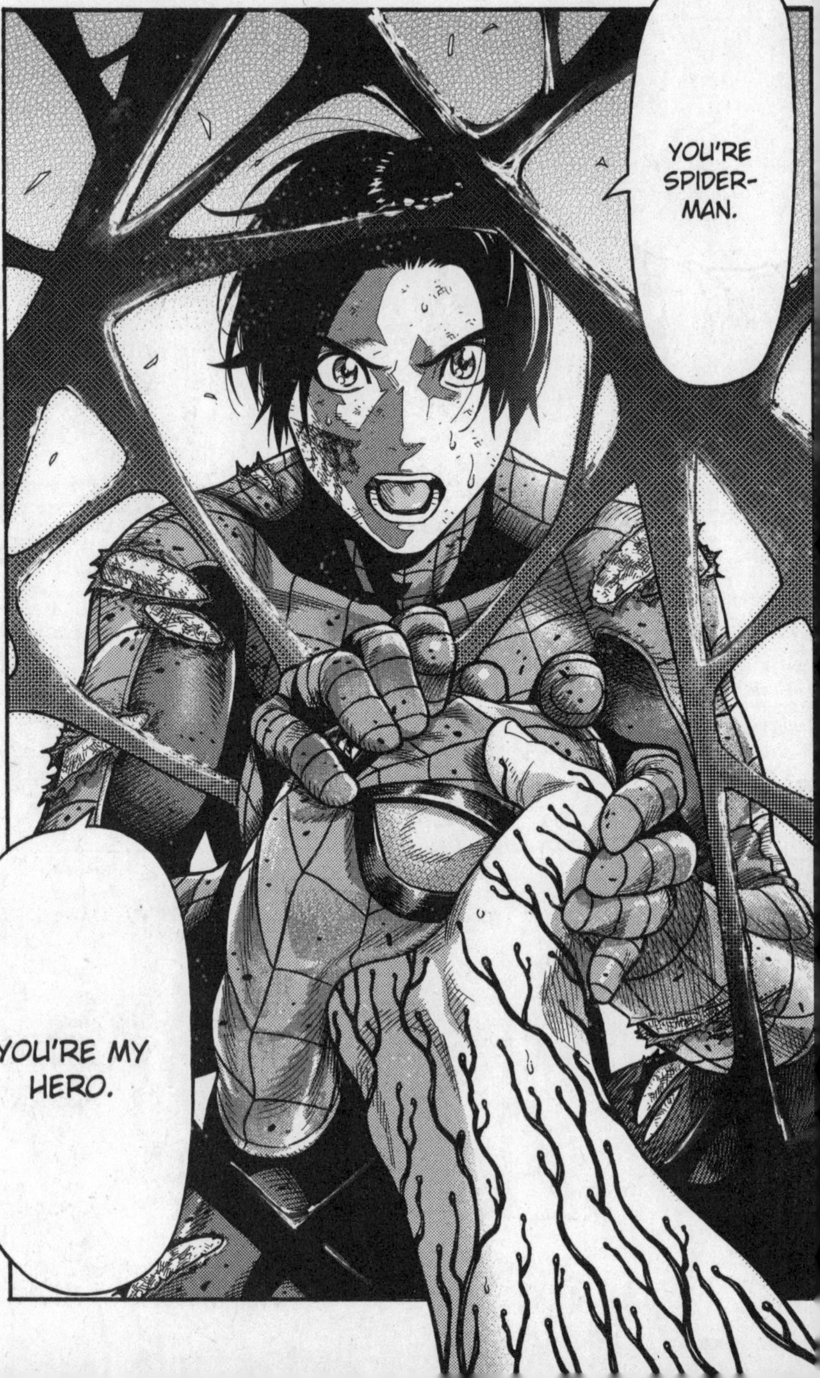
YOU'RE SPIDER-MAN.
YOU'RE MY HERO.

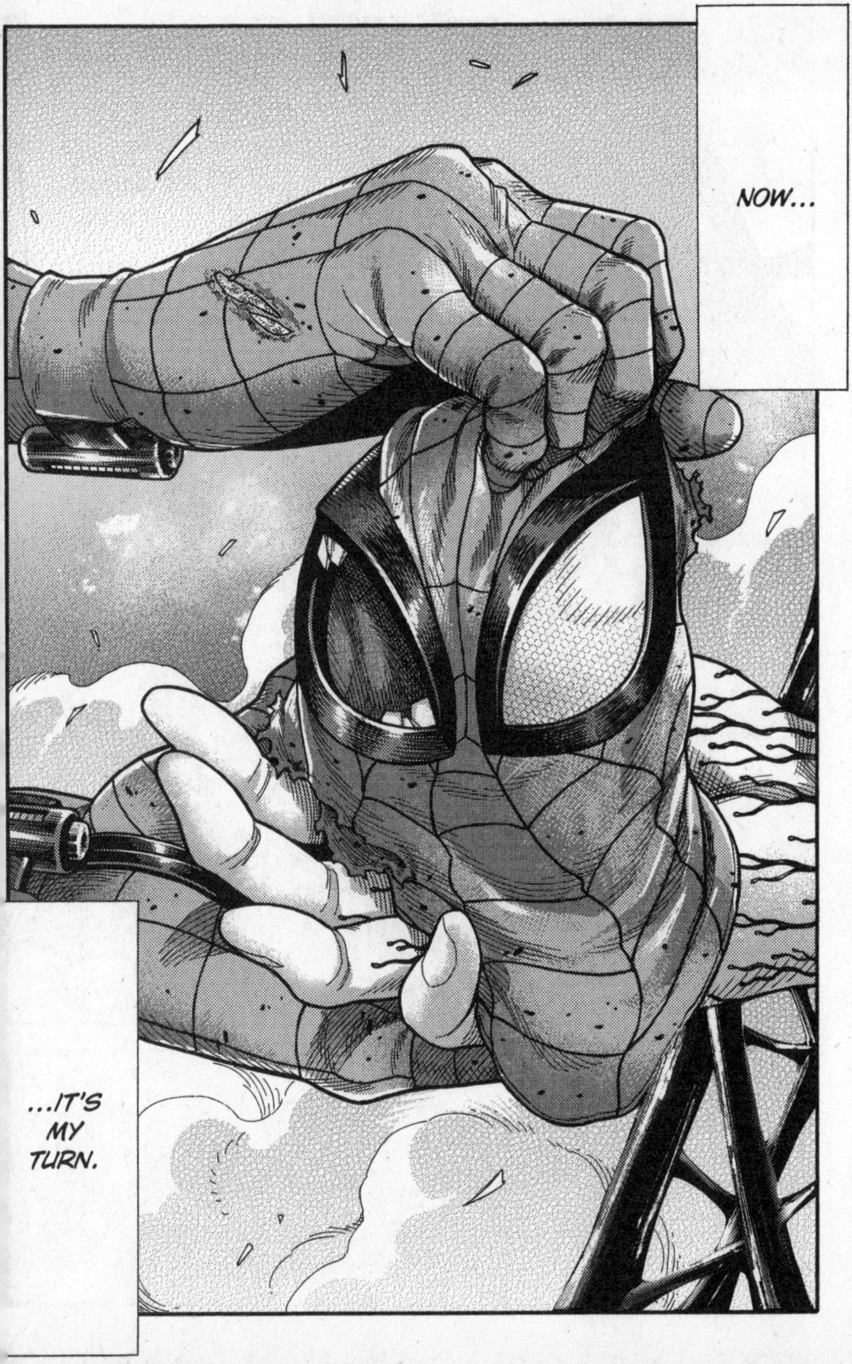
NOW...
...IT'S MY TURN.

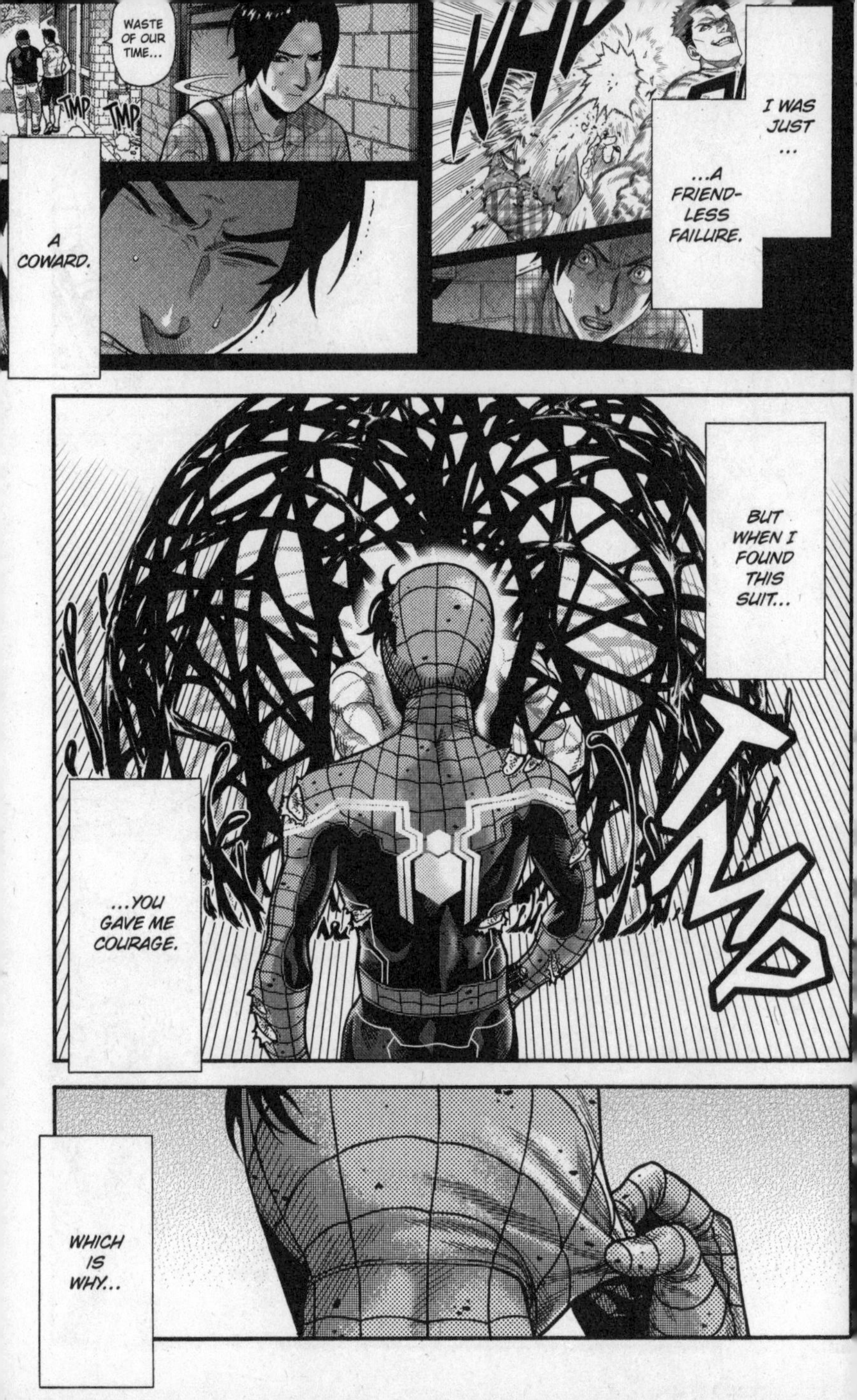
KH
I WAS JUST...
...A FRIEND-LESS FAILURE.
WASTE OF OUR TIME...
TMP
TMP
A COWARD.
BUT WHEN I FOUND THIS SUIT...
TMP
...YOU GAVE ME COURAGE.
WHICH IS WHY...

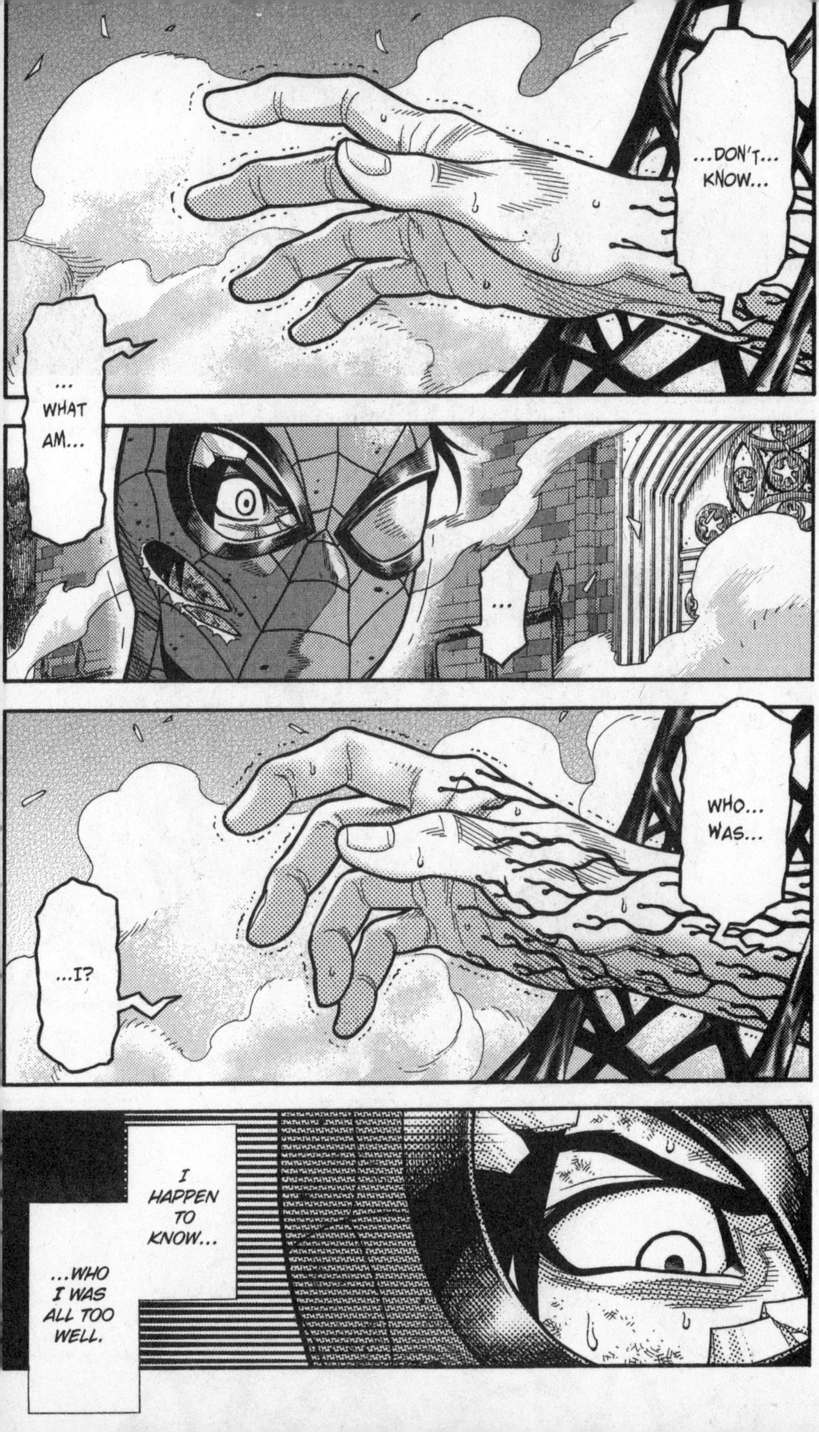
...DON'T... KNOW...
... WHAT AM...
...
WHO... WAS...
...I?
I HAPPEN TO KNOW...
...WHO I WAS ALL TOO WELL.

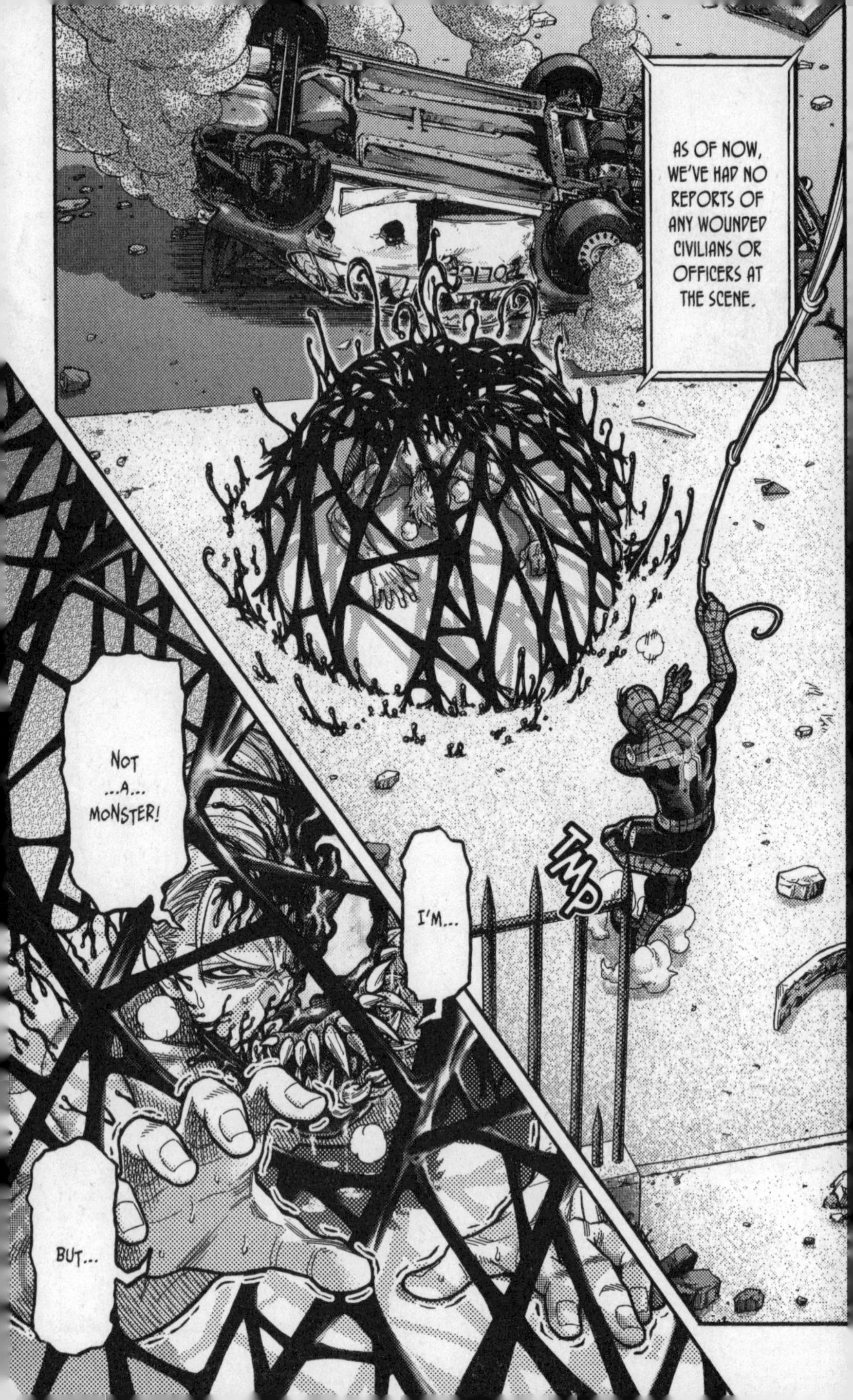
AS OF NOW, WE'VE HAD NO REPORTS OF ANY WOUNDED CIVILIANS OR OFFICERS AT THE SCENE.
TMP
I'M...
NOT ...A... MONSTER!
BUT...

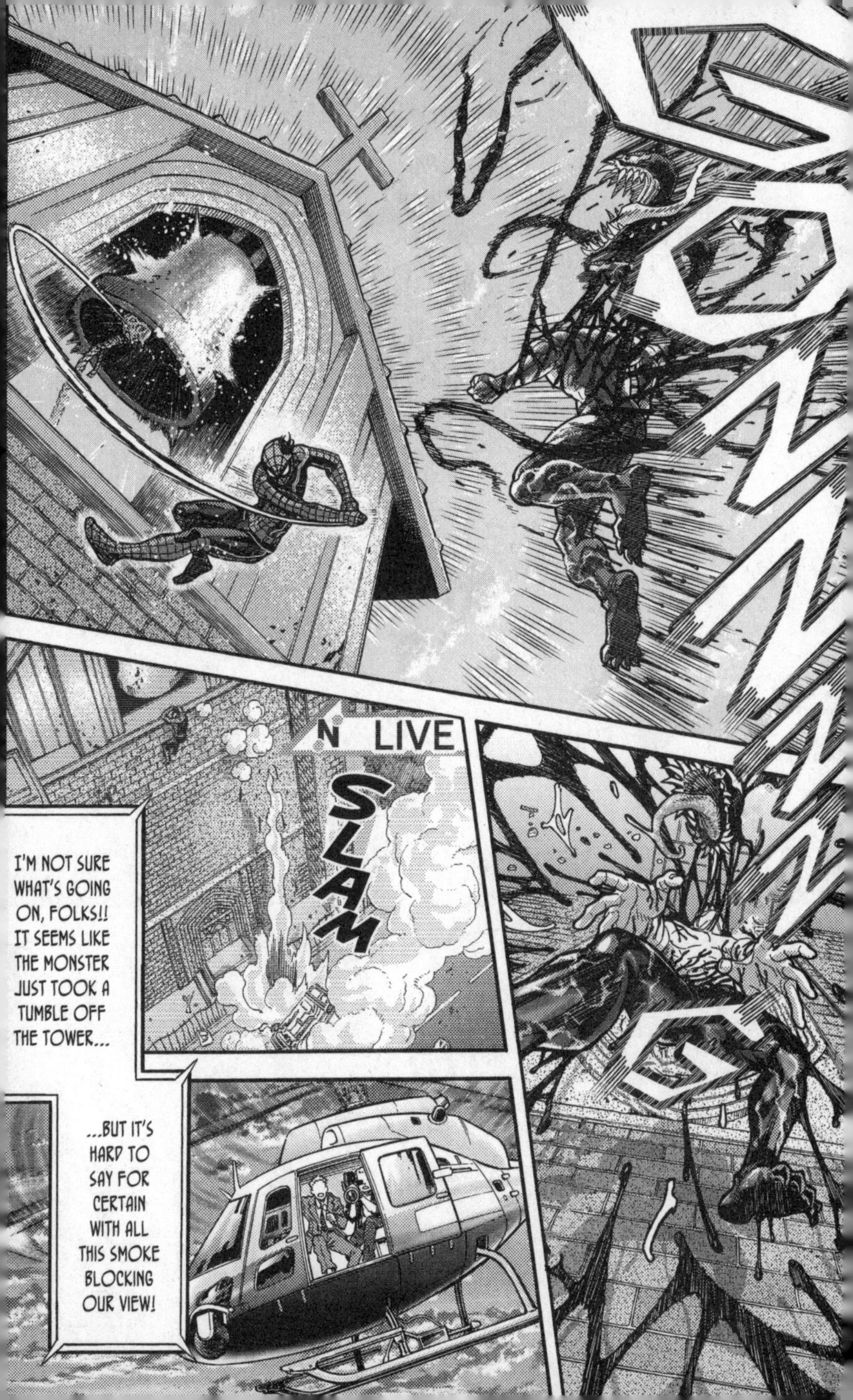
N LIVE
SLAM
I'M NOT SURE WHAT'S GOING ON, FOLKS!! IT SEEMS LIKE THE MONSTER JUST TOOK A TUMBLE OFF THE TOWER...
...BUT IT'S HARD TO SAY FOR CERTAIN WITH ALL THIS SMOKE BLOCKING OUR VIEW!

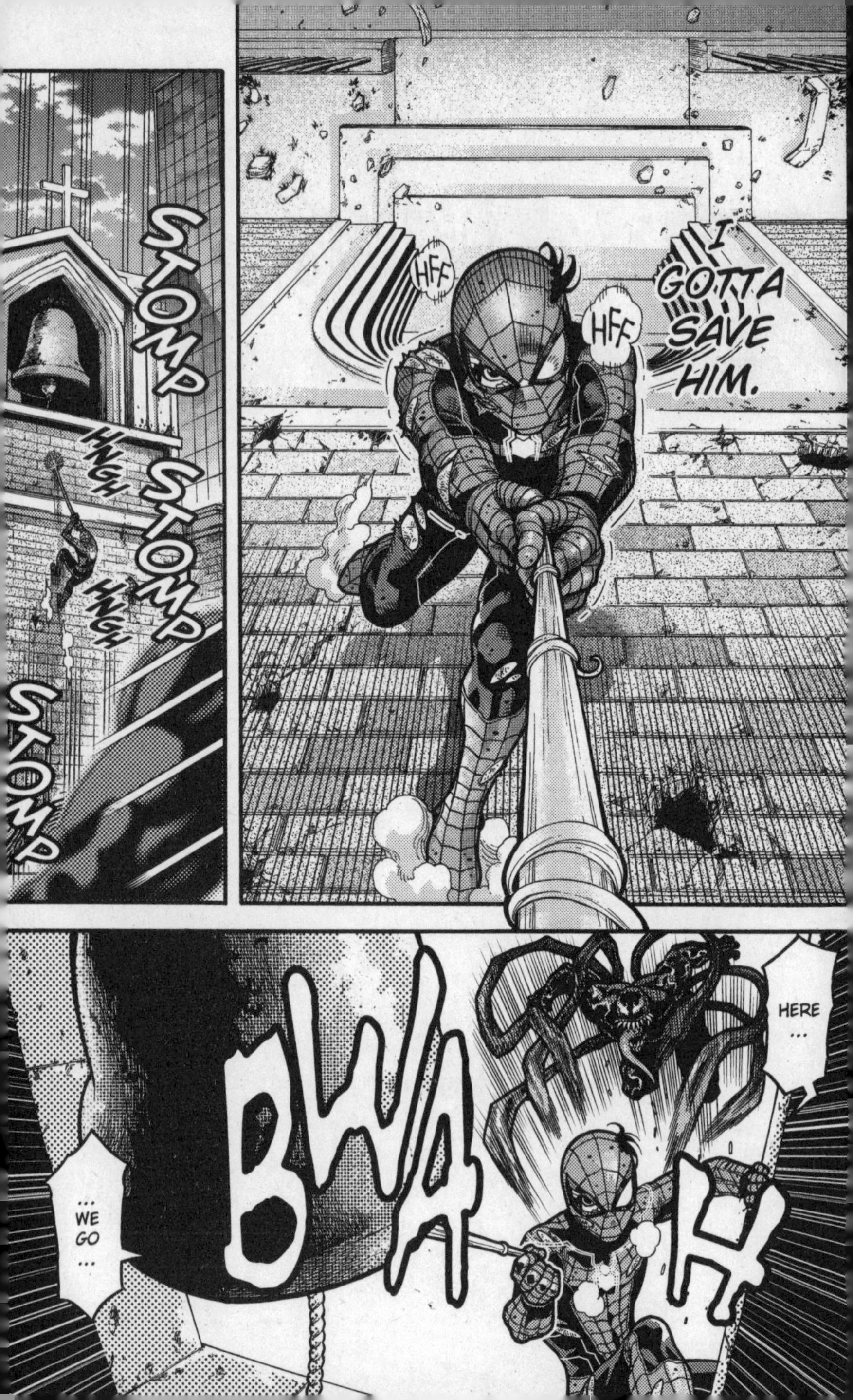
HFF
HFF
I GOTTA SAVE HIM.
STOMP
STOMP
HNGH
HNGH
STOMP
HERE ...
... WE GO ...
BWAH

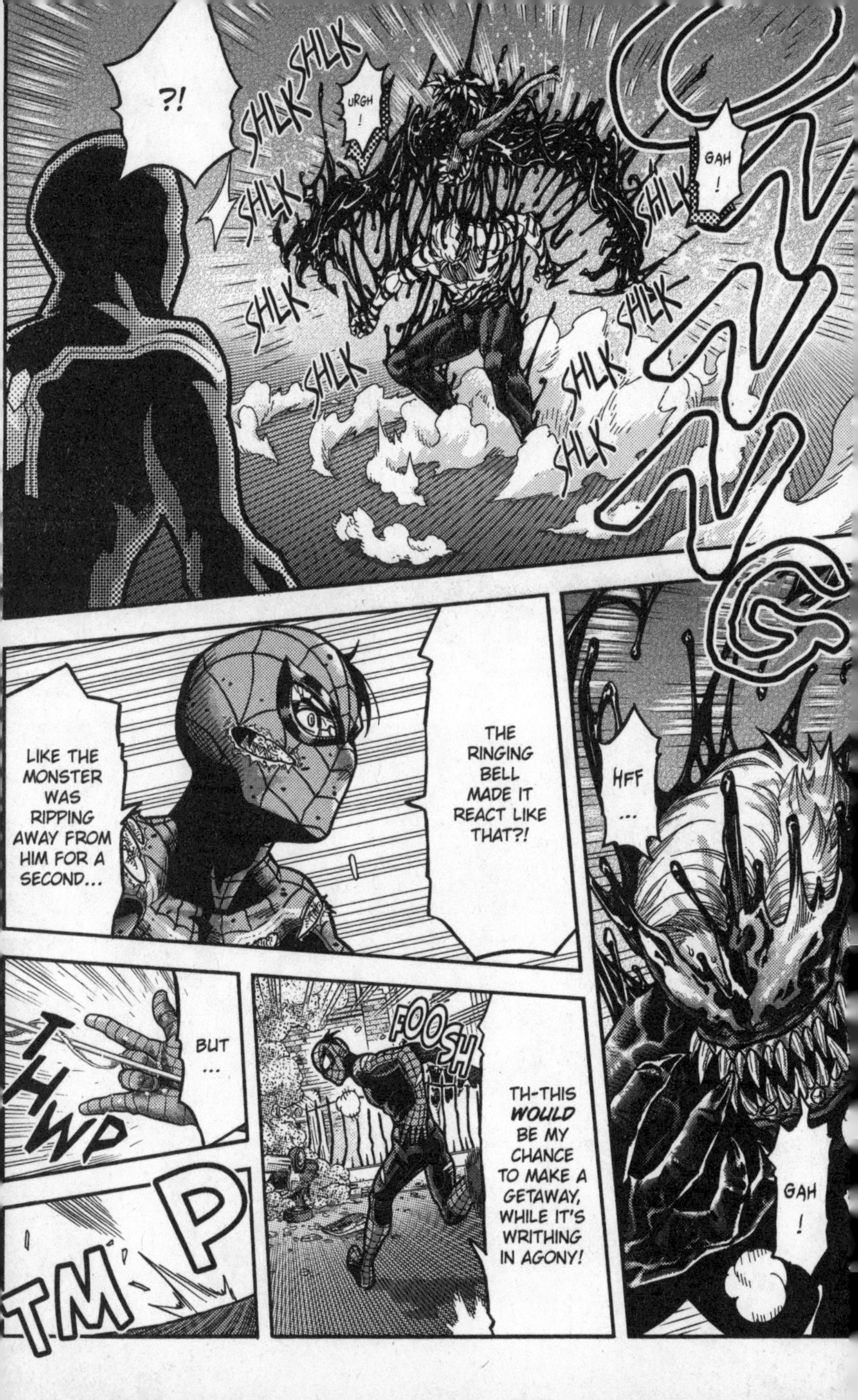
GAH!
SHLK SHLK SHLK SHLK SHLK SHLK SHLK SHLK SHLK
URGH!
?!
HFF...
GAH!
THE RINGING BELL MADE IT REACT LIKE THAT?!
LIKE THE MONSTER WAS RIPPING AWAY FROM HIM FOR A SECOND...
FOOSH
TH-THIS *WOULD* BE MY CHANCE TO MAKE A GETAWAY, WHILE IT'S WRITHING IN AGONY!
BUT...
THWP
TMP

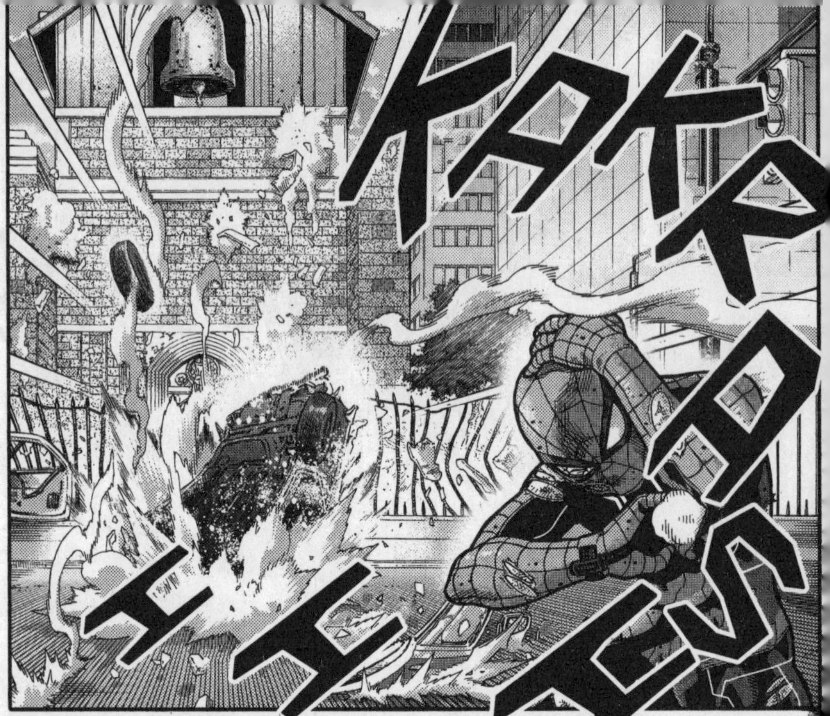
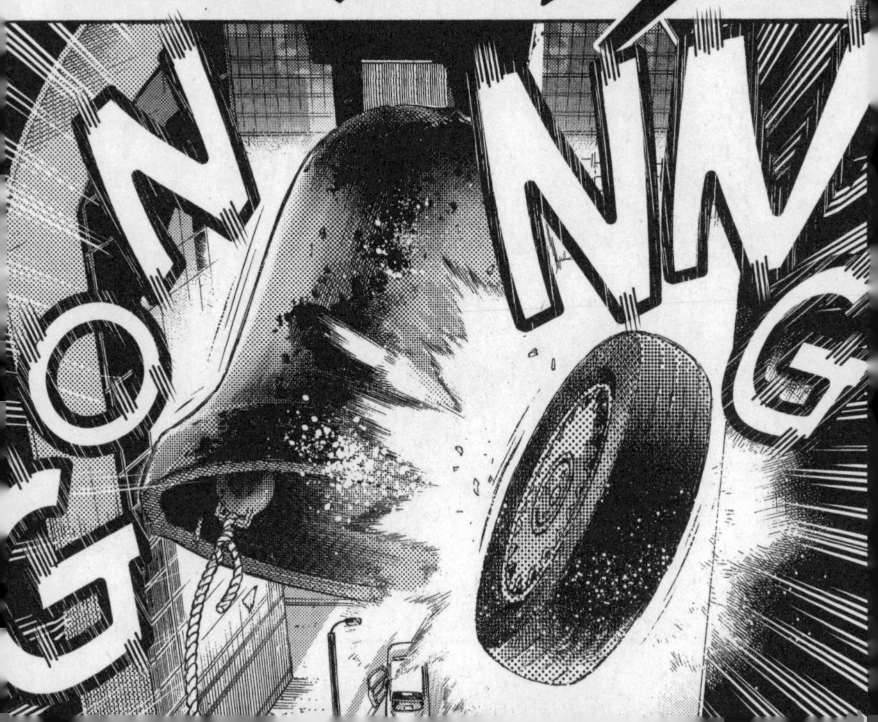

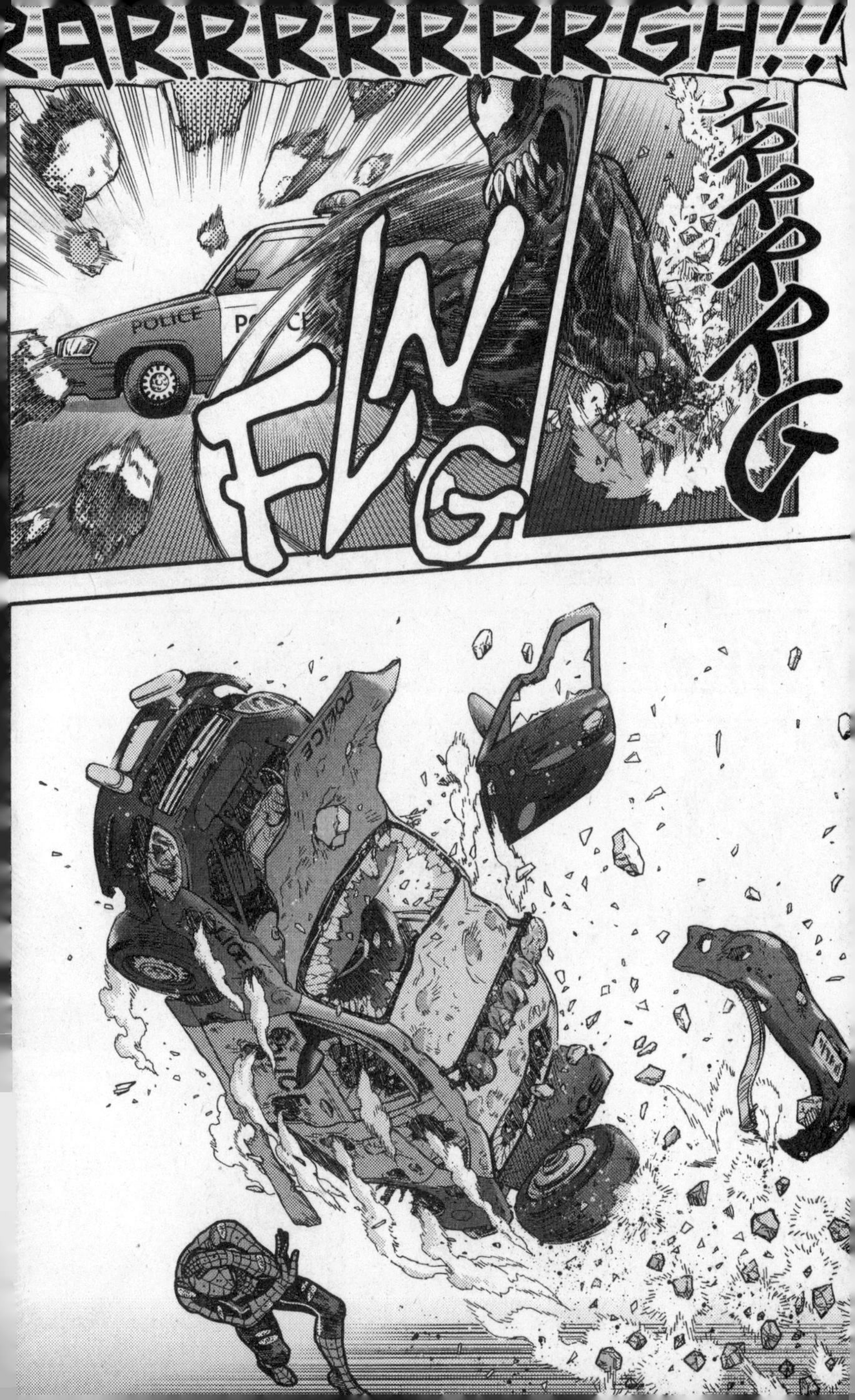
RARRRRRRGH!!
SKRRRG
FWG

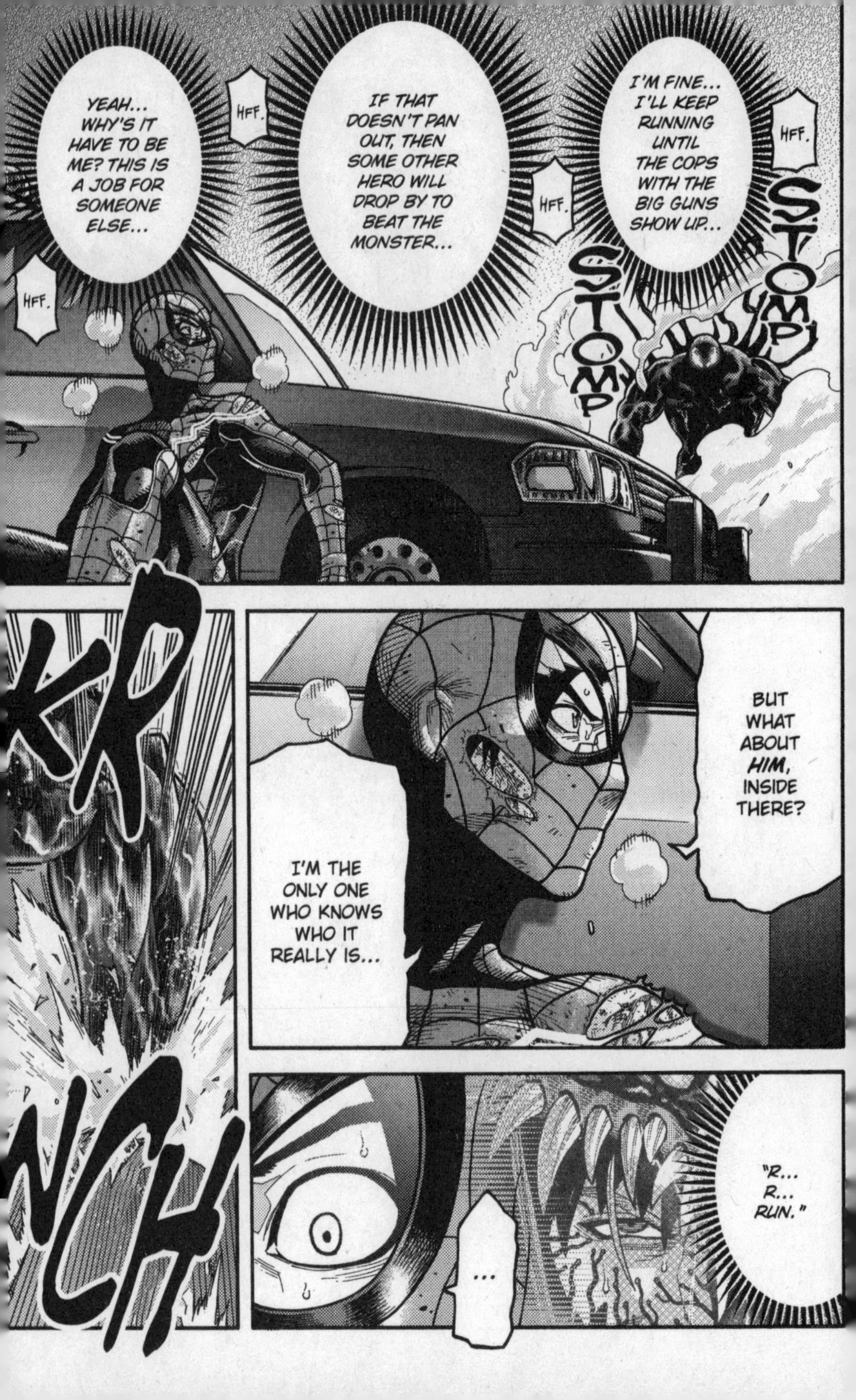
HFF.
I'M FINE... I'LL KEEP RUNNING UNTIL THE COPS WITH THE BIG GUNS SHOW UP...
STOMP
STOMP
HFF.
IF THAT DOESN'T PAN OUT, THEN SOME OTHER HERO WILL DROP BY TO BEAT THE MONSTER...
HFF.
YEAH... WHY'S IT HAVE TO BE ME? THIS IS A JOB FOR SOMEONE ELSE...
HFF.
BUT WHAT ABOUT *HIM*, INSIDE THERE?
I'M THE ONLY ONE WHO KNOWS WHO IT REALLY IS...
"R... R... RUN."
...
KR
NCH

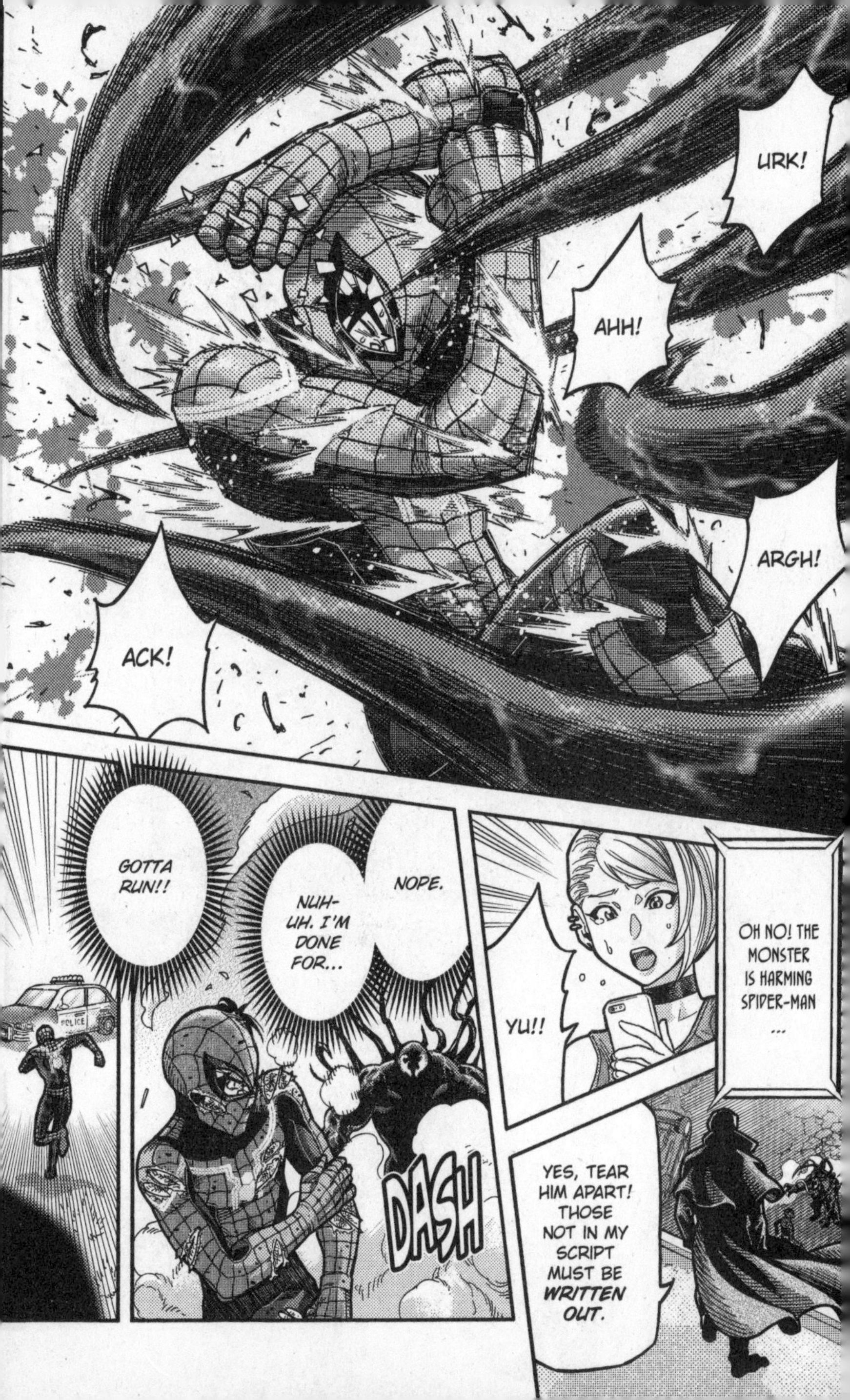
URK!
AHH!
ARGH!
ACK!
OH NO! THE MONSTER IS HARMING SPIDER-MAN ...
YU!!
YES, TEAR HIM APART! THOSE NOT IN MY SCRIPT MUST BE WRITTEN OUT.
NOPE.
NUH-UH. I'M DONE FOR...
GOTTA RUN!!
DASH

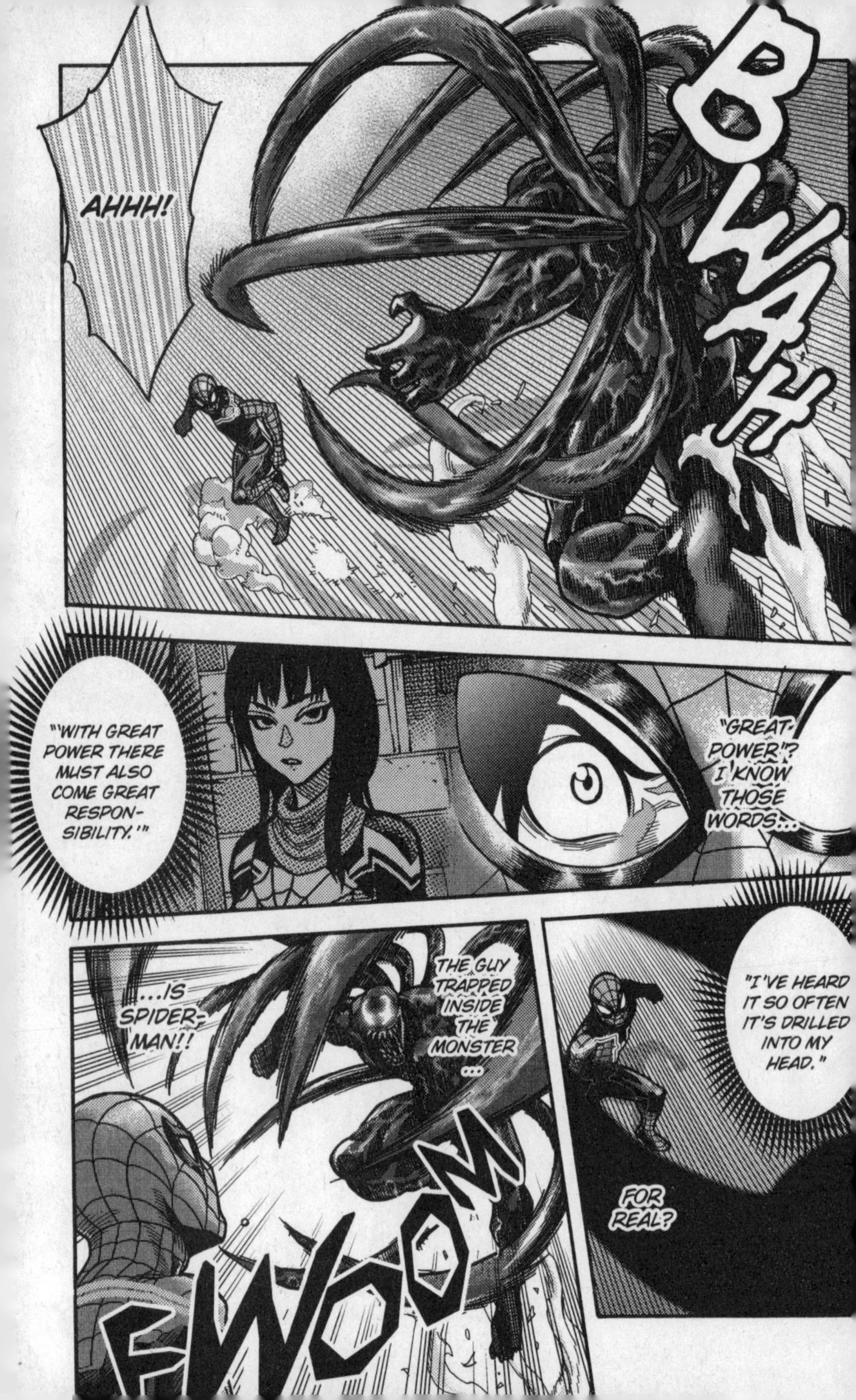
BWAH
AHHH!
"GREAT POWER"? I KNOW THOSE WORDS...
"'WITH GREAT POWER THERE MUST ALSO COME GREAT RESPONSIBILITY.'"
"I'VE HEARD IT SO OFTEN IT'S DRILLED INTO MY HEAD."
FOR REAL?
THE GUY TRAPPED INSIDE THE MONSTER...
...IS SPIDER-MAN!!
FWOOM

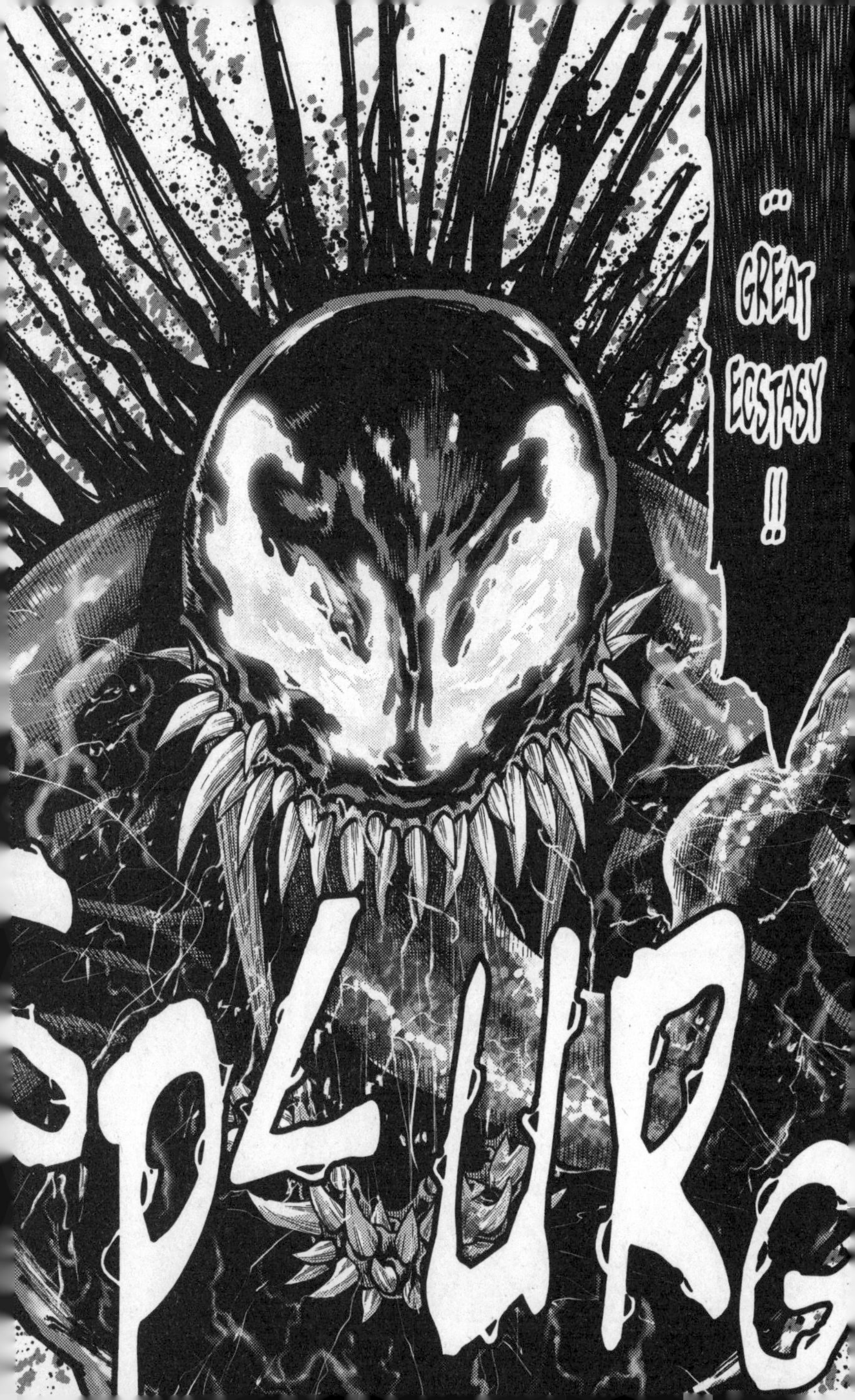
...GREAT ECSTASY!!
SPLURG

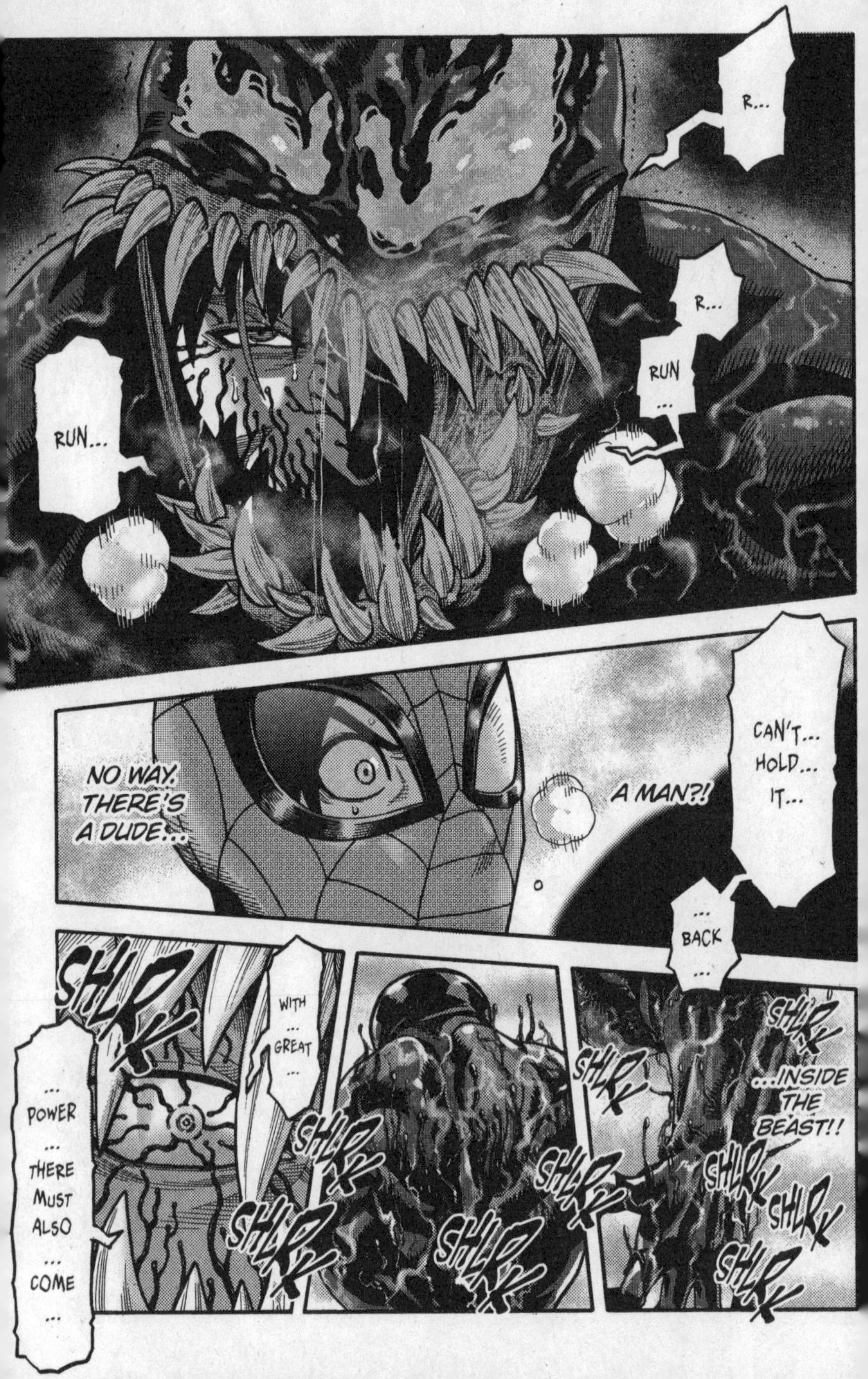

R...
R...
RUN
...
RUN...
CAN'T... HOLD... IT...
... BACK ...
A MAN?!
NO WAY. THERE'S A DUDE...
SHLRK
SHLRK
...INSIDE THE BEAST!!
SHLRK
SHLRK
SHLRK
SHLRK
SHLRK
SHLRK
SHLRK
SHLRK
WITH ... GREAT ...
... POWER ... THERE MUST ALSO ... COME ...

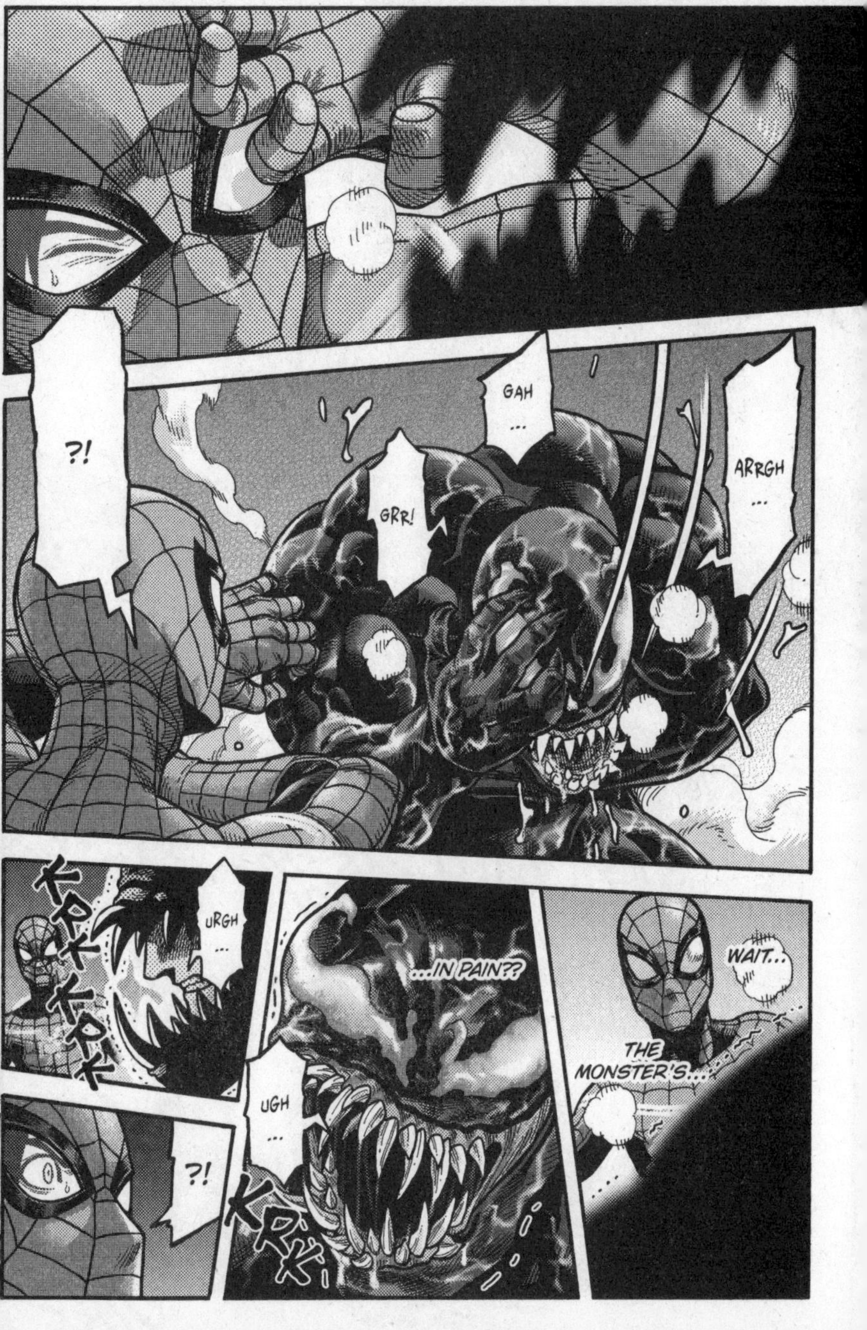
ARRGH ...
GAH ...
GRR!
?!
WAIT...
THE MONSTER'S...
...IN PAIN??
UGH ...
KRK
URGH ...
KRK KRK KRK
?!

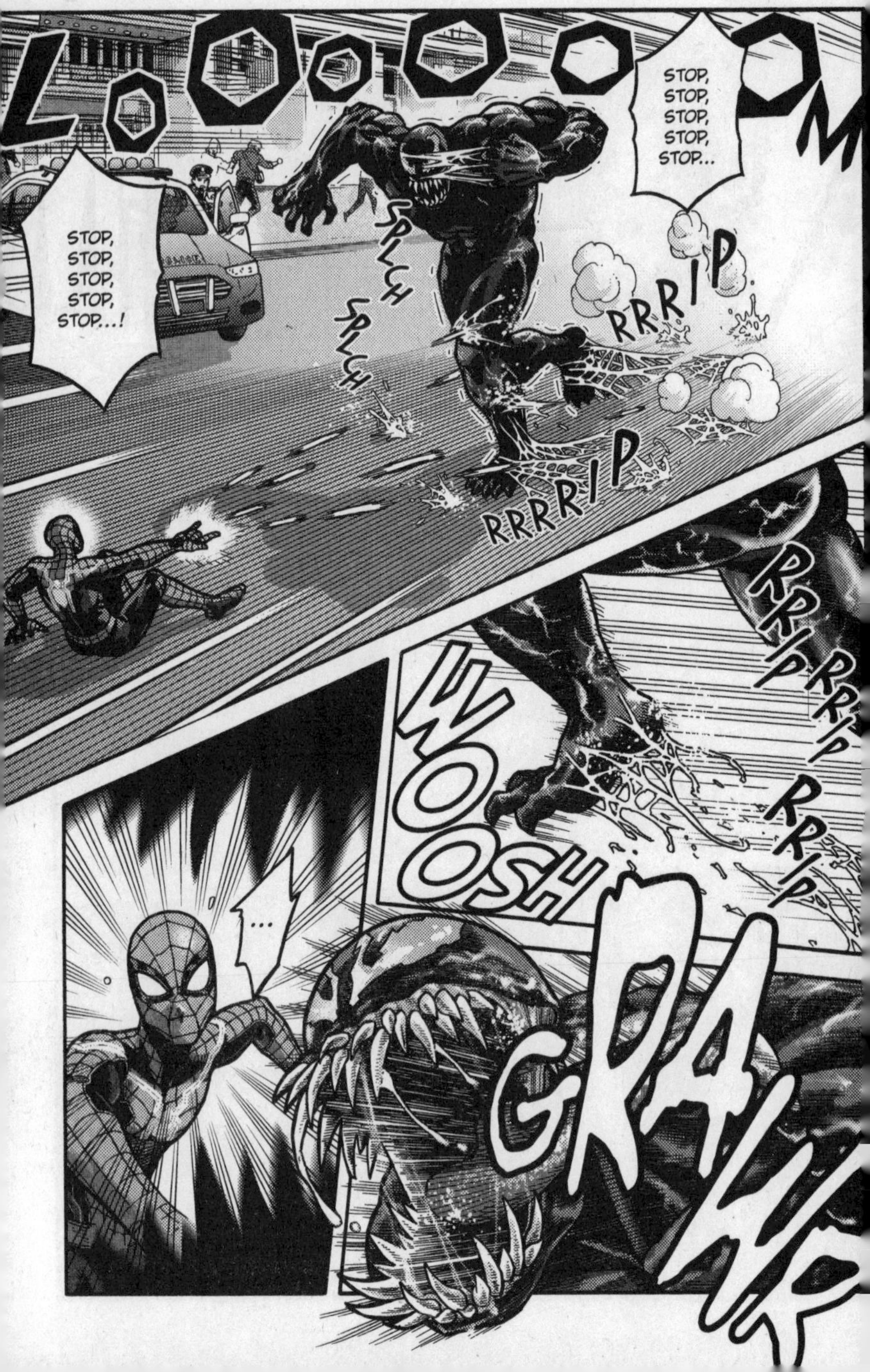
LOOOOOOOM
STOP, STOP, STOP, STOP, STOP...
STOP, STOP, STOP, STOP, STOP...!
SPLCH SPLCH
RRRIP
RRRRIP
RRRIP RRRIP RRRIP RRRIP
WOOSH
...
GRA

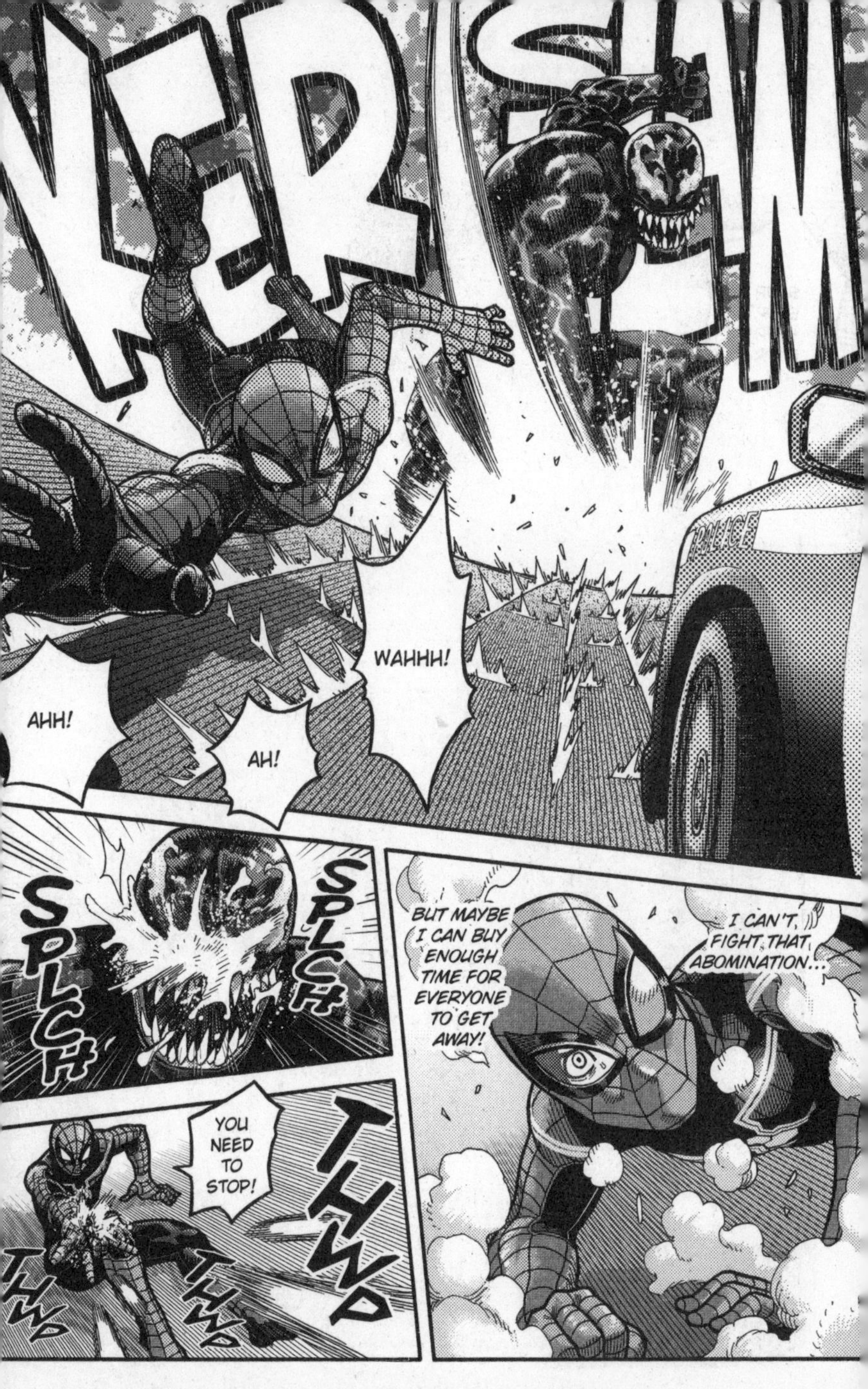
WAHHH!
AH!
AHH!
I CAN'T FIGHT THAT ABOMINATION...
BUT MAYBE I CAN BUY ENOUGH TIME FOR EVERYONE TO GET AWAY!
SPLCH
SPLCH
THWP
YOU NEED TO STOP!
THWP
THWP

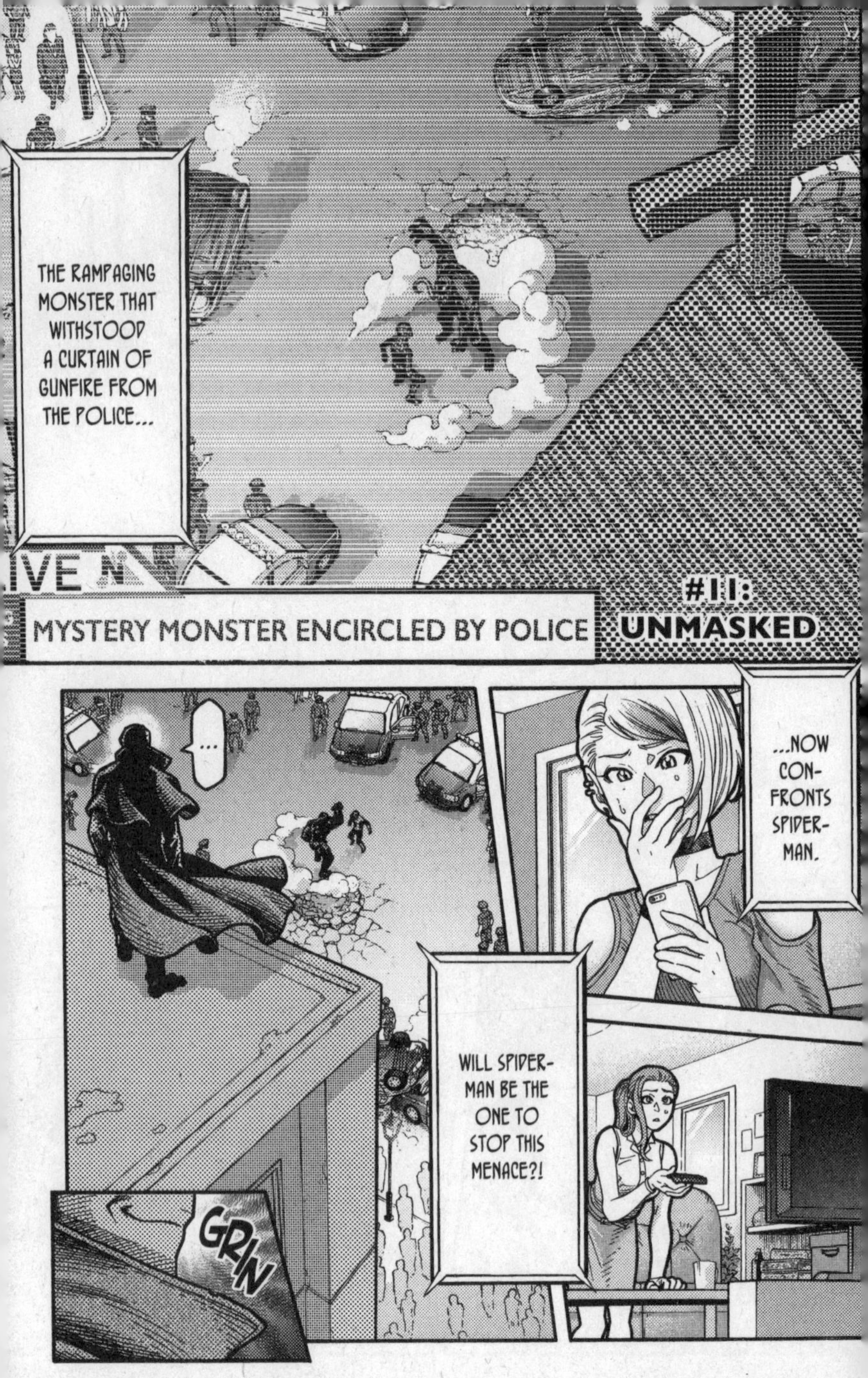
THE RAMPAGING MONSTER THAT WITHSTOOD A CURTAIN OF GUNFIRE FROM THE POLICE...
IVE N
MYSTERY MONSTER ENCIRCLED BY POLICE
#11: UNMASKED
...NOW CON-FRONTS SPIDER-MAN.
WILL SPIDER-MAN BE THE ONE TO STOP THIS MENACE?!
...
GRIN

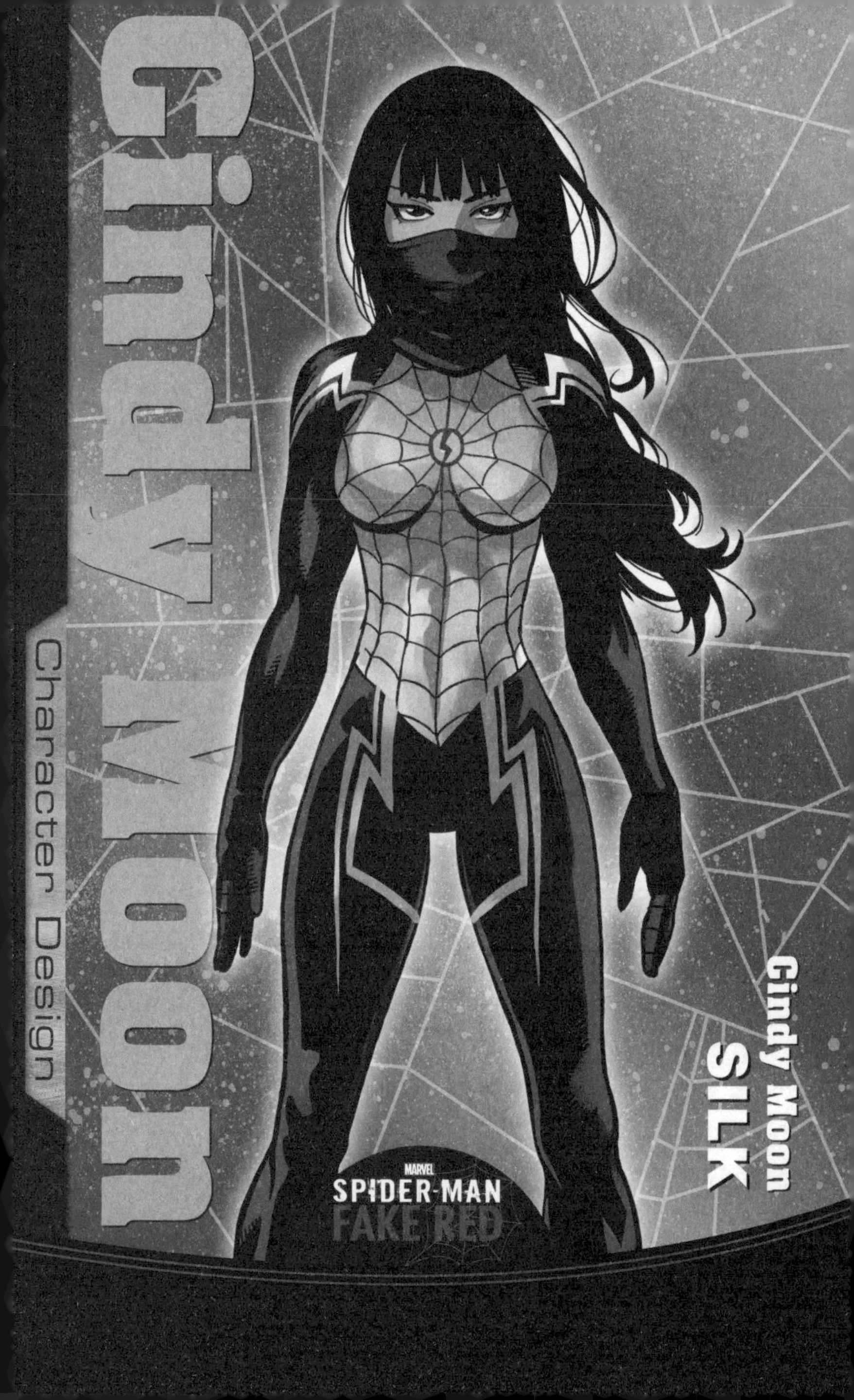
Cindy Moon
Character Design
Cindy Moon
SILK
MARVEL
SPIDER-MAN
FAKE RED

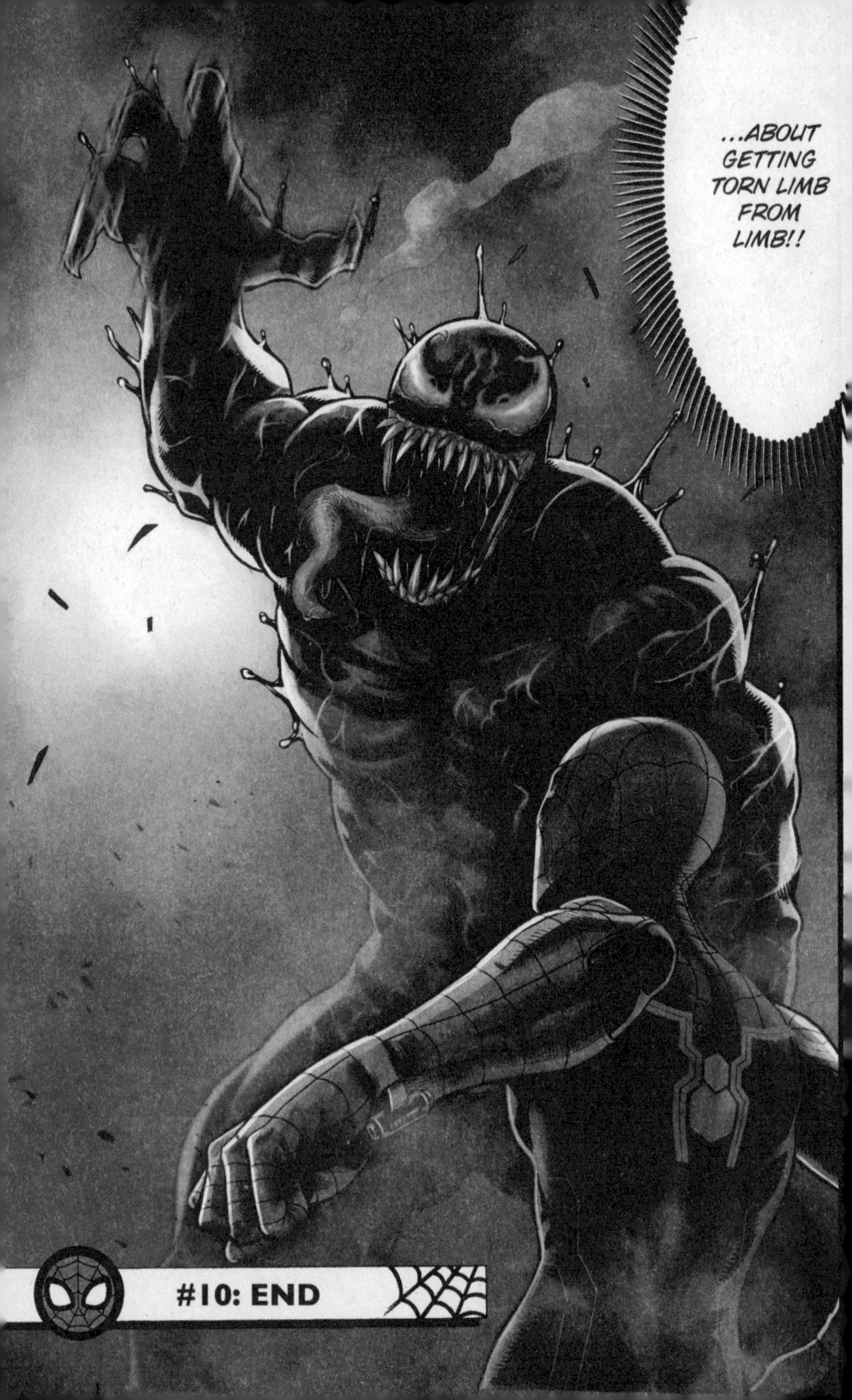
...ABOUT GETTING TORN LIMB FROM LIMB!!
#10: END

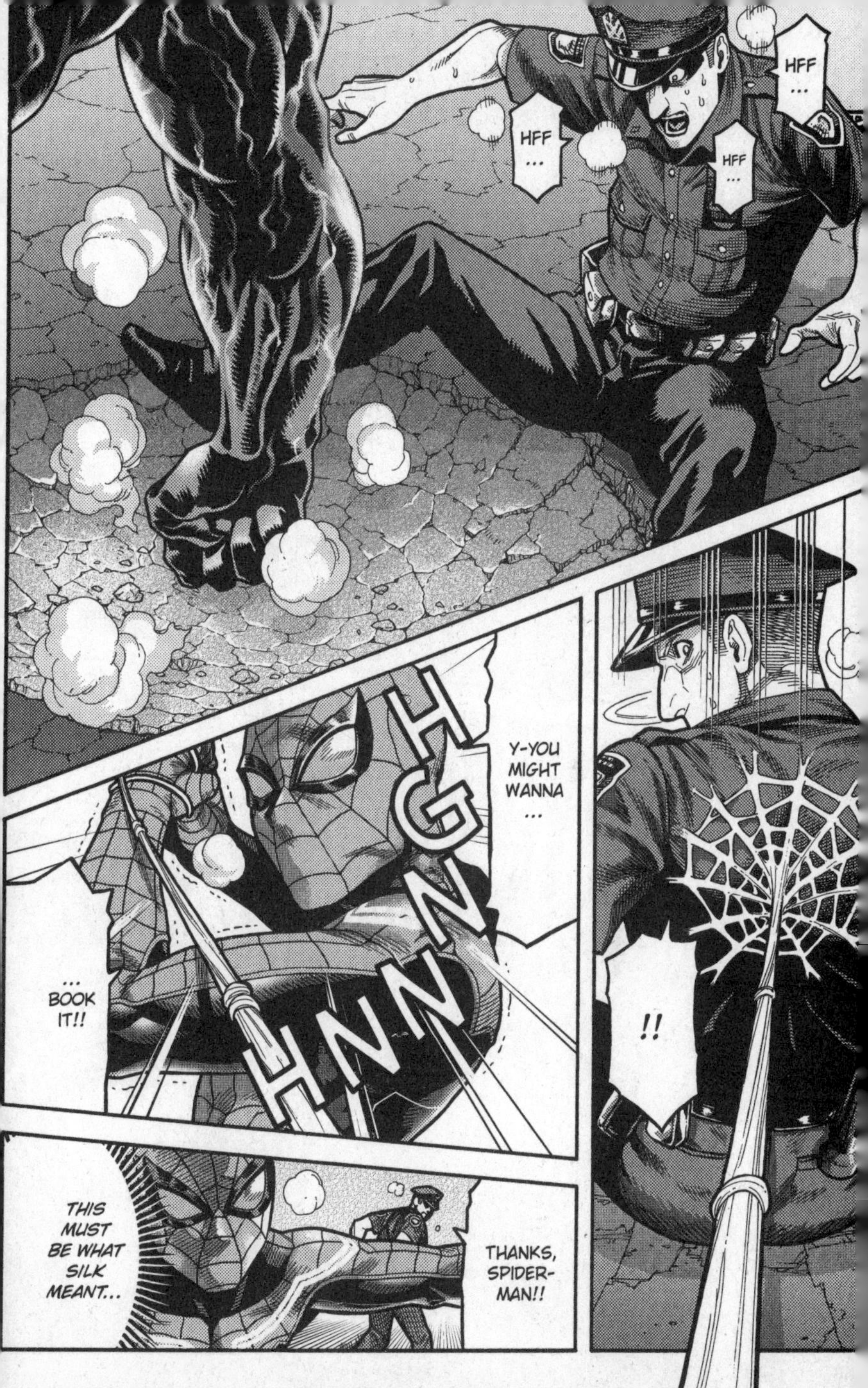
HFF ...
HFF ...
HFF ...
!!
HNNNGH
Y-YOU MIGHT WANNA ...
... BOOK IT!!
THANKS, SPIDER-MAN!!
THIS MUST BE WHAT SILK MEANT...

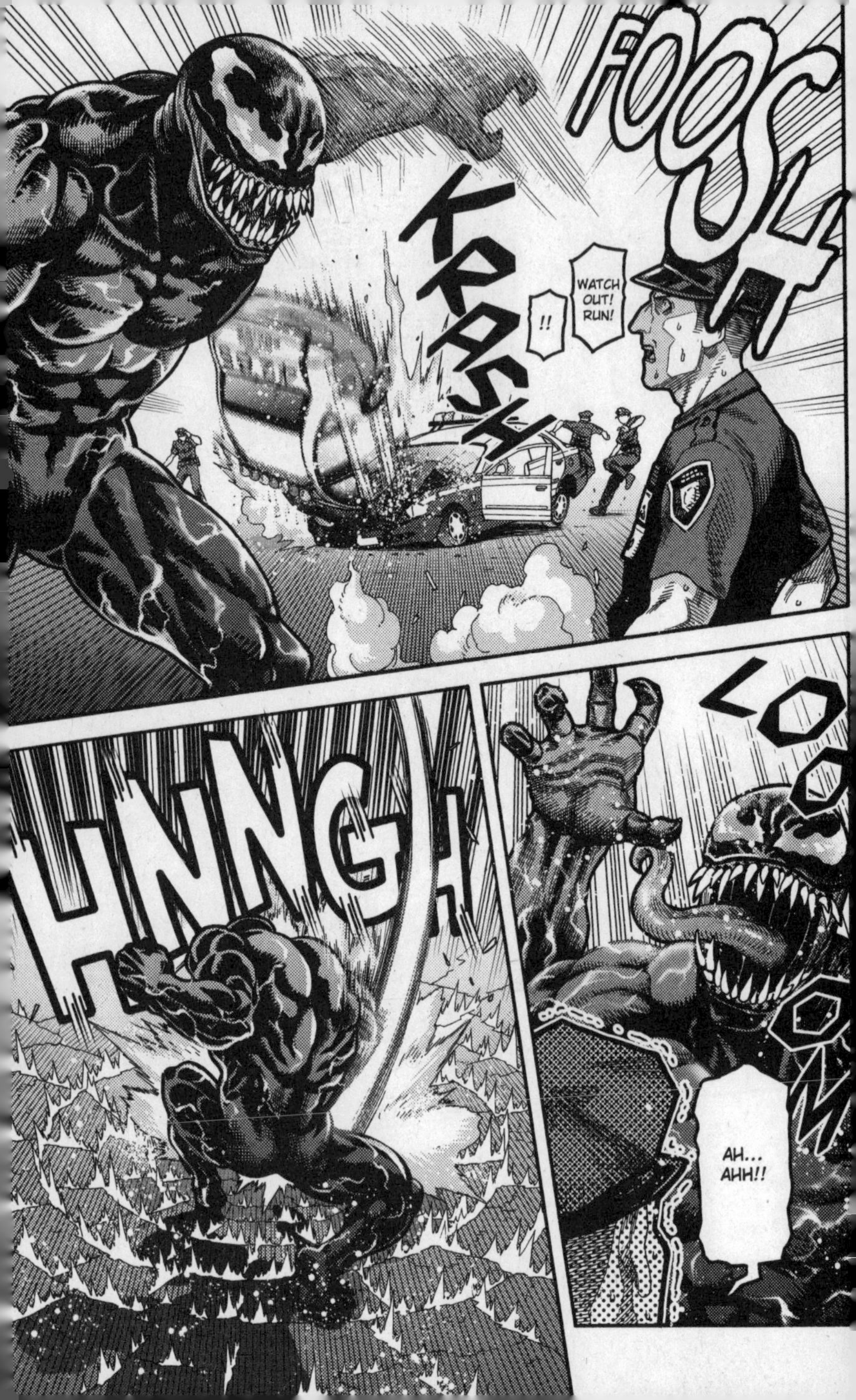
FOOSH
WATCH OUT! RUN!
!!
KRASH
LOOOM
AH... AHH!!
HNNGH

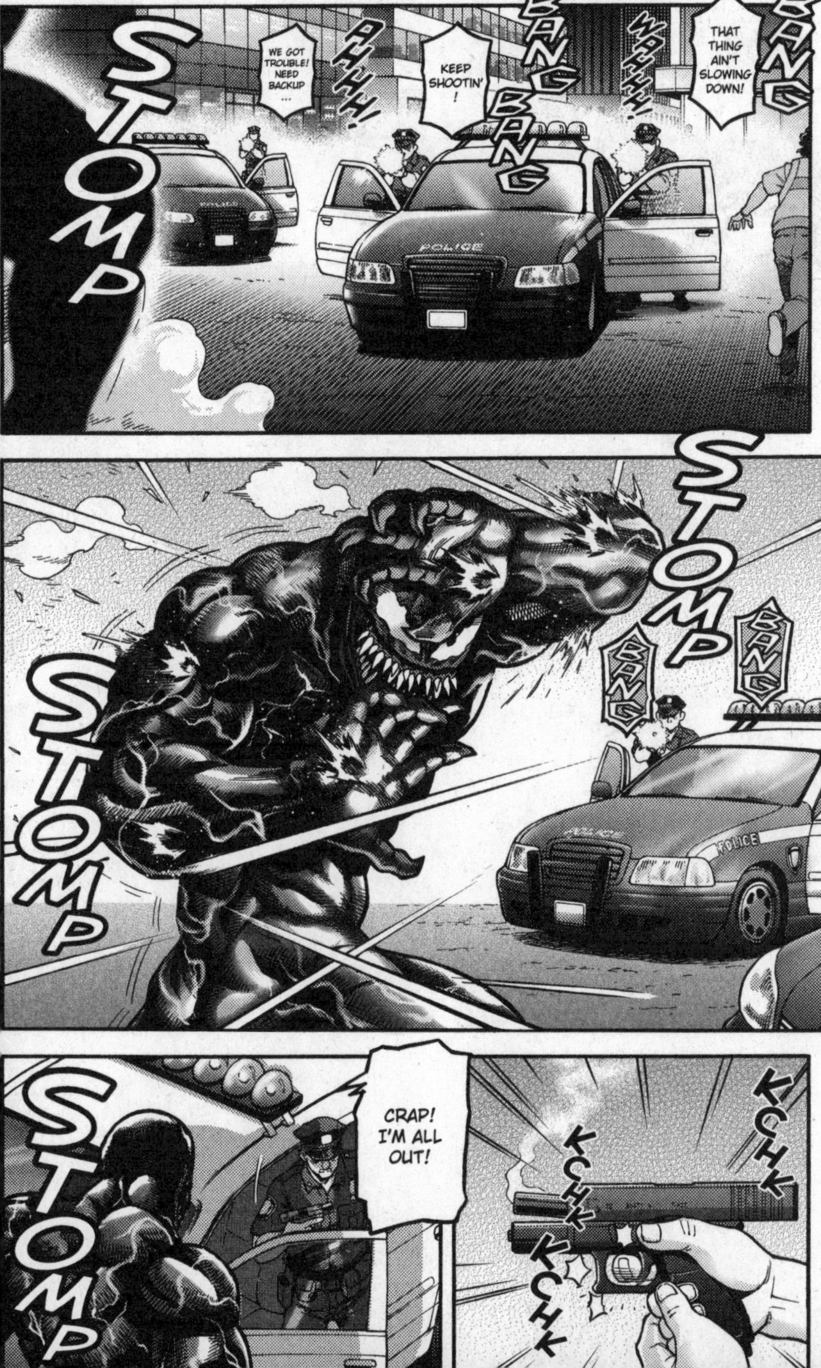
BANG
THAT THING AIN'T SLOWING DOWN!
WAHHHH!
BANG
BANG
BANG
KEEP SHOOTIN'!
AHHHH!
WE GOT TROUBLE! NEED BACKUP...
STOMP
STOMP
BANG
BANG
STOMP
KCHK
KCHK
KCHK
KCHK
CRAP! I'M ALL OUT!
STOMP

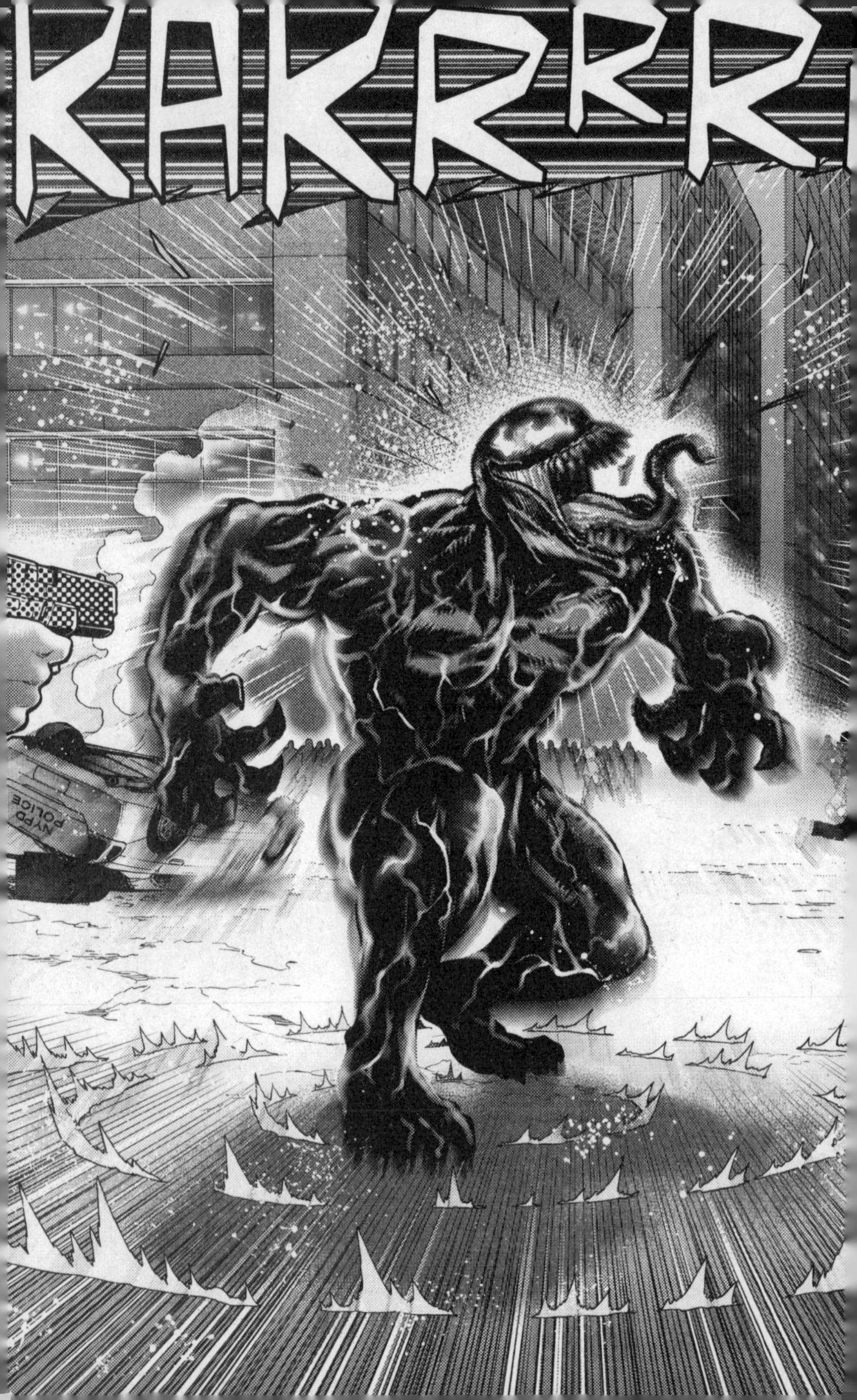
KAKRRR
NYPD
POLICE

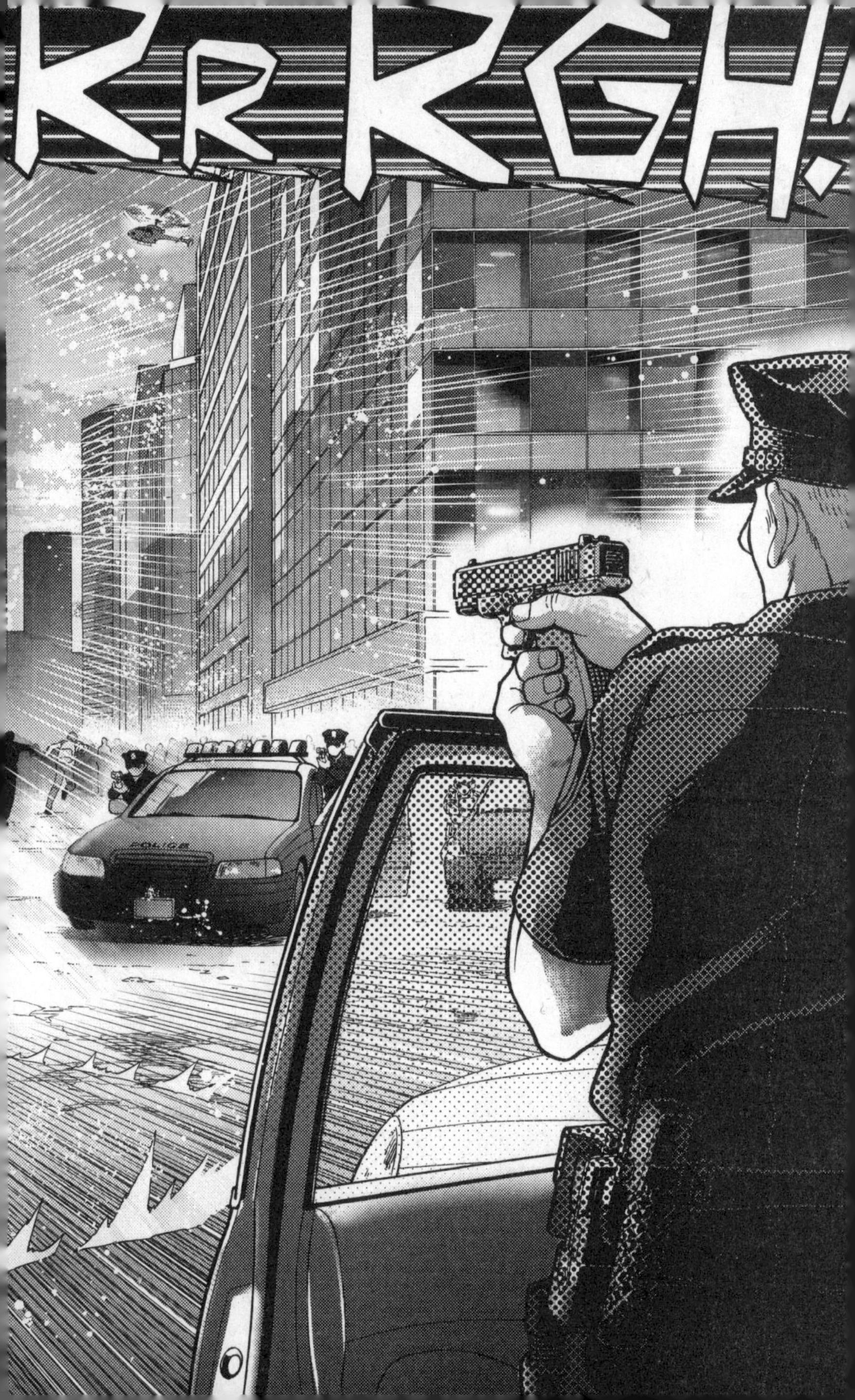
KRRGH!
POLICE

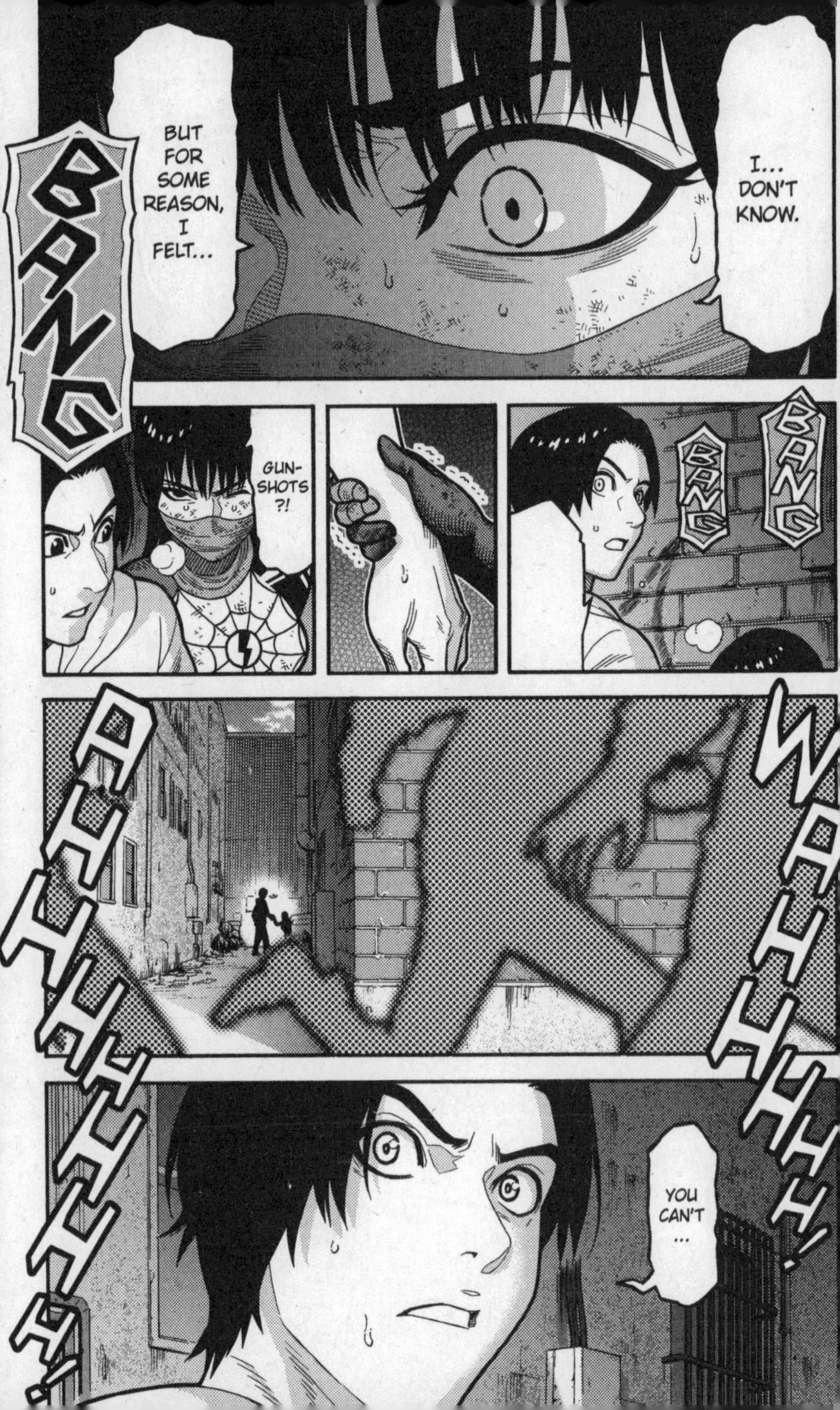
I... DON'T KNOW.
BUT FOR SOME REASON, I FELT...
BANG
BANG
BANG
GUN-SHOTS?!
WAHHHHHH!
AHHHHHHH!
YOU CAN'T ...

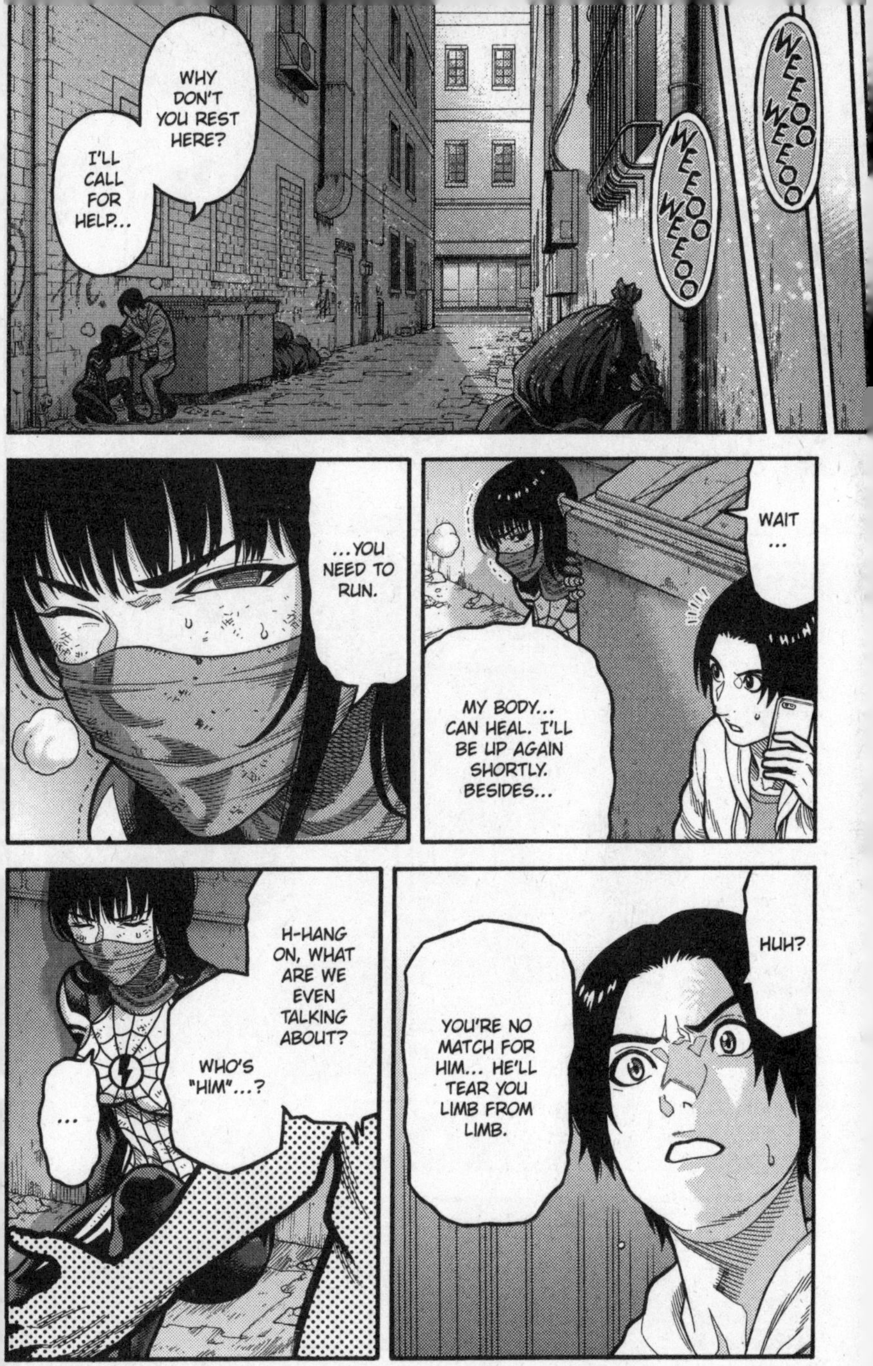
WEEOO WEEOO
WEEOO WEEOO
WHY DON'T YOU REST HERE?
I'LL CALL FOR HELP...
WAIT...
MY BODY... CAN HEAL. I'LL BE UP AGAIN SHORTLY. BESIDES...
...YOU NEED TO RUN.
HUH?
YOU'RE NO MATCH FOR HIM... HE'LL TEAR YOU LIMB FROM LIMB.
H-HANG ON, WHAT ARE WE EVEN TALKING ABOUT?
WHO'S "HIM"...?
...

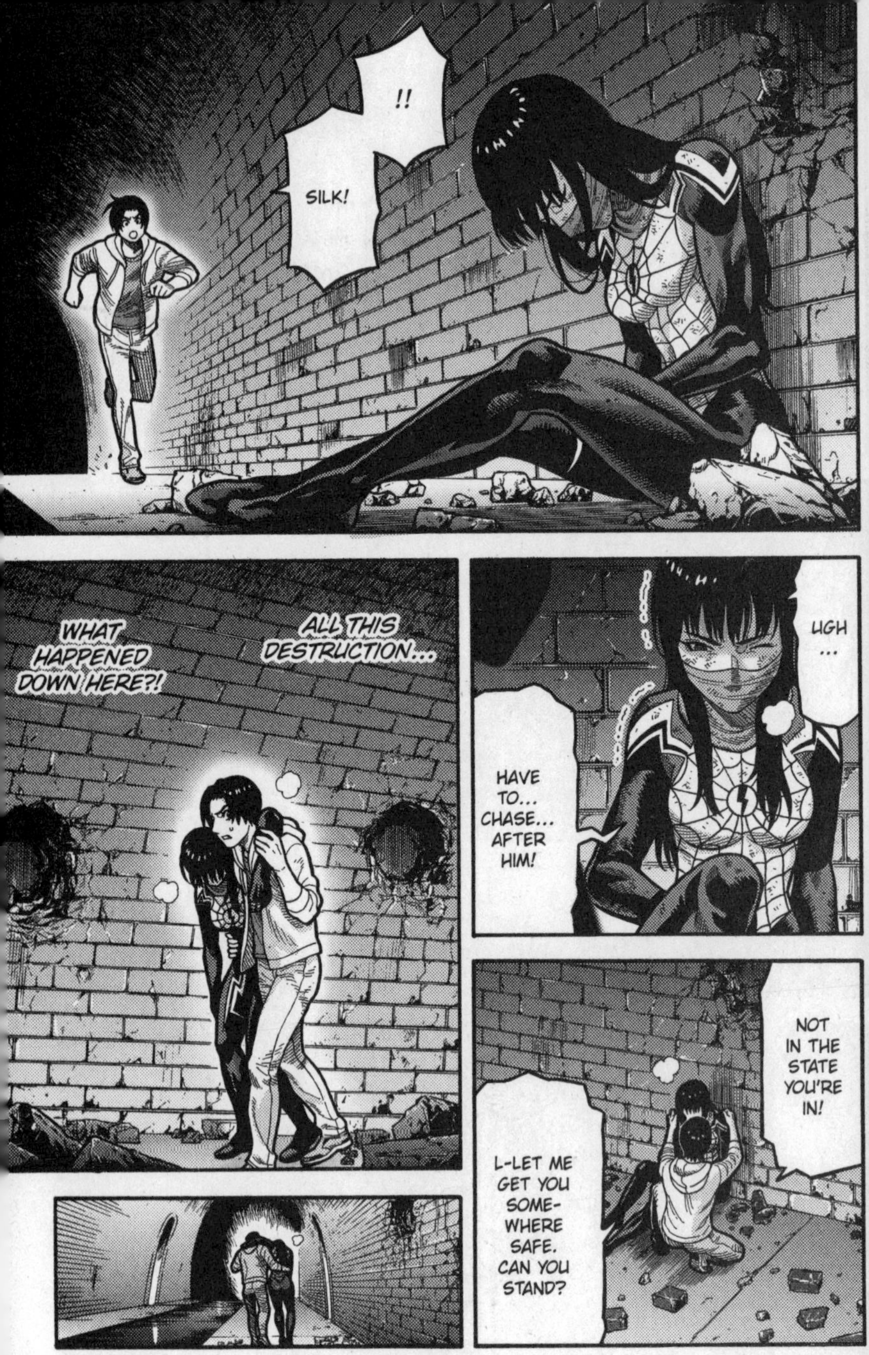
!!
SILK!
UGH...
HAVE TO... CHASE... AFTER HIM!
NOT IN THE STATE YOU'RE IN!
L-LET ME GET YOU SOME-WHERE SAFE. CAN YOU STAND?
ALL THIS DESTRUCTION...
WHAT HAPPENED DOWN HERE?!

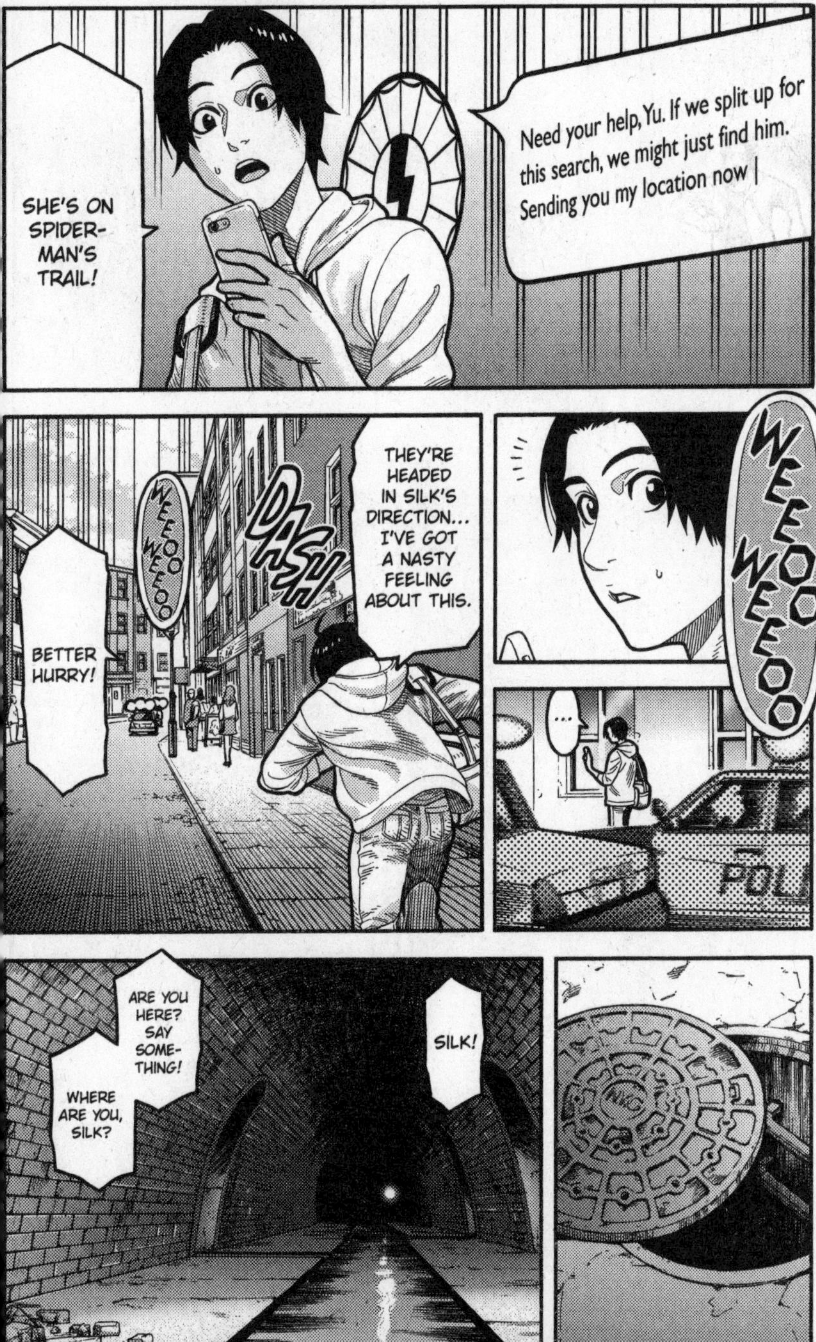
Need your help, Yu. If we split up for this search, we might just find him. Sending you my location now
SHE'S ON SPIDER-MAN'S TRAIL!
WEEEOO WEEEOO
...
THEY'RE HEADED IN SILK'S DIRECTION... I'VE GOT A NASTY FEELING ABOUT THIS.
DASH
WEEOO WEEOO
BETTER HURRY!
SILK!
ARE YOU HERE? SAY SOME-THING!
WHERE ARE YOU, SILK?

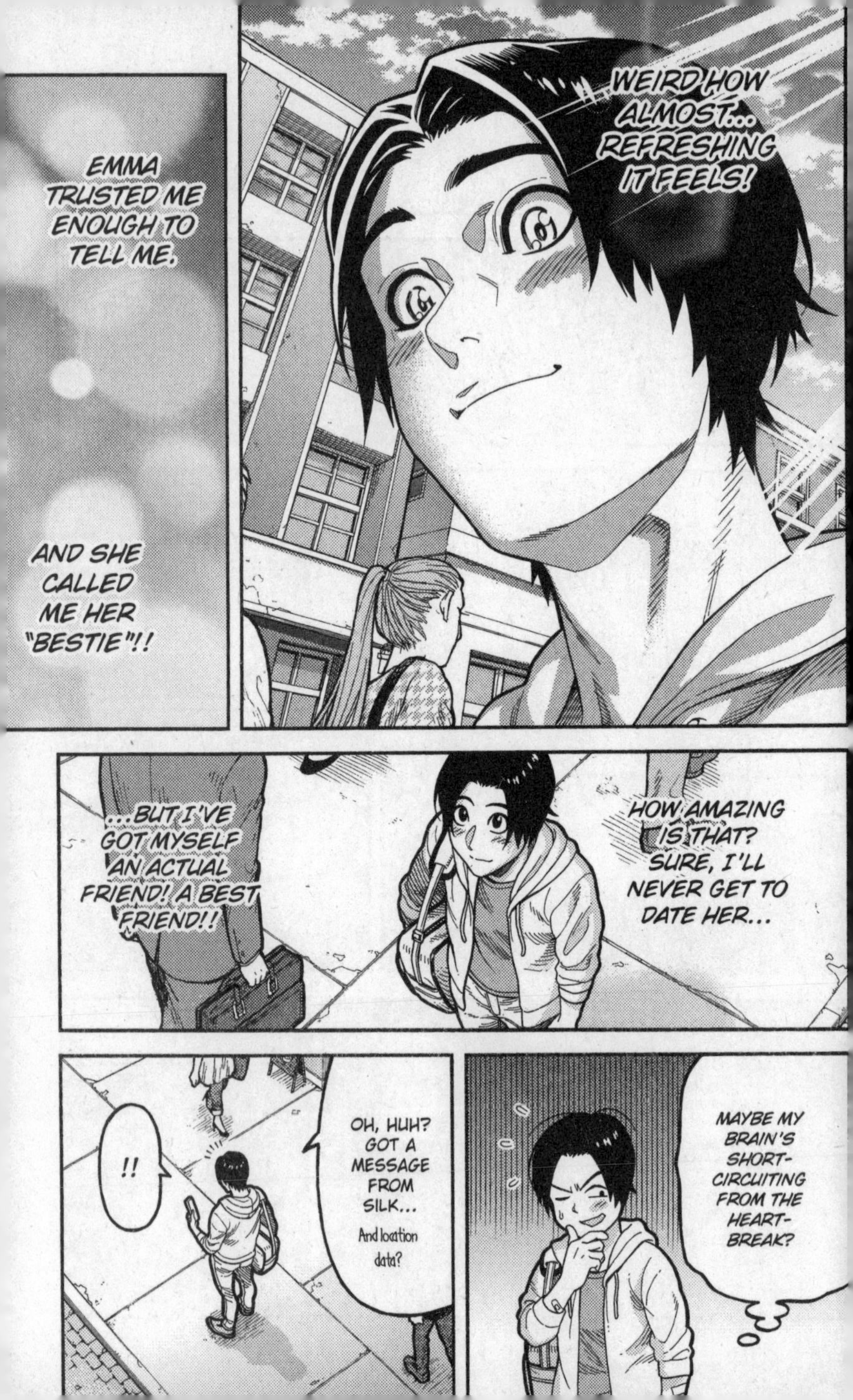
WEIRD HOW ALMOST... REFRESHING IT FEELS!
EMMA TRUSTED ME ENOUGH TO TELL ME.
AND SHE CALLED ME HER "BESTIE"!!
HOW AMAZING IS THAT? SURE, I'LL NEVER GET TO DATE HER...
...BUT I'VE GOT MYSELF AN ACTUAL FRIEND! A BEST FRIEND!!
MAYBE MY BRAIN'S SHORT-CIRCUITING FROM THE HEART-BREAK?
OH, HUH? GOT A MESSAGE FROM SILK...
And location data?
!!

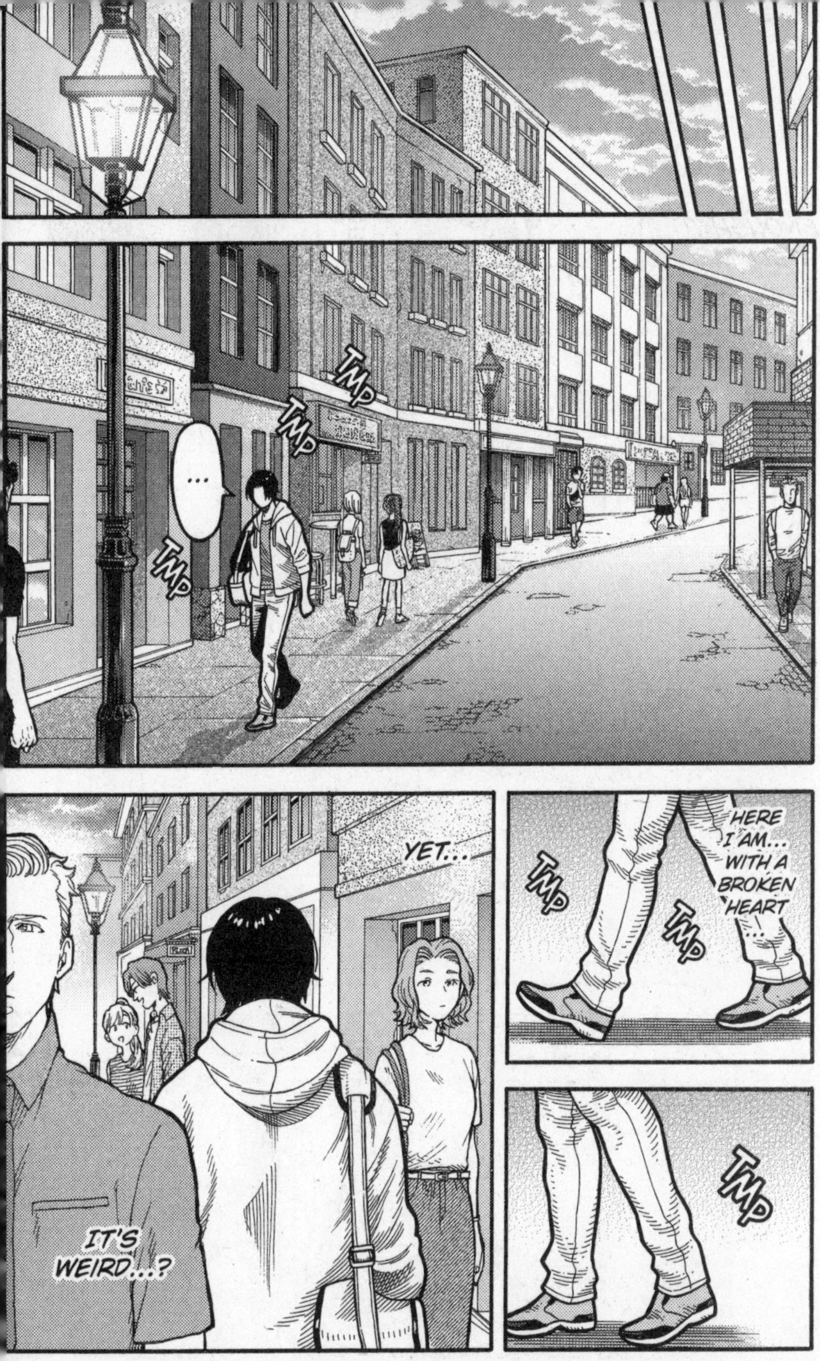
TMP
TMP
...
TMP
HERE I AM... WITH A BROKEN HEART...
TMP
TMP
TMP
YET...
IT'S WEIRD...?

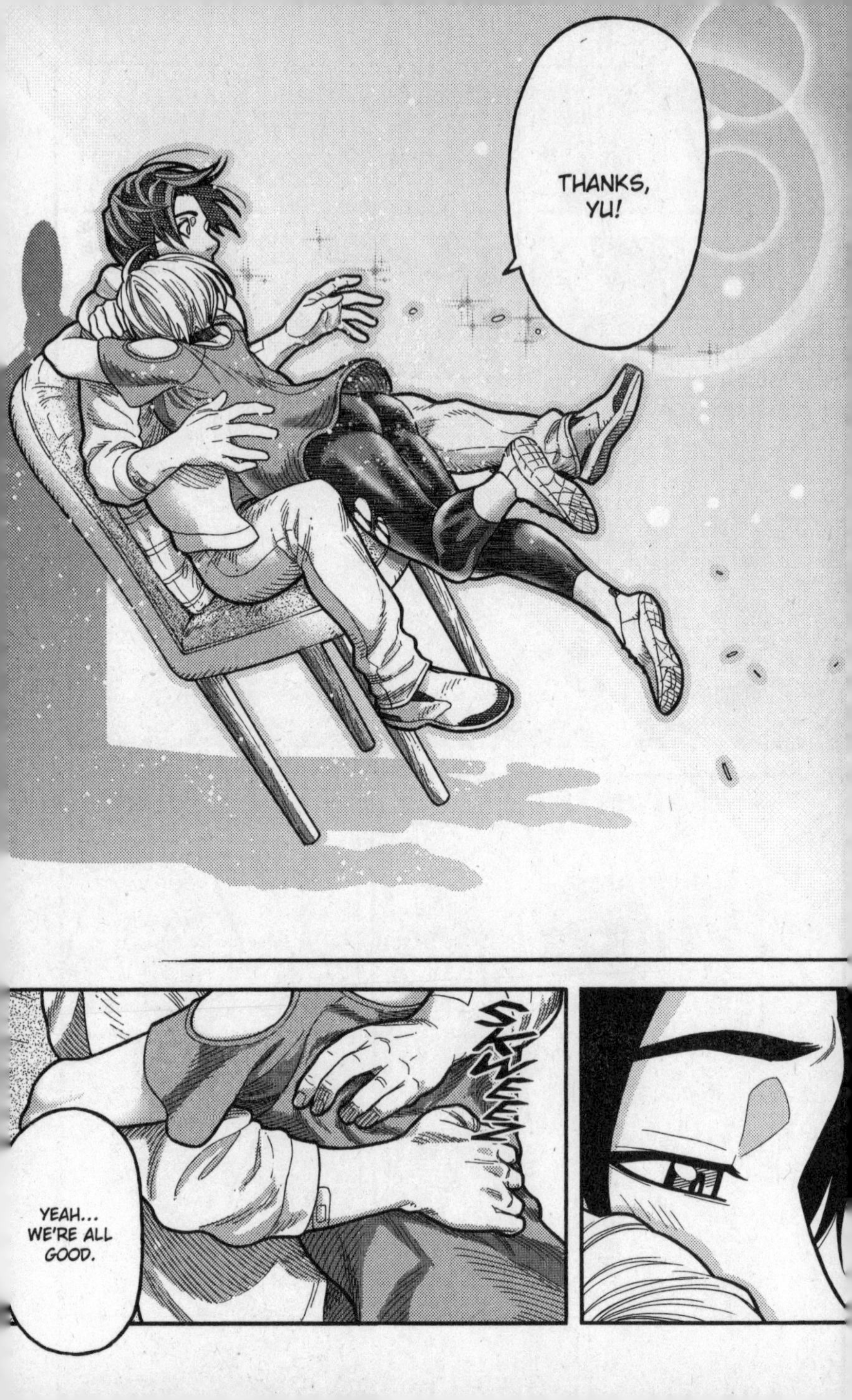
THANKS, YU!
YEAH... WE'RE ALL GOOD.

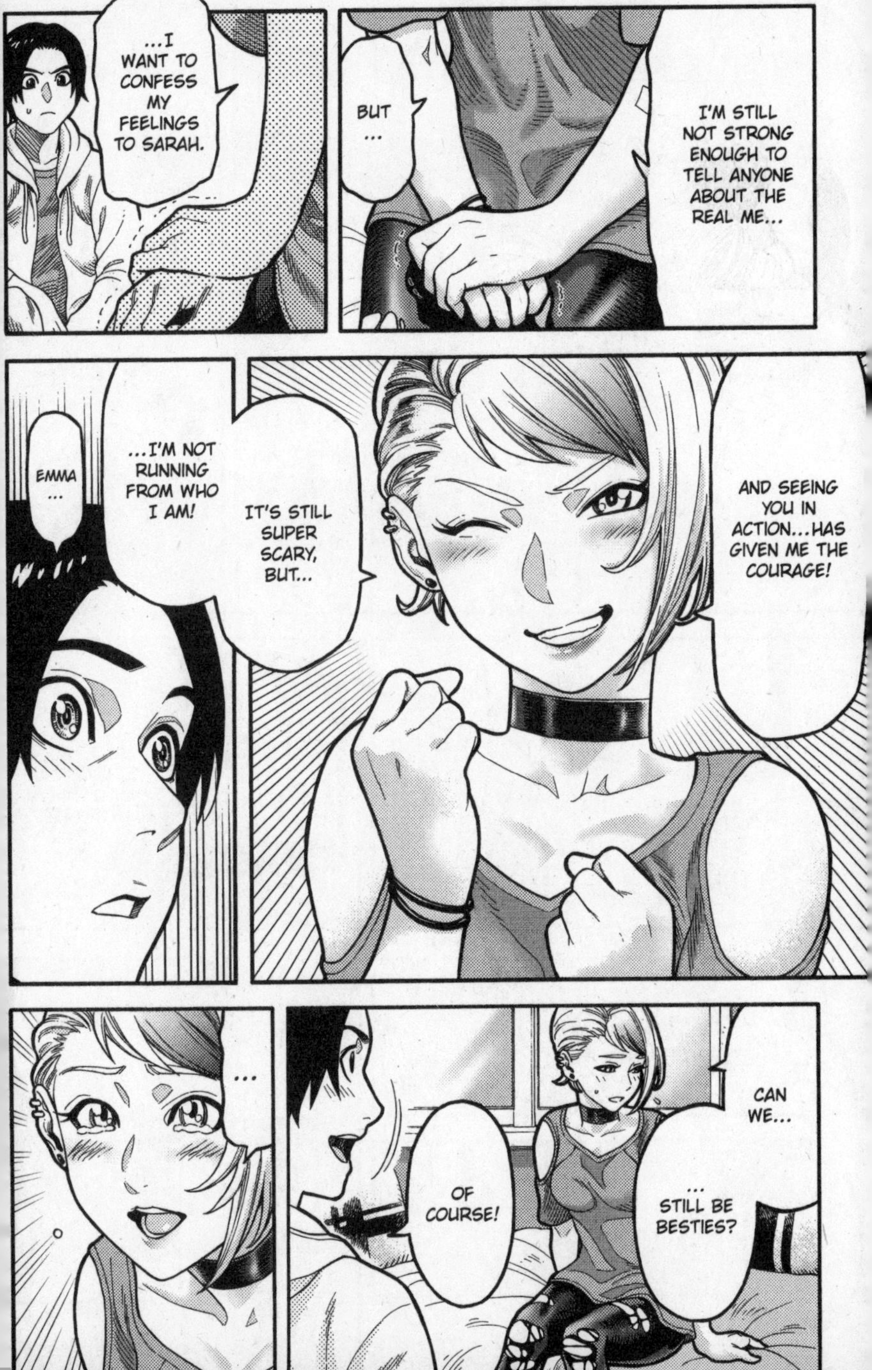
BUT ...
I'M STILL NOT STRONG ENOUGH TO TELL ANYONE ABOUT THE REAL ME...
...I WANT TO CONFESS MY FEELINGS TO SARAH.
AND SEEING YOU IN ACTION...HAS GIVEN ME THE COURAGE!
IT'S STILL SUPER SCARY, BUT...
...I'M NOT RUNNING FROM WHO I AM!
EMMA ...
CAN WE...
... STILL BE BESTIES?
OF COURSE!
...

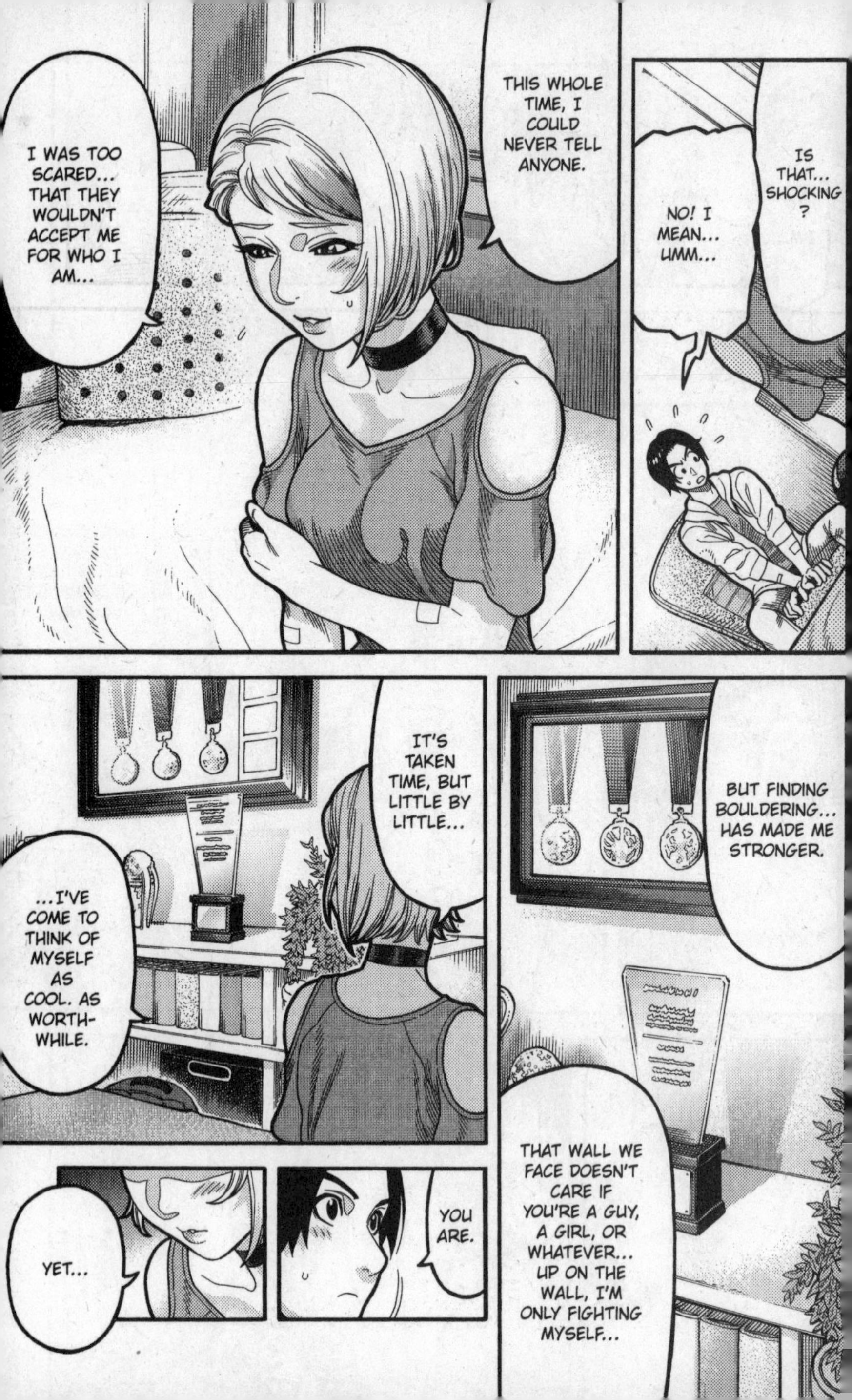
IS THAT... SHOCKING?
NO! I MEAN... UMM...
THIS WHOLE TIME, I COULD NEVER TELL ANYONE.
I WAS TOO SCARED... THAT THEY WOULDN'T ACCEPT ME FOR WHO I AM...
BUT FINDING BOULDERING... HAS MADE ME STRONGER.
THAT WALL WE FACE DOESN'T CARE IF YOU'RE A GUY, A GIRL, OR WHATEVER... UP ON THE WALL, I'M ONLY FIGHTING MYSELF...
IT'S TAKEN TIME, BUT LITTLE BY LITTLE...
...I'VE COME TO THINK OF MYSELF AS COOL. AS WORTH-WHILE.
YOU ARE.
YET...

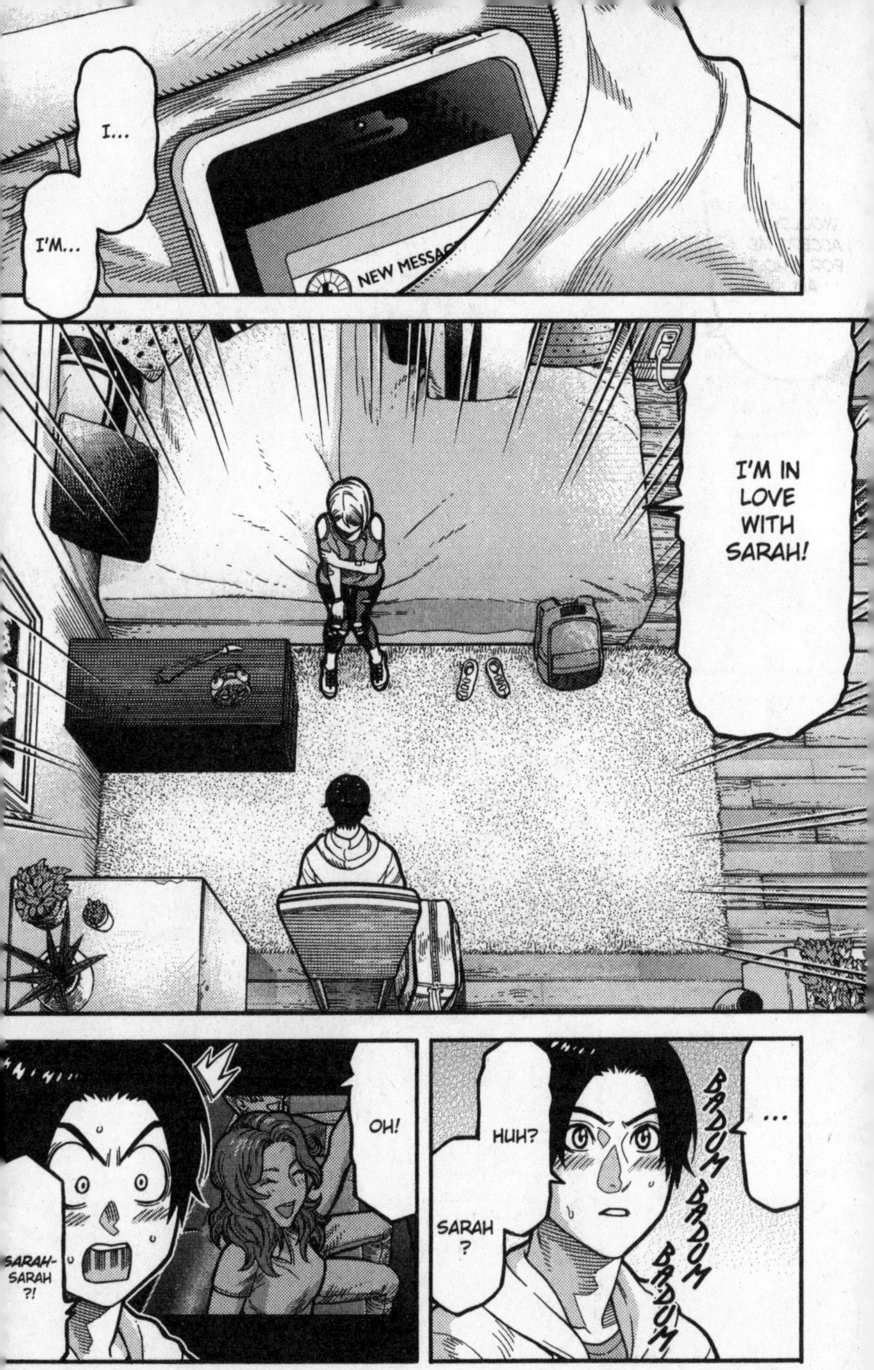
I...
I'M...
I'M IN LOVE WITH SARAH!
...
BADUM BADUM BADUM
HUH?
SARAH?
OH!
SARAH-SARAH?!

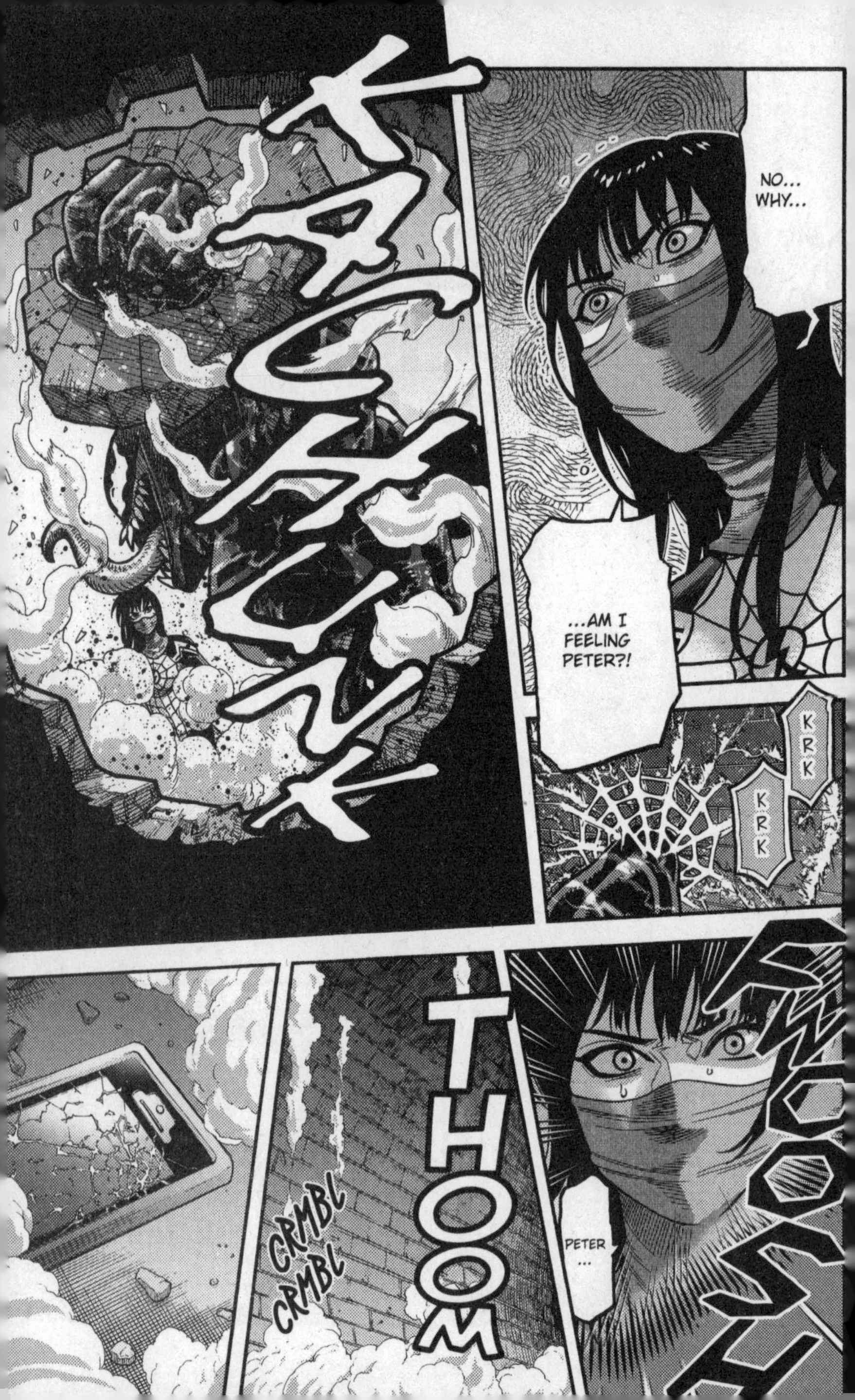
NO... WHY...
...AM I FEELING PETER?!
KRK
KRK
KACHUNK
WHOOSH
PETER ...
THOOM
CRMBL CRMBL

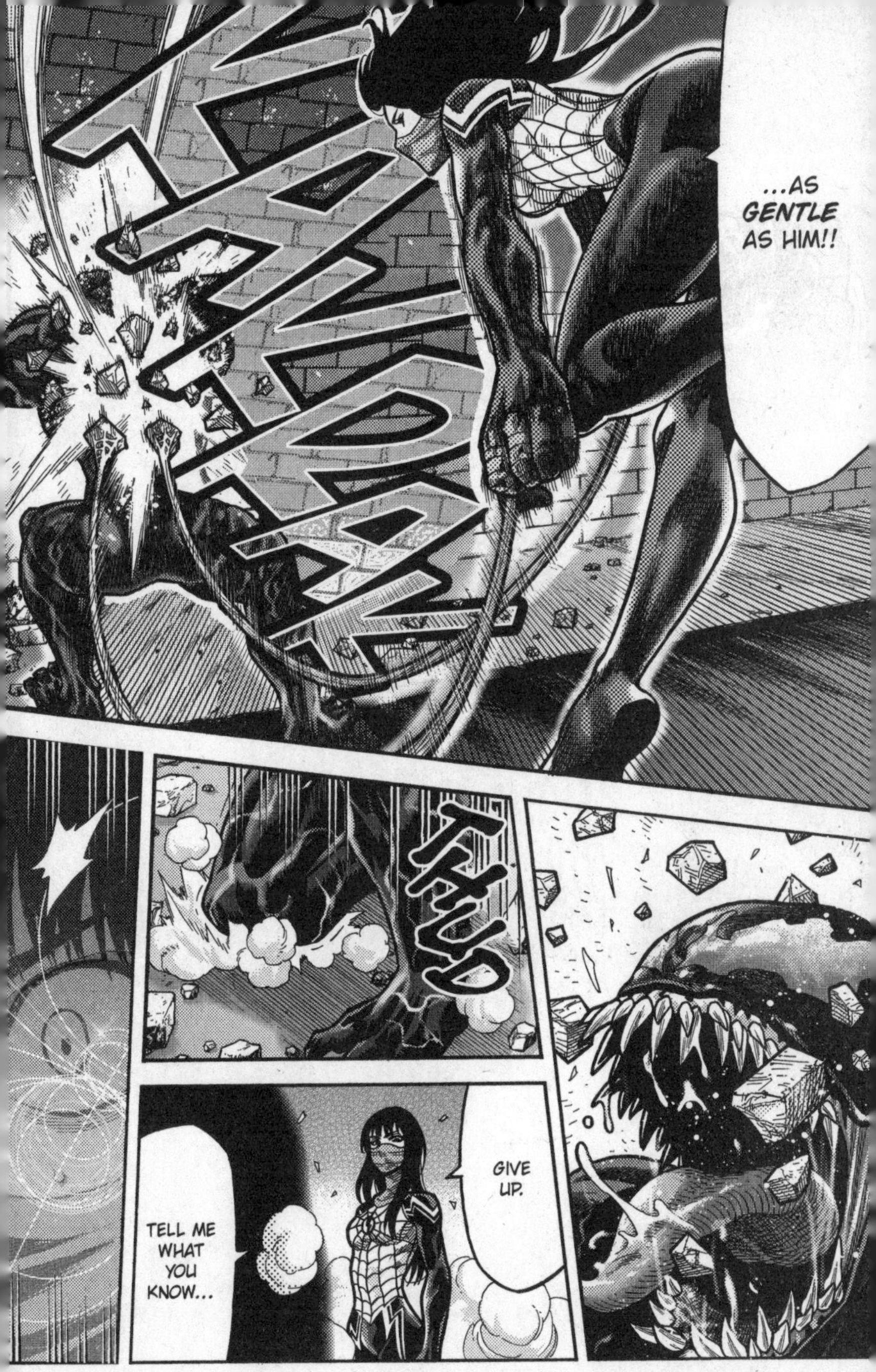
...AS GENTLE AS HIM!!
THUD
GIVE UP.
TELL ME WHAT YOU KNOW...

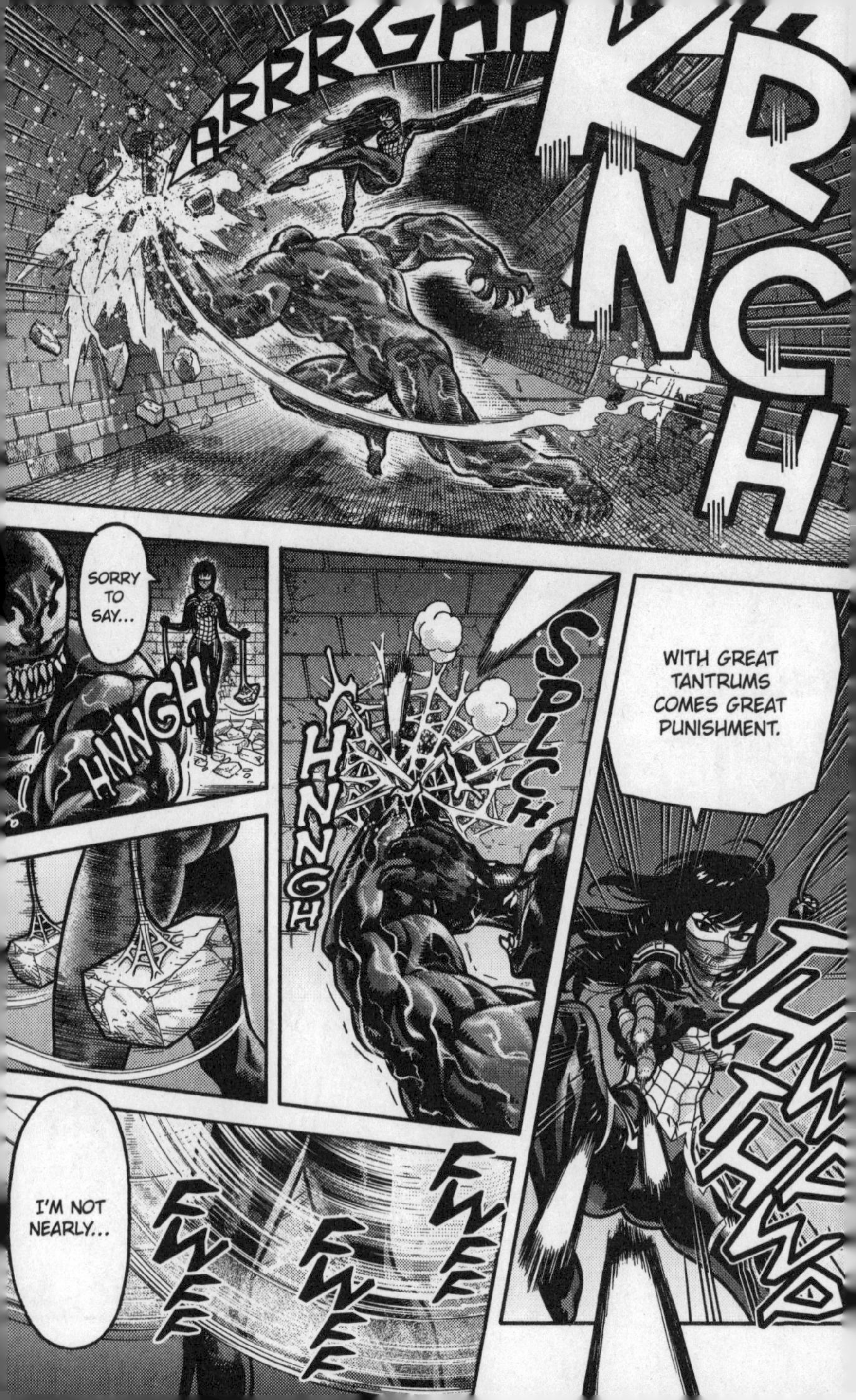
KRNCH
ARRRGH
WITH GREAT TANTRUMS COMES GREAT PUNISHMENT.
SPLCH
HNNGH
SORRY TO SAY...
HNNGH
I'M NOT NEARLY...
FWEE
FWEE
FWEE

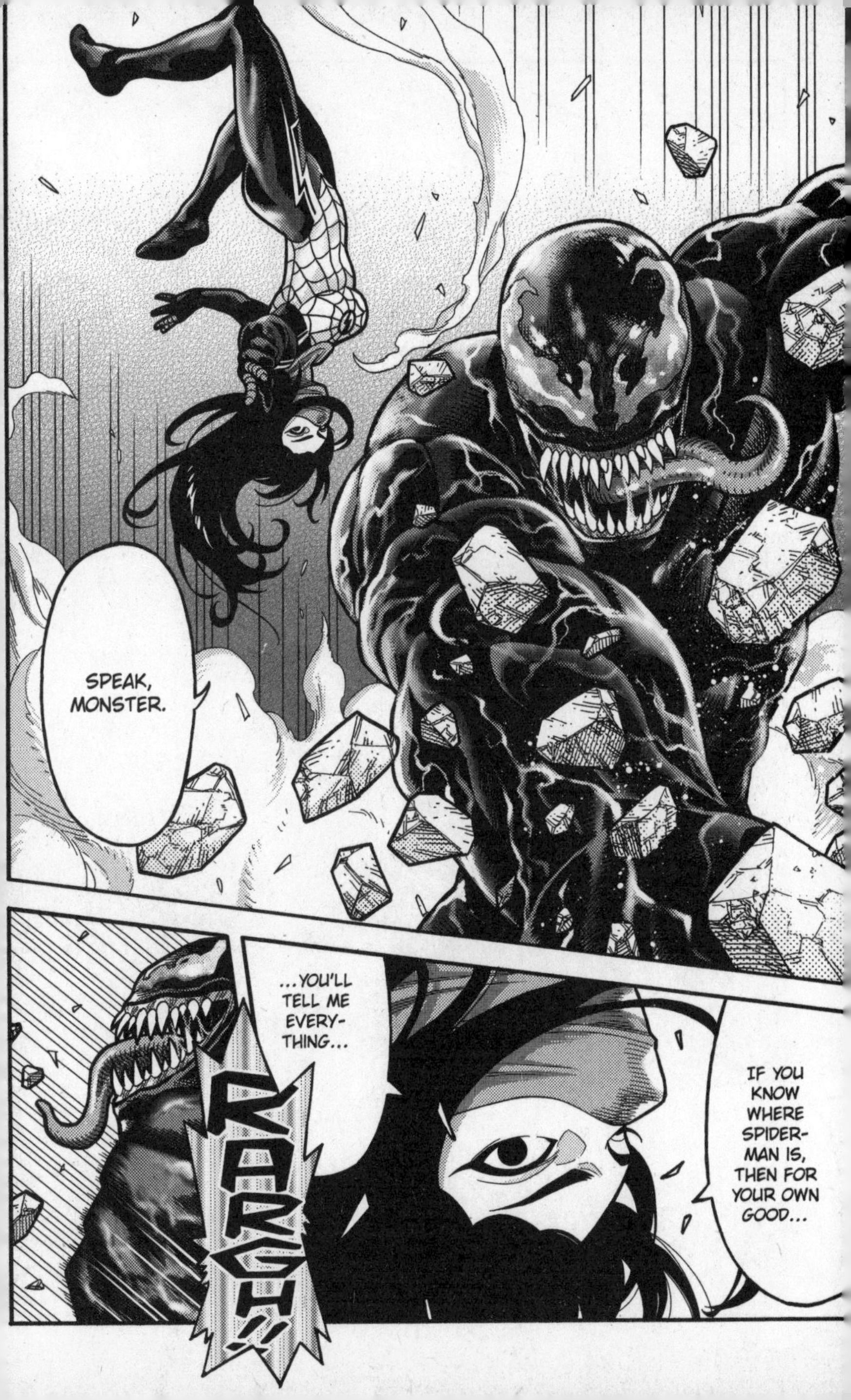
SPEAK, MONSTER.
IF YOU KNOW WHERE SPIDER-MAN IS, THEN FOR YOUR OWN GOOD...
...YOU'LL TELL ME EVERYTHING...
RARGH!!

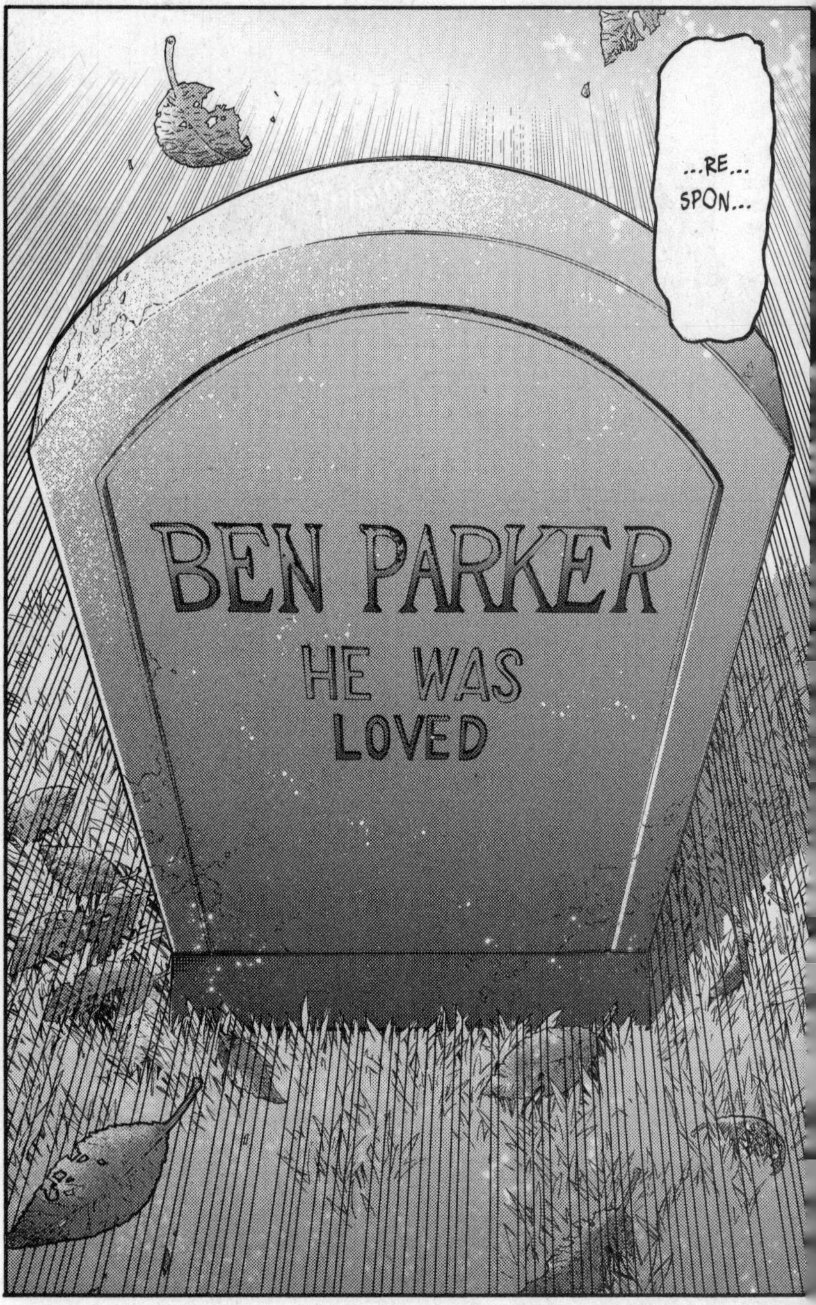
...RE...
SPON...
BEN PARKER
HE WAS
LOVED

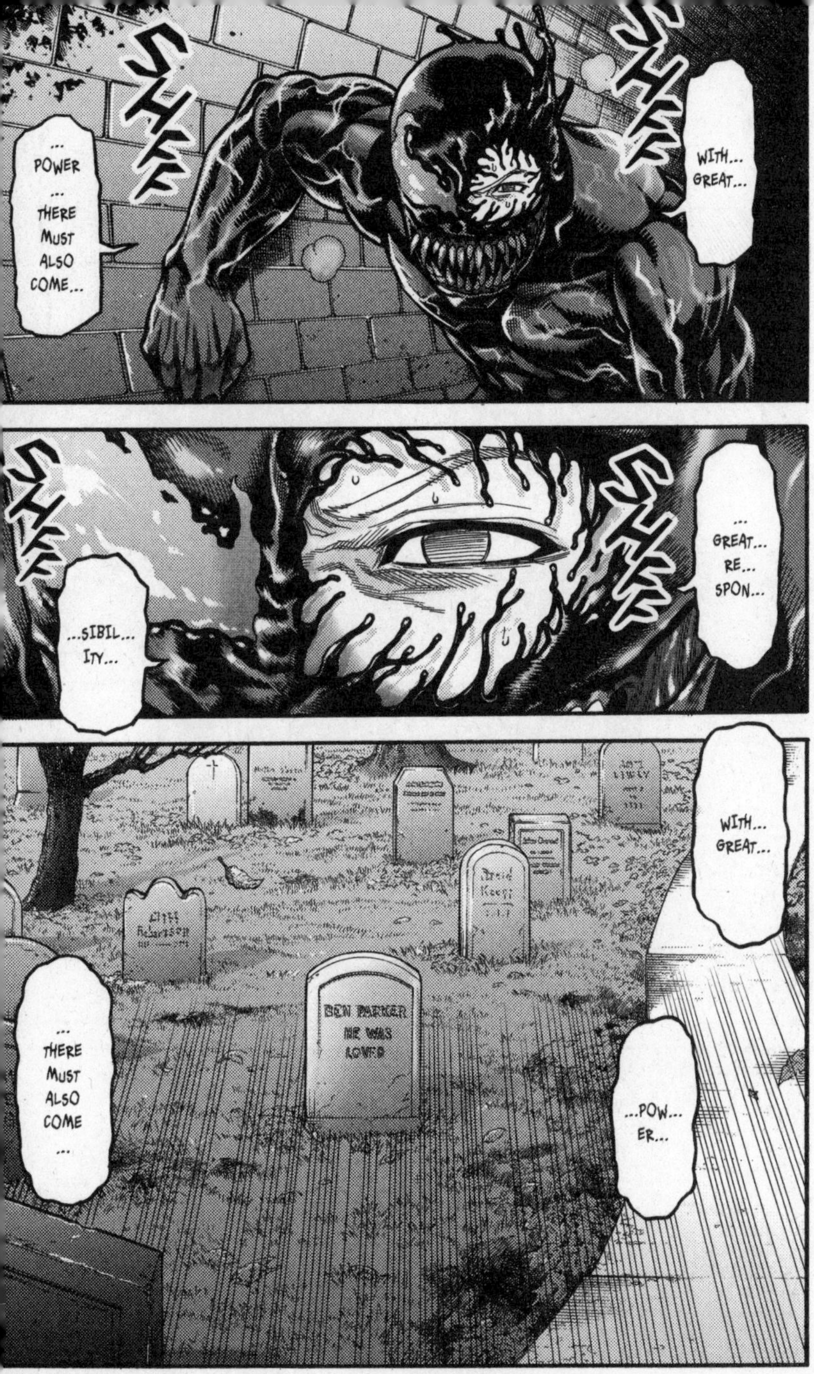
SHKK
WITH... GREAT...
SHKK
... POWER ... THERE MUST ALSO COME...
SHKK
... GREAT... RE... SPON...
SHKK
...SIBIL... ITY...
WITH... GREAT...
BEN PARKER HE WAS LOVED
...POW... ER...
... THERE MUST ALSO COME ...

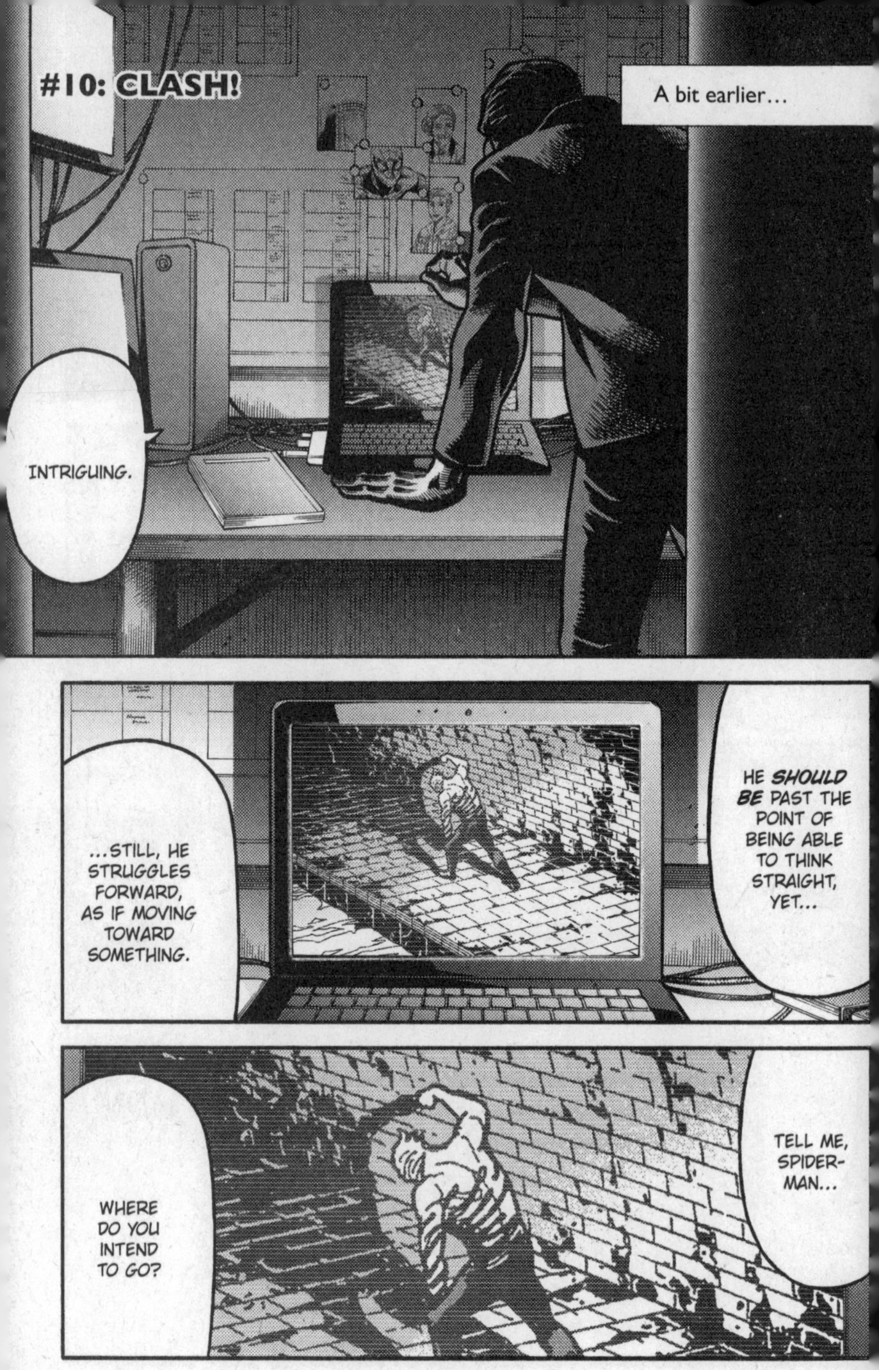
#10: CLASH!
A bit earlier…
INTRIGUING.
HE SHOULD BE PAST THE POINT OF BEING ABLE TO THINK STRAIGHT, YET…
…STILL, HE STRUGGLES FORWARD, AS IF MOVING TOWARD SOMETHING.
TELL ME, SPIDER-MAN…
WHERE DO YOU INTEND TO GO?

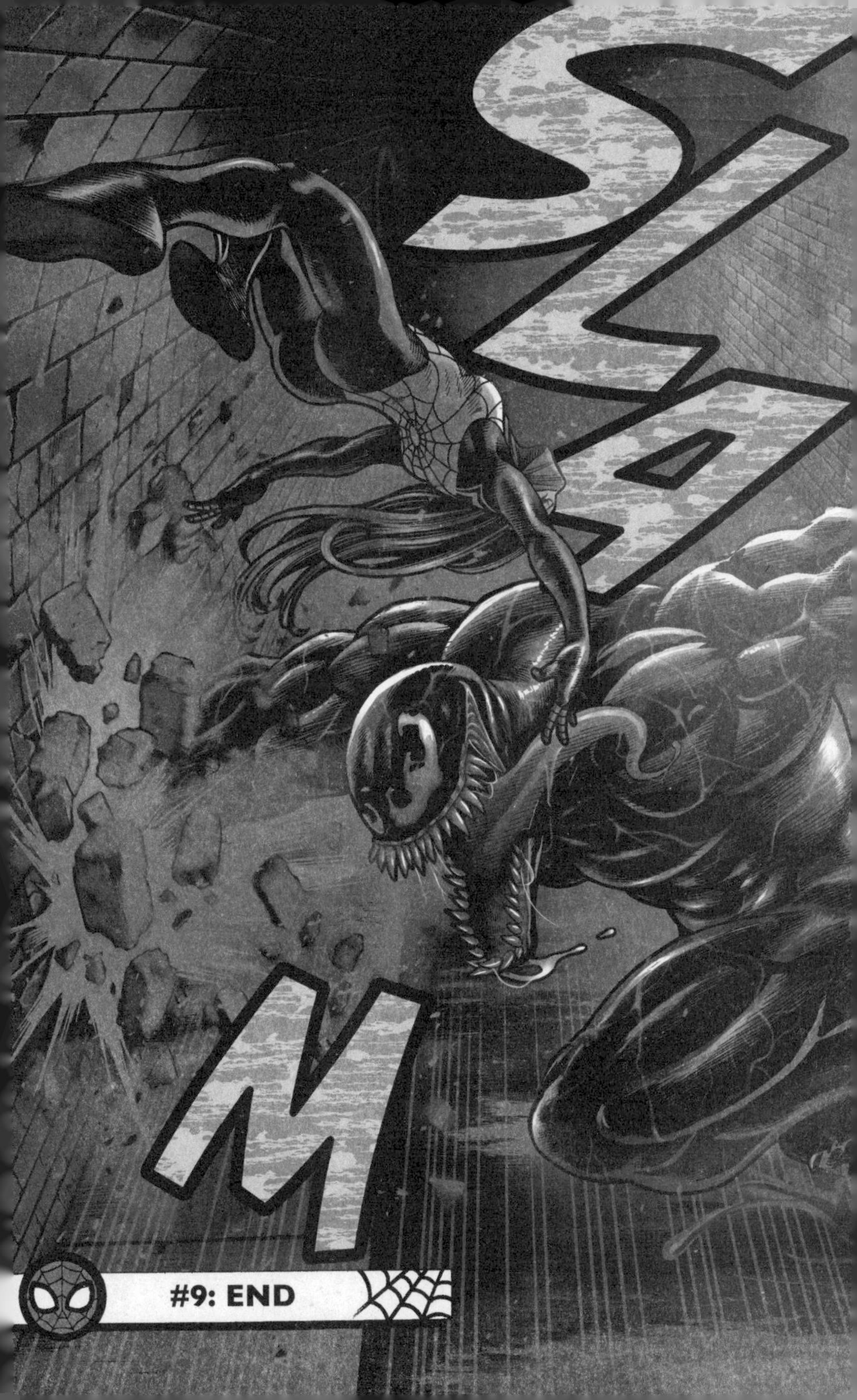
SLAM
#9: END

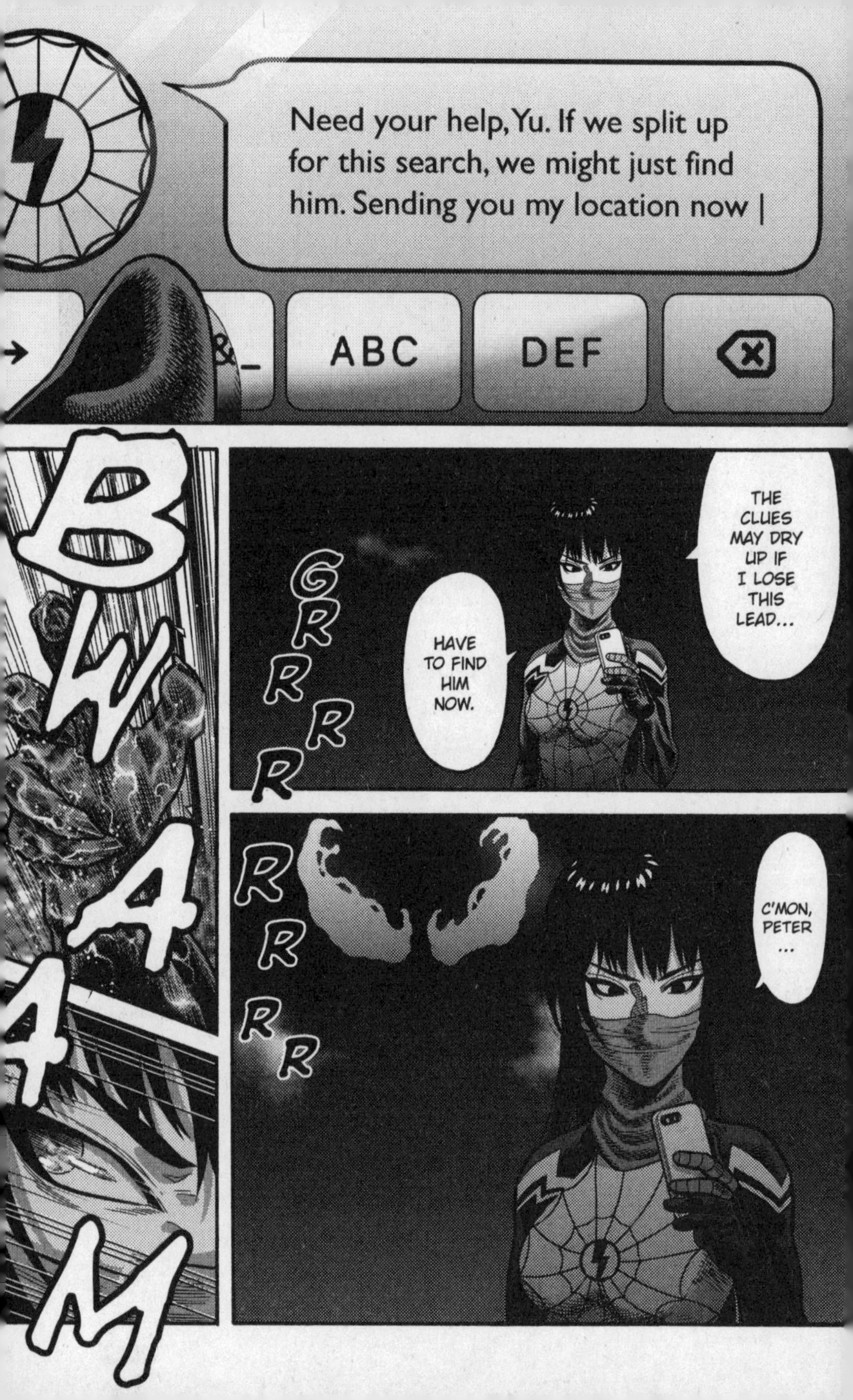
Need your help, Yu. If we split up for this search, we might just find him. Sending you my location now |
&_
ABC
DEF
THE CLUES MAY DRY UP IF I LOSE THIS LEAD...
HAVE TO FIND HIM NOW.
GRRRRRRRRR
C'MON, PETER...
BWAAAM

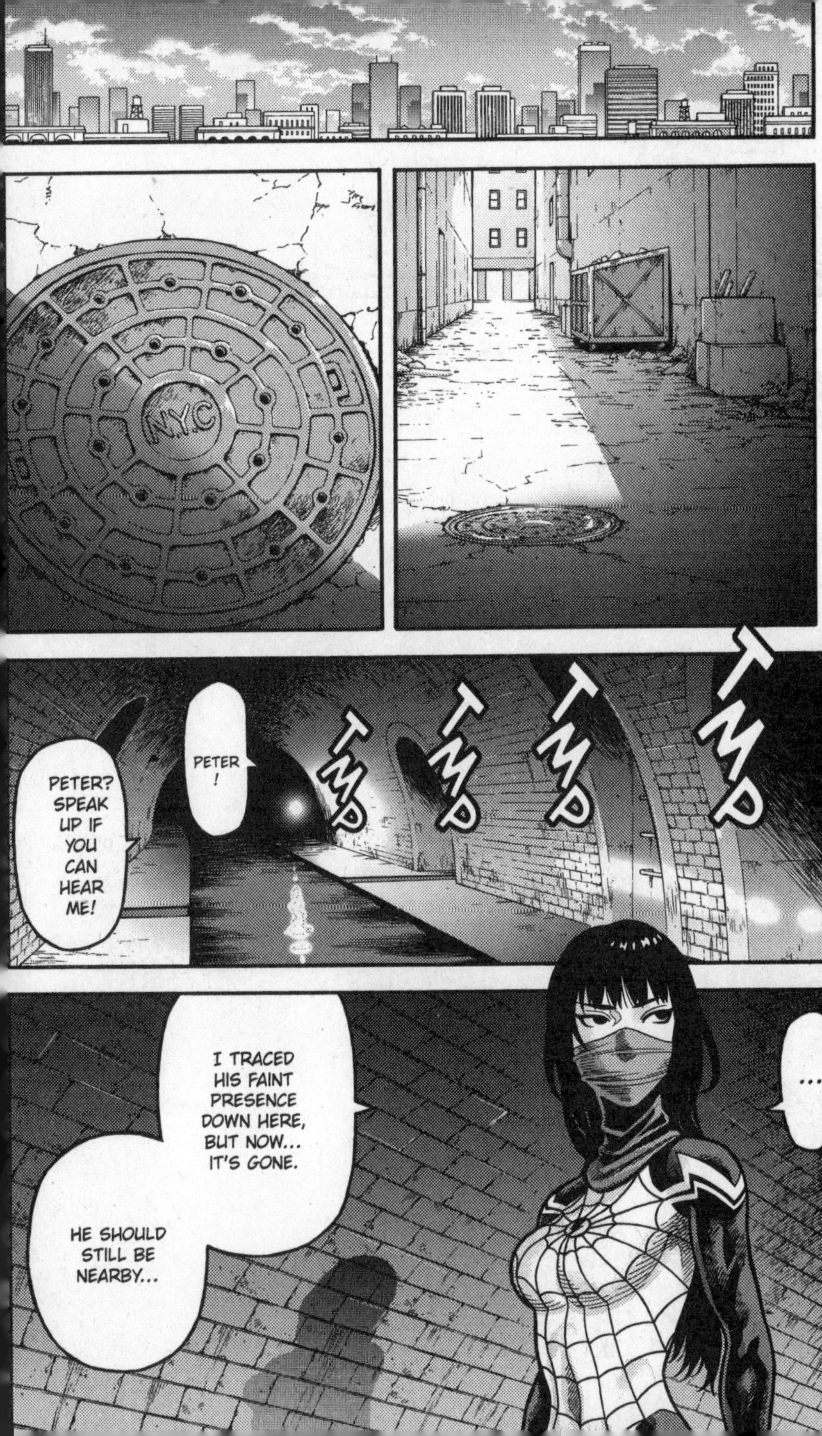
TMP
TMP
TMP
TMP
PETER!
PETER? SPEAK UP IF YOU CAN HEAR ME!
...
I TRACED HIS FAINT PRESENCE DOWN HERE, BUT NOW... IT'S GONE.
HE SHOULD STILL BE NEARBY...

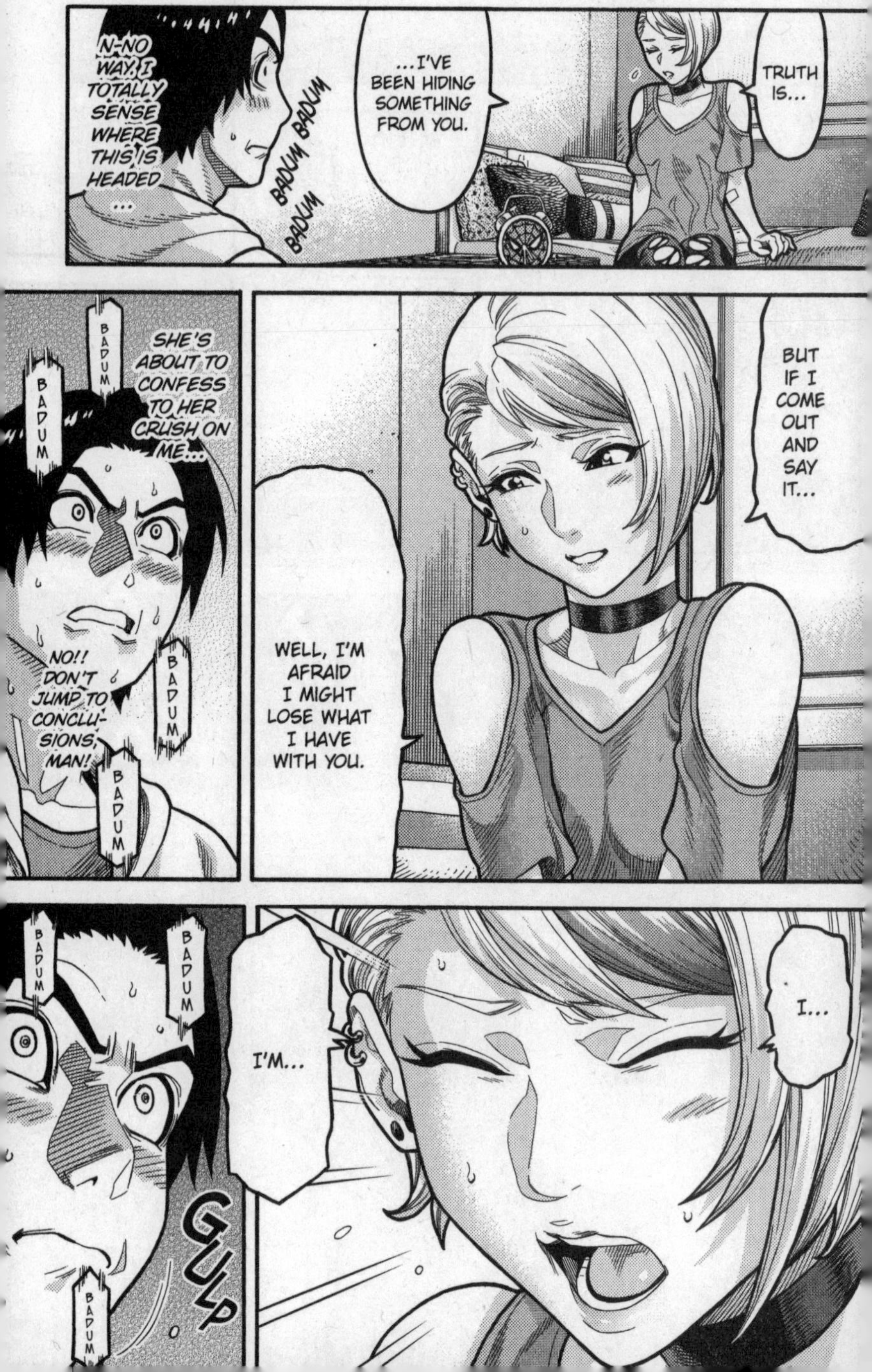
TRUTH IS...
...I'VE BEEN HIDING SOMETHING FROM YOU.
N-NO WAY. I TOTALLY SENSE WHERE THIS IS HEADED ...
BADUM BADUM
BADUM
BUT IF I COME OUT AND SAY IT...
WELL, I'M AFRAID I MIGHT LOSE WHAT I HAVE WITH YOU.
BADUM
SHE'S ABOUT TO CONFESS TO HER CRUSH ON ME...
BADUM
BADUM
NO!! DON'T JUMP TO CONCLU-SIONS, MAN!
BADUM
I...
I'M...
BADUM
BADUM
GULP
BADUM

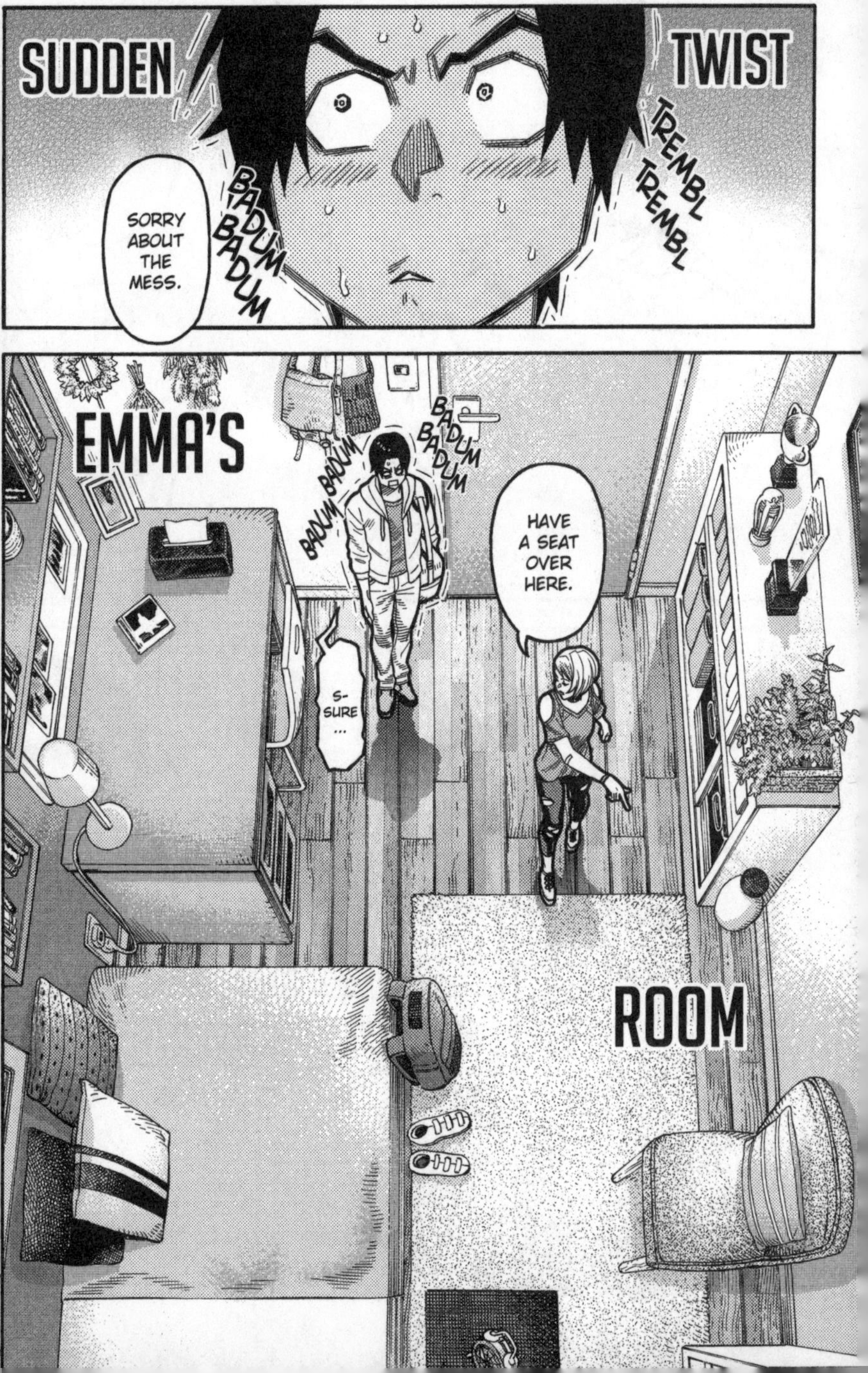
SUDDEN TWIST
TREMBL TREMBL
BADUM BADUM
SORRY ABOUT THE MESS.
EMMA'S ROOM
BADUM BADUM
HAVE A SEAT OVER HERE.
BADUM BADUM BADUM
S-SURE ...

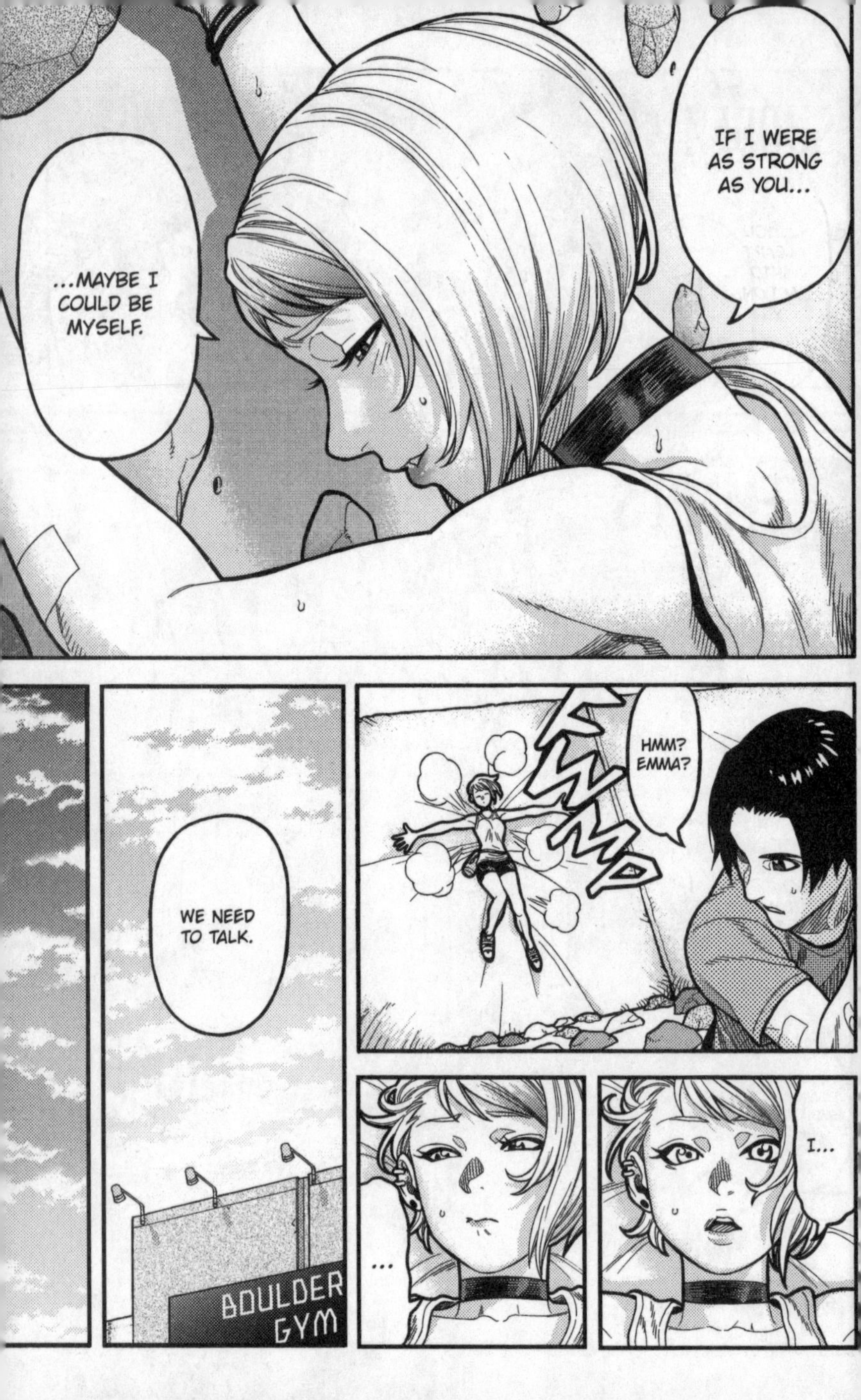
IF I WERE AS STRONG AS YOU...
...MAYBE I COULD BE MYSELF.
HMM? EMMA?
KWMP
I...
...
WE NEED TO TALK.
BOULDER GYM

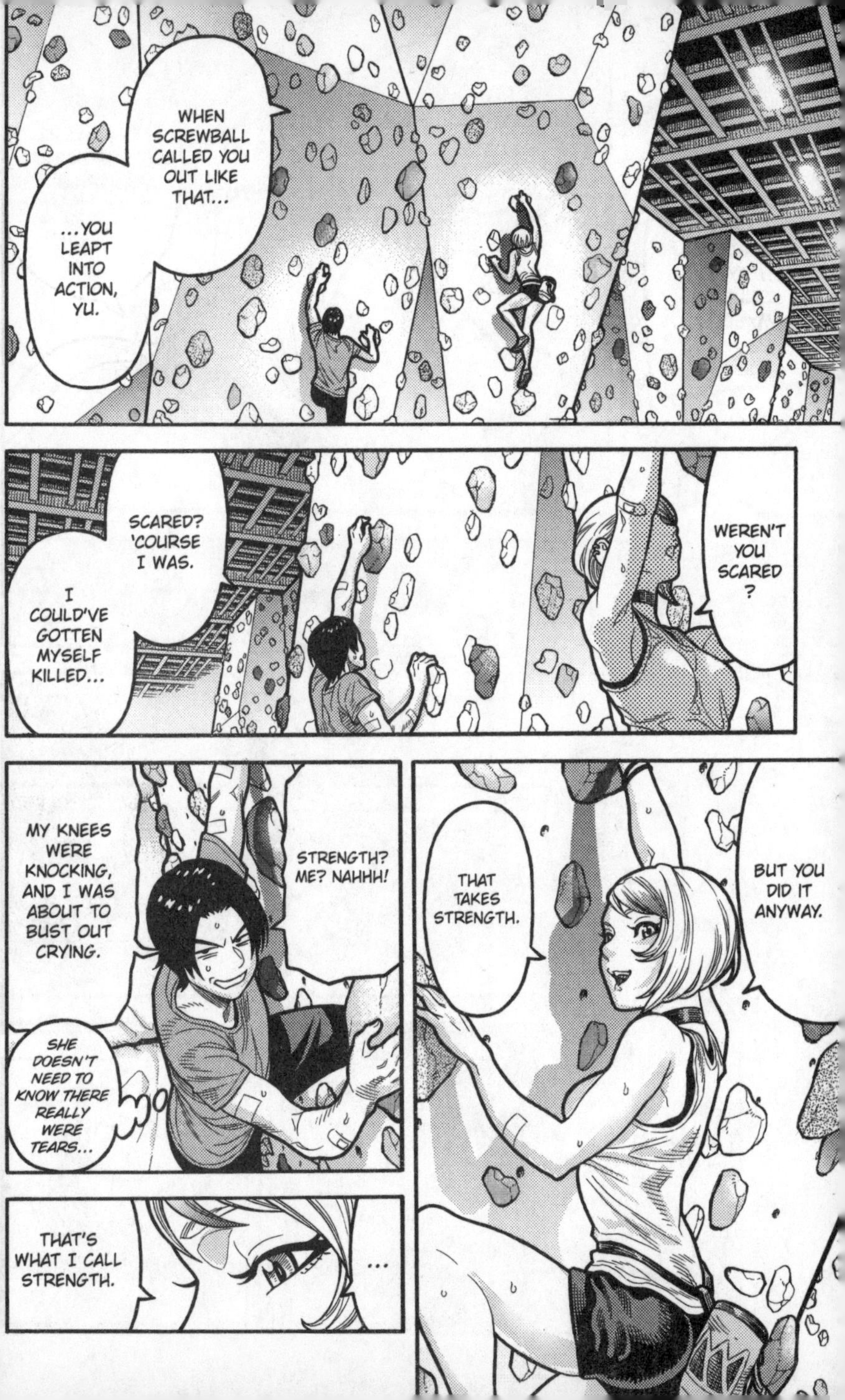
WHEN SCREWBALL CALLED YOU OUT LIKE THAT...
...YOU LEAPT INTO ACTION, YU.
WEREN'T YOU SCARED?
SCARED? 'COURSE I WAS.
I COULD'VE GOTTEN MYSELF KILLED...
BUT YOU DID IT ANYWAY.
THAT TAKES STRENGTH.
STRENGTH? ME? NAHHH!
MY KNEES WERE KNOCKING, AND I WAS ABOUT TO BUST OUT CRYING.
SHE DOESN'T NEED TO KNOW THERE REALLY WERE TEARS...
...
THAT'S WHAT I CALL STRENGTH.

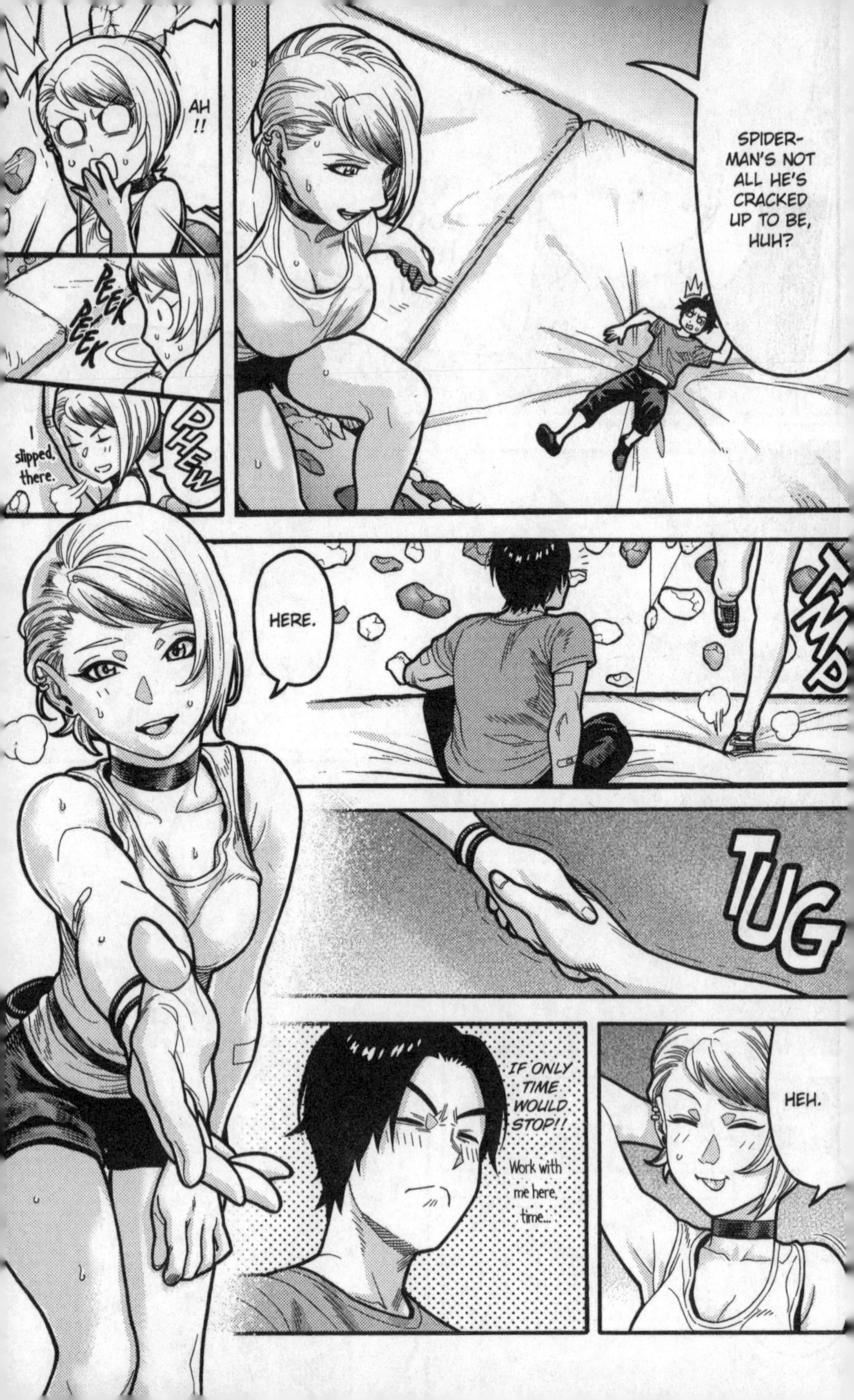
SPIDER-MAN'S NOT ALL HE'S CRACKED UP TO BE, HUH?
AH !!
PEEK PEEK
PHEW
I slipped, there.
TMP
HERE.
TUG
HEH.
IF ONLY TIME WOULD STOP!!
Work with me here, time...

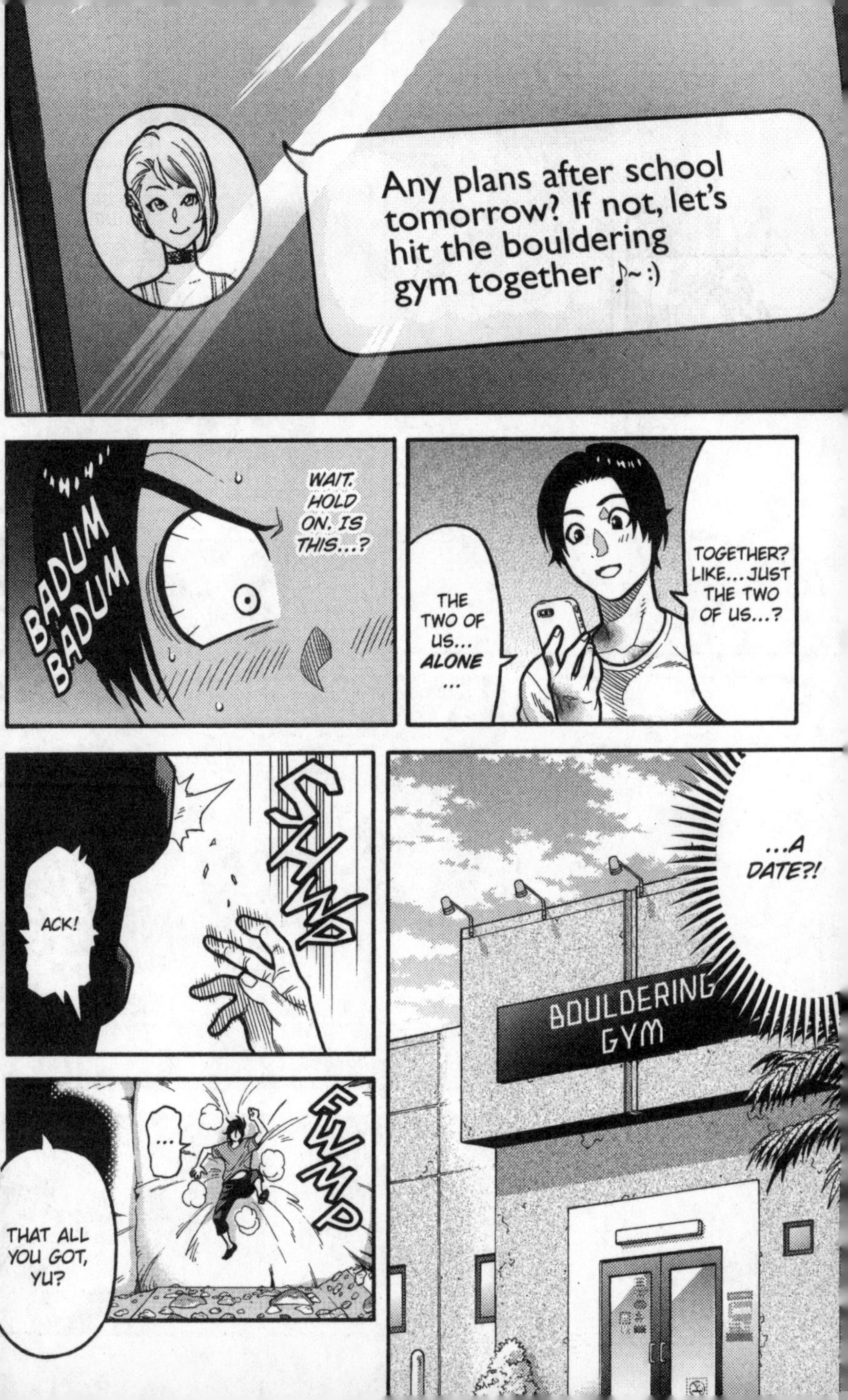
Any plans after school tomorrow? If not, let's hit the bouldering gym together ♪~ :)
TOGETHER? LIKE... JUST THE TWO OF US...?
THE TWO OF US... ALONE ...
WAIT. HOLD ON. IS THIS...?
BADUM BADUM
...A DATE?!
BOULDERING GYM
SHWP
ACK!
FWMP
...
THAT ALL YOU GOT, YU?

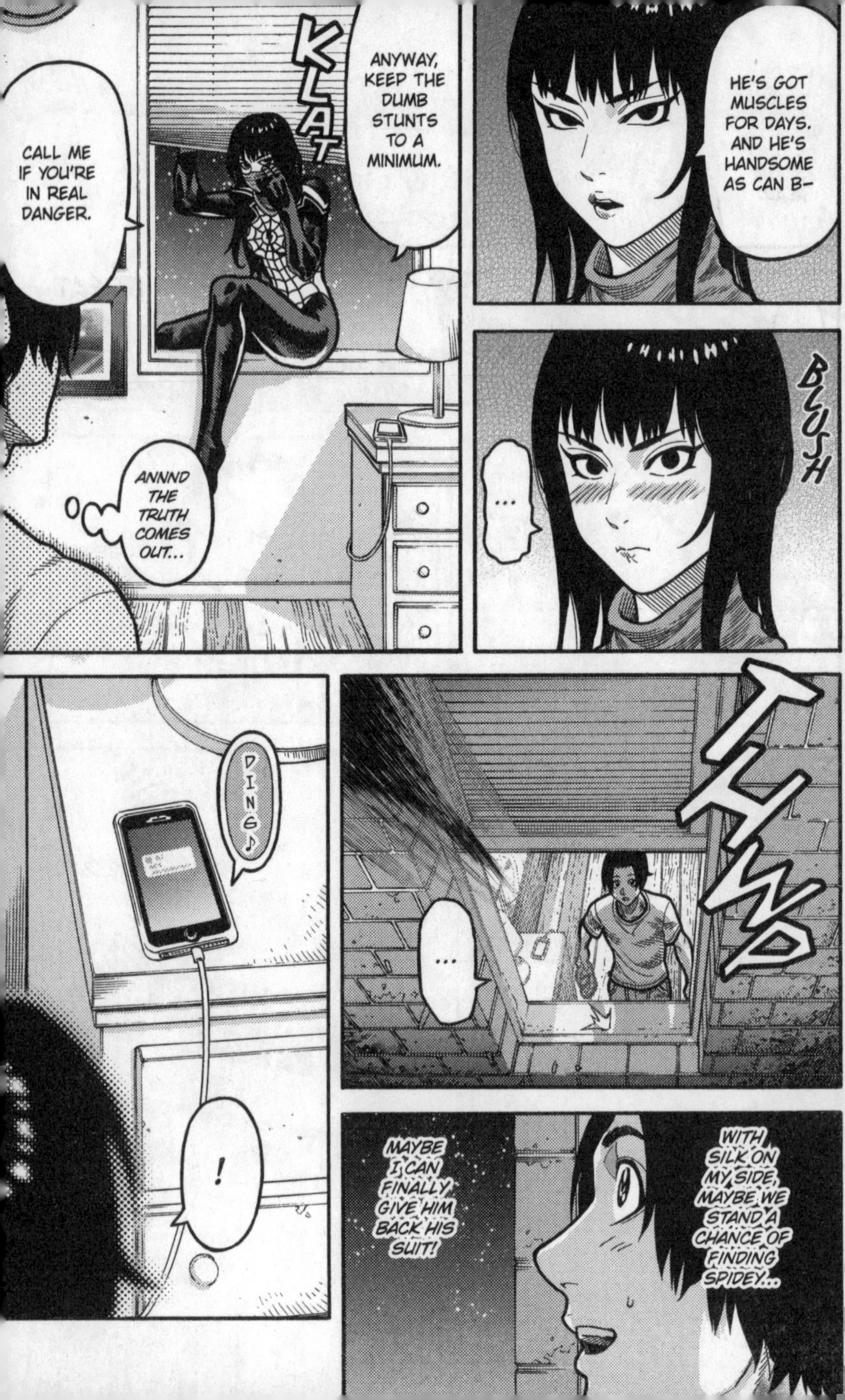
HE'S GOT MUSCLES FOR DAYS. AND HE'S HANDSOME AS CAN B-
BLUSH
...
KLAT
ANYWAY, KEEP THE DUMB STUNTS TO A MINIMUM.
CALL ME IF YOU'RE IN REAL DANGER.
ANNND THE TRUTH COMES OUT...
THWP
...
WITH SILK ON MY SIDE, MAYBE WE STAND A CHANCE OF FINDING SPIDEY...
MAYBE I CAN FINALLY GIVE HIM BACK HIS SUIT!
DING♪
!

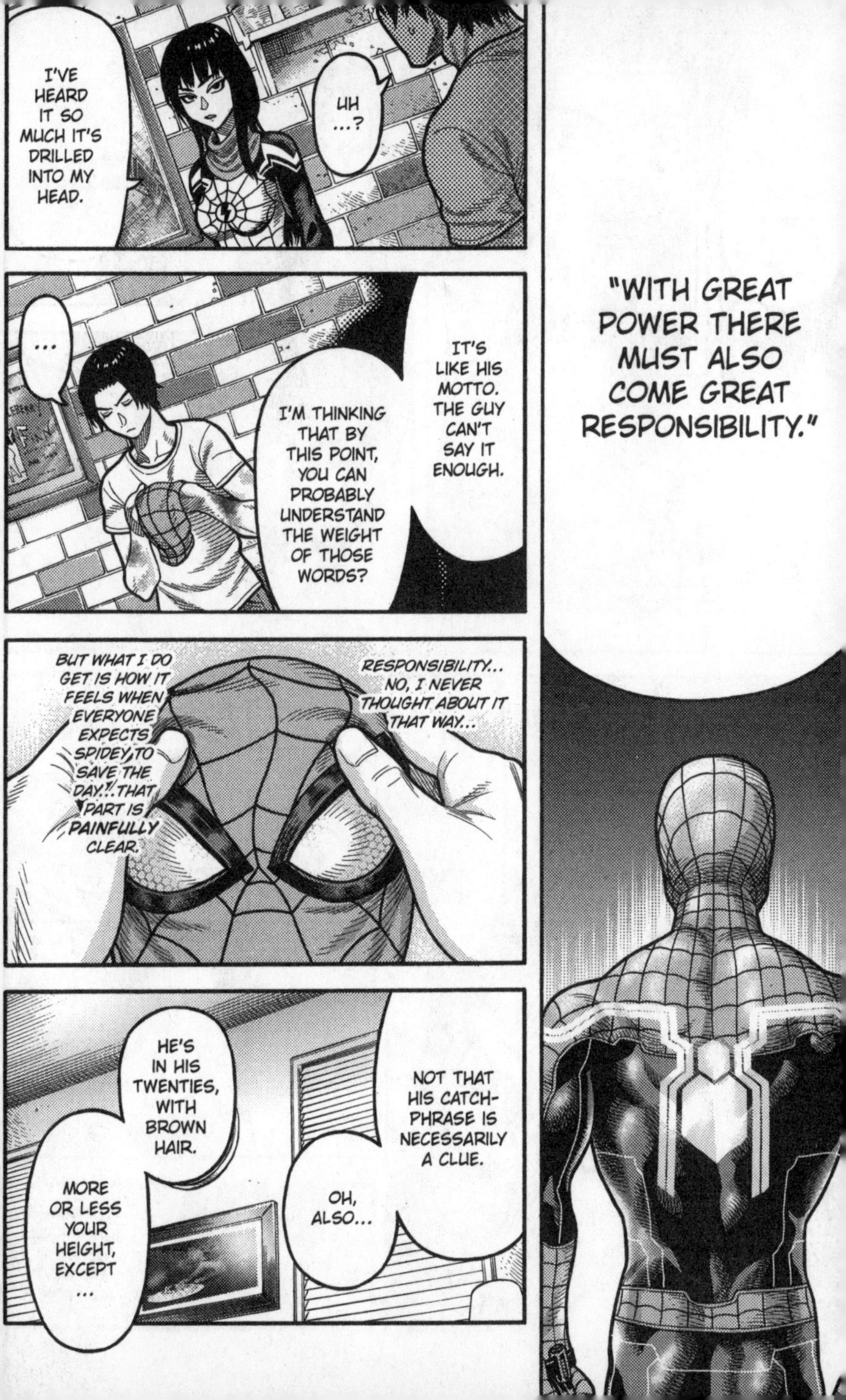
"WITH GREAT POWER THERE MUST ALSO COME GREAT RESPONSIBILITY."
I'VE HEARD IT SO MUCH IT'S DRILLED INTO MY HEAD.
UH ...?
IT'S LIKE HIS MOTTO. THE GUY CAN'T SAY IT ENOUGH.
I'M THINKING THAT BY THIS POINT, YOU CAN PROBABLY UNDERSTAND THE WEIGHT OF THOSE WORDS?
...
RESPONSIBILITY... NO, I NEVER THOUGHT ABOUT IT THAT WAY...
BUT WHAT I DO GET IS HOW IT FEELS WHEN EVERYONE EXPECTS SPIDEY TO SAVE THE DAY... THAT PART IS PAINFULLY CLEAR.
NOT THAT HIS CATCH-PHRASE IS NECESSARILY A CLUE.
OH, ALSO...
HE'S IN HIS TWENTIES, WITH BROWN HAIR.
MORE OR LESS YOUR HEIGHT, EXCEPT ...

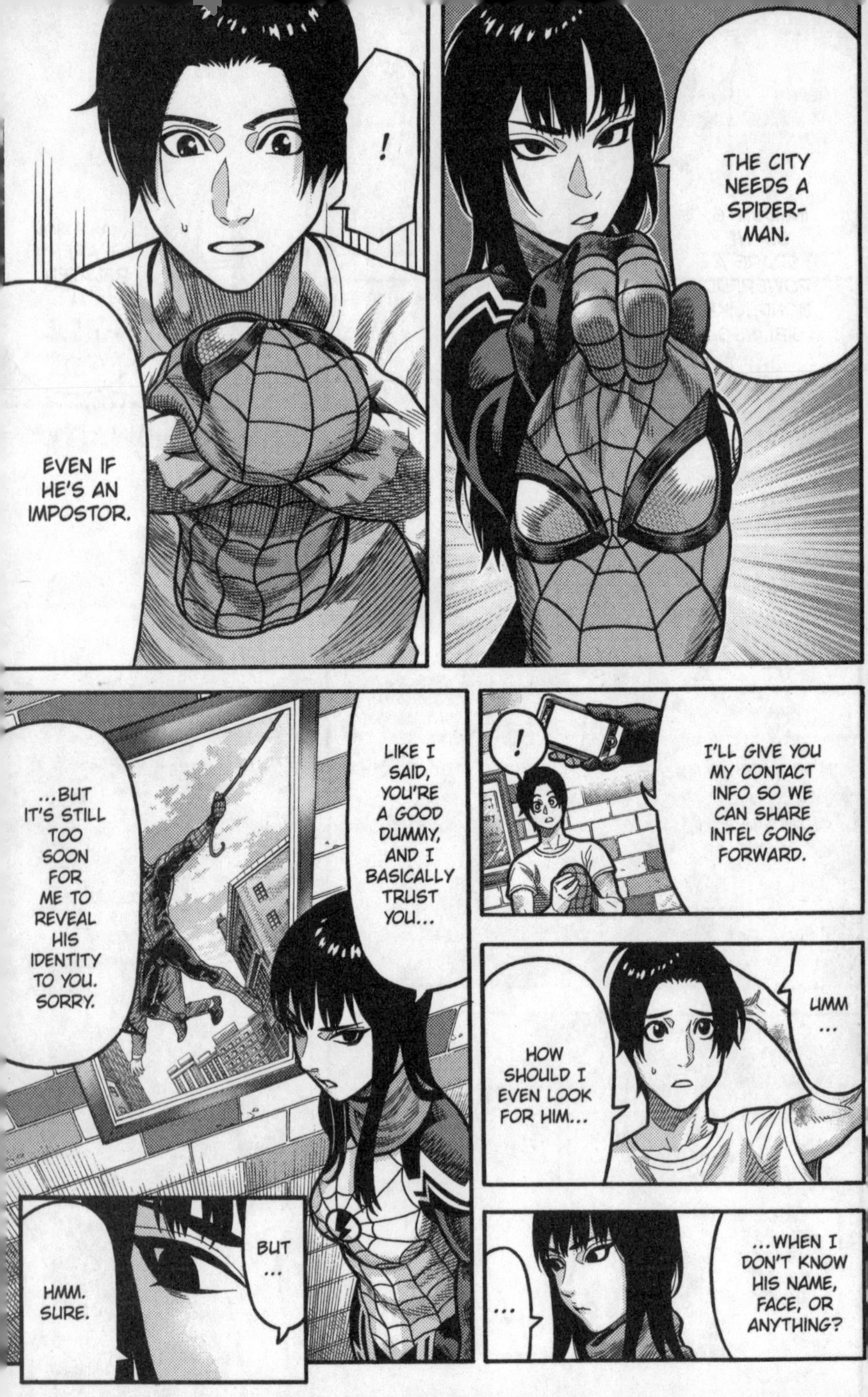
THE CITY NEEDS A SPIDER-MAN.
!
EVEN IF HE'S AN IMPOSTOR.
!
I'LL GIVE YOU MY CONTACT INFO SO WE CAN SHARE INTEL GOING FORWARD.
UMM ...
HOW SHOULD I EVEN LOOK FOR HIM...
...WHEN I DON'T KNOW HIS NAME, FACE, OR ANYTHING?
...
LIKE I SAID, YOU'RE A GOOD DUMMY, AND I BASICALLY TRUST YOU...
...BUT IT'S STILL TOO SOON FOR ME TO REVEAL HIS IDENTITY TO YOU. SORRY.
BUT ...
HMM. SURE.

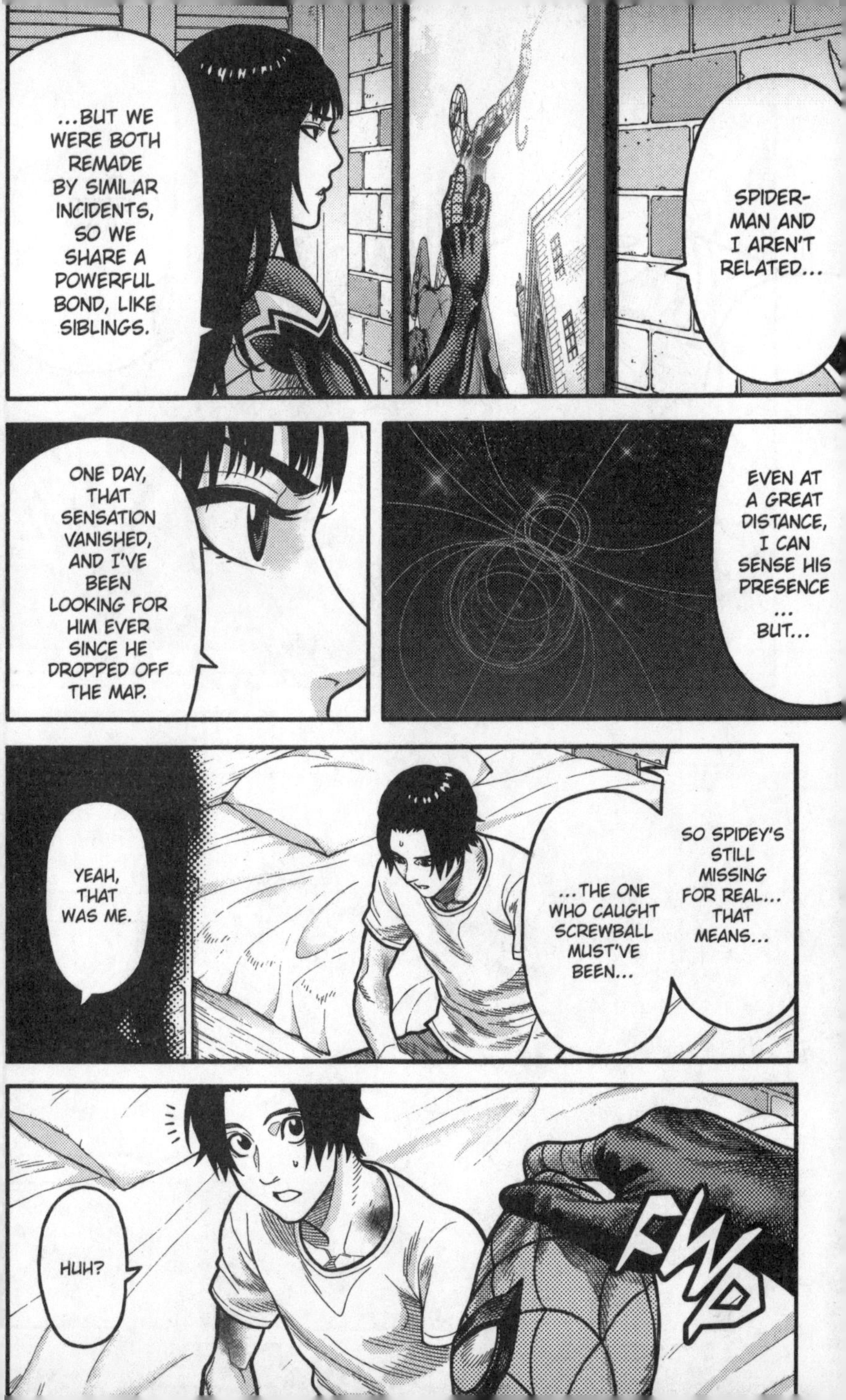
SPIDER-MAN AND I AREN'T RELATED...
...BUT WE WERE BOTH REMADE BY SIMILAR INCIDENTS, SO WE SHARE A POWERFUL BOND, LIKE SIBLINGS.
EVEN AT A GREAT DISTANCE, I CAN SENSE HIS PRESENCE ... BUT...
ONE DAY, THAT SENSATION VANISHED, AND I'VE BEEN LOOKING FOR HIM EVER SINCE HE DROPPED OFF THE MAP.
SO SPIDEY'S STILL MISSING FOR REAL... THAT MEANS...
...THE ONE WHO CAUGHT SCREWBALL MUST'VE BEEN...
YEAH, THAT WAS ME.
FWP
HUH?

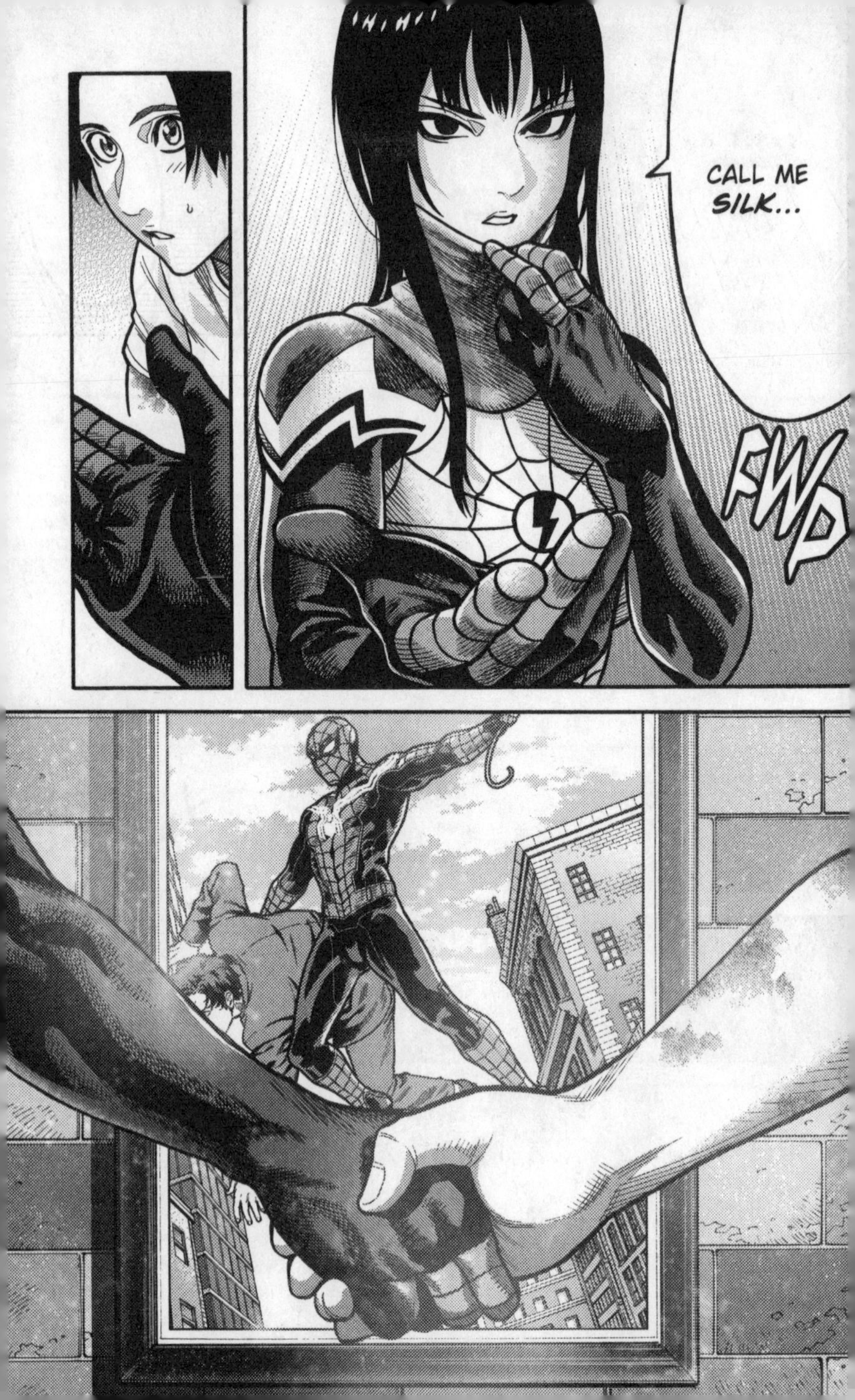
CALL ME SILK...
FWD

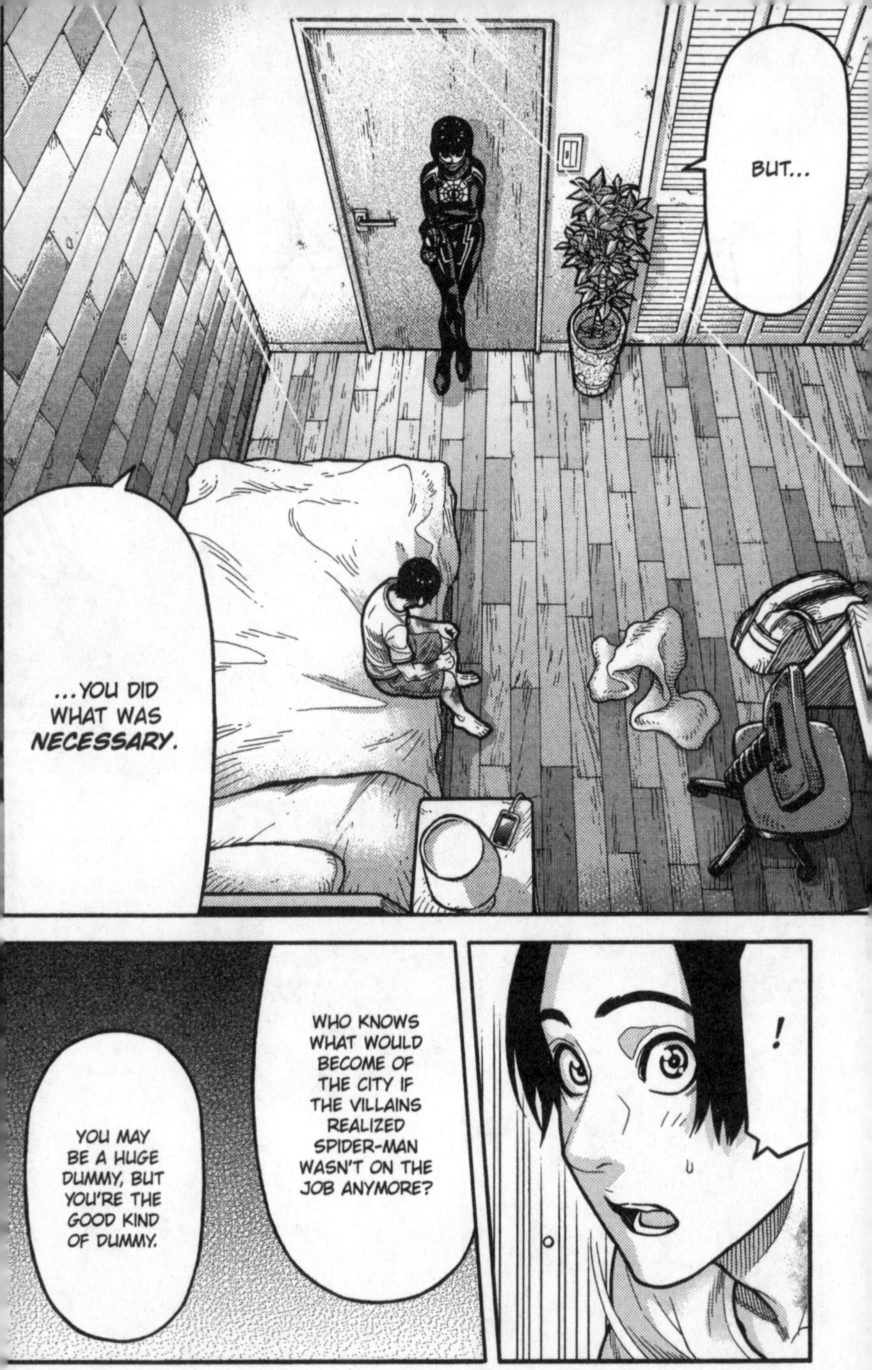
BUT...
...YOU DID WHAT WAS NECESSARY.
!
WHO KNOWS WHAT WOULD BECOME OF THE CITY IF THE VILLAINS REALIZED SPIDER-MAN WASN'T ON THE JOB ANYMORE?
YOU MAY BE A HUGE DUMMY, BUT YOU'RE THE GOOD KIND OF DUMMY.

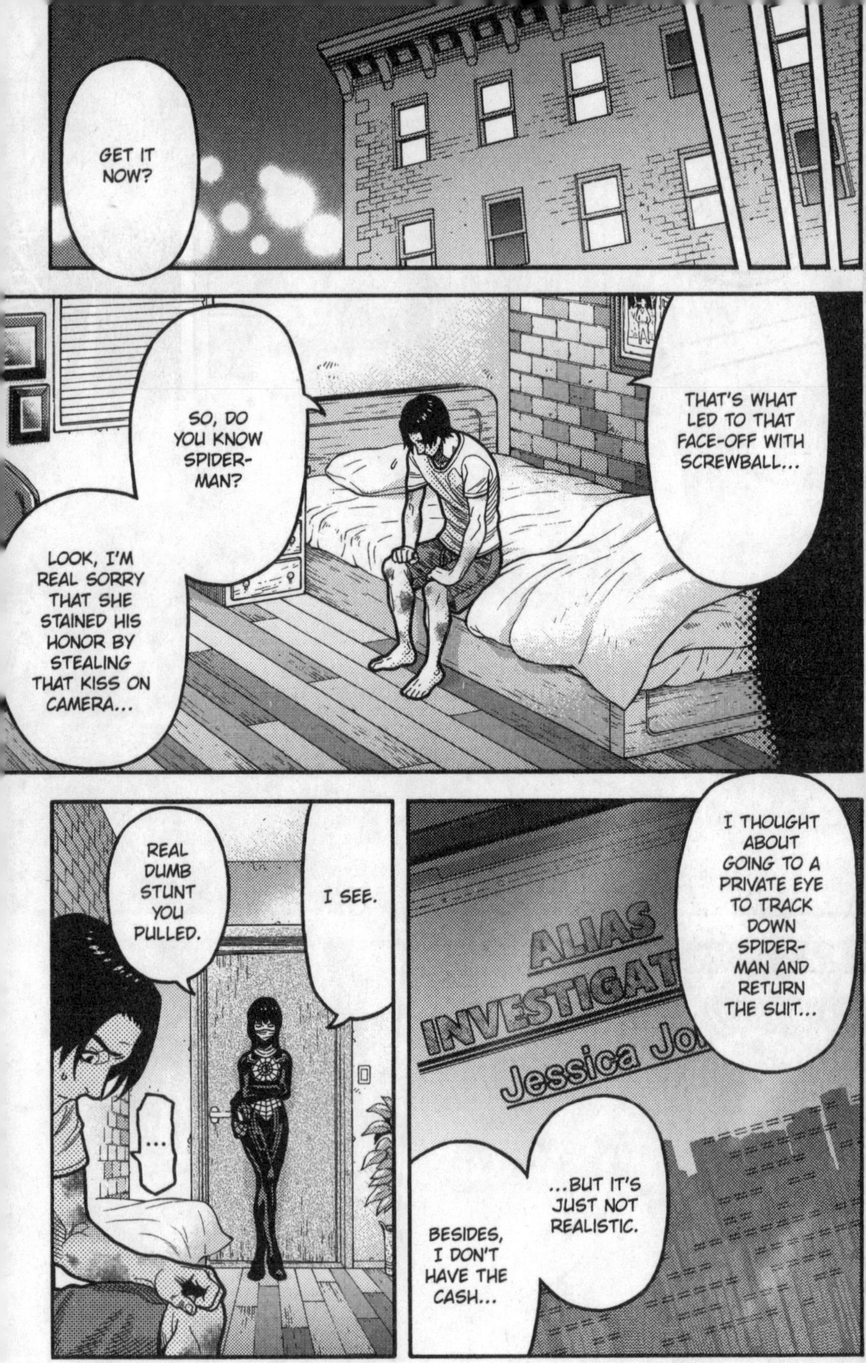
GET IT NOW?
THAT'S WHAT LED TO THAT FACE-OFF WITH SCREWBALL...
SO, DO YOU KNOW SPIDER-MAN?
LOOK, I'M REAL SORRY THAT SHE STAINED HIS HONOR BY STEALING THAT KISS ON CAMERA...
I THOUGHT ABOUT GOING TO A PRIVATE EYE TO TRACK DOWN SPIDER-MAN AND RETURN THE SUIT...
ALIAS INVESTIGAT
Jessica Jo
...BUT IT'S JUST NOT REALISTIC.
BESIDES, I DON'T HAVE THE CASH...
I SEE.
REAL DUMB STUNT YOU PULLED.
...

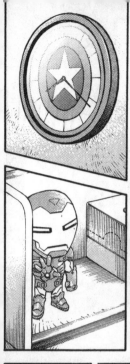

STARE

SIGH

...

!

FINE.
I'LL
FREE
YOU.

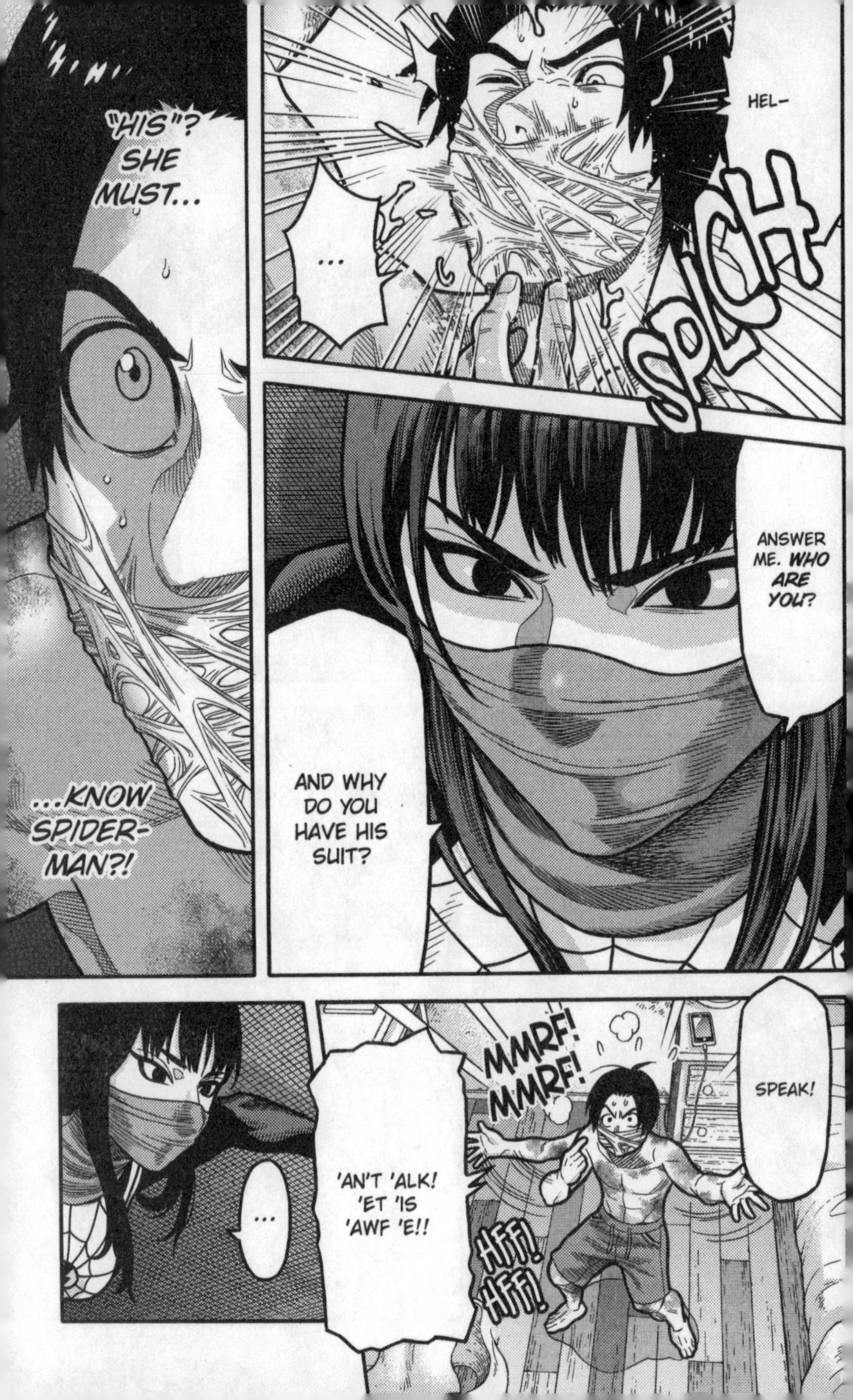
HEL-
SPLCH
...
ANSWER ME. WHO ARE YOU?
AND WHY DO YOU HAVE HIS SUIT?
"HIS"? SHE MUST...
...KNOW SPIDER-MAN?!
SPEAK!
MMRF! MMRF!
'AN'T 'ALK! 'ET 'IS 'AWF 'E!!
HFF! HFF!
...

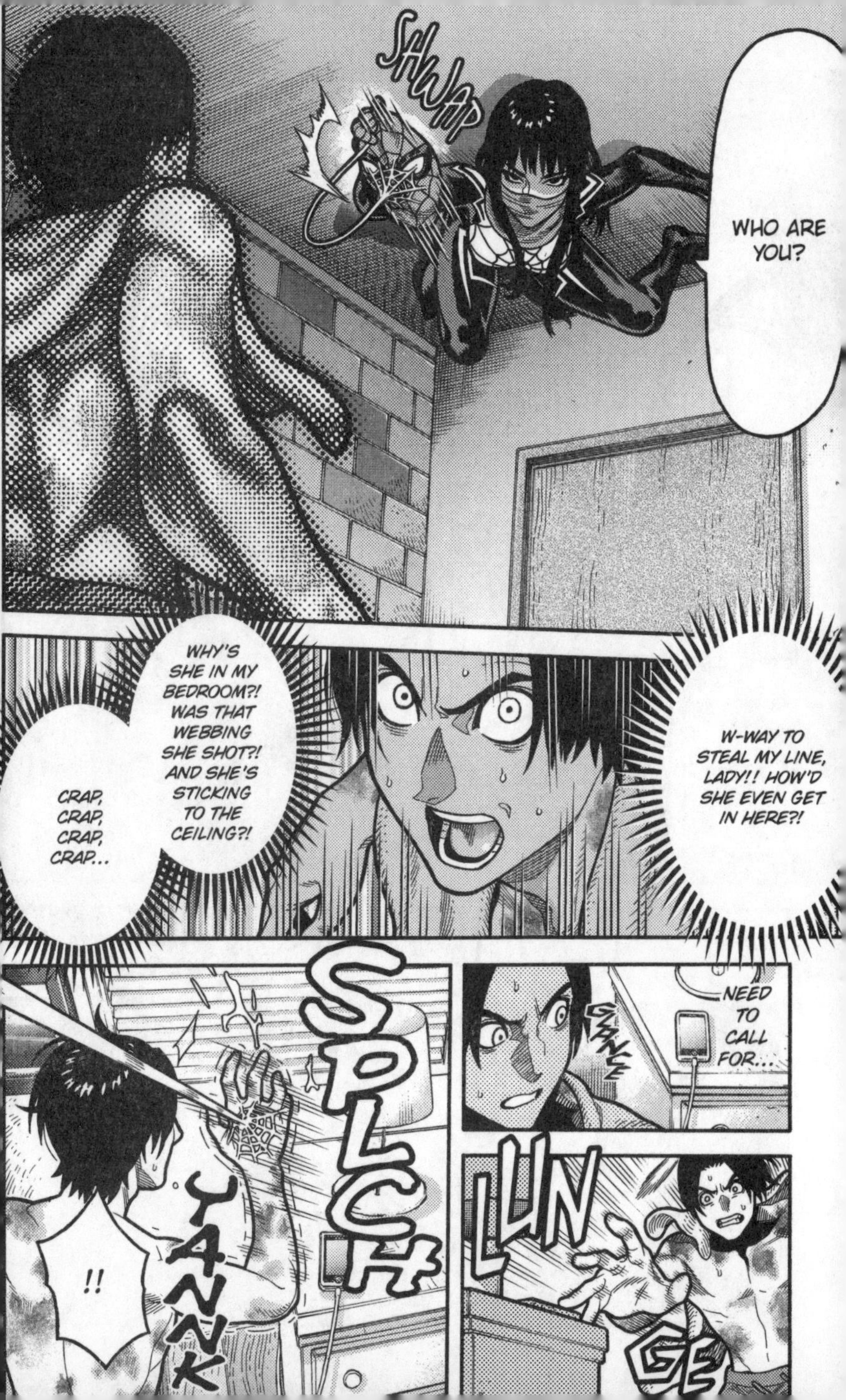
WHO ARE YOU?
SHWAP
W-WAY TO STEAL MY LINE, LADY!! HOW'D SHE EVEN GET IN HERE?!
WHY'S SHE IN MY BEDROOM?! WAS THAT WEBBING SHE SHOT?! AND SHE'S STICKING TO THE CEILING?!
CRAP, CRAP, CRAP, CRAP...
NEED TO CALL FOR...
GLANCE
LUNGE
SPLCH
YANNK
!!

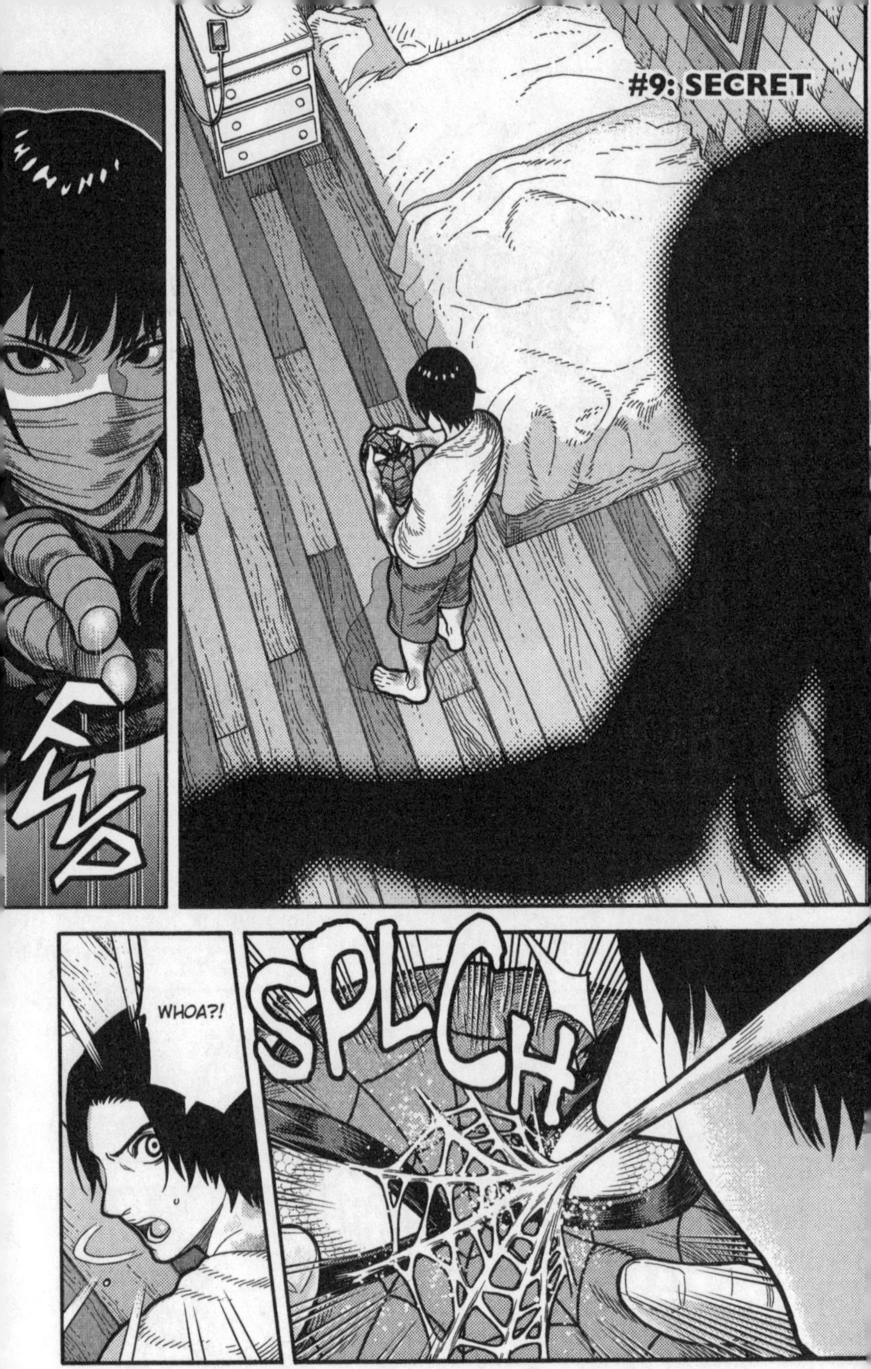
#9: SECRET
FWP
SPLCH
WHOA?!

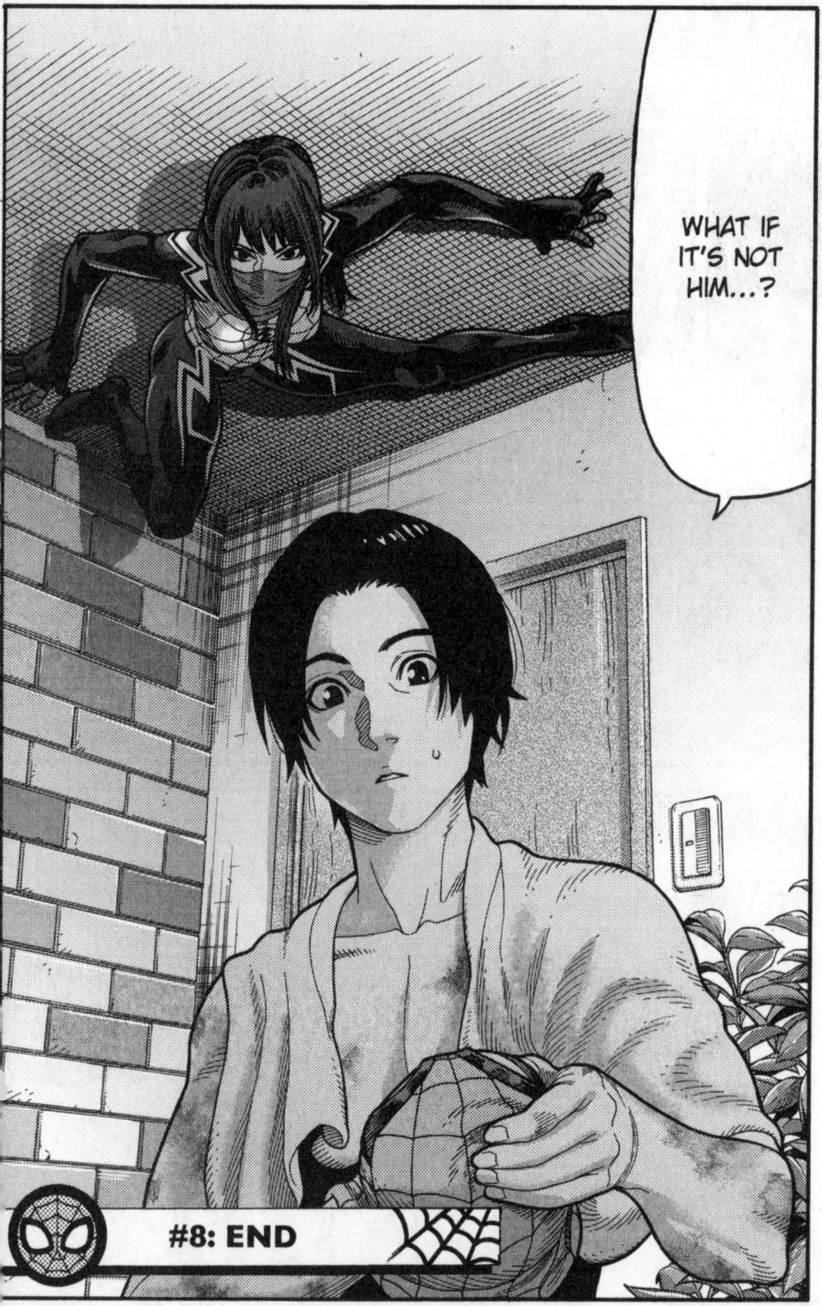
WHAT IF IT'S NOT HIM...?
#8: END

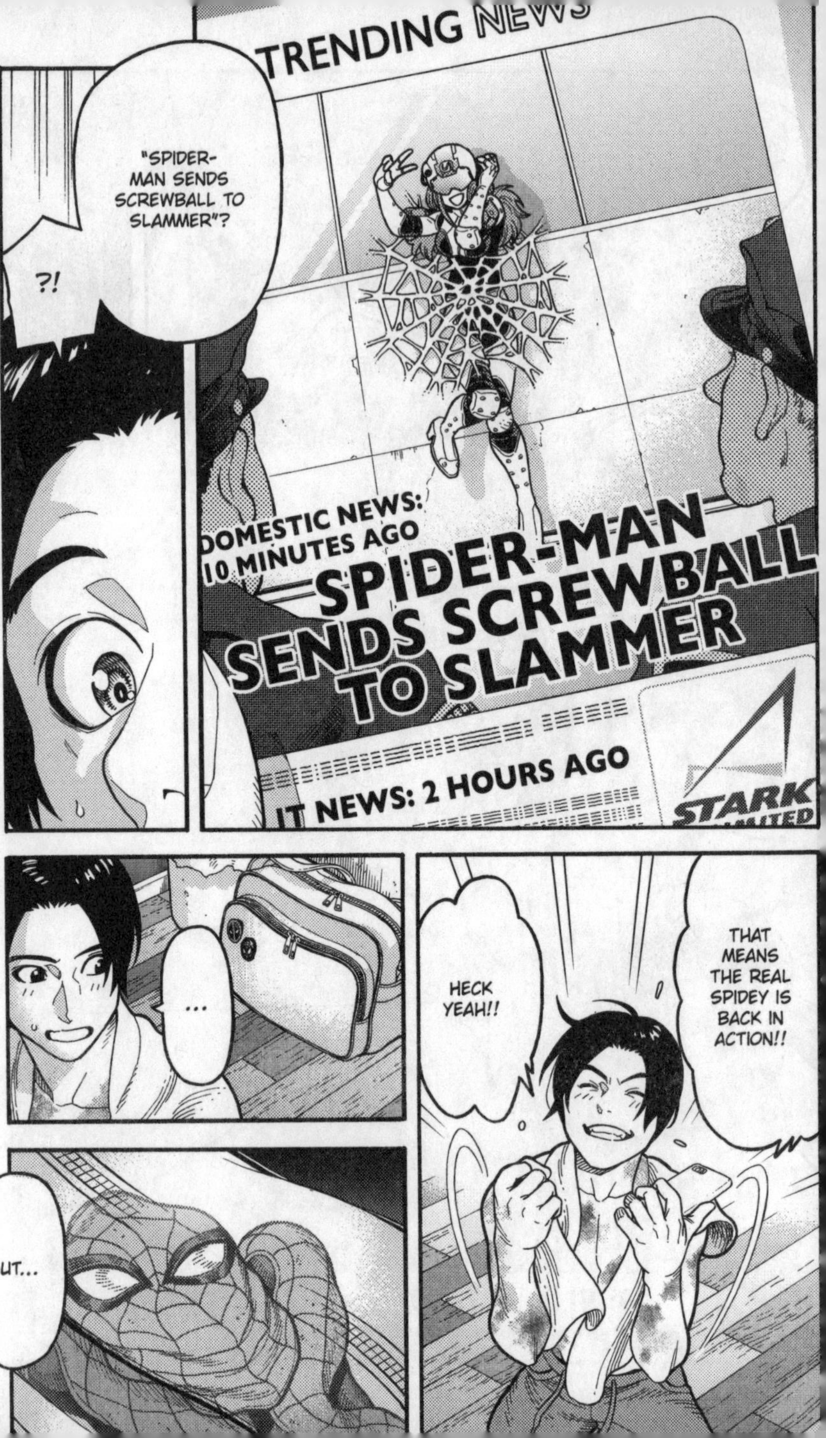
TRENDING NEWS
DOMESTIC NEWS: 10 MINUTES AGO
SPIDER-MAN SENDS SCREWBALL TO SLAMMER
IT NEWS: 2 HOURS AGO
STARK
"SPIDER-MAN SENDS SCREWBALL TO SLAMMER"?
?!
THAT MEANS THE REAL SPIDEY IS BACK IN ACTION!!
HECK YEAH!!
...
BUT...

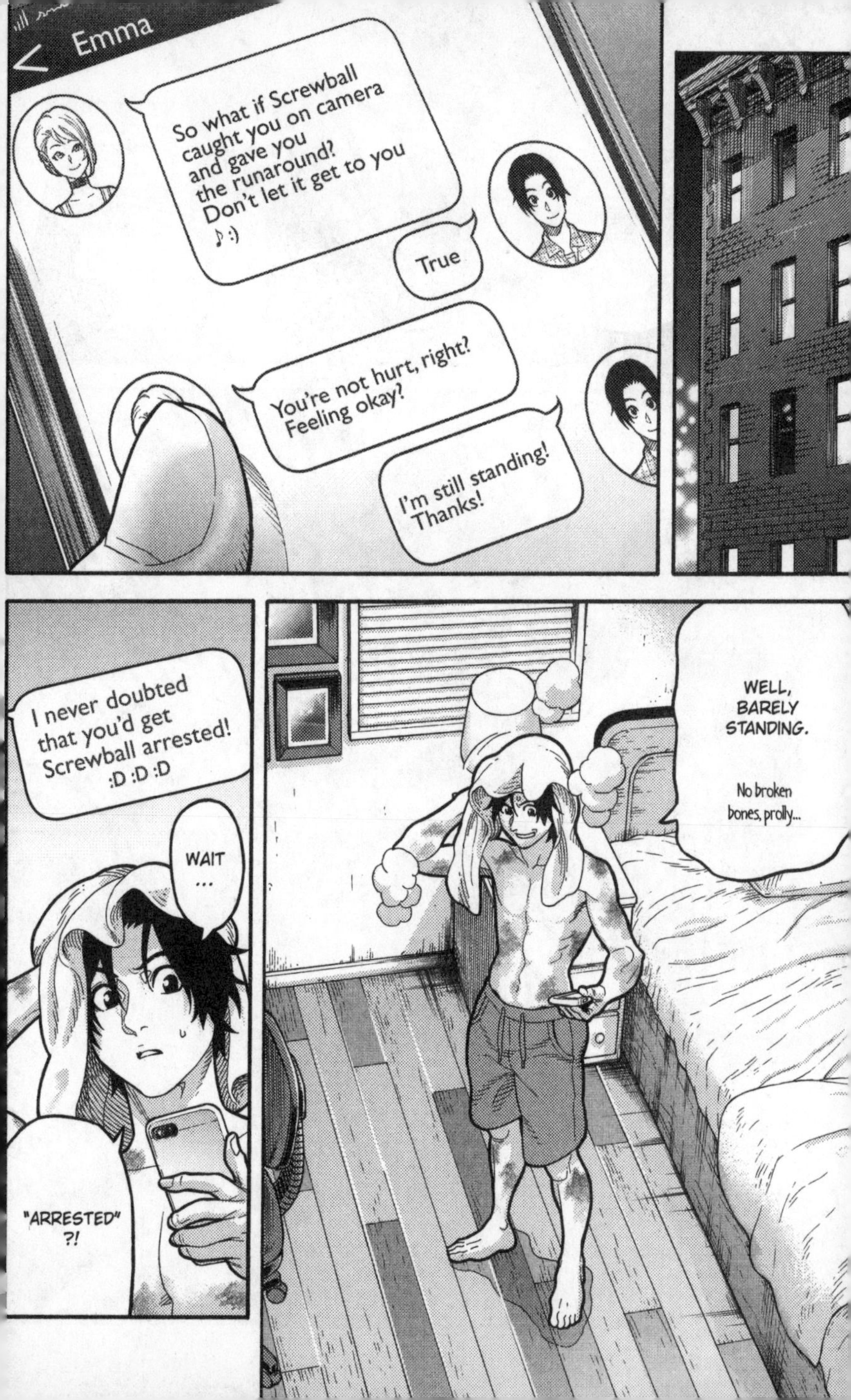
Emma
So what if Screwball caught you on camera and gave you the runaround? Don't let it get to you ♪ :)
True
You're not hurt, right? Feeling okay?
I'm still standing! Thanks!
WELL, BARELY STANDING.
No broken bones, prolly...
I never doubted that you'd get Screwball arrested! :D :D :D
WAIT ...
"ARRESTED" ?!

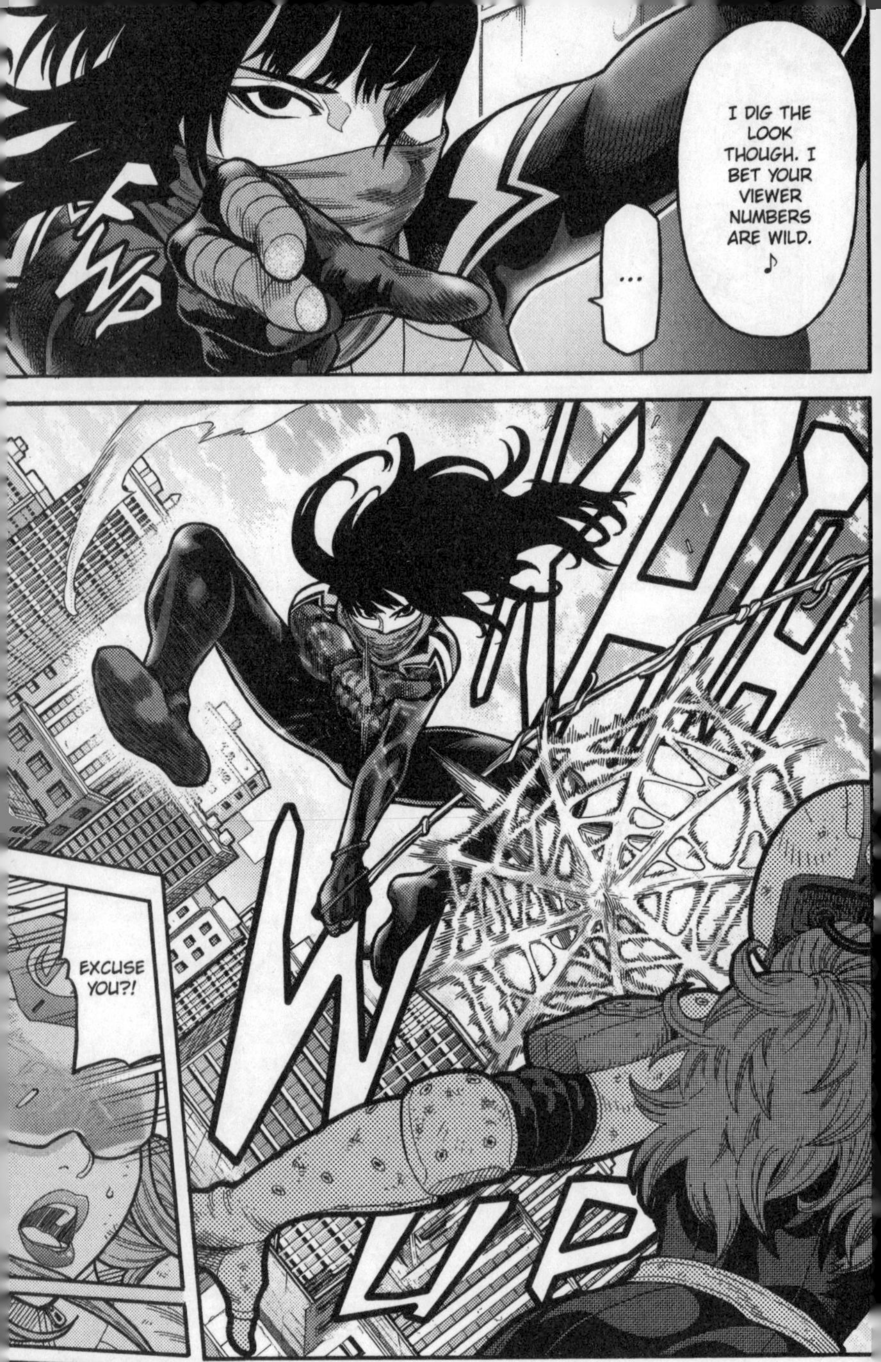
I DIG THE LOOK THOUGH. I BET YOUR VIEWER NUMBERS ARE WILD. ♪
...
FWP
EXCUSE YOU?!

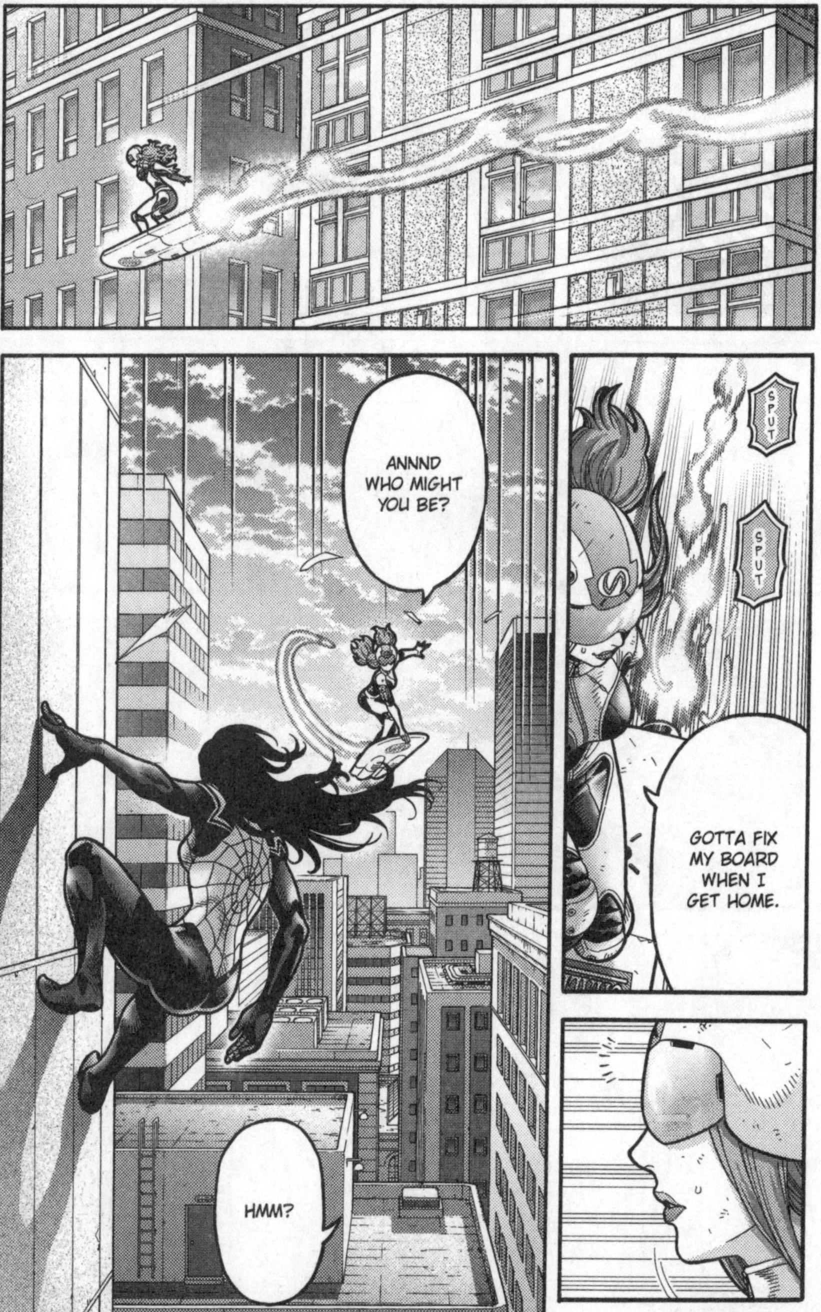
SPUT
SPUT
GOTTA FIX MY BOARD WHEN I GET HOME.
ANNND WHO MIGHT YOU BE?
HMM?

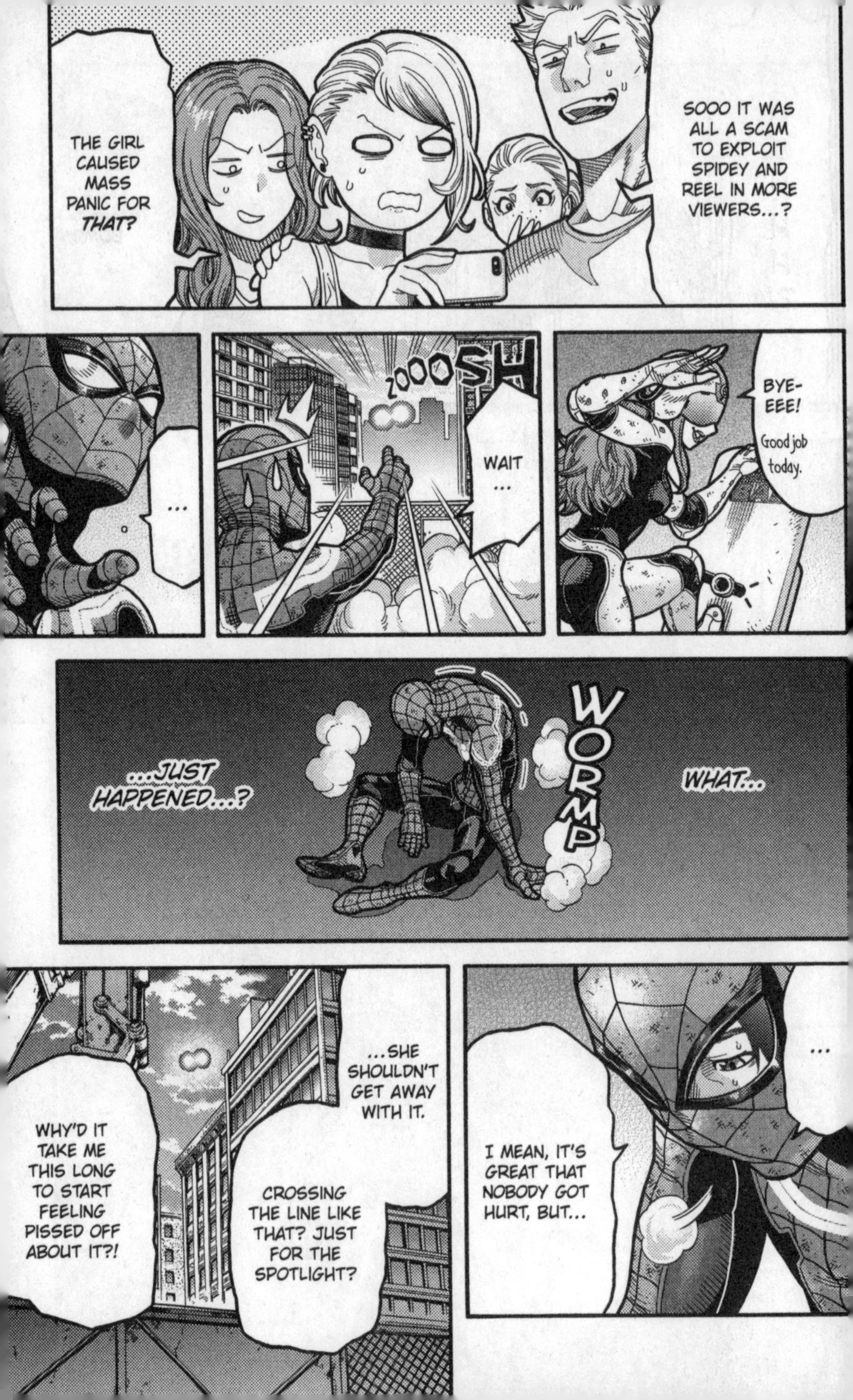
SOOO IT WAS ALL A SCAM TO EXPLOIT SPIDEY AND REEL IN MORE VIEWERS...?
THE GIRL CAUSED MASS PANIC FOR *THAT?*
BYE-EEE!
Good job today.
ZOOOSH
WAIT ...
...
WHAT...
WORMP
...JUST HAPPENED...?
...
I MEAN, IT'S GREAT THAT NOBODY GOT HURT, BUT...
...SHE SHOULDN'T GET AWAY WITH IT.
CROSSING THE LINE LIKE THAT? JUST FOR THE SPOTLIGHT?
WHY'D IT TAKE ME THIS LONG TO START FEELING PISSED OFF ABOUT IT?!

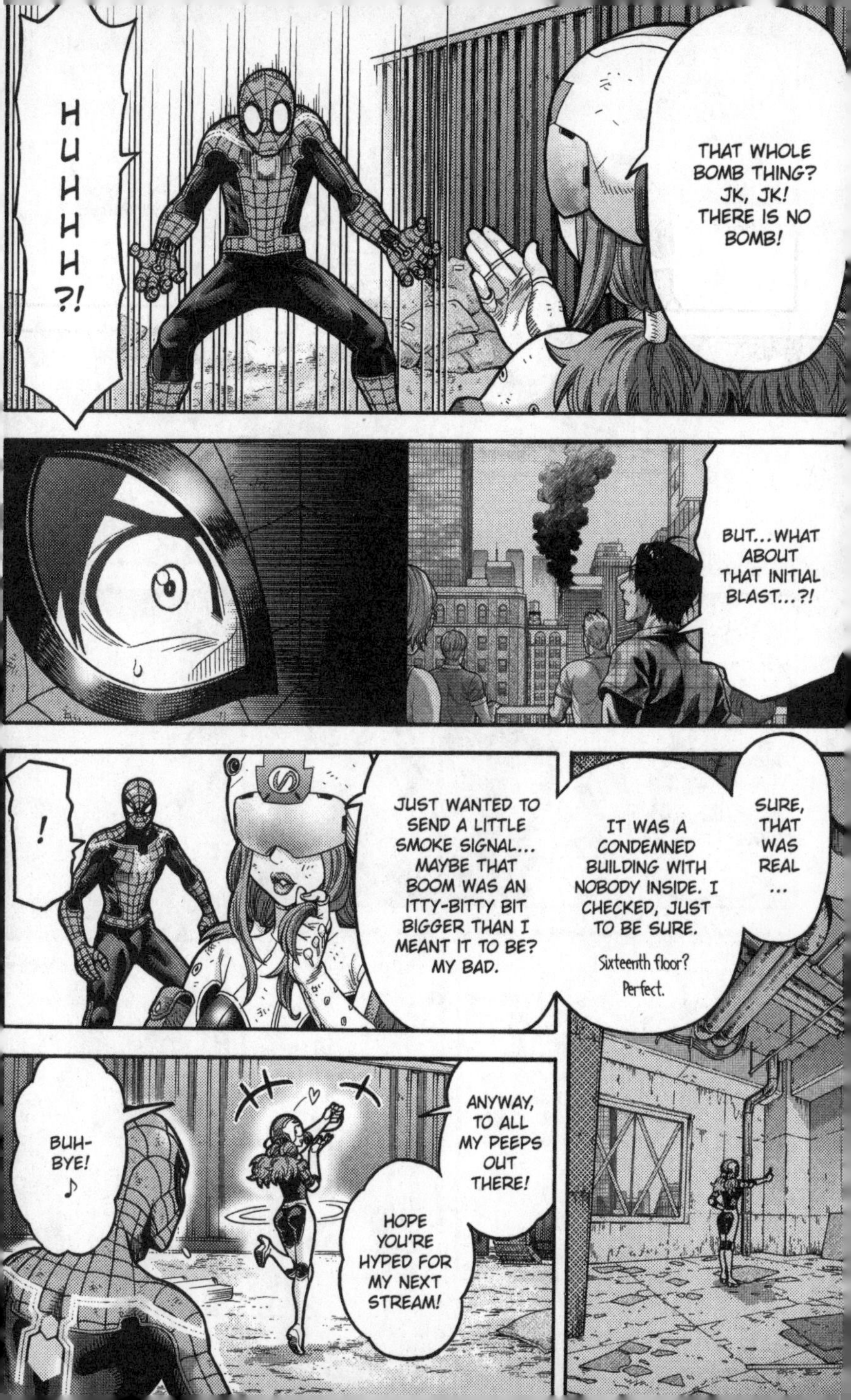
THAT WHOLE BOMB THING? JK, JK! THERE IS NO BOMB!
HUHHHH?!
BUT...WHAT ABOUT THAT INITIAL BLAST...?!
SURE, THAT WAS REAL ...
IT WAS A CONDEMNED BUILDING WITH NOBODY INSIDE. I CHECKED, JUST TO BE SURE.
Sixteenth floor? Perfect.
JUST WANTED TO SEND A LITTLE SMOKE SIGNAL... MAYBE THAT BOOM WAS AN ITTY-BITTY BIT BIGGER THAN I MEANT IT TO BE? MY BAD.
!
ANYWAY, TO ALL MY PEEPS OUT THERE!
HOPE YOU'RE HYPED FOR MY NEXT STREAM!
BUH-BYE! ♪

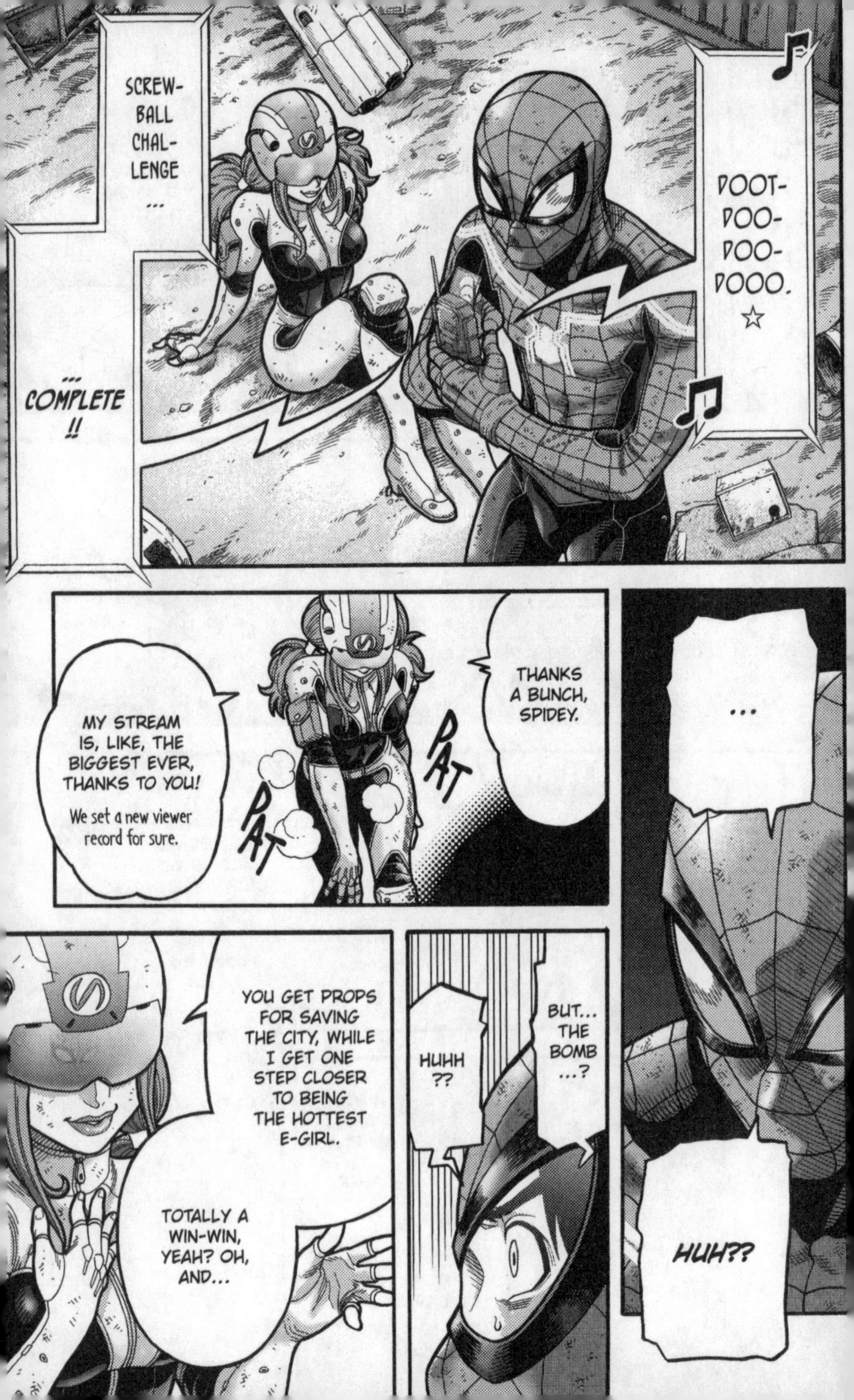
DOOT-DOO-DOO-DOOO. ☆
SCREW-BALL CHAL-LENGE ...
... COMPLETE !!
...
HUH??
THANKS A BUNCH, SPIDEY.
PAT
PAT
MY STREAM IS, LIKE, THE BIGGEST EVER, THANKS TO YOU!
We set a new viewer record for sure.
BUT... THE BOMB ...?
HUHH ??
YOU GET PROPS FOR SAVING THE CITY, WHILE I GET ONE STEP CLOSER TO BEING THE HOTTEST E-GIRL.
TOTALLY A WIN-WIN, YEAH? OH, AND...

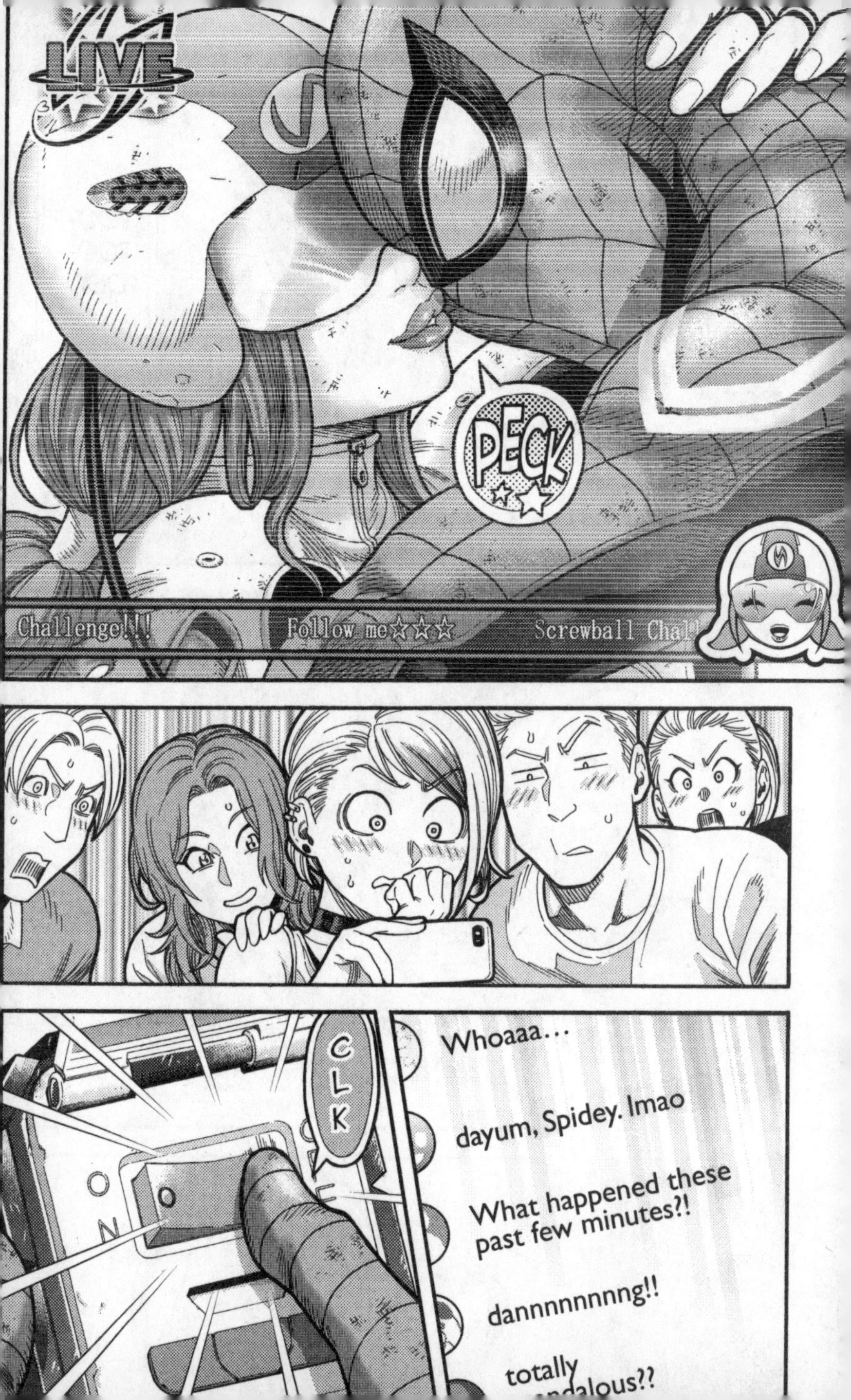
LIVE
PECK
Challenge!!!
Follow me☆☆☆
Screwball Chal
Whoaaa…
dayum, Spidey. lmao
What happened these past few minutes?!
dannnnnnnng!!
totally
CLK
ON

YDNK

NOW I CAN...

YES!!

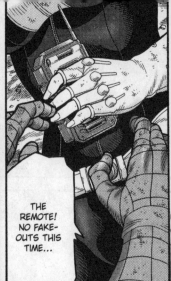

THE REMOTE! NO FAKE-OUTS THIS TIME...

HUH ?!

SHK

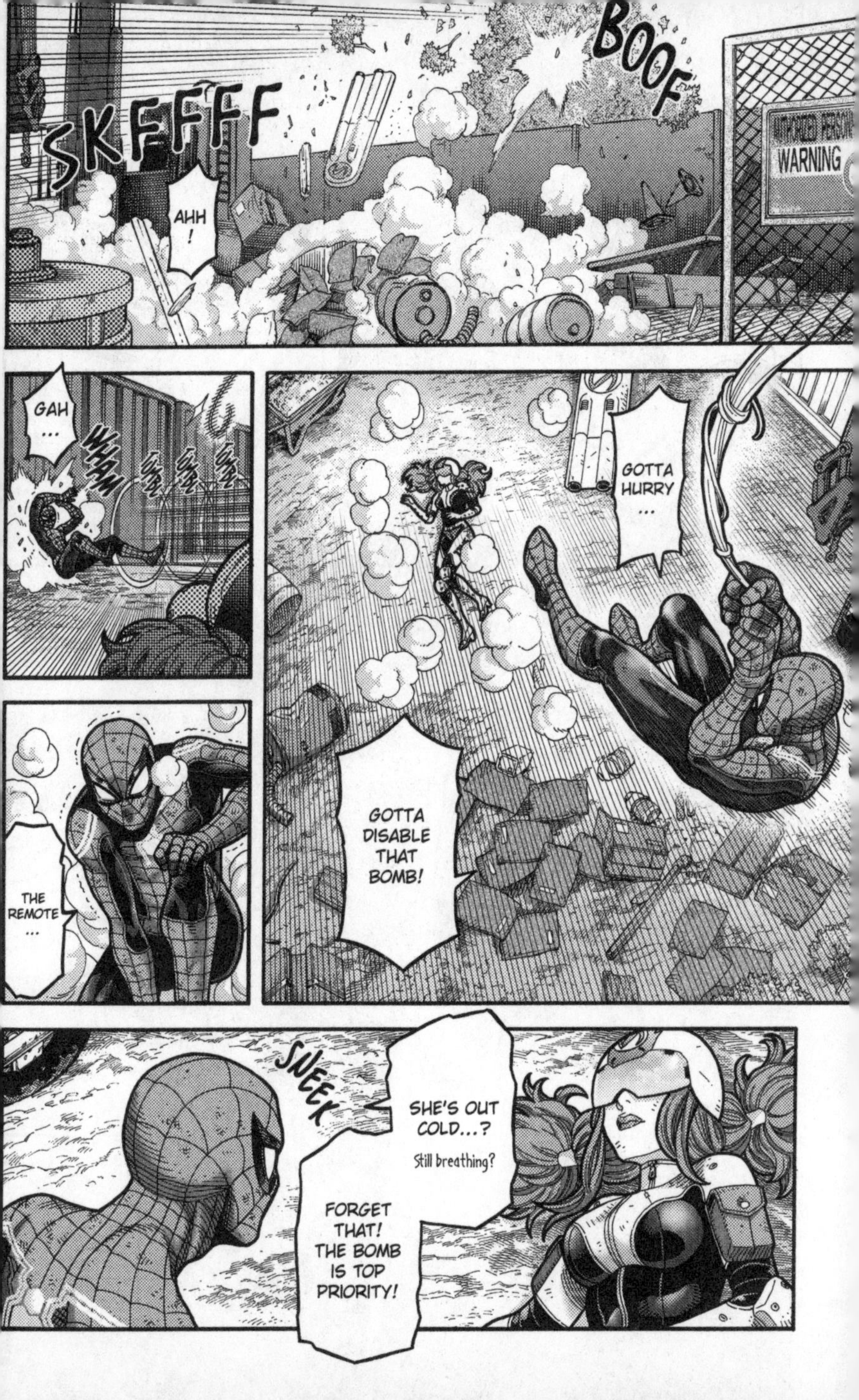
BOOF
WARNING
SKFFFF
AHH!
GOTTA HURRY...
GOTTA DISABLE THAT BOMB!
GAH...
WHAM
THE REMOTE...
SNEEK
SHE'S OUT COLD...?
Still breathing?
FORGET THAT! THE BOMB IS TOP PRIORITY!

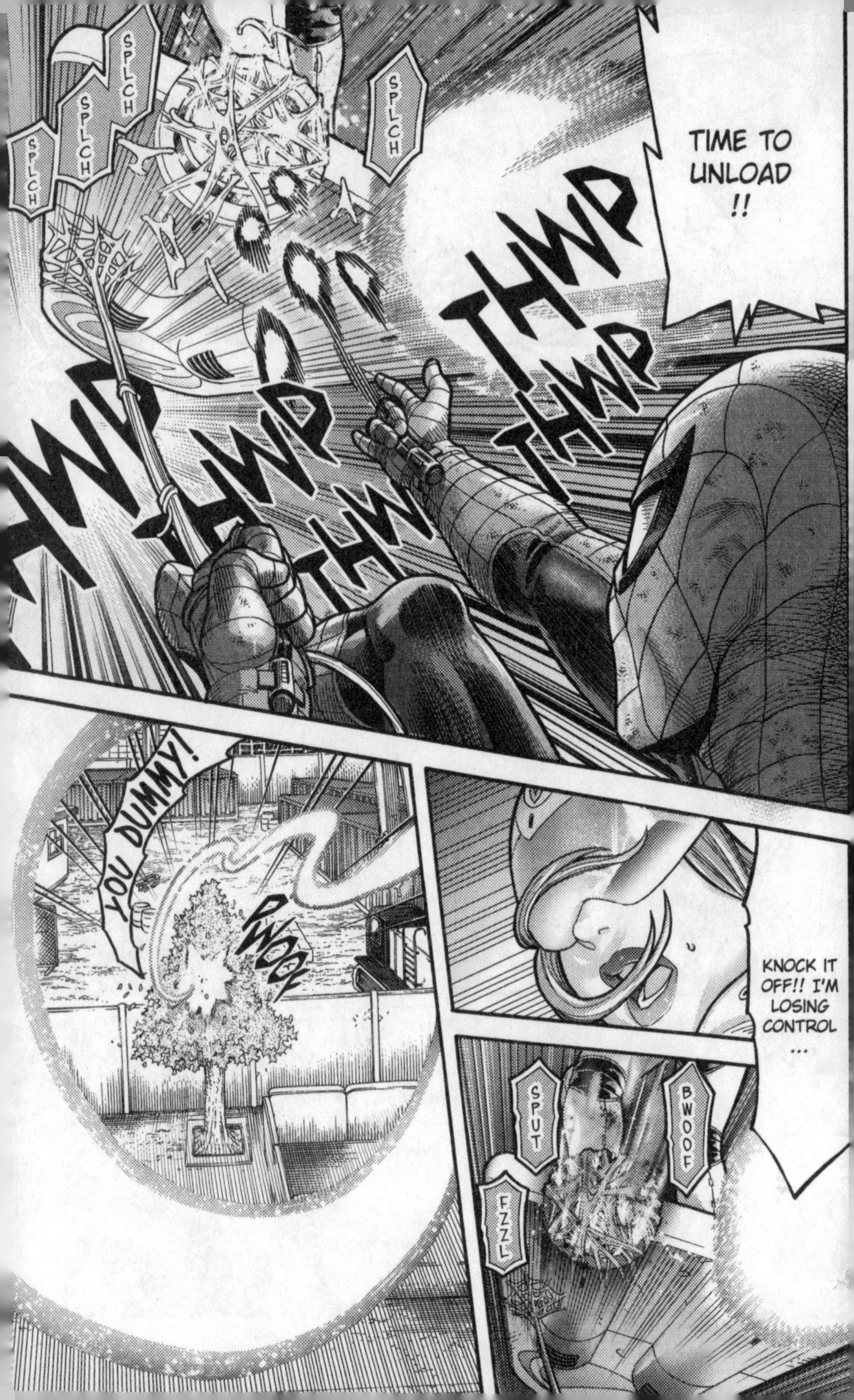
TIME TO UNLOAD !!
THWP
THWP
THWP
THWP
SPLCH
SPLCH
SPLCH
SPLCH
KNOCK IT OFF!! I'M LOSING CONTROL ...
BWOOF
SPUT
FZZL
YOU DUMMY!
DWOOK

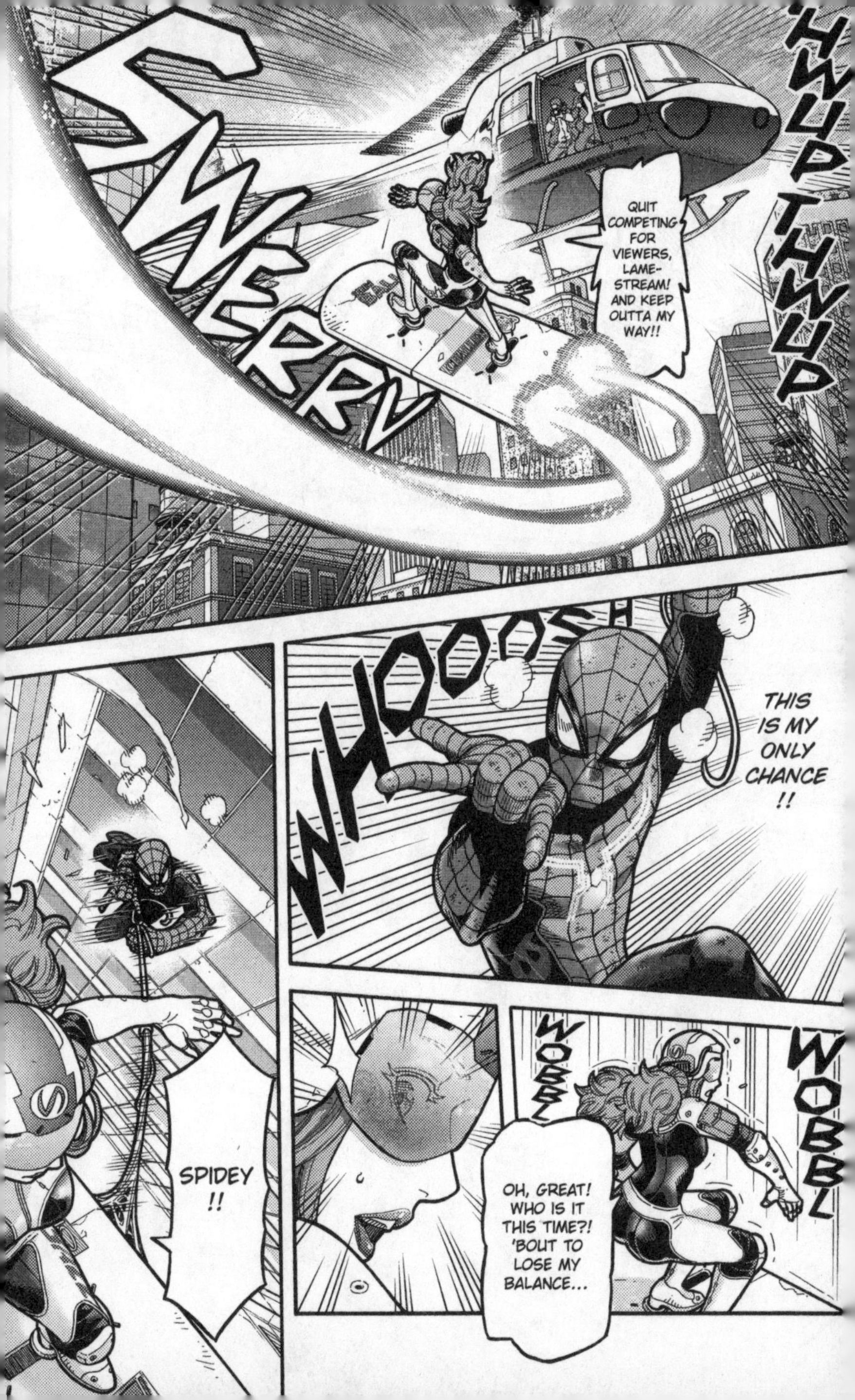
'HWUP THWUP
SWERRV
QUIT COMPETING FOR VIEWERS, LAME-STREAM! AND KEEP OUTTA MY WAY!!
THIS IS MY ONLY CHANCE!!
WHOOOSH
WOBBL
WOBBL
OH, GREAT! WHO IS IT THIS TIME?! 'BOUT TO LOSE MY BALANCE...
SPIDEY!!

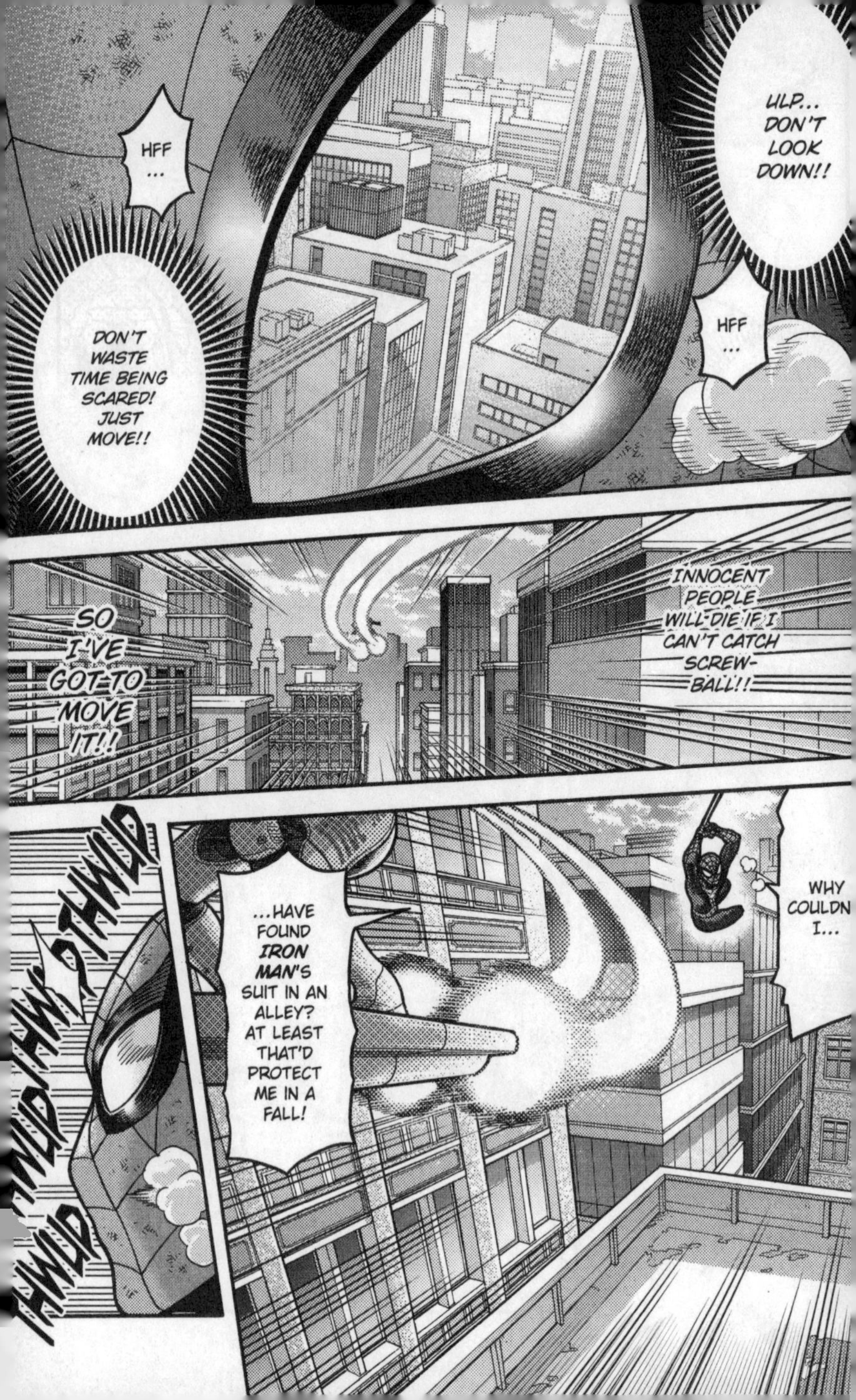
ULP... DON'T LOOK DOWN!!
HFF ...
HFF ...
DON'T WASTE TIME BEING SCARED! JUST MOVE!!
INNOCENT PEOPLE WILL DIE IF I CAN'T CATCH SCREW-BALL!!
SO I'VE GOT TO MOVE IT!!
WHY COULDN I...
...HAVE FOUND IRON MAN'S SUIT IN AN ALLEY? AT LEAST THAT'D PROTECT ME IN A FALL!
THWIP THWIP THWIP THWIP

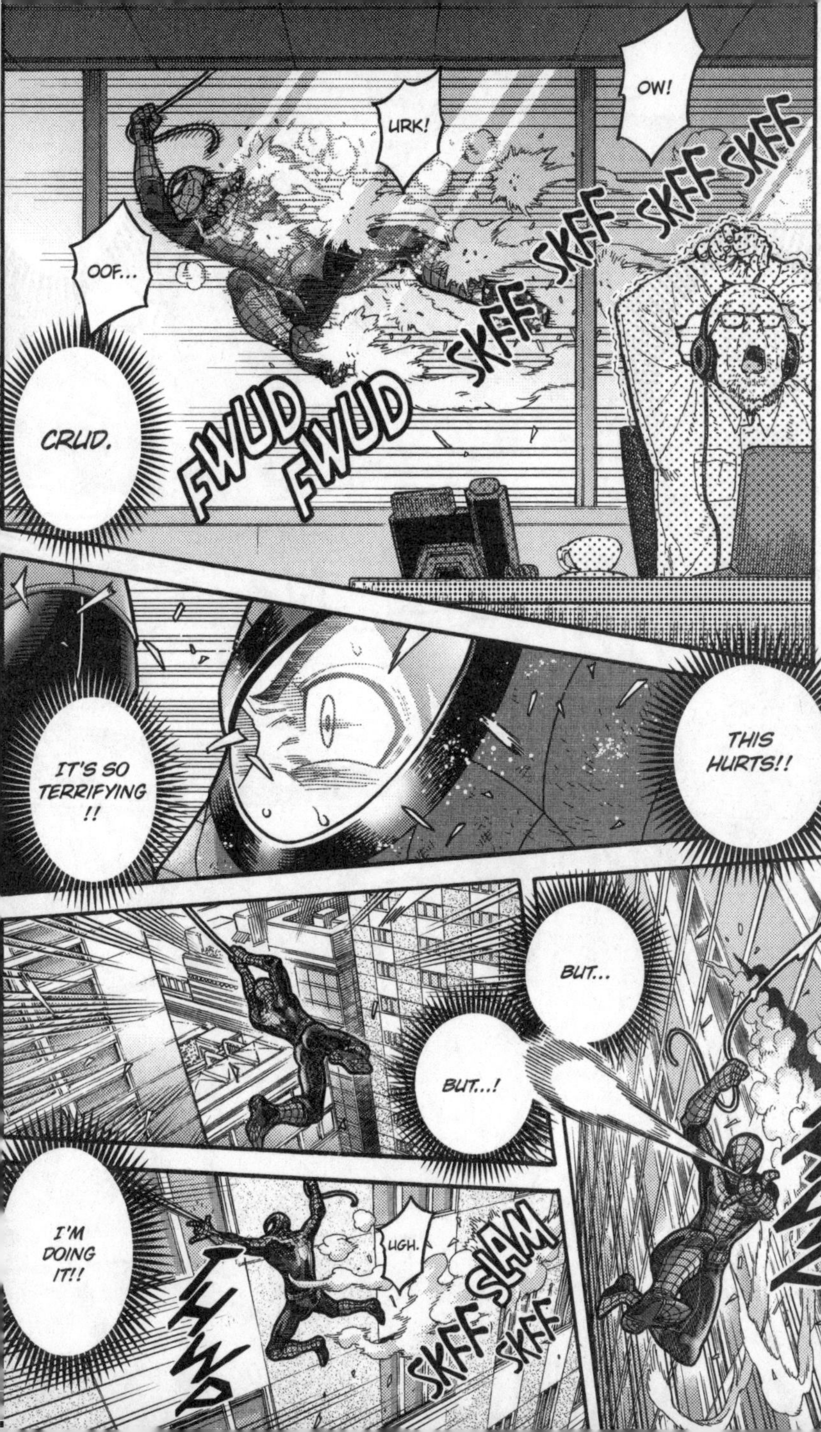
OW!
SKFF SKFF SKFF SKFF
URK!
OOF...
FWUD FWUD
CRUD.
THIS HURTS!!
IT'S SO TERRIFYING!!
BUT...
BUT...!
THWP
UGH.
SKFF SLAM
SKFF
I'M DOING IT!!
THWP

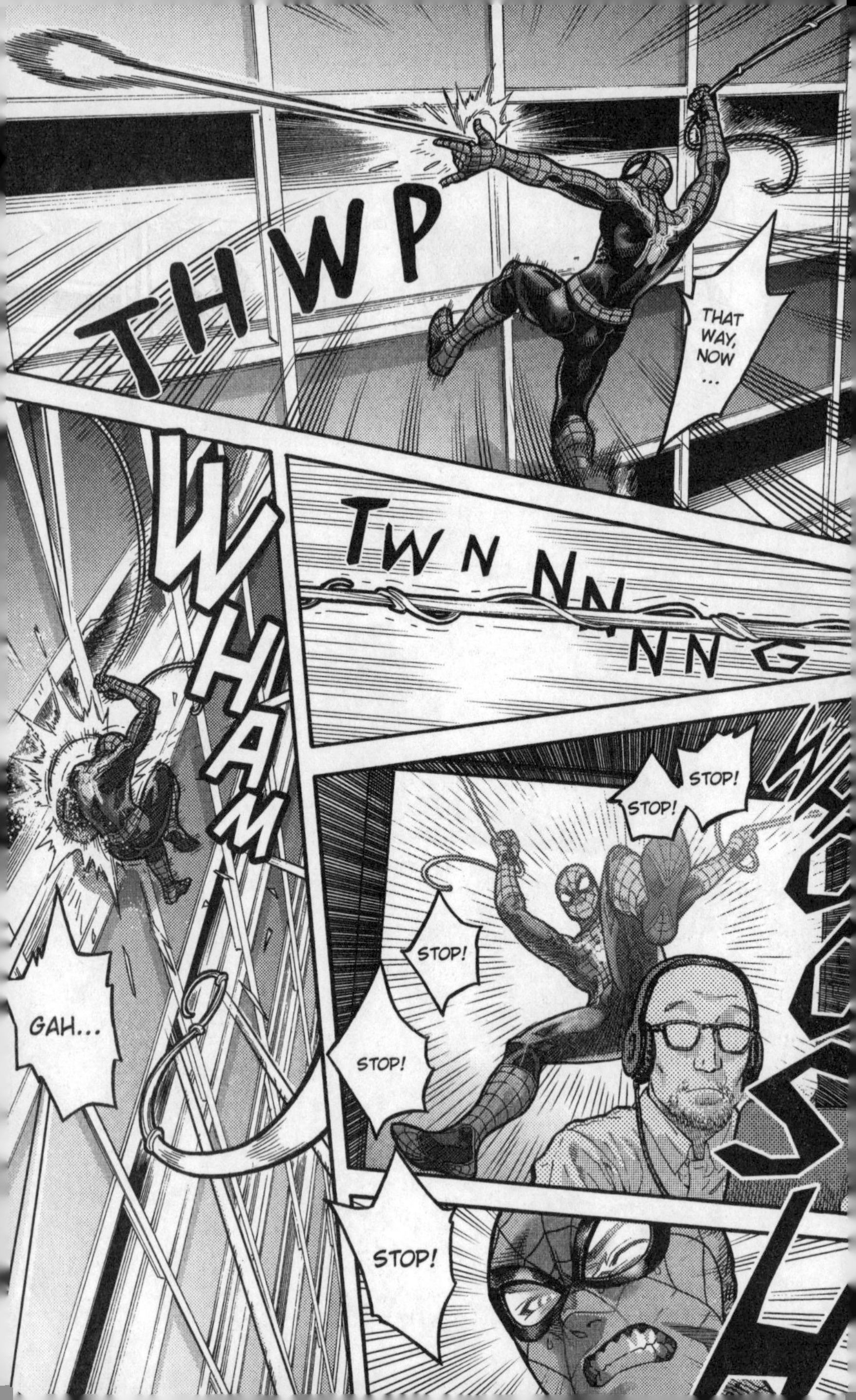
THAT WAY, NOW ...
THWP
TWNNNNNNG
STOP!
STOP!
WHOOSH
STOP!
STOP!
STOP!
WHAM
GAH...

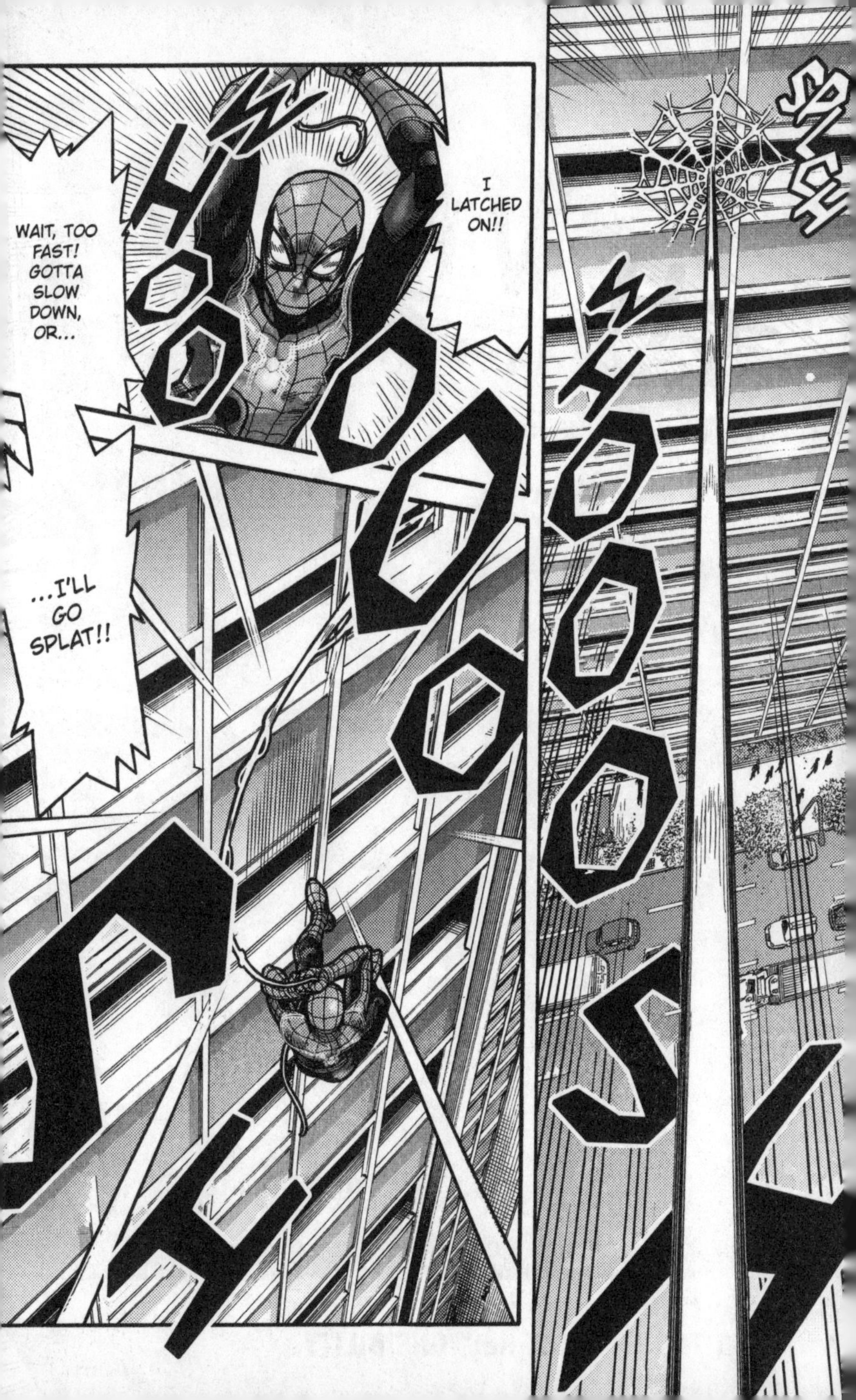
SPLCH
WHOOOOSH
WHOOOOSH
I LATCHED ON!!
WAIT, TOO FAST! GOTTA SLOW DOWN, OR...
...I'LL GO SPLAT!!

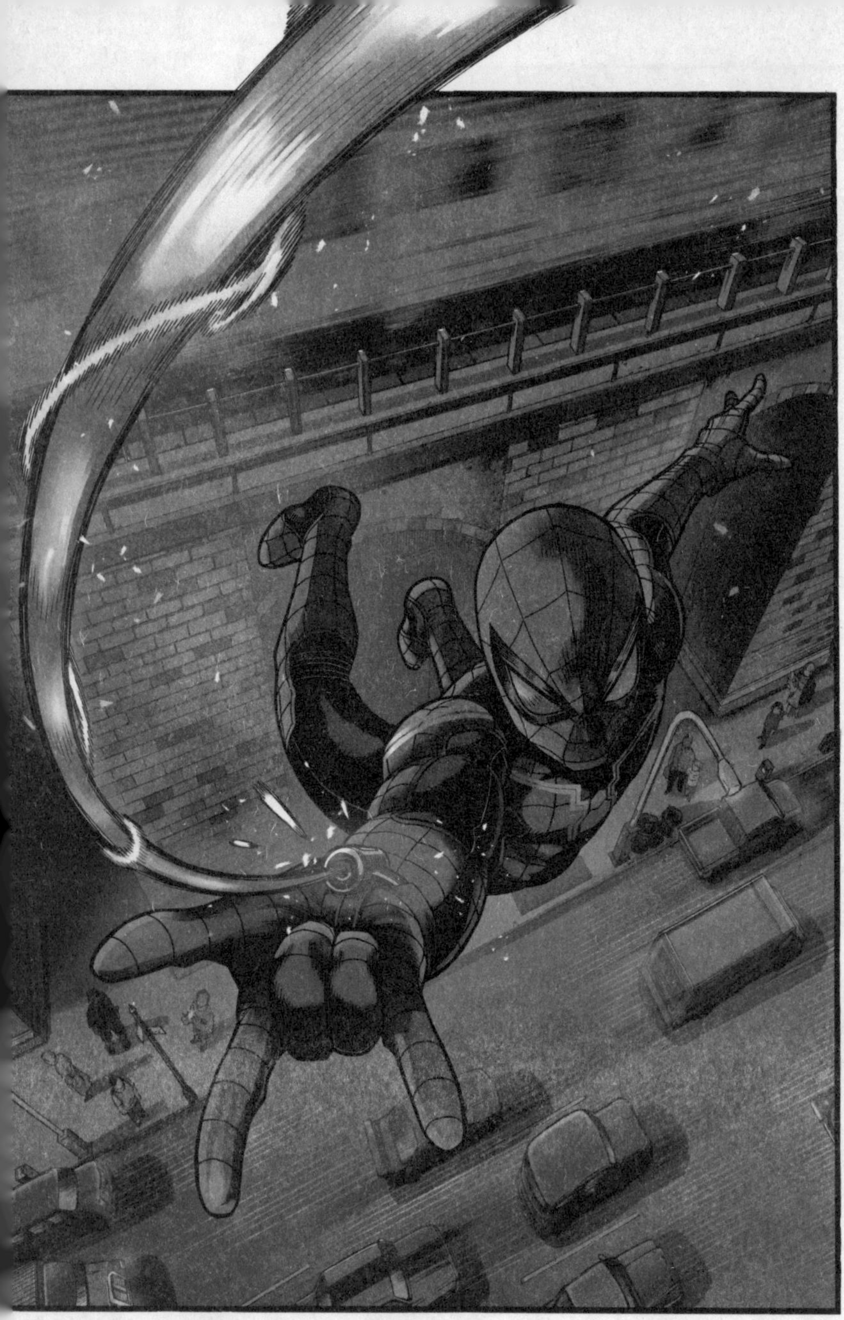

#8 WITHOUT GREAT POWER, WITHOUT GREAT RESPONSIBILITY

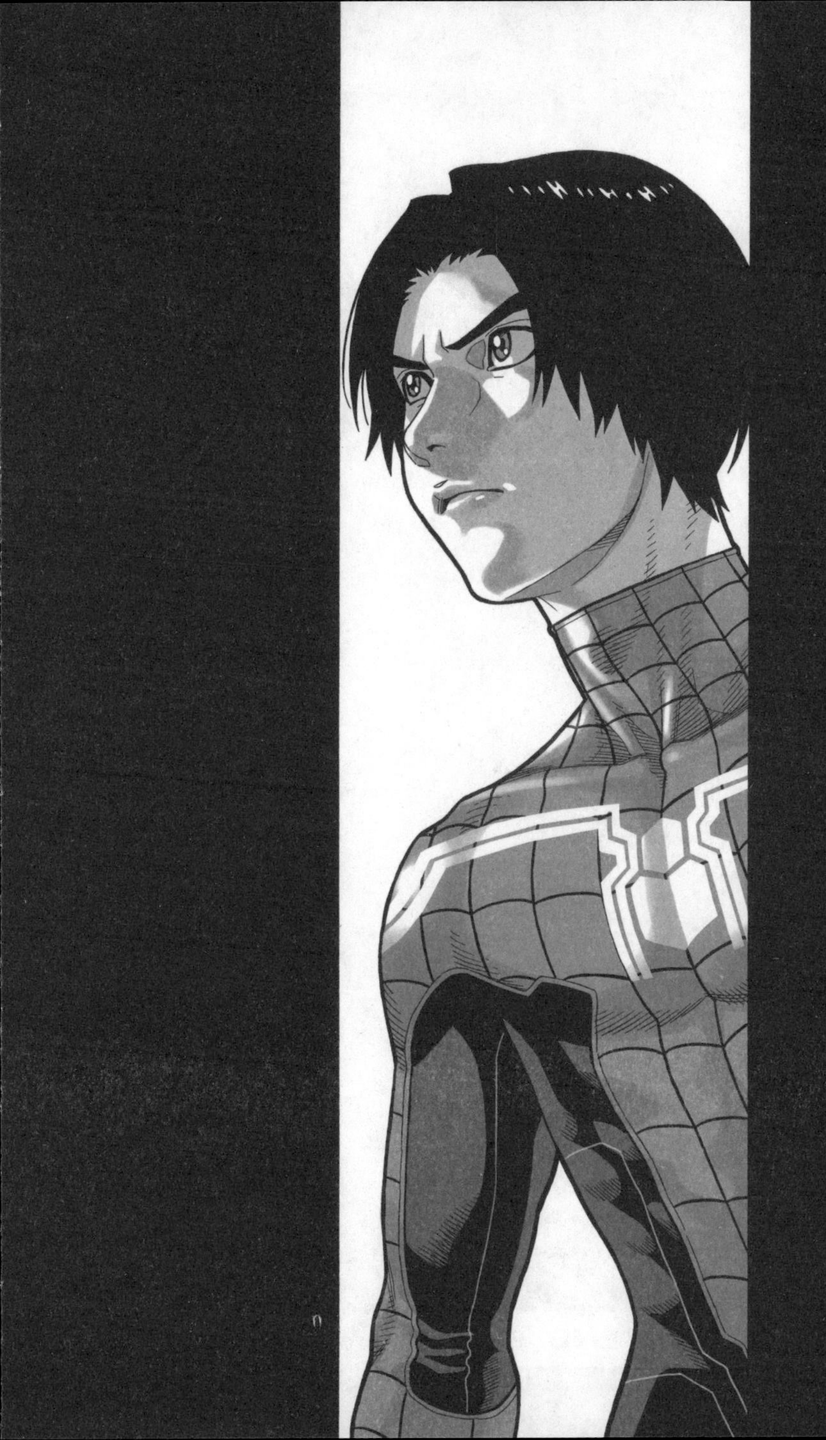

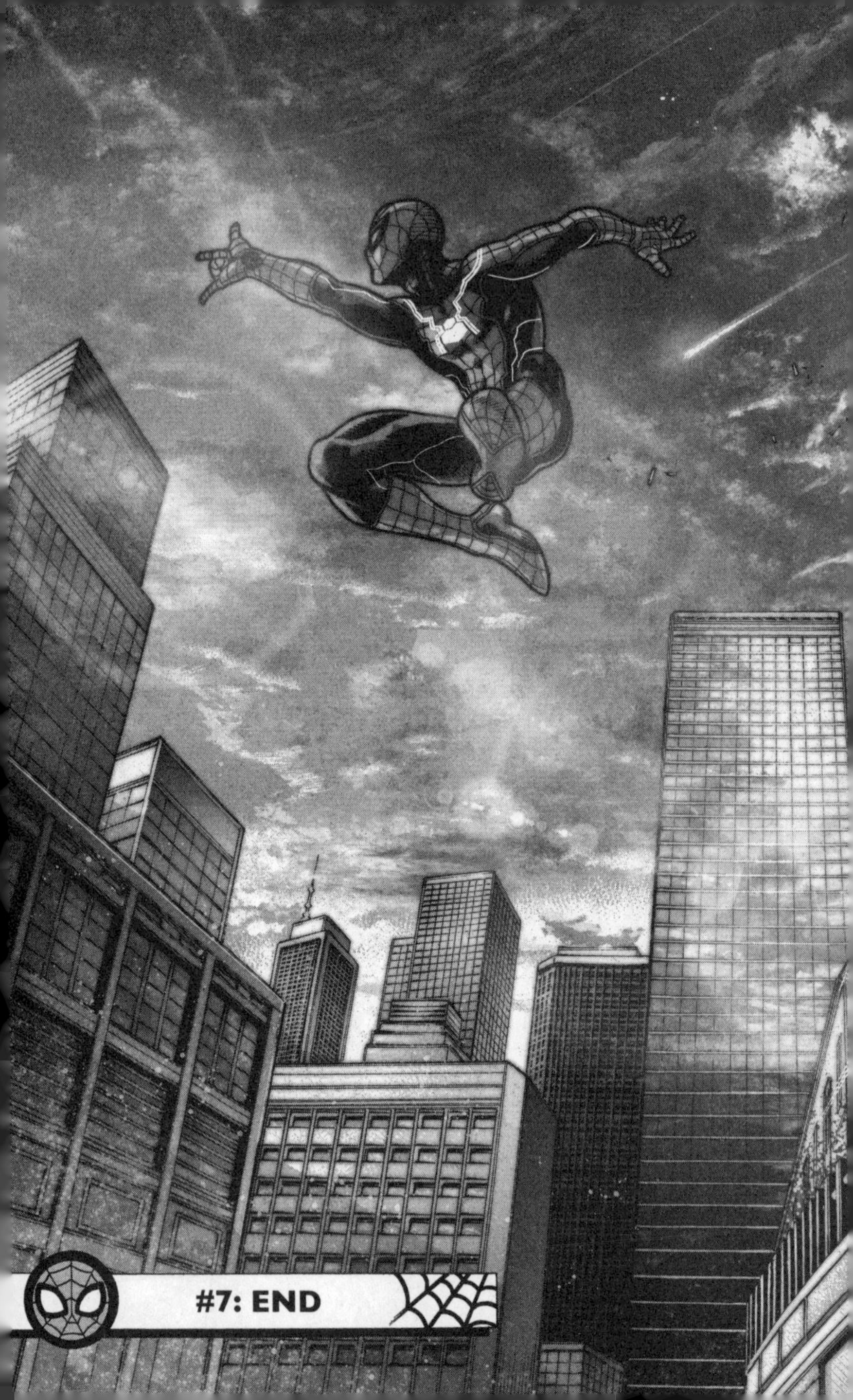
#7: END

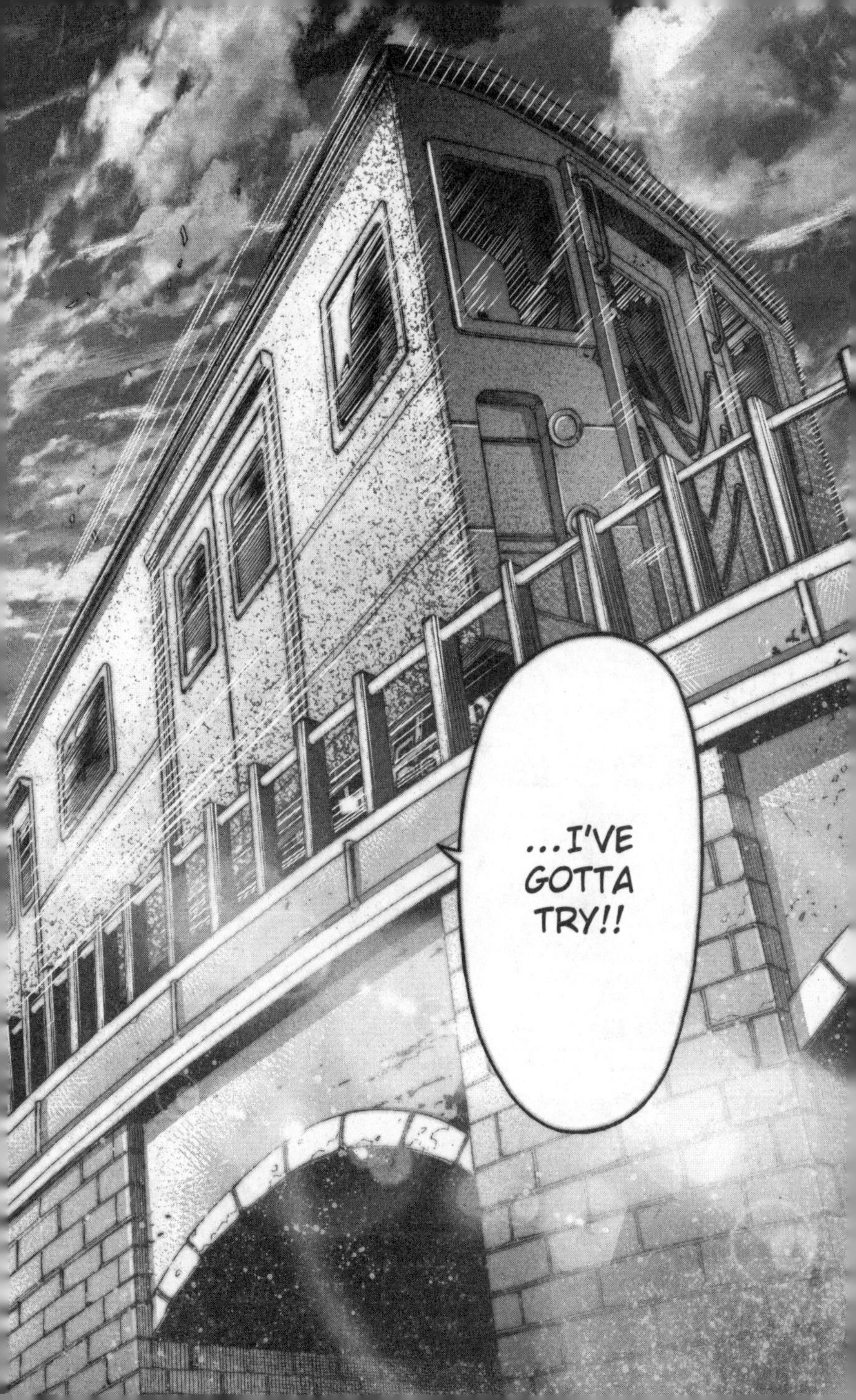
...I'VE GOTTA TRY!!

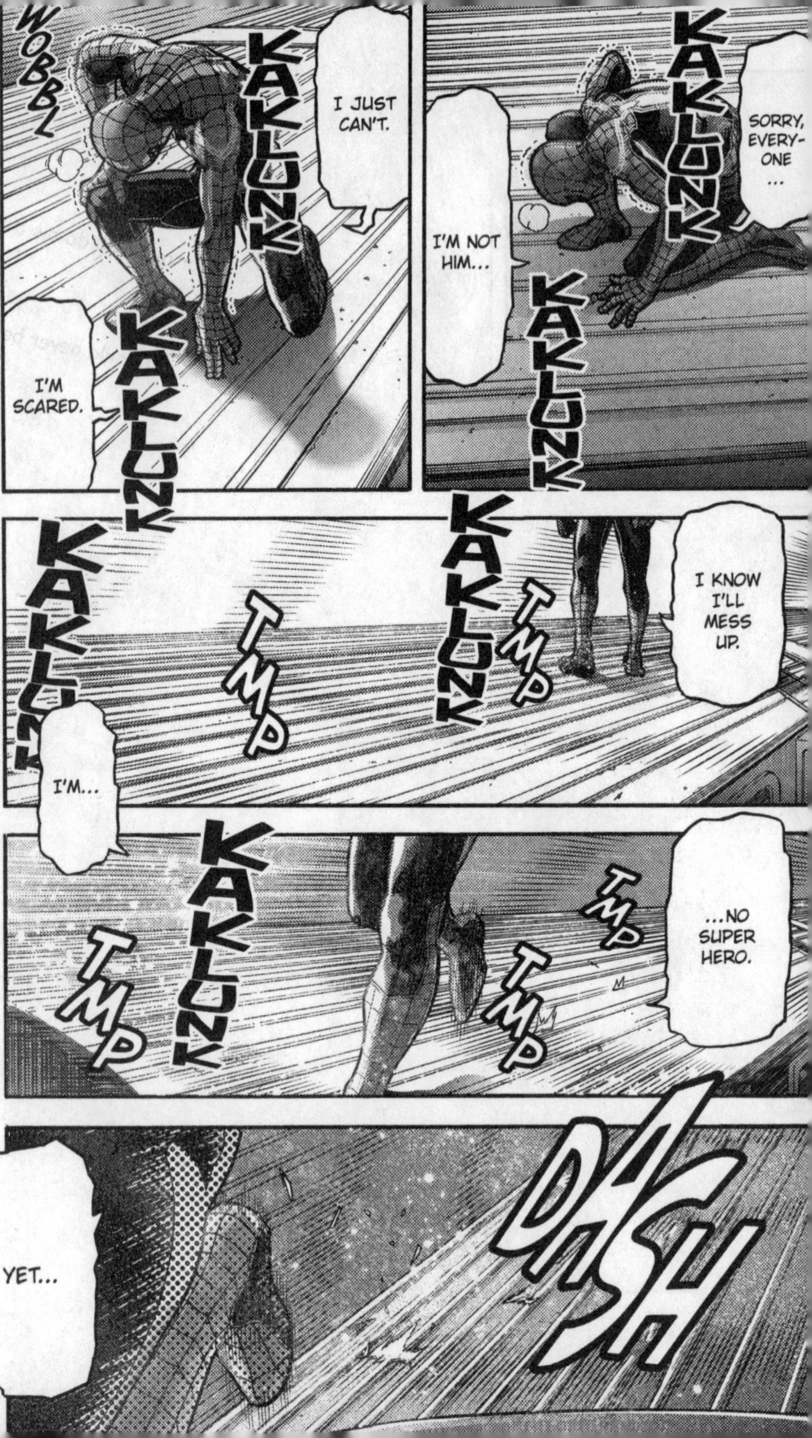

SORRY, EVERY-ONE ...
KAKLUNK
I'M NOT HIM...
KAKLUNK
I JUST CAN'T.
KAKLUNK
WOBBL
I'M SCARED.
KAKLUNK
I KNOW I'LL MESS UP.
KAKLUNK
TMP
TMP
KAKLUNK
I'M...
...NO SUPER HERO.
TMP
TMP
KAKLUNK
TMP
DASH
YET...

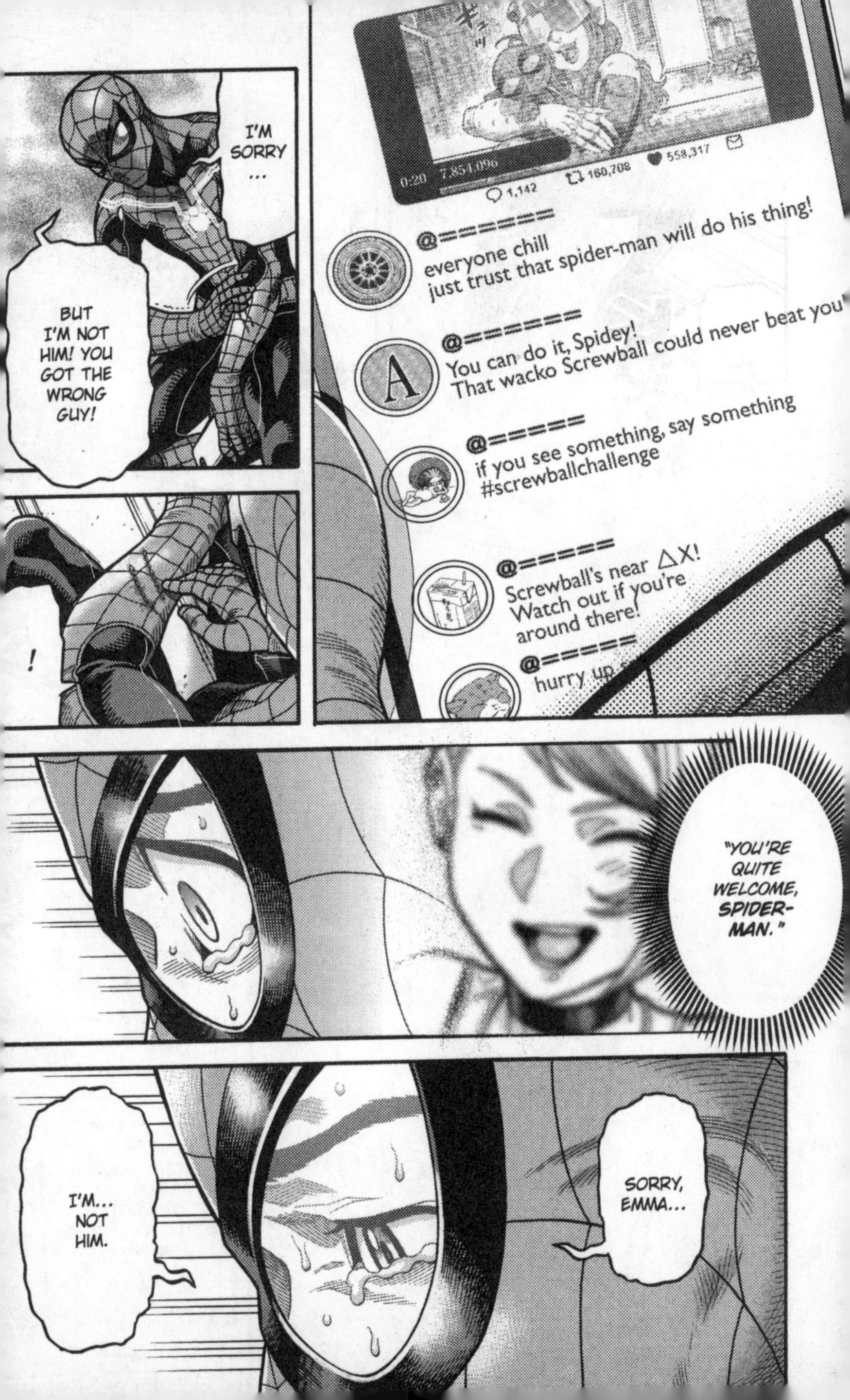
0:20 7,854,096
1,142
160,708
558,317
@======
everyone chill
just trust that spider-man will do his thing!
@======
You can do it, Spidey!
That wacko Screwball could never beat you
@=====
if you see something, say something
#screwballchallenge
@=====
Screwball's near △X!
Watch out if you're
around there!
@=====
hurry up
I'M SORRY...
BUT I'M NOT HIM! YOU GOT THE WRONG GUY!
!
"YOU'RE QUITE WELCOME, SPIDER-MAN."
SORRY, EMMA...
I'M... NOT HIM.

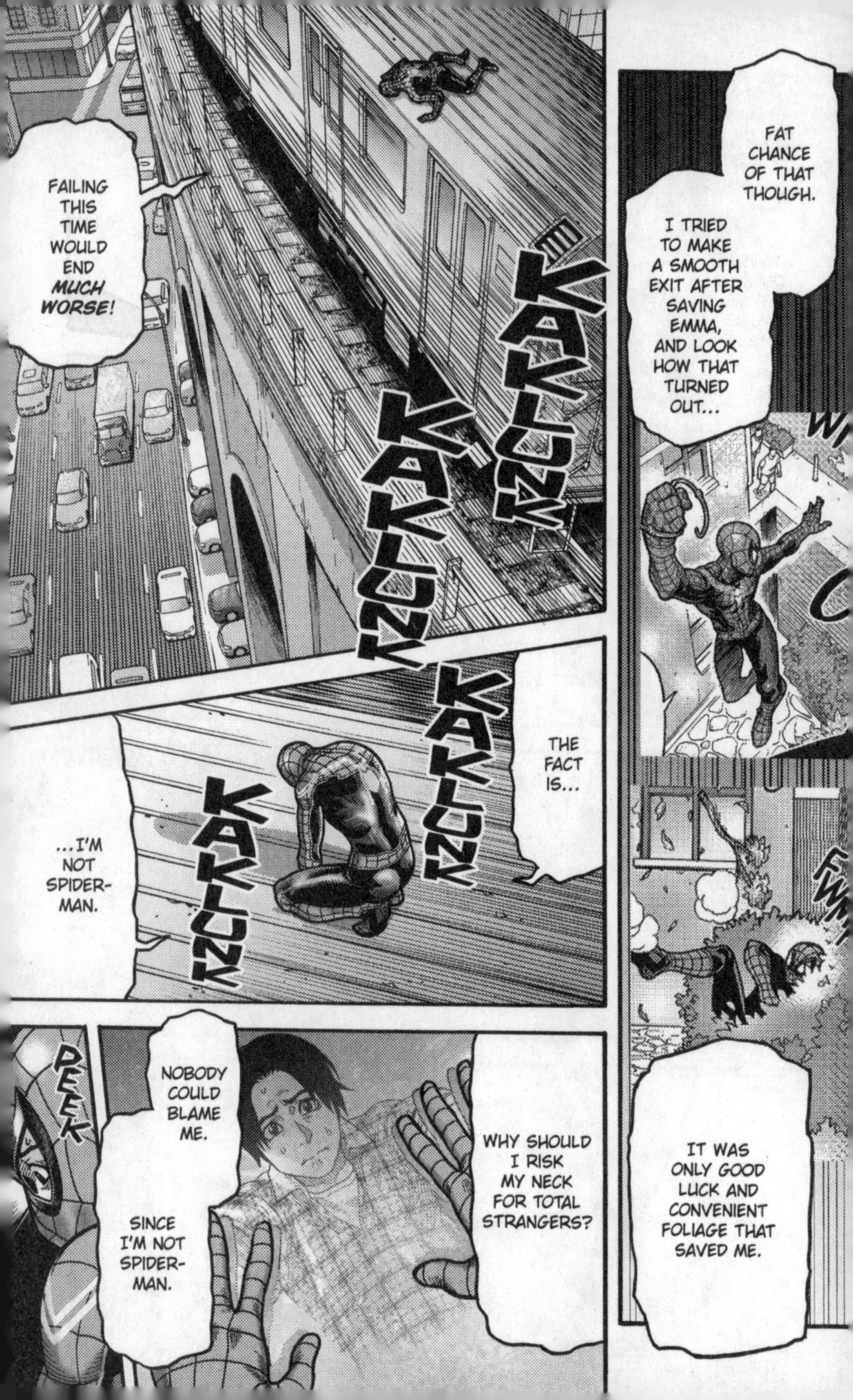

FAT CHANCE OF THAT THOUGH.
I TRIED TO MAKE A SMOOTH EXIT AFTER SAVING EMMA, AND LOOK HOW THAT TURNED OUT...
IT WAS ONLY GOOD LUCK AND CONVENIENT FOLIAGE THAT SAVED ME.
FAILING THIS TIME WOULD END MUCH WORSE!
KAKLUNK
KAKLUNK
THE FACT IS...
KAKLUNK
KAKLUNK
...I'M NOT SPIDER-MAN.
WHY SHOULD I RISK MY NECK FOR TOTAL STRANGERS?
NOBODY COULD BLAME ME.
SINCE I'M NOT SPIDER-MAN.
PEEK

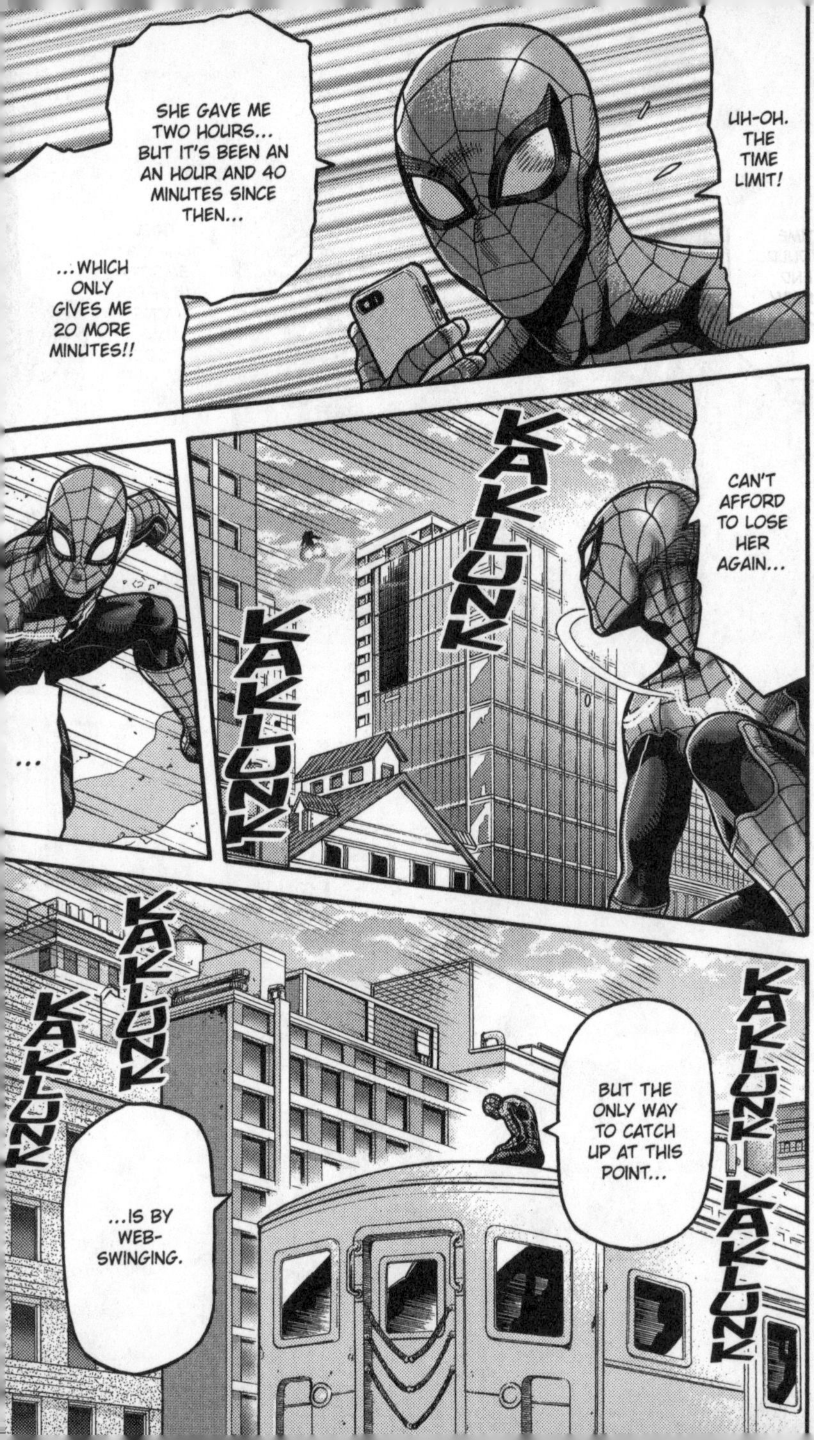
UH-OH. THE TIME LIMIT!
SHE GAVE ME TWO HOURS... BUT IT'S BEEN AN AN HOUR AND 40 MINUTES SINCE THEN...
...WHICH ONLY GIVES ME 20 MORE MINUTES!!
CAN'T AFFORD TO LOSE HER AGAIN...
KAKLUNK
KAKLUNK
...
KAKLUNK
KAKLUNK
BUT THE ONLY WAY TO CATCH UP AT THIS POINT...
...IS BY WEB-SWINGING.
KAKLUNK
KAKLUNK

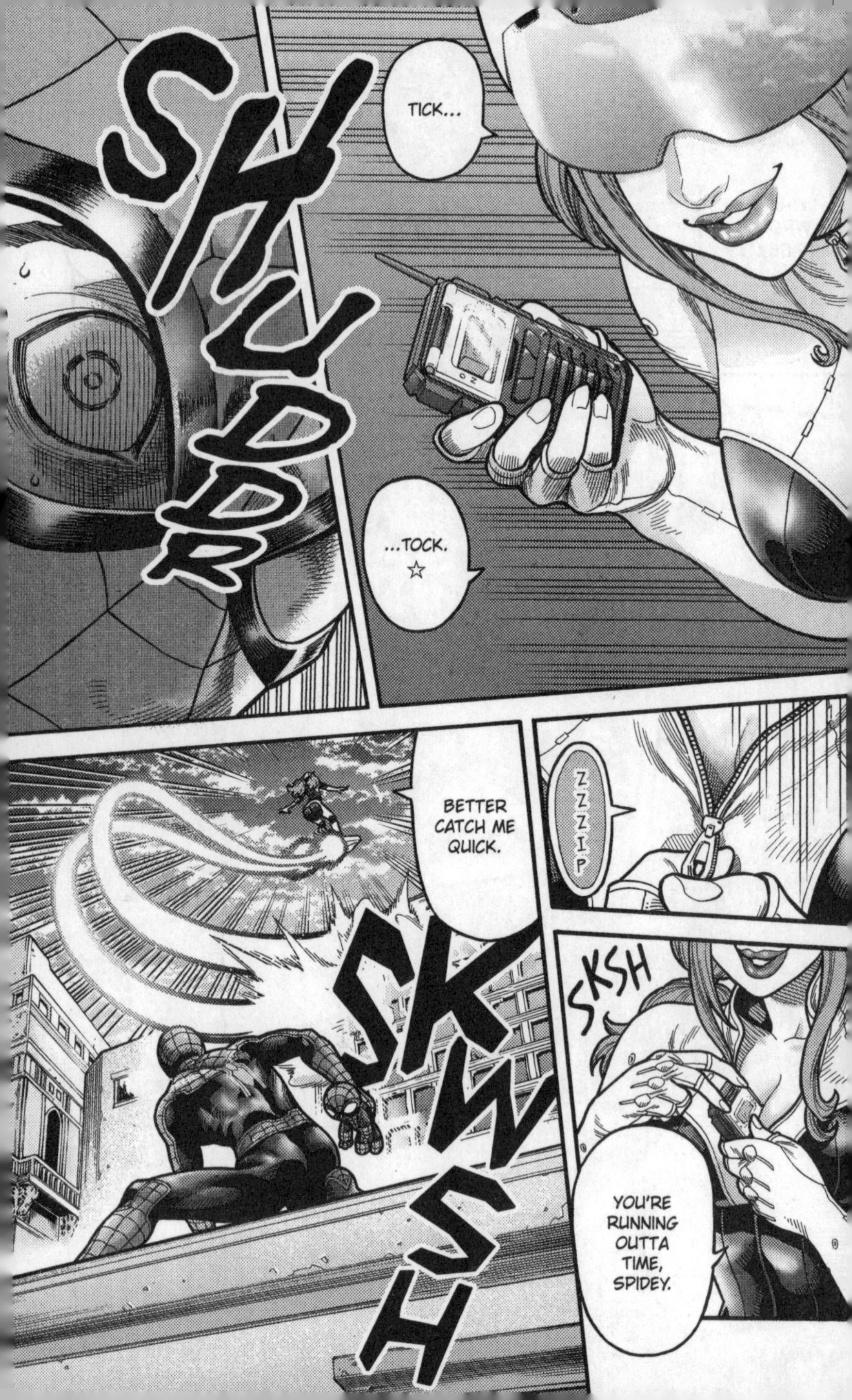
TICK...
...TOCK. ☆
SHUDDR
ZZZIP
SKSH
YOU'RE RUNNING OUTTA TIME, SPIDEY.
BETTER CATCH ME QUICK.
SKWSH

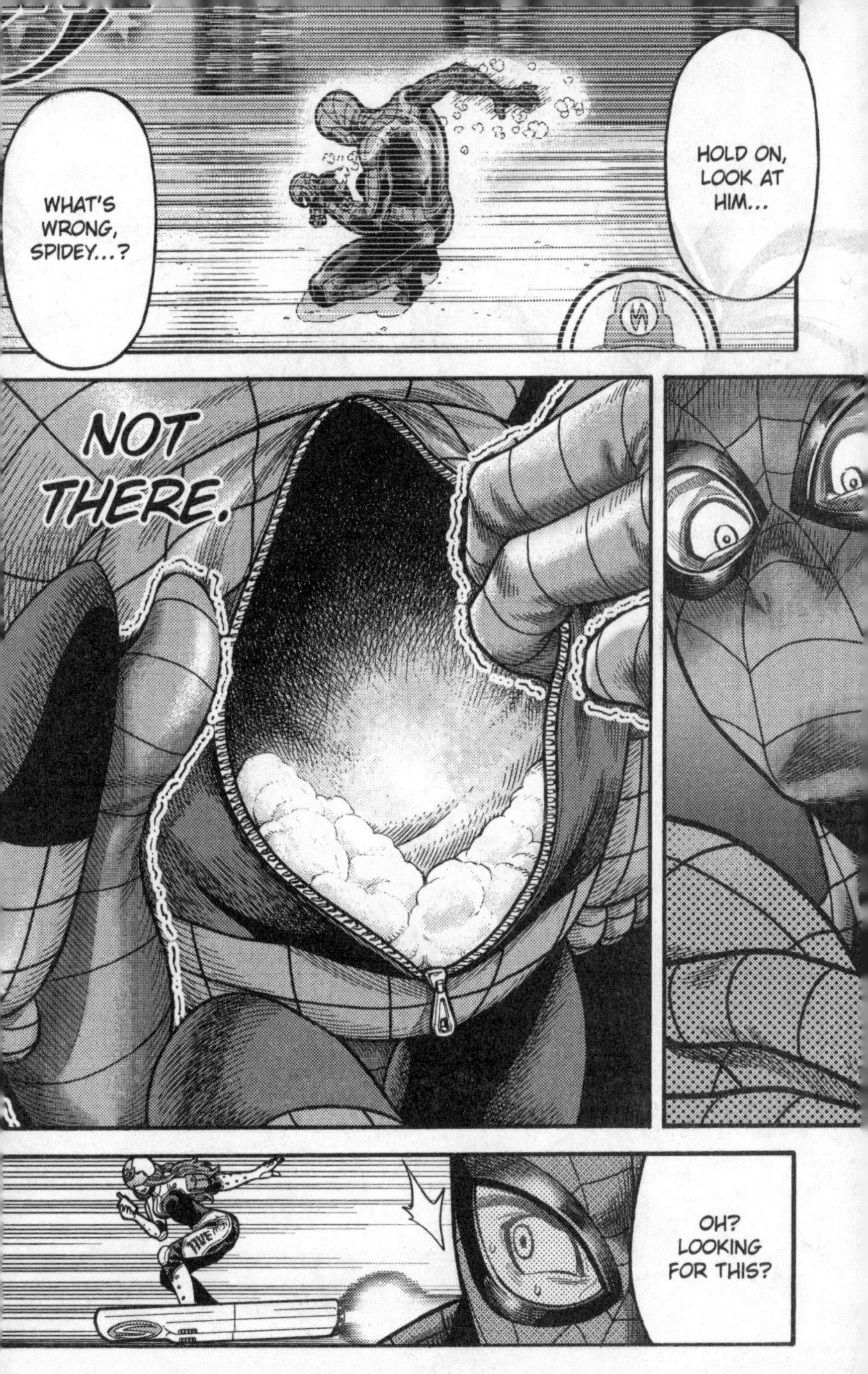
HOLD ON, LOOK AT HIM...
WHAT'S WRONG, SPIDEY...?
NOT THERE.
OH? LOOKING FOR THIS?

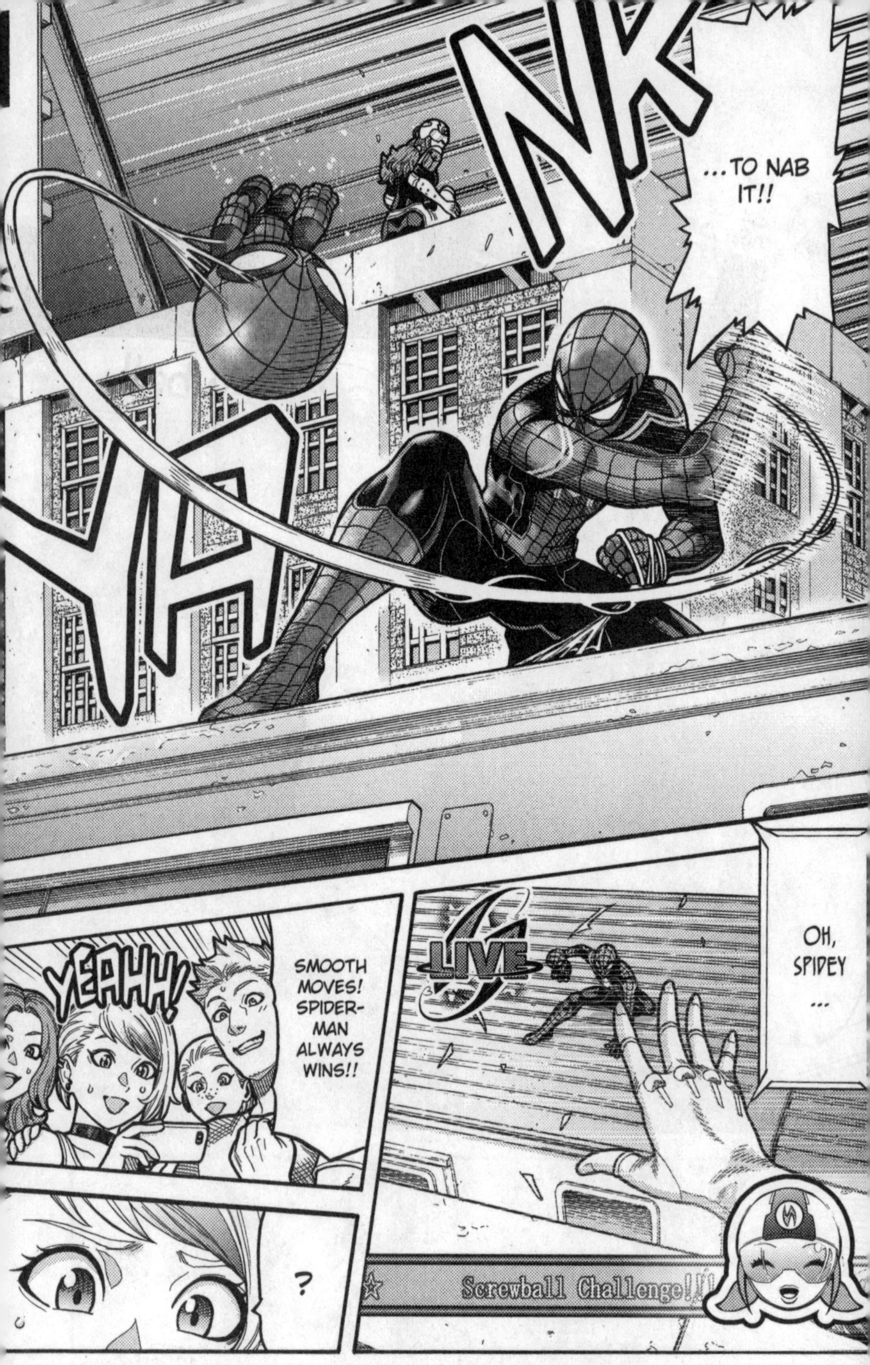

...TO NAB IT!!
YANK
OH, SPIDEY ...
LIVE
Screwball Challenge!!
YEAHH!
SMOOTH MOVES! SPIDER-MAN ALWAYS WINS!!
?

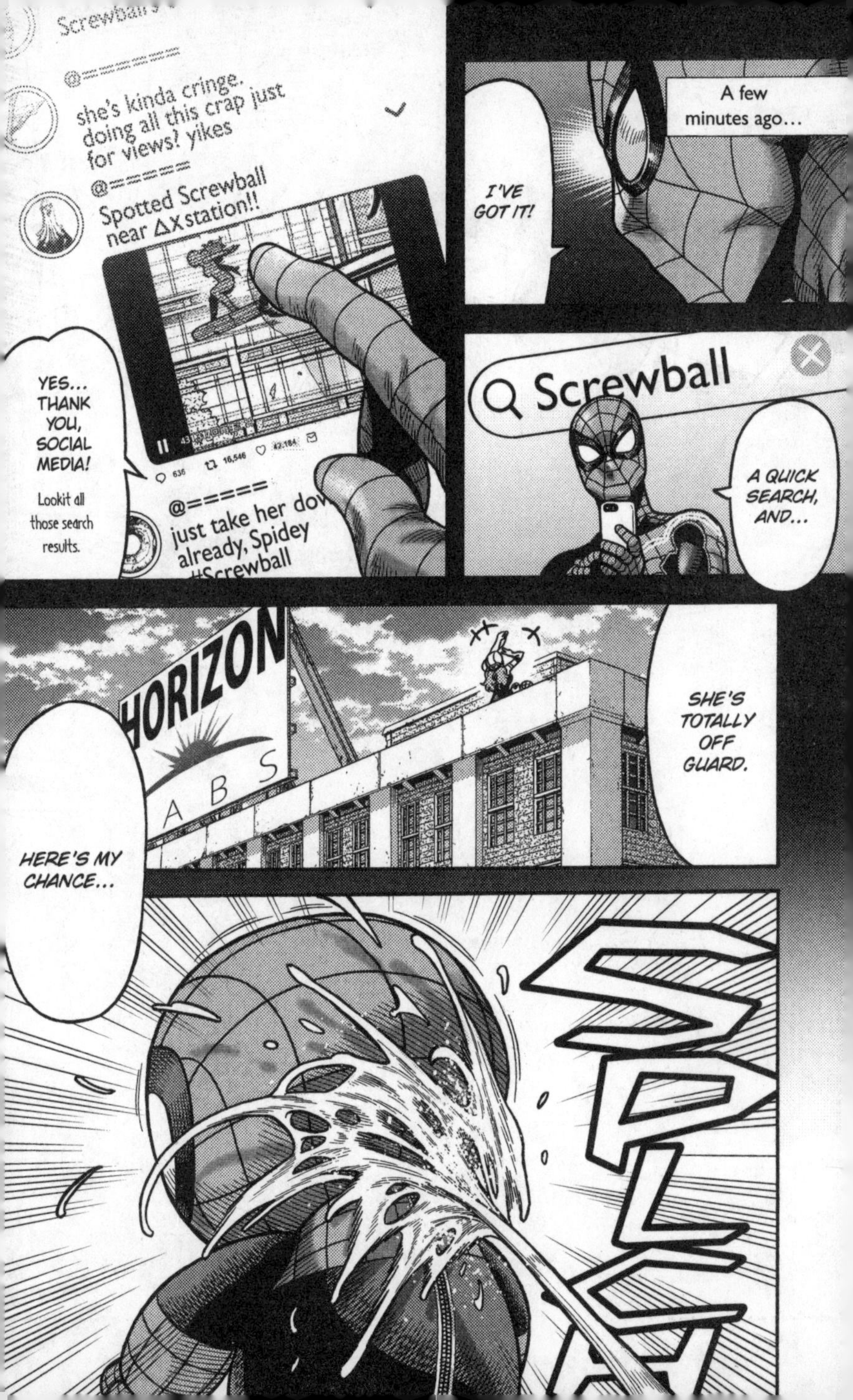
A few minutes ago…
I'VE GOT IT!
Screwball
A QUICK SEARCH, AND…
Screwball's
@======
she's kinda cringe. doing all this crap just for views? yikes
@======
Spotted Screwball near ΔX station!!
636
16,546
42,184
@======
just take her dow already, Spidey #Screwball
YES… THANK YOU, SOCIAL MEDIA!
Lookit all those search results.
SHE'S TOTALLY OFF GUARD.
HORIZON LABS
HERE'S MY CHANCE…
SPLA

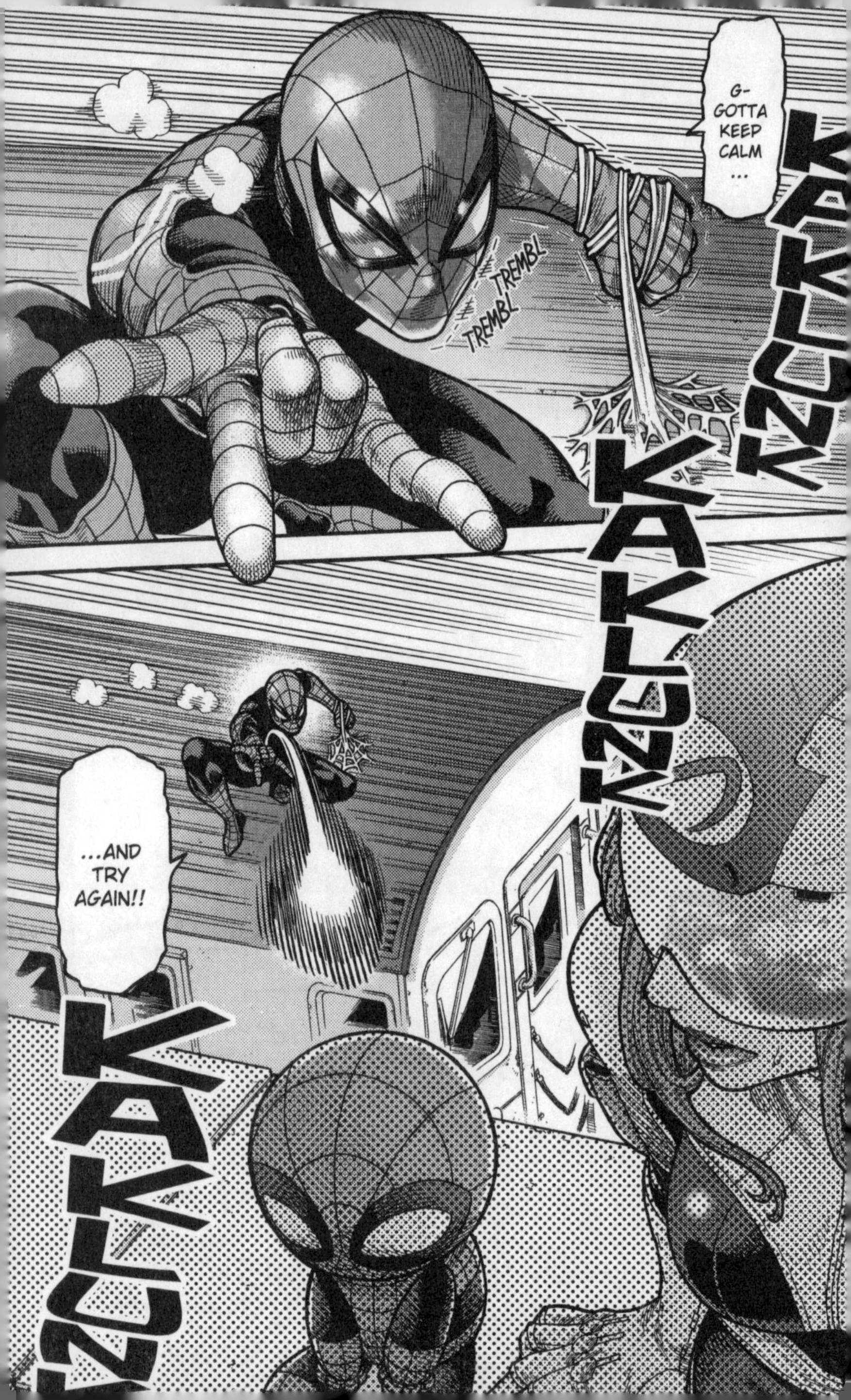
G- GOTTA KEEP CALM ...
KAKLUNK
TREMBL
TREMBL
TREMBL
KAKLUNK
...AND TRY AGAIN!!
KAKLUNK

SOME MEN JUST CAN'T KEEP UP, HUH?

Sorry, peeps.

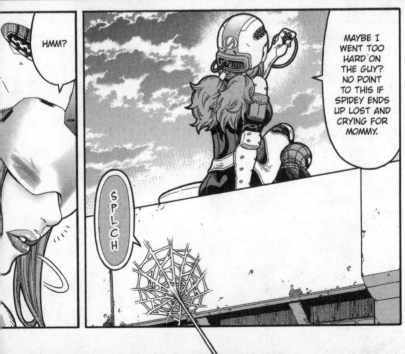

HMM?

MAYBE I WENT TOO HARD ON THE GUY? NO POINT TO THIS IF SPIDEY ENDS UP LOST AND CRYING FOR MOMMY.

SPLCH

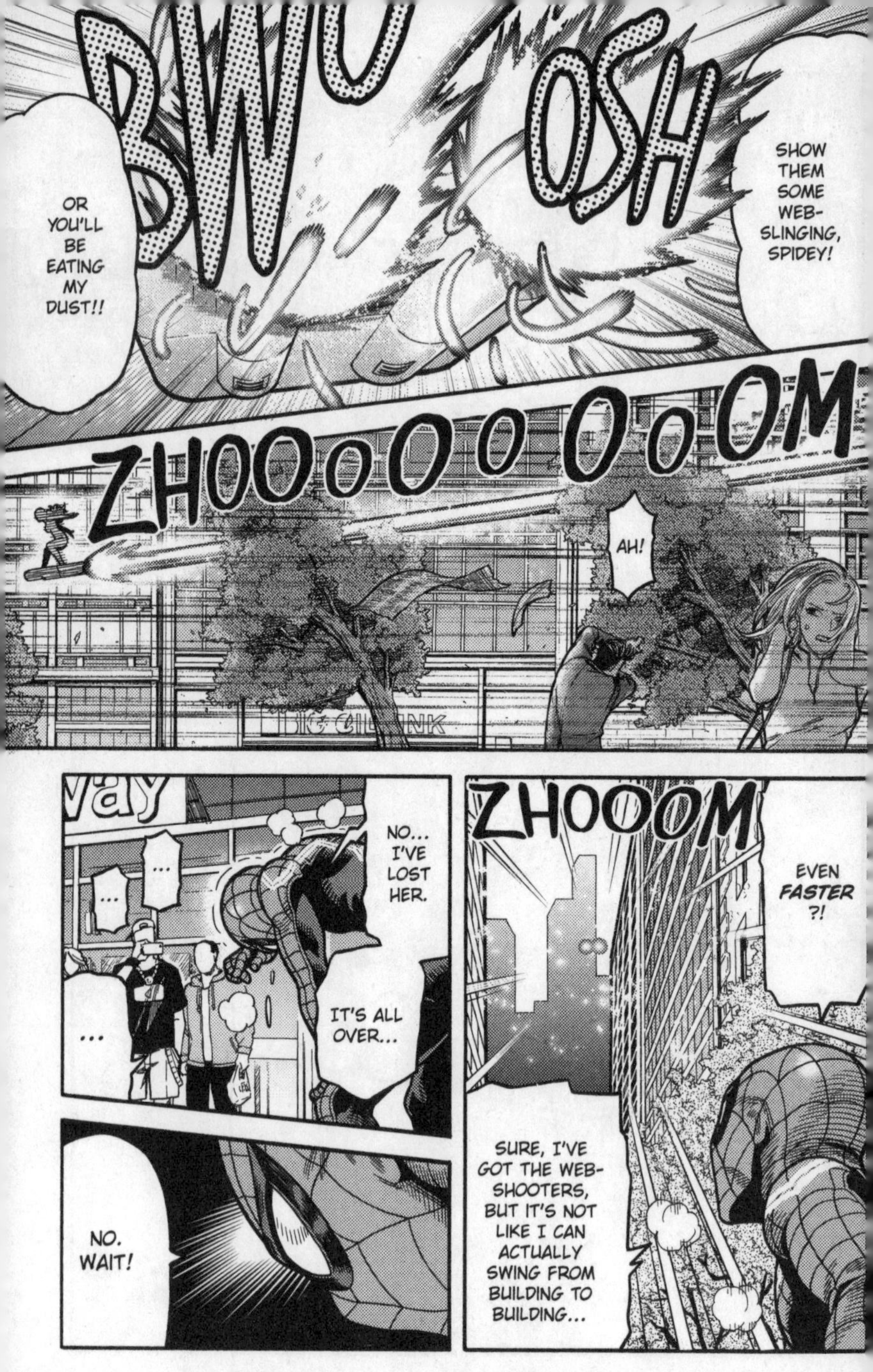
BWUOSH
SHOW THEM SOME WEB-SLINGING, SPIDEY!
OR YOU'LL BE EATING MY DUST!!
ZHOOOOOOOOOOM
AH!
ZHOOOM
EVEN *FASTER* ?!
SURE, I'VE GOT THE WEB-SHOOTERS, BUT IT'S NOT LIKE I CAN ACTUALLY SWING FROM BUILDING TO BUILDING...
NO... I'VE LOST HER.
...
...
IT'S ALL OVER...
...
NO. WAIT!

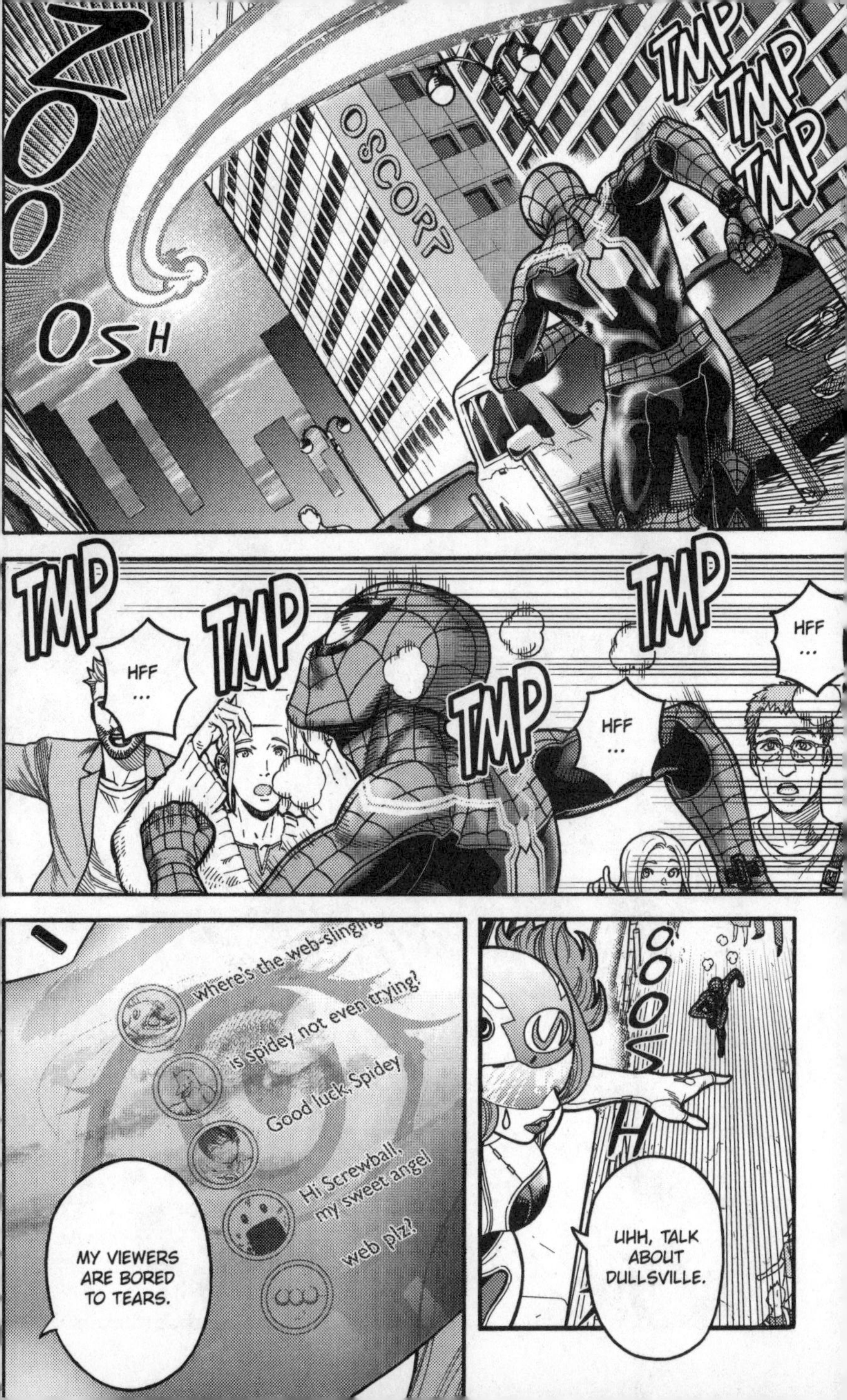
ZOOOSH
OSCORP
TMP TMP TMP
TMP
HFF ...
TMP
HFF ...
TMP
TMP
HFF ...
WOOOOSH
UHH, TALK ABOUT DULLSVILLE.
where's the web-slinging
where's the web-slinging
is spidey not even trying?
Good luck, Spidey
Hi Screwball, my sweet angel
web plz?
MY VIEWERS ARE BORED TO TEARS.

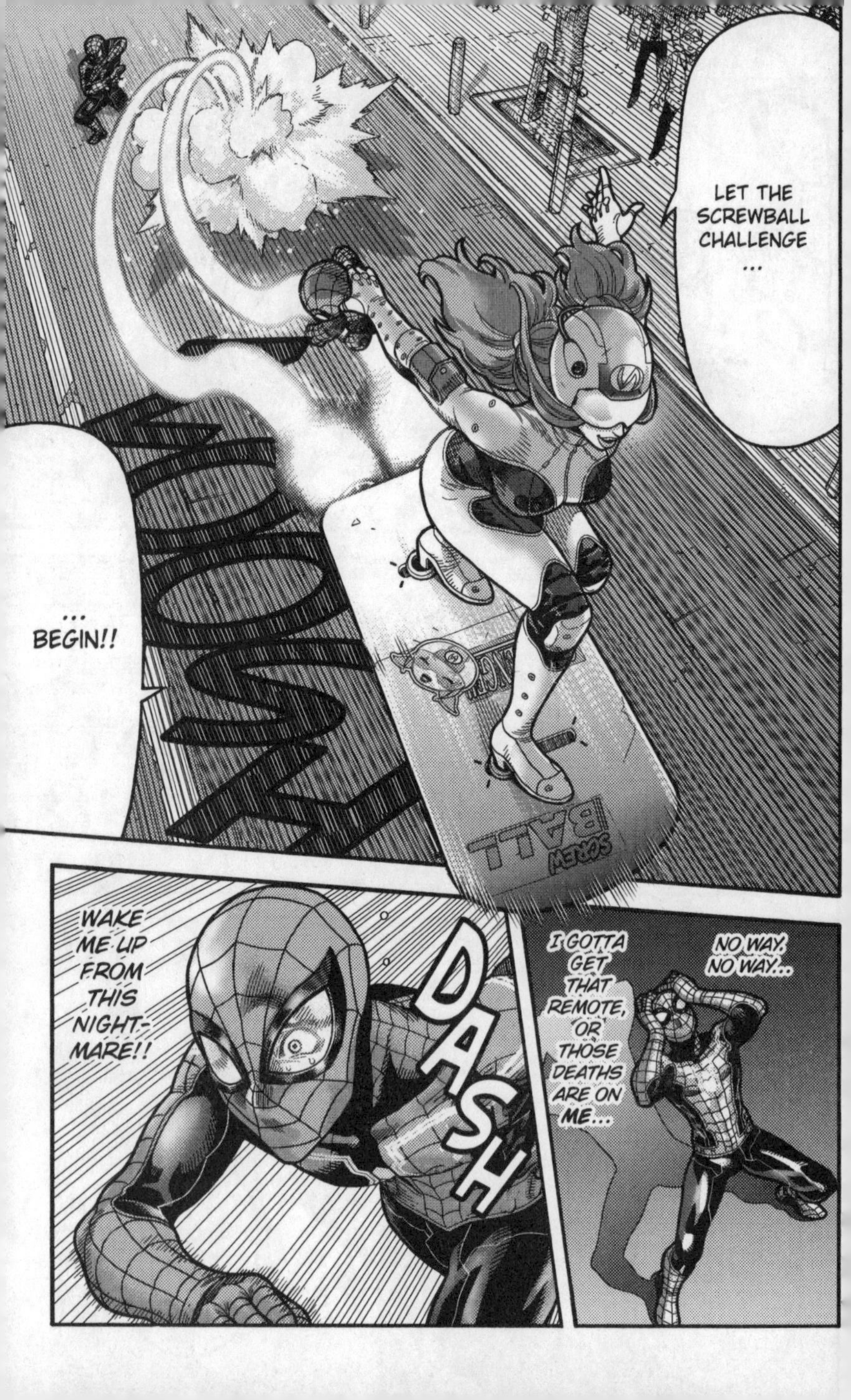
LET THE SCREWBALL CHALLENGE ...
... BEGIN!!
NO WAY. NO WAY...
I GOTTA GET THAT REMOTE, OR THOSE DEATHS ARE ON ME...
DASH
WAKE ME UP FROM THIS NIGHT-MARE!!

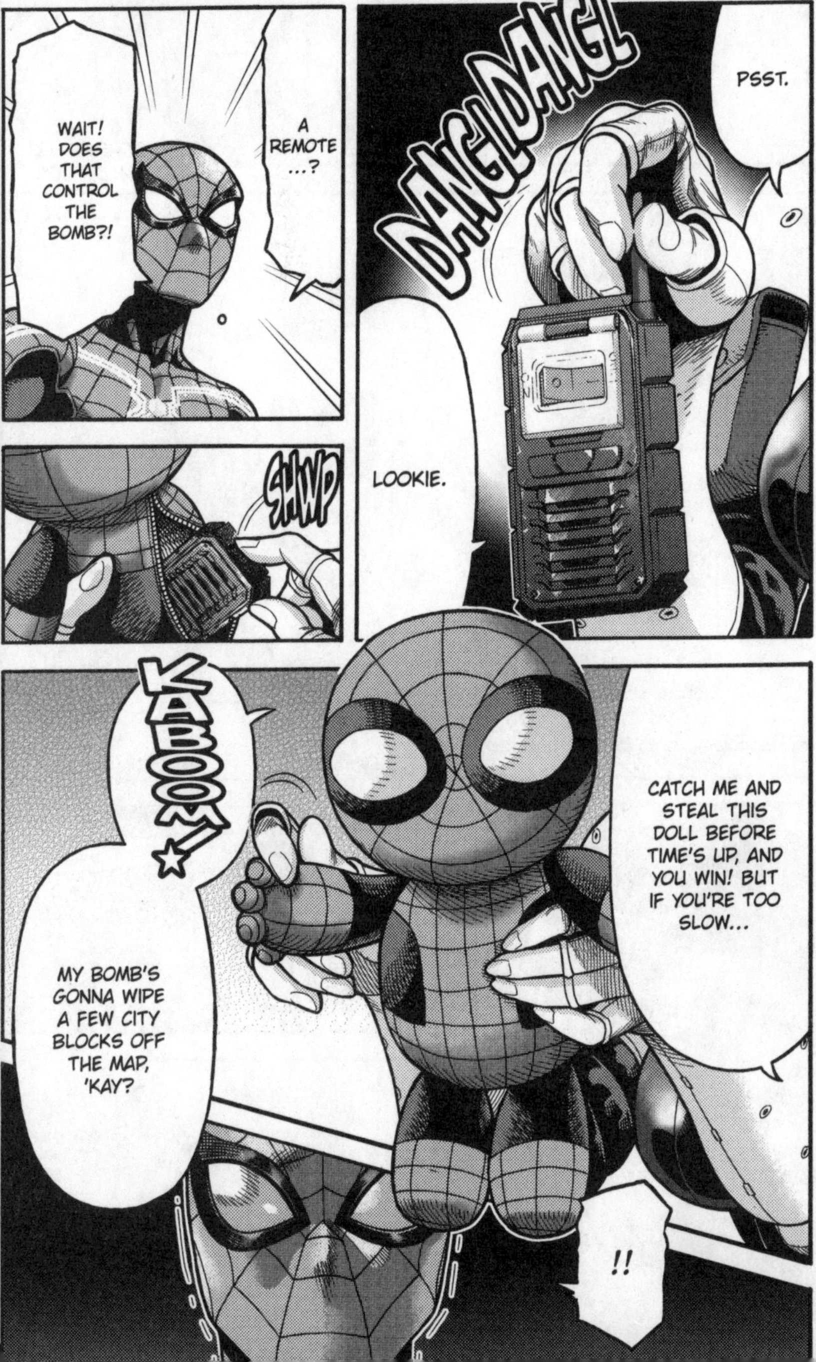
PSST.
DANGL DANGL
LOOKIE.
A REMOTE …?
WAIT! DOES THAT CONTROL THE BOMB?!
SHWP
CATCH ME AND STEAL THIS DOLL BEFORE TIME'S UP, AND YOU WIN! BUT IF YOU'RE TOO SLOW…
KABOOM!☆
MY BOMB'S GONNA WIPE A FEW CITY BLOCKS OFF THE MAP, 'KAY?
!!

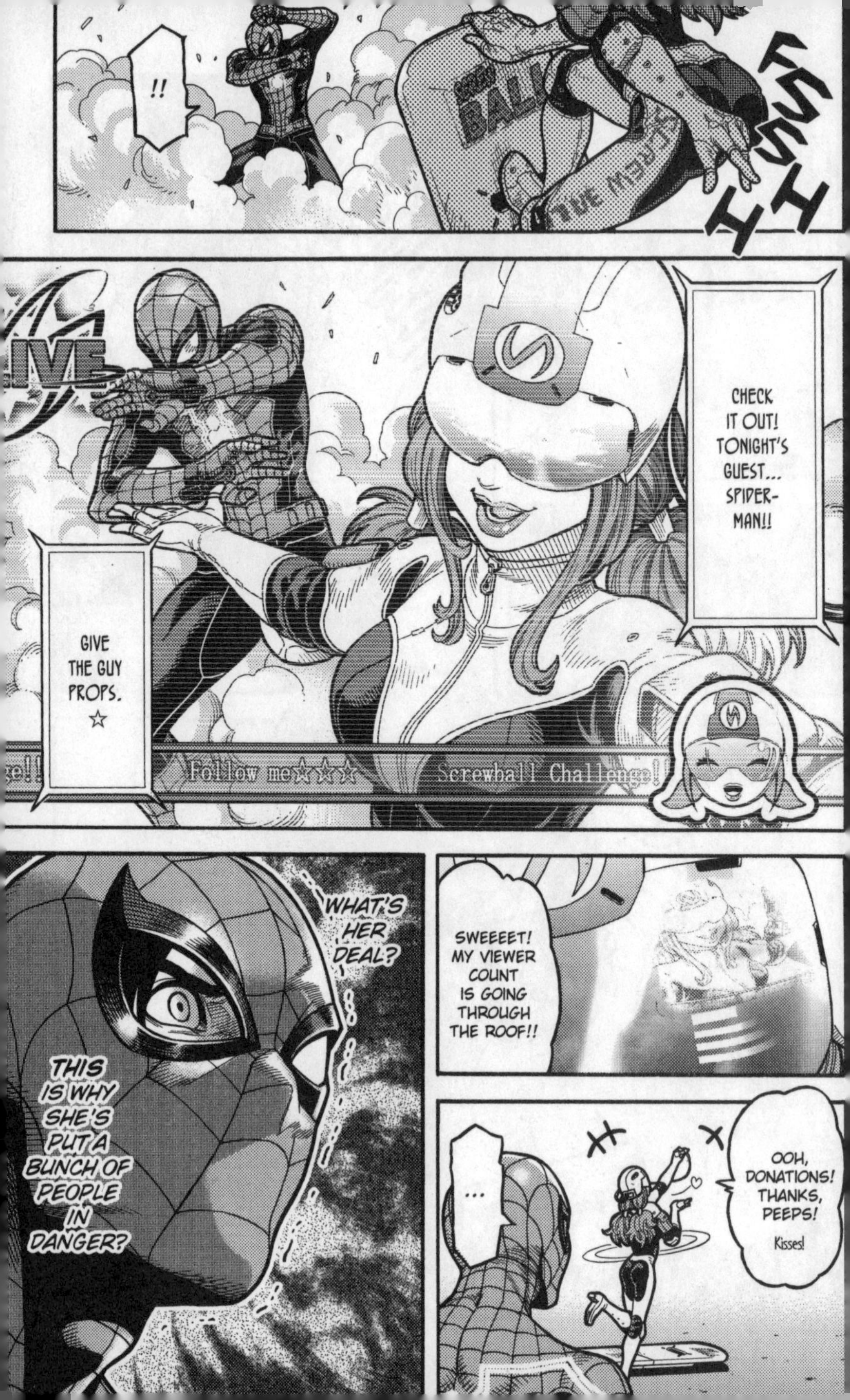
FSSHH
!!
CHECK IT OUT! TONIGHT'S GUEST... SPIDER-MAN!!
GIVE THE GUY PROPS. ☆
Follow me☆☆☆
Screwball Challenge!!
SWEEEET! MY VIEWER COUNT IS GOING THROUGH THE ROOF!!
OOH, DONATIONS! THANKS, PEEPS!
Kisses!
...
WHAT'S HER DEAL?
THIS IS WHY SHE'S PUT A BUNCH OF PEOPLE IN DANGER?

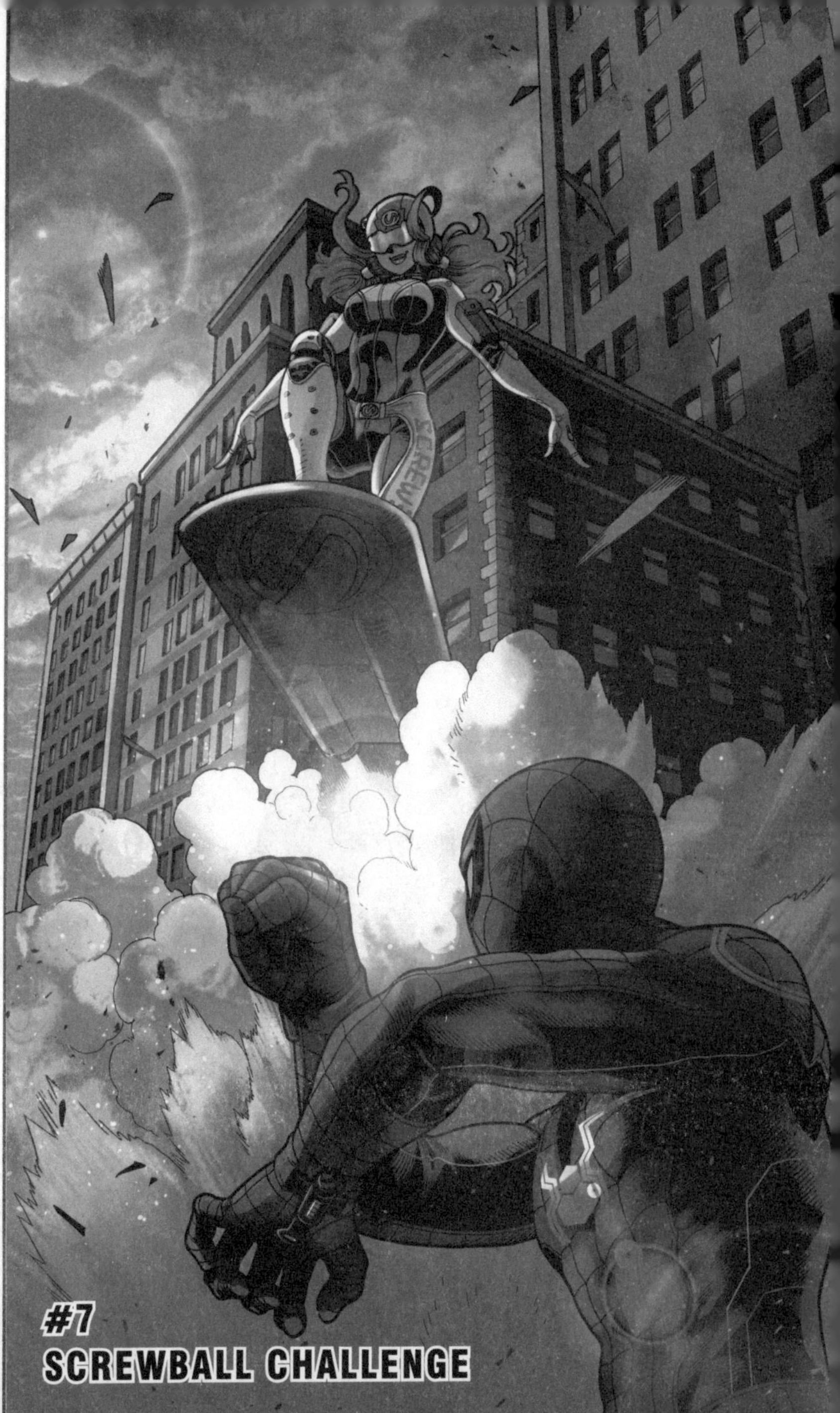
#7
SCREWBALL CHALLENGE

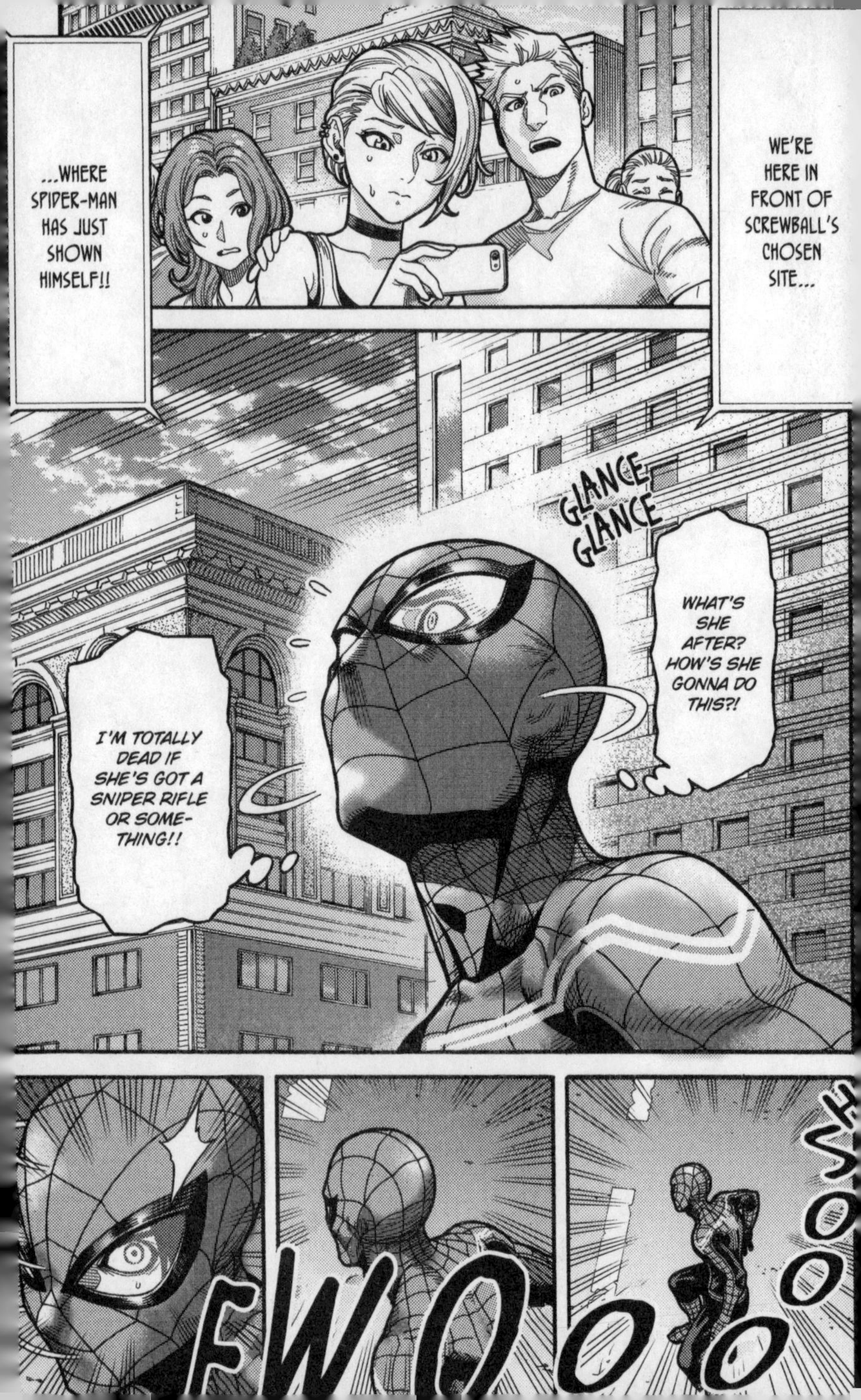
WE'RE HERE IN FRONT OF SCREWBALL'S CHOSEN SITE...
...WHERE SPIDER-MAN HAS JUST SHOWN HIMSELF!!
GLANCE GLANCE
WHAT'S SHE AFTER? HOW'S SHE GONNA DO THIS?!
I'M TOTALLY DEAD IF SHE'S GOT A SNIPER RIFLE OR SOME-THING!!
FWOOooooOOSH

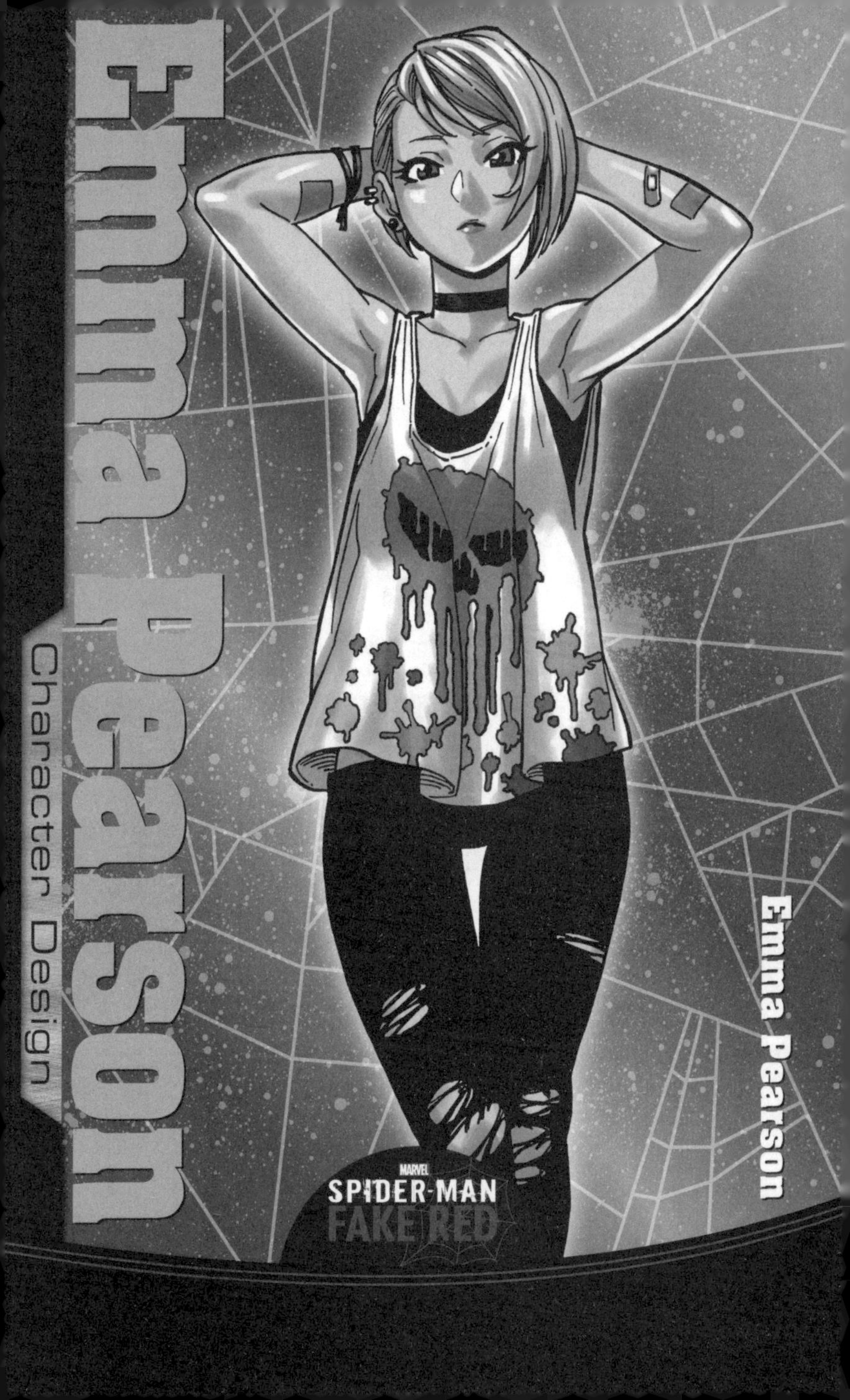
Emma Pearson
Character Design
Emma Pearson
MARVEL
SPIDER-MAN
FAKE RED

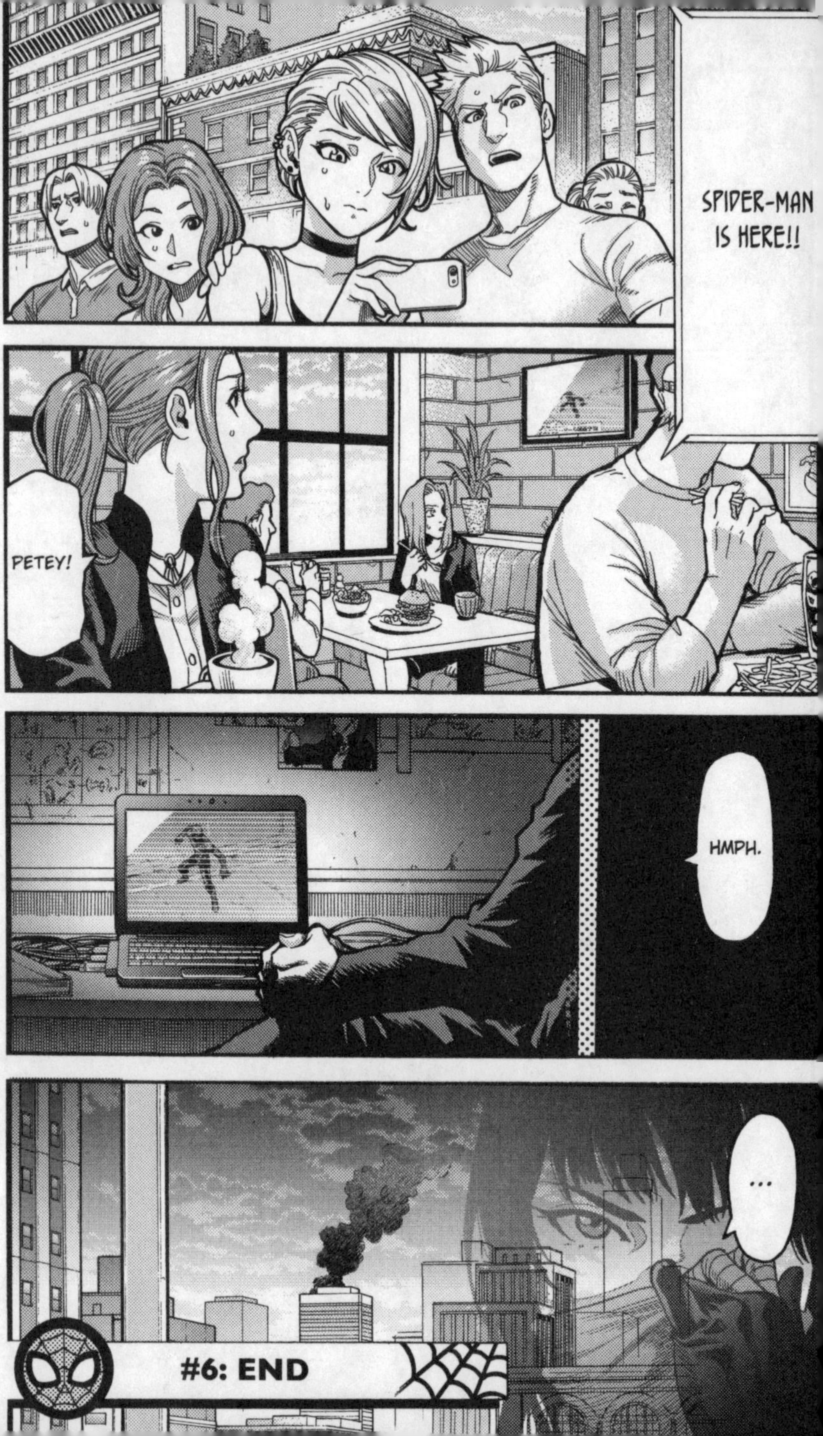
SPIDER-MAN IS HERE!!
PETEY!
HMPH.
...
#6: END

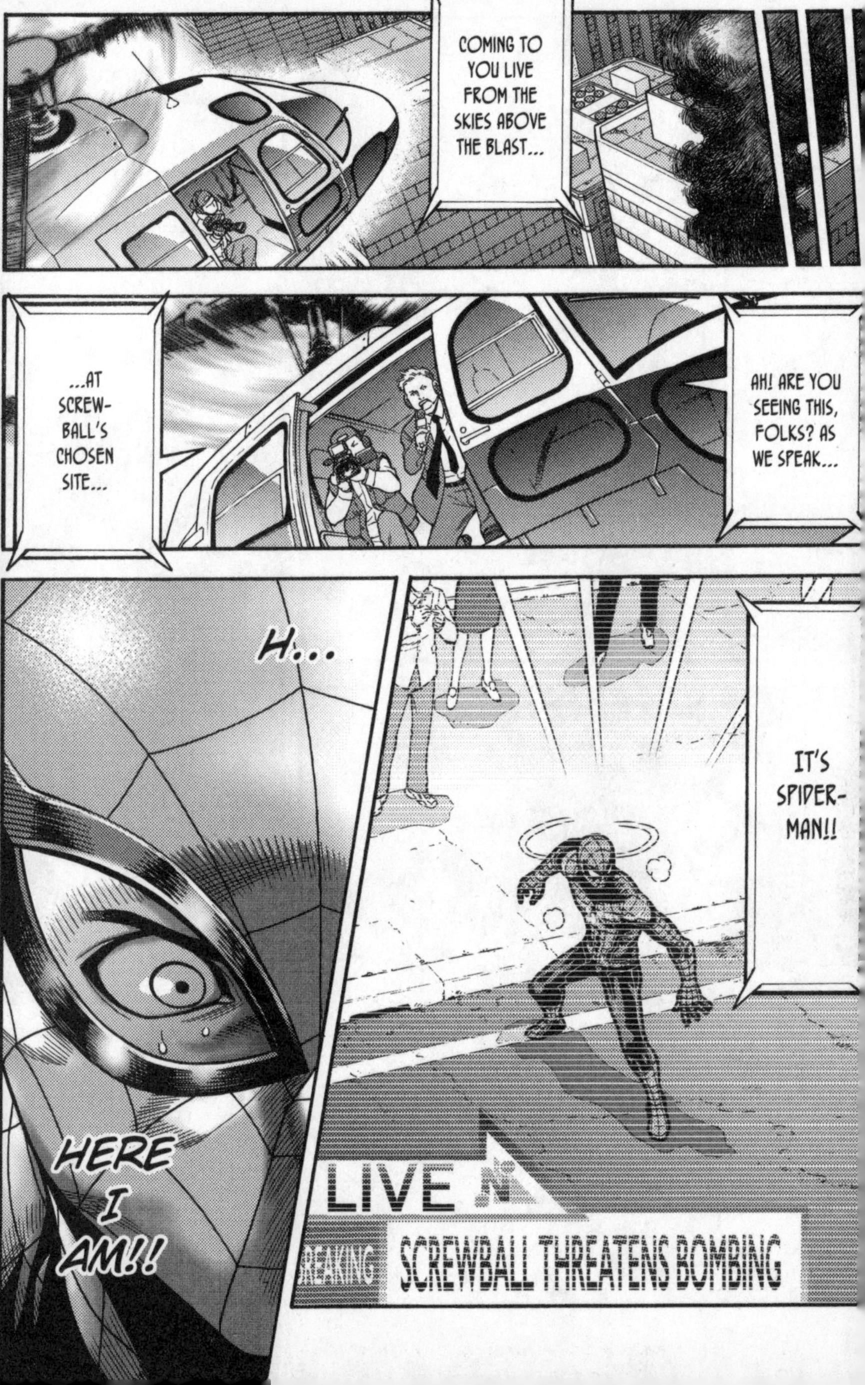
COMING TO YOU LIVE FROM THE SKIES ABOVE THE BLAST...
...AT SCREW-BALL'S CHOSEN SITE...
AH! ARE YOU SEEING THIS, FOLKS? AS WE SPEAK...
IT'S SPIDER-MAN!!
LIVE
REAKING
SCREWBALL THREATENS BOMBING
H...
HERE I AM!!

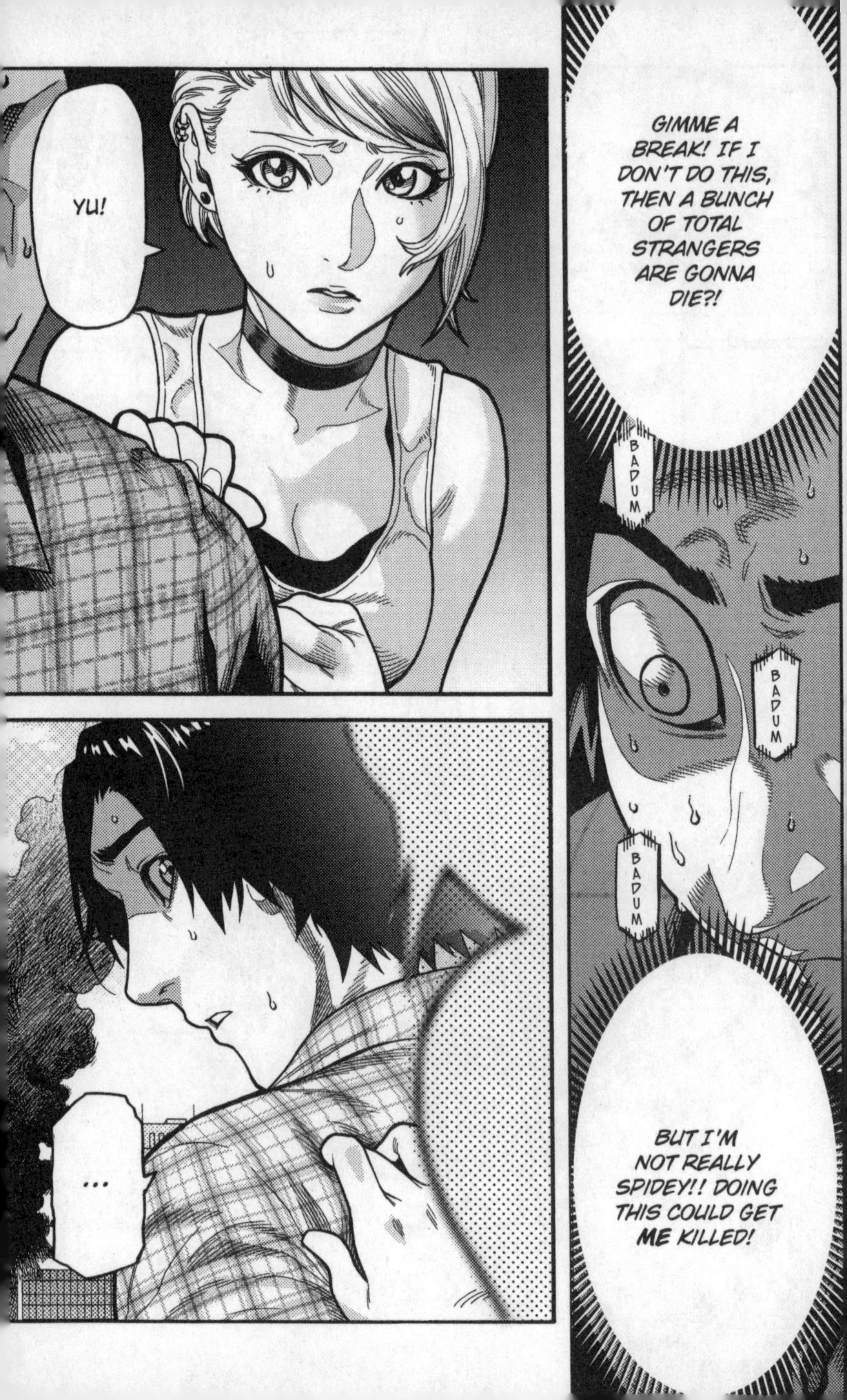
GIMME A BREAK! IF I DON'T DO THIS, THEN A BUNCH OF TOTAL STRANGERS ARE GONNA DIE?!
BADUM
BADUM
BADUM
BUT I'M NOT REALLY SPIDEY!! DOING THIS COULD GET ME KILLED!
YU!
...

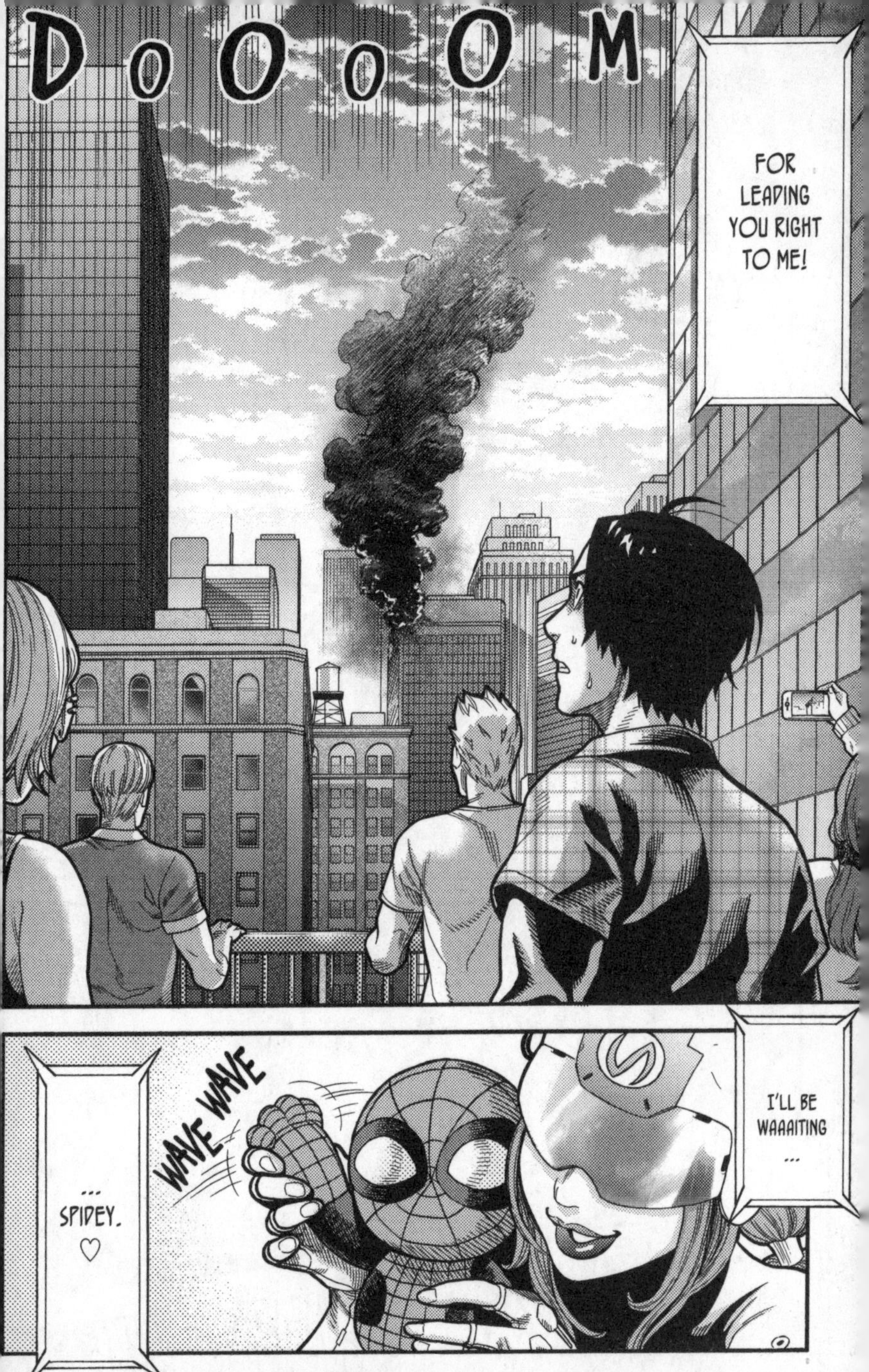
FOR LEADING YOU RIGHT TO ME!
DoOoOOM
I'LL BE WAAAITING ...
WAVE WAVE
... SPIDEY. ♡

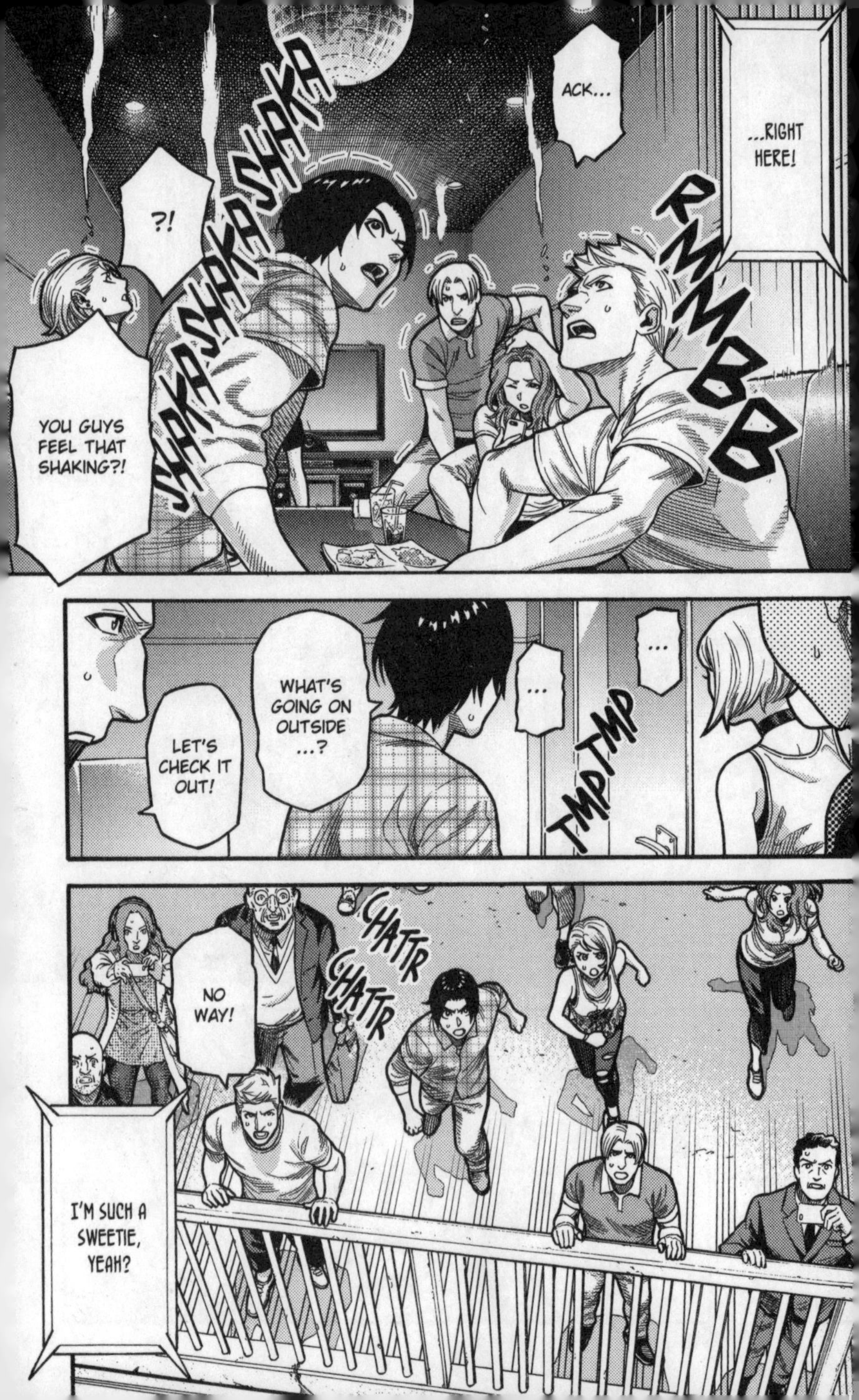
...RIGHT HERE!
RMMBB
ACK...
SHAKASHAKASHAKA
?!
YOU GUYS FEEL THAT SHAKING?!
...
...
TMP TMP
WHAT'S GOING ON OUTSIDE ...?
LET'S CHECK IT OUT!
CHATTR CHATTR
NO WAY!
I'M SUCH A SWEETIE, YEAH?

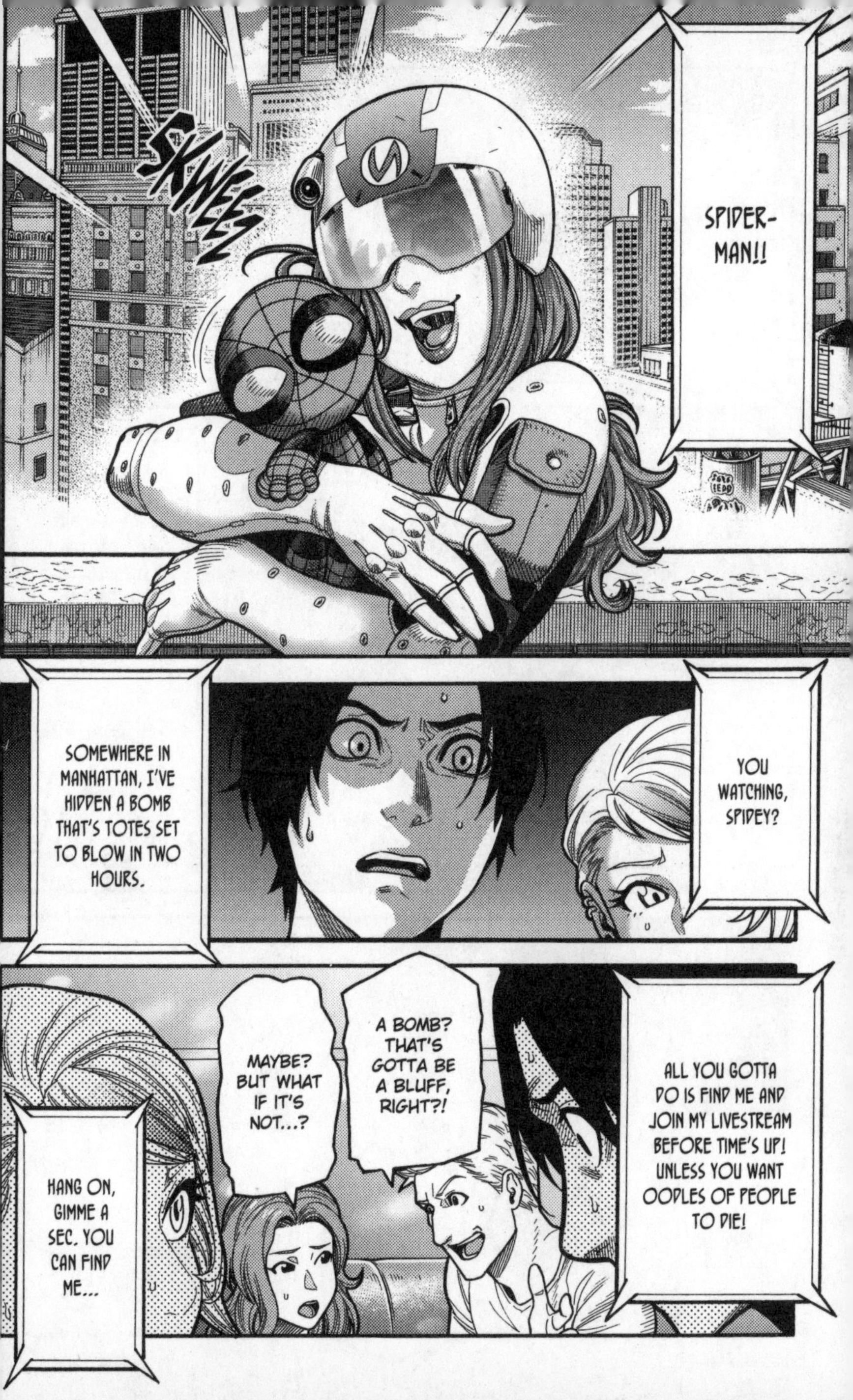
SPIDER-MAN!!
SKWEEE
YOU WATCHING, SPIDEY?
SOMEWHERE IN MANHATTAN, I'VE HIDDEN A BOMB THAT'S TOTES SET TO BLOW IN TWO HOURS.
ALL YOU GOTTA DO IS FIND ME AND JOIN MY LIVESTREAM BEFORE TIME'S UP! UNLESS YOU WANT OODLES OF PEOPLE TO DIE!
A BOMB? THAT'S GOTTA BE A BLUFF, RIGHT?!
MAYBE? BUT WHAT IF IT'S NOT...?
HANG ON, GIMME A SEC. YOU CAN FIND ME...

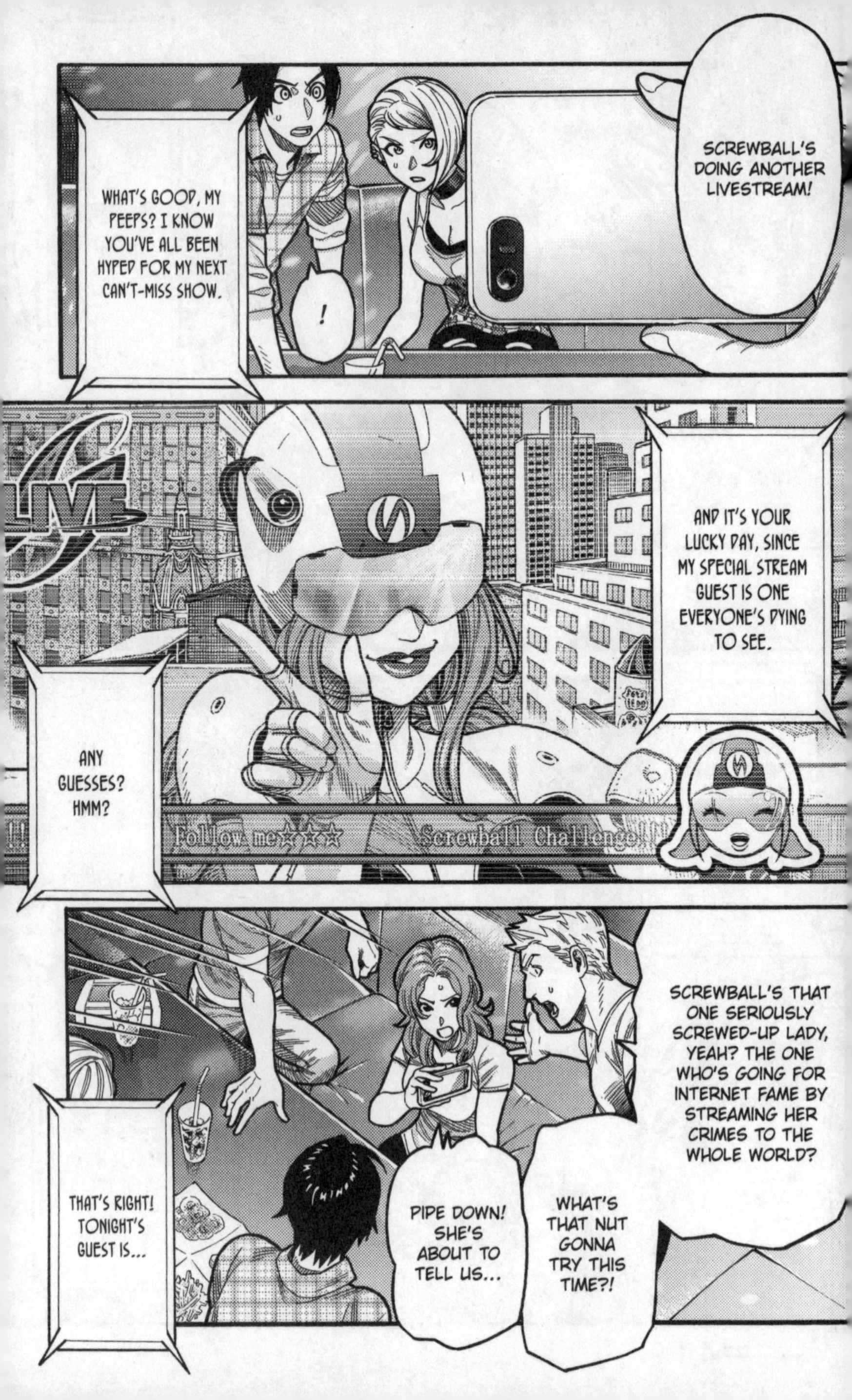
SCREWBALL'S DOING ANOTHER LIVESTREAM!
!
WHAT'S GOOD, MY PEEPS? I KNOW YOU'VE ALL BEEN HYPED FOR MY NEXT CAN'T-MISS SHOW.
LIVE
AND IT'S YOUR LUCKY DAY, SINCE MY SPECIAL STREAM GUEST IS ONE EVERYONE'S DYING TO SEE.
Follow me☆☆☆
Screwball Challenge
ANY GUESSES? HMM?
SCREWBALL'S THAT ONE SERIOUSLY SCREWED-UP LADY, YEAH? THE ONE WHO'S GOING FOR INTERNET FAME BY STREAMING HER CRIMES TO THE WHOLE WORLD?
WHAT'S THAT NUT GONNA TRY THIS TIME?!
PIPE DOWN! SHE'S ABOUT TO TELL US...
THAT'S RIGHT! TONIGHT'S GUEST IS...

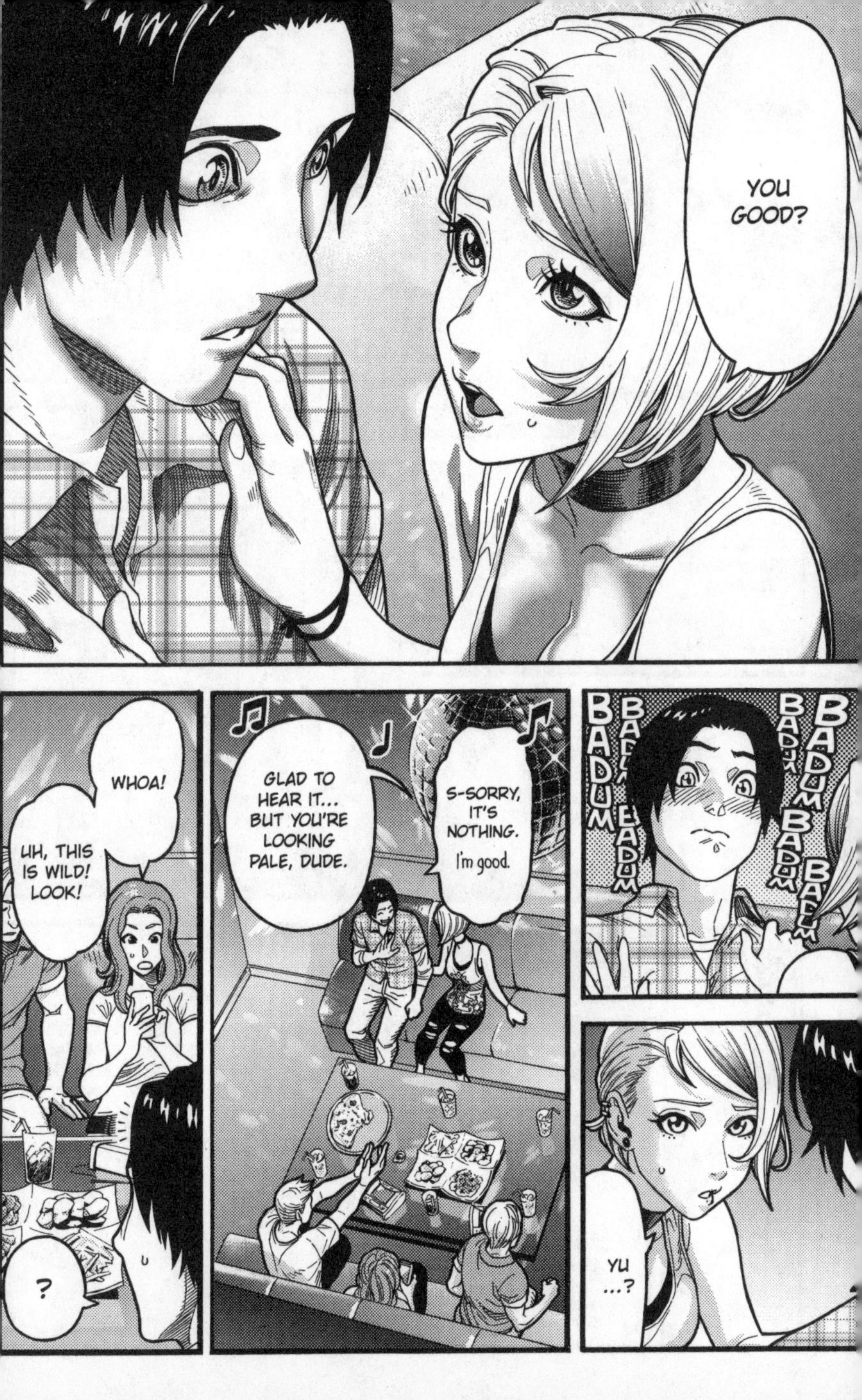
YOU GOOD?
BADUM BADUM BADUM
BADUM BADUM BADUM
BADUM
BADUM BADUM
YU ...?
S-SORRY, IT'S NOTHING. I'm good.
GLAD TO HEAR IT... BUT YOU'RE LOOKING PALE, DUDE.
WHOA!
UH, THIS IS WILD! LOOK!
?

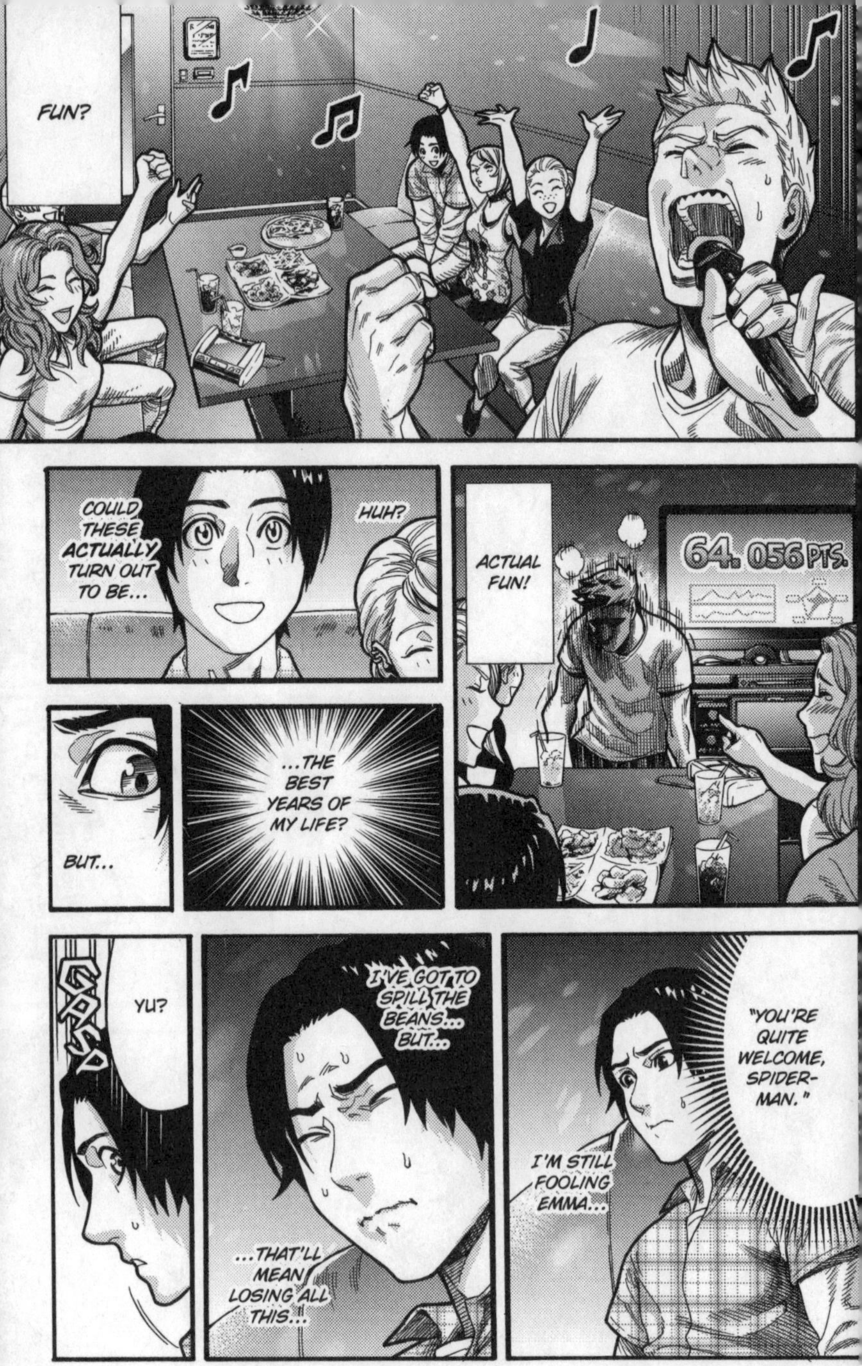
FUN?
ACTUAL FUN!
64.056 PTS.
HUH?
COULD THESE ACTUALLY TURN OUT TO BE...
...THE BEST YEARS OF MY LIFE?
BUT...
"YOU'RE QUITE WELCOME, SPIDER-MAN."
I'M STILL FOOLING EMMA...
I'VE GOT TO SPILL THE BEANS... BUT...
...THAT'LL MEAN LOSING ALL THIS...!
GASP
YU?

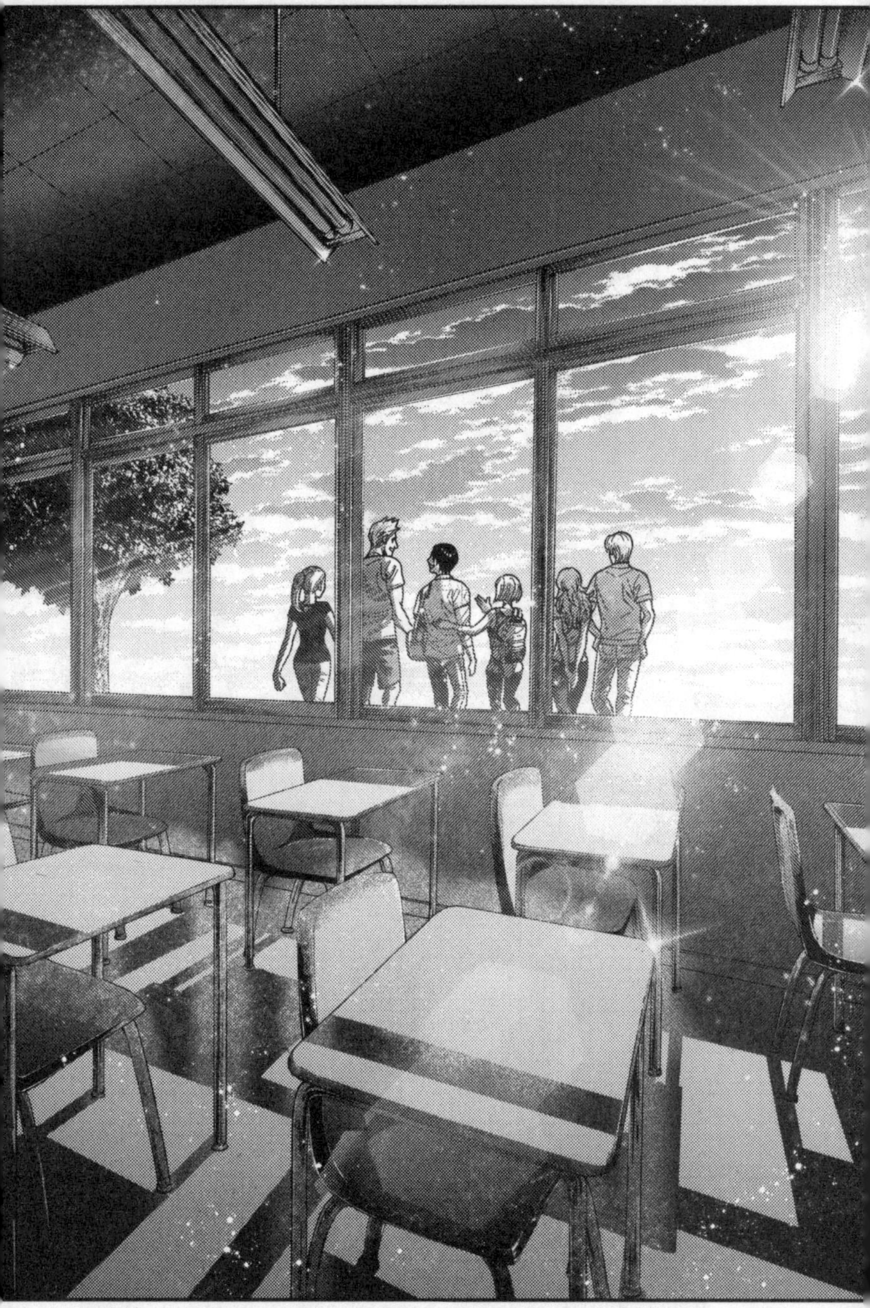

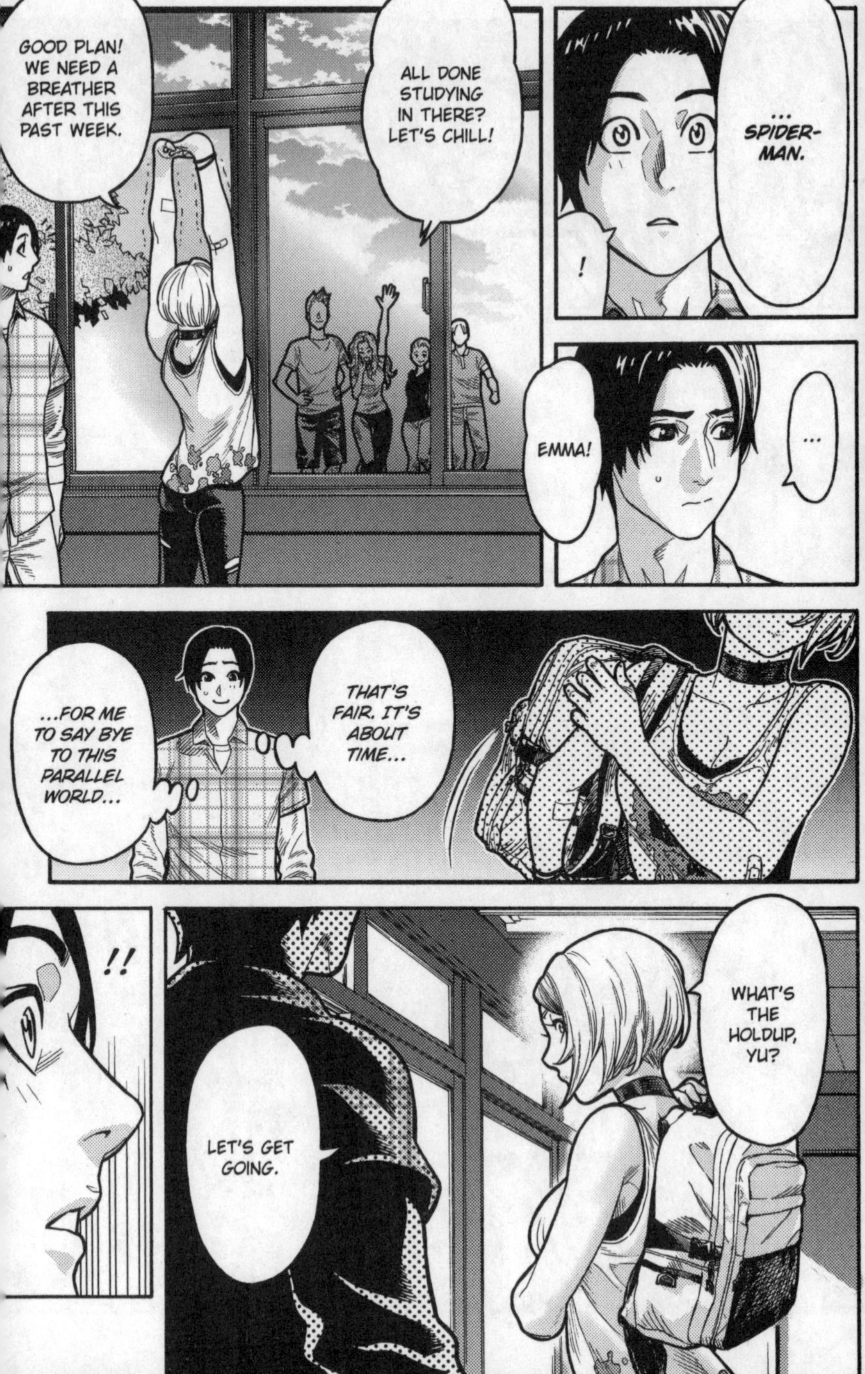
...SPIDER-MAN.
!
...
EMMA!
ALL DONE STUDYING IN THERE? LET'S CHILL!
GOOD PLAN! WE NEED A BREATHER AFTER THIS PAST WEEK.
THAT'S FAIR. IT'S ABOUT TIME...
...FOR ME TO SAY BYE TO THIS PARALLEL WORLD...
WHAT'S THE HOLDUP, YU?
LET'S GET GOING.
!!

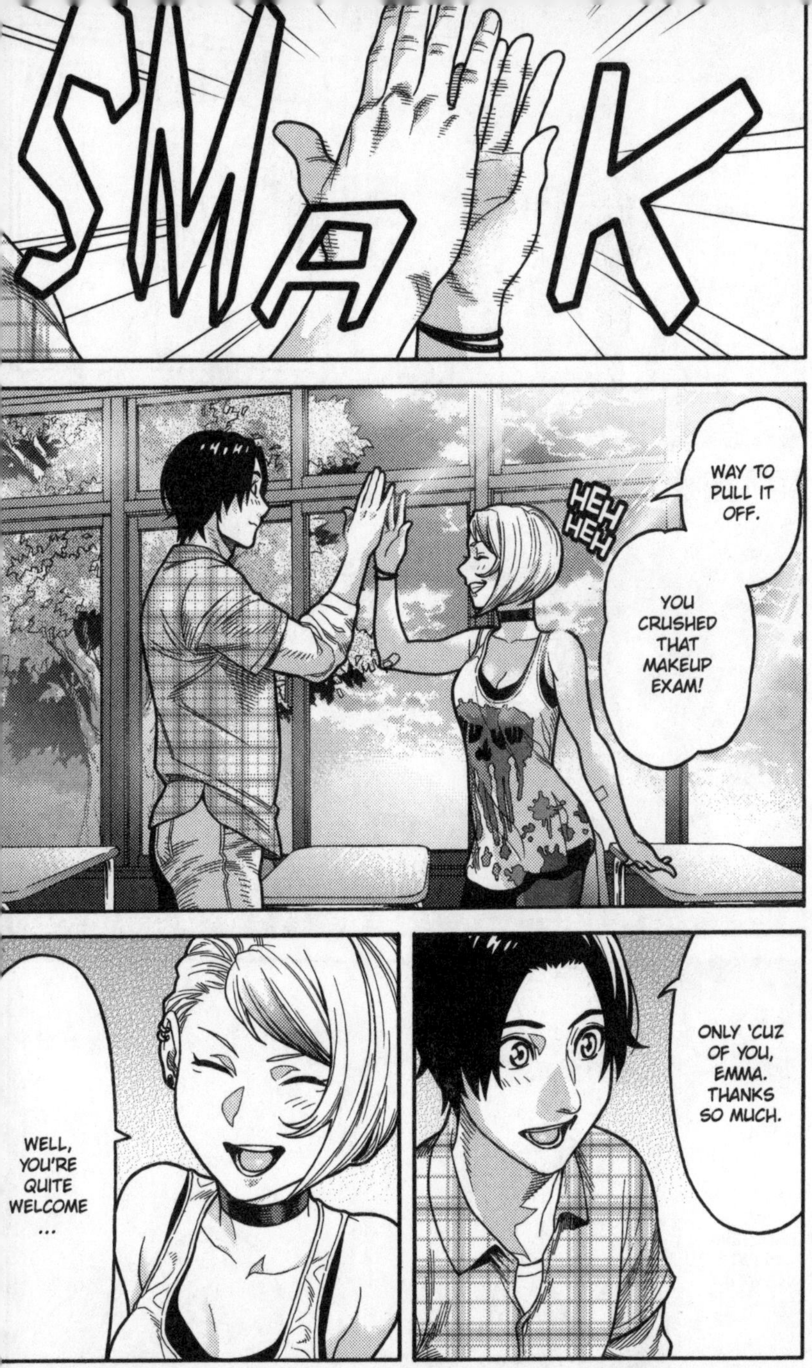
SMAK
WAY TO PULL IT OFF.
HEH HEH
YOU CRUSHED THAT MAKEUP EXAM!
ONLY 'CUZ OF YOU, EMMA. THANKS SO MUCH.
WELL, YOU'RE QUITE WELCOME ...

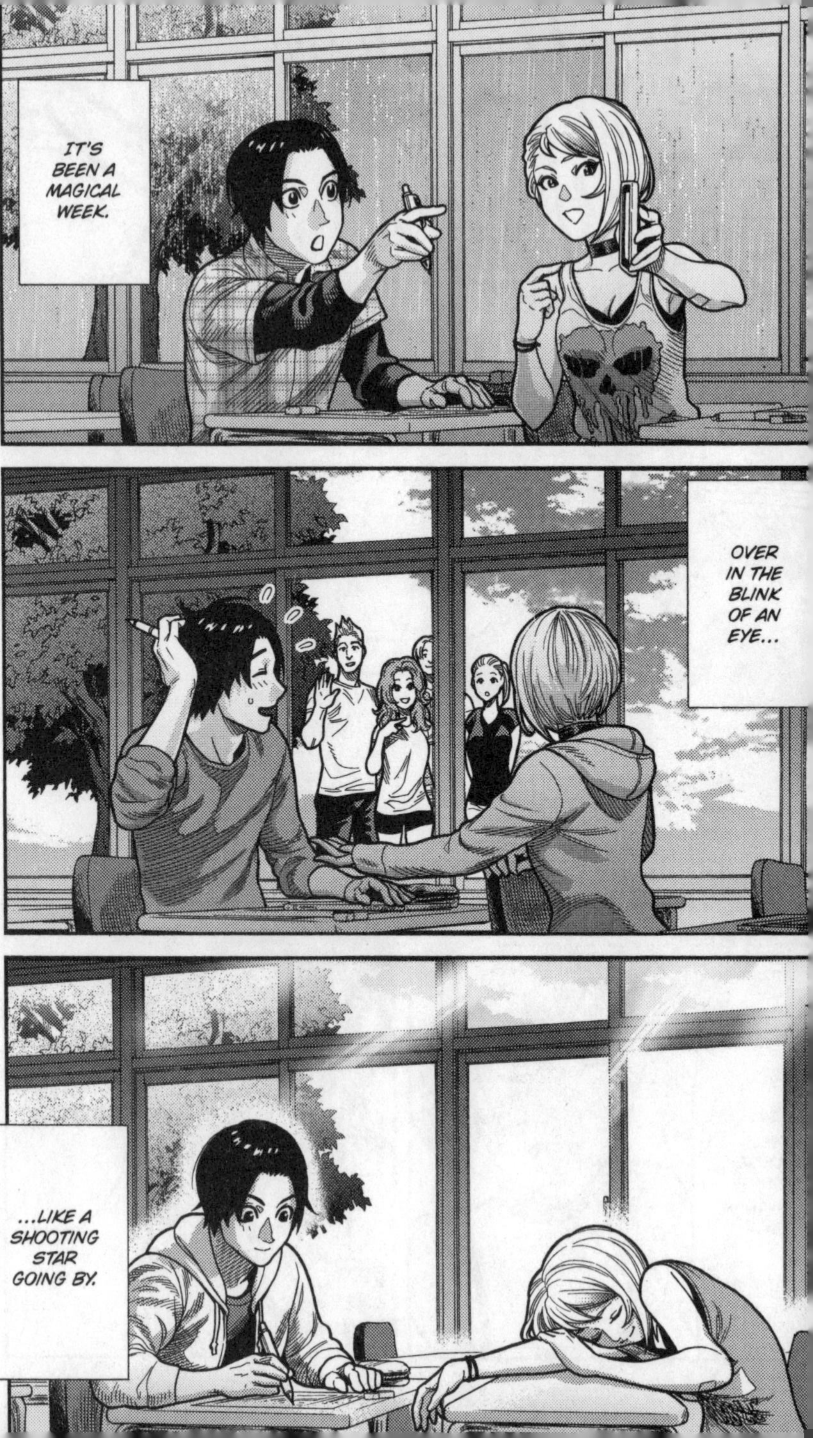
IT'S BEEN A MAGICAL WEEK.
OVER IN THE BLINK OF AN EYE...
...LIKE A SHOOTING STAR GOING BY.

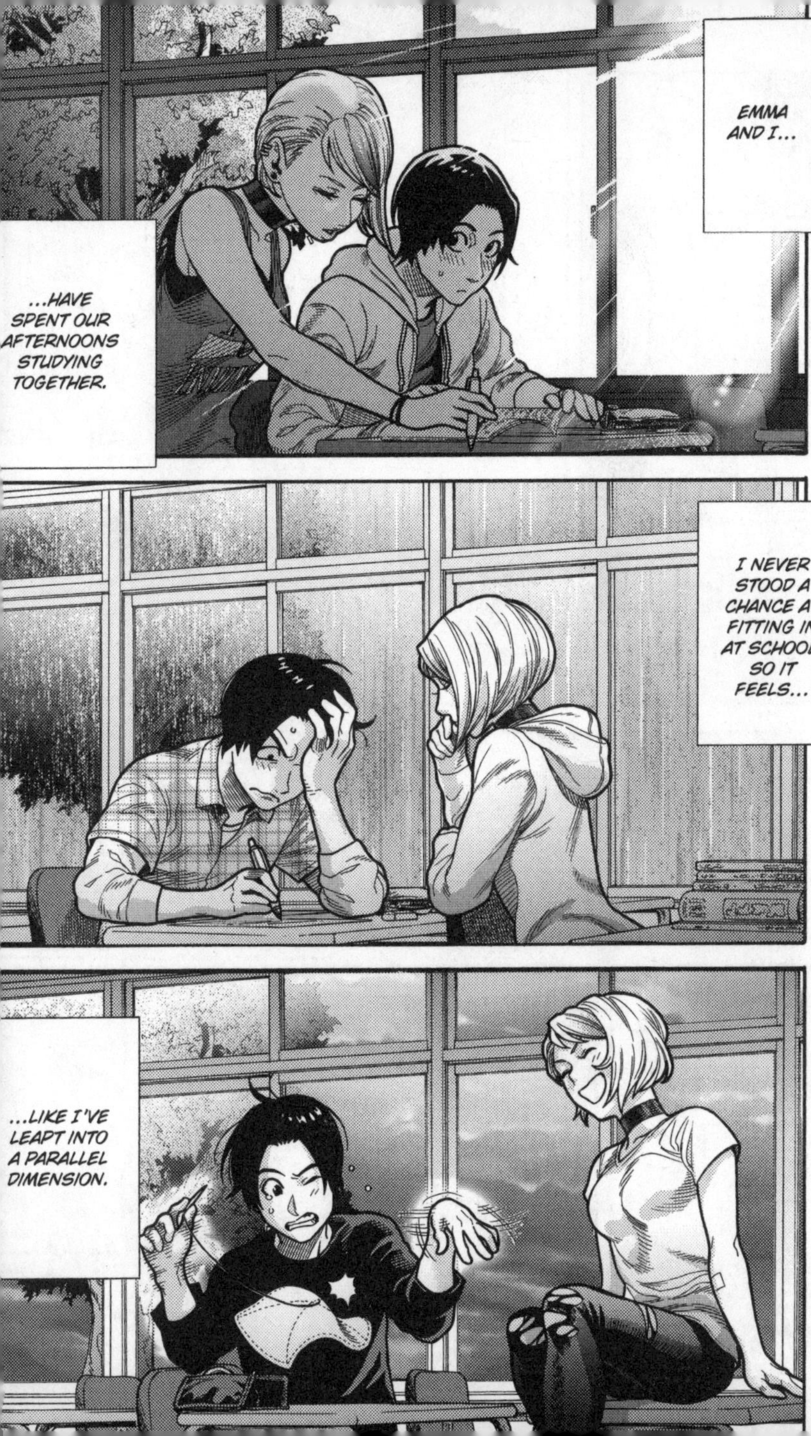
EMMA AND I...
...HAVE SPENT OUR AFTERNOONS STUDYING TOGETHER.
I NEVER STOOD A CHANCE AT FITTING IN AT SCHOOL, SO IT FEELS...
...LIKE I'VE LEAPT INTO A PARALLEL DIMENSION.

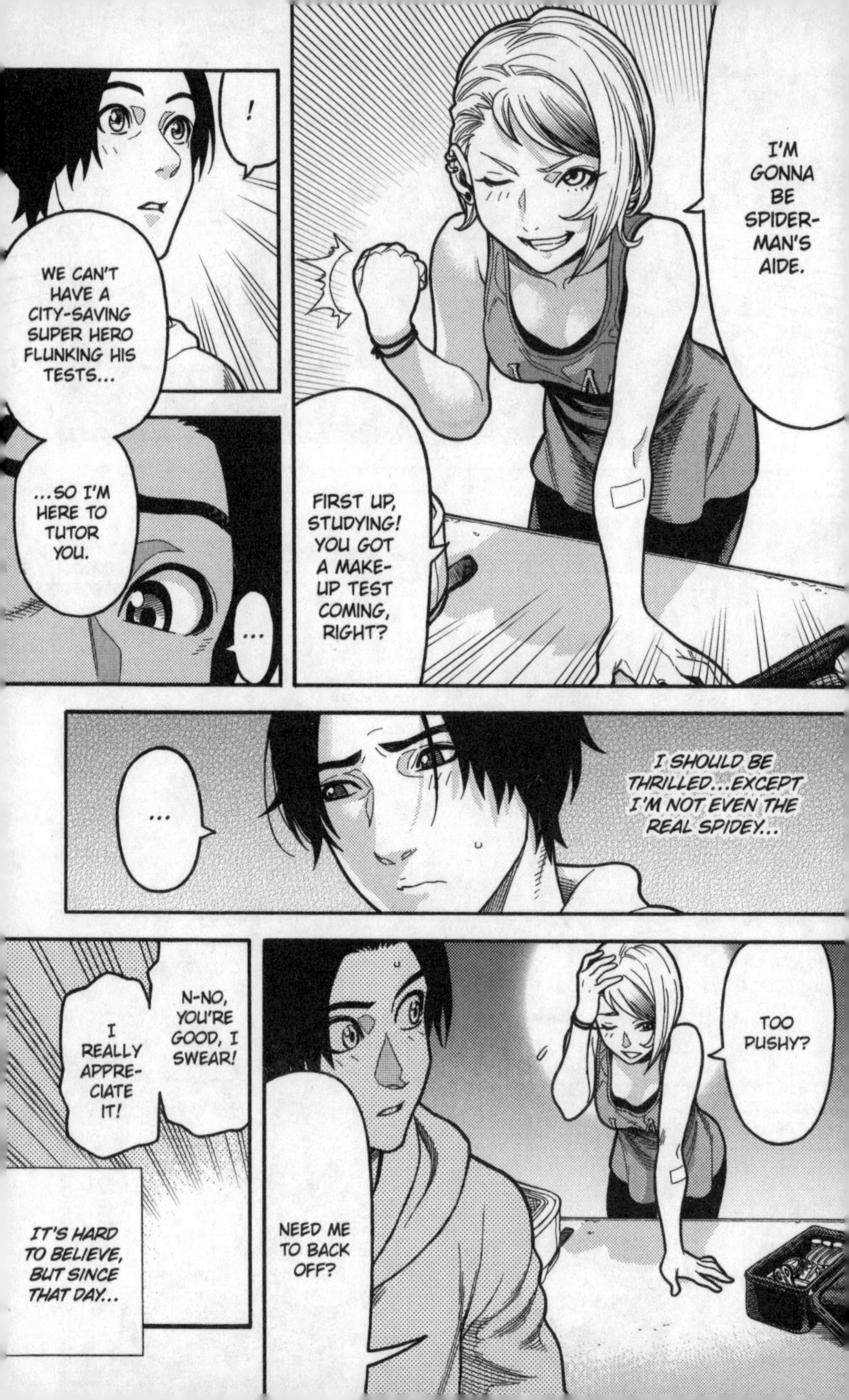
I'M GONNA BE SPIDER-MAN'S AIDE.
FIRST UP, STUDYING! YOU GOT A MAKE-UP TEST COMING, RIGHT?
!
WE CAN'T HAVE A CITY-SAVING SUPER HERO FLUNKING HIS TESTS...
...SO I'M HERE TO TUTOR YOU.
...
I SHOULD BE THRILLED...EXCEPT I'M NOT EVEN THE REAL SPIDEY...
...
TOO PUSHY?
NEED ME TO BACK OFF?
N-NO, YOU'RE GOOD, I SWEAR!
I REALLY APPRE-CIATE IT!
IT'S HARD TO BELIEVE, BUT SINCE THAT DAY...

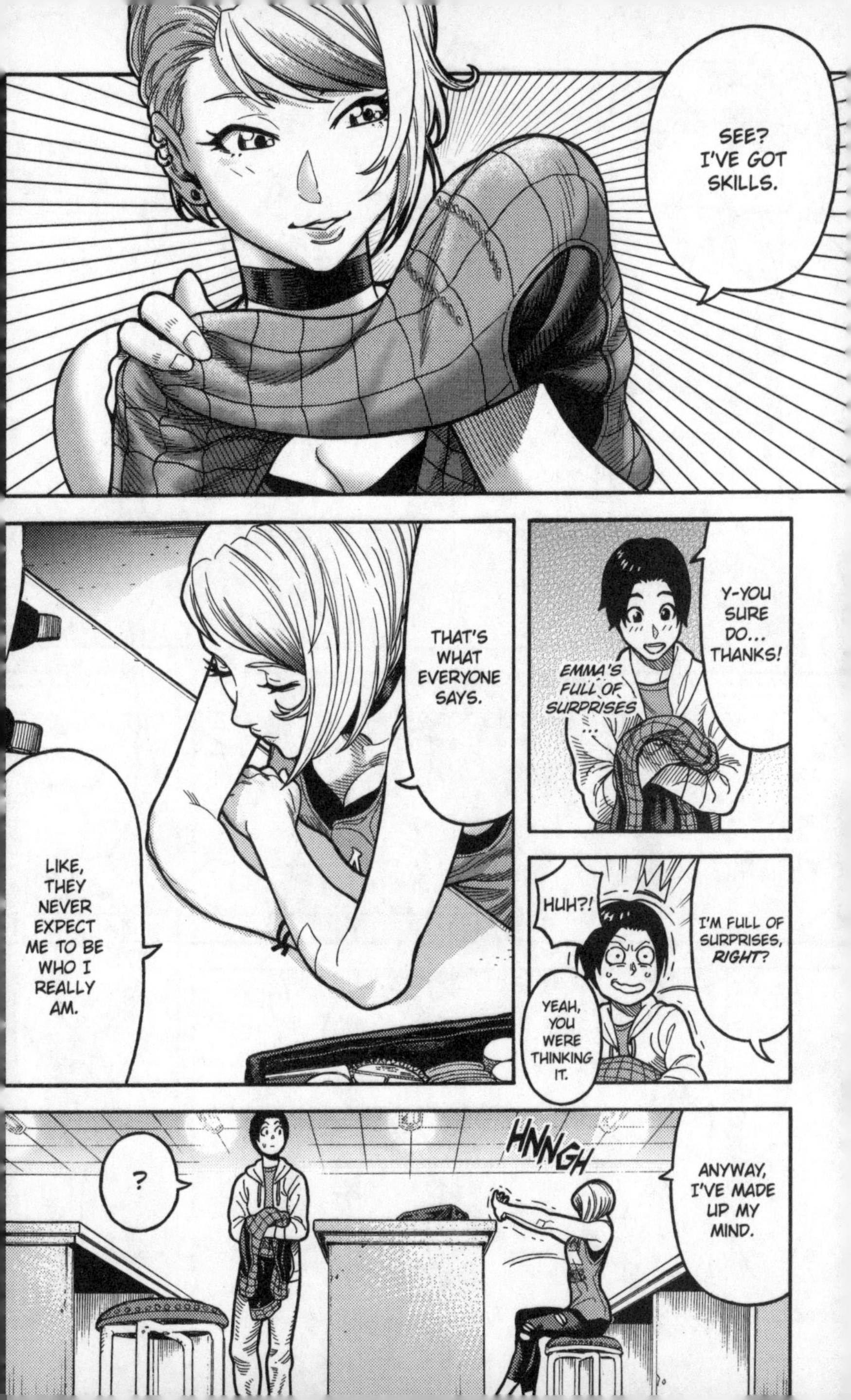
SEE? I'VE GOT SKILLS.
Y-YOU SURE DO... THANKS!
EMMA'S FULL OF SURPRISES...
I'M FULL OF SURPRISES, RIGHT?
HUH?!
YEAH, YOU WERE THINKING IT.
THAT'S WHAT EVERYONE SAYS.
LIKE, THEY NEVER EXPECT ME TO BE WHO I REALLY AM.
ANYWAY, I'VE MADE UP MY MIND.
HNNGH
?

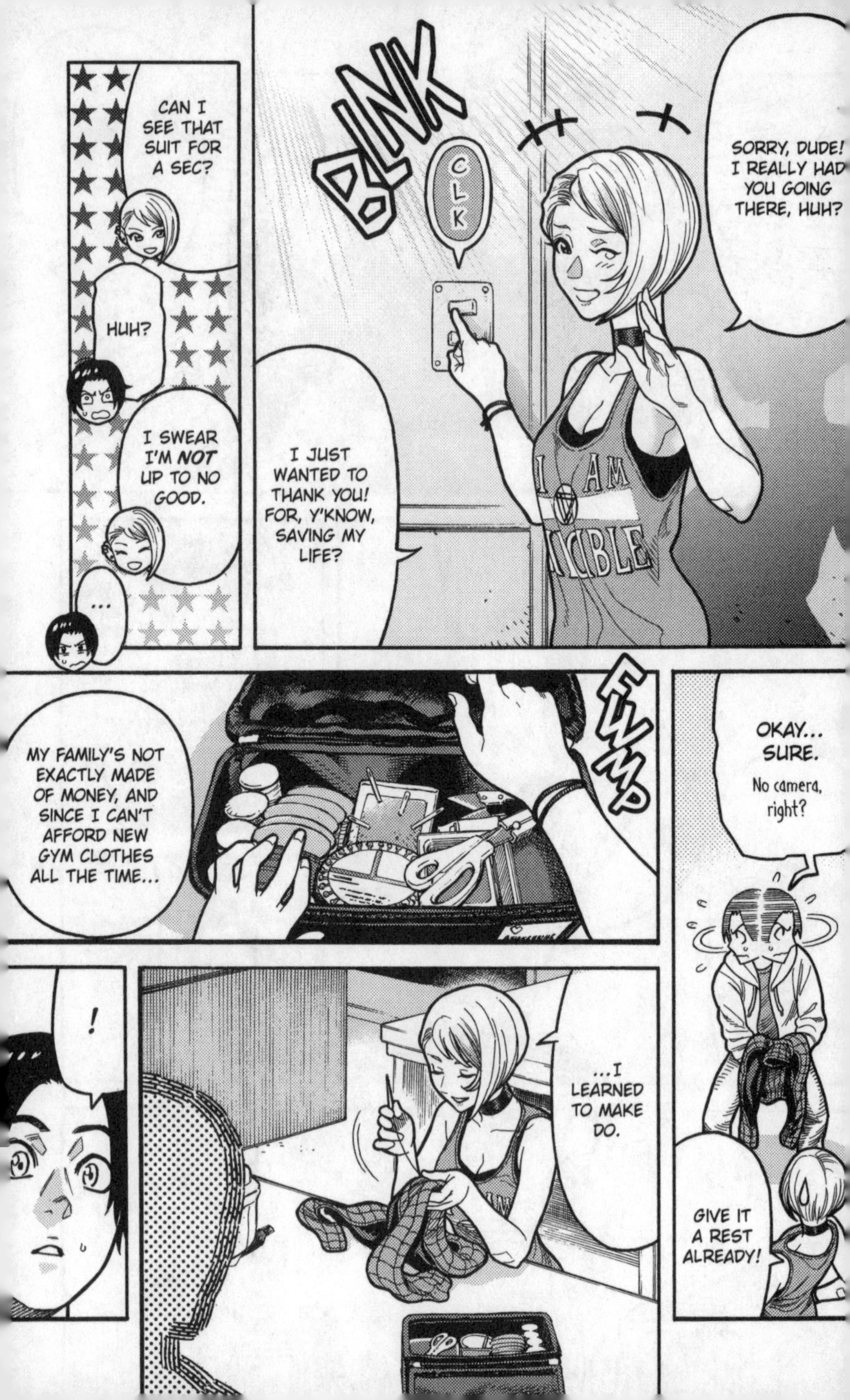
BLINK
CLK
SORRY, DUDE! I REALLY HAD YOU GOING THERE, HUH?
I JUST WANTED TO THANK YOU! FOR, Y'KNOW, SAVING MY LIFE?
CAN I SEE THAT SUIT FOR A SEC?
HUH?
I SWEAR I'M ***NOT*** UP TO NO GOOD.
...
OKAY... SURE.
No camera, right?
GIVE IT A REST ALREADY!
FWMP
MY FAMILY'S NOT EXACTLY MADE OF MONEY, AND SINCE I CAN'T AFFORD NEW GYM CLOTHES ALL THE TIME...
...I LEARNED TO MAKE DO.
!

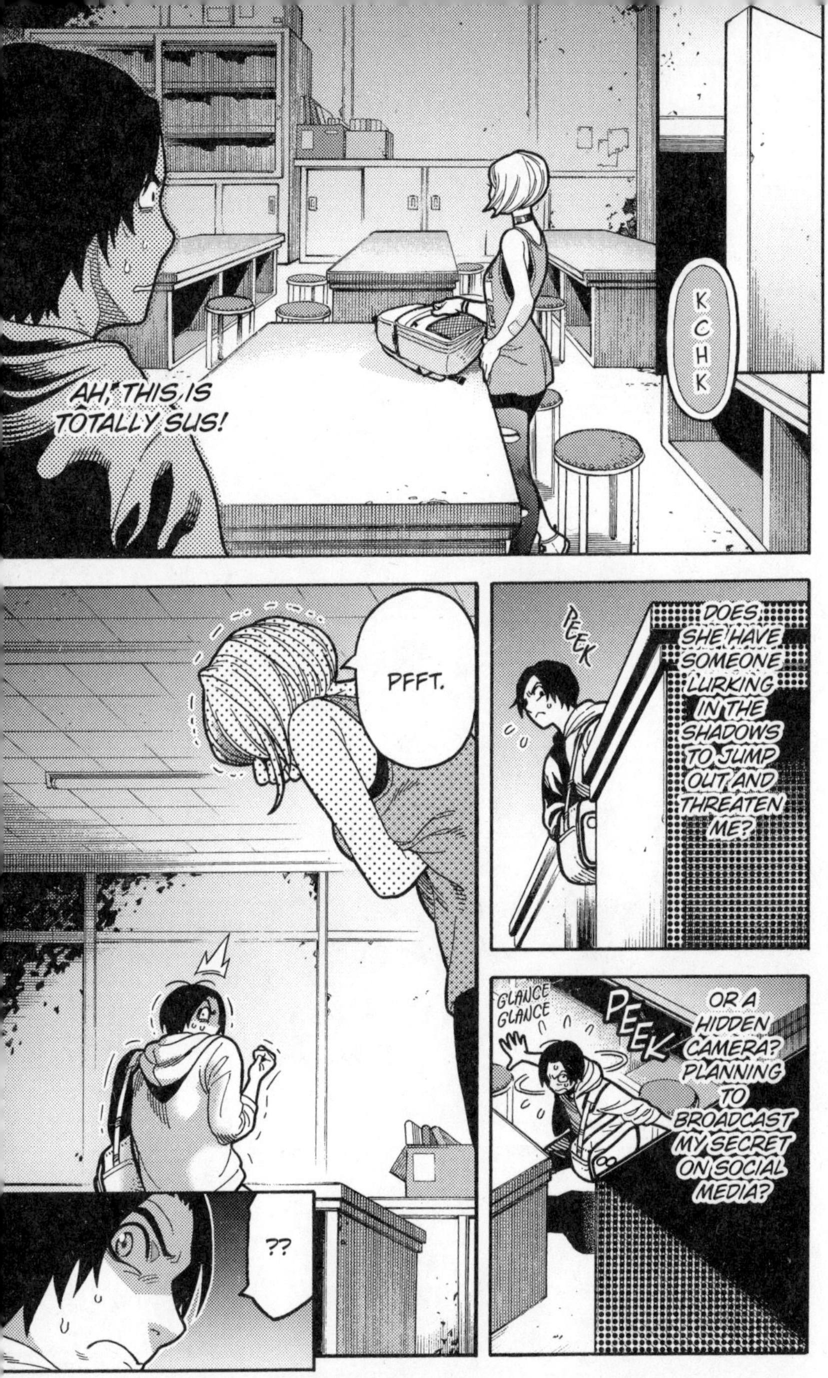
KCHK
AH, THIS IS TOTALLY SUS!
PEEK
DOES SHE HAVE SOMEONE LURKING IN THE SHADOWS TO JUMP OUT AND THREATEN ME?
OR A HIDDEN CAMERA? PLANNING TO BROADCAST MY SECRET ON SOCIAL MEDIA?
PEEK
GLANCE GLANCE
PFFT.
??

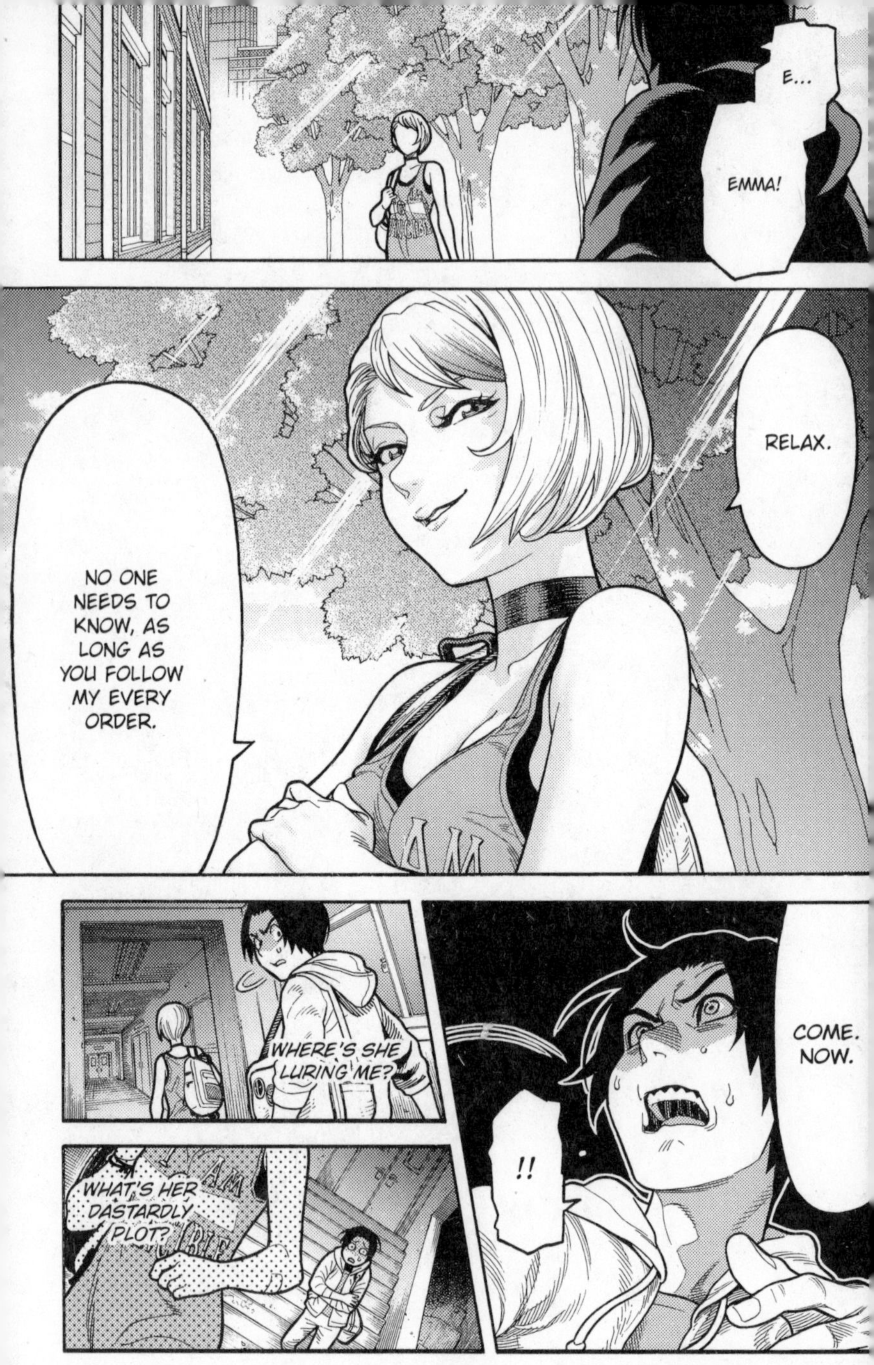
E...
EMMA!
RELAX.
NO ONE NEEDS TO KNOW, AS LONG AS YOU FOLLOW MY EVERY ORDER.
COME. NOW.
!!
WHERE'S SHE LURING ME?
WHAT'S HER DASTARDLY PLOT?

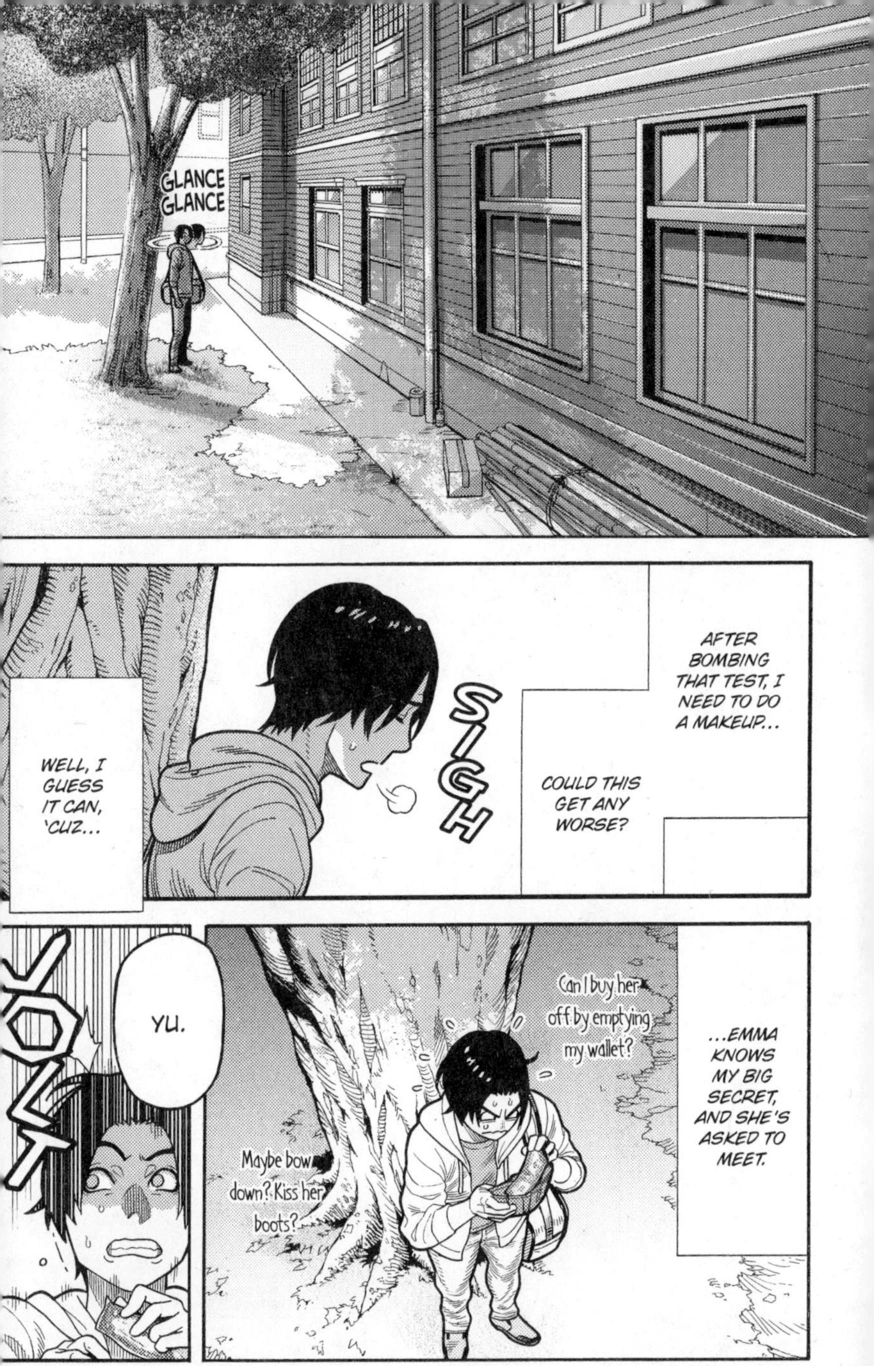
GLANCE GLANCE
AFTER BOMBING THAT TEST, I NEED TO DO A MAKEUP...
COULD THIS GET ANY WORSE?
SIGH
WELL, I GUESS IT CAN, 'CUZ...
...EMMA KNOWS MY BIG SECRET, AND SHE'S ASKED TO MEET.
Can I buy her off by emptying my wallet?
Maybe bow down? Kiss her boots?
YU.
JOLT

#6 CALLED OUT

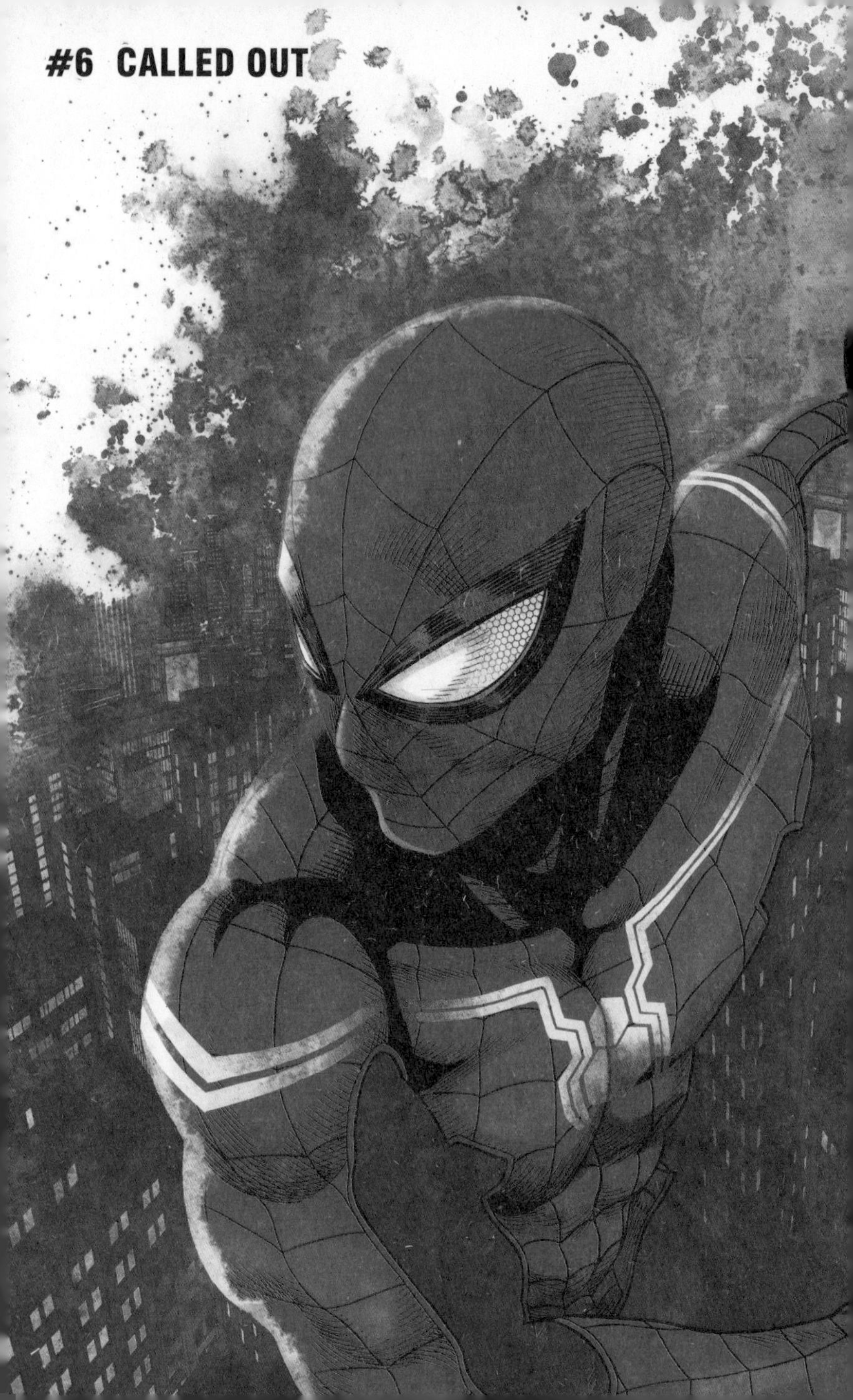

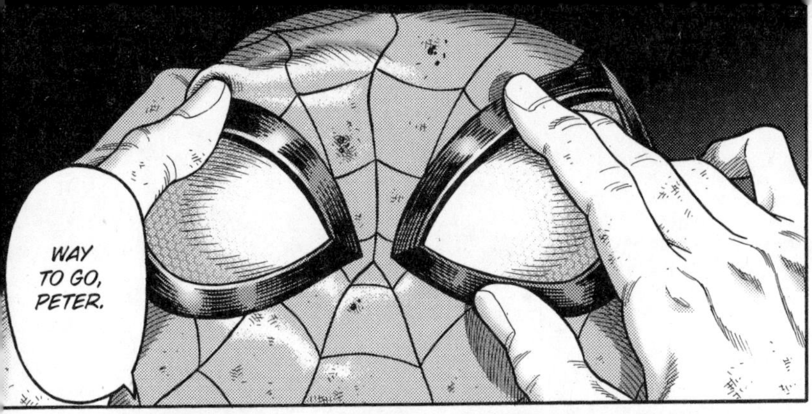
WAY TO GO, PETER.

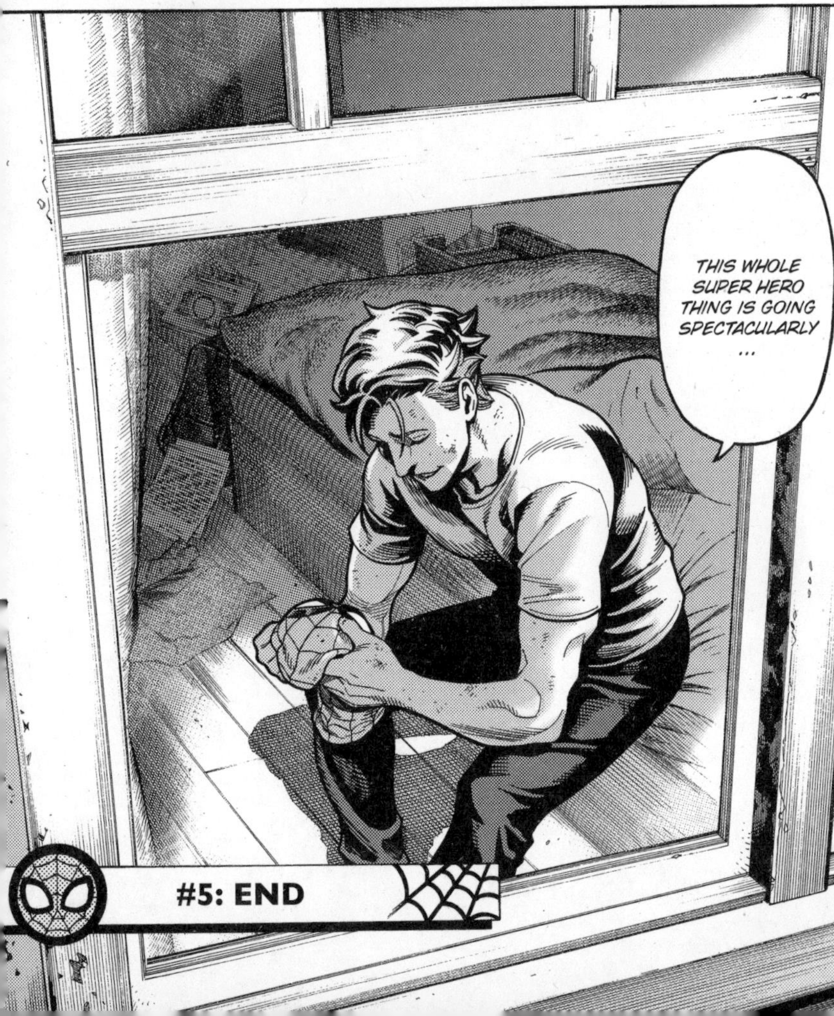
THIS WHOLE SUPER HERO THING IS GOING SPECTACULARLY ...

#5: END

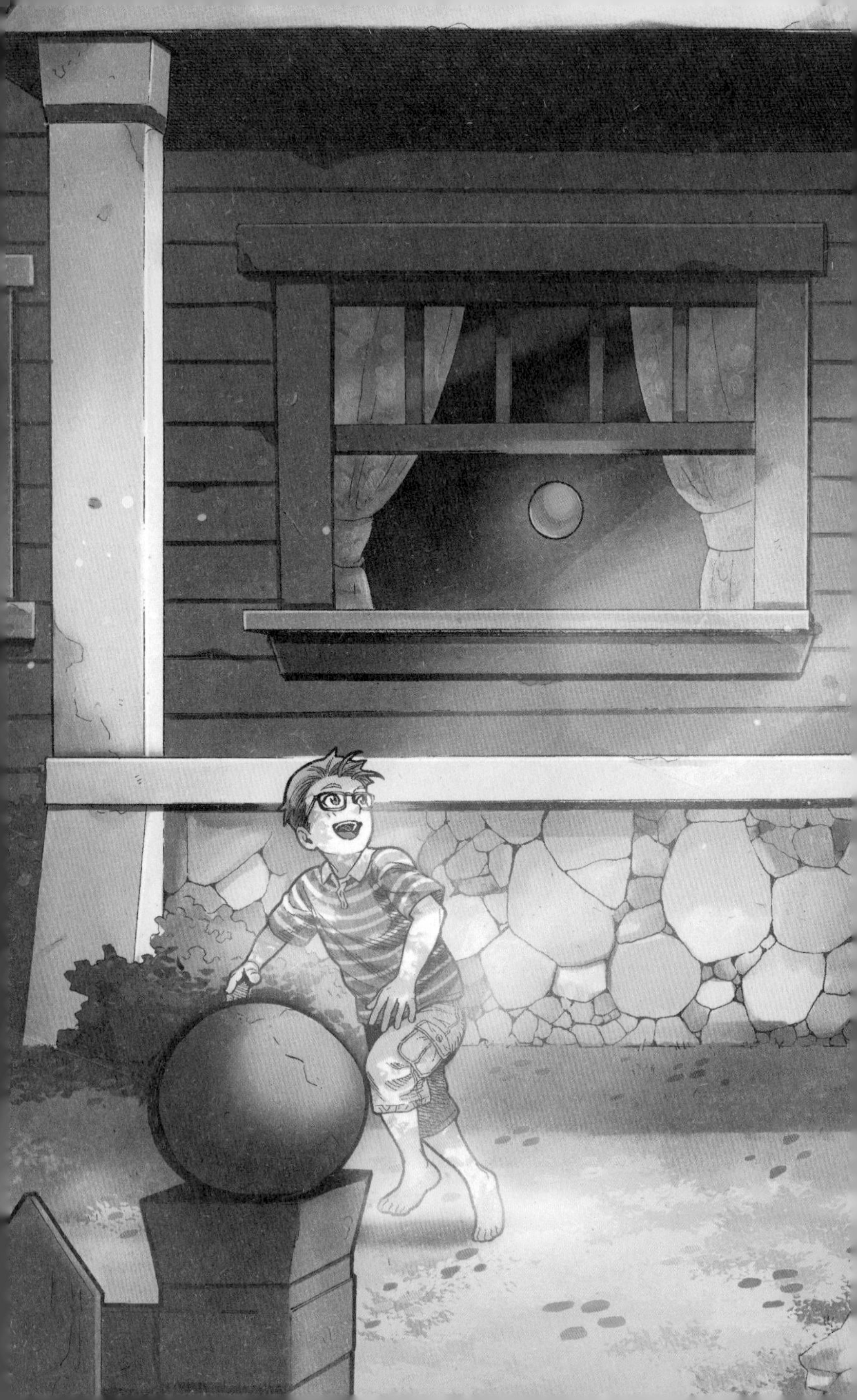

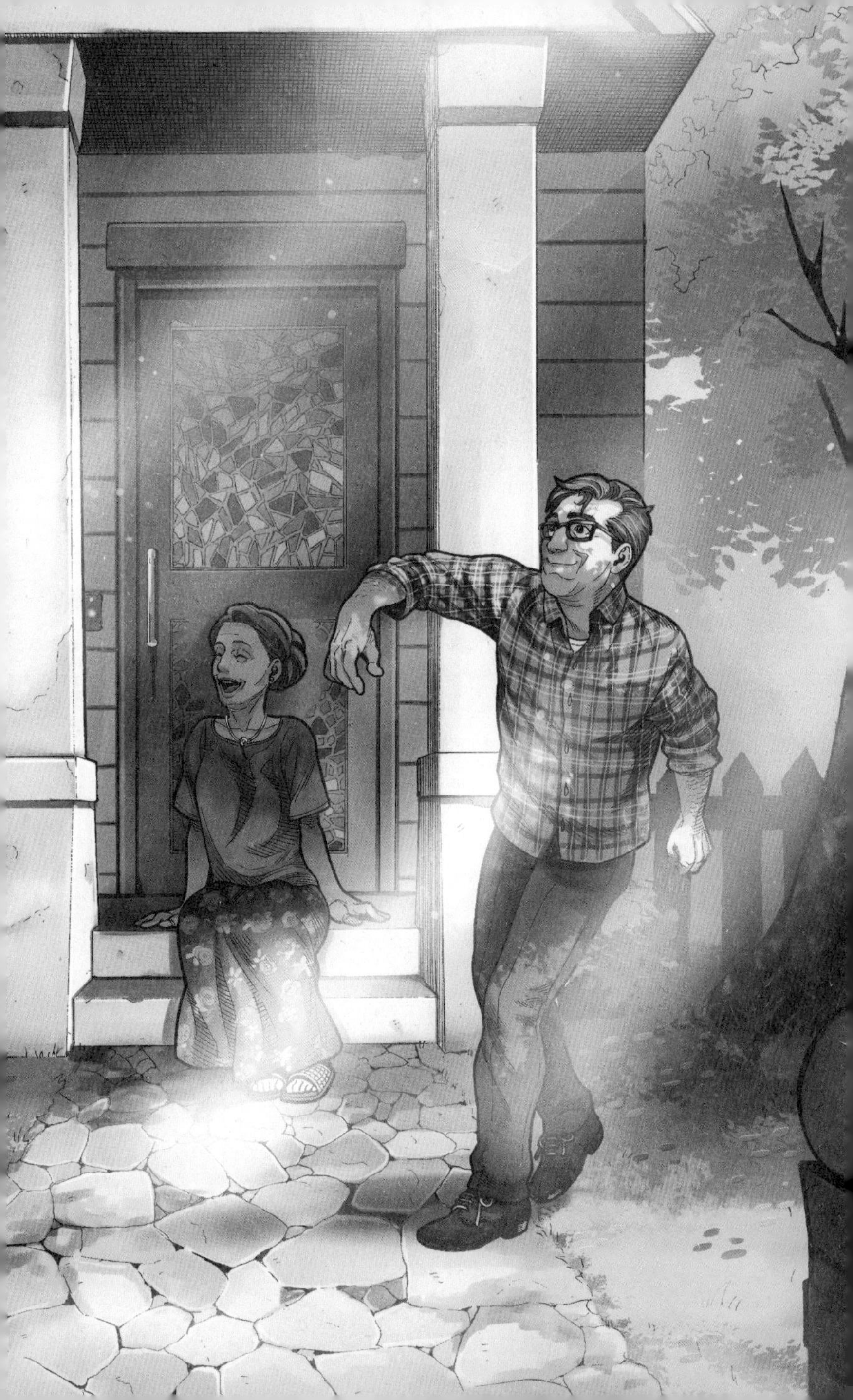

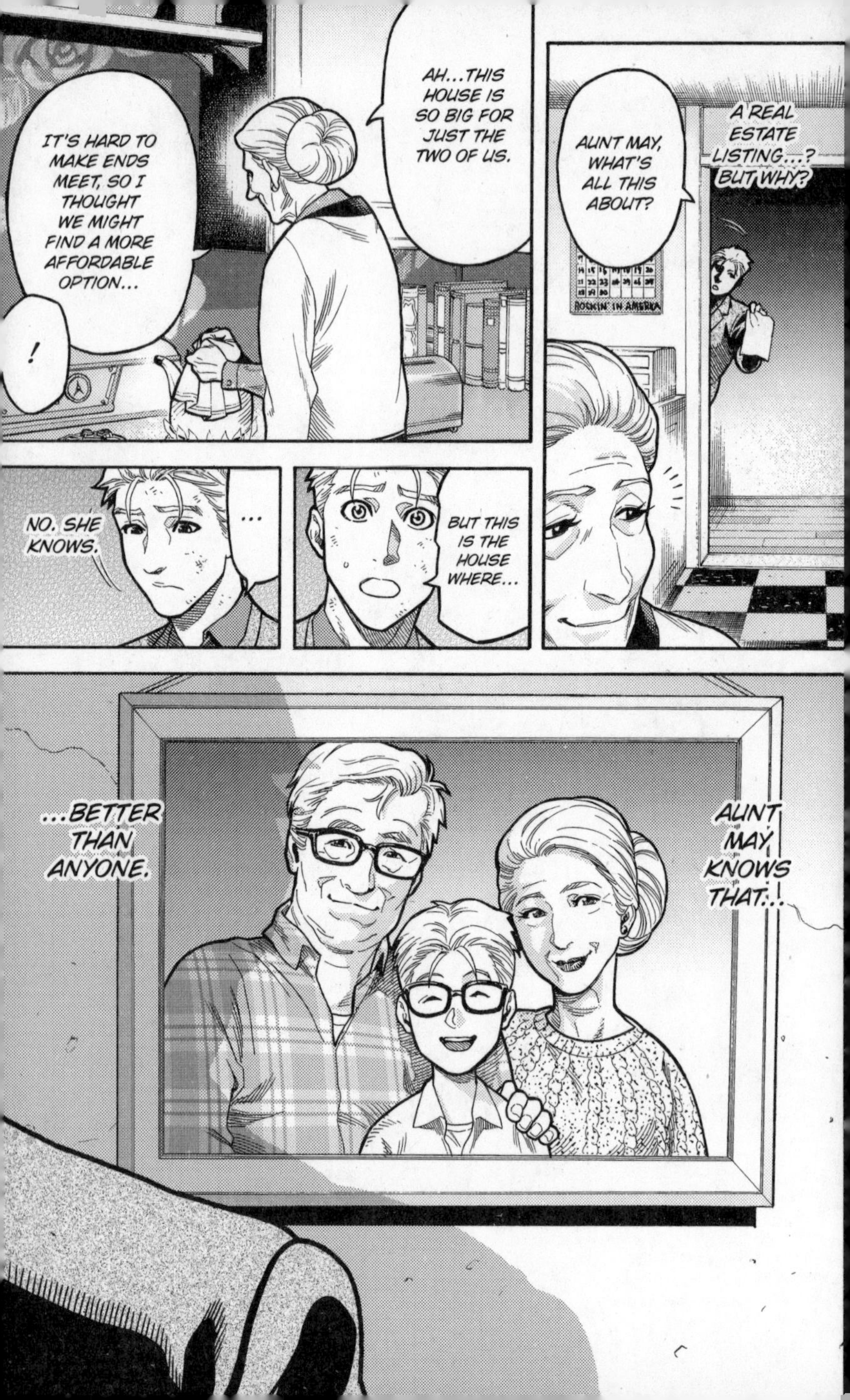
A REAL ESTATE LISTING...? BUT WHY?
AUNT MAY, WHAT'S ALL THIS ABOUT?
ROCKIN' IN AMERICA
AH...THIS HOUSE IS SO BIG FOR JUST THE TWO OF US.
IT'S HARD TO MAKE ENDS MEET, SO I THOUGHT WE MIGHT FIND A MORE AFFORDABLE OPTION...
!
BUT THIS IS THE HOUSE WHERE...
...
NO. SHE KNOWS.
AUNT MAY KNOWS THAT...
...BETTER THAN ANYONE.

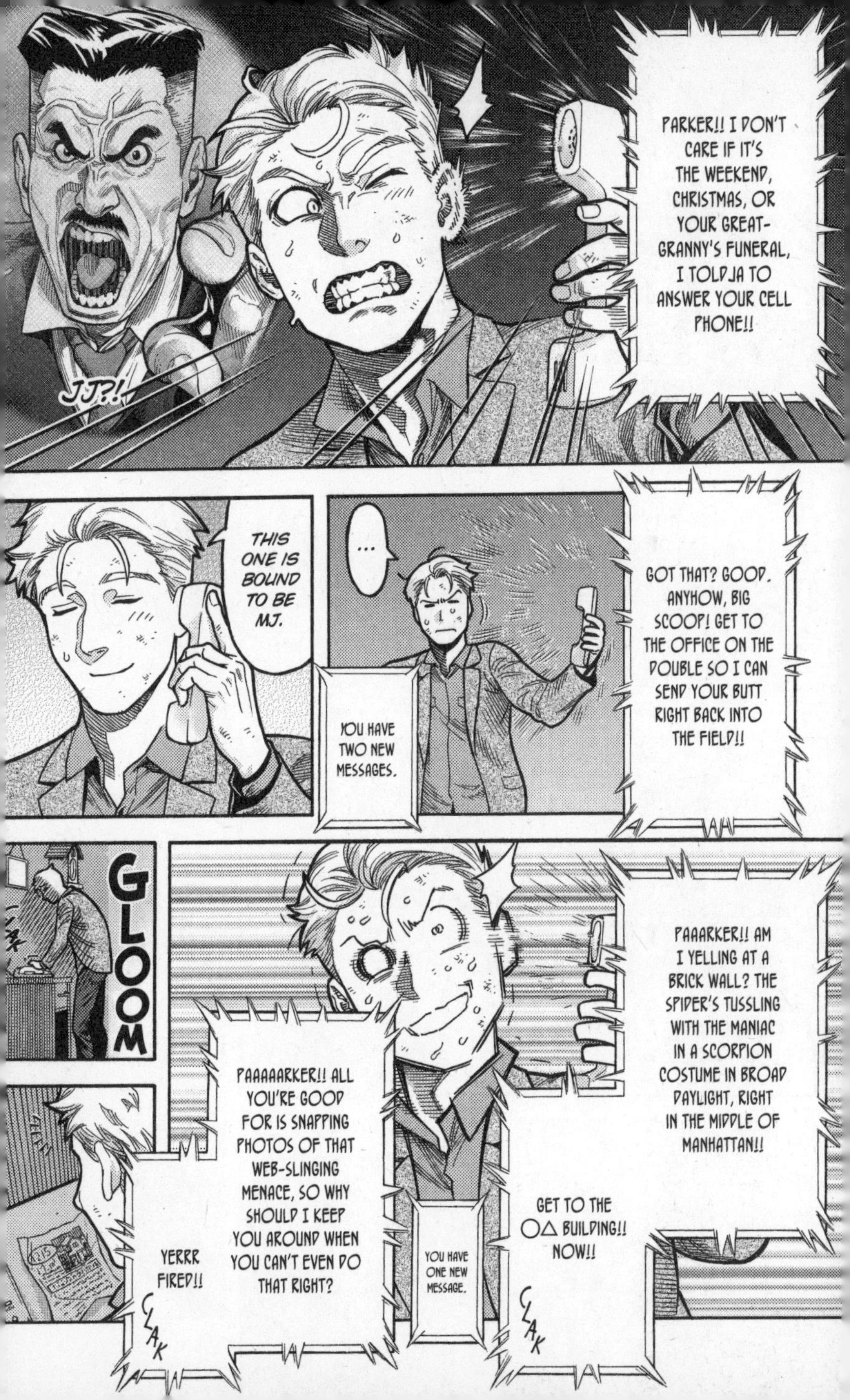
PARKER!! I DON'T CARE IF IT'S THE WEEKEND, CHRISTMAS, OR YOUR GREAT-GRANNY'S FUNERAL, I TOLDJA TO ANSWER YOUR CELL PHONE!!
JJ?!
GOT THAT? GOOD. ANYHOW, BIG SCOOP! GET TO THE OFFICE ON THE DOUBLE SO I CAN SEND YOUR BUTT RIGHT BACK INTO THE FIELD!!
...
YOU HAVE TWO NEW MESSAGES.
THIS ONE IS BOUND TO BE MJ.
PAAARKER!! AM I YELLING AT A BRICK WALL? THE SPIDER'S TUSSLING WITH THE MANIAC IN A SCORPION COSTUME IN BROAD DAYLIGHT, RIGHT IN THE MIDDLE OF MANHATTAN!!
GET TO THE ○△ BUILDING!! NOW!!
CLAK
YOU HAVE ONE NEW MESSAGE.
PAAAAARKER!! ALL YOU'RE GOOD FOR IS SNAPPING PHOTOS OF THAT WEB-SLINGING MENACE, SO WHY SHOULD I KEEP YOU AROUND WHEN YOU CAN'T EVEN DO THAT RIGHT?
YERRR FIRED!!
CLAK
GLOOM

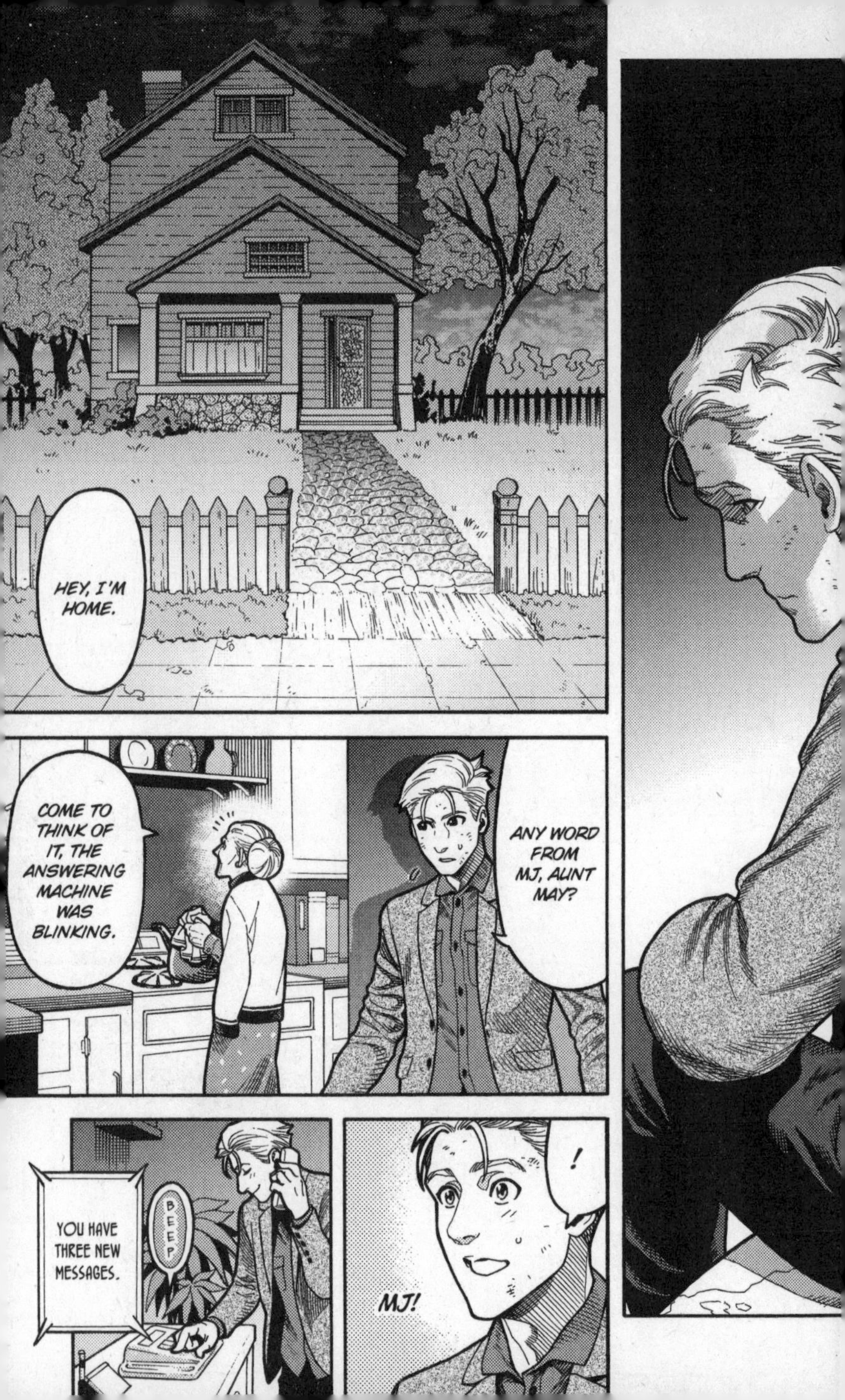
HEY, I'M HOME.
ANY WORD FROM MJ, AUNT MAY?
COME TO THINK OF IT, THE ANSWERING MACHINE WAS BLINKING.
!
MJ!
BEEP
YOU HAVE THREE NEW MESSAGES.

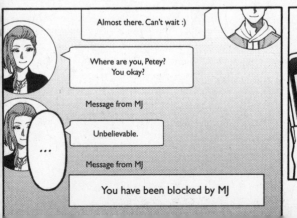

Almost there. Can't wait :)

Where are you, Petey?
You okay?

Message from MJ

Unbelievable.

...

Message from MJ

You have been blocked by MJ

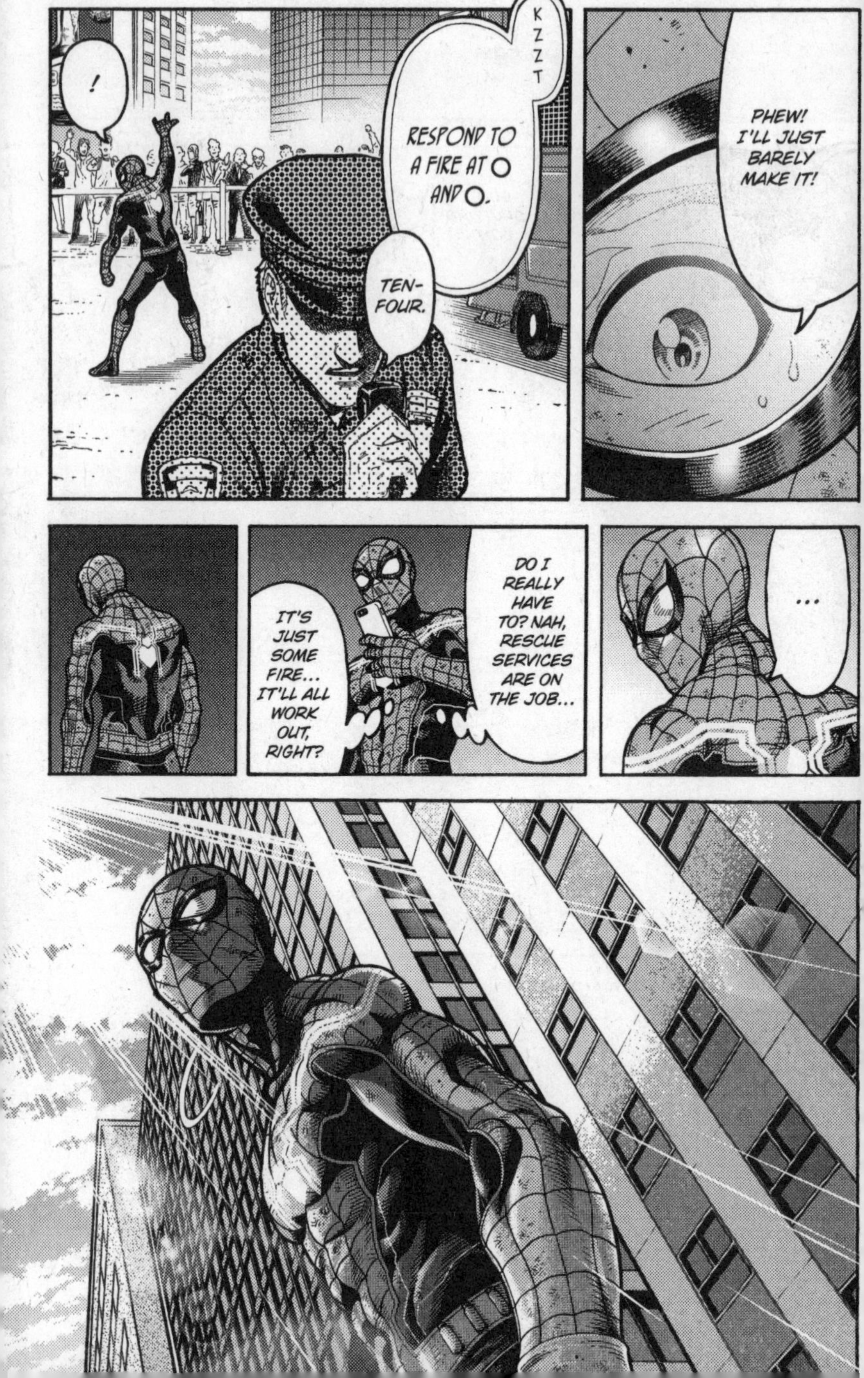
PHEW! I'LL JUST BARELY MAKE IT!
KZZT
RESPOND TO A FIRE AT ○ AND ○.
TEN-FOUR.
!
...
DO I REALLY HAVE TO? NAH, RESCUE SERVICES ARE ON THE JOB...
IT'S JUST SOME FIRE... IT'LL ALL WORK OUT, RIGHT?

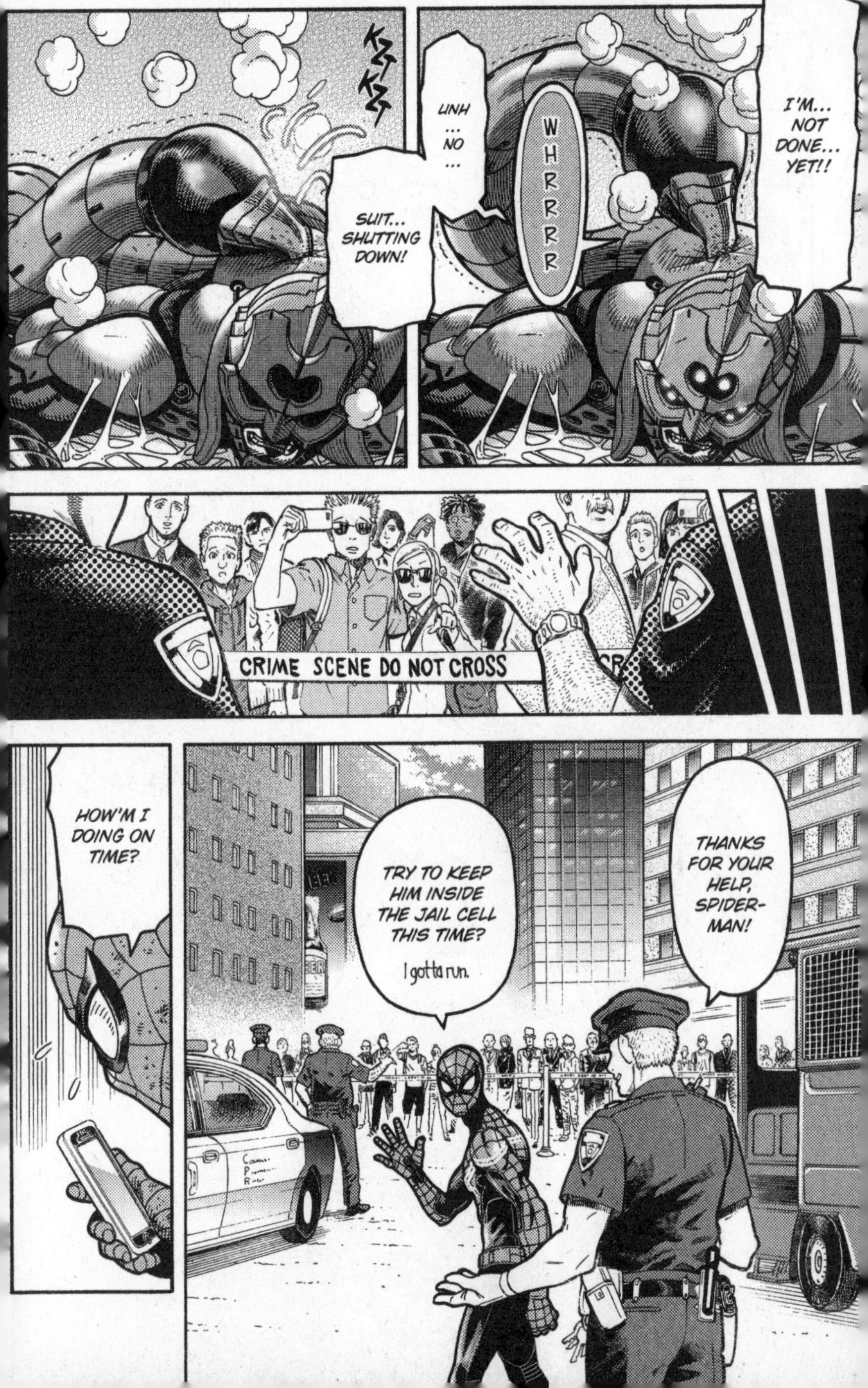
I'M... NOT DONE... YET!!
WHRRRR
UNH ... NO ...
SUIT... SHUTTING DOWN!
KZT KZT
CRIME SCENE DO NOT CROSS
THANKS FOR YOUR HELP, SPIDER-MAN!
TRY TO KEEP HIM INSIDE THE JAIL CELL THIS TIME?
I gotta run.
HOW'M I DOING ON TIME?

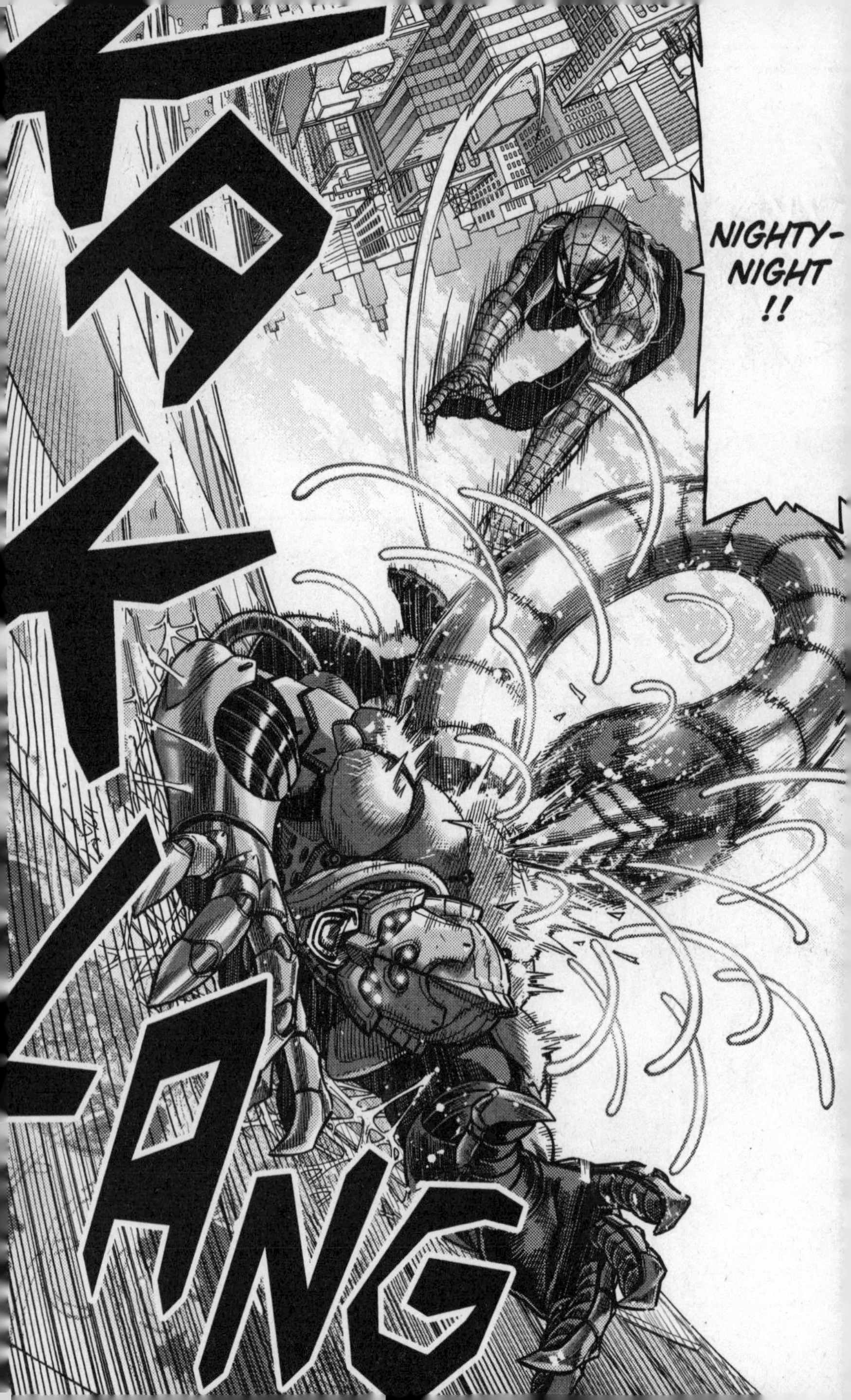
NIGHTY-NIGHT!!

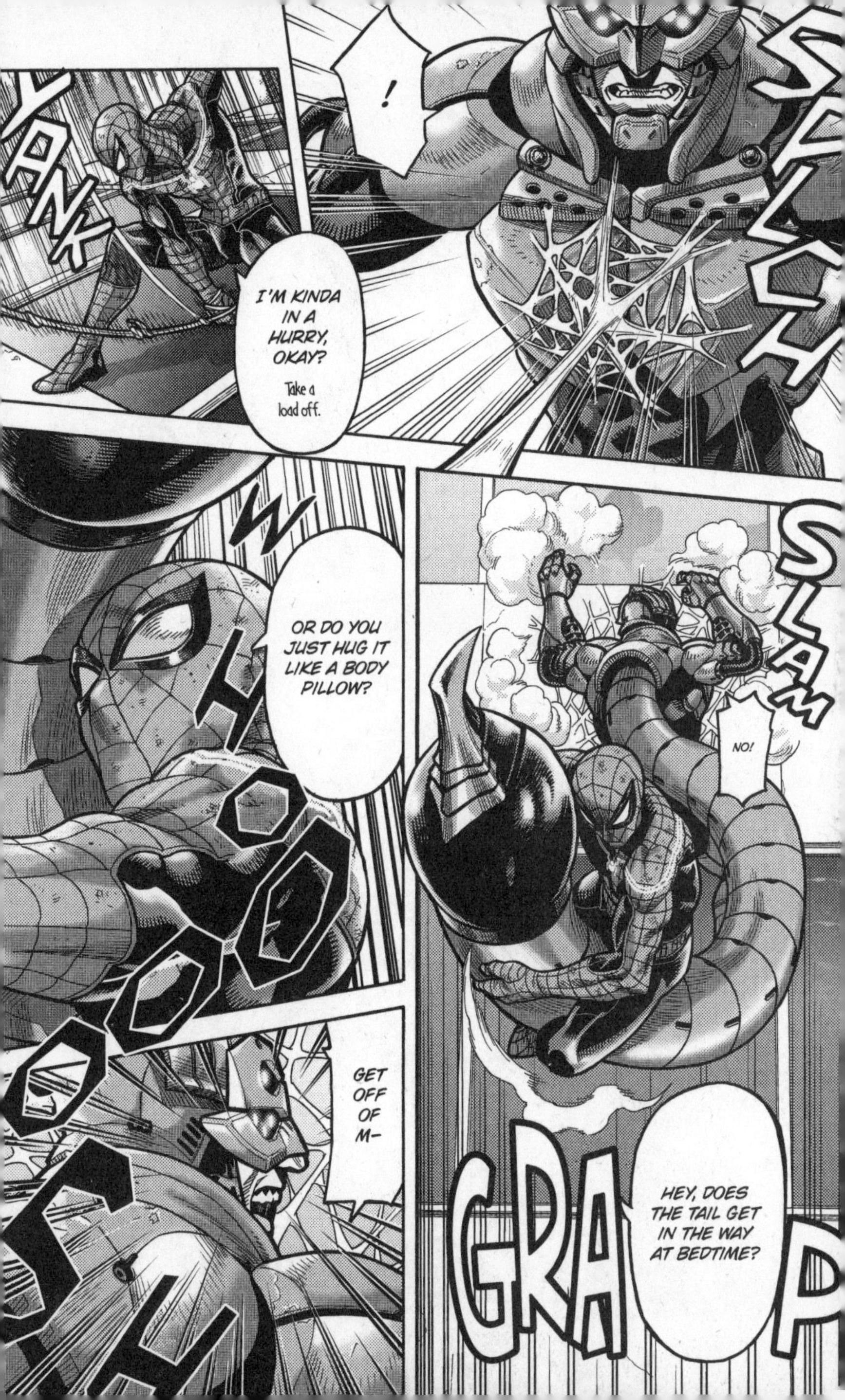
!
I'M KINDA IN A HURRY, OKAY?
Take a load off.
YANK
SLAM
NO!
GRAP
HEY, DOES THE TAIL GET IN THE WAY AT BEDTIME?
OR DO YOU JUST HUG IT LIKE A BODY PILLOW?
GET OFF OF M-

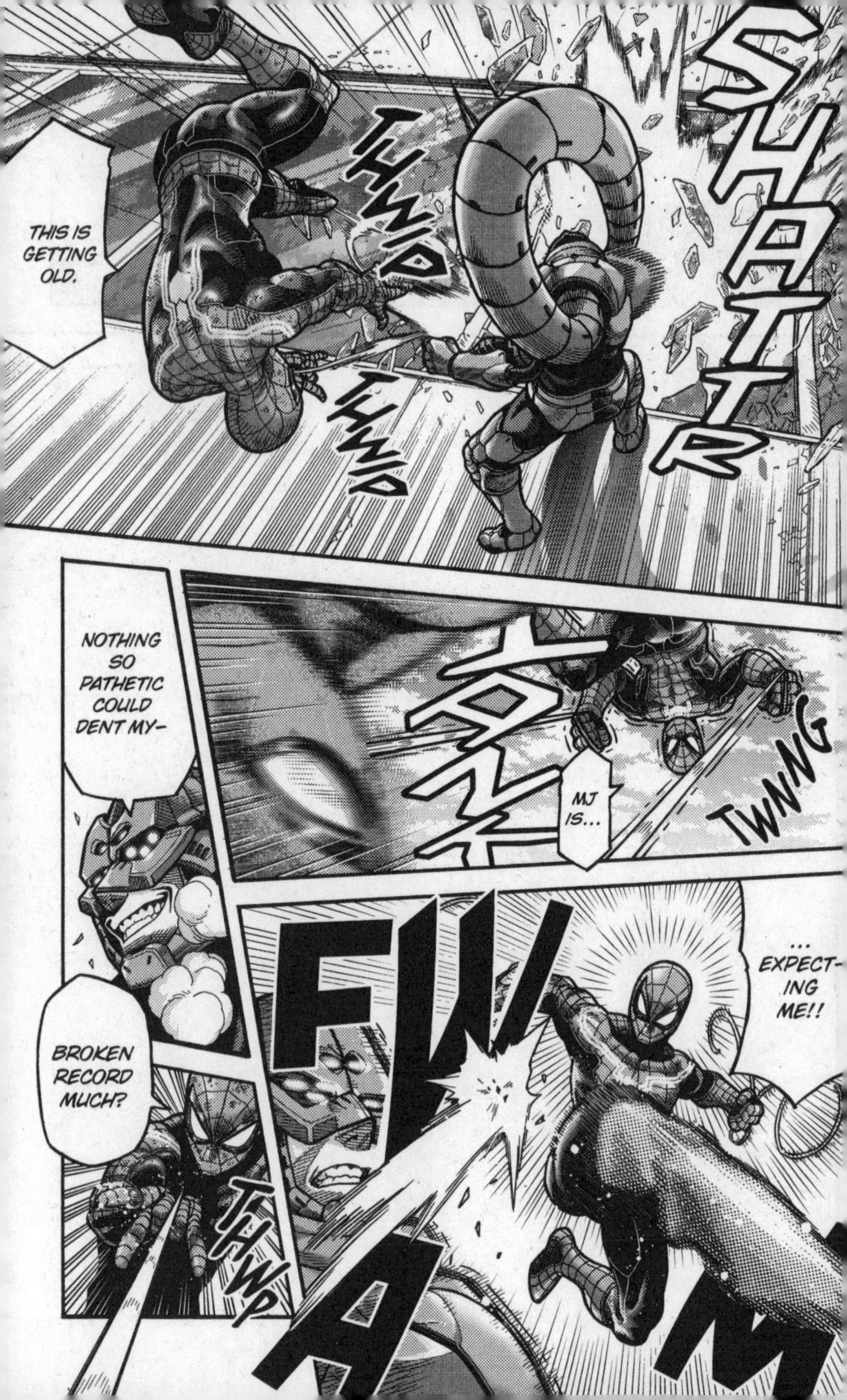
SHATTR
THWIP
THWIP
THIS IS GETTING OLD.
TWNNG
MJ IS...
YANK
NOTHING SO PATHETIC COULD DENT MY-
... EXPECTING ME!!
FWAM
BROKEN RECORD MUCH?
THWP

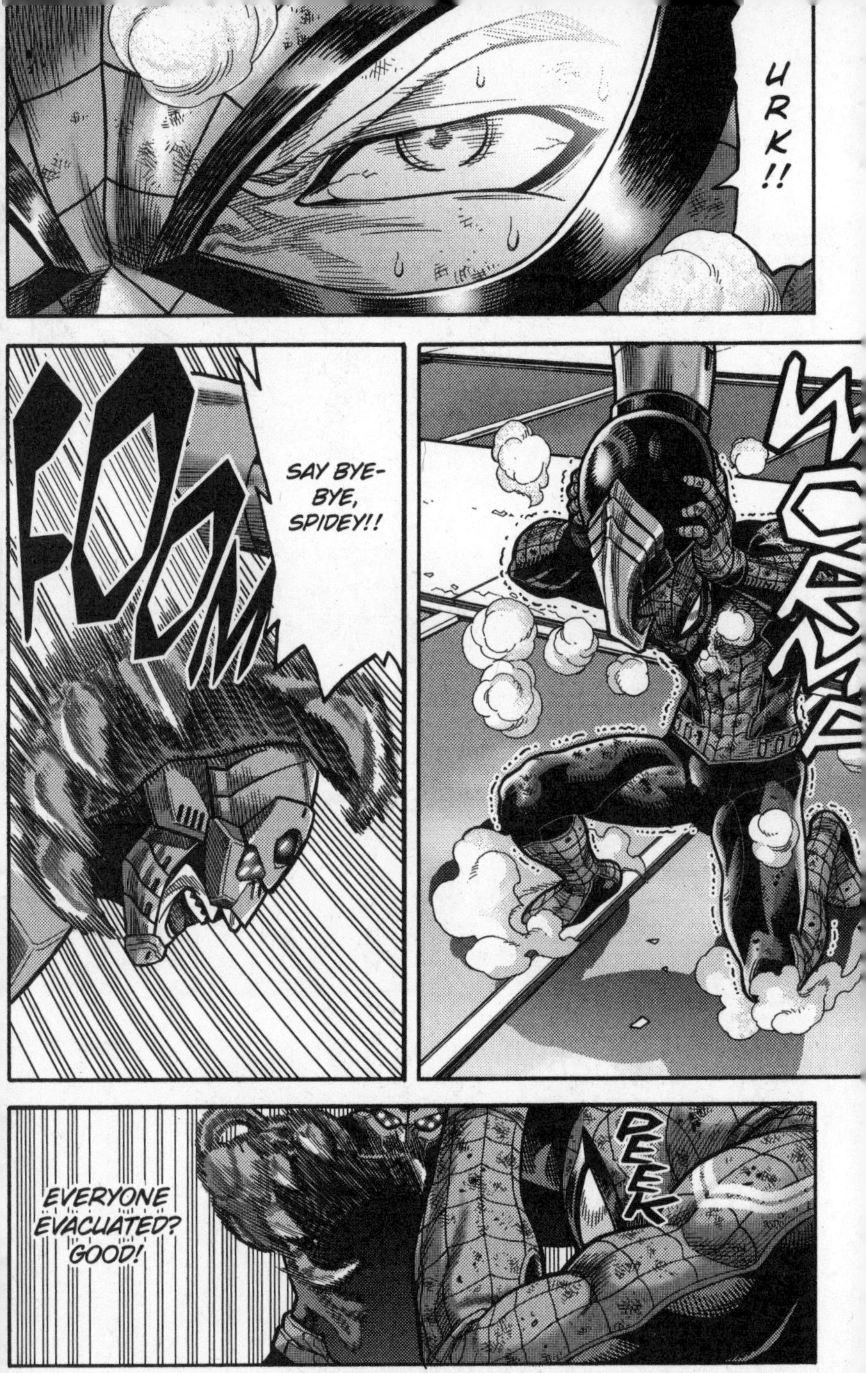
URK!!
SAY BYE-BYE, SPIDEY!!
FOOM
PEEK
EVERYONE EVACUATED? GOOD!

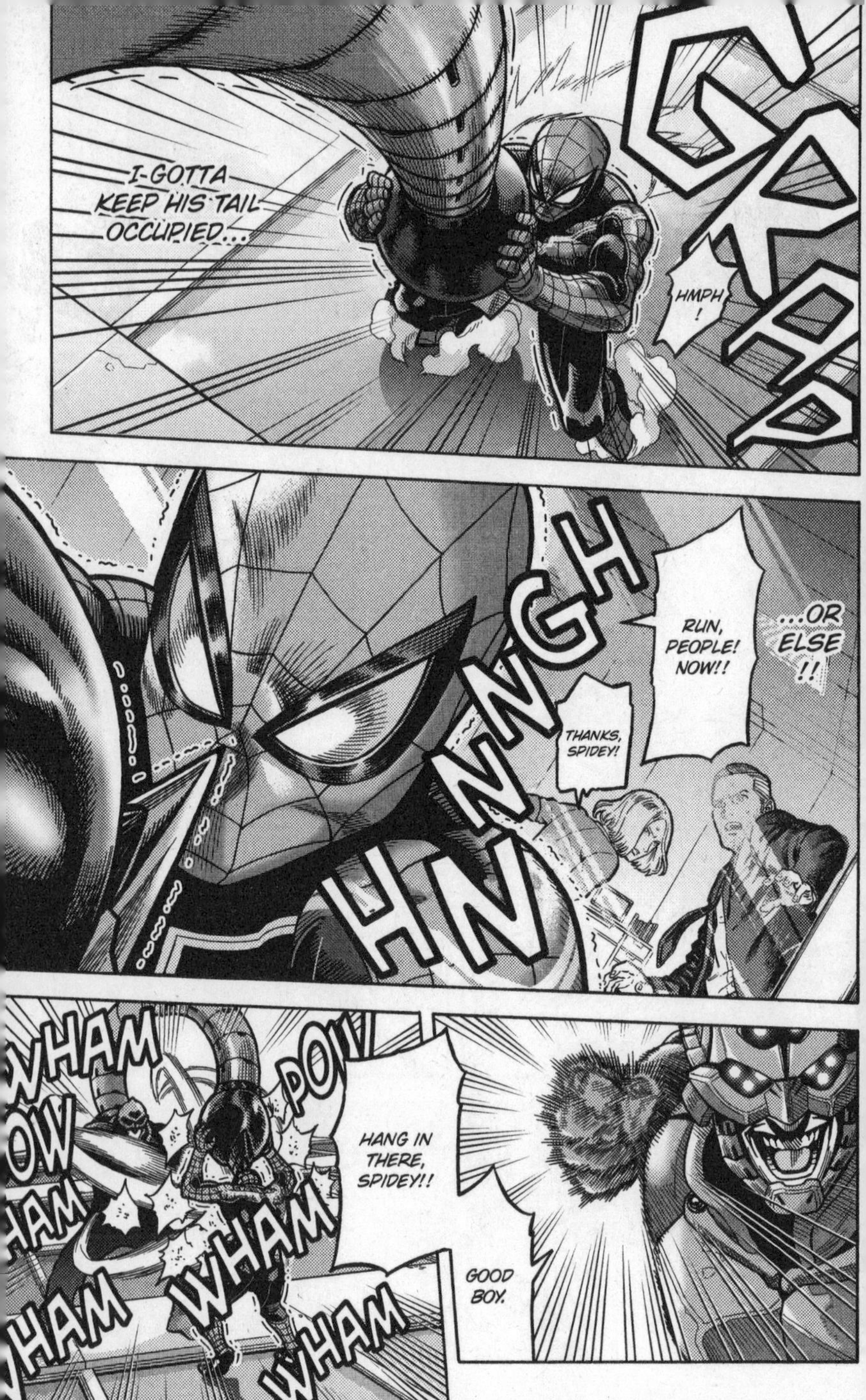
HMPH!
I-GOTTA KEEP HIS TAIL OCCUPIED...
...OR ELSE!!
RUN, PEOPLE! NOW!!
THANKS, SPIDEY!
HNNNGH
HANG IN THERE, SPIDEY!!
GOOD BOY.
POW
WHAM
POW
WHAM
WHAM
WHAM
WHAM
WHAM

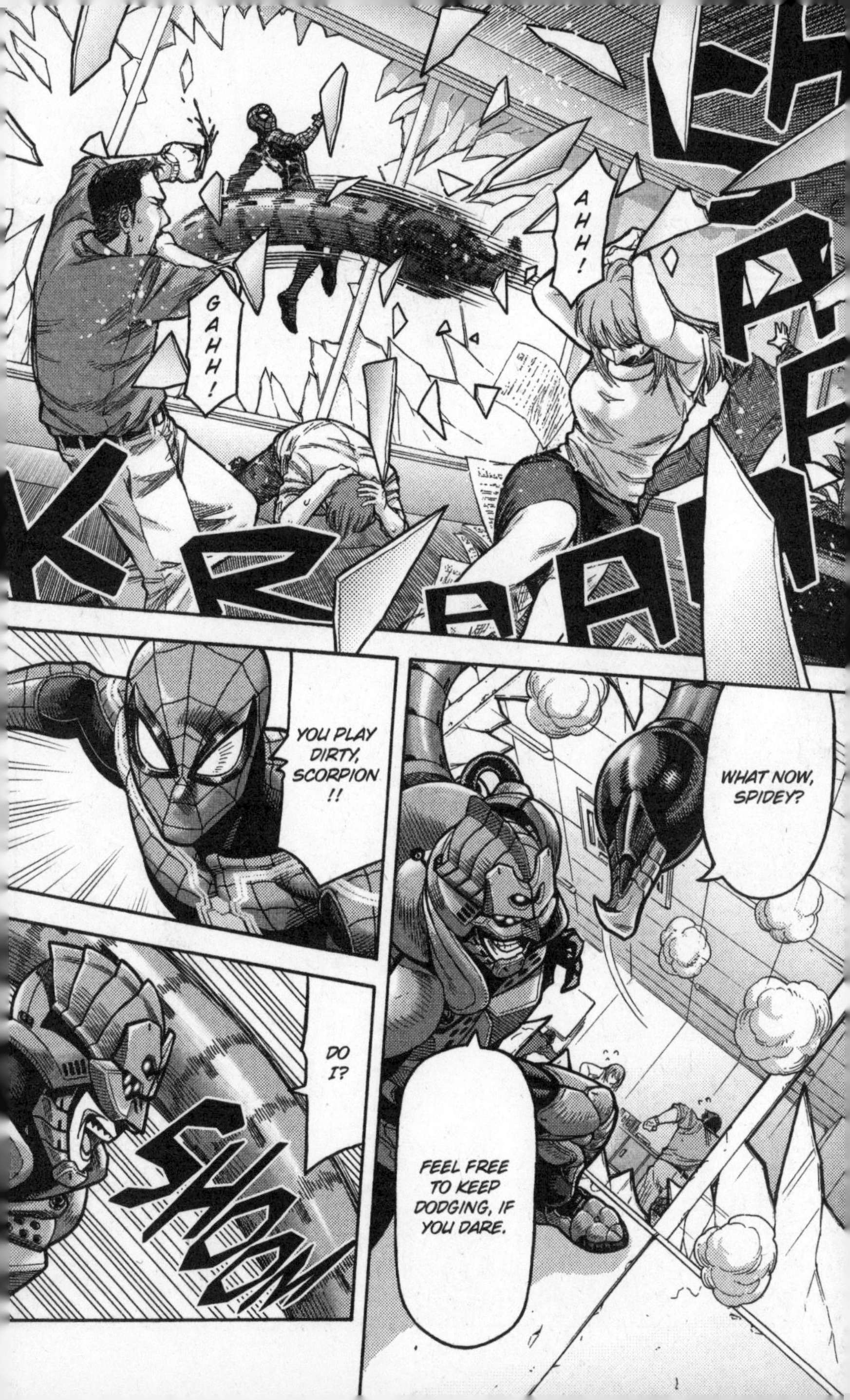
AHH!
GAHH!
WHAT NOW, SPIDEY?
FEEL FREE TO KEEP DODGING, IF YOU DARE.
YOU PLAY DIRTY, SCORPION!!
DO I?

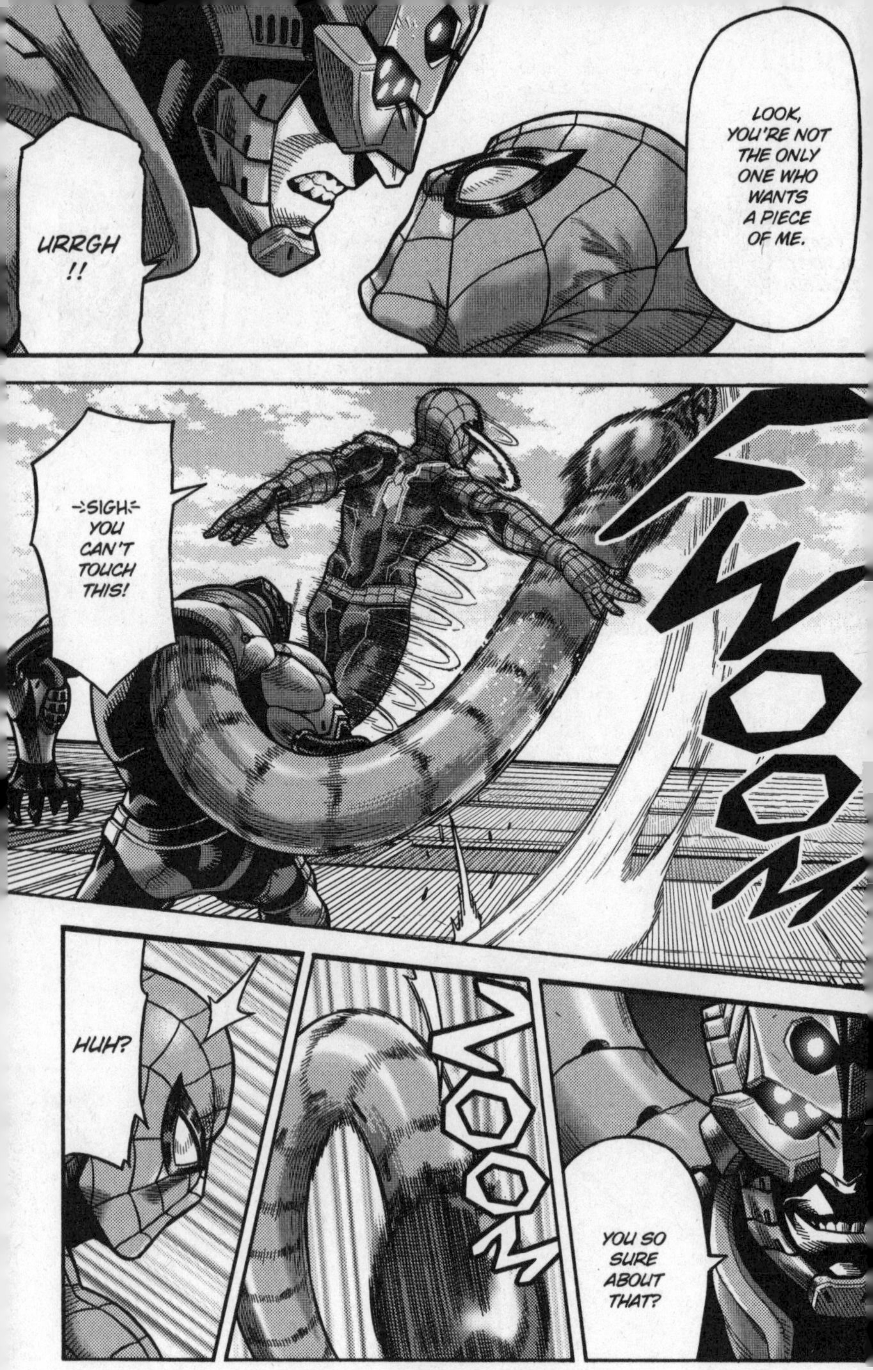
LOOK, YOU'RE NOT THE ONLY ONE WHO WANTS A PIECE OF ME.
URRGH !!
KWOOM
-SIGH- YOU CAN'T TOUCH THIS!
YOU SO SURE ABOUT THAT?
VOOOM
HUH?

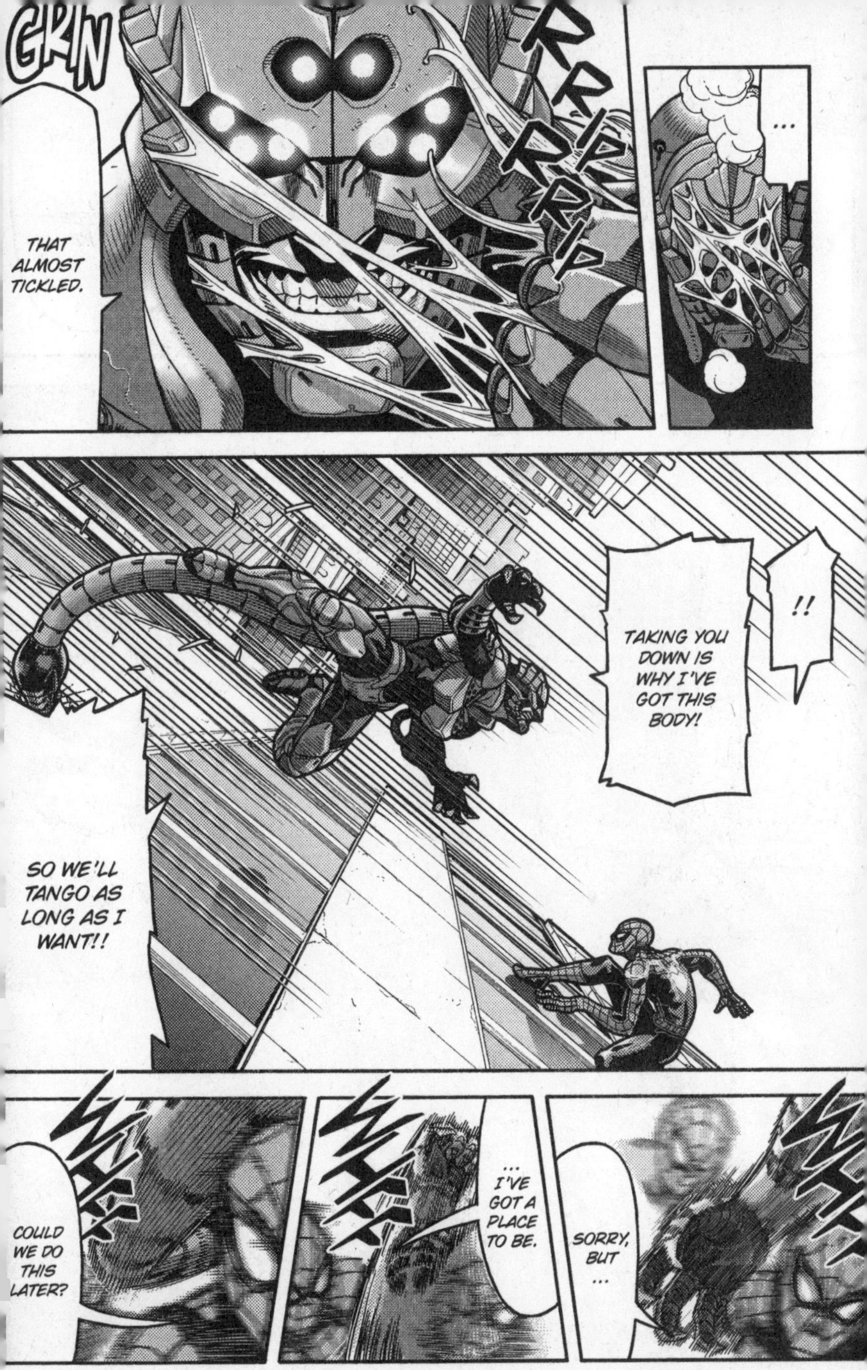
...
RRIP RRIP RRIP
GRIN
THAT ALMOST TICKLED.
!!
TAKING YOU DOWN IS WHY I'VE GOT THIS BODY!
SO WE'LL TANGO AS LONG AS I WANT!!
SORRY, BUT ...
... I'VE GOT A PLACE TO BE.
COULD WE DO THIS LATER?

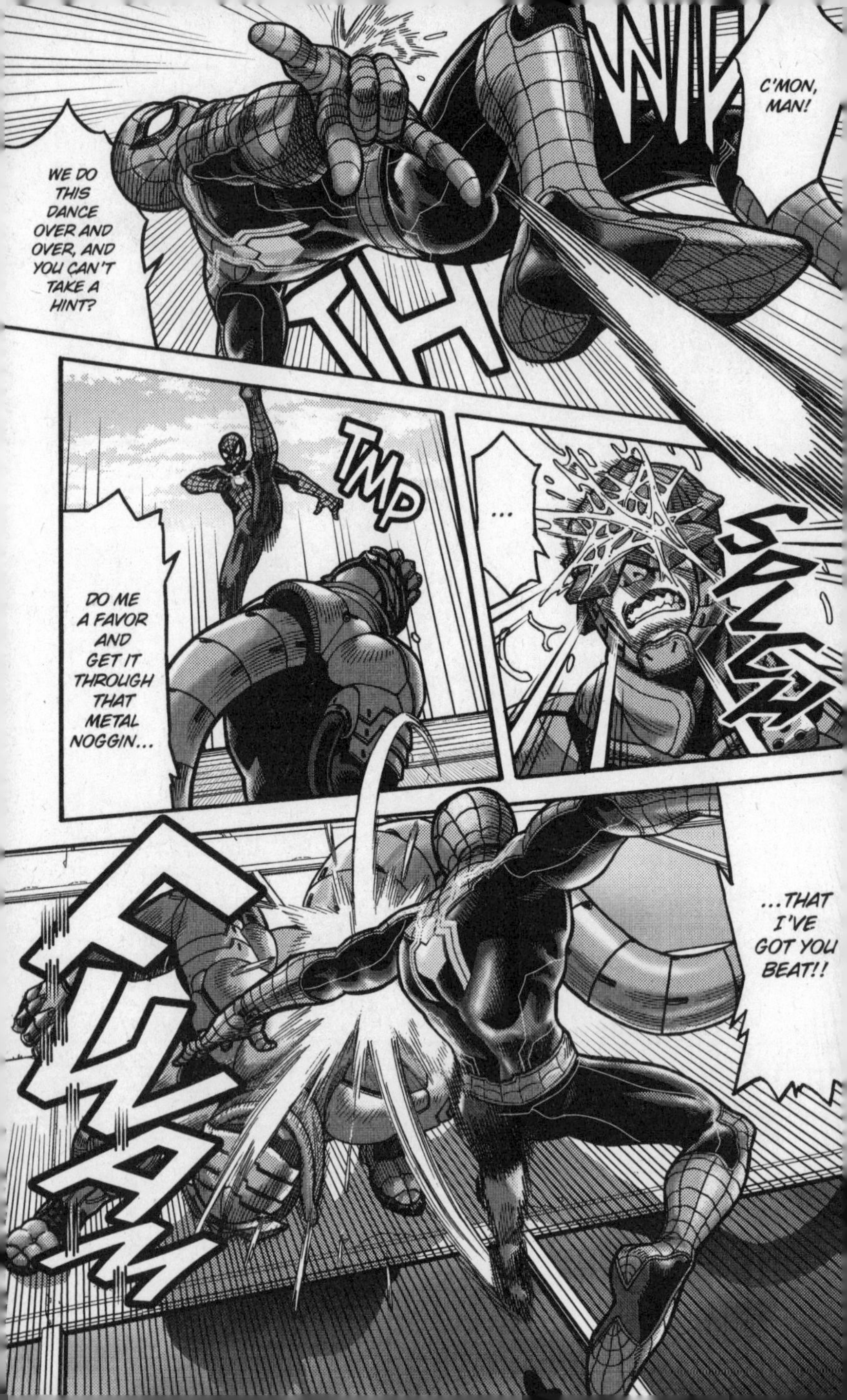
C'MON, MAN!
THWIP
WE DO THIS DANCE OVER AND OVER, AND YOU CAN'T TAKE A HINT?
...
TMP
DO ME A FAVOR AND GET IT THROUGH THAT METAL NOGGIN...
...THAT I'VE GOT YOU BEAT!!

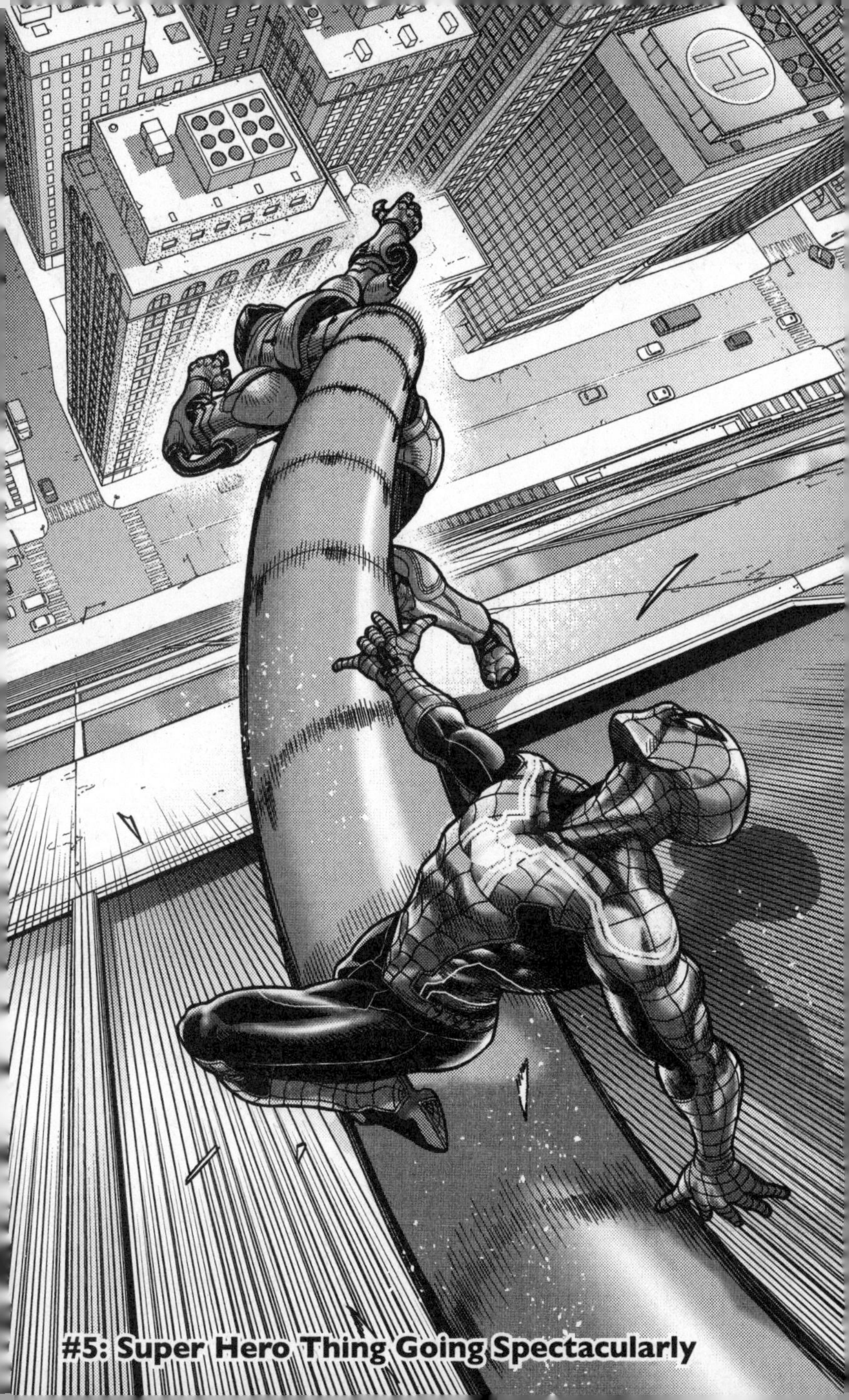

#5: Super Hero Thing Going Spectacularly

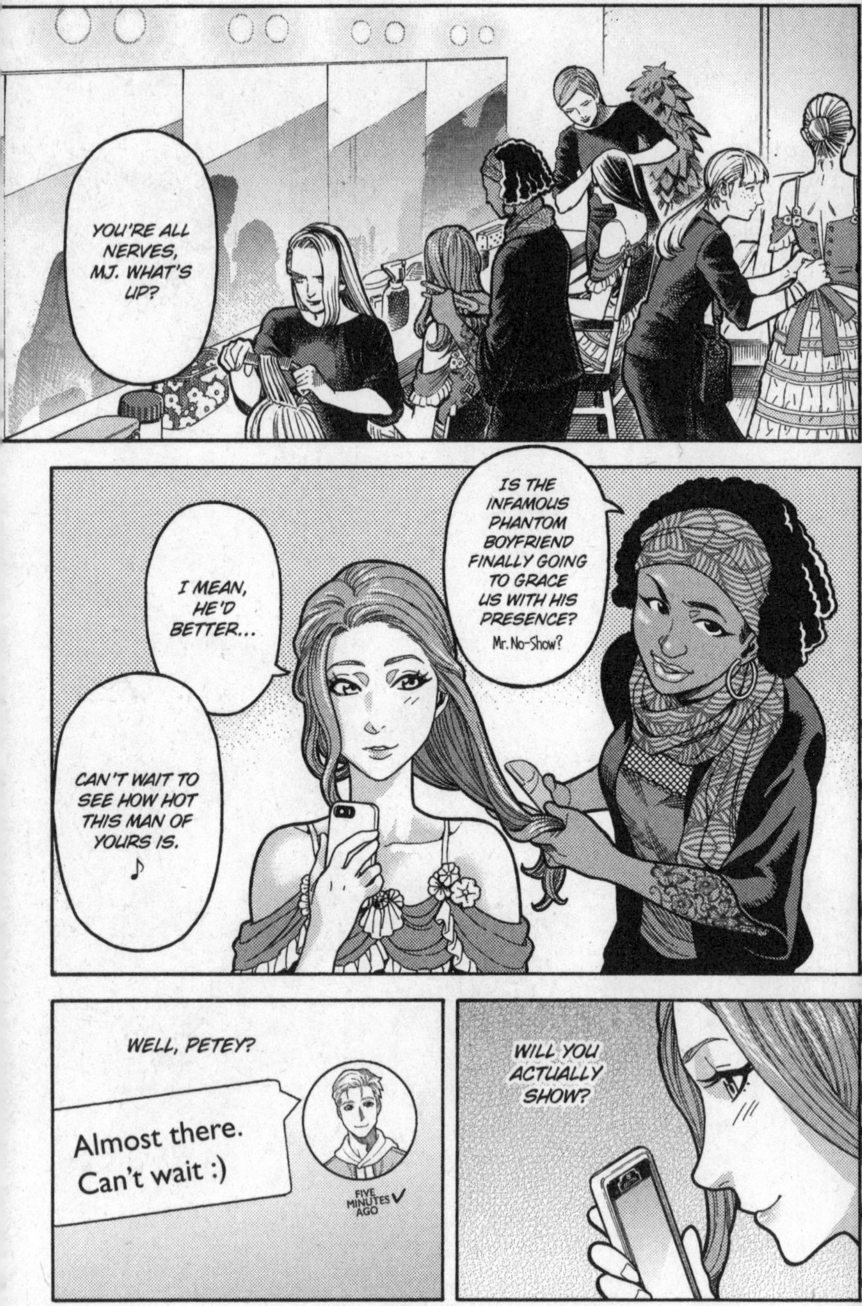
YOU'RE ALL NERVES, MJ. WHAT'S UP?
IS THE INFAMOUS PHANTOM BOYFRIEND FINALLY GOING TO GRACE US WITH HIS PRESENCE?
Mr. No-Show?
I MEAN, HE'D BETTER...
CAN'T WAIT TO SEE HOW HOT THIS MAN OF YOURS IS. ♪
WILL YOU ACTUALLY SHOW?
WELL, PETEY?
Almost there. Can't wait :)
FIVE MINUTES AGO

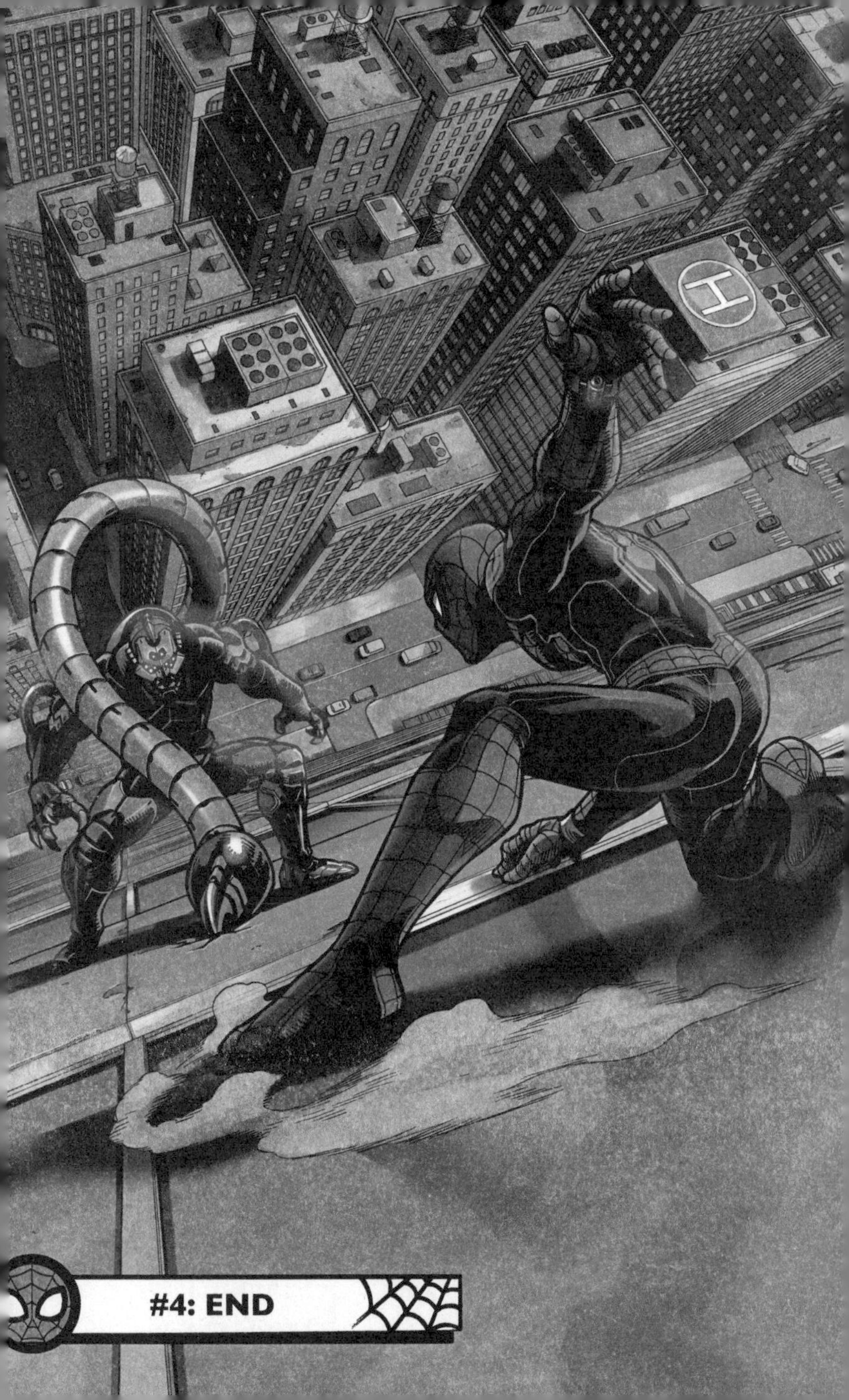
#4: END

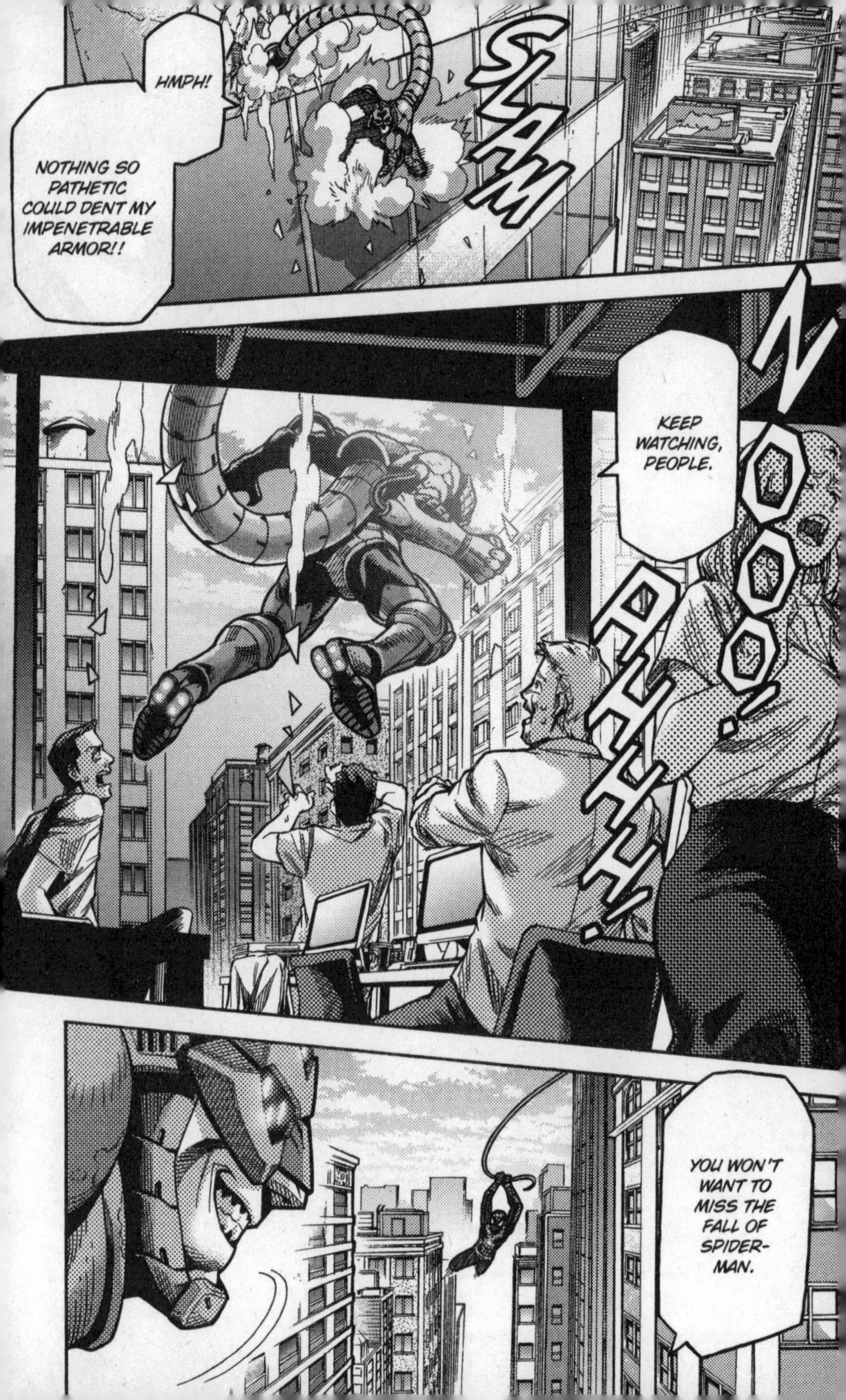
SLAM
HMPH!
NOTHING SO PATHETIC COULD DENT MY IMPENETRABLE ARMOR!!
NOOOO! AHHHH!
KEEP WATCHING, PEOPLE.
YOU WON'T WANT TO MISS THE FALL OF SPIDER-MAN.

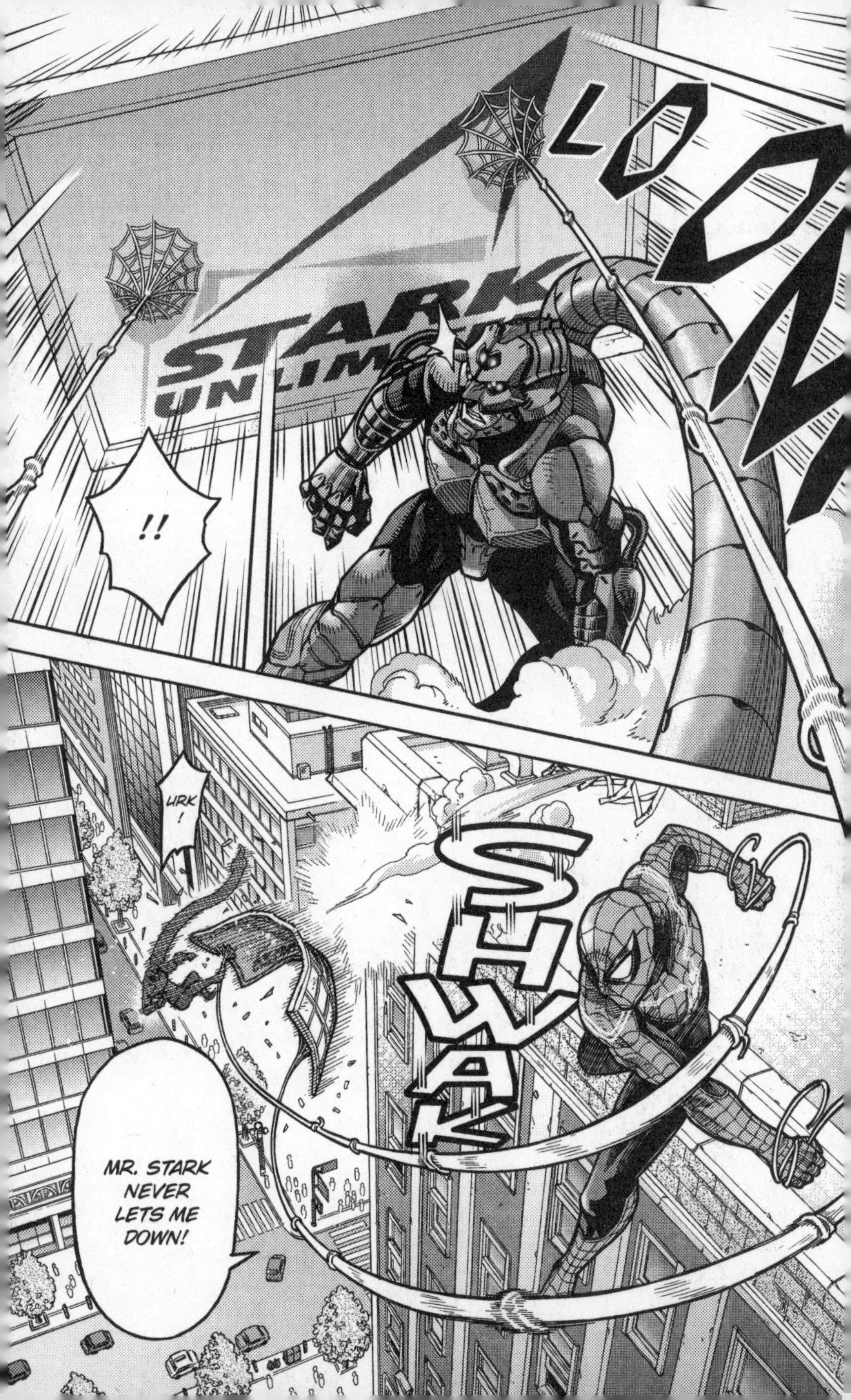
LOOM
STARK
!!
SHWAK
URK!
MR. STARK NEVER LETS ME DOWN!

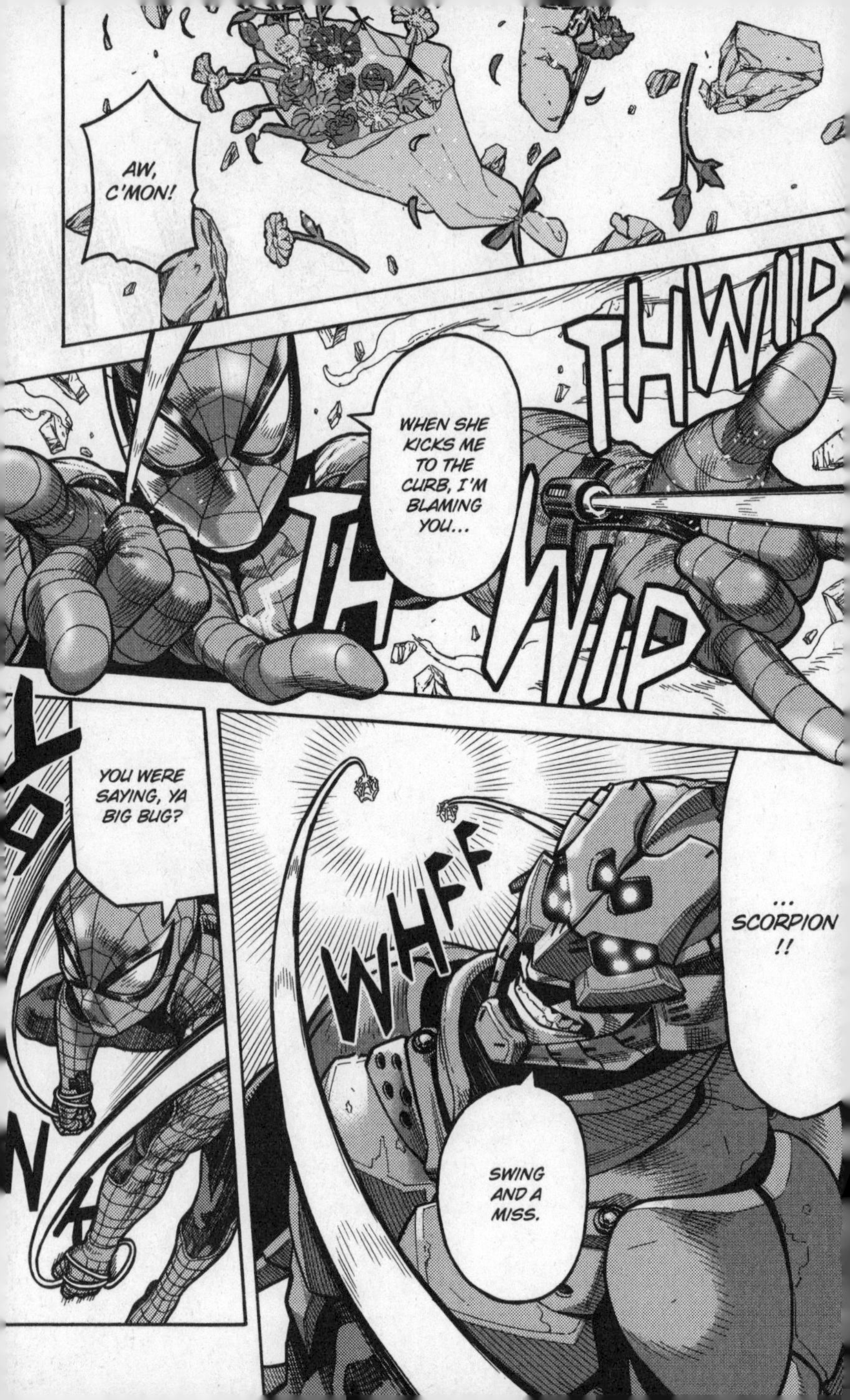
AW, C'MON!
THWIP
WHEN SHE KICKS ME TO THE CURB, I'M BLAMING YOU...
THWIP
... SCORPION !!
WHFF
SWING AND A MISS.
YOU WERE SAYING, YA BIG BUG?

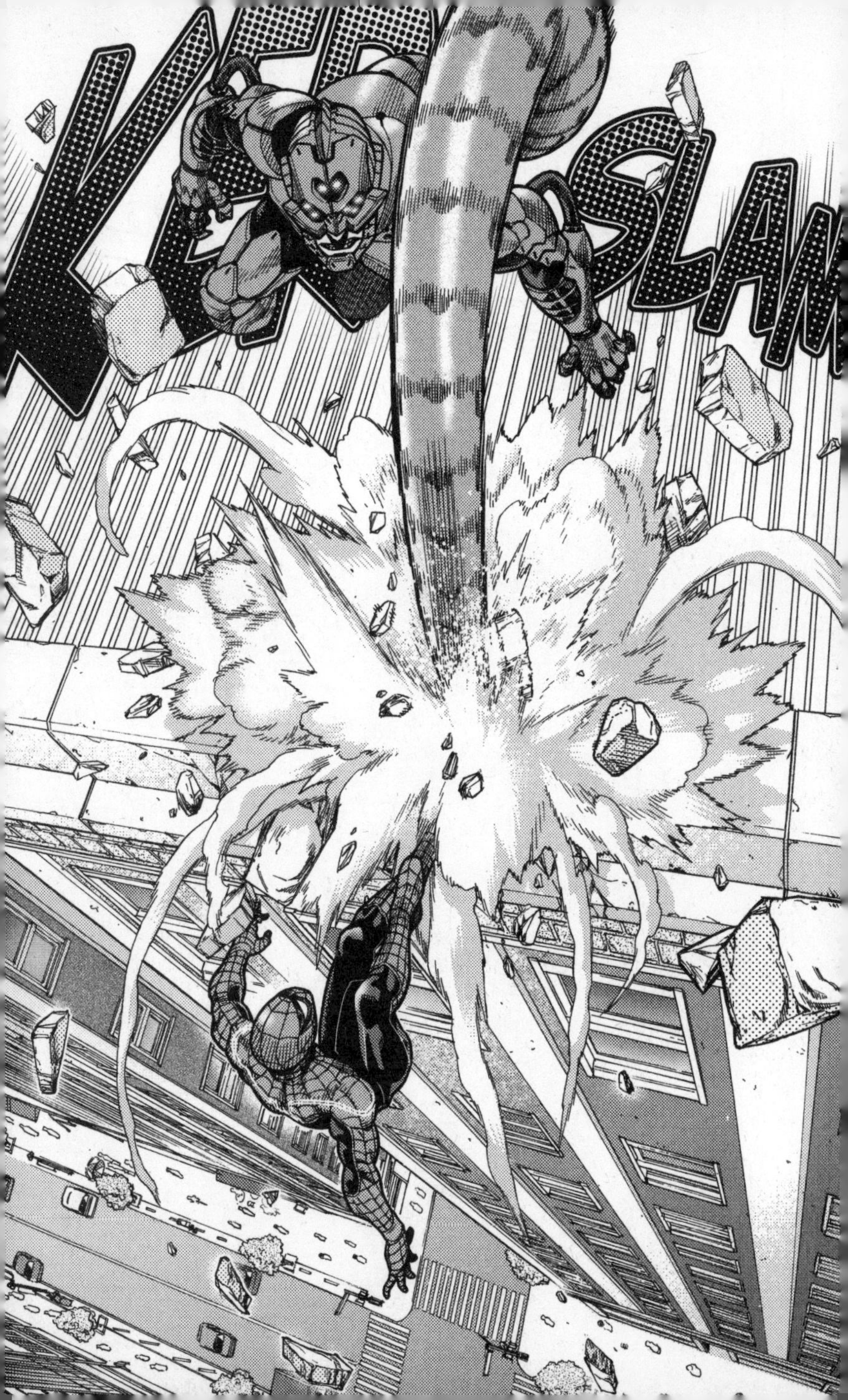
SLAM

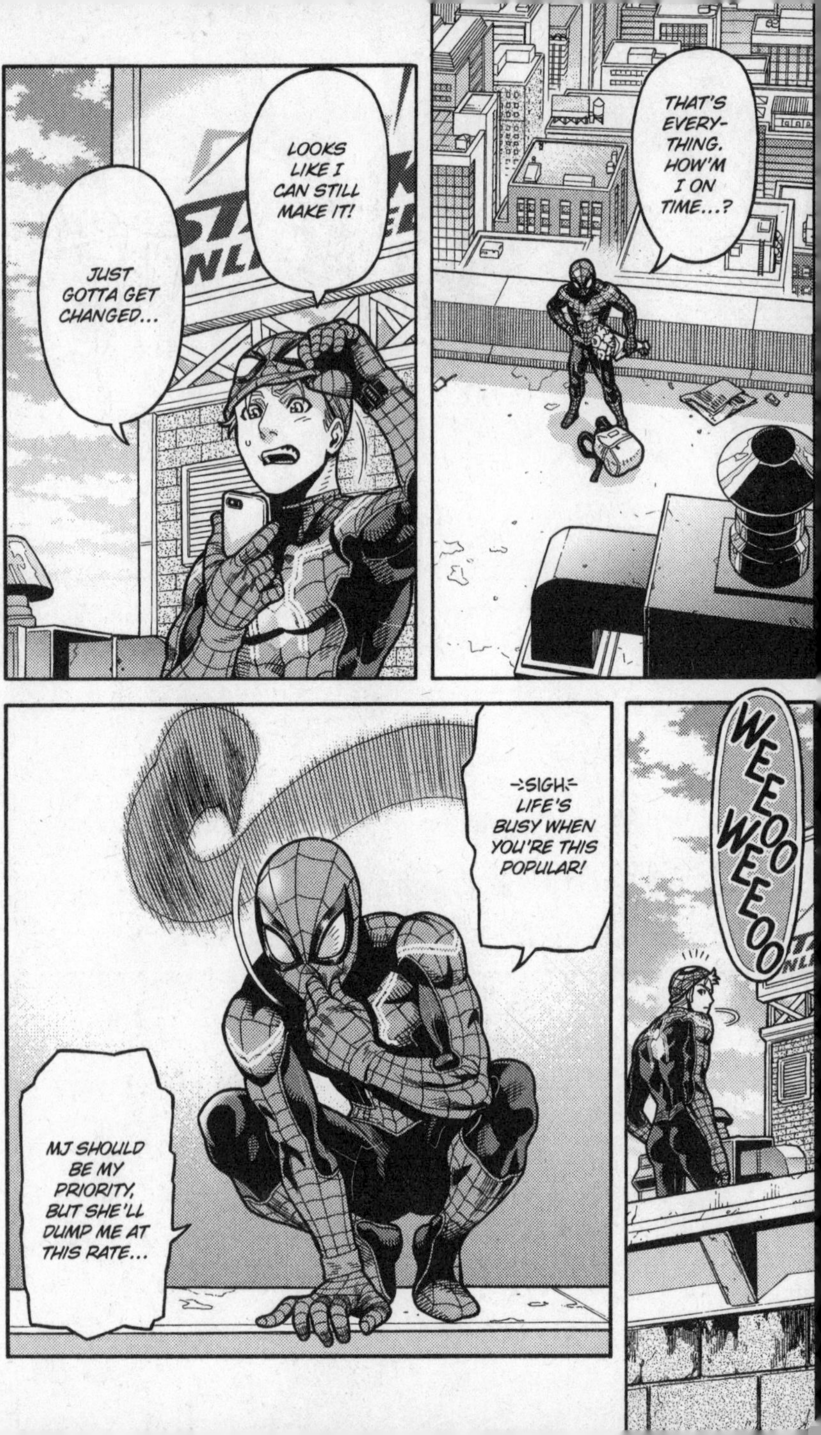
THAT'S EVERY-THING. HOW'M I ON TIME...?
LOOKS LIKE I CAN STILL MAKE IT!
JUST GOTTA GET CHANGED...
WEEOO WEEOO
-SIGH- LIFE'S BUSY WHEN YOU'RE THIS POPULAR!
MJ SHOULD BE MY PRIORITY, BUT SHE'LL DUMP ME AT THIS RATE...

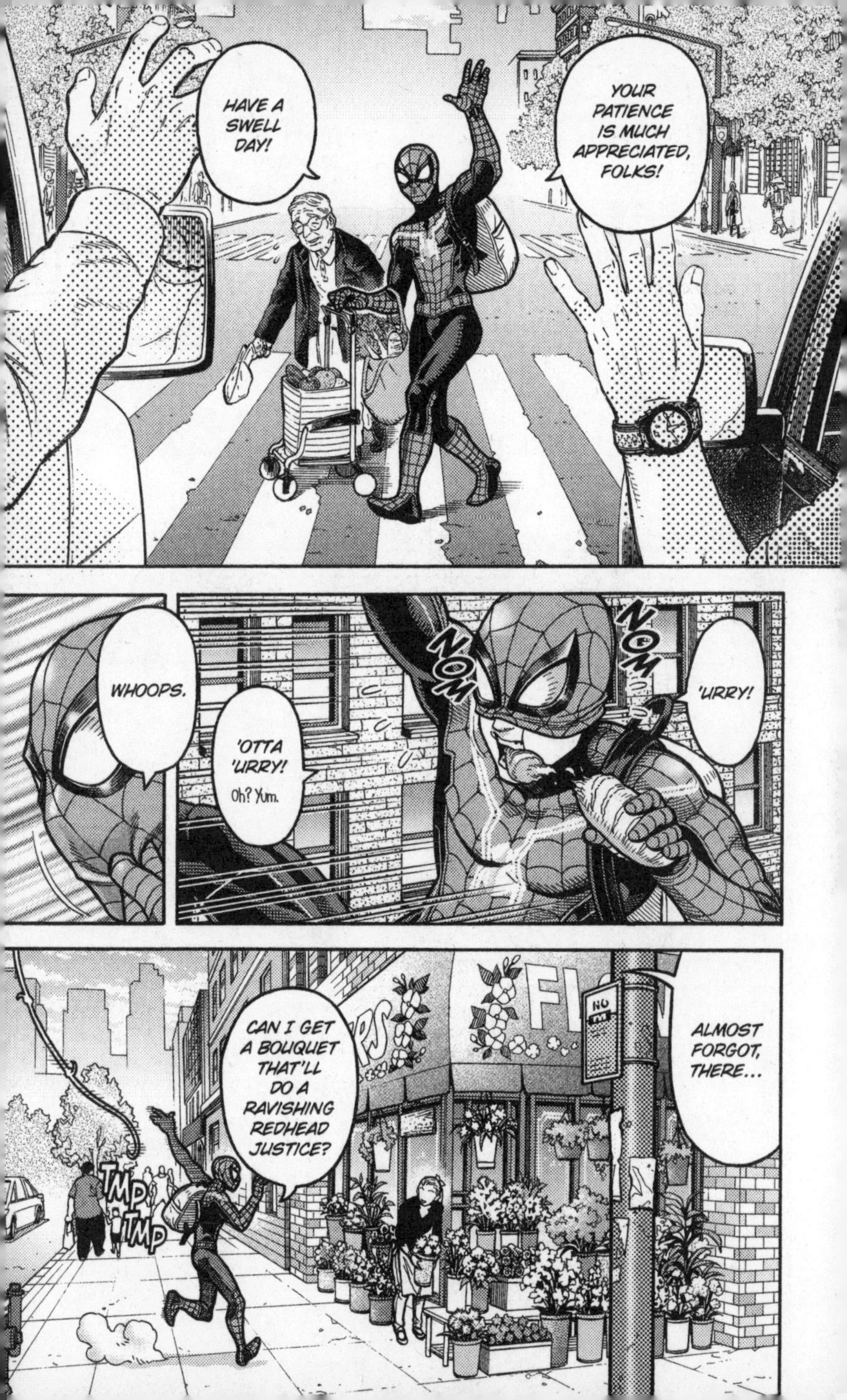
YOUR PATIENCE IS MUCH APPRECIATED, FOLKS!
HAVE A SWELL DAY!
NOM
NOM
'URRY!
'OTTA 'URRY!
Oh? Yum.
WHOOPS.
ALMOST FORGOT, THERE...
NO
FL
CAN I GET A BOUQUET THAT'LL DO A RAVISHING REDHEAD JUSTICE?
TMP
TMP

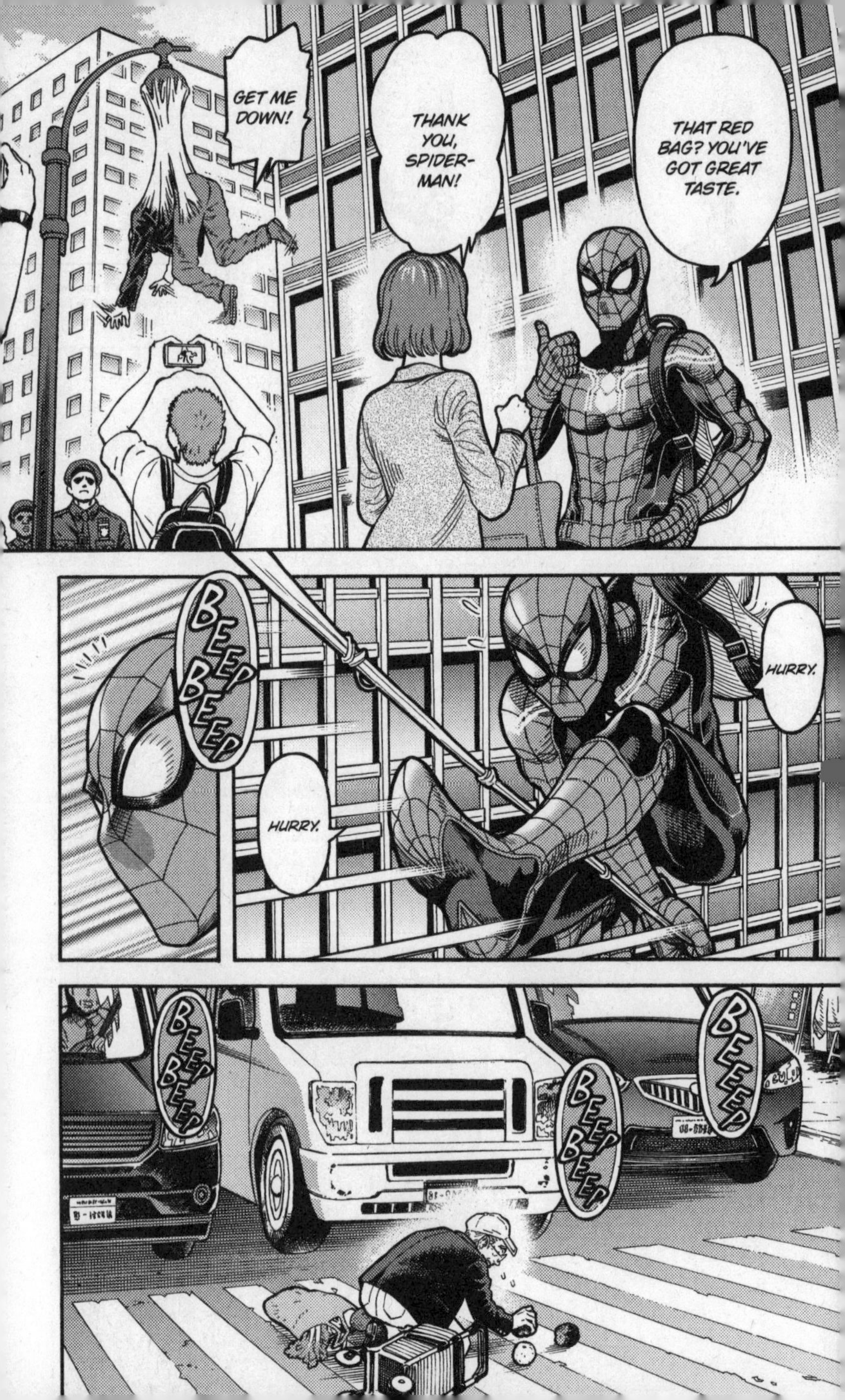

THAT RED BAG? YOU'VE GOT GREAT TASTE.
THANK YOU, SPIDER-MAN!
GET ME DOWN!
HURRY.
HURRY.
BEEP BEEP
BEEEP
BEEP BEEP
BEEP BEEP

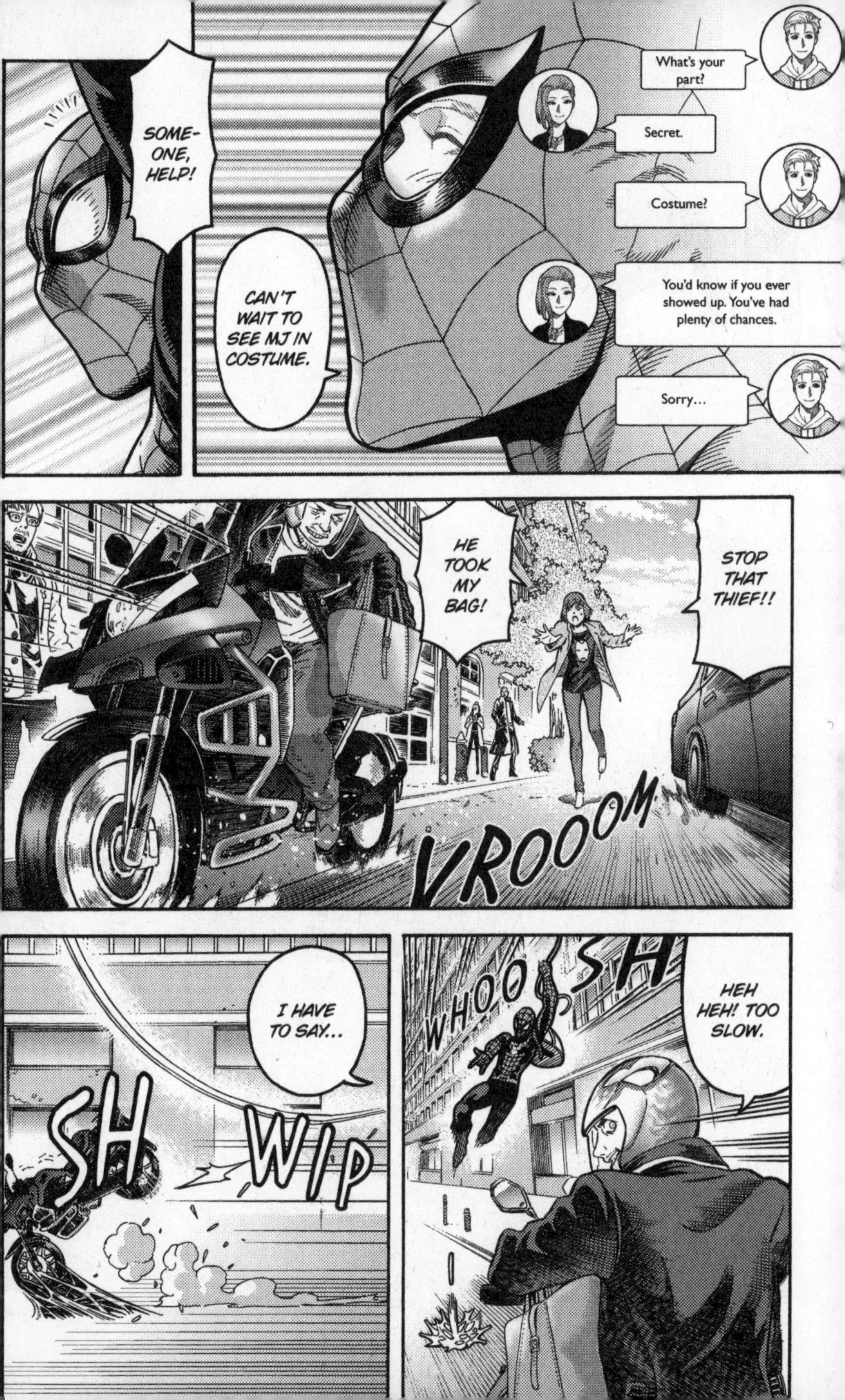
What's your part?
Secret.
Costume?
You'd know if you ever showed up. You've had plenty of chances.
Sorry...
CAN'T WAIT TO SEE MJ IN COSTUME.
SOME-ONE, HELP!
STOP THAT THIEF!!
HE TOOK MY BAG!
VROOOM
WHOOSH
HEH HEH! TOO SLOW.
I HAVE TO SAY...
SH WIP

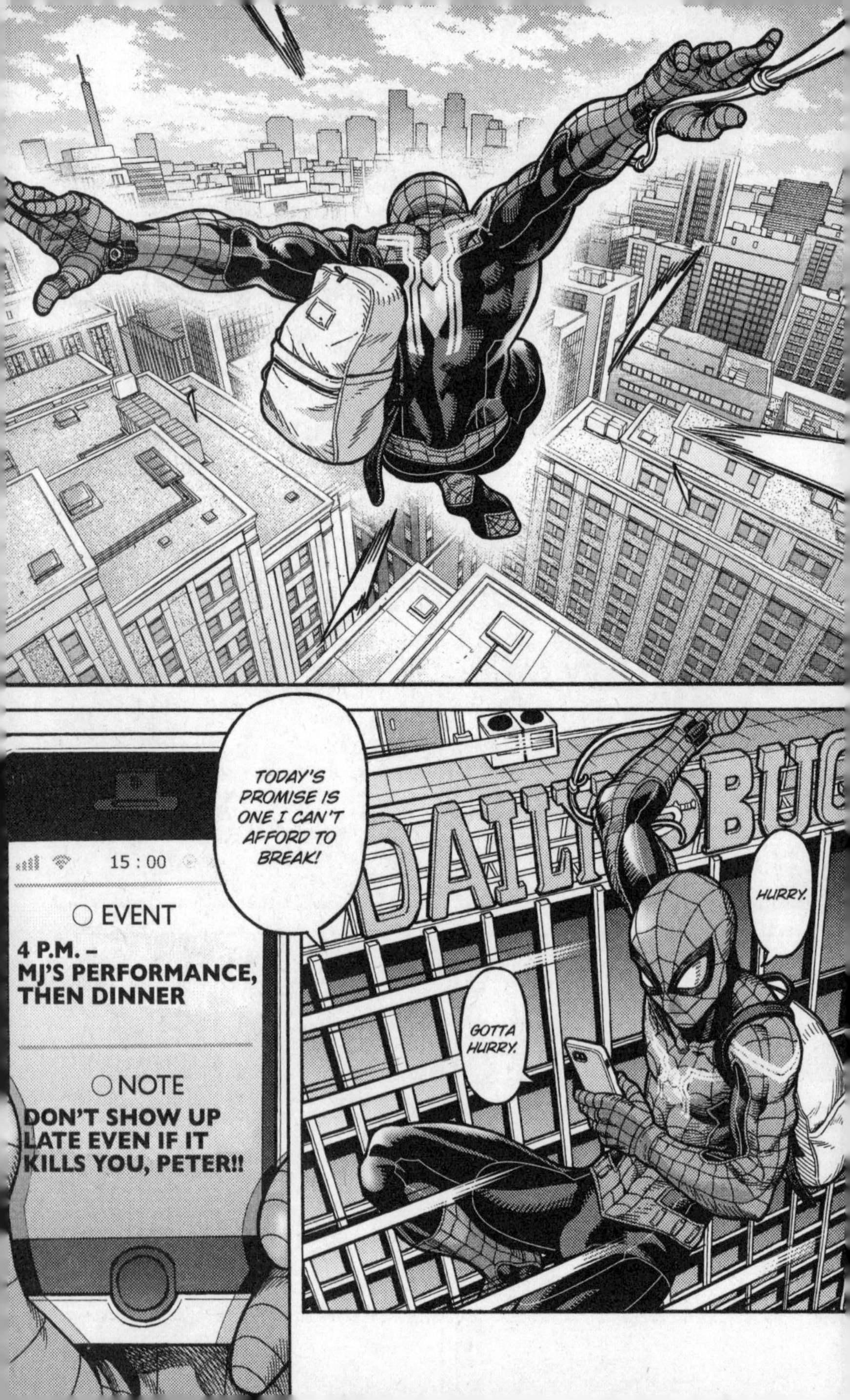
TODAY'S PROMISE IS ONE I CAN'T AFFORD TO BREAK!
HURRY.
GOTTA HURRY.
15 : 00
EVENT
4 P.M. – MJ'S PERFORMANCE, THEN DINNER
NOTE
DON'T SHOW UP LATE EVEN IF IT KILLS YOU, PETER!!

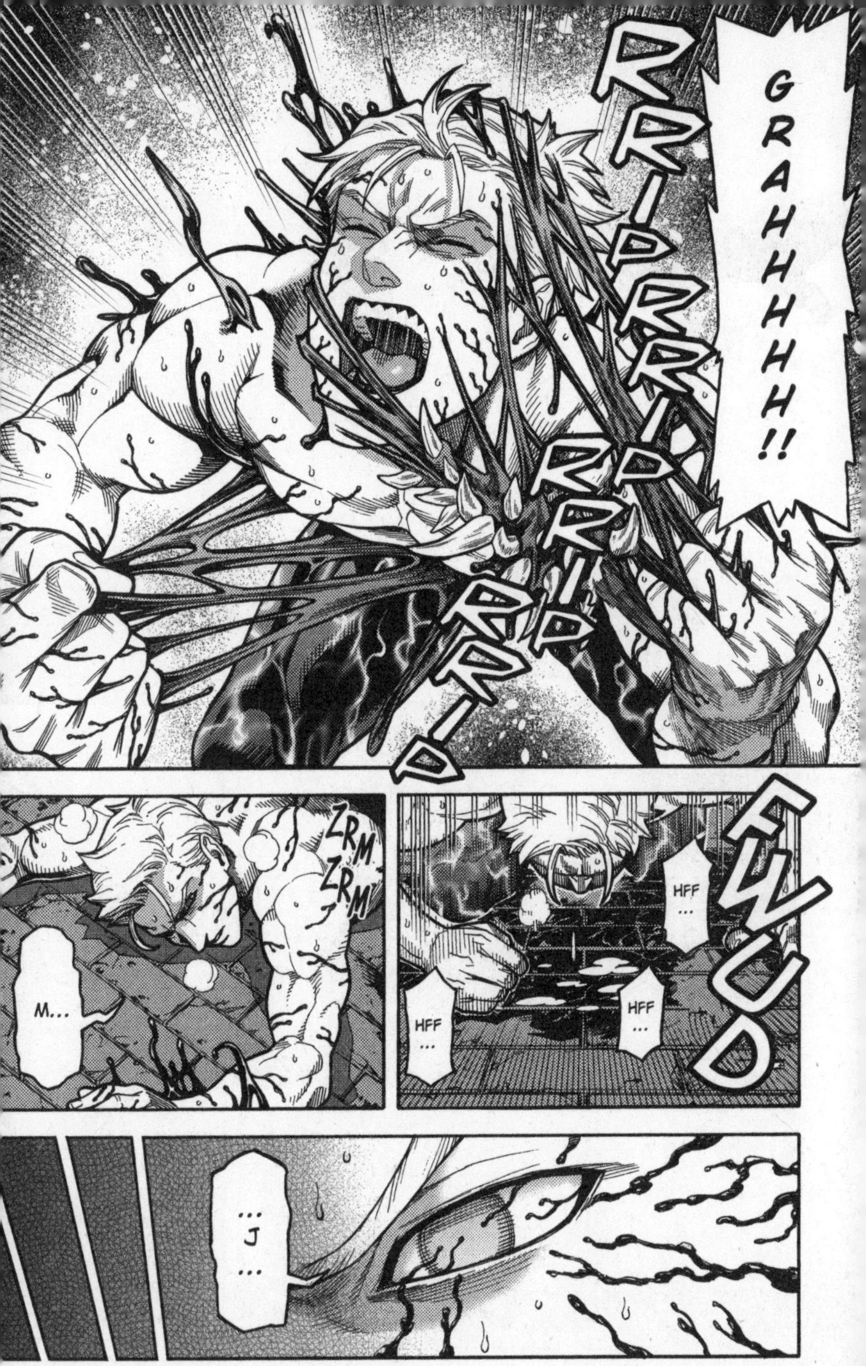
GRAHHHHHH!!
RRRIPPRRRIPPRRRIPPRRRIPP
FWUD
HFF...
HFF...
HFF...
ZRM ZRM
M...
...J...

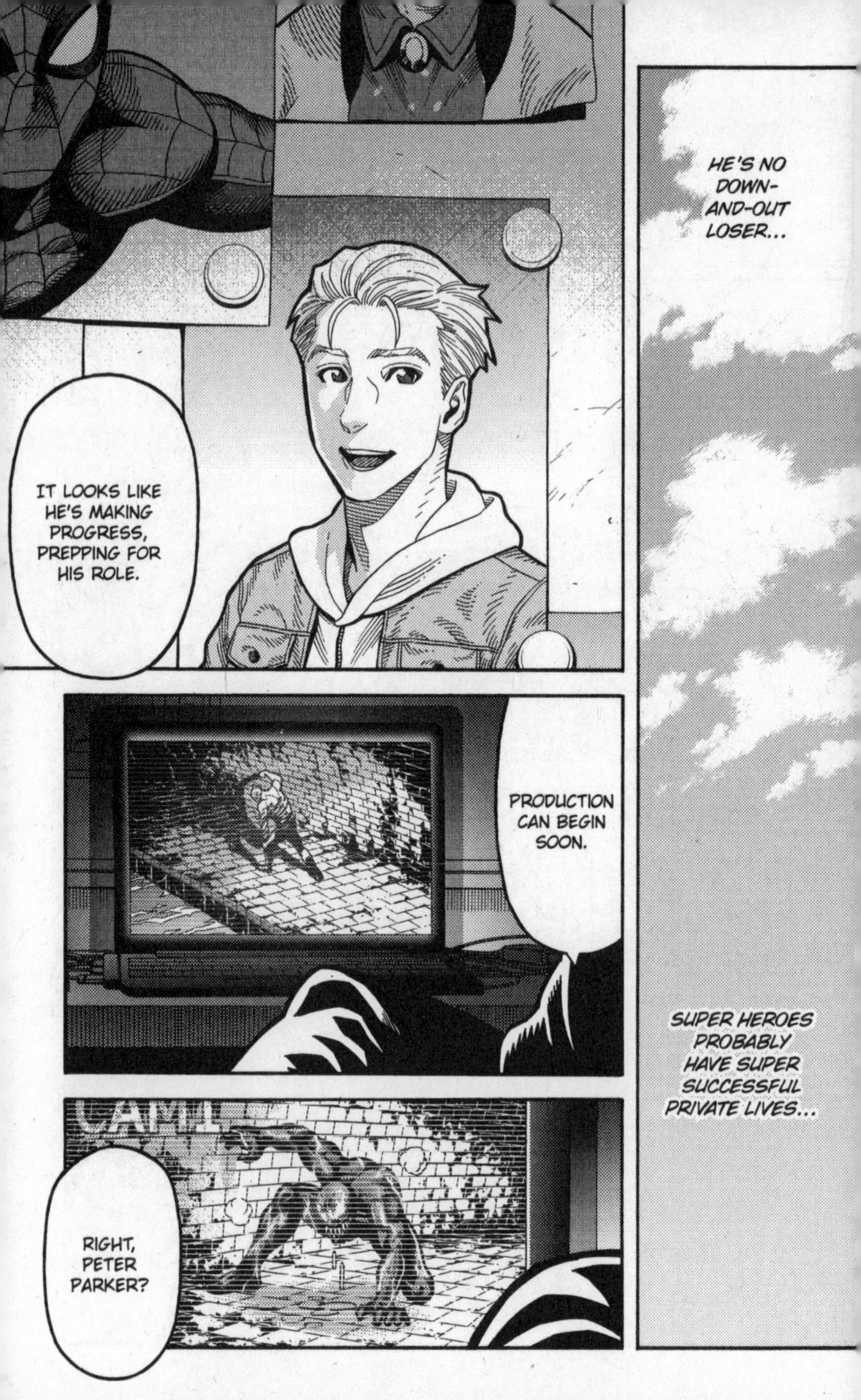
HE'S NO DOWN-AND-OUT LOSER...
SUPER HEROES PROBABLY HAVE SUPER SUCCESSFUL PRIVATE LIVES...
IT LOOKS LIKE HE'S MAKING PROGRESS, PREPPING FOR HIS ROLE.
PRODUCTION CAN BEGIN SOON.
RIGHT, PETER PARKER?

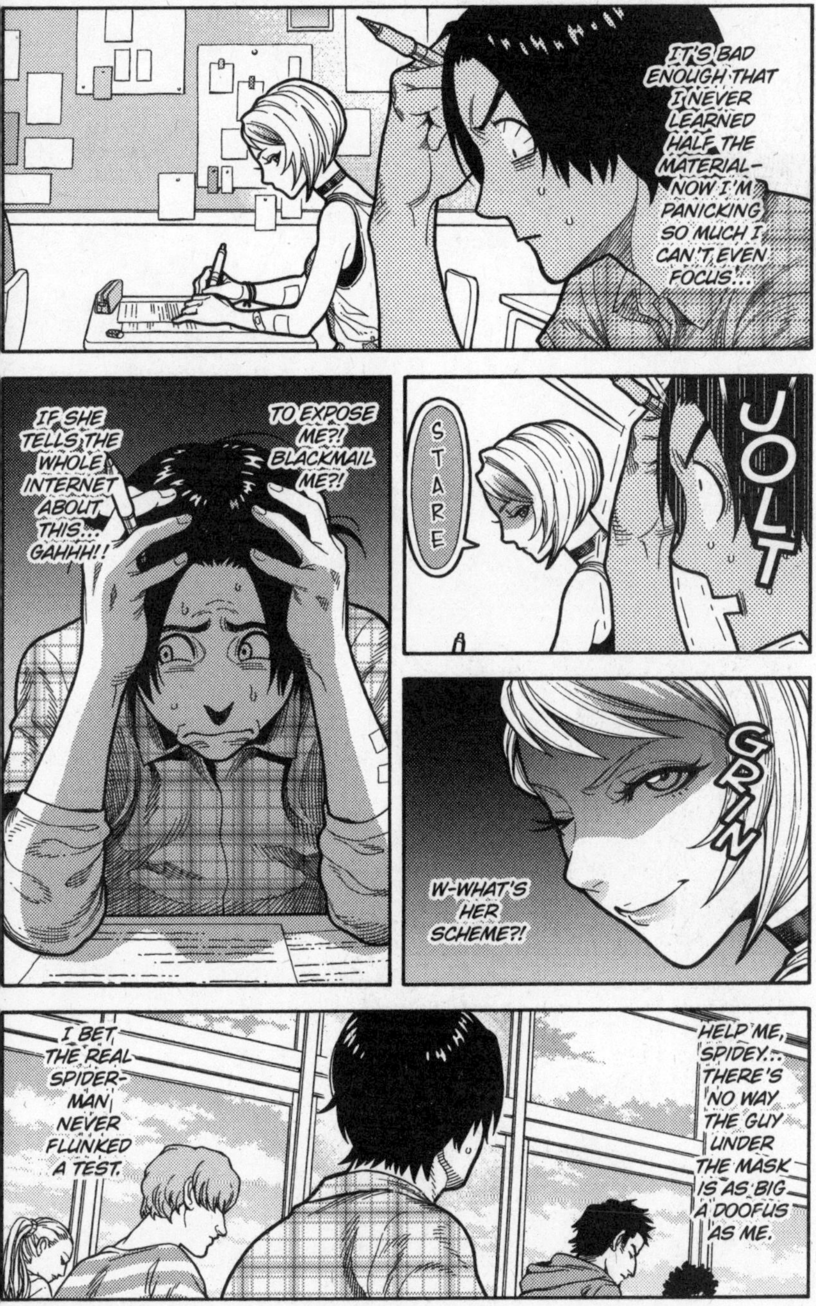
IT'S BAD ENOUGH THAT I NEVER LEARNED HALF THE MATERIAL— NOW I'M PANICKING SO MUCH I CAN'T EVEN FOCUS...
JOLT
STARE
GRIN
W-WHAT'S HER SCHEME?!
TO EXPOSE ME?! BLACKMAIL ME?!
IF SHE TELLS THE WHOLE INTERNET ABOUT THIS... GAHHH!!
HELP ME, SPIDEY... THERE'S NO WAY THE GUY UNDER THE MASK IS AS BIG A DOOFUS AS ME.
I BET THE REAL SPIDER-MAN NEVER FLUNKED A TEST.

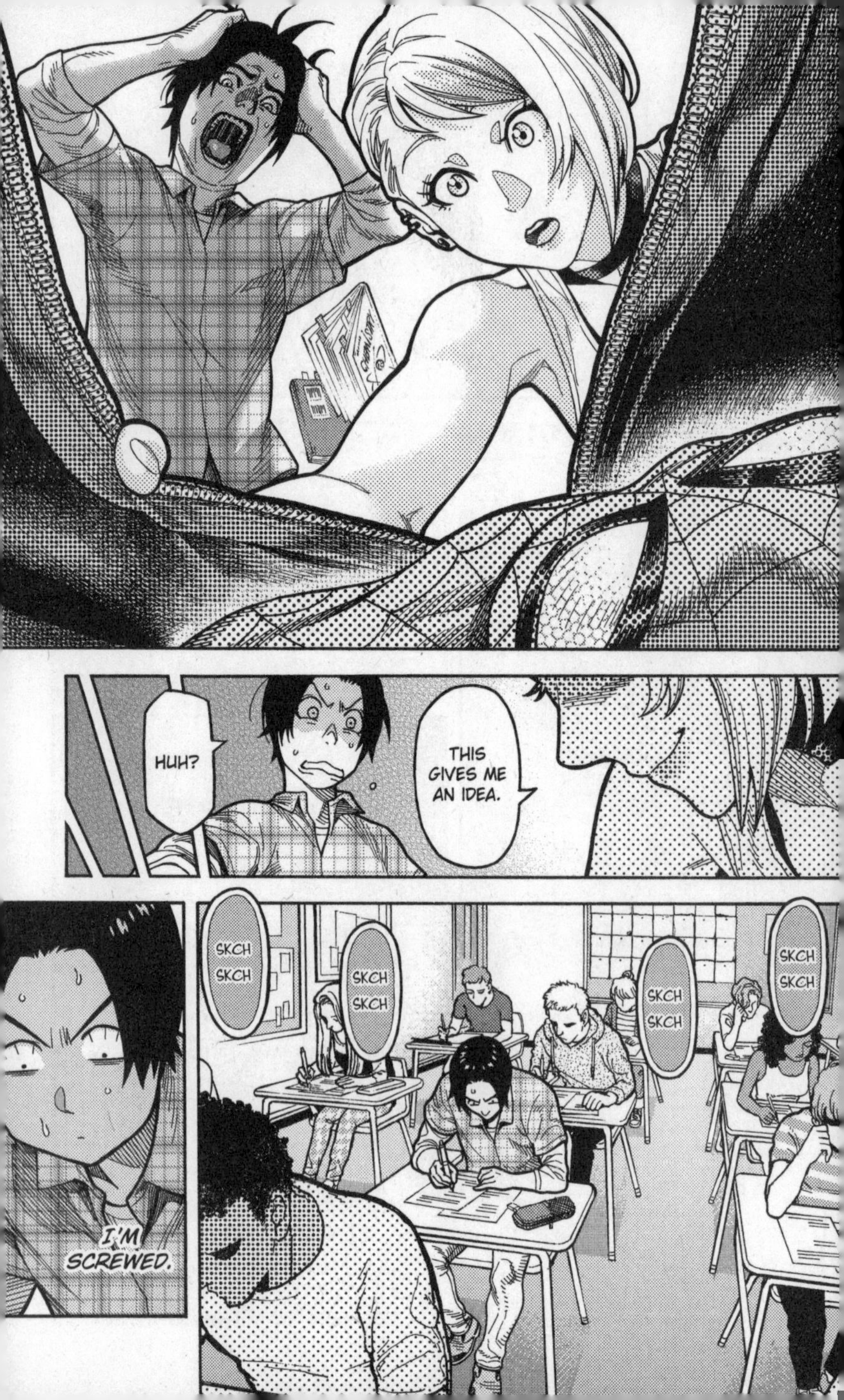
THIS GIVES ME AN IDEA.
HUH?
SKCH SKCH
SKCH SKCH
SKCH SKCH
SKCH SKCH
I'M SCREWED.

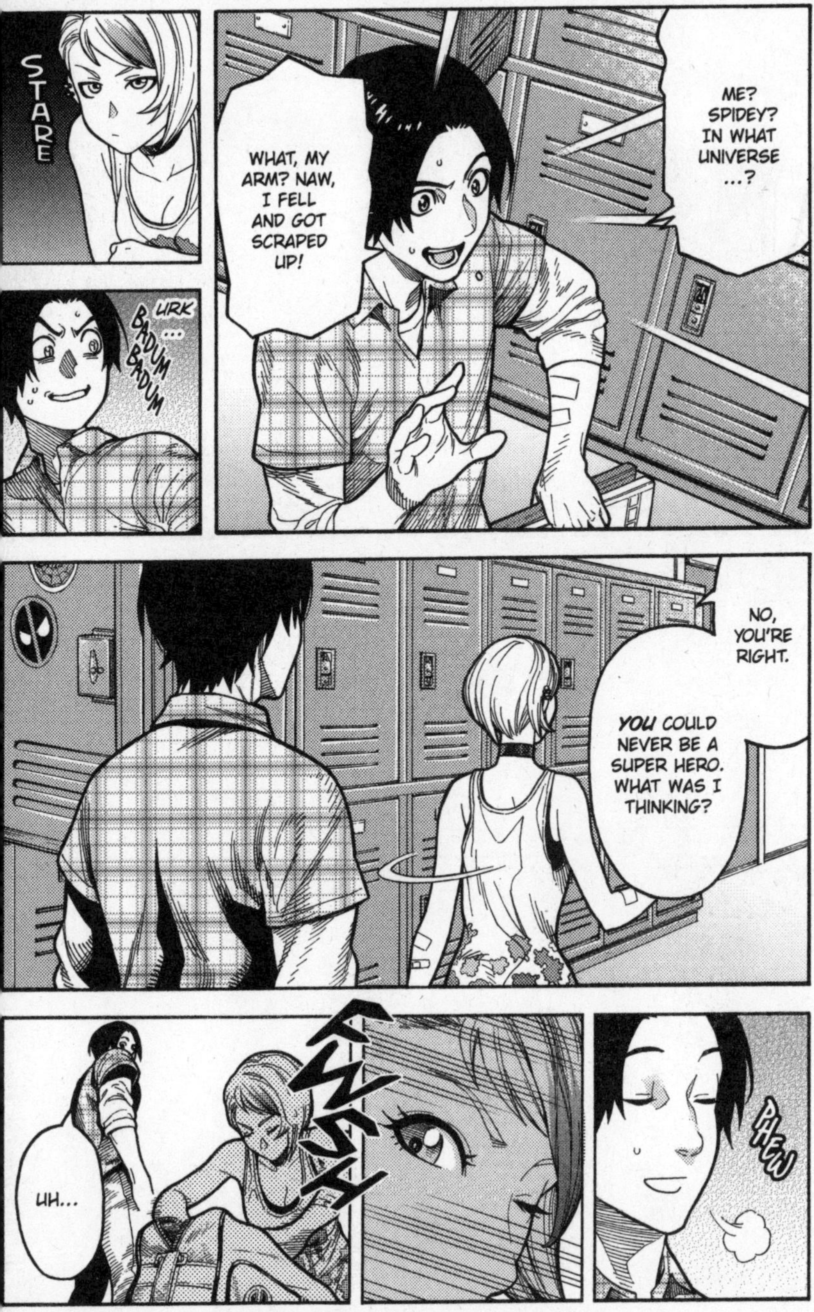
ME? SPIDEY? IN WHAT UNIVERSE ...?
WHAT, MY ARM? NAW, I FELL AND GOT SCRAPED UP!
STARE
URK ...
BADUM BADUM
NO, YOU'RE RIGHT.
YOU COULD NEVER BE A SUPER HERO. WHAT WAS I THINKING?
PHEW
SWSH
UH...

#4 PETER PARKER

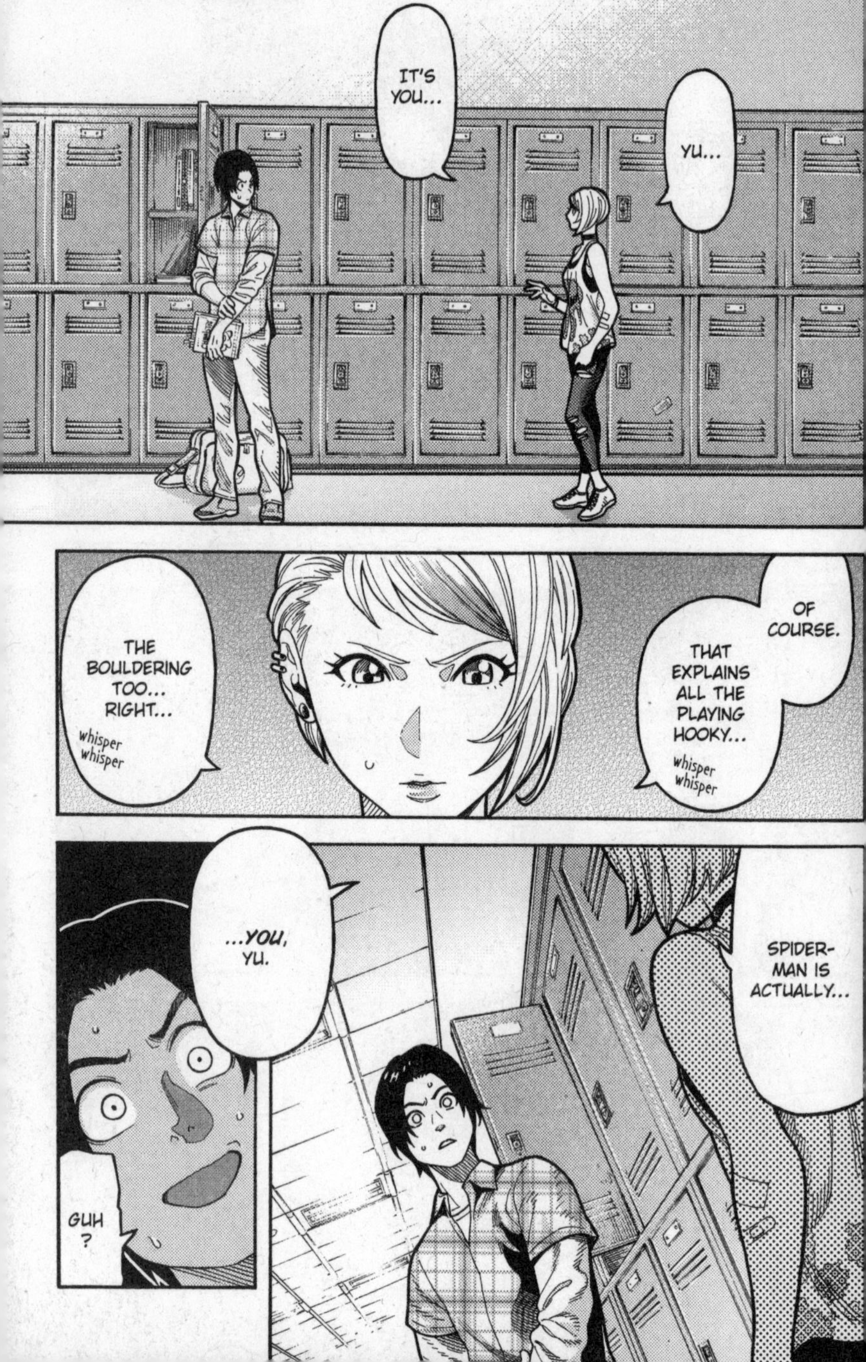
YU...
IT'S YOU...
OF COURSE.
THAT EXPLAINS ALL THE PLAYING HOOKY...
whisper whisper
THE BOULDERING TOO... RIGHT...
whisper whisper
SPIDER-MAN IS ACTUALLY...
...YOU, YU.
GUH?

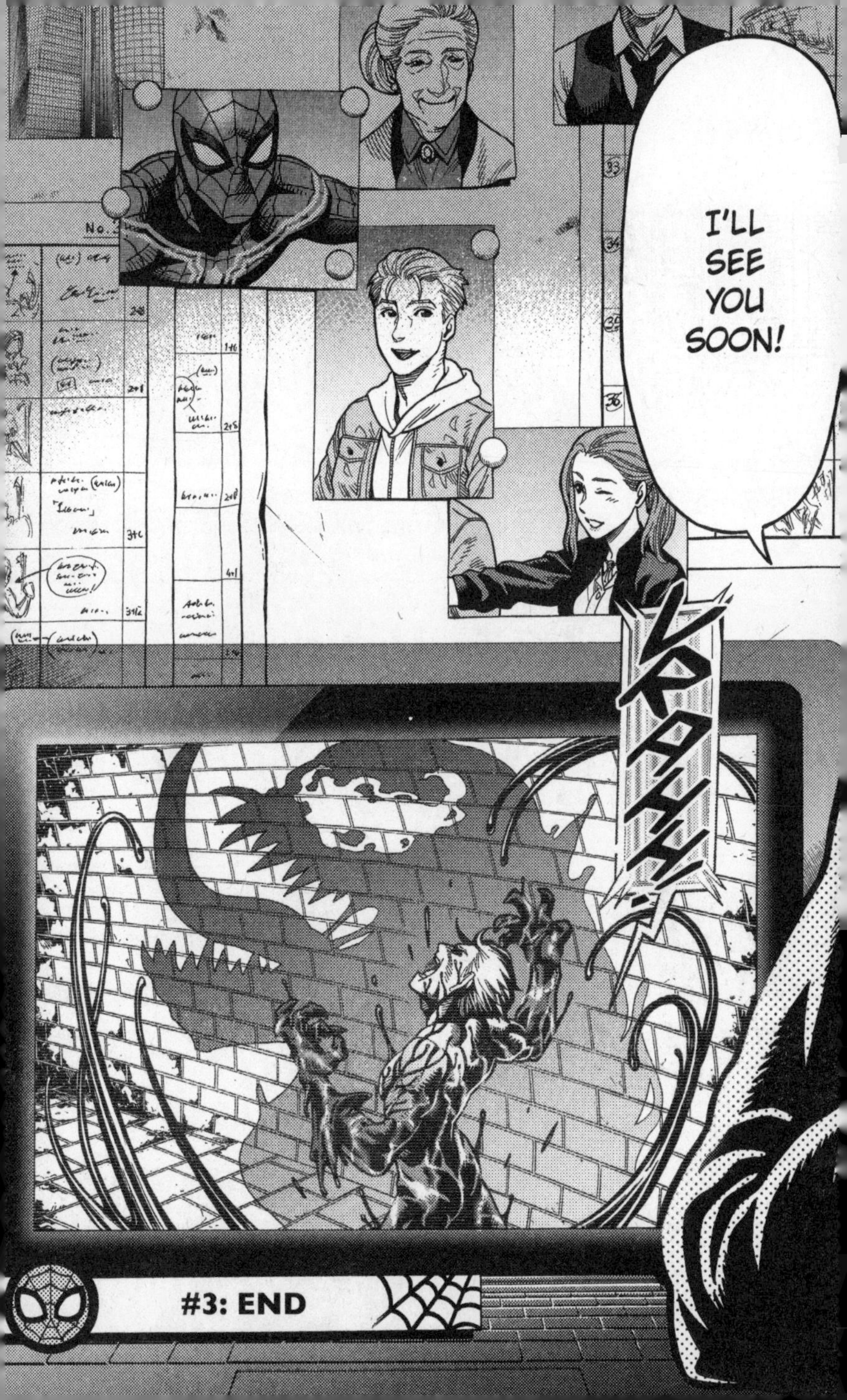
I'LL SEE YOU SOON!
VRAHH!
#3: END

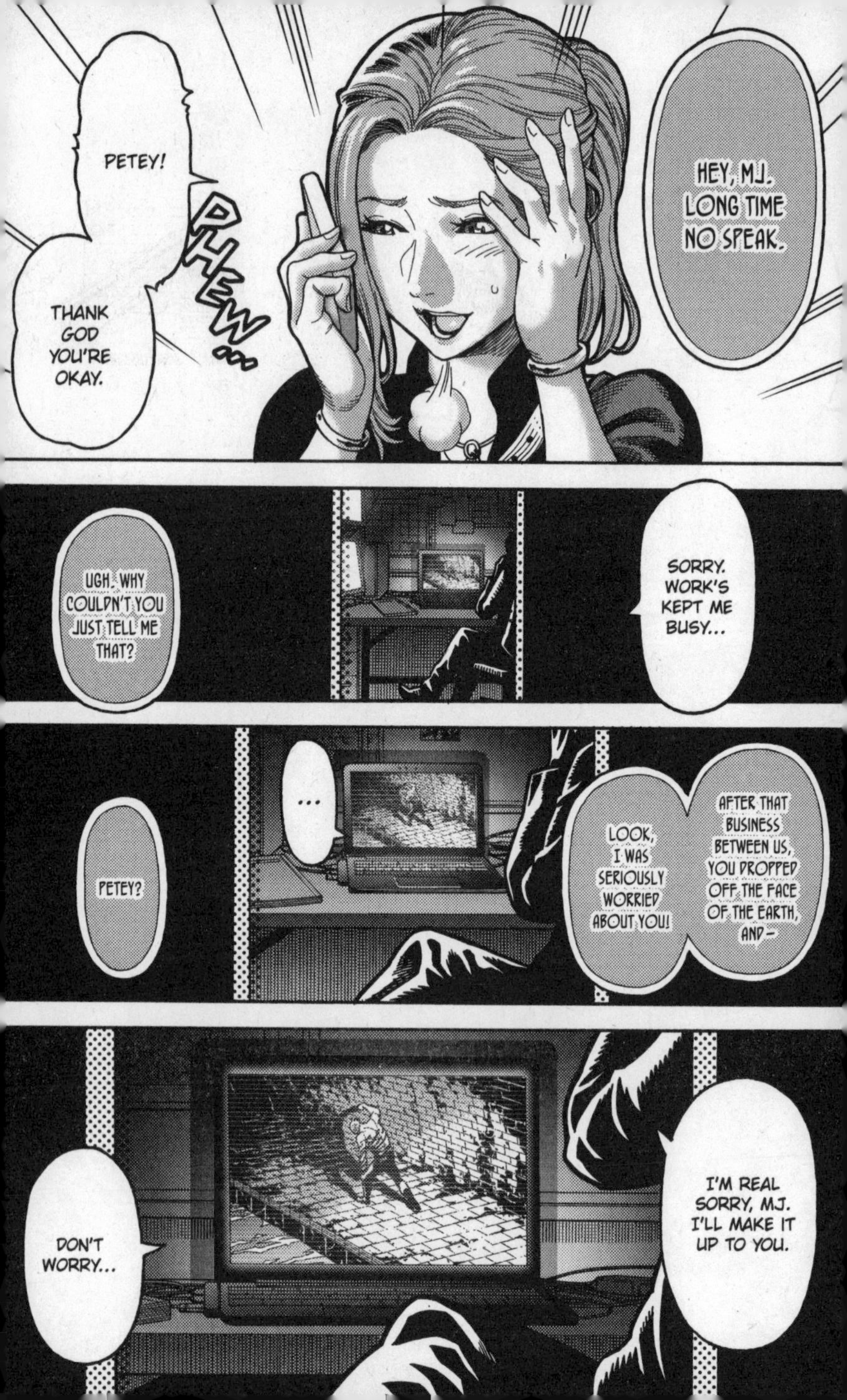
HEY, MJ. LONG TIME NO SPEAK.
PETEY!
PHEW...
THANK GOD YOU'RE OKAY.
SORRY. WORK'S KEPT ME BUSY...
UGH. WHY COULDN'T YOU JUST TELL ME THAT?
AFTER THAT BUSINESS BETWEEN US, YOU DROPPED OFF THE FACE OF THE EARTH, AND—
LOOK, I WAS SERIOUSLY WORRIED ABOUT YOU!
...
PETEY?
I'M REAL SORRY, MJ. I'LL MAKE IT UP TO YOU.
DON'T WORRY...

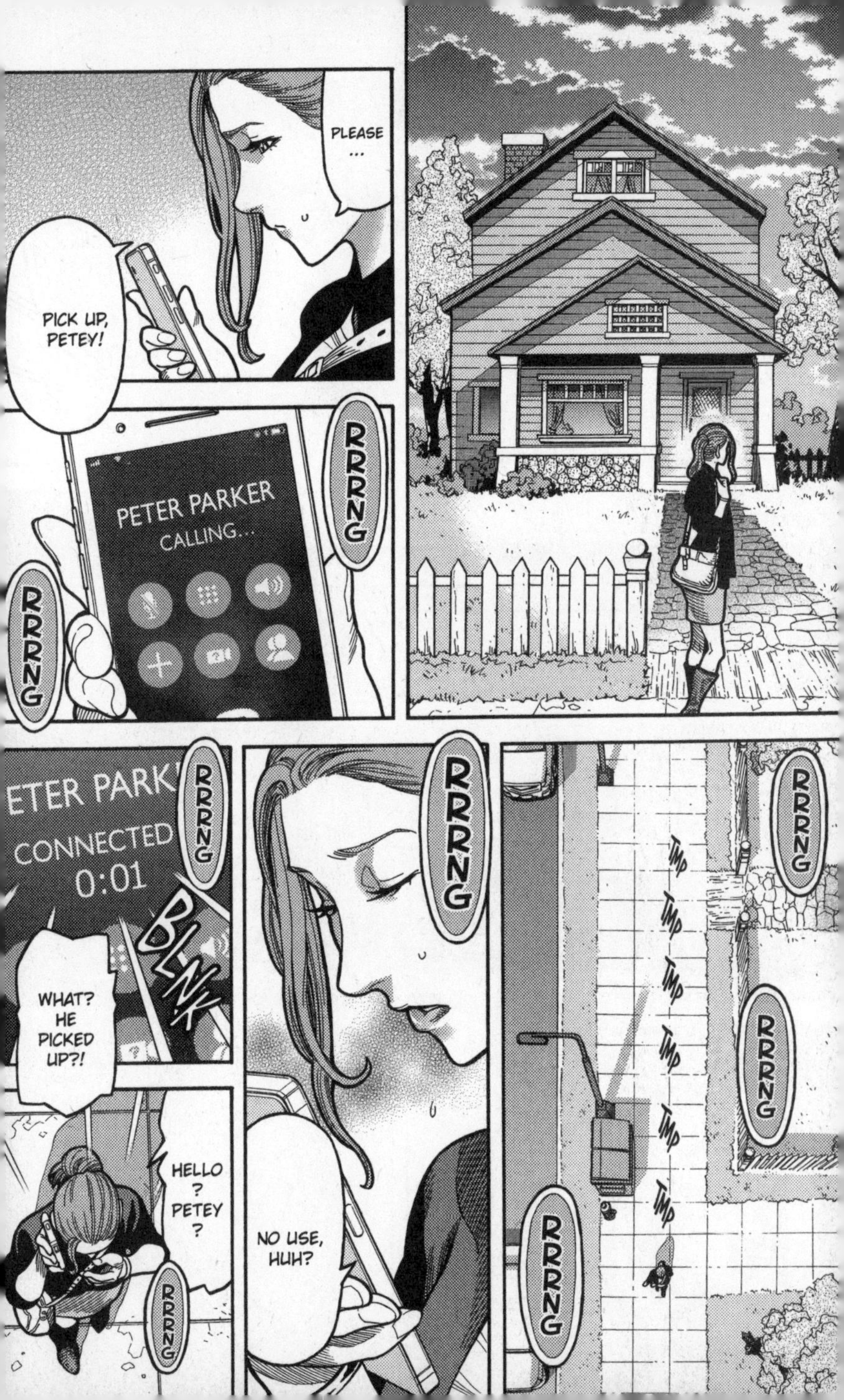
PLEASE ...
PICK UP, PETEY!
RRRNG
PETER PARKER
CALLING...
RRRNG
RRRNG
TMP
TMP
TMP
TMP
TMP
TMP
TMP
RRRNG
RRRNG
RRRNG
NO USE, HUH?
RRRNG
ETER PARK
CONNECTED
0:01
BLNK
WHAT? HE PICKED UP?!
HELLO? PETEY?
RRRNG

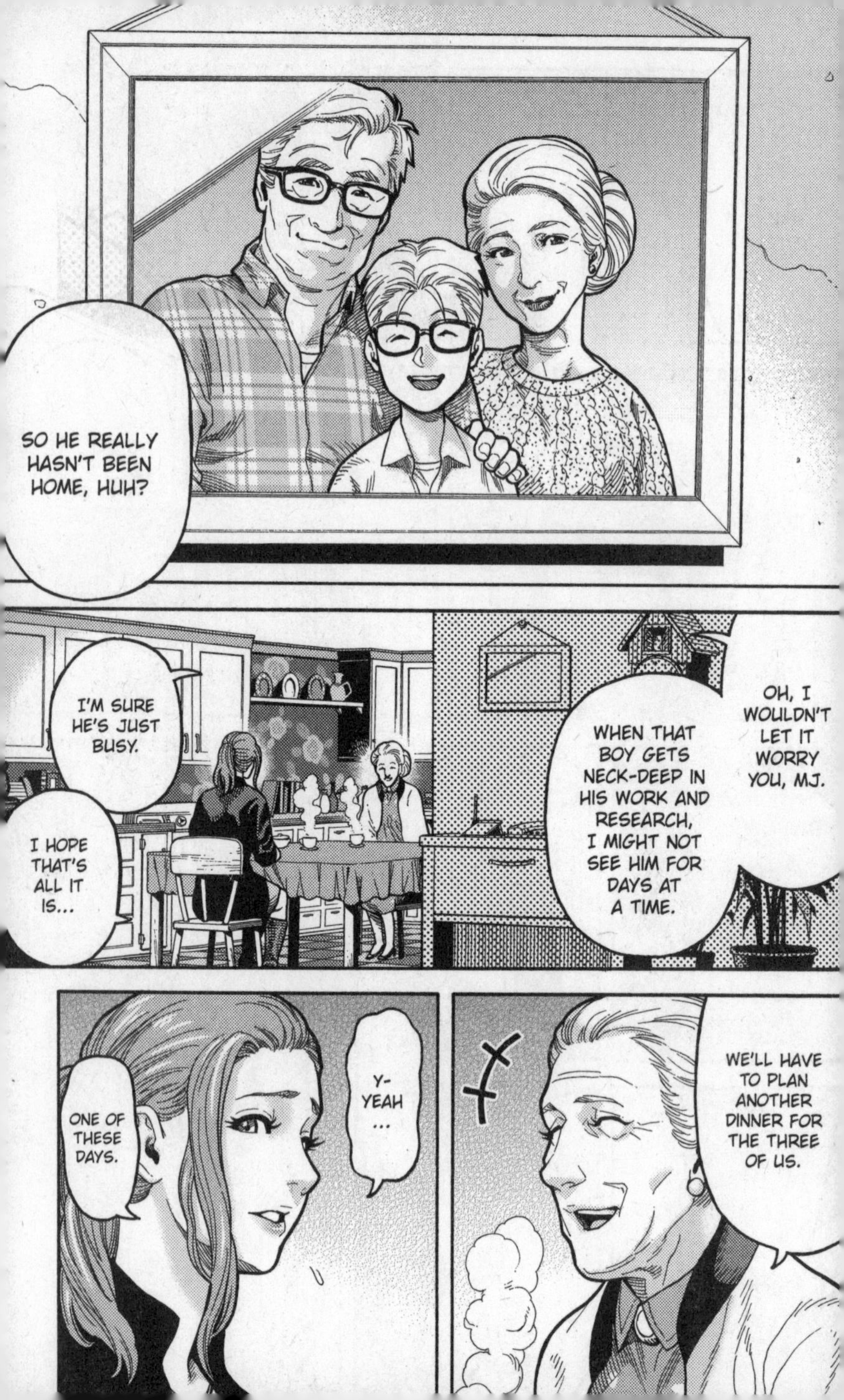
SO HE REALLY HASN'T BEEN HOME, HUH?
OH, I WOULDN'T LET IT WORRY YOU, MJ.
WHEN THAT BOY GETS NECK-DEEP IN HIS WORK AND RESEARCH, I MIGHT NOT SEE HIM FOR DAYS AT A TIME.
I'M SURE HE'S JUST BUSY.
I HOPE THAT'S ALL IT IS...
WE'LL HAVE TO PLAN ANOTHER DINNER FOR THE THREE OF US.
Y-YEAH...
ONE OF THESE DAYS.

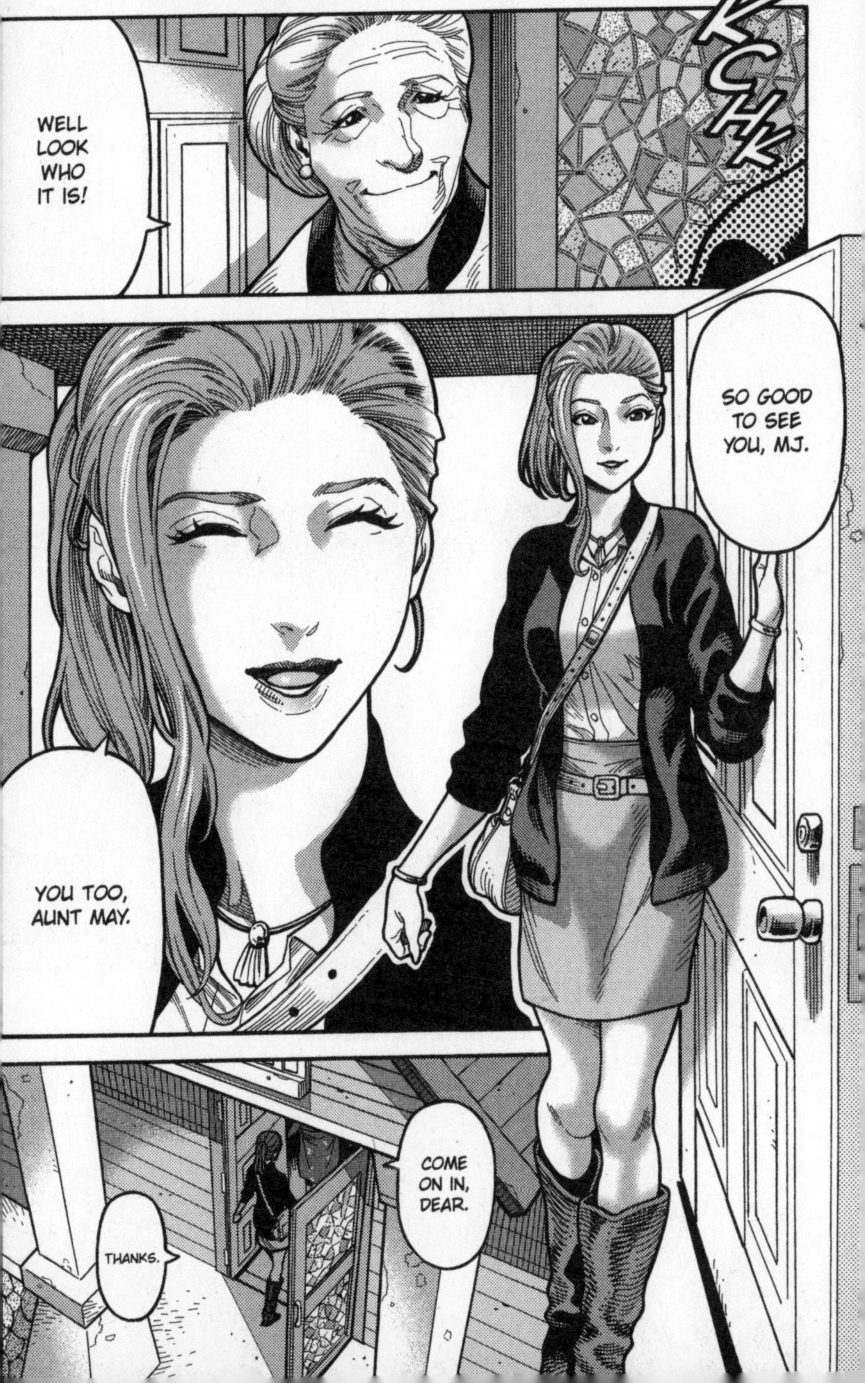
KCHK
WELL LOOK WHO IT IS!
SO GOOD TO SEE YOU, MJ.
YOU TOO, AUNT MAY.
COME ON IN, DEAR.
THANKS.

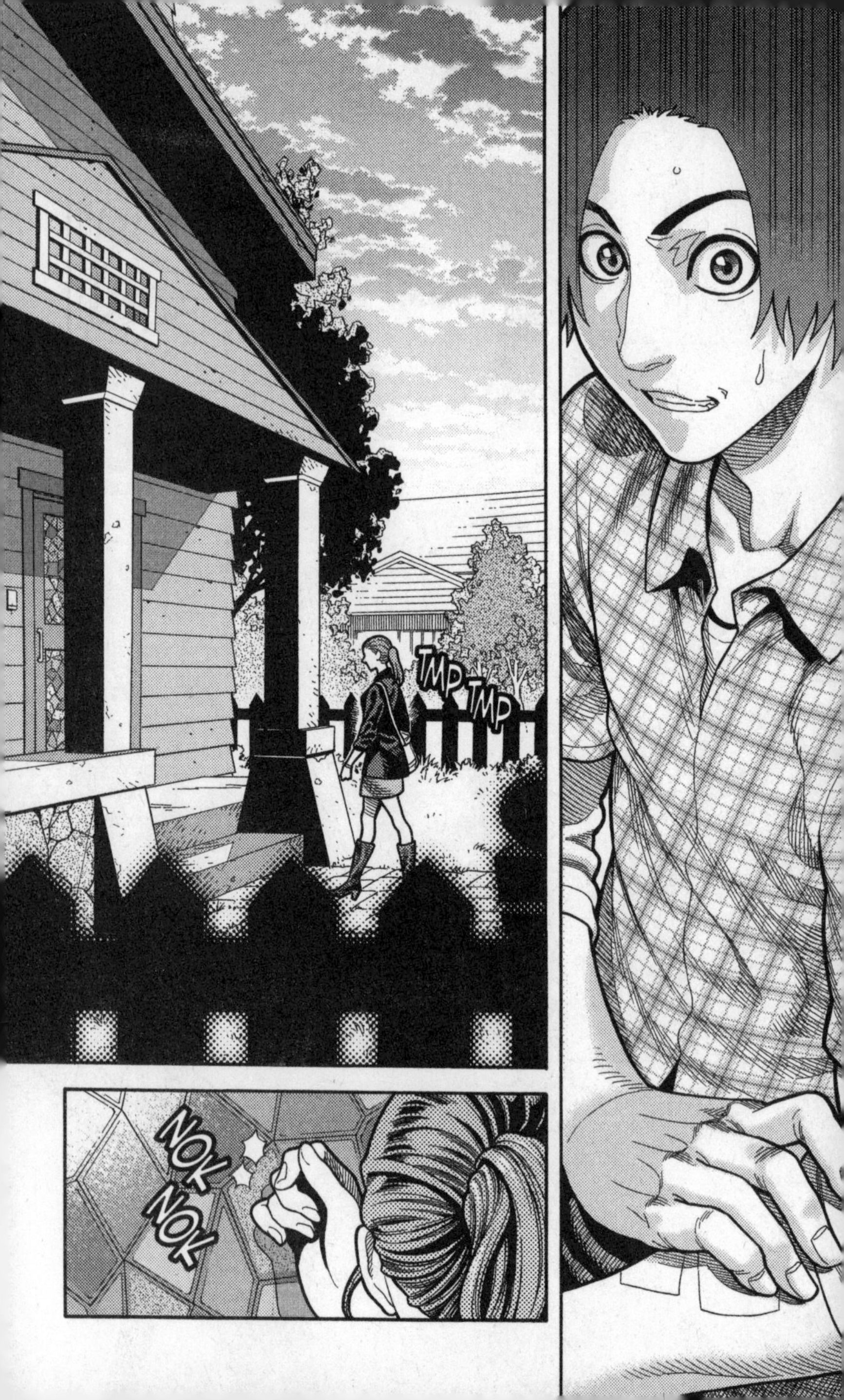
TMP TMP
NOK NOK

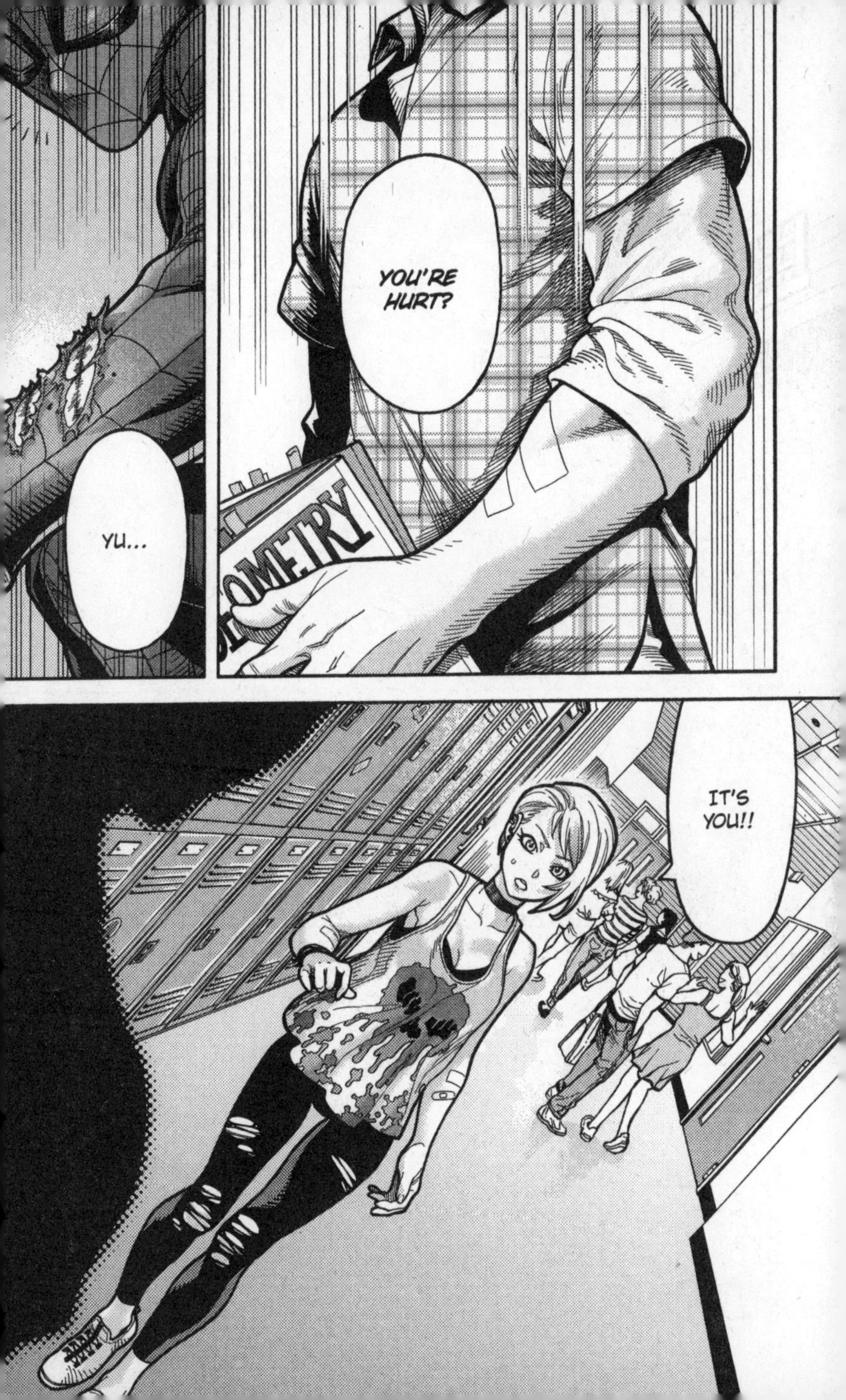
YOU'RE HURT?
YU...
IT'S YOU!!

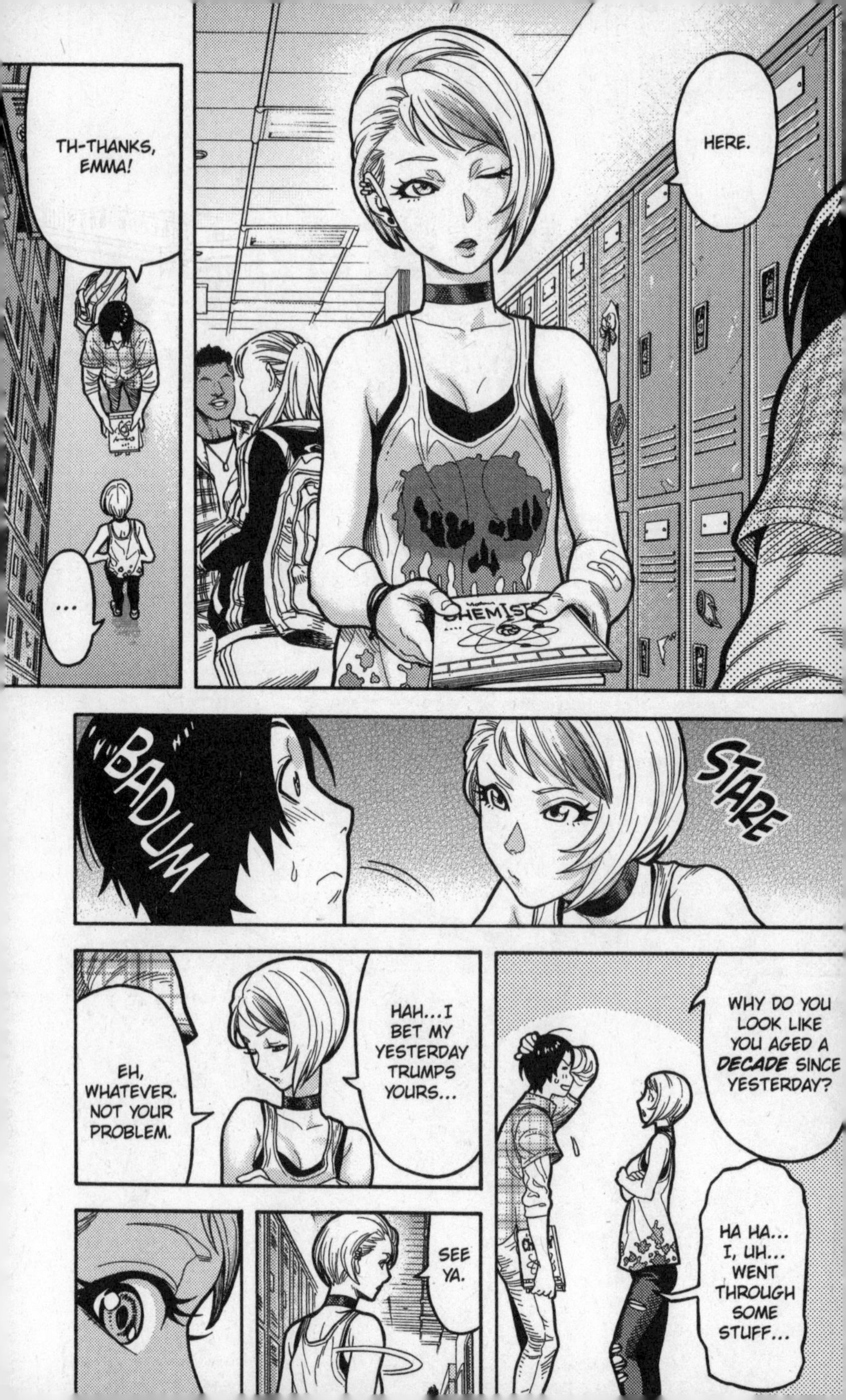
HERE.
TH-THANKS, EMMA!
...
STARE
BADUM
WHY DO YOU LOOK LIKE YOU AGED A DECADE SINCE YESTERDAY?
HA HA... I, UH... WENT THROUGH SOME STUFF...
HAH...I BET MY YESTERDAY TRUMPS YOURS...
EH, WHATEVER. NOT YOUR PROBLEM.
SEE YA.

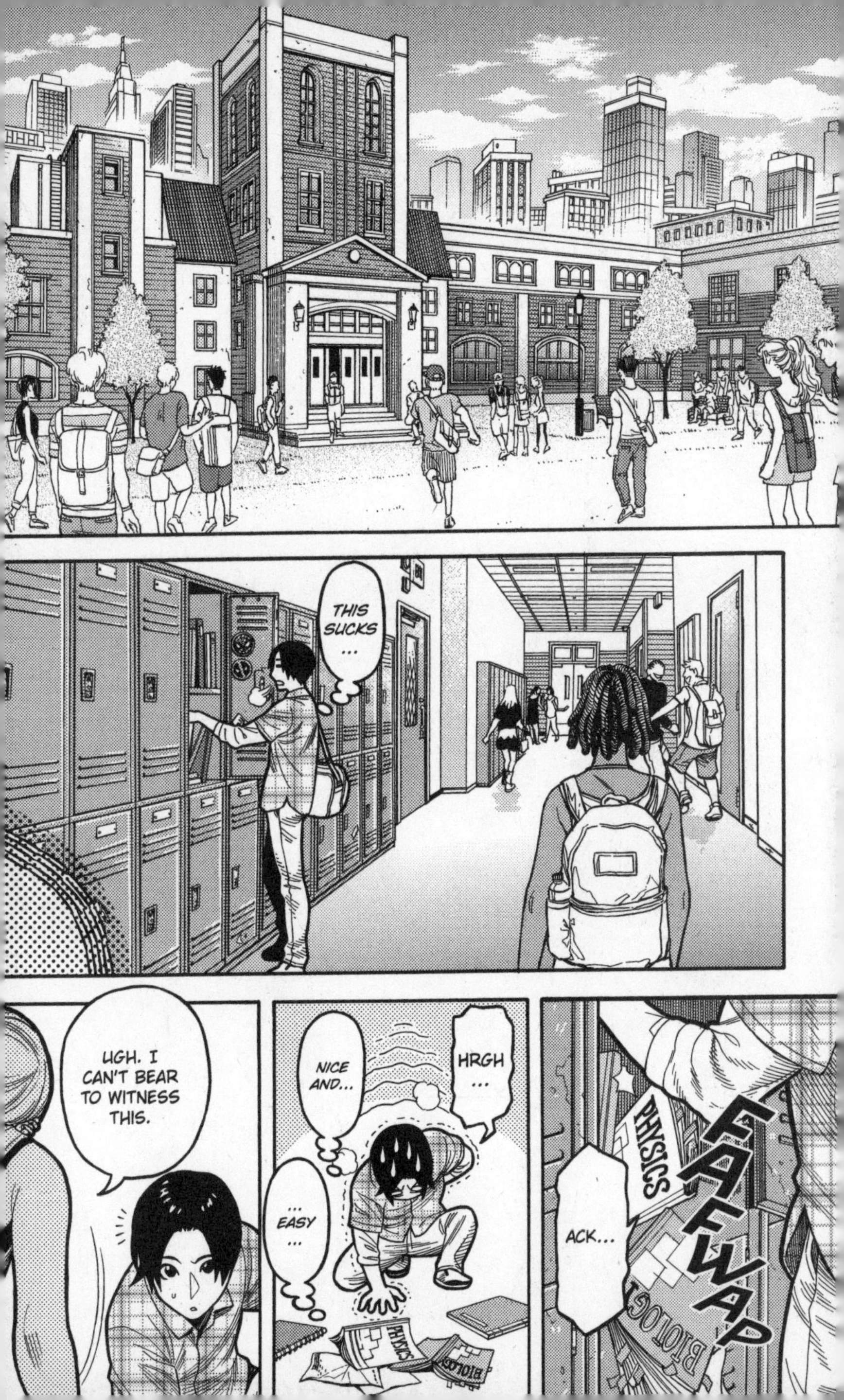
THIS SUCKS ...
ACK...
FAFWAP
PHYSICS
HRGH ...
NICE AND...
... EASY ...
PHYSICS
UGH. I CAN'T BEAR TO WITNESS THIS.

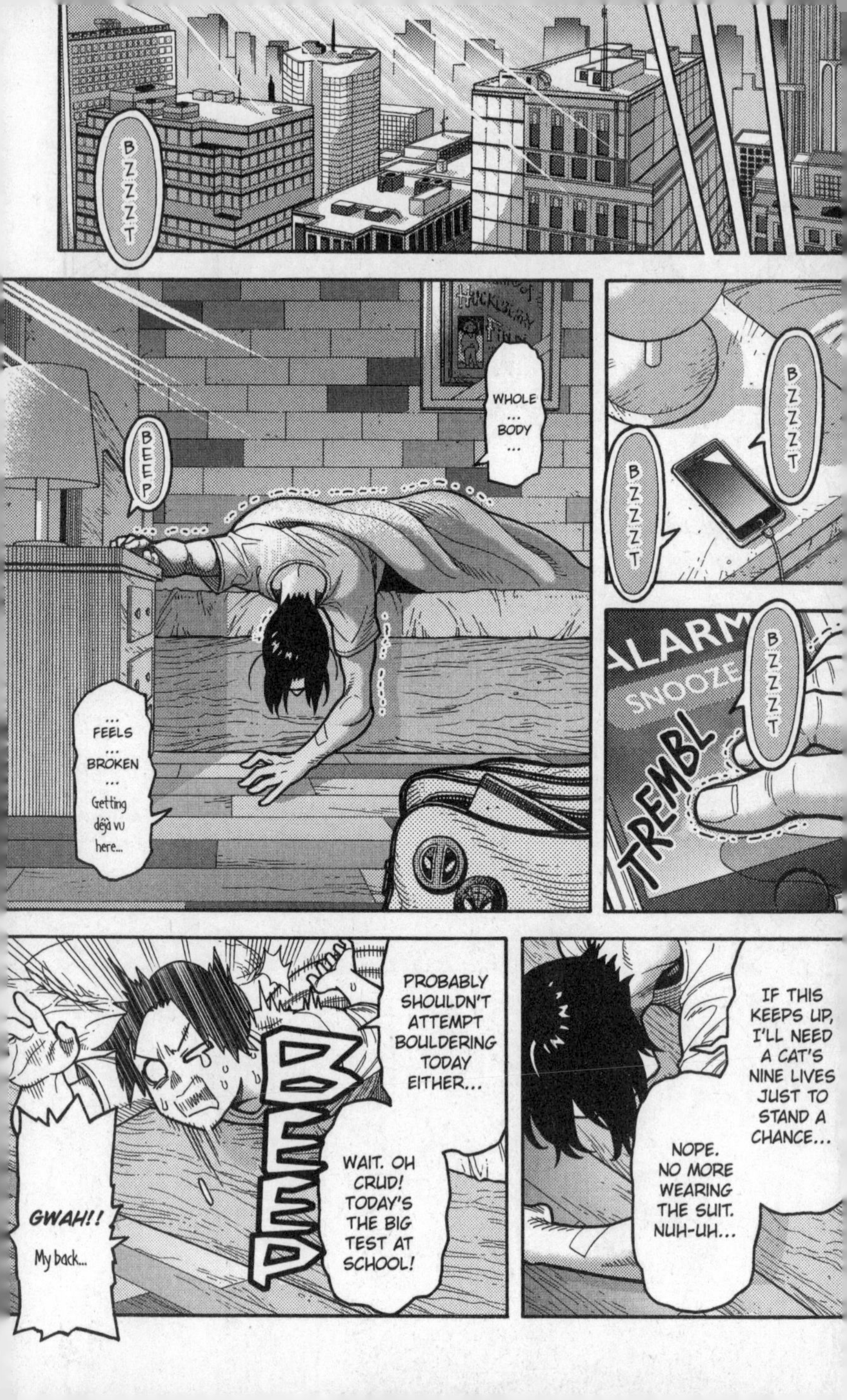
BZZZT
BZZZT
BZZZT
ALARM
SNOOZE
BZZZT
TREMBL
WHOLE... BODY...
BEEP
... FEELS ... BROKEN ...
Getting déjà vu here...
IF THIS KEEPS UP, I'LL NEED A CAT'S NINE LIVES JUST TO STAND A CHANCE...
NOPE. NO MORE WEARING THE SUIT. NUH-UH...
PROBABLY SHOULDN'T ATTEMPT BOULDERING TODAY EITHER...
BEEP
WAIT. OH CRUD! TODAY'S THE BIG TEST AT SCHOOL!
GWAH!!
My back...

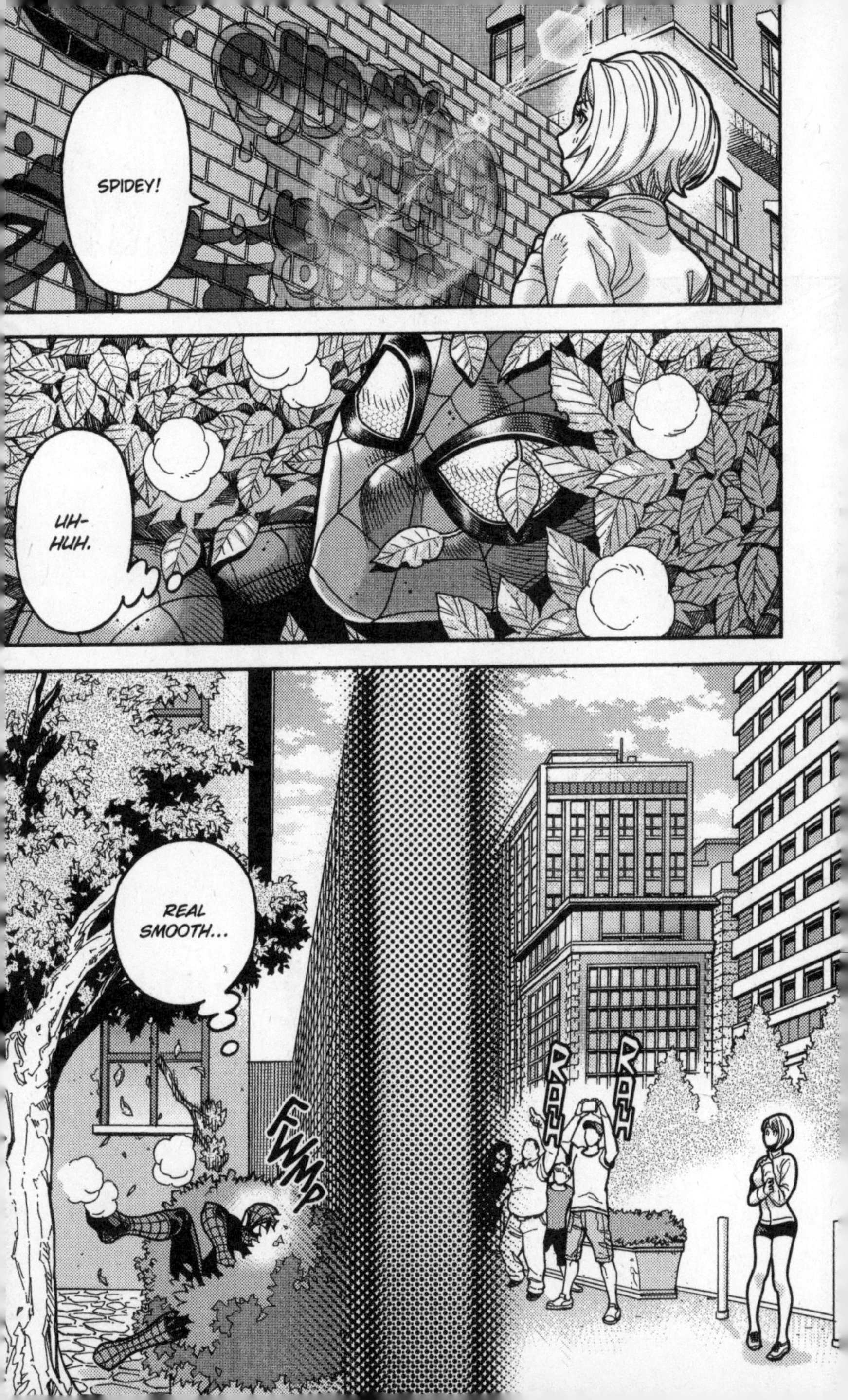
SPIDEY!
UH-HUH.
REAL SMOOTH...
RAAH
RAAH
FWMP

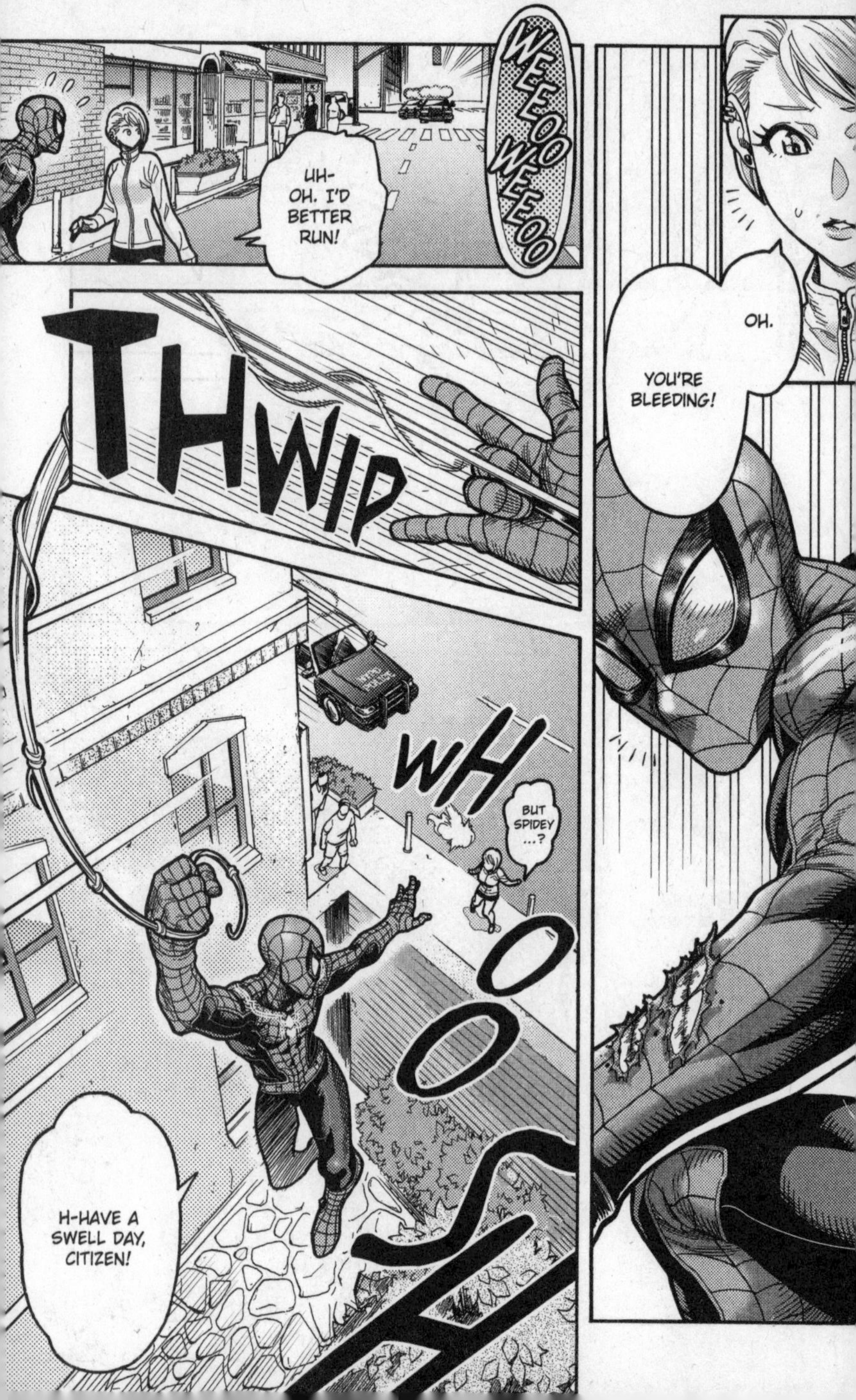
OH.
YOU'RE BLEEDING!
WEEOOWEEOO
UH-OH. I'D BETTER RUN!
THWIP
WHOOSH
BUT SPIDEY ...?
H-HAVE A SWELL DAY, CITIZEN!

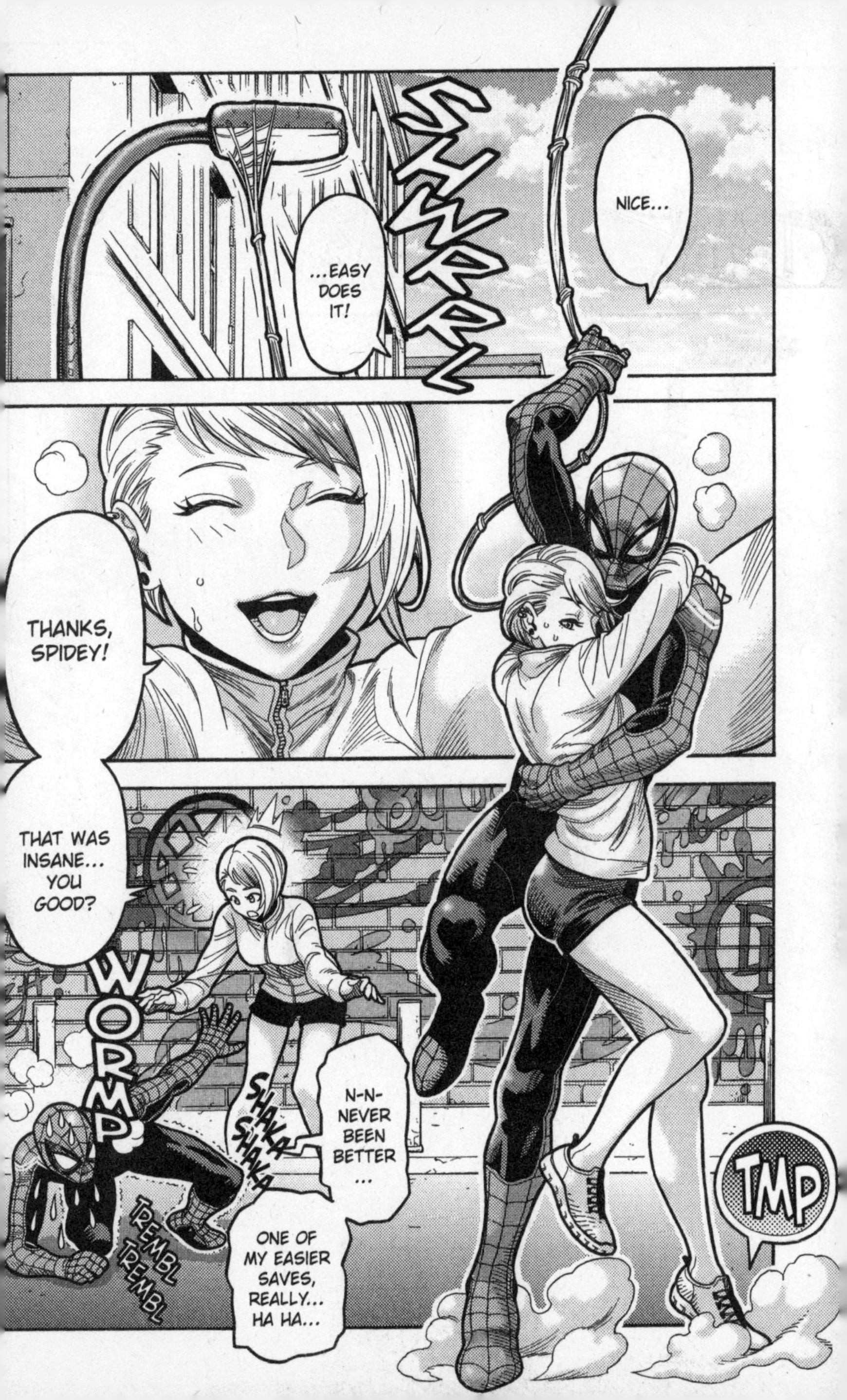
SHWAPL
NICE...
...EASY DOES IT!
THANKS, SPIDEY!
TMP
THAT WAS INSANE... YOU GOOD?
WORMP
N-N-NEVER BEEN BETTER...
SHAKA SHAKA
ONE OF MY EASIER SAVES, REALLY... HA HA...
TREMBL TREMBL

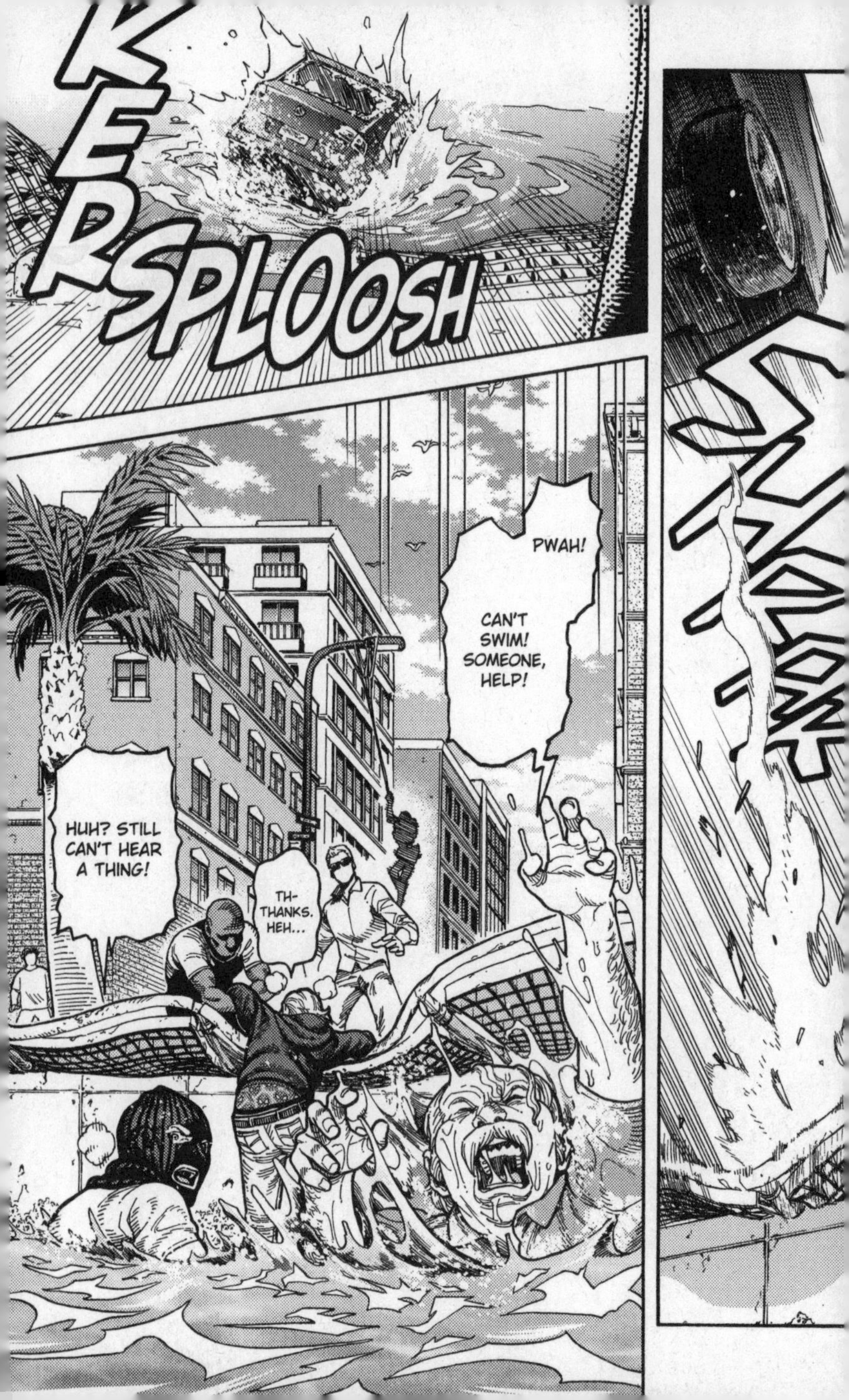
KERSPLOOSH
PWAH!
CAN'T SWIM! SOMEONE, HELP!
TH- THANKS, HEH...
HUH? STILL CAN'T HEAR A THING!

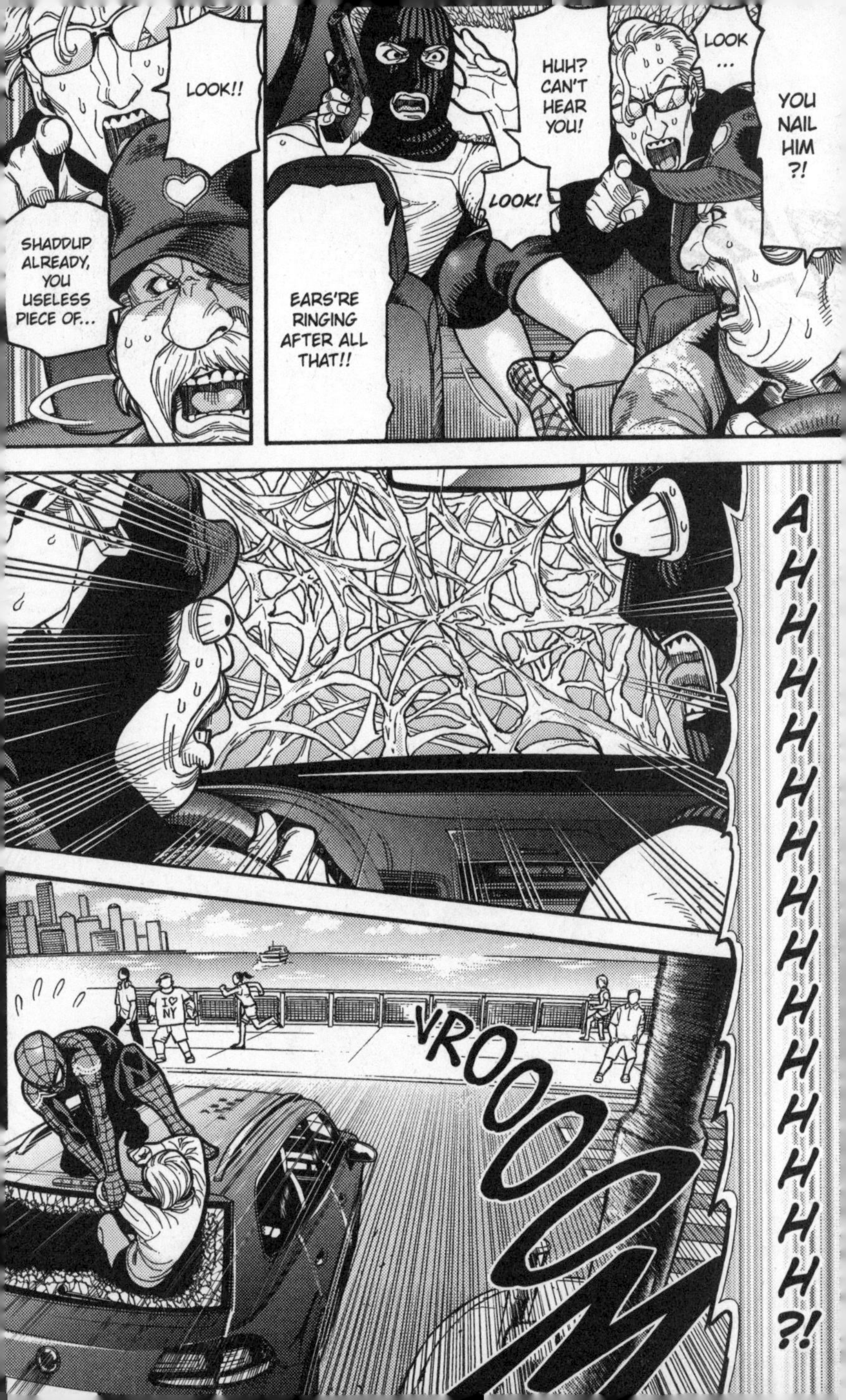
LOOK ...
YOU NAIL HIM?!
HUH? CAN'T HEAR YOU!
LOOK!
EARS'RE RINGING AFTER ALL THAT!!
LOOK!!
SHADDUP ALREADY, YOU USELESS PIECE OF...
AHHHHHHHHHHHHHHHH?!
VROOOOM

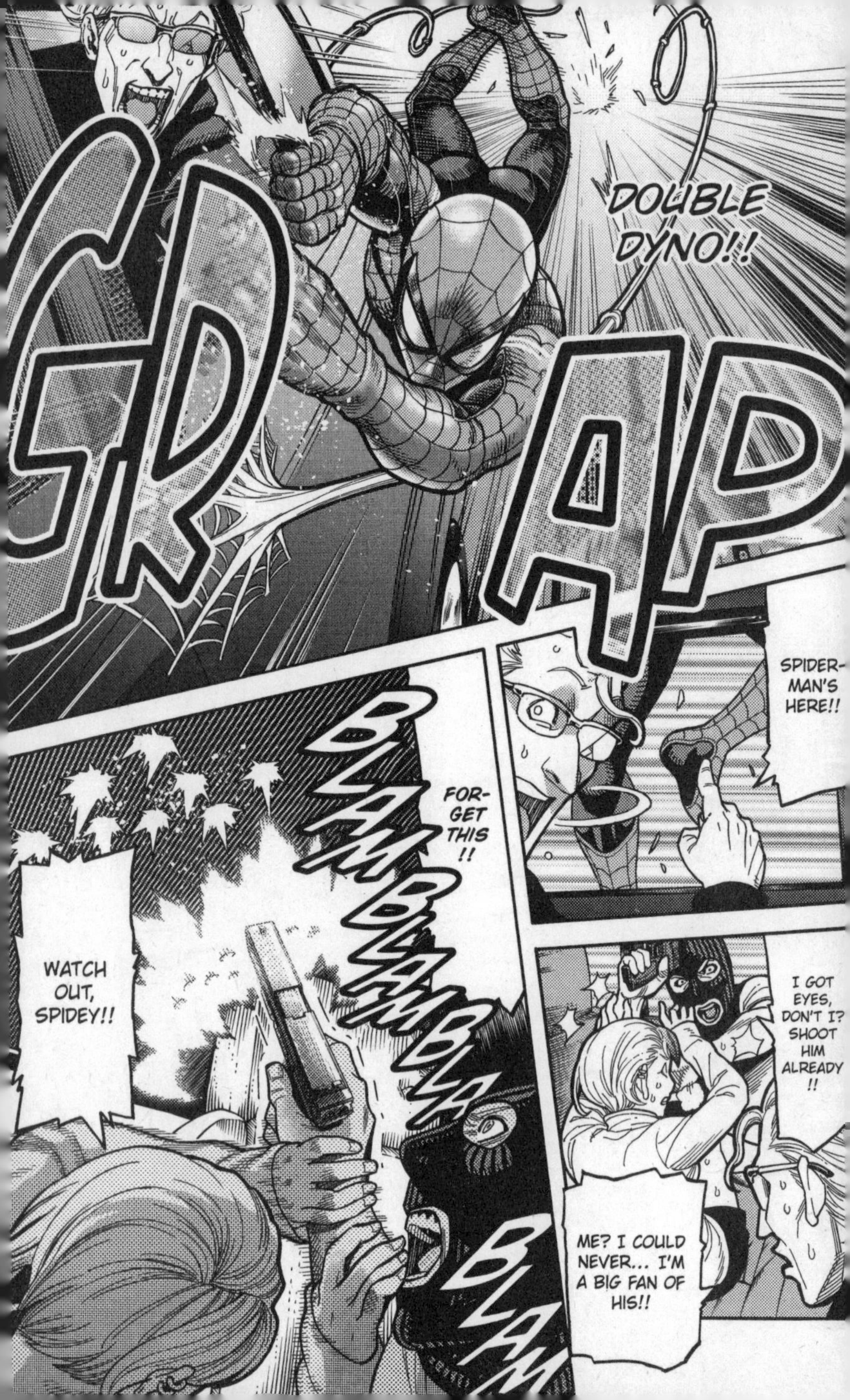
DOUBLE DYNO!!
SPIDER-MAN'S HERE!!
I GOT EYES, DON'T I? SHOOT HIM ALREADY!!
ME? I COULD NEVER... I'M A BIG FAN OF HIS!!
FOR-GET THIS!!
BLAMBLAMBLAM
WATCH OUT, SPIDEY!!
BLAM

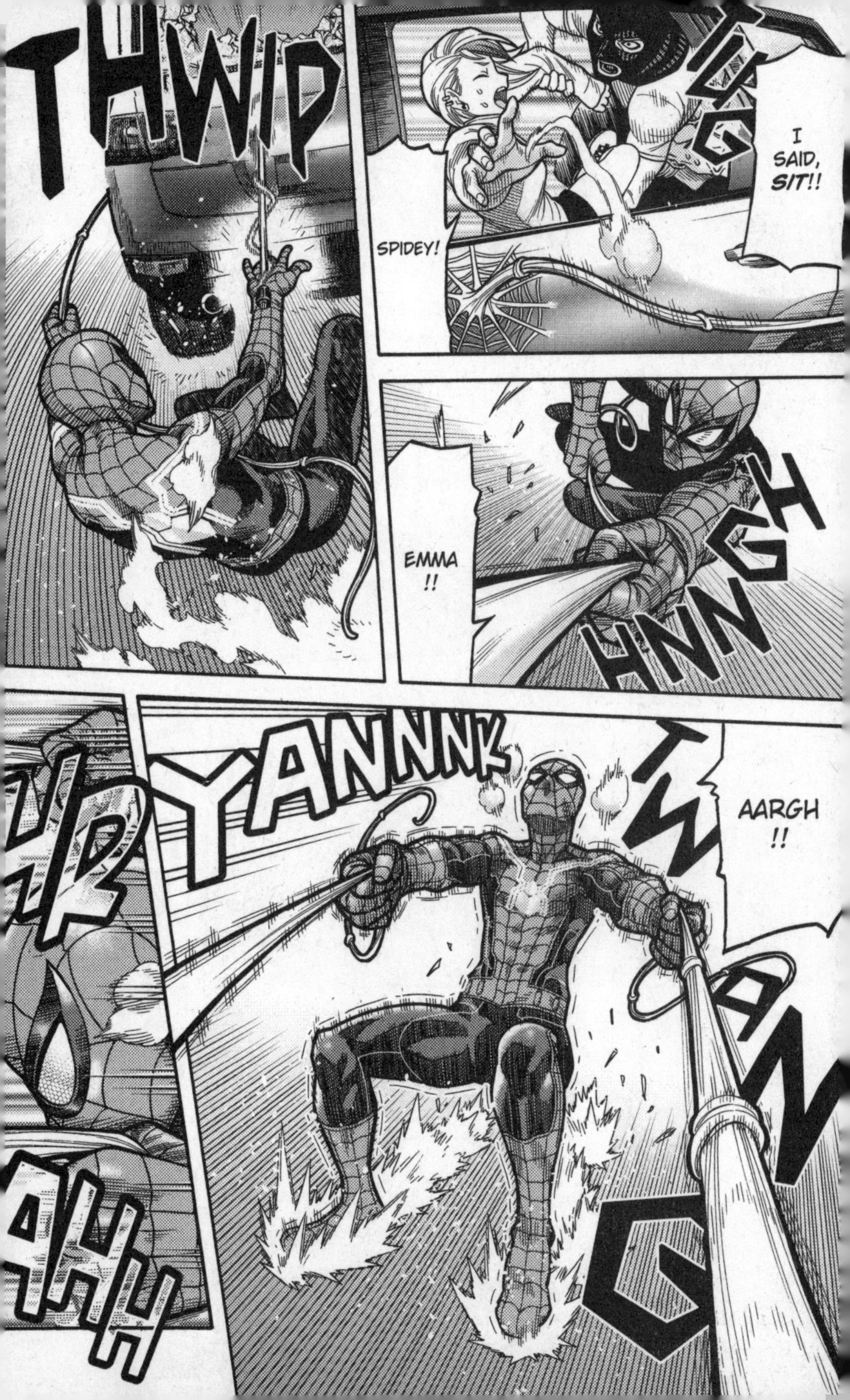
I SAID, SIT!!
SPIDEY!
EMMA !!
HNNGH
THWIP
TWANG
AARGH !!
YANNNK

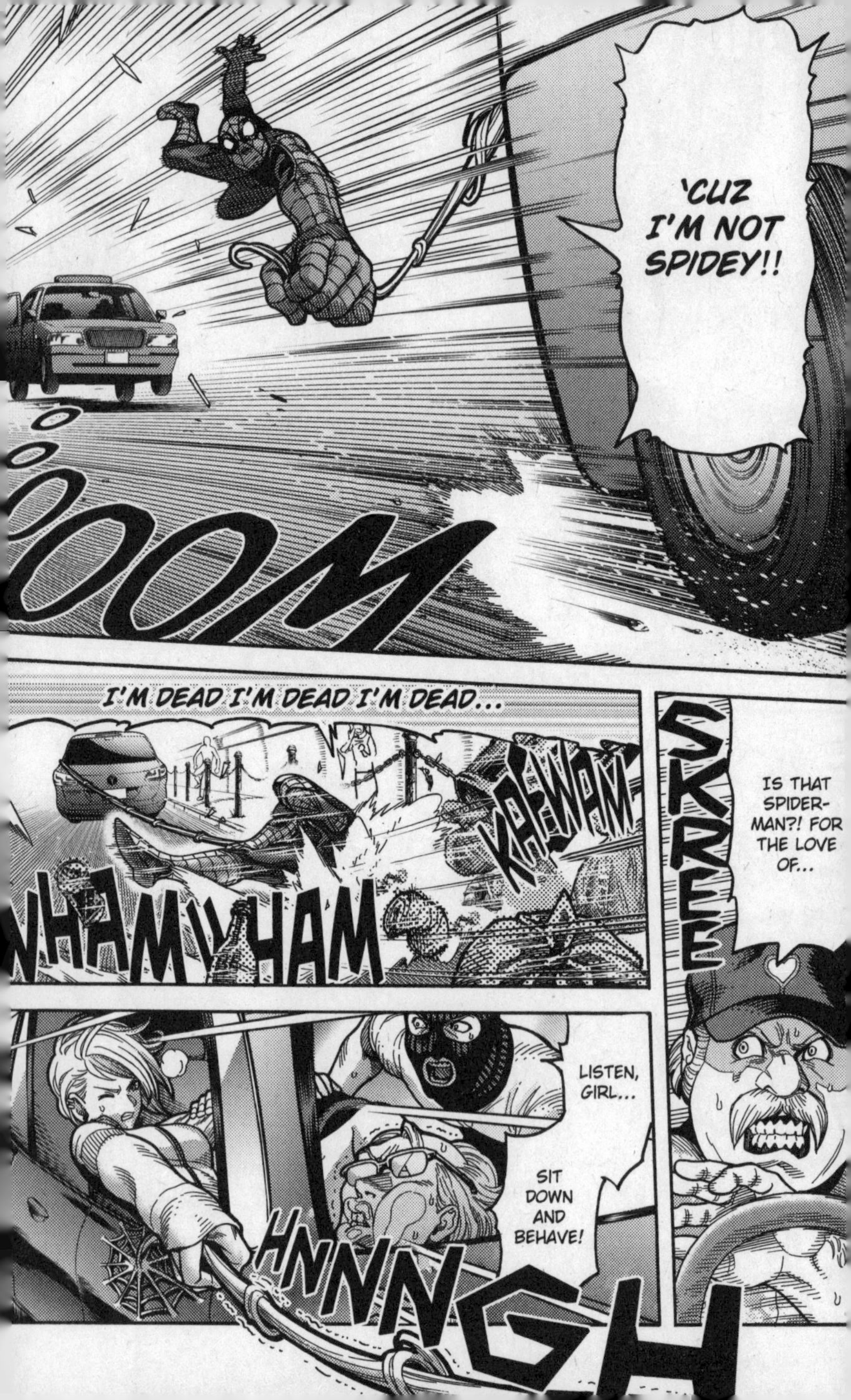
'CUZ I'M NOT SPIDEY!!
VOOOM
SKREE
IS THAT SPIDER-MAN?! FOR THE LOVE OF...
I'M DEAD I'M DEAD I'M DEAD...
KRAWAM
LISTEN, GIRL...
SIT DOWN AND BEHAVE!
HNNNNGH

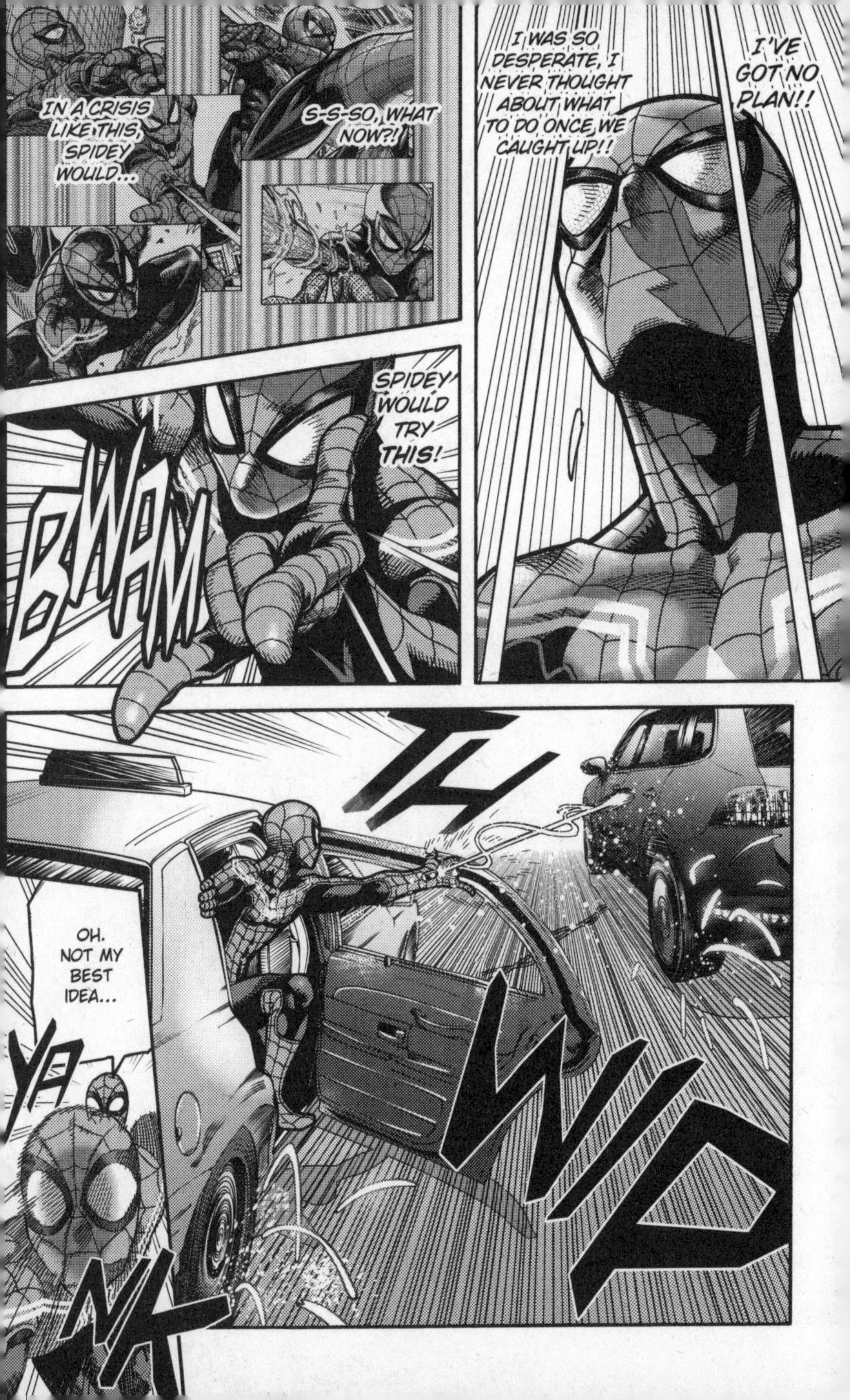

I'VE GOT NO PLAN!!
I WAS SO DESPERATE, I NEVER THOUGHT ABOUT WHAT TO DO ONCE WE CAUGHT UP!!
S-S-SO, WHAT NOW?!
IN A CRISIS LIKE THIS, SPIDEY WOULD...
SPIDEY WOULD TRY THIS!
BWAM
THWIP
OH. NOT MY BEST IDEA...
YANK

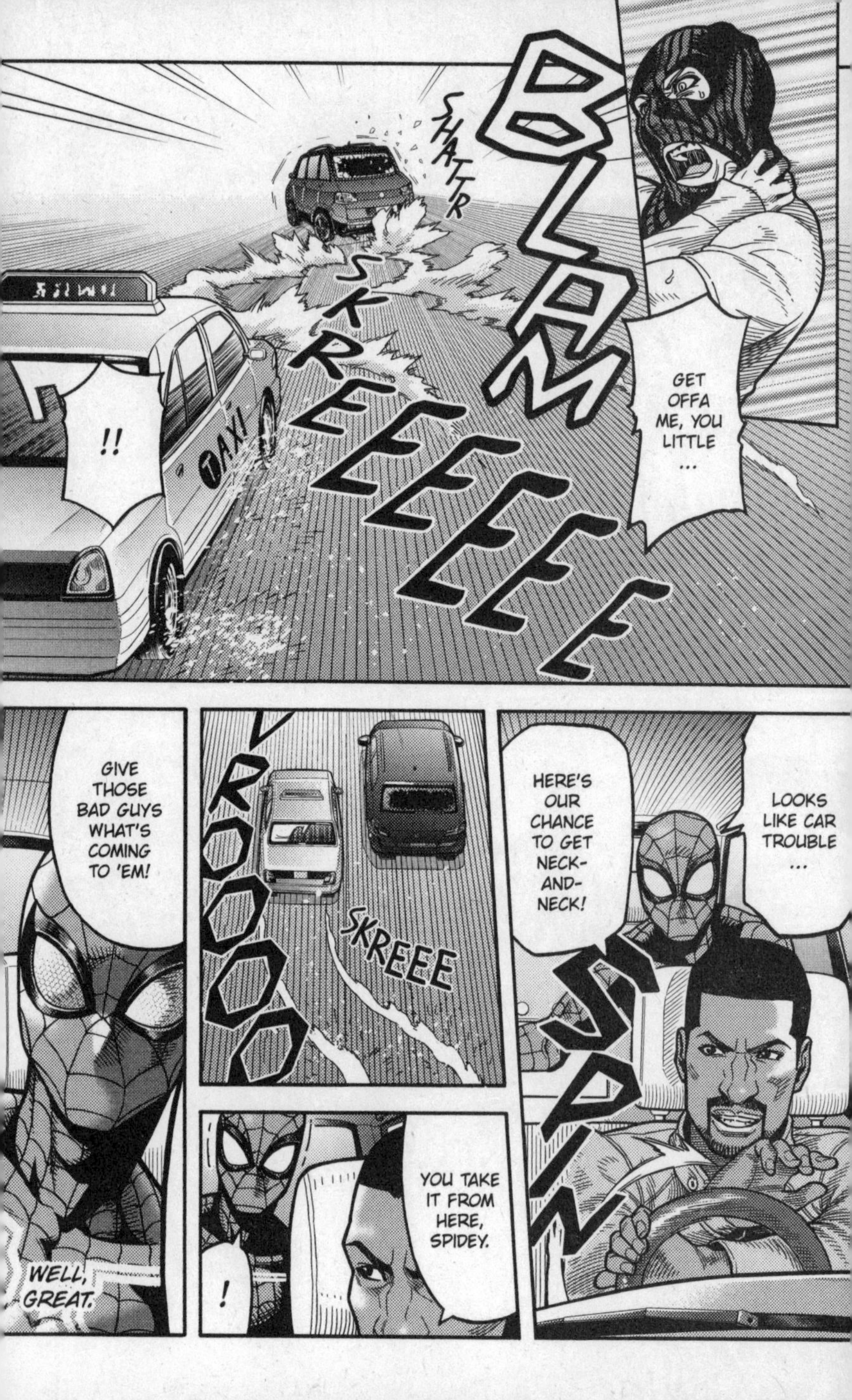
BLAM
GET OFFA ME, YOU LITTLE ...
SHATTR
SKREEEEEE
!!
LOOKS LIKE CAR TROUBLE ...
HERE'S OUR CHANCE TO GET NECK-AND-NECK!
SPIN
VROOOOO
SKREEE
YOU TAKE IT FROM HERE, SPIDEY.
!
GIVE THOSE BAD GUYS WHAT'S COMING TO 'EM!
WELL, GREAT.

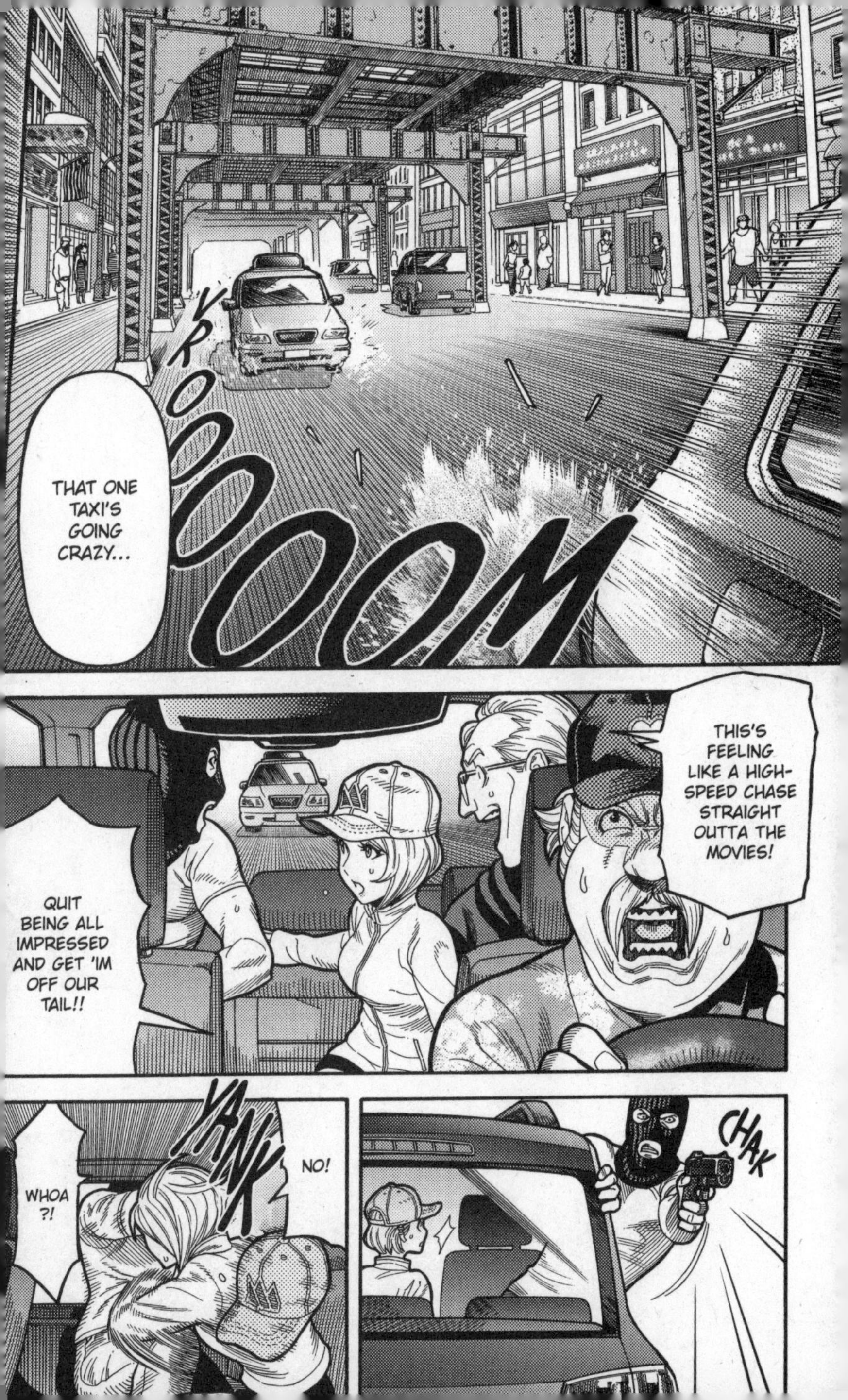
VROOOOOOM
THAT ONE TAXI'S GOING CRAZY...
THIS'S FEELING LIKE A HIGH-SPEED CHASE STRAIGHT OUTTA THE MOVIES!
QUIT BEING ALL IMPRESSED AND GET 'IM OFF OUR TAIL!!
CHAK
YANK
NO!
WHOA?!

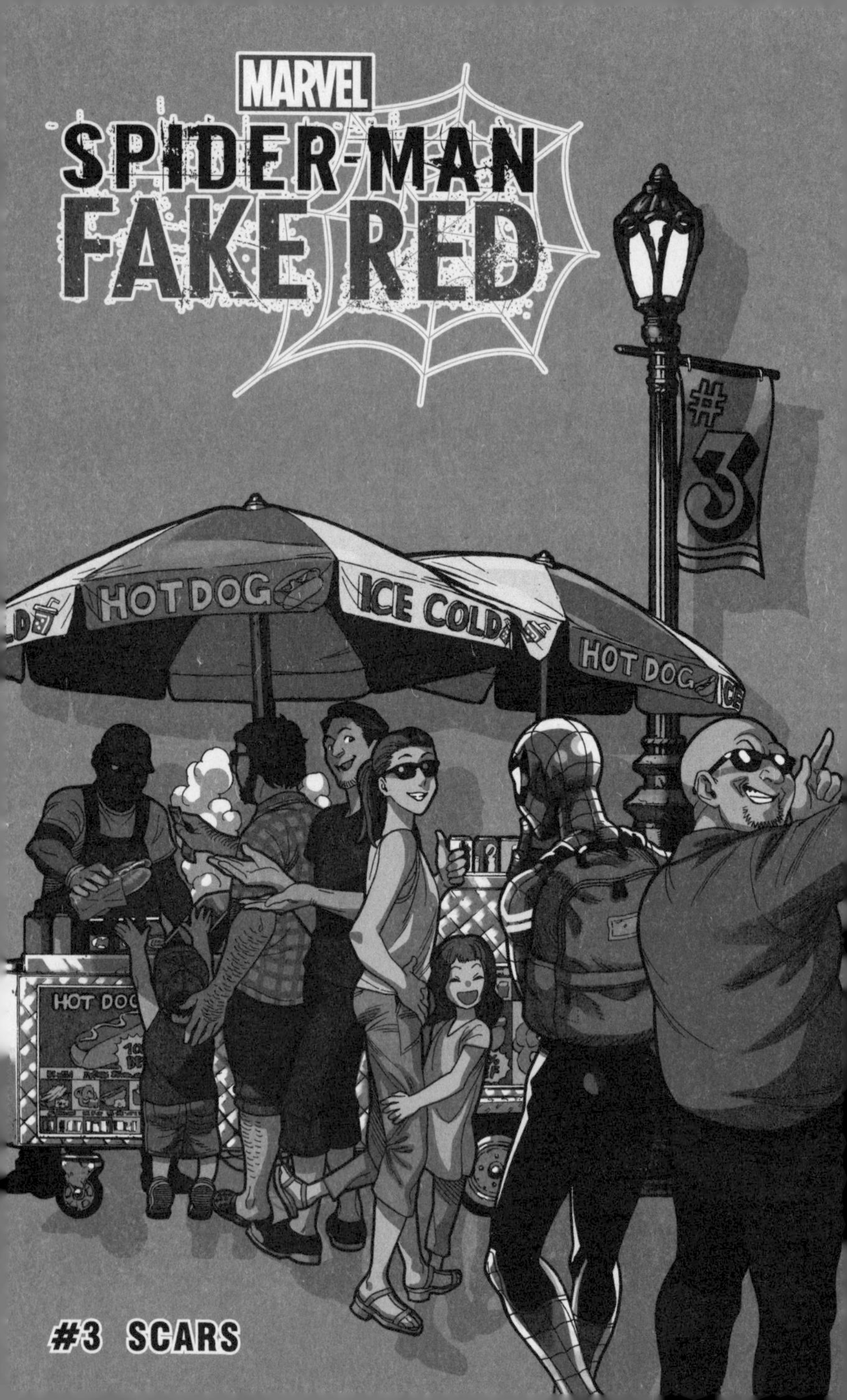
MARVEL
SPIDER-MAN
FAKE RED
#3
HOT DOG
ICE COLD
HOT DOG
HOT DOG
#3 SCARS

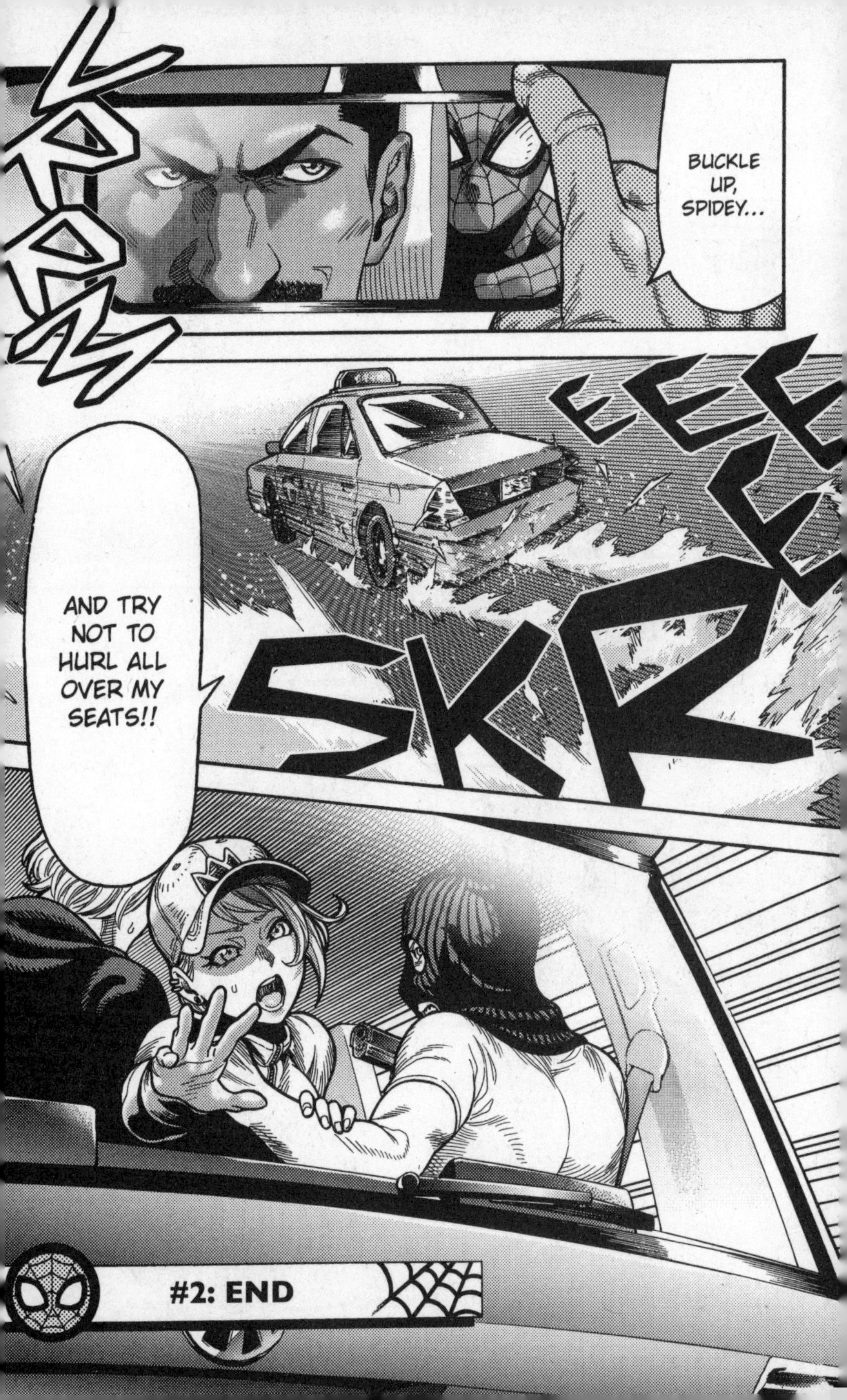
BUCKLE UP, SPIDEY...
AND TRY NOT TO HURL ALL OVER MY SEATS!!
#2: END

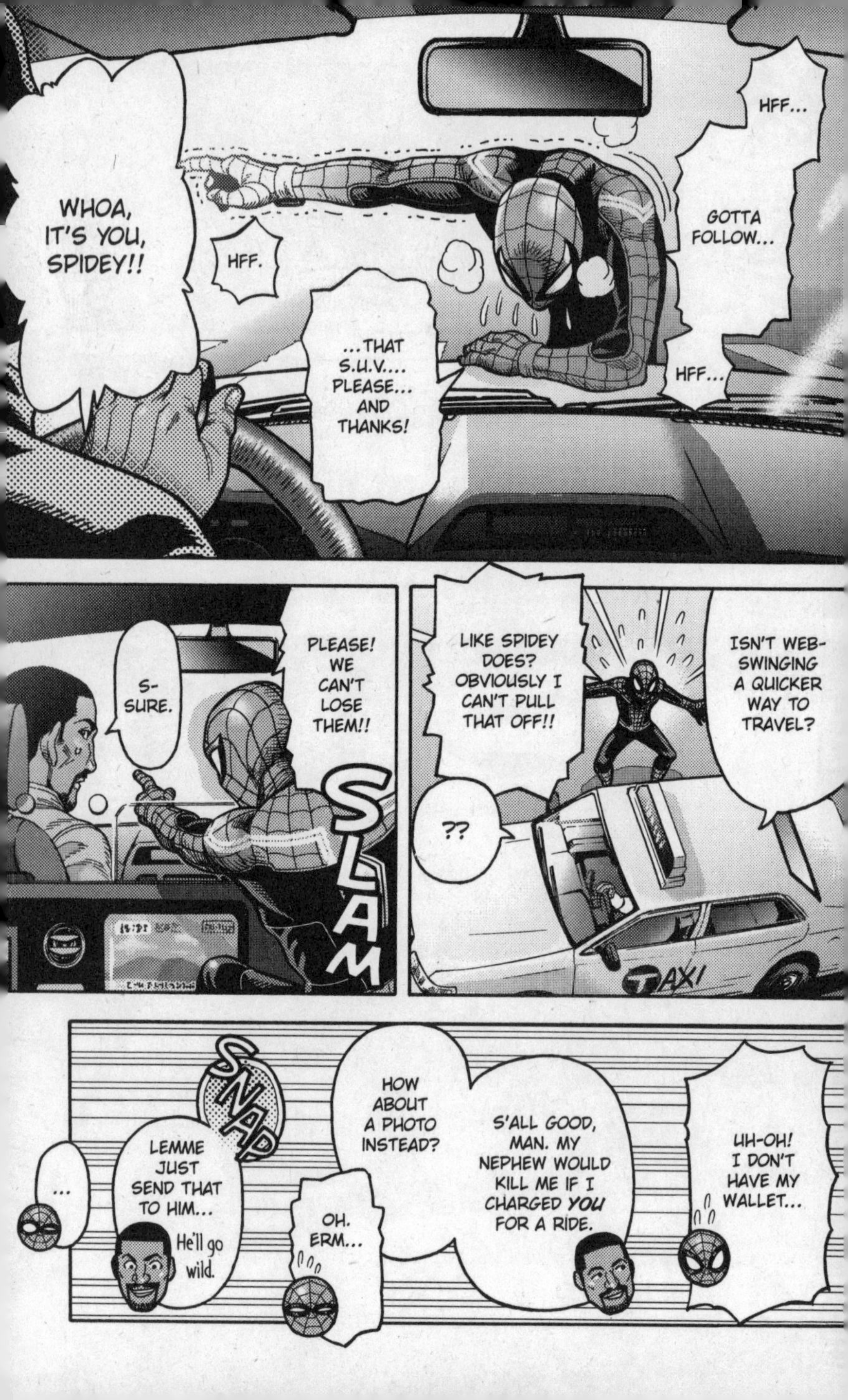
HFF...
GOTTA FOLLOW...
HFF...
WHOA, IT'S YOU, SPIDEY!!
HFF.
...THAT S.U.V.... PLEASE... AND THANKS!
ISN'T WEB-SWINGING A QUICKER WAY TO TRAVEL?
LIKE SPIDEY DOES? OBVIOUSLY I CAN'T PULL THAT OFF!!
??
TAXI
PLEASE! WE CAN'T LOSE THEM!!
S-SURE.
SLAM
UH-OH! I DON'T HAVE MY WALLET...
S'ALL GOOD, MAN. MY NEPHEW WOULD KILL ME IF I CHARGED *YOU* FOR A RIDE.
HOW ABOUT A PHOTO INSTEAD?
OH. ERM...
SNAP
LEMME JUST SEND THAT TO HIM...
He'll go wild.
...

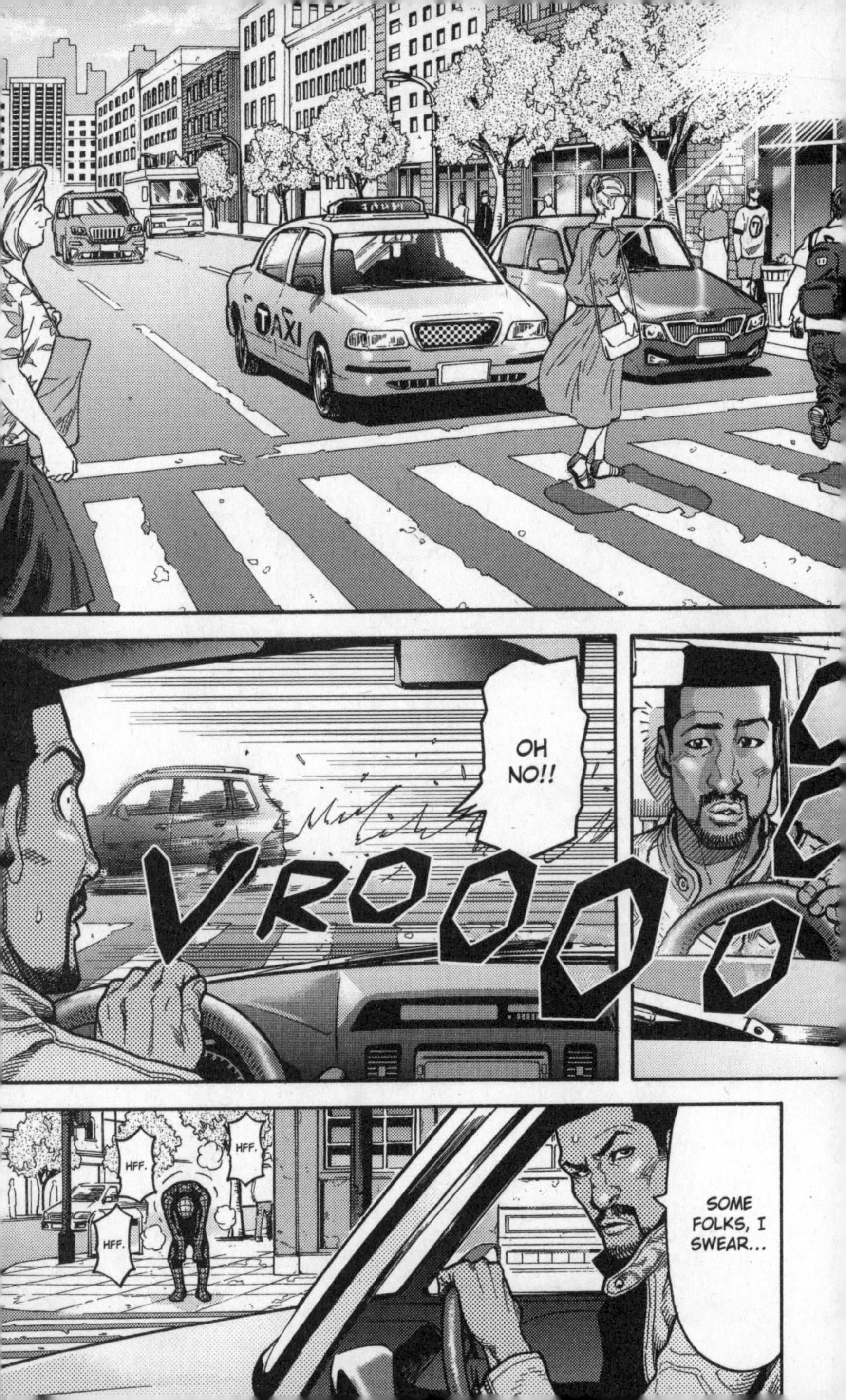
TAXI
VROOOOO
OH NO!!
SOME FOLKS, I SWEAR...
HFF.
HFF.
HFF.

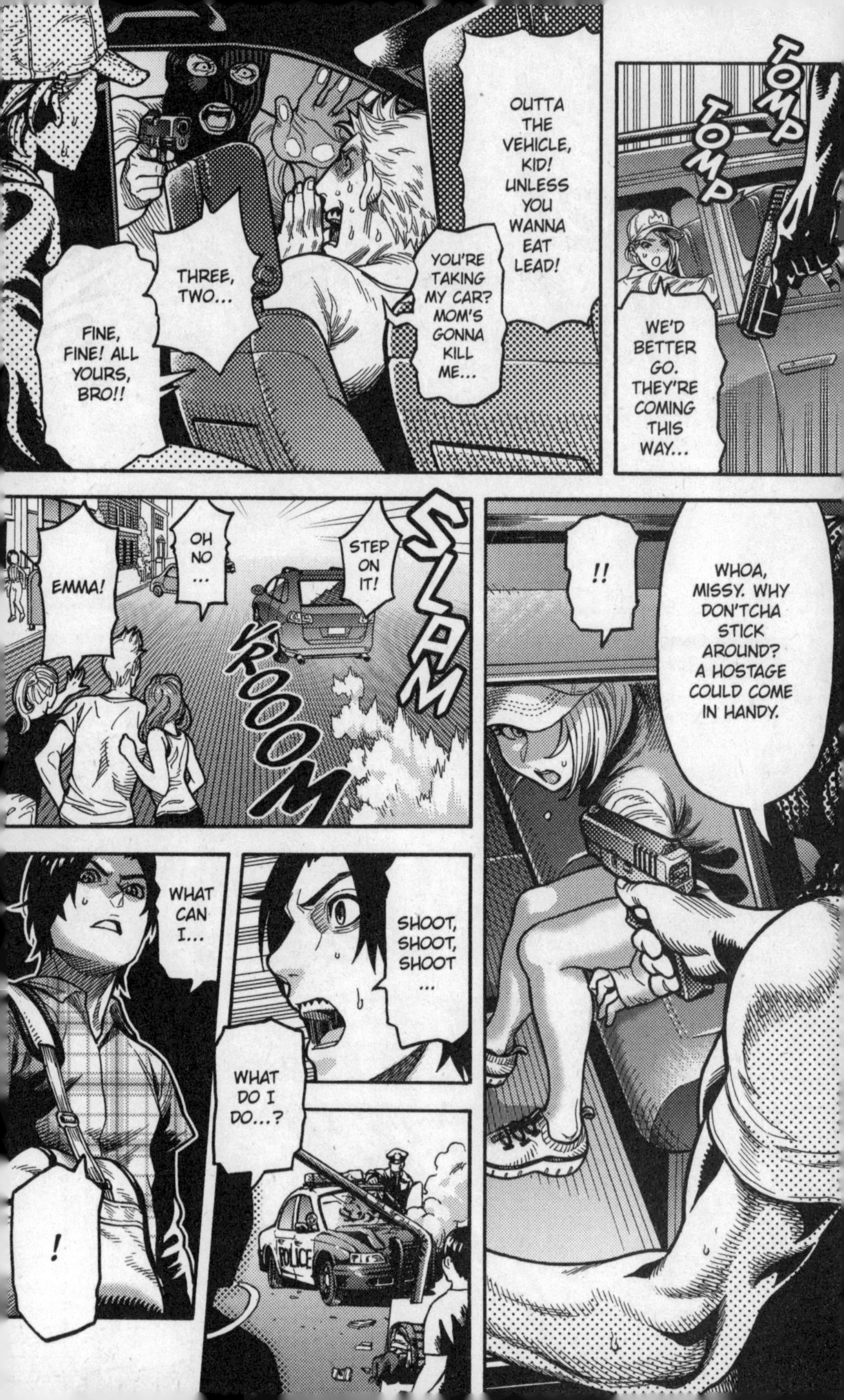
TOMP
TOMP
TOMP
WE'D BETTER GO. THEY'RE COMING THIS WAY...
OUTTA THE VEHICLE, KID! UNLESS YOU WANNA EAT LEAD!
YOU'RE TAKING MY CAR? MOM'S GONNA KILL ME...
THREE, TWO...
FINE, FINE! ALL YOURS, BRO!!
!!
WHOA, MISSY. WHY DON'TCHA STICK AROUND? A HOSTAGE COULD COME IN HANDY.
STEP ON IT!
SLAM
OH NO ...
EMMA!
VROOOM
SHOOT, SHOOT, SHOOT ...
WHAT DO I DO...?
POLICE
WHAT CAN I...
!

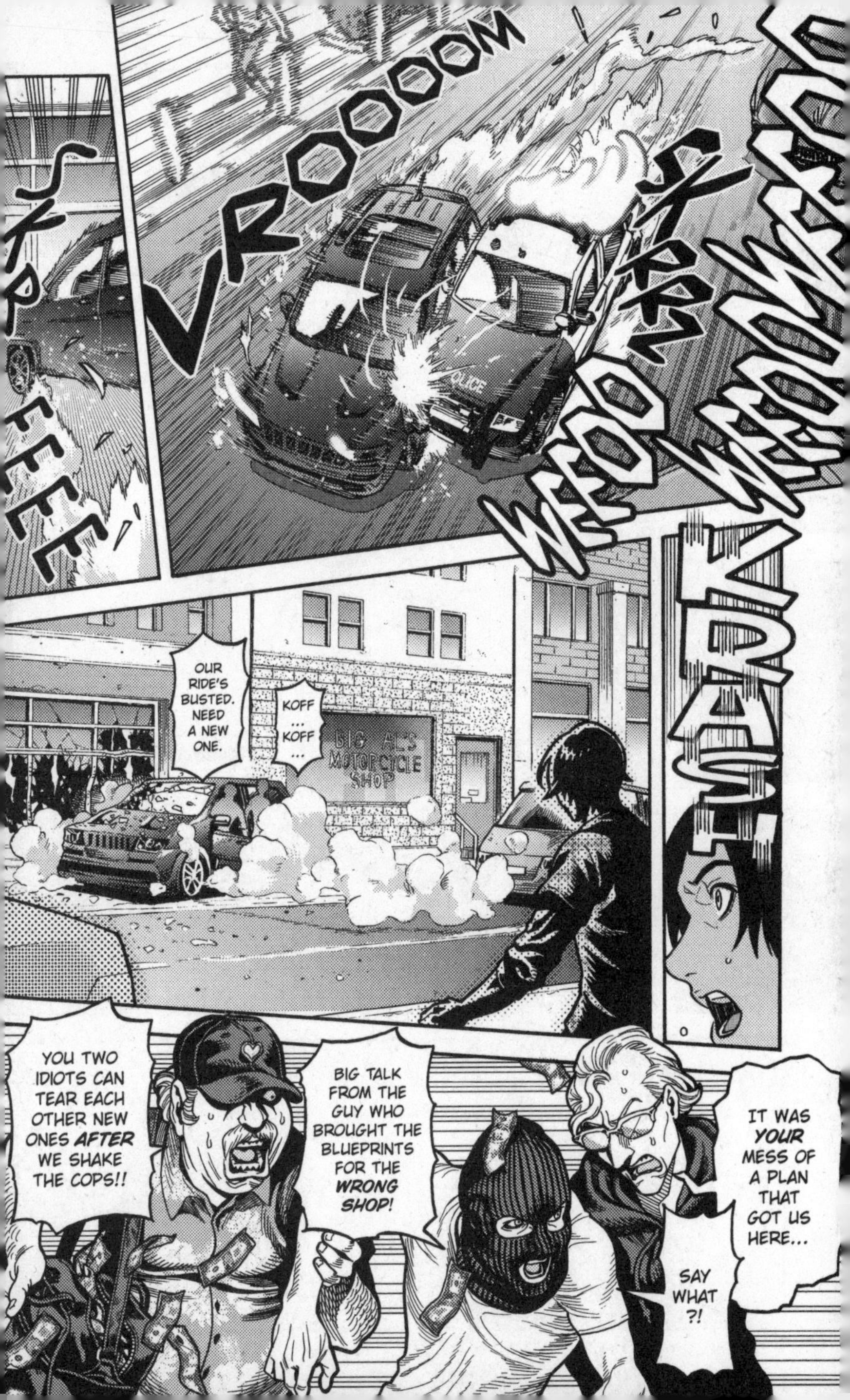
VROOOOOM
SKRK
WEEOO WEEOO WEEOO
SKREEEE
OUR RIDE'S BUSTED. NEED A NEW ONE.
KOFF ... KOFF ...
BIG AL'S MOTORCYCLE SHOP
IT WAS *YOUR* MESS OF A PLAN THAT GOT US HERE...
SAY WHAT ?!
BIG TALK FROM THE GUY WHO BROUGHT THE BLUEPRINTS FOR THE *WRONG* SHOP!
YOU TWO IDIOTS CAN TEAR EACH OTHER NEW ONES *AFTER* WE SHAKE THE COPS!!

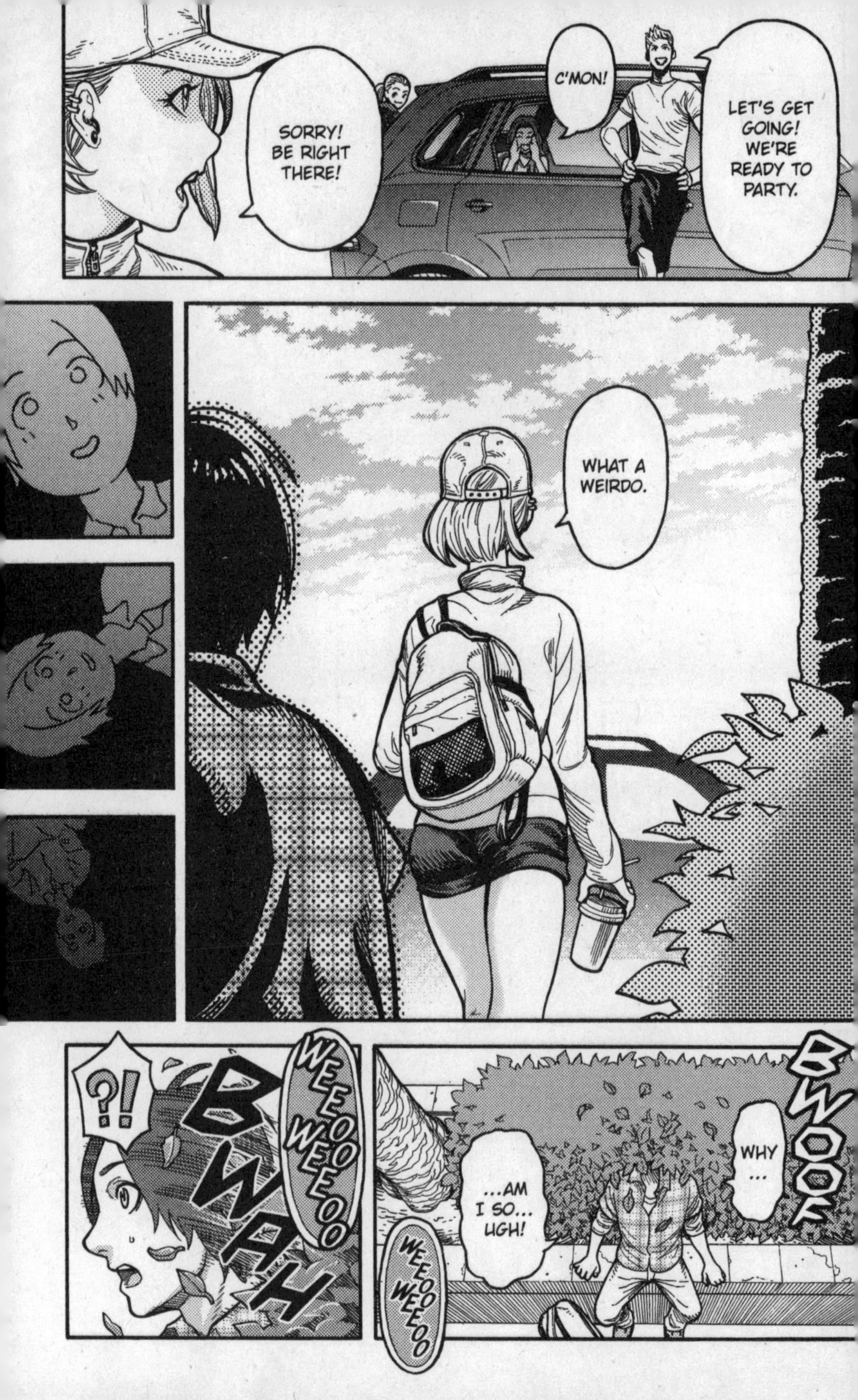
LET'S GET GOING! WE'RE READY TO PARTY.
C'MON!
SORRY! BE RIGHT THERE!
WHAT A WEIRDO.
BWOOF
WHY...
...AM I SO... UGH!
WEEOO WEEOO
WEEOOWEEOO
BWAH
?!!

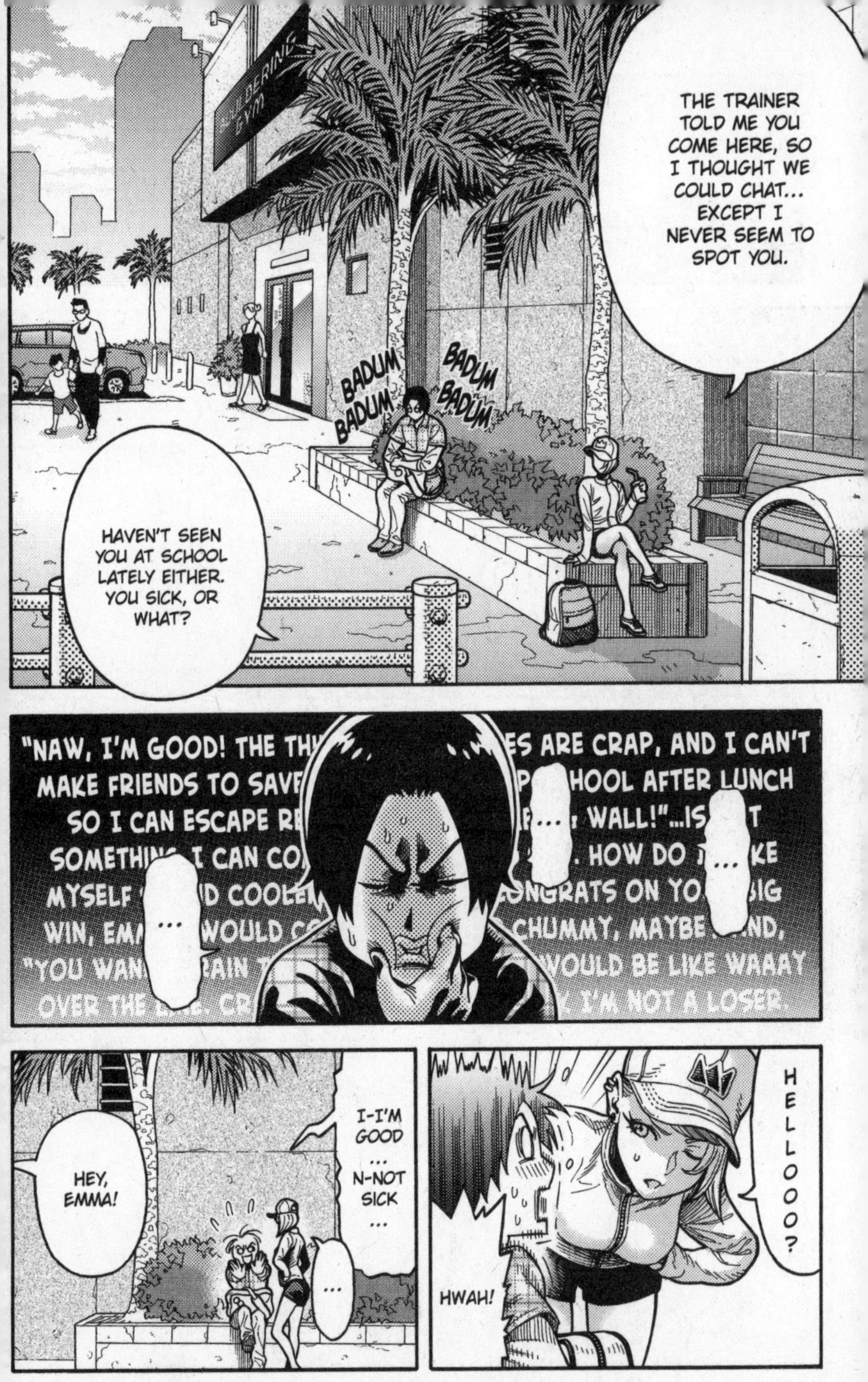
THE TRAINER TOLD ME YOU COME HERE, SO I THOUGHT WE COULD CHAT... EXCEPT I NEVER SEEM TO SPOT YOU.
BADUM BADUM
BADUM BADUM
HAVEN'T SEEN YOU AT SCHOOL LATELY EITHER. YOU SICK, OR WHAT?
"NAW, I'M GOOD! THE TH ES ARE CRAP, AND I CAN'T
MAKE FRIENDS TO SAVE HOOL AFTER LUNCH
SO I CAN ESCAPE RE WALL!"...IS T
SOMETHIN I CAN CO . HOW DO KE
MYSELF D COOLE ONGRATS ON YO BIG
WIN, EMM WOULD C CHUMMY, MAYBE ND,
"YOU WAN RAIN T WOULD BE LIKE WAAAY
OVER THE CR I'M NOT A LOSER.
...
...
...
HELLOOOO?
HWAH!
I-I'M GOOD... N-NOT SICK...
HEY, EMMA!
...

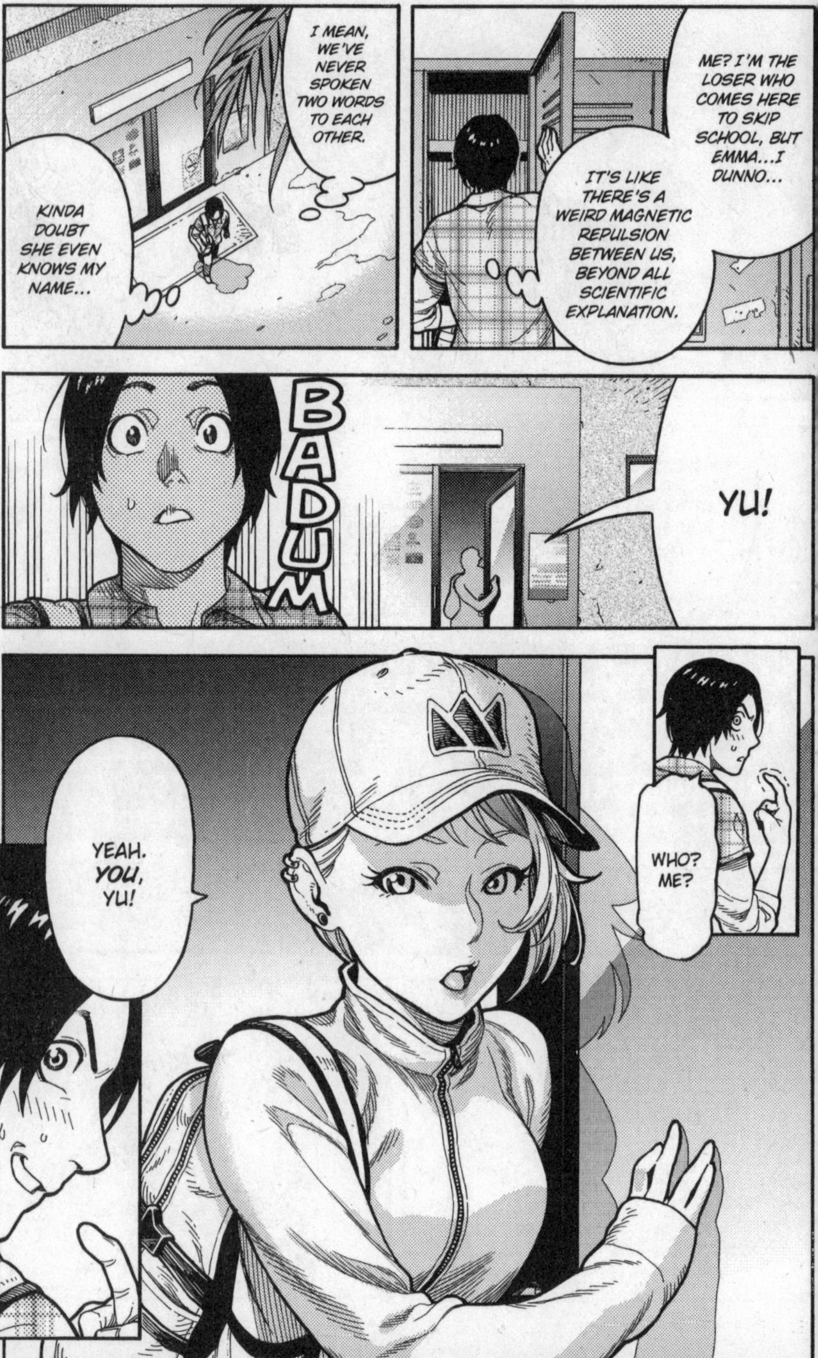
ME? I'M THE LOSER WHO COMES HERE TO SKIP SCHOOL, BUT EMMA...I DUNNO...
IT'S LIKE THERE'S A WEIRD MAGNETIC REPULSION BETWEEN US, BEYOND ALL SCIENTIFIC EXPLANATION.
I MEAN, WE'VE NEVER SPOKEN TWO WORDS TO EACH OTHER.
KINDA DOUBT SHE EVEN KNOWS MY NAME...
YU!
BADUM
WHO? ME?
YEAH. ***YOU***, YU!

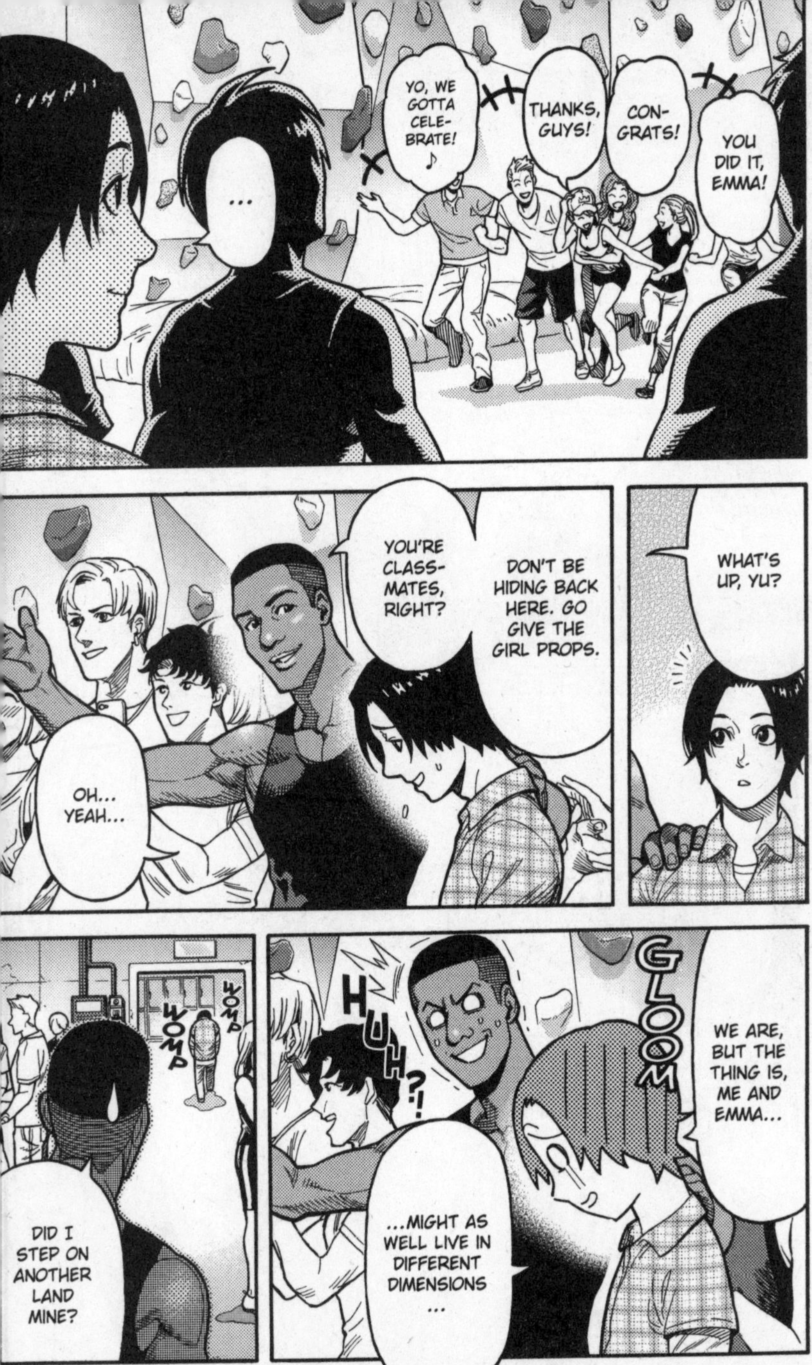
YOU DID IT, EMMA!
CON-GRATS!
THANKS, GUYS!
YO, WE GOTTA CELE-BRATE! ♪
...
WHAT'S UP, YU?
DON'T BE HIDING BACK HERE. GO GIVE THE GIRL PROPS.
YOU'RE CLASS-MATES, RIGHT?
OH... YEAH...
GLOOM
WE ARE, BUT THE THING IS, ME AND EMMA...
HUH?!
...MIGHT AS WELL LIVE IN DIFFERENT DIMENSIONS ...
WOMP
WOMP
WOMP
DID I STEP ON ANOTHER LAND MINE?

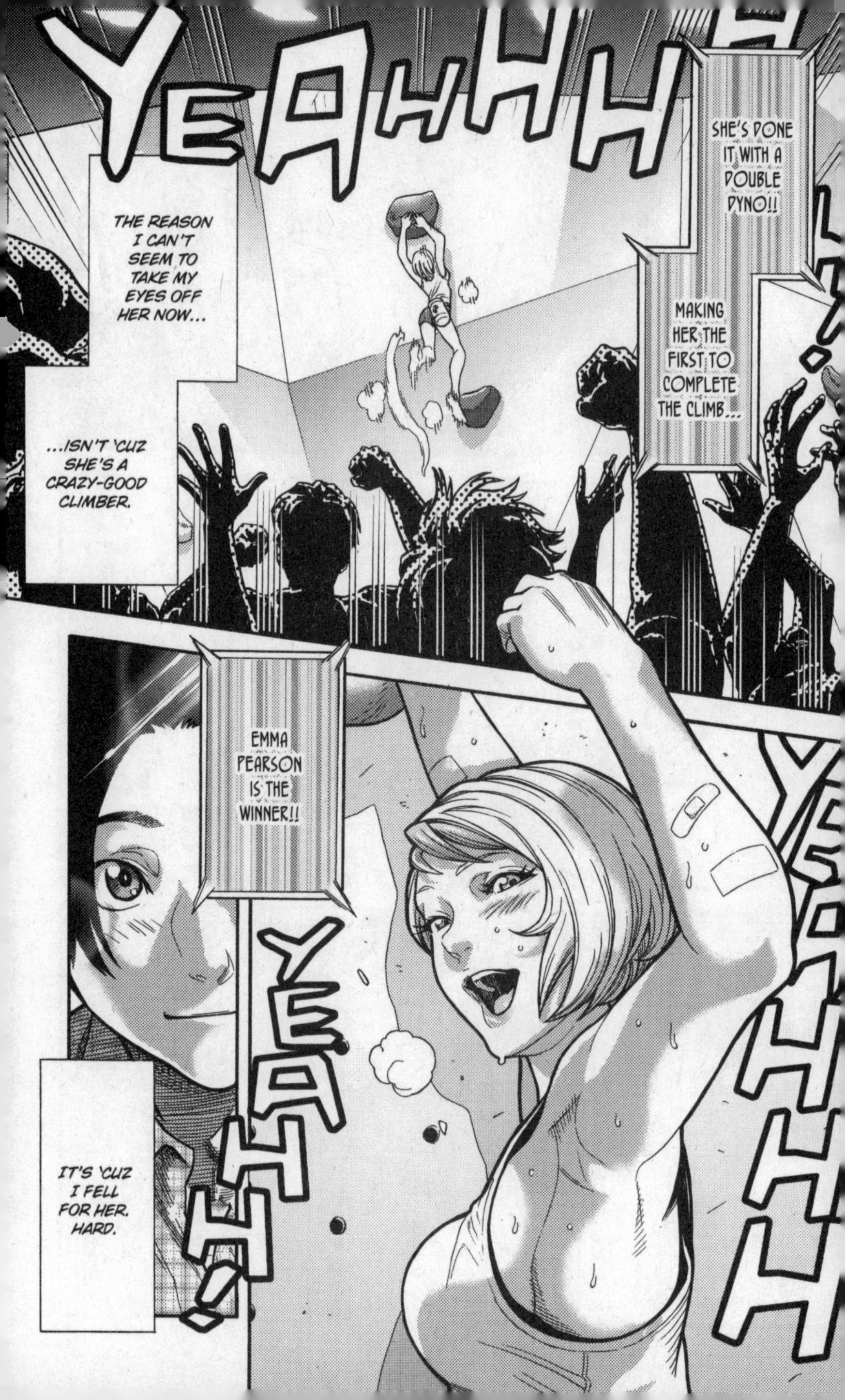
YEAHHHH
SHE'S DONE IT WITH A DOUBLE DYNO!!
MAKING HER THE FIRST TO COMPLETE THE CLIMB...
THE REASON I CAN'T SEEM TO TAKE MY EYES OFF HER NOW...
...ISN'T 'CUZ SHE'S A CRAZY-GOOD CLIMBER.
YEAHHHHH
EMMA PEARSON IS THE WINNER!!
YEAHH!
IT'S 'CUZ I FELL FOR HER. HARD.

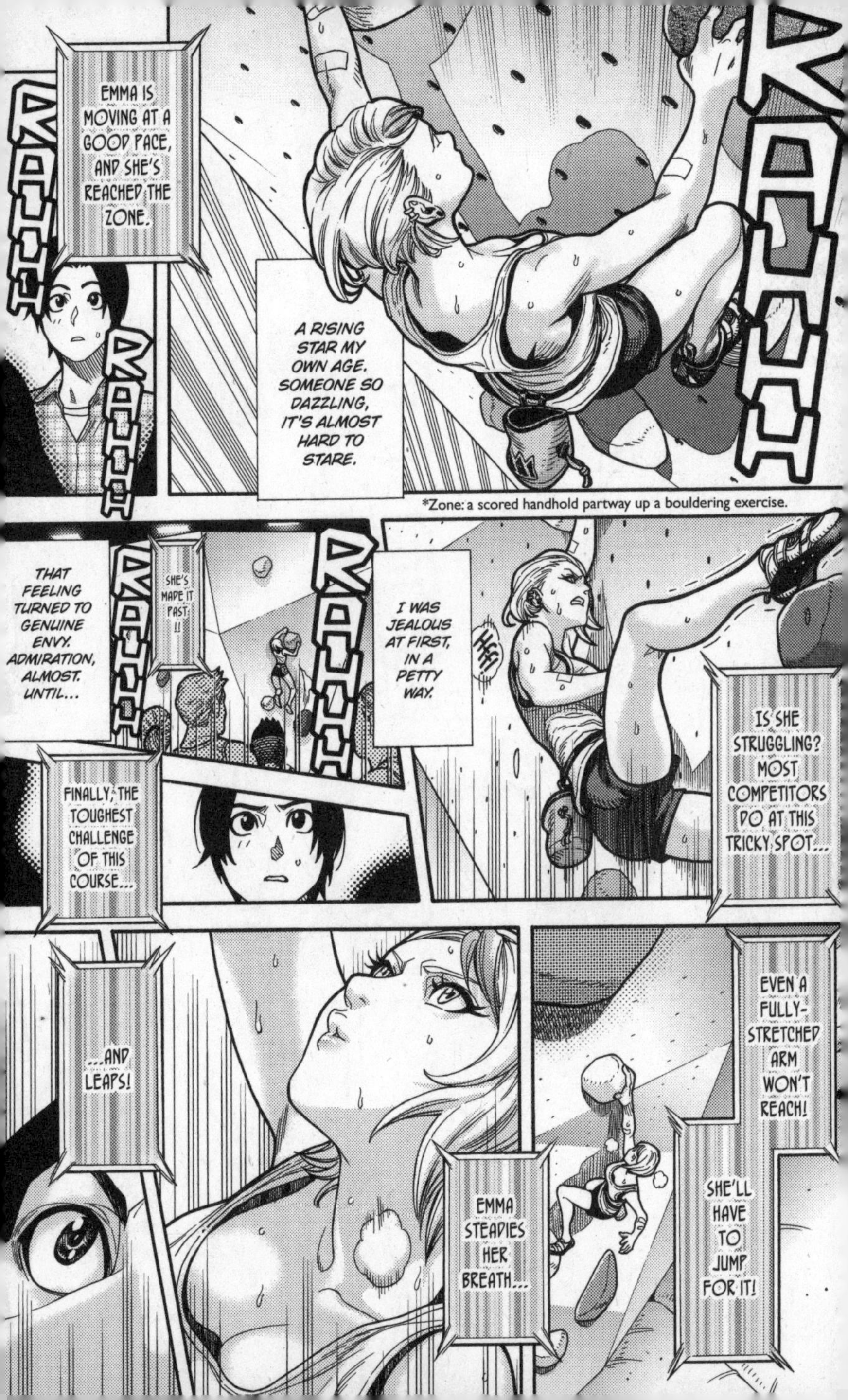

A RISING STAR MY OWN AGE. SOMEONE SO DAZZLING, IT'S ALMOST HARD TO STARE.
EMMA IS MOVING AT A GOOD PACE, AND SHE'S REACHED THE ZONE.
I WAS JEALOUS AT FIRST, IN A PETTY WAY.
HFF!
IS SHE STRUGGLING? MOST COMPETITORS DO AT THIS TRICKY SPOT...
SHE'S MADE IT PAST!!
THAT FEELING TURNED TO GENUINE ENVY. ADMIRATION, ALMOST. UNTIL...
FINALLY, THE TOUGHEST CHALLENGE OF THIS COURSE...
EVEN A FULLY-STRETCHED ARM WON'T REACH!
SHE'LL HAVE TO JUMP FOR IT!
EMMA STEADIES HER BREATH...
...AND LEAPS!

*Zone: a scored handhold partway up a bouldering exercise.

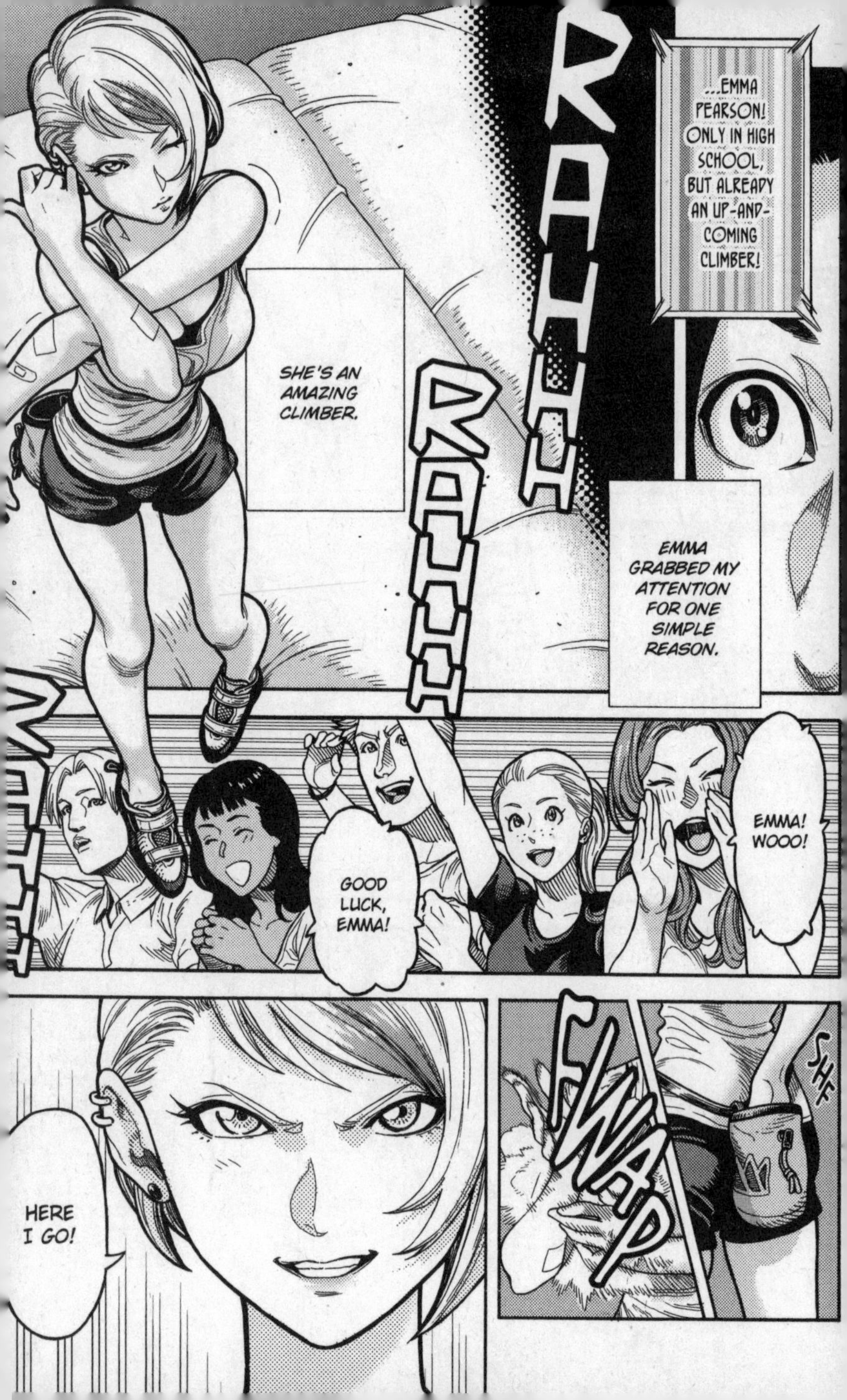
...EMMA PEARSON! ONLY IN HIGH SCHOOL, BUT ALREADY AN UP-AND-COMING CLIMBER!
EMMA GRABBED MY ATTENTION FOR ONE SIMPLE REASON.
RAUHH
RAUUHH
SHE'S AN AMAZING CLIMBER.
EMMA! WOOO!
GOOD LUCK, EMMA!
SHF
FWAP
HERE I GO!

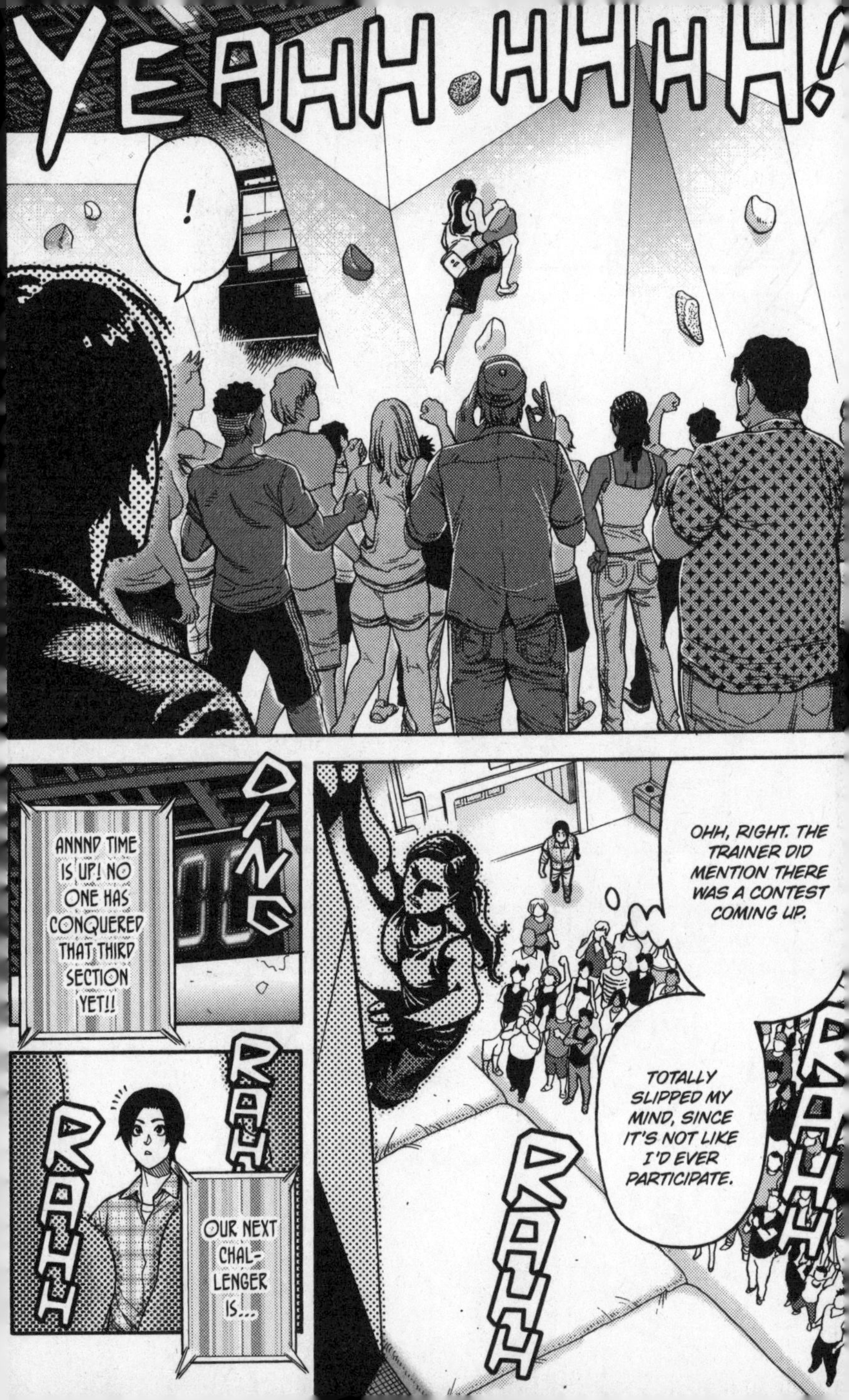
YEAHH-HHHHH!
!
OHH, RIGHT. THE TRAINER DID MENTION THERE WAS A CONTEST COMING UP.
TOTALLY SLIPPED MY MIND, SINCE IT'S NOT LIKE I'D EVER PARTICIPATE.
RAUH
RAUH
DING
ANNND TIME IS UP! NO ONE HAS CONQUERED THAT THIRD SECTION YET!!
RAUH
RAUH
OUR NEXT CHAL-LENGER IS...

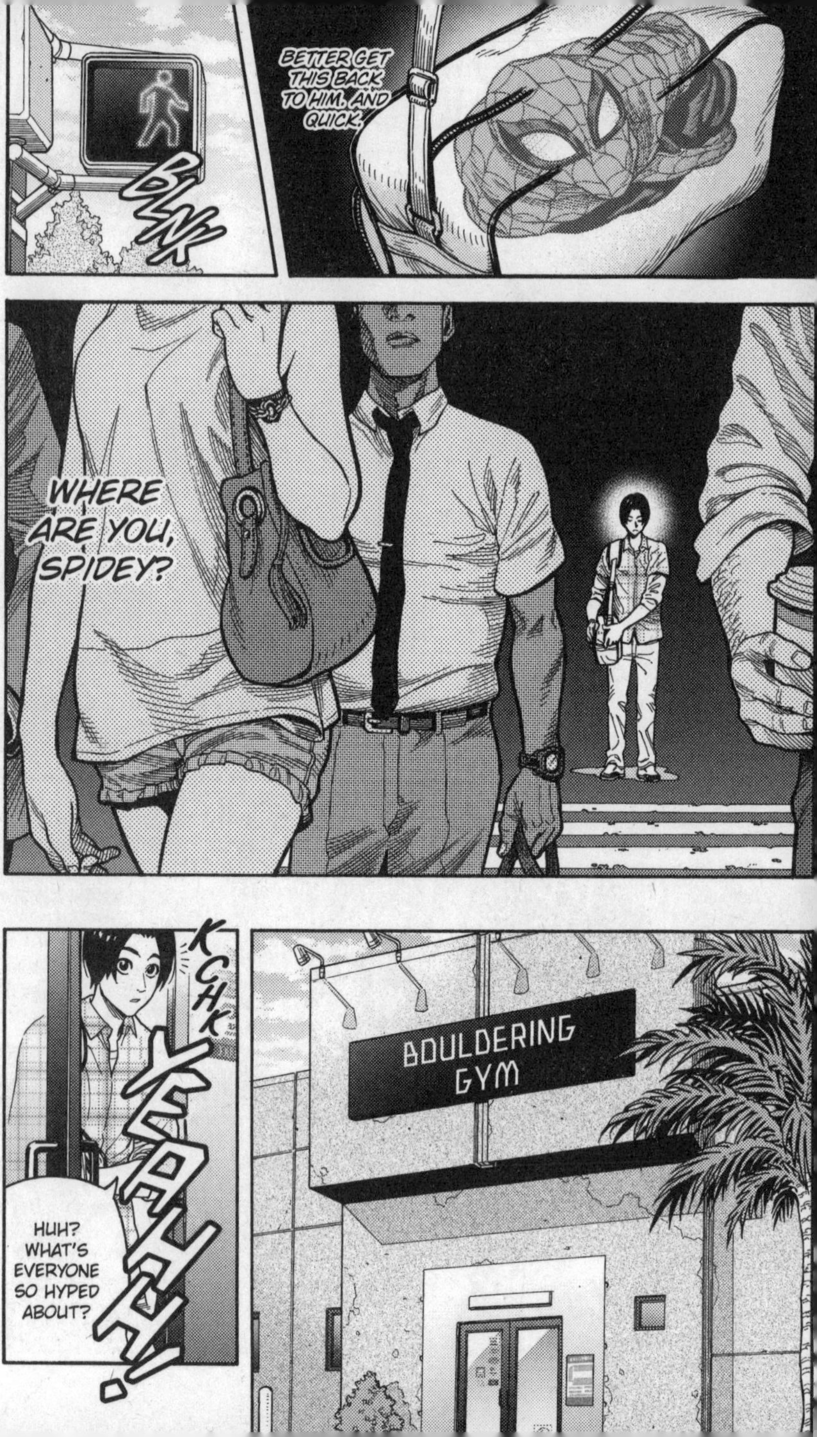
BETTER GET THIS BACK TO HIM, AND QUICK.
BLNK
WHERE ARE YOU, SPIDEY?
BOULDERING GYM
KCHK
YEAHHH!
HUH? WHAT'S EVERYONE SO HYPED ABOUT?

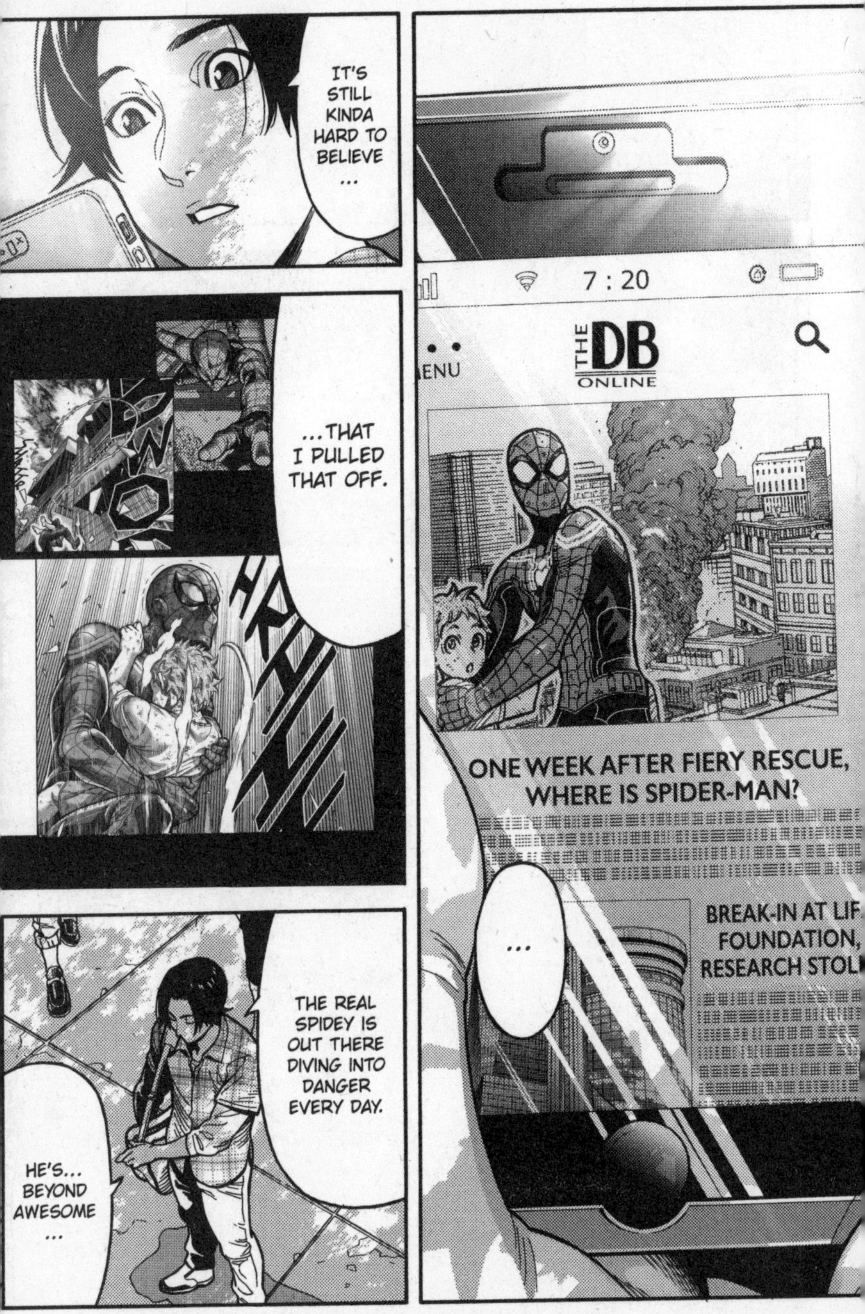
7:20
THE DB ONLINE
ENU
ONE WEEK AFTER FIERY RESCUE, WHERE IS SPIDER-MAN?
...
BREAK-IN AT LIF
FOUNDATION,
RESEARCH STOL
IT'S STILL KINDA HARD TO BELIEVE...
...THAT I PULLED THAT OFF.
THE REAL SPIDEY IS OUT THERE DIVING INTO DANGER EVERY DAY.
HE'S... BEYOND AWESOME...

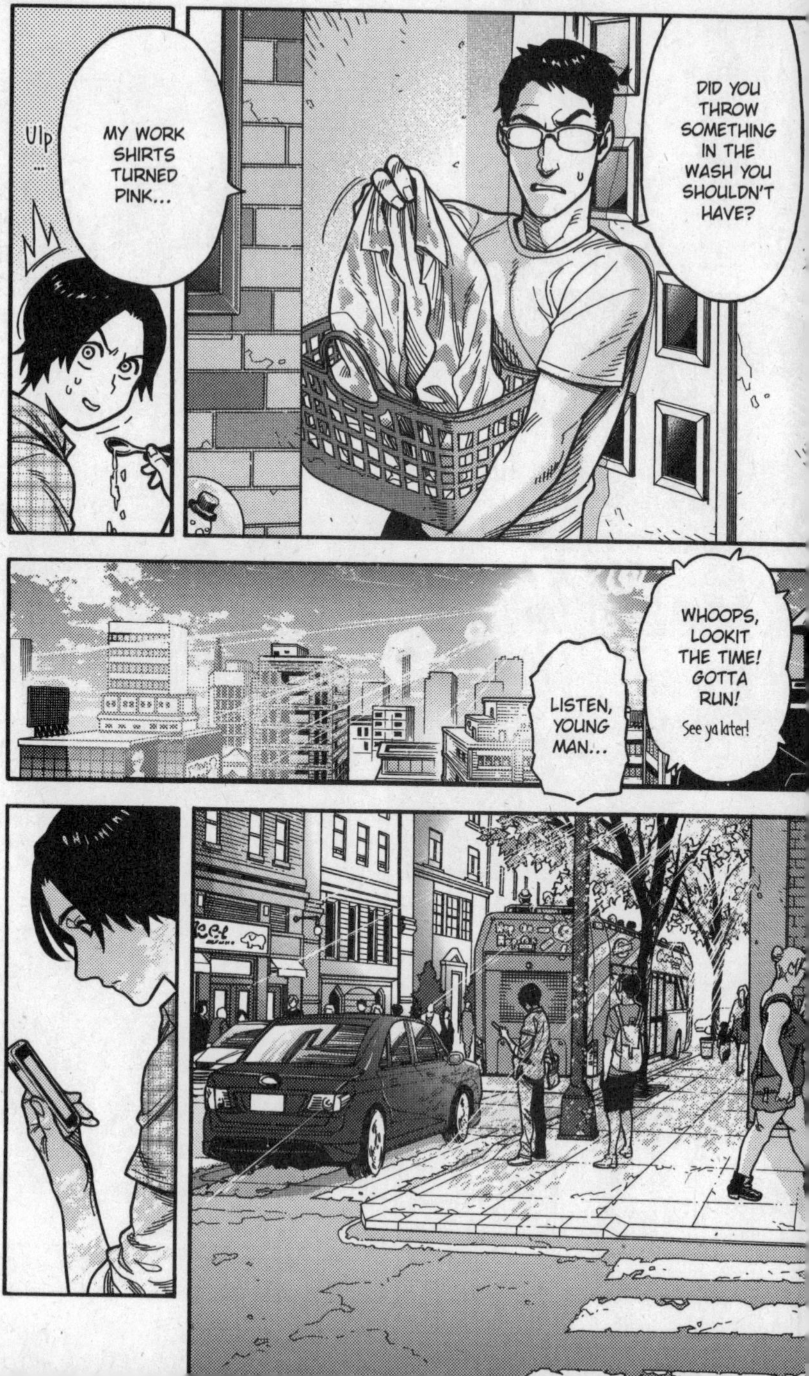
DID YOU THROW SOMETHING IN THE WASH YOU SHOULDN'T HAVE?
MY WORK SHIRTS TURNED PINK...
Ulp...
WHOOPS, LOOKIT THE TIME! GOTTA RUN!
See ya later!
LISTEN, YOUNG MAN...

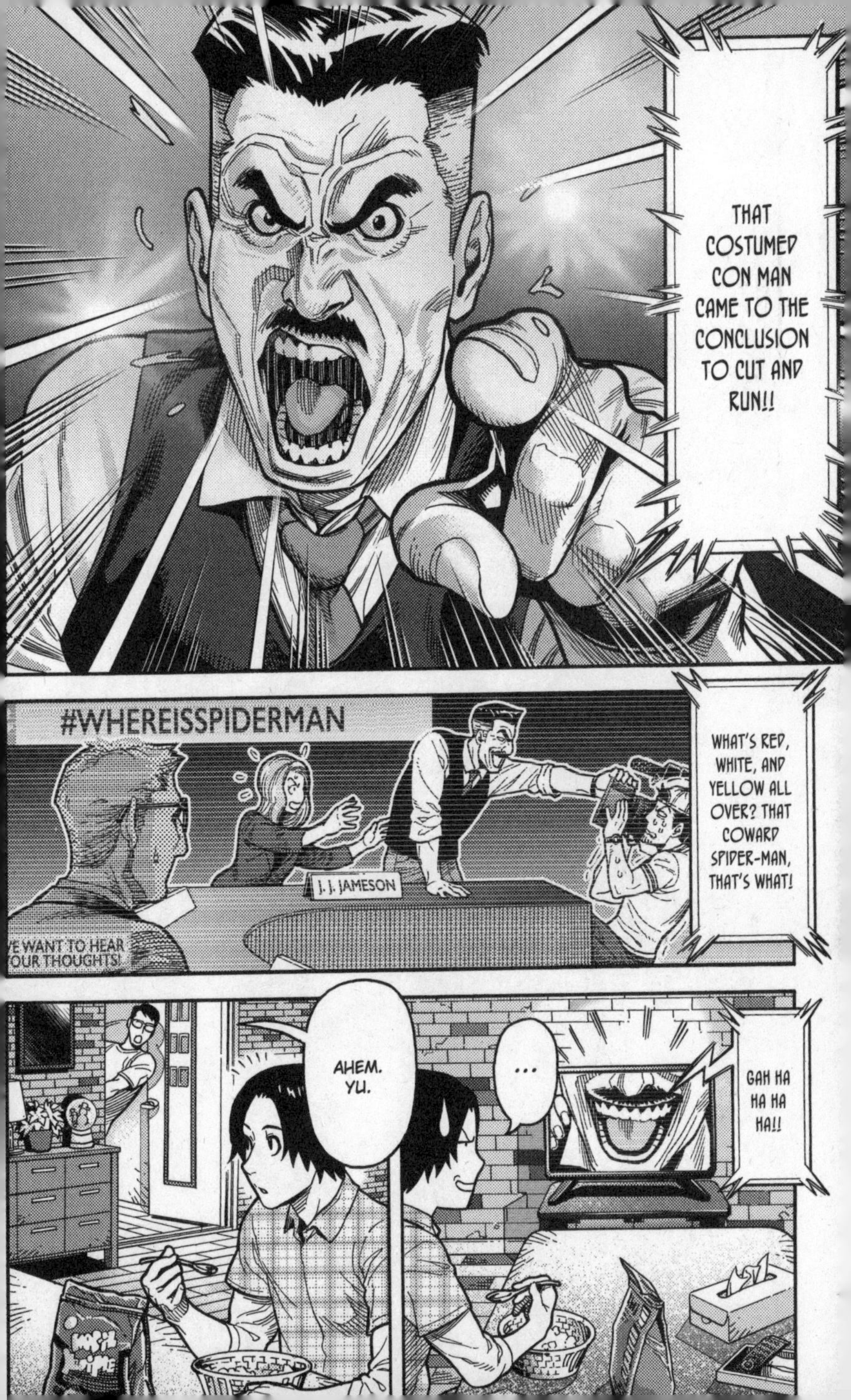
THAT COSTUMED CON MAN CAME TO THE CONCLUSION TO CUT AND RUN!!
WHAT'S RED, WHITE, AND YELLOW ALL OVER? THAT COWARD SPIDER-MAN, THAT'S WHAT!
#WHEREISSPIDERMAN
J. J. JAMESON
E WANT TO HEAR
OUR THOUGHTS!
GAH HA HA HA HA!!
...
AHEM. YU.

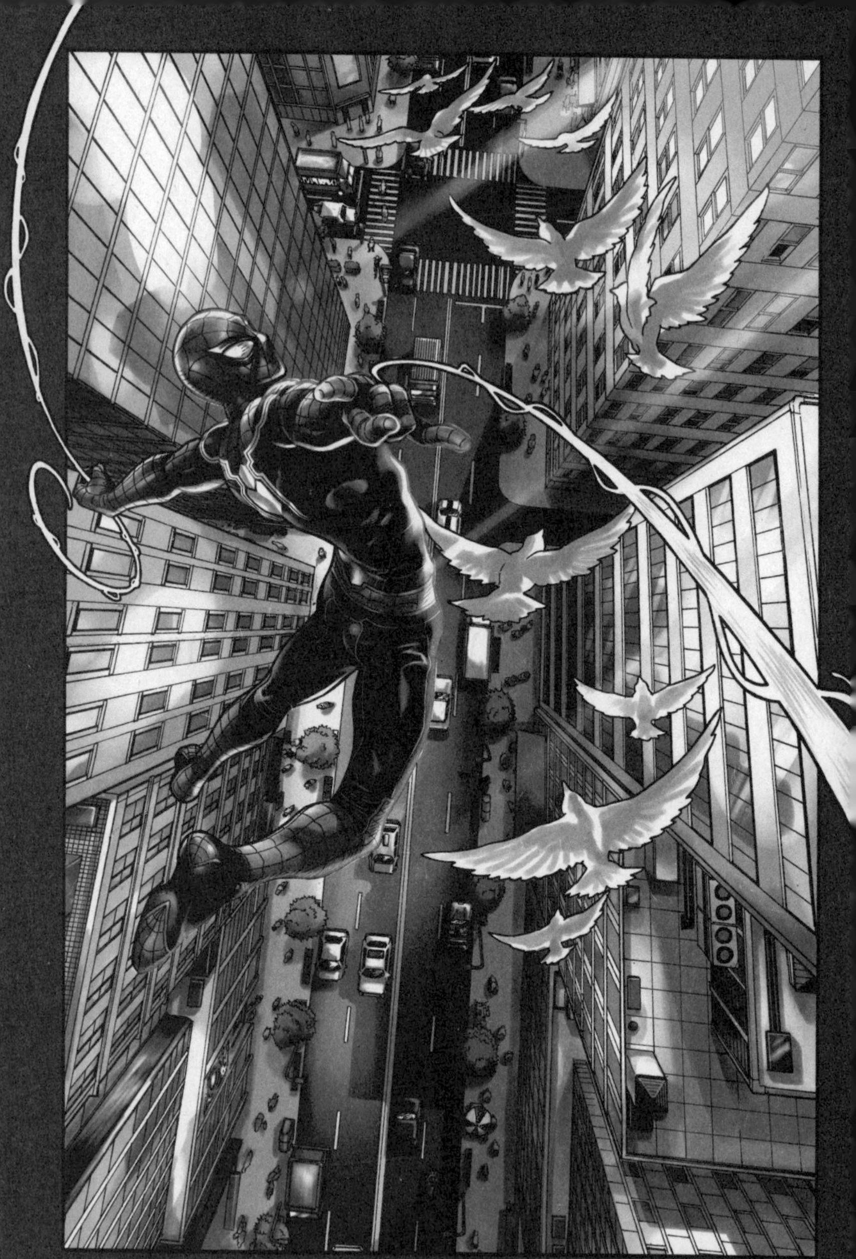

#2 #whereisspiderman

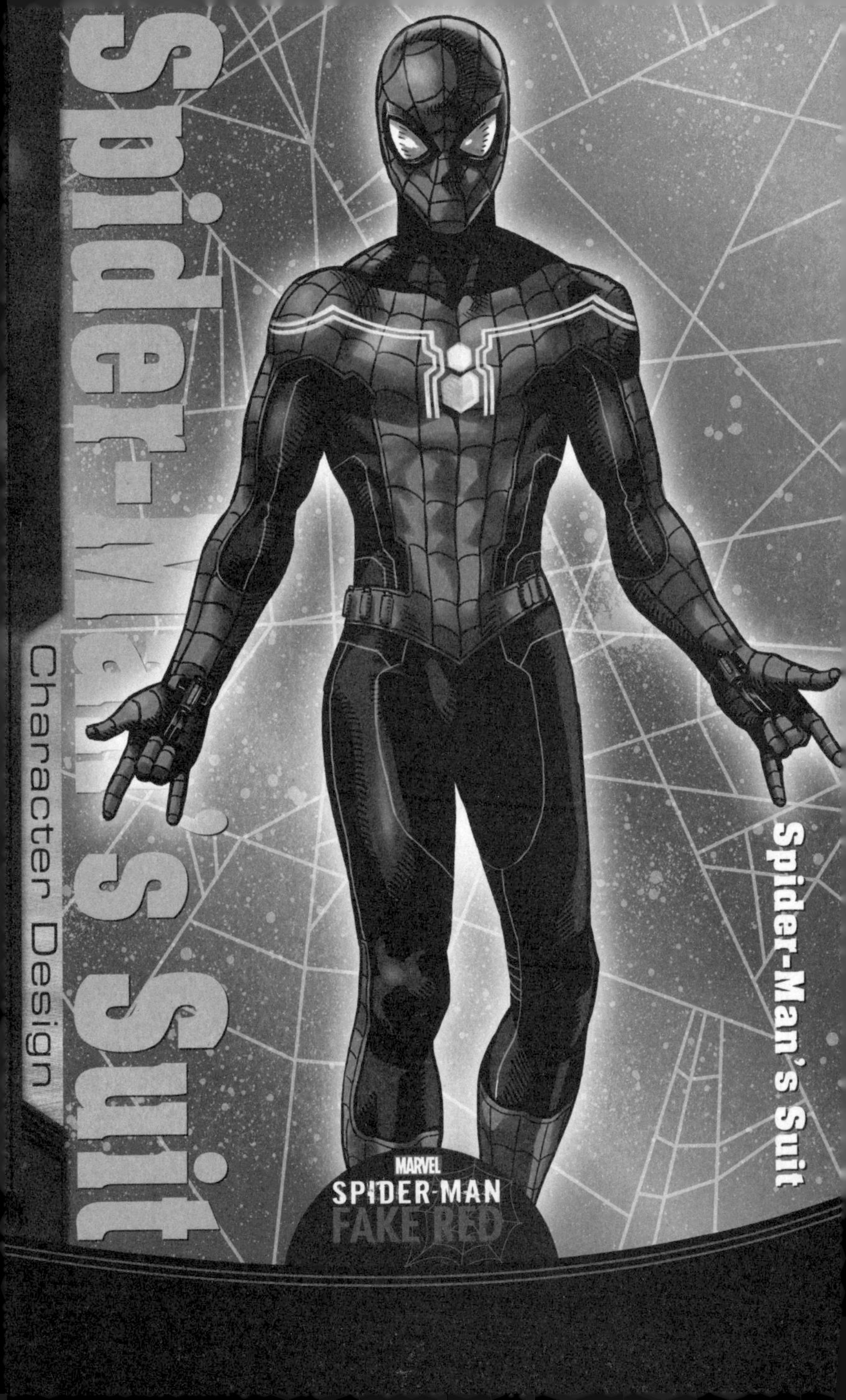
Spider-Man's Suit
Character Design
Spider-Man's Suit
MARVEL
SPIDER-MAN
FAKE RED

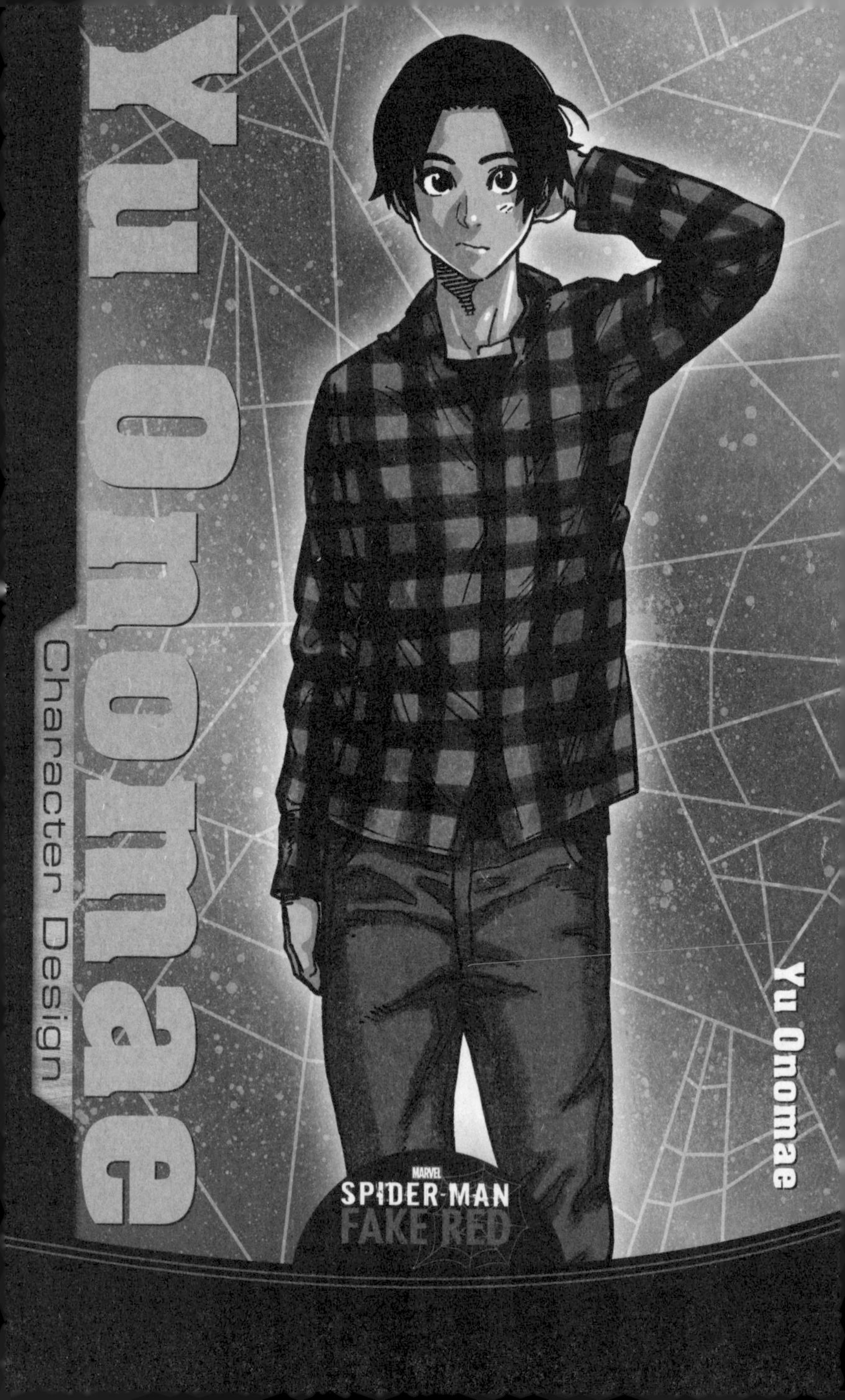
Yu Onomae
Character Design
Yu Onomae
MARVEL
SPIDER-MAN
FAKE RED

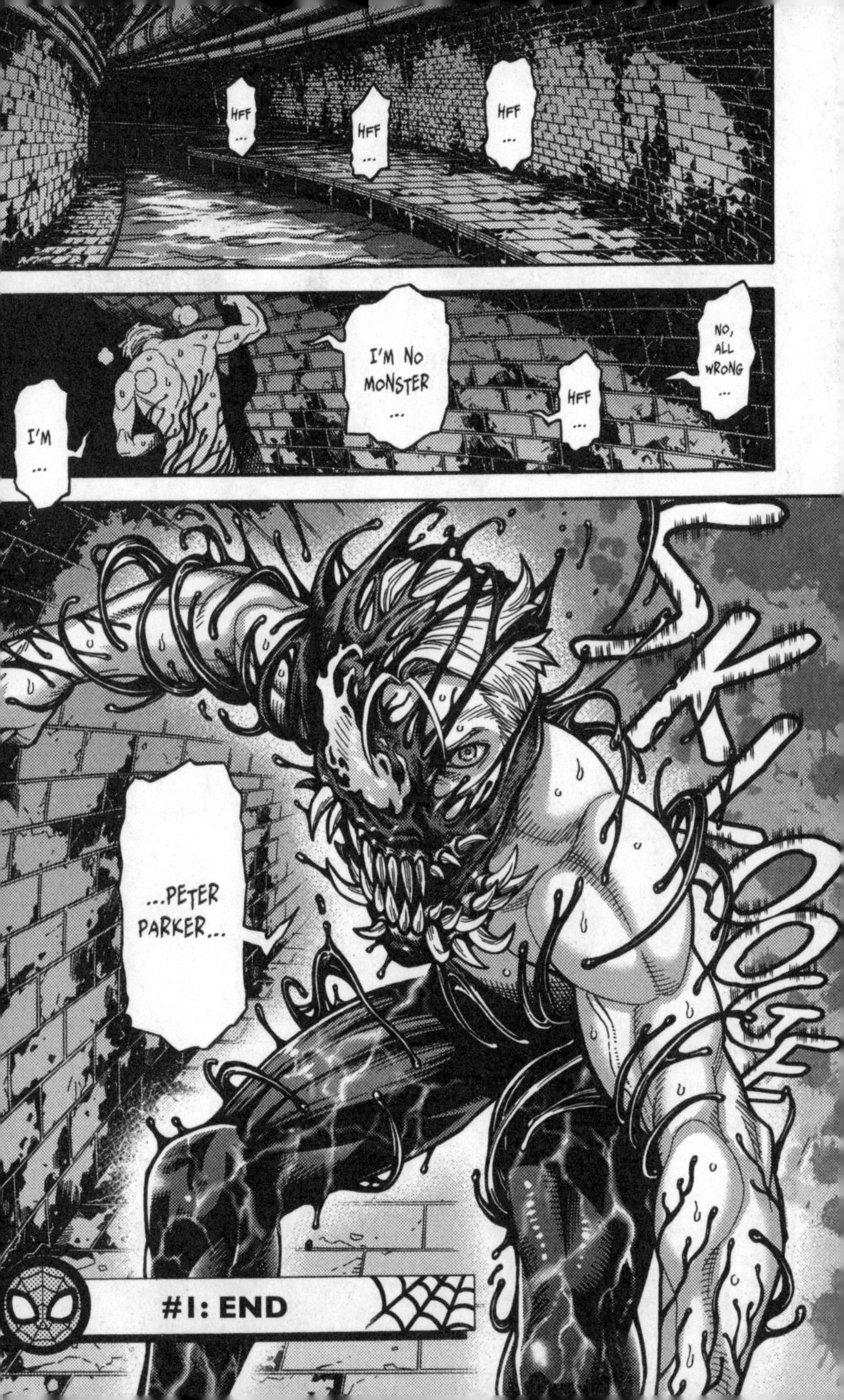
HFF ...
HFF ...
HFF ...
NO, ALL WRONG ...
HFF ...
I'M NO MONSTER ...
I'M ...
...PETER PARKER...
#1: END

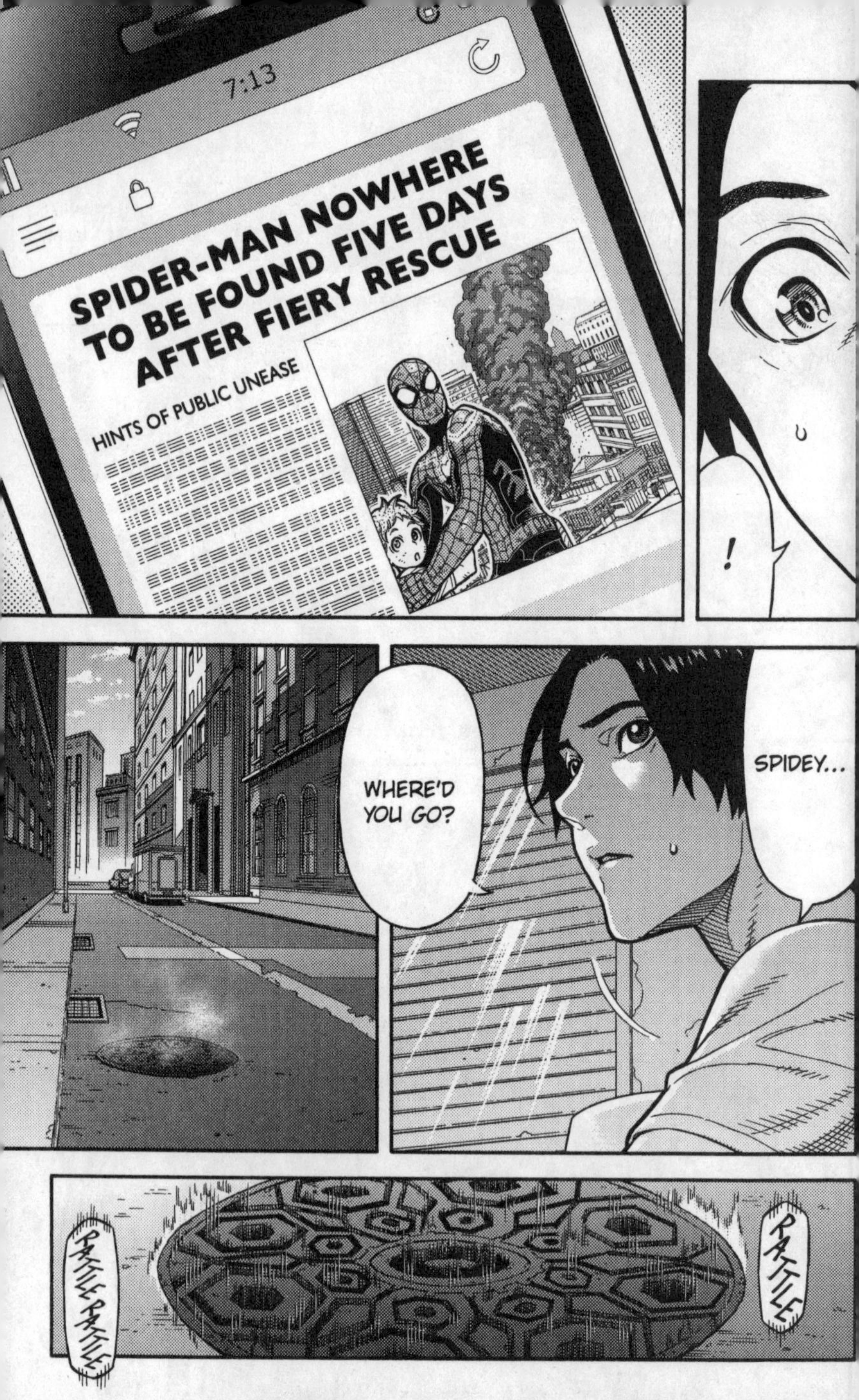
!
7:13
SPIDER-MAN NOWHERE TO BE FOUND FIVE DAYS AFTER FIERY RESCUE
HINTS OF PUBLIC UNEASE
SPIDEY...
WHERE'D YOU GO?
RATTLE
RATTLE RATTLE

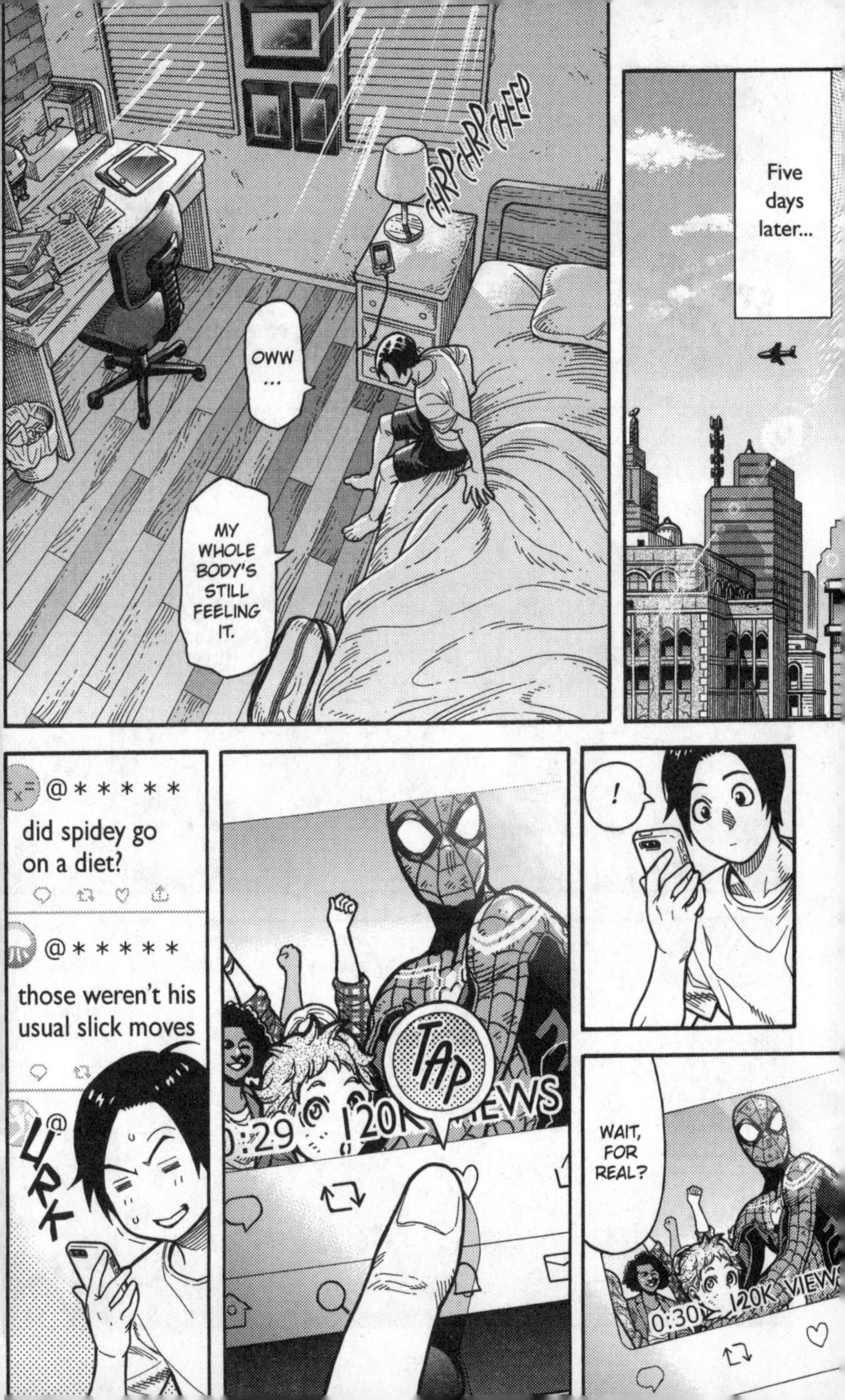
Five days later...
CHRP CHRP CHEEP
OWW ...
MY WHOLE BODY'S STILL FEELING IT.
!
WAIT, FOR REAL?
0:30
120K VIEWS
TAP
0:29
120K
@*****
did spidey go on a diet?
@*****
those weren't his usual slick moves
URK

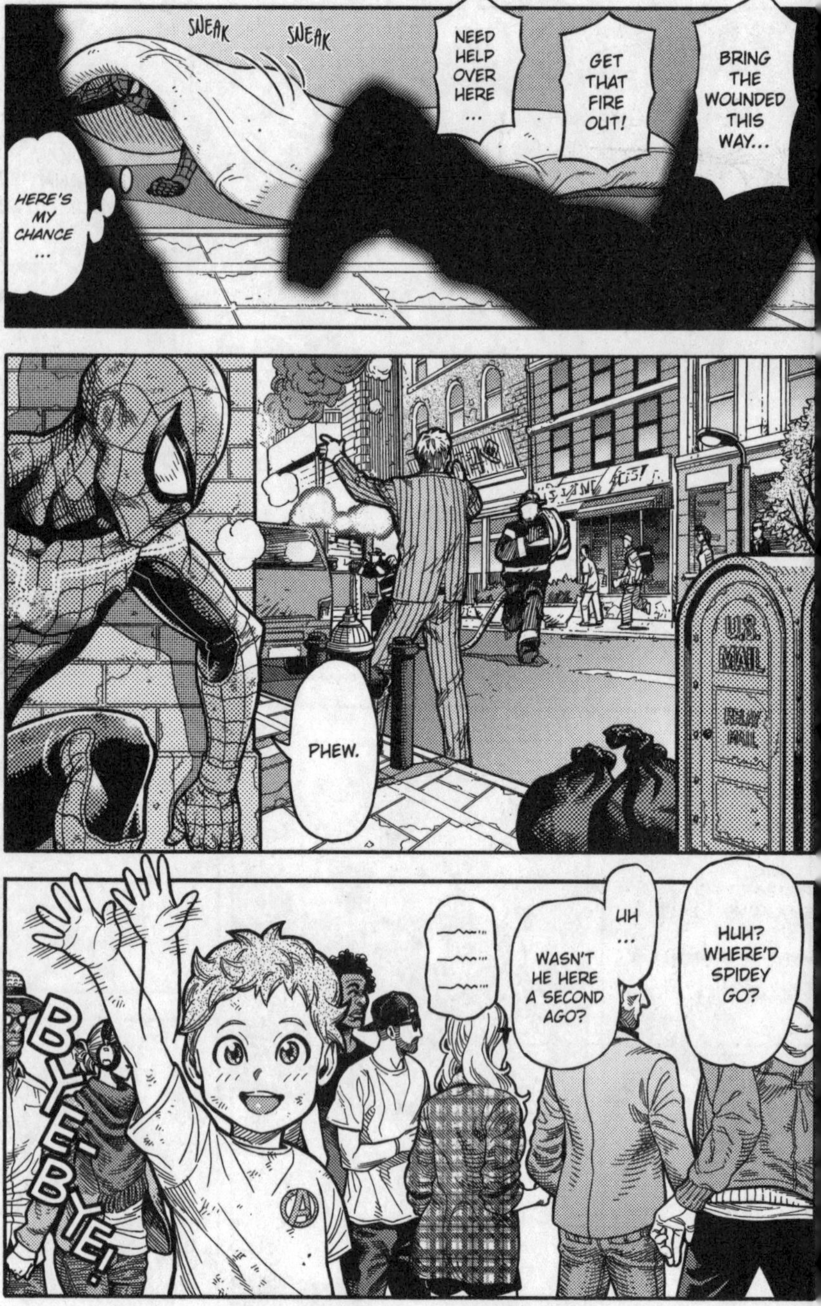
BRING THE WOUNDED THIS WAY...
GET THAT FIRE OUT!
NEED HELP OVER HERE ...
SNEAK
SNEAK
HERE'S MY CHANCE ...
PHEW.
HUH? WHERE'D SPIDEY GO?
UH ...
WASN'T HE HERE A SECOND AGO?
BYE-BYE!

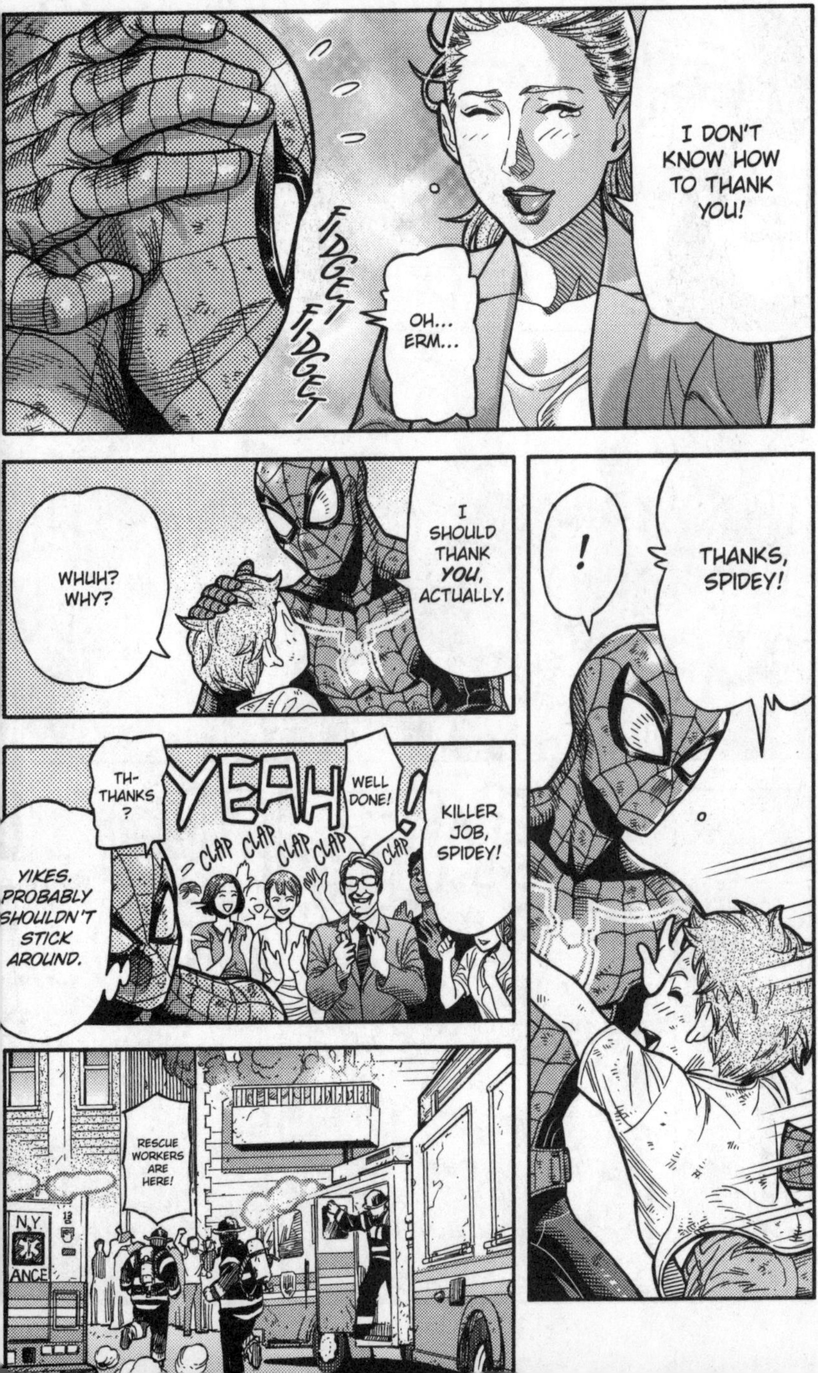
I DON'T KNOW HOW TO THANK YOU!
OH... ERM...
FIDGET FIDGET
THANKS, SPIDEY!
!
I SHOULD THANK *YOU*, ACTUALLY.
WHUH? WHY?
KILLER JOB, SPIDEY!
WELL DONE!
YEAH!
CLAP CLAP CLAP CLAP CLAP
TH-THANKS?
YIKES. PROBABLY SHOULDN'T STICK AROUND.
RESCUE WORKERS ARE HERE!
N.Y.
ANCE

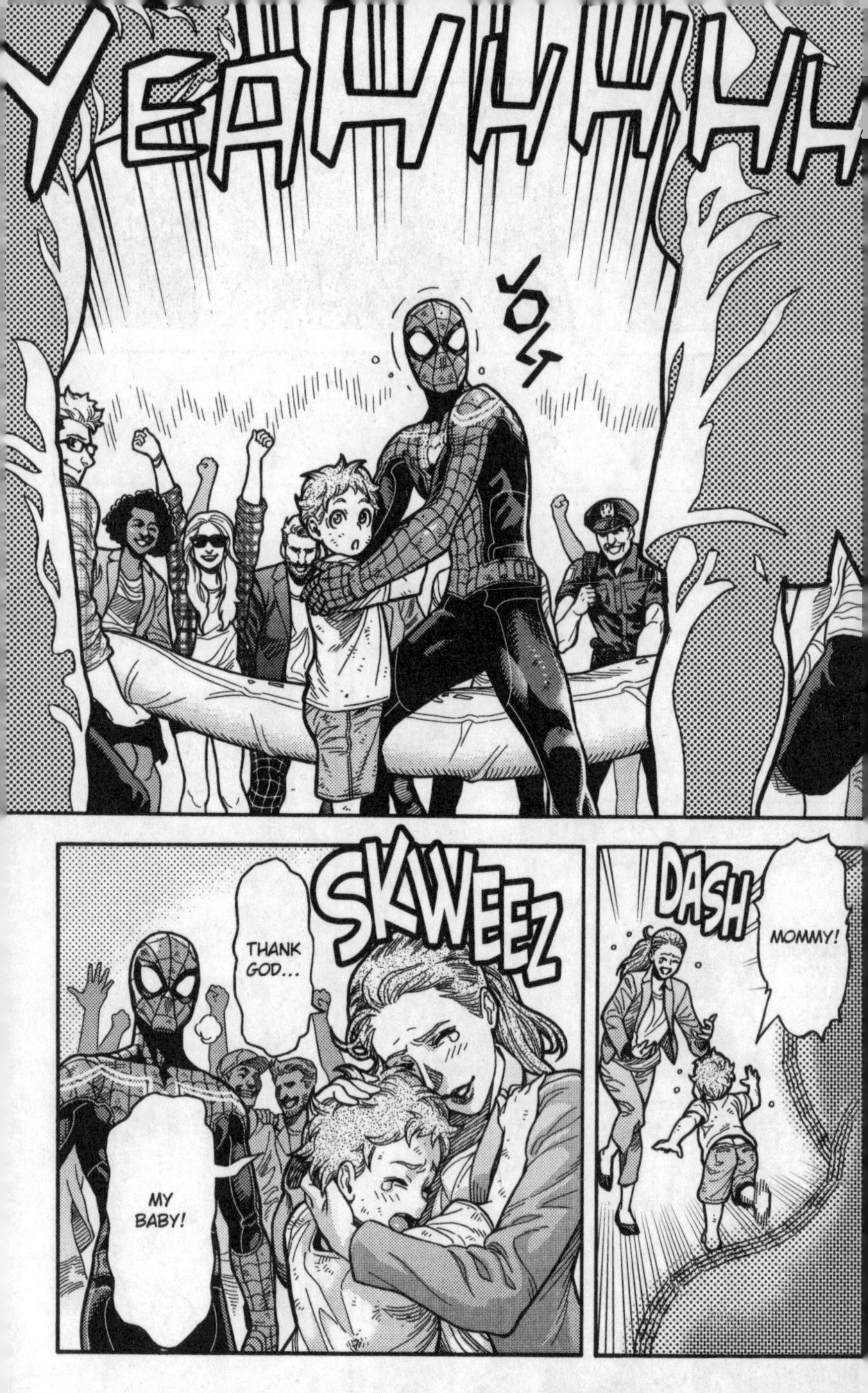
YEAHHHHHH
JOLT
DASH
MOMMY!
SKWEEZ
THANK GOD...
MY BABY!

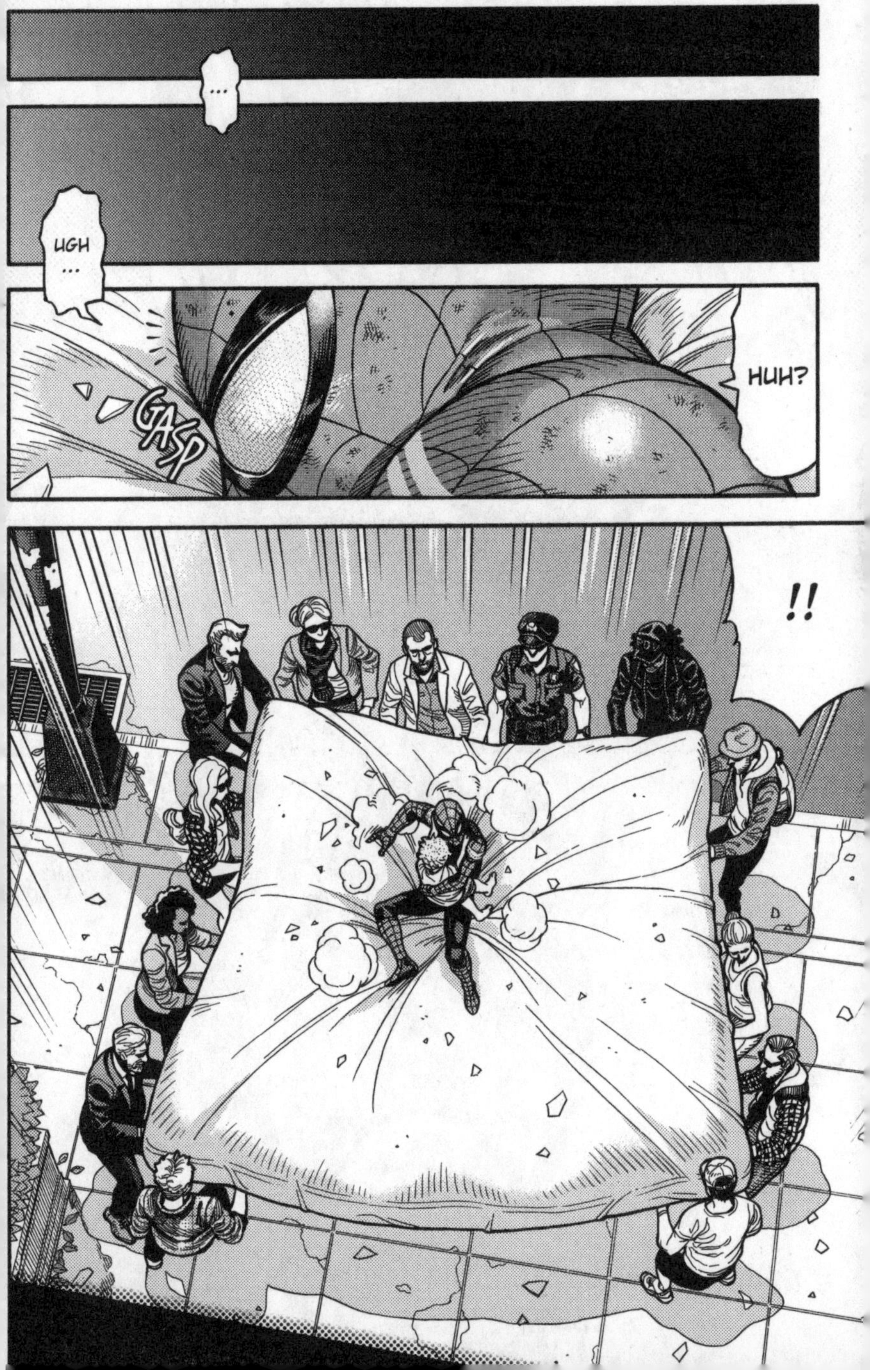
...
UGH ...
HUH?
GASP
!!

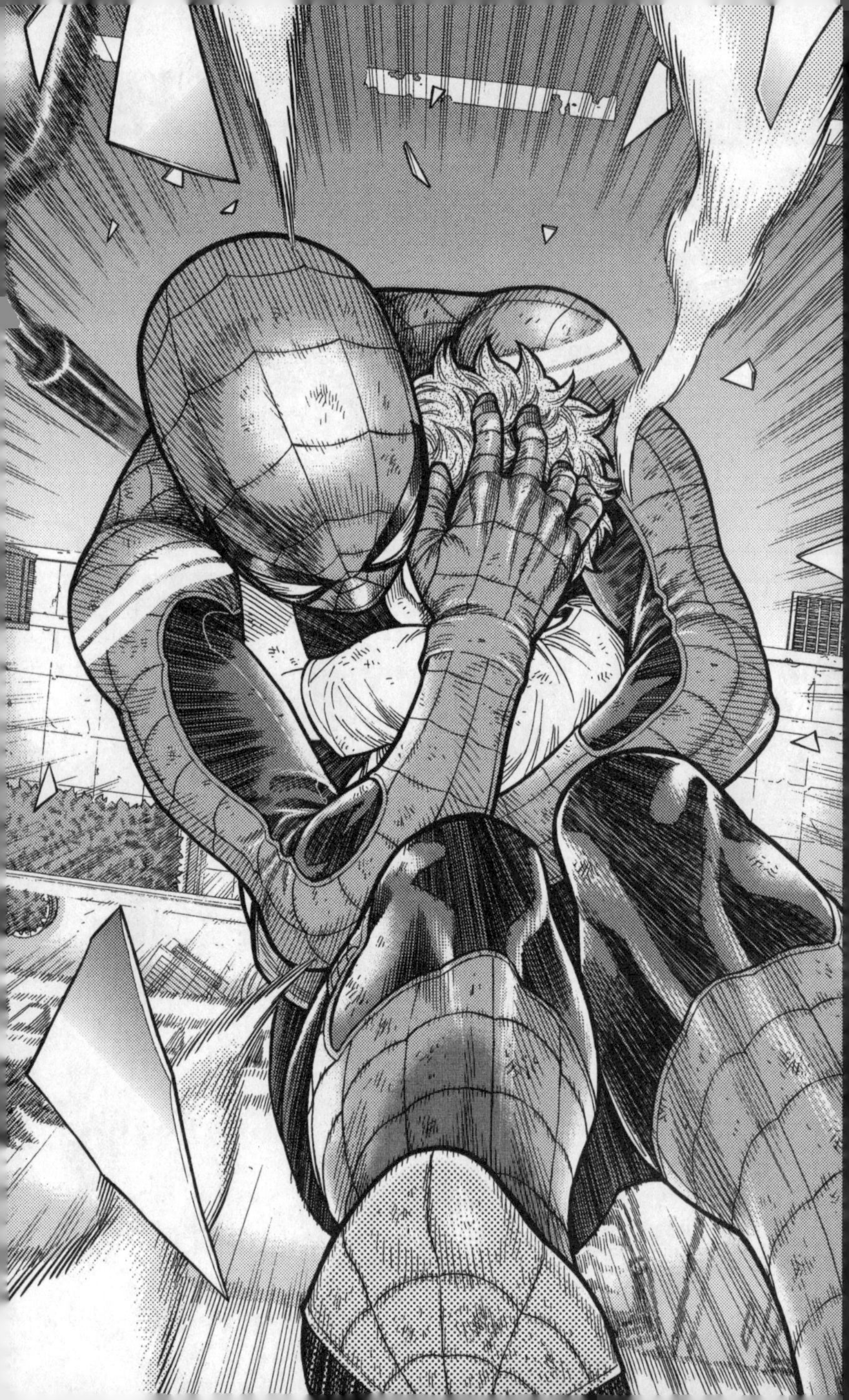

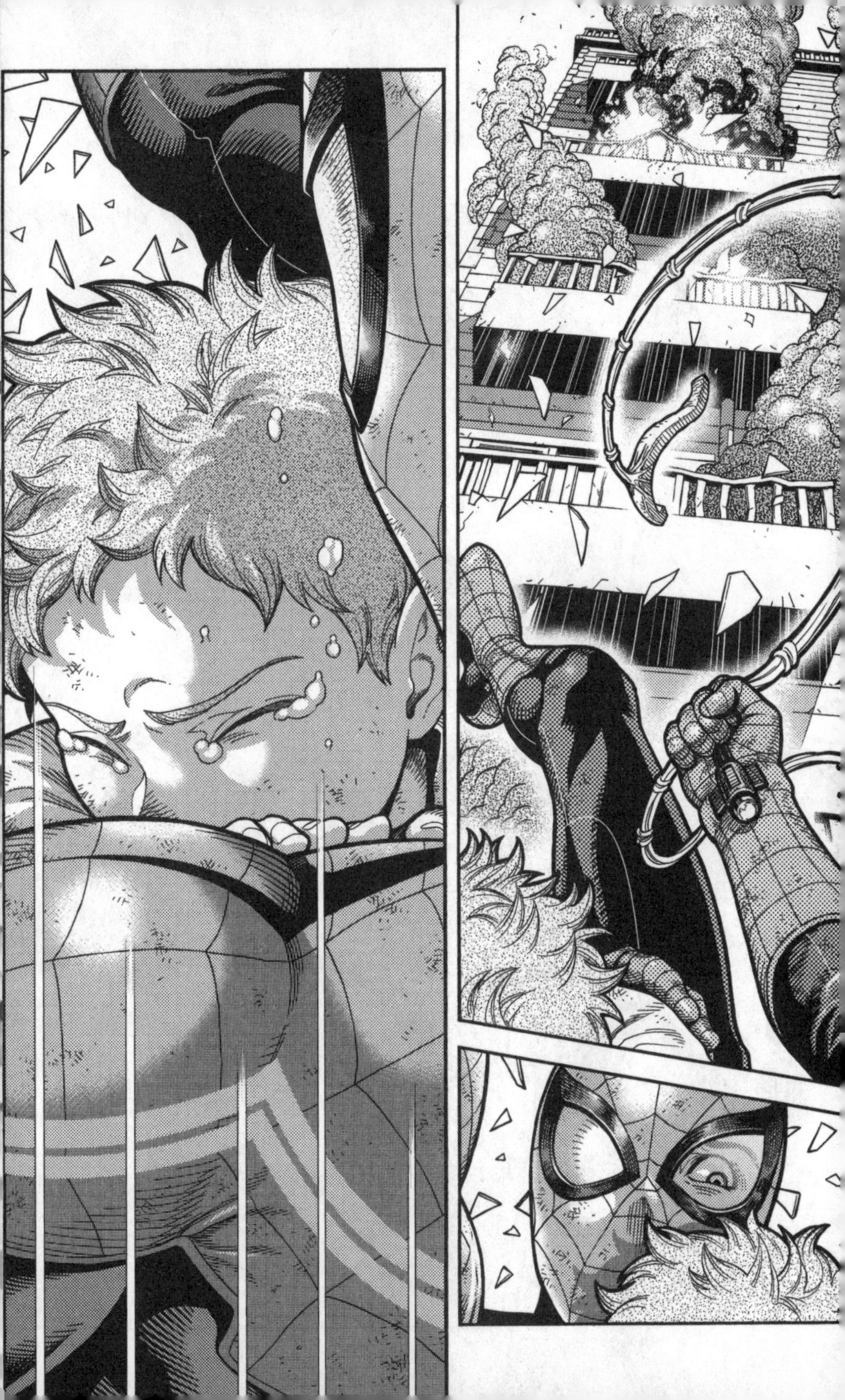

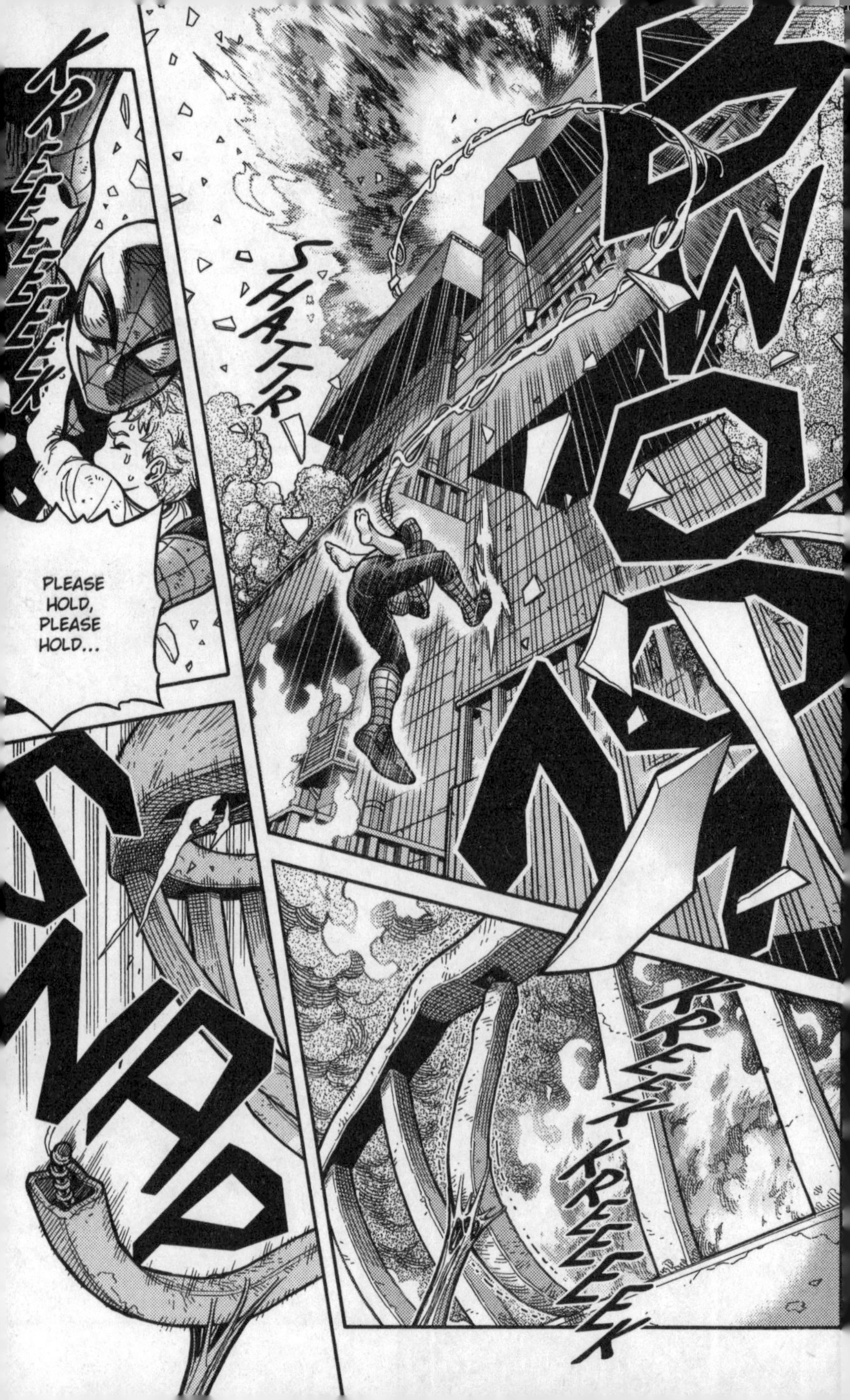

SHATTR
KREEEEEEEEK
PLEASE HOLD, PLEASE HOLD...
KREEET KREEEEEEK
SNAP

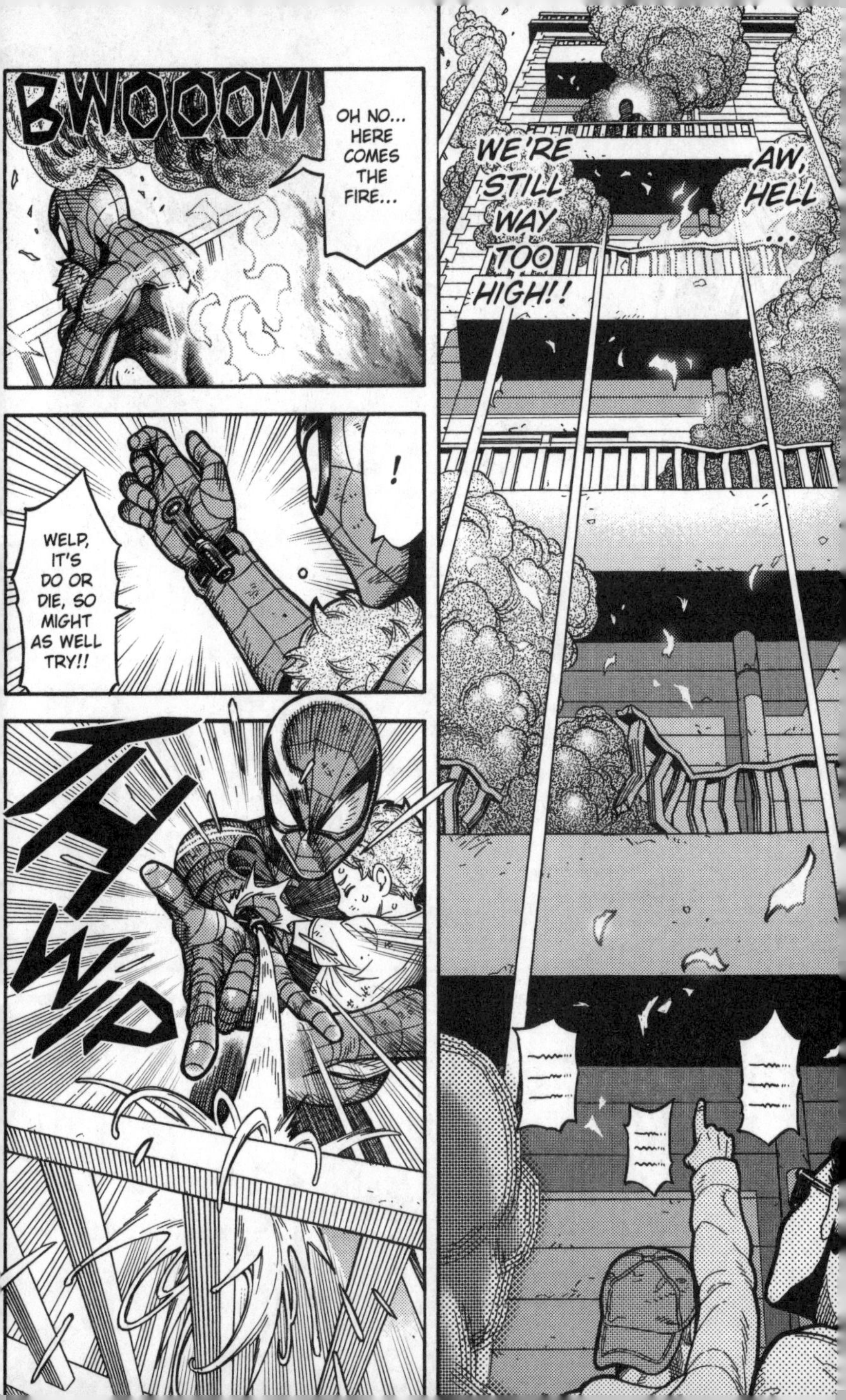
AW, HELL...
WE'RE STILL WAY TOO HIGH!!
OH NO... HERE COMES THE FIRE...
BWOOOM
!
WELP, IT'S DO OR DIE, SO MIGHT AS WELL TRY!!
THWIP

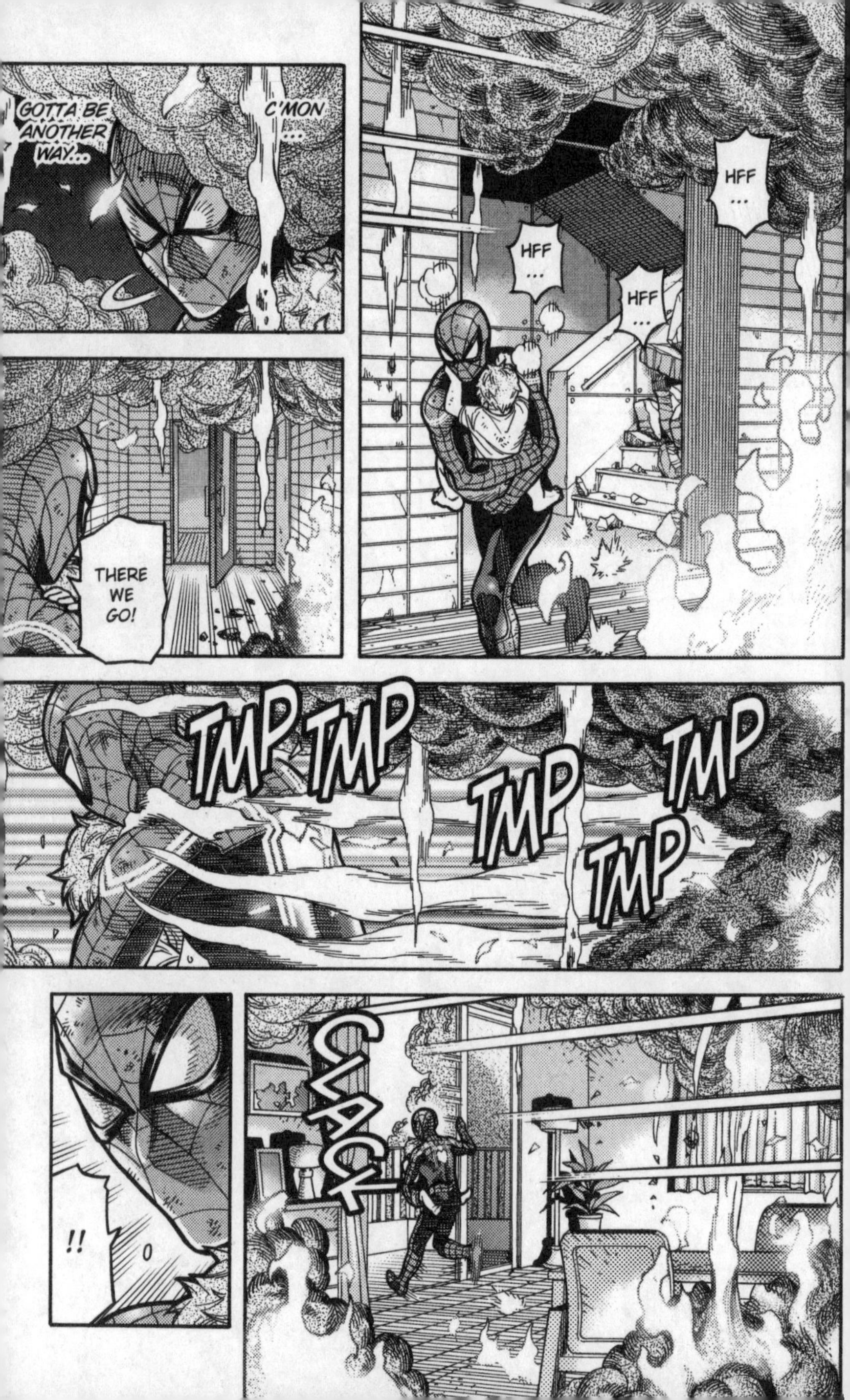
HFF ...
HFF ...
HFF ...
C'MON ...
GOTTA BE ANOTHER WAY...
THERE WE GO!
TMP TMP
TMP TMP
TMP
CLACK
!!

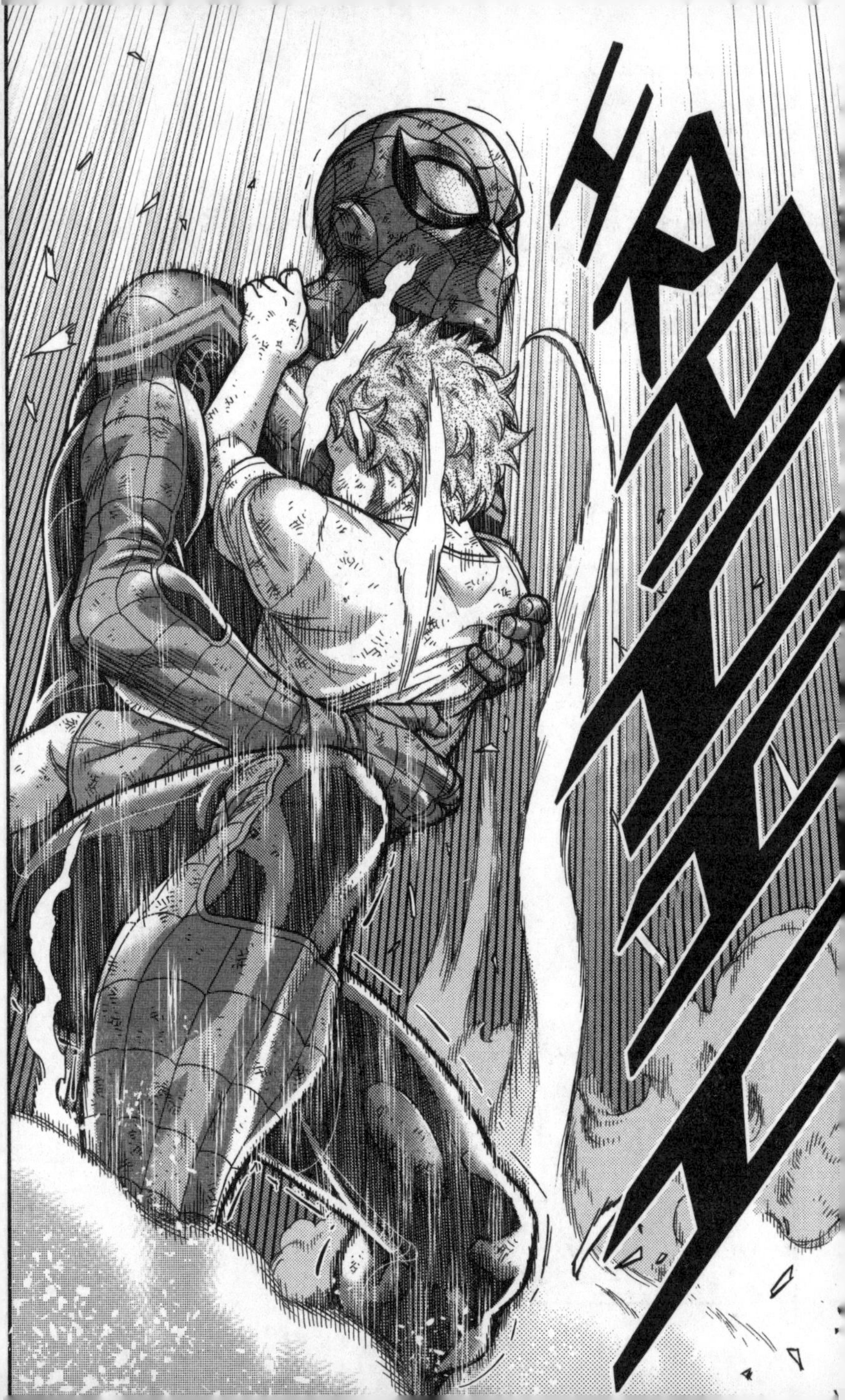

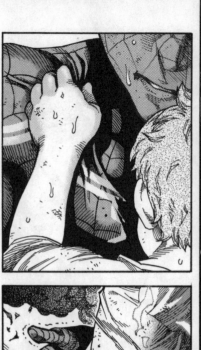

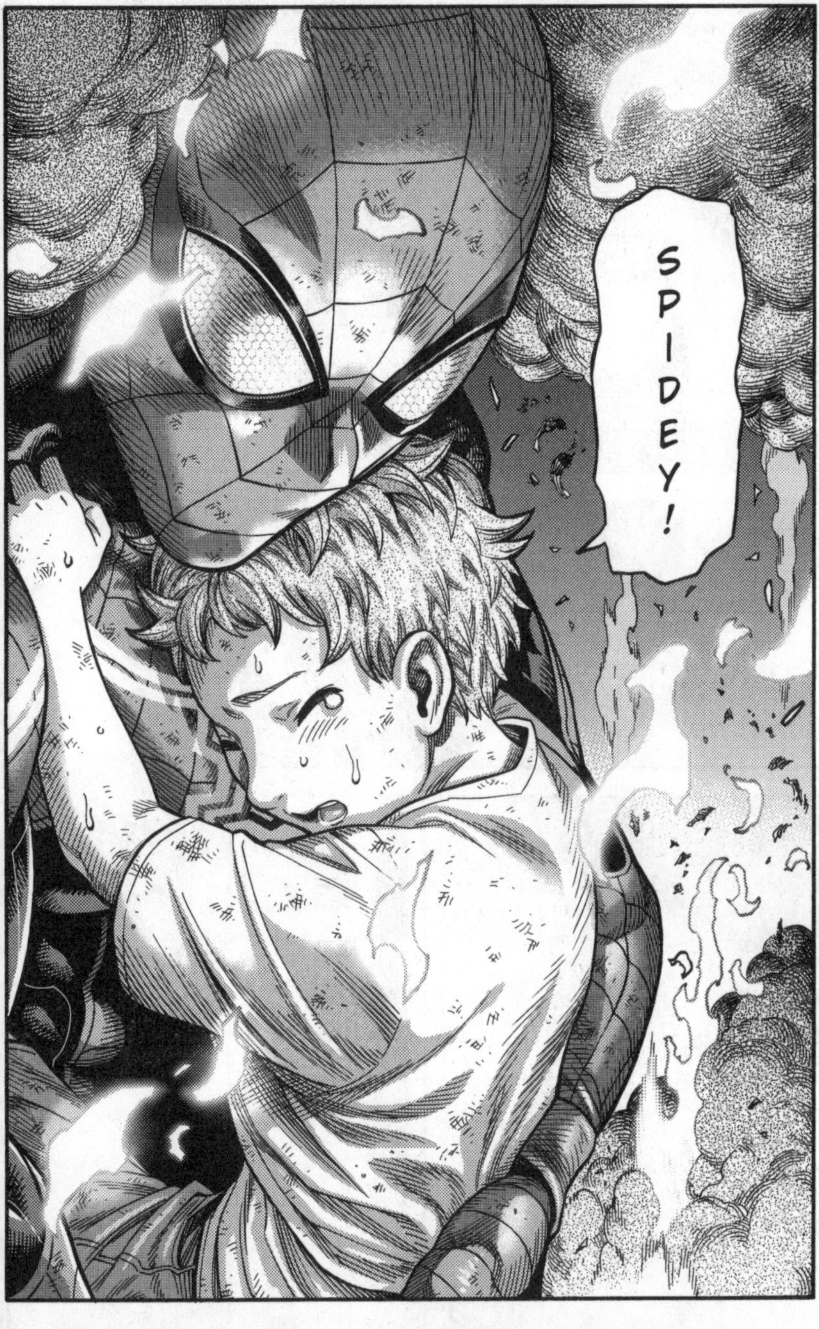
SPIDEY!

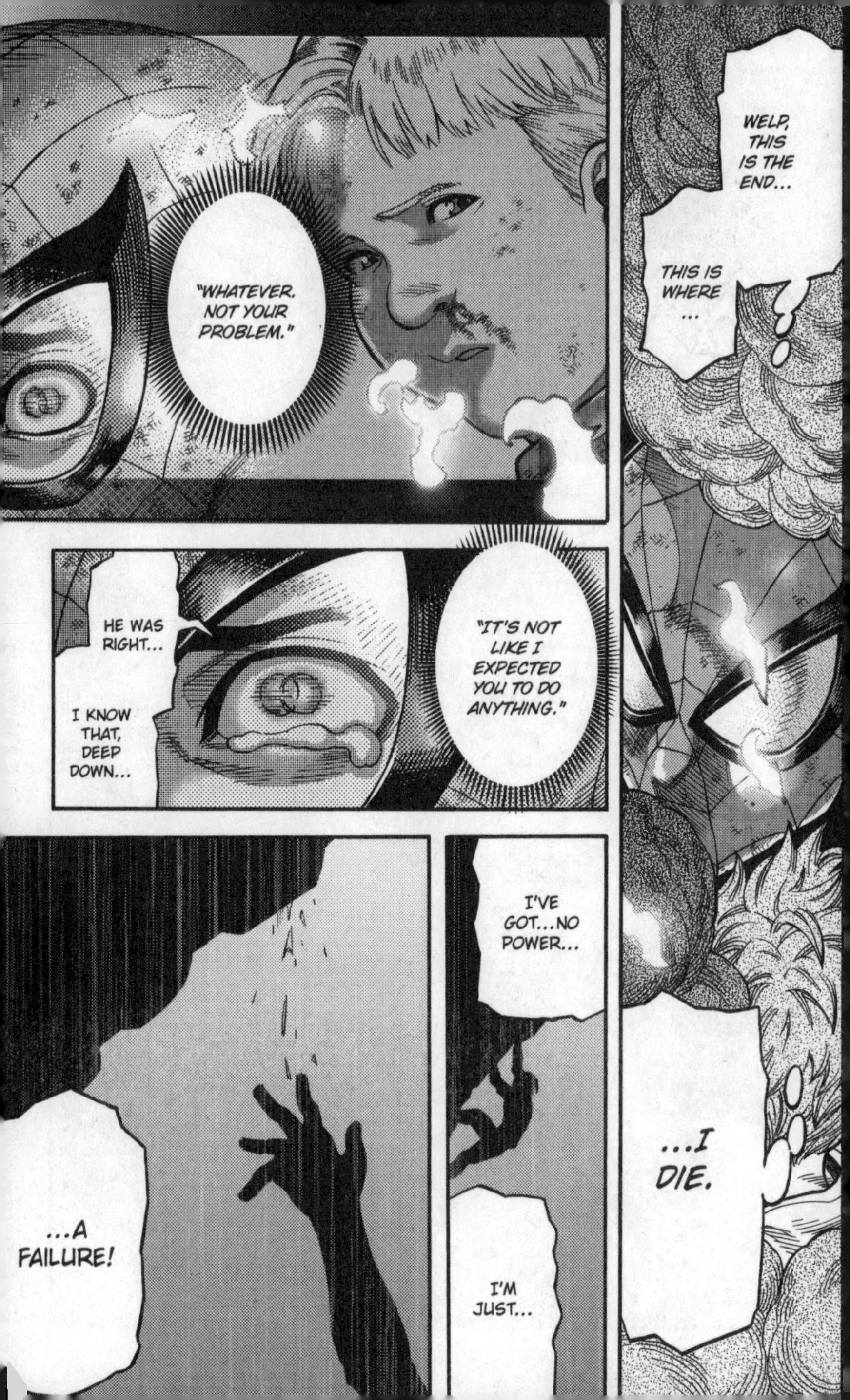
WELP, THIS IS THE END...
THIS IS WHERE ...
...I DIE.
"WHATEVER. NOT YOUR PROBLEM."
"IT'S NOT LIKE I EXPECTED YOU TO DO ANYTHING."
HE WAS RIGHT...
I KNOW THAT, DEEP DOWN...
I'VE GOT...NO POWER...
I'M JUST...
...A FAILURE!

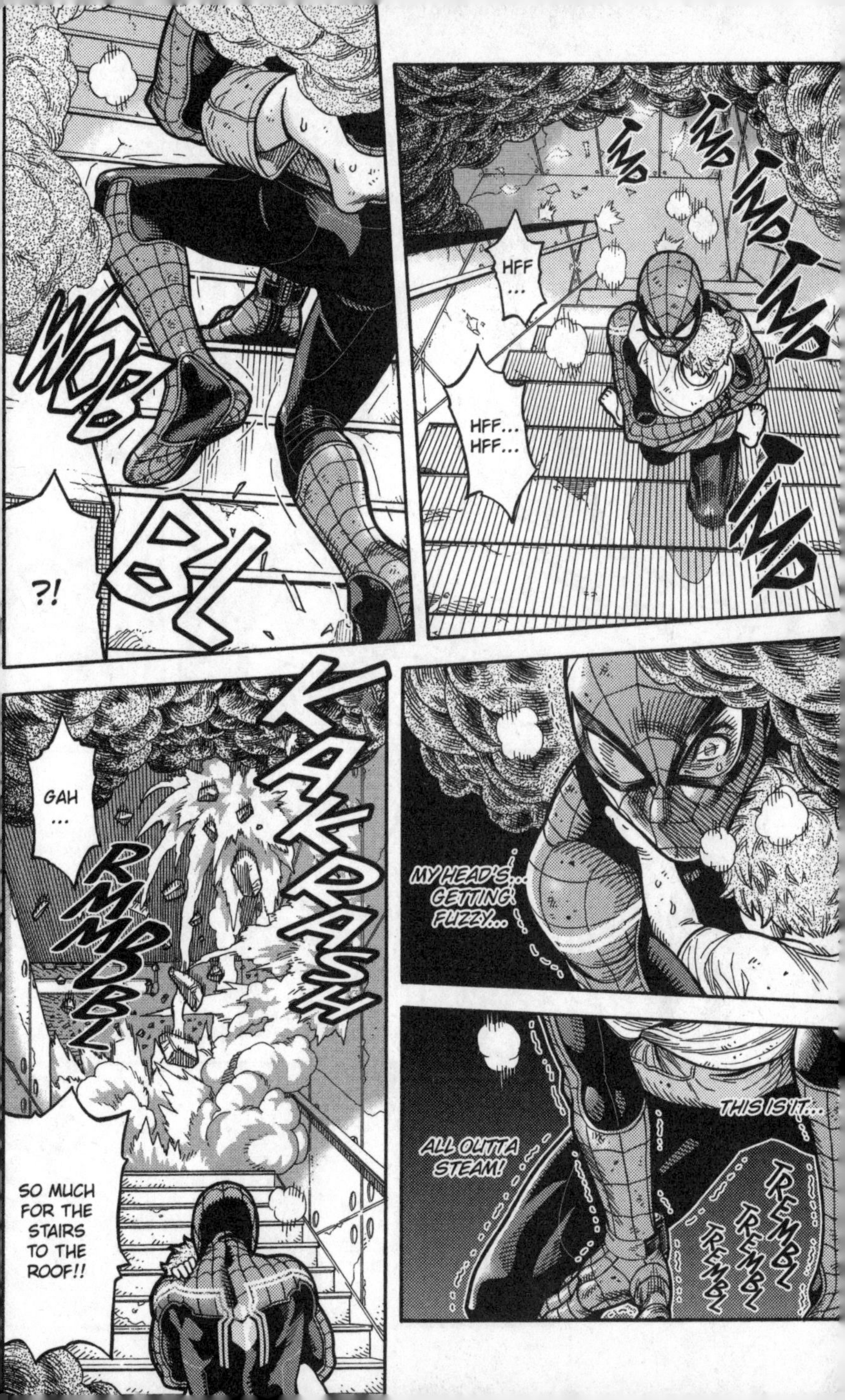
TMP TMP TMP TMP TMP TMP
HFF...
HFF... HFF...
WOBBBL
?!
MY HEAD'S... GETTING FUZZY...
THIS IS IT...
ALL OUTTA STEAM!
TREMBL TREMBL TREMBL
KAKRASH
GAH...
RMMBL
SO MUCH FOR THE STAIRS TO THE ROOF!!

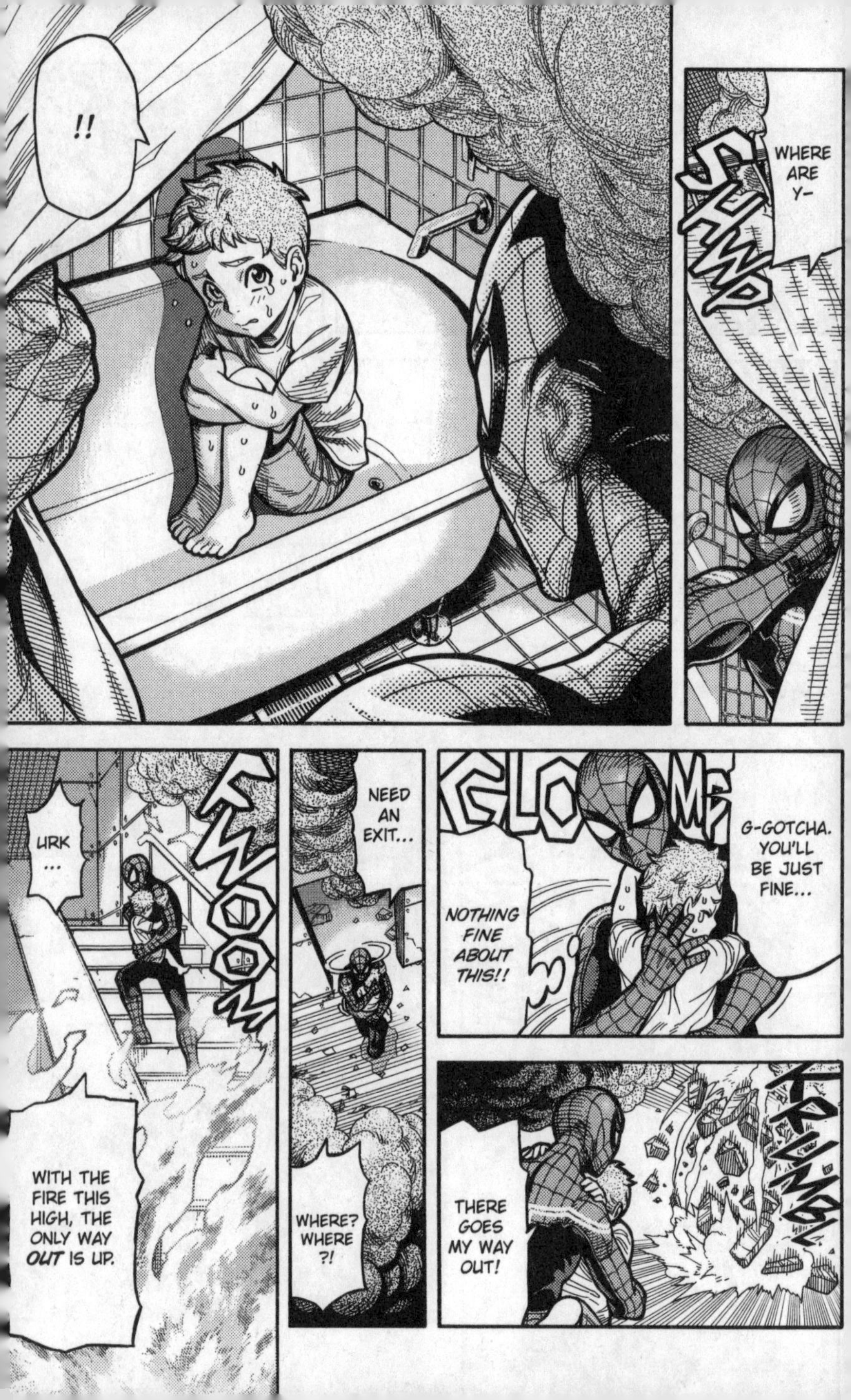
SHWP
WHERE ARE Y-
!!
CLO MF
G-GOTCHA. YOU'LL BE JUST FINE...
NOTHING FINE ABOUT THIS!!
KRUMBL
THERE GOES MY WAY OUT!
NEED AN EXIT...
WHERE? WHERE?!
FWOOOM
URK...
WITH THE FIRE THIS HIGH, THE ONLY WAY *OUT* IS UP.

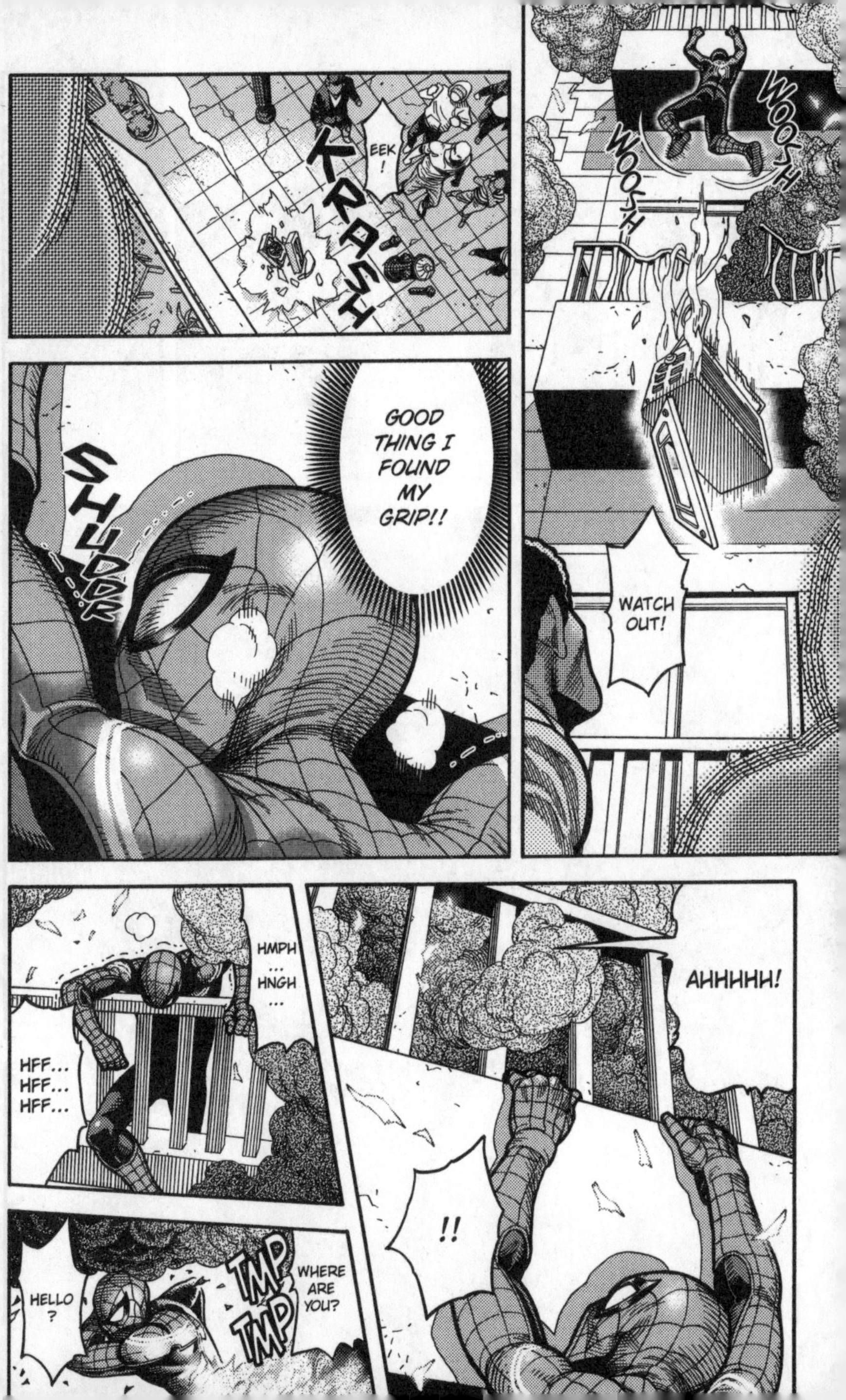
WOOSH
WOOSH
WATCH OUT!
EEK!
KRASH
GOOD THING I FOUND MY GRIP!!
SHUDDR
AHHHHH!
!!
HMPH... HNGH...
HFF... HFF... HFF...
WHERE ARE YOU?
TMP TMP
HELLO?

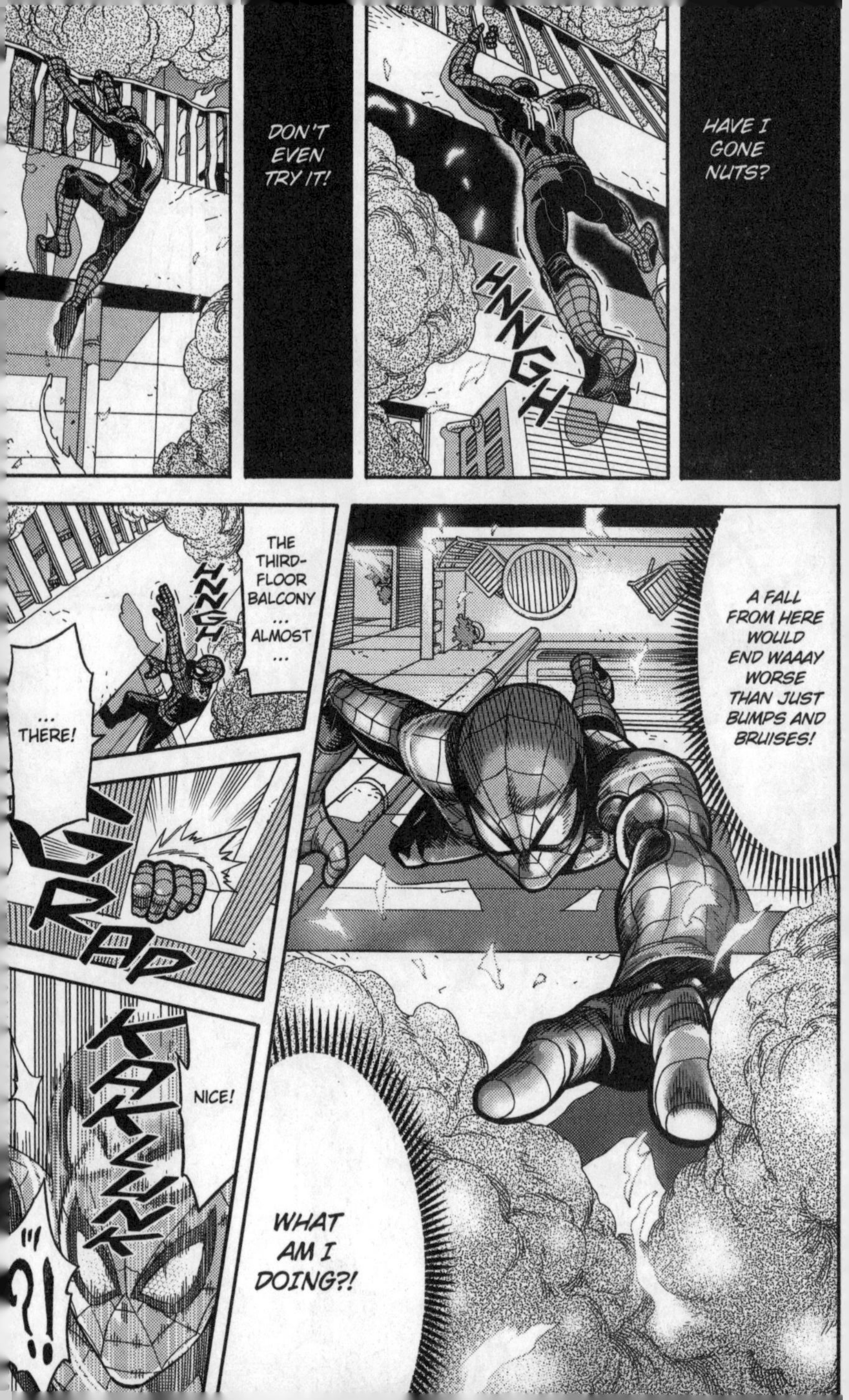
HAVE I GONE NUTS?
HNNGH
DON'T EVEN TRY IT!
A FALL FROM HERE WOULD END WAAAY WORSE THAN JUST BUMPS AND BRUISES!
WHAT AM I DOING?!
THE THIRD-FLOOR BALCONY ... ALMOST ...
HNNGH
... THERE!
KAKLUNK
NICE!
?!

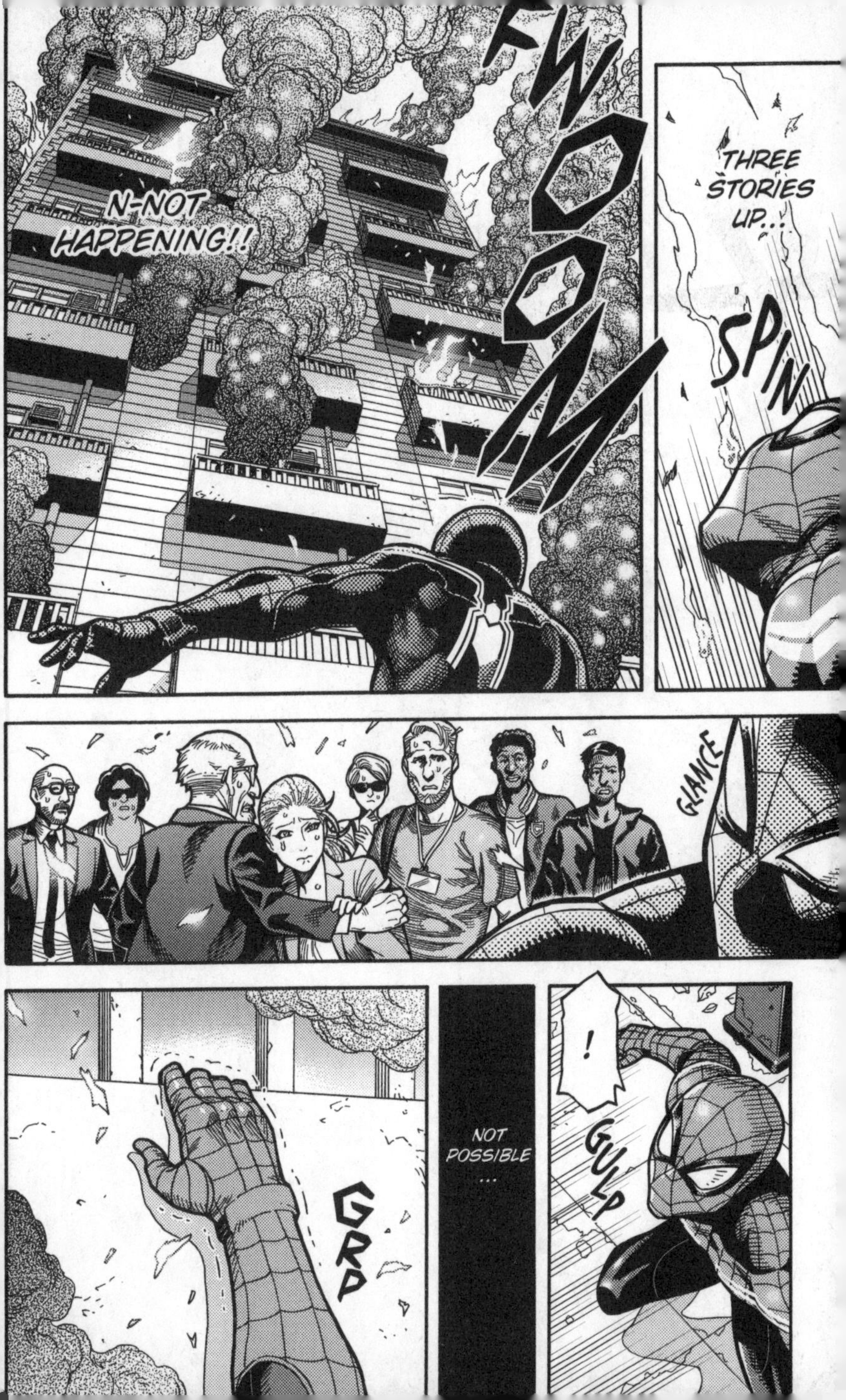
THREE STORIES UP...
SPIN
FWOOOM
N-NOT HAPPENING!!
GLANCE
!
GULP
NOT POSSIBLE ...
GRP

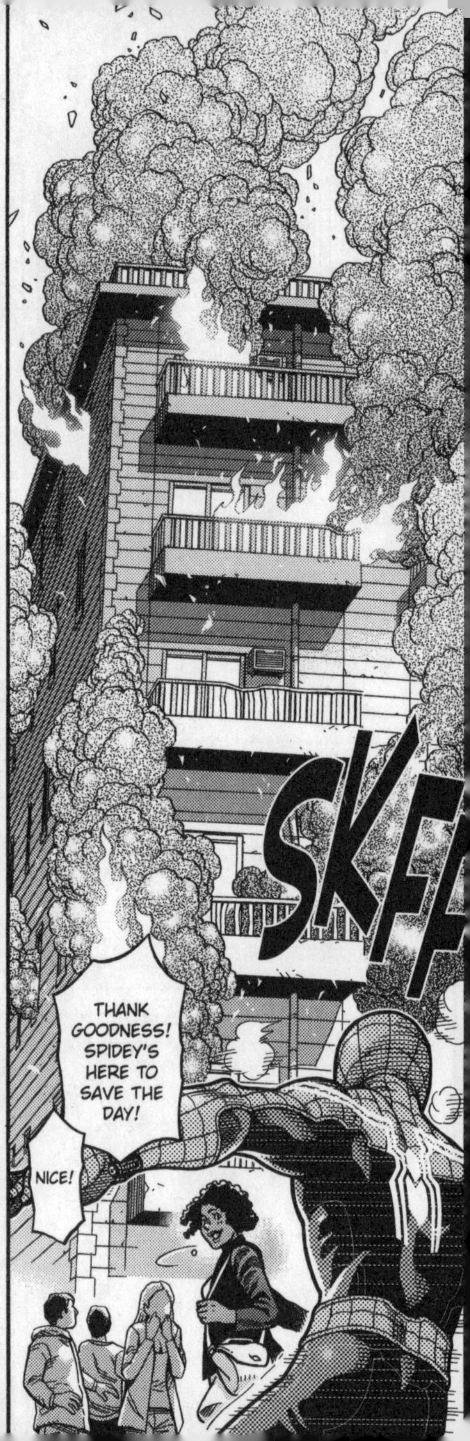
SKFF
THANK GOODNESS! SPIDEY'S HERE TO SAVE THE DAY!
NICE!

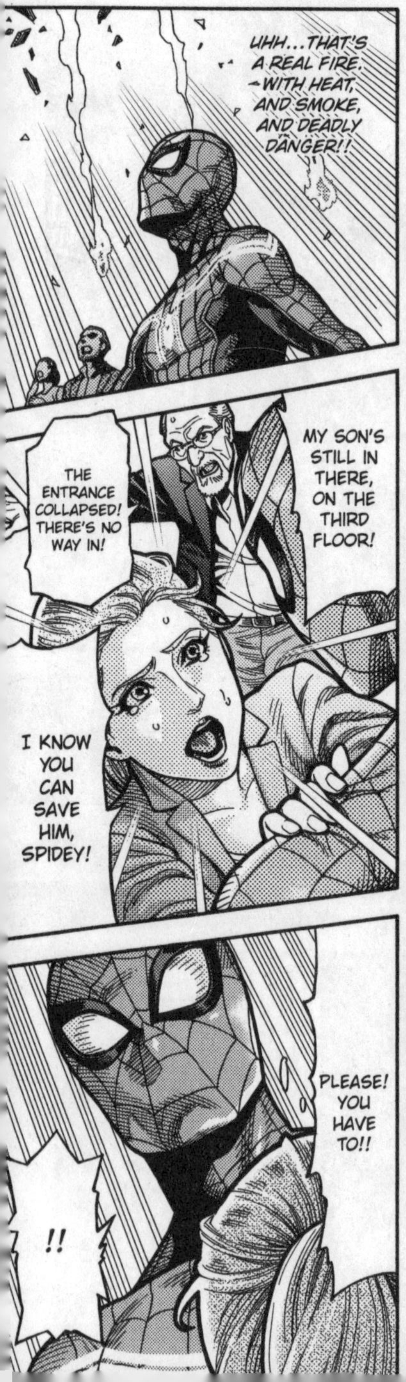
UHH...THAT'S A REAL FIRE. —WITH HEAT, AND SMOKE, AND DEADLY DANGER!!
MY SON'S STILL IN THERE, ON THE THIRD FLOOR!
THE ENTRANCE COLLAPSED! THERE'S NO WAY IN!
I KNOW YOU CAN SAVE HIM, SPIDEY!
PLEASE! YOU HAVE TO!!
!!

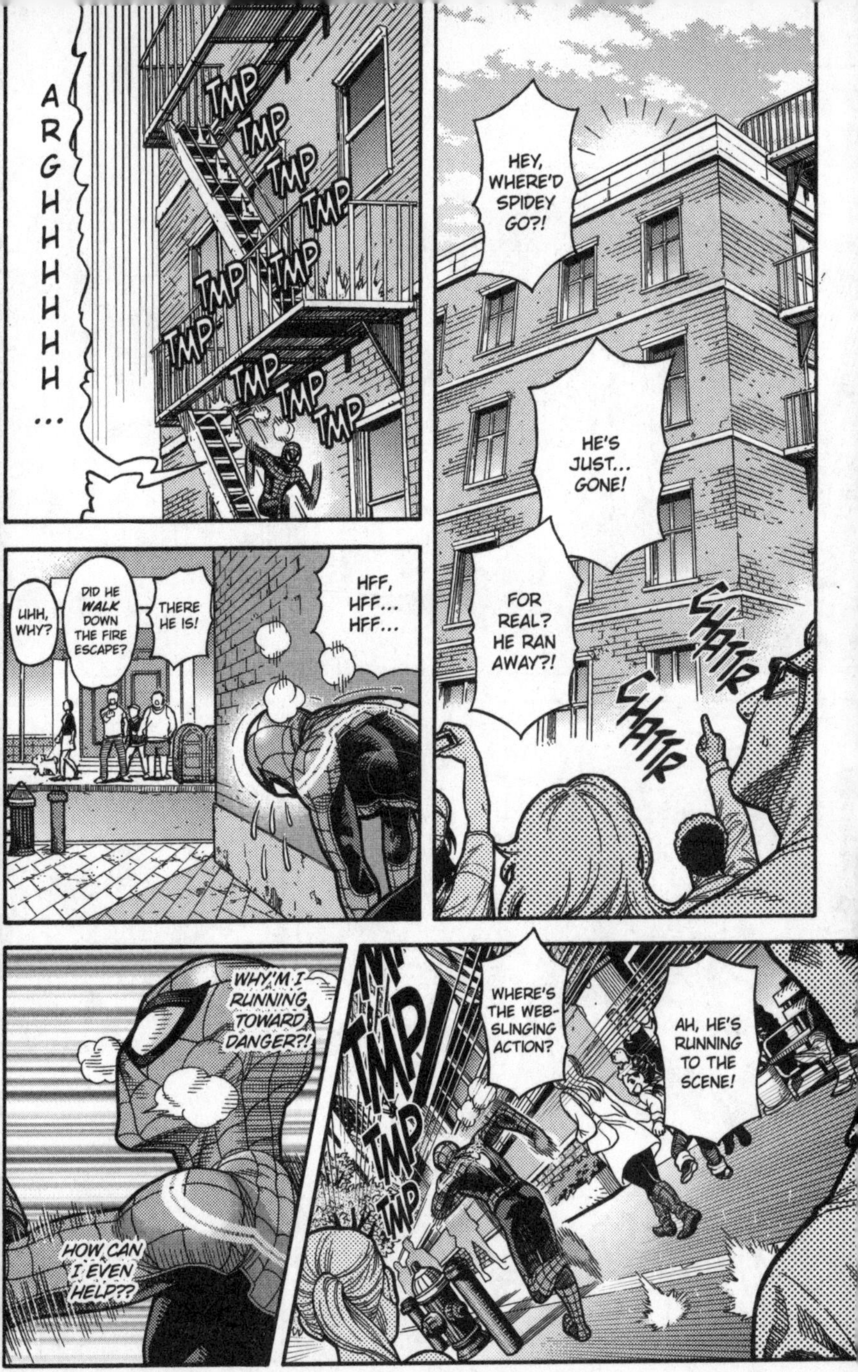
HEY, WHERE'D SPIDEY GO?!
HE'S JUST... GONE!
FOR REAL? HE RAN AWAY?!
CHATTR
CHATTR
TMP TMP TMP TMP TMP TMP TMP TMP TMP TMP
ARGHHHHHH...
HFF, HFF... HFF...
THERE HE IS!
DID HE WALK DOWN THE FIRE ESCAPE?
UHH, WHY?
AH, HE'S RUNNING TO THE SCENE!
WHERE'S THE WEB-SLINGING ACTION?
TMP
TMP
TMP
TMP
WHY'M I RUNNING TOWARD DANGER?!
HOW CAN I EVEN HELP??

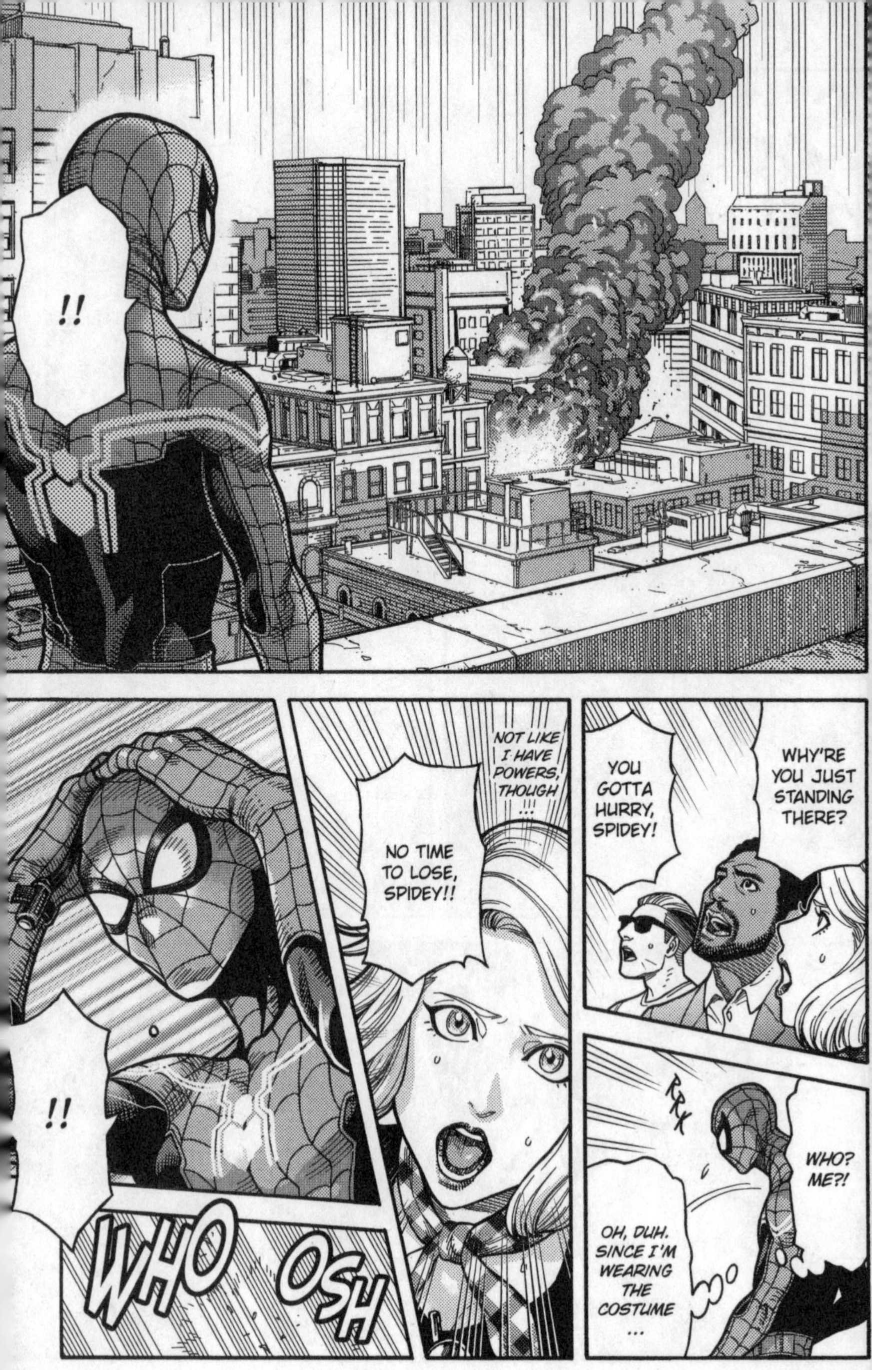
!!
WHY'RE YOU JUST STANDING THERE?
YOU GOTTA HURRY, SPIDEY!
WHO? ME?!
RRK
OH, DUH. SINCE I'M WEARING THE COSTUME ...
NOT LIKE I HAVE POWERS, THOUGH ...
NO TIME TO LOSE, SPIDEY!!
!!
WHOOSH

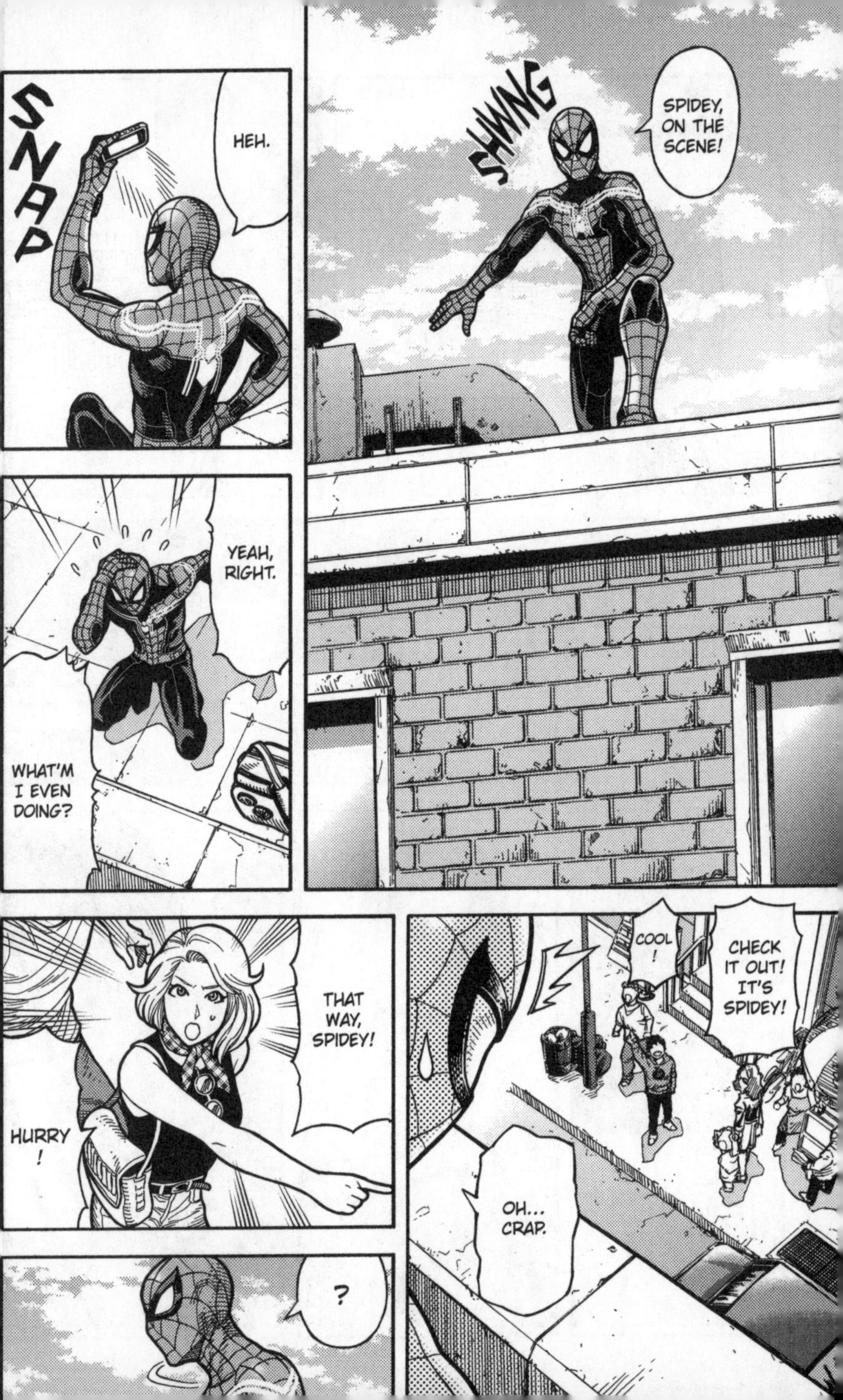
SHWNG
SPIDEY, ON THE SCENE!
SNAP
HEH.
YEAH, RIGHT.
WHAT'M I EVEN DOING?
CHECK IT OUT! IT'S SPIDEY!
COOL!
OH... CRAP.
THAT WAY, SPIDEY!
HURRY!
?

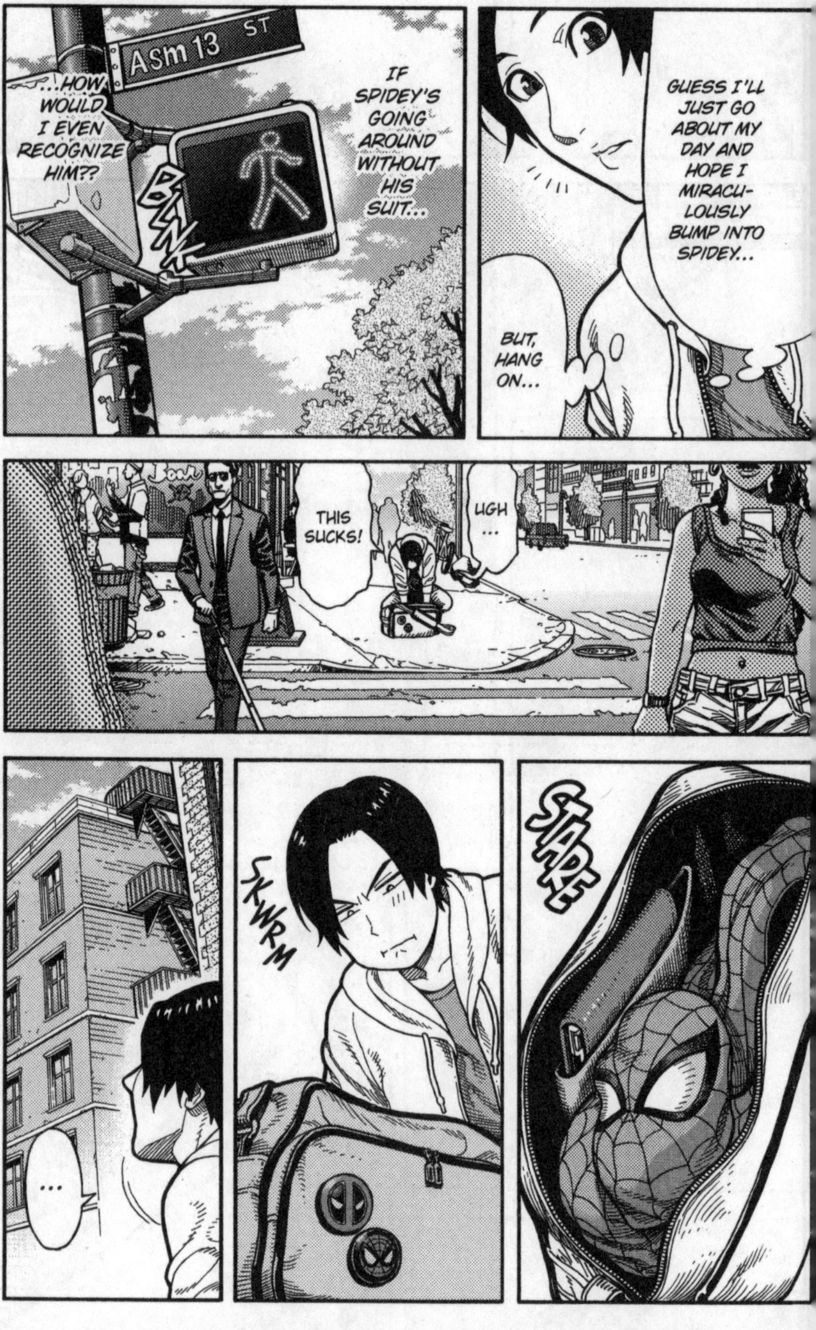
GUESS I'LL JUST GO ABOUT MY DAY AND HOPE I MIRACULOUSLY BUMP INTO SPIDEY...
BUT, HANG ON...
ASm 13 ST
IF SPIDEY'S GOING AROUND WITHOUT HIS SUIT...
...HOW WOULD I EVEN RECOGNIZE HIM??
BLINK
UGH ...
THIS SUCKS!
STARE
SKWRM
...

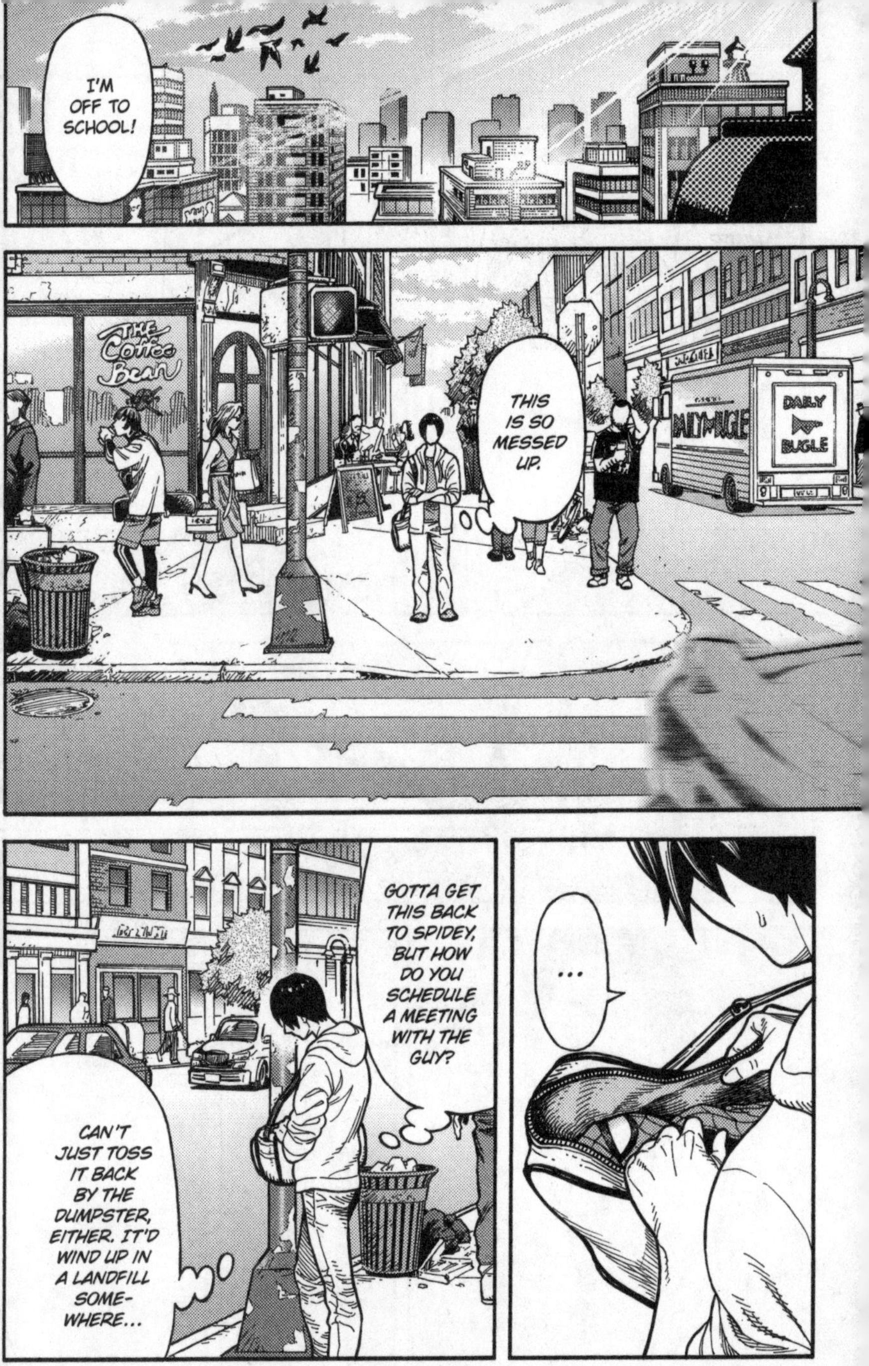
I'M OFF TO SCHOOL!
THE Coffee Bean
DAILY BUGLE
DAILY BUGLE
THIS IS SO MESSED UP.
...
GOTTA GET THIS BACK TO SPIDEY, BUT HOW DO YOU SCHEDULE A MEETING WITH THE GUY?
CAN'T JUST TOSS IT BACK BY THE DUMPSTER, EITHER. IT'D WIND UP IN A LANDFILL SOME-WHERE...

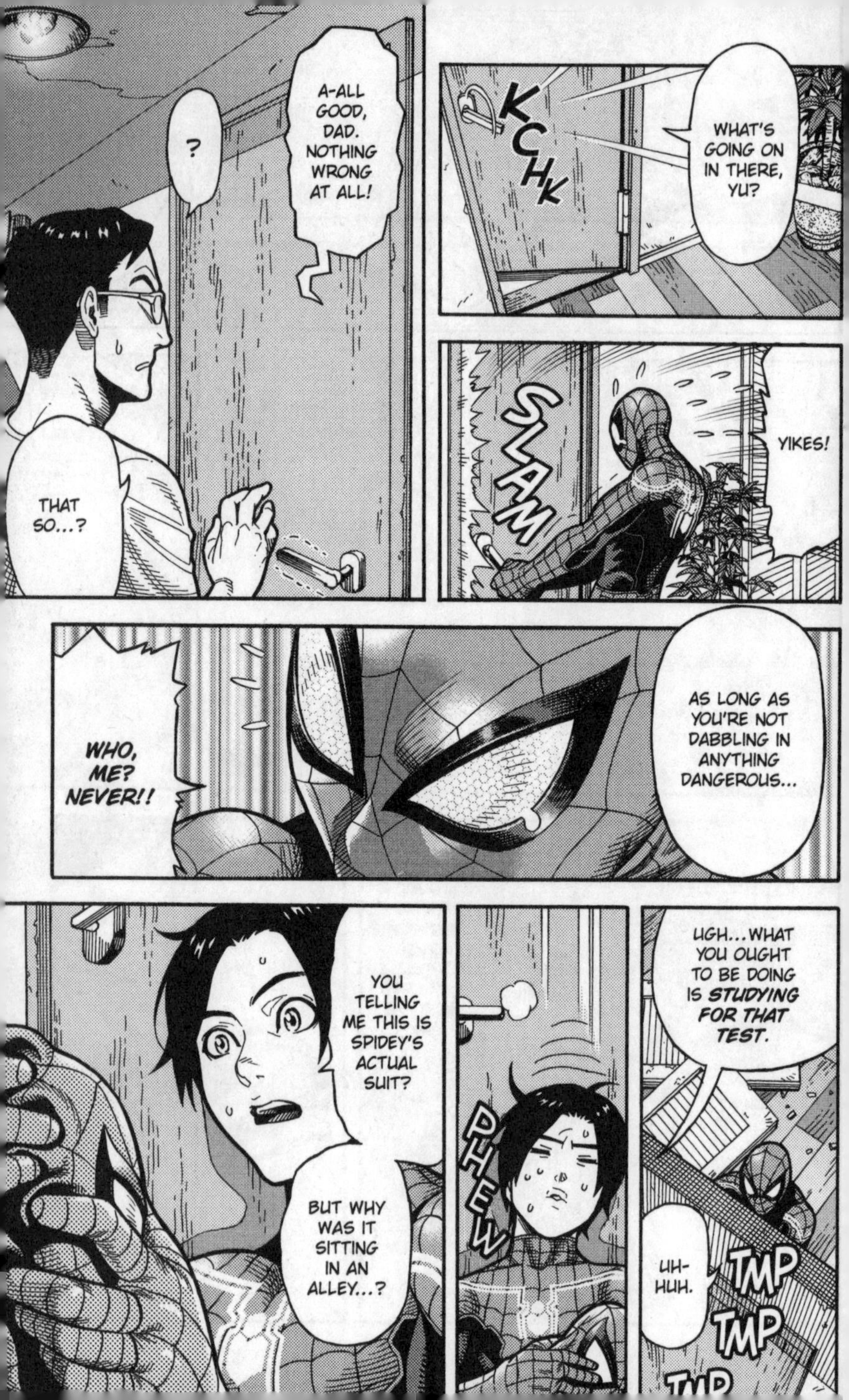
KCHK
WHAT'S GOING ON IN THERE, YU?
YIKES!
SLAM
A-ALL GOOD, DAD. NOTHING WRONG AT ALL!
?
THAT SO...?
AS LONG AS YOU'RE NOT DABBLING IN ANYTHING DANGEROUS...
WHO, ME? NEVER!!
UGH...WHAT YOU OUGHT TO BE DOING IS STUDYING FOR THAT TEST.
UH-HUH.
TMP
TMP
PHEW
YOU TELLING ME THIS IS SPIDEY'S ACTUAL SUIT?
BUT WHY WAS IT SITTING IN AN ALLEY...?

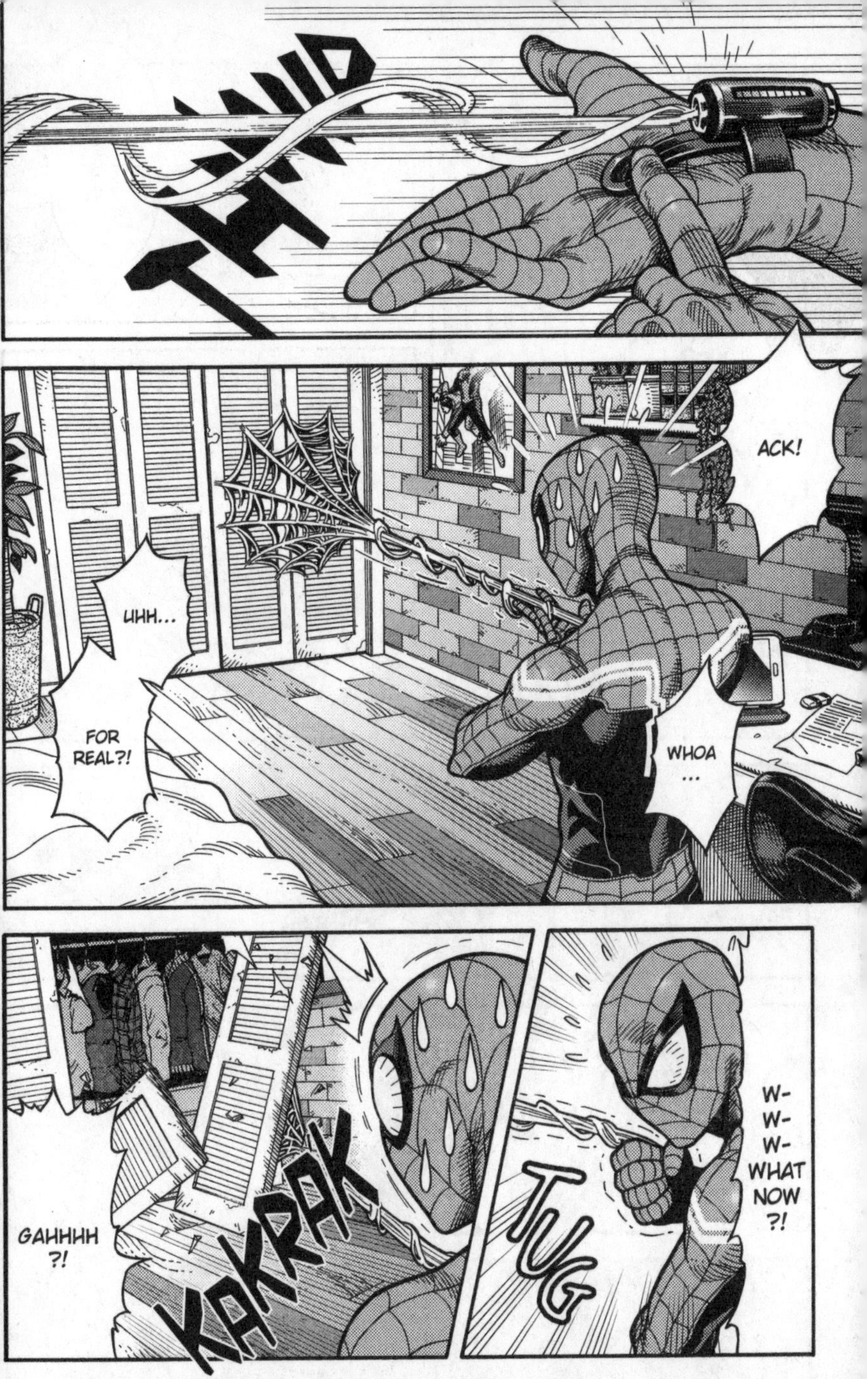
THWIP
ACK!
WHOA...
UHH...
FOR REAL?!
W-W-W-WHAT NOW?!
TUG
KAKRAK
GAHHHH?!

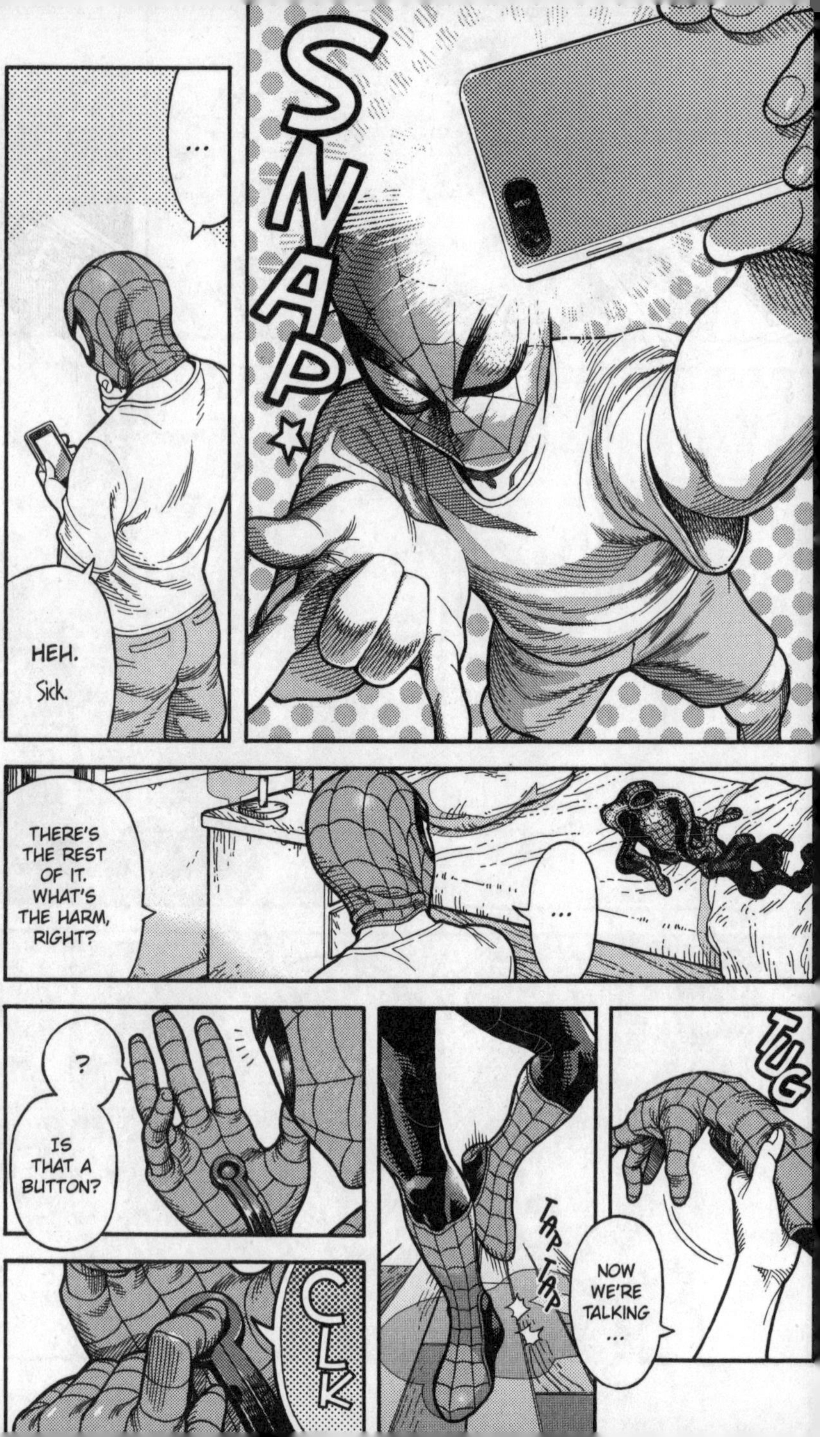
SNAP★
...
HEH.
Sick.
...
THERE'S THE REST OF IT. WHAT'S THE HARM, RIGHT?
TUG
NOW WE'RE TALKING ...
TAP TAP
?
IS THAT A BUTTON?
CLK

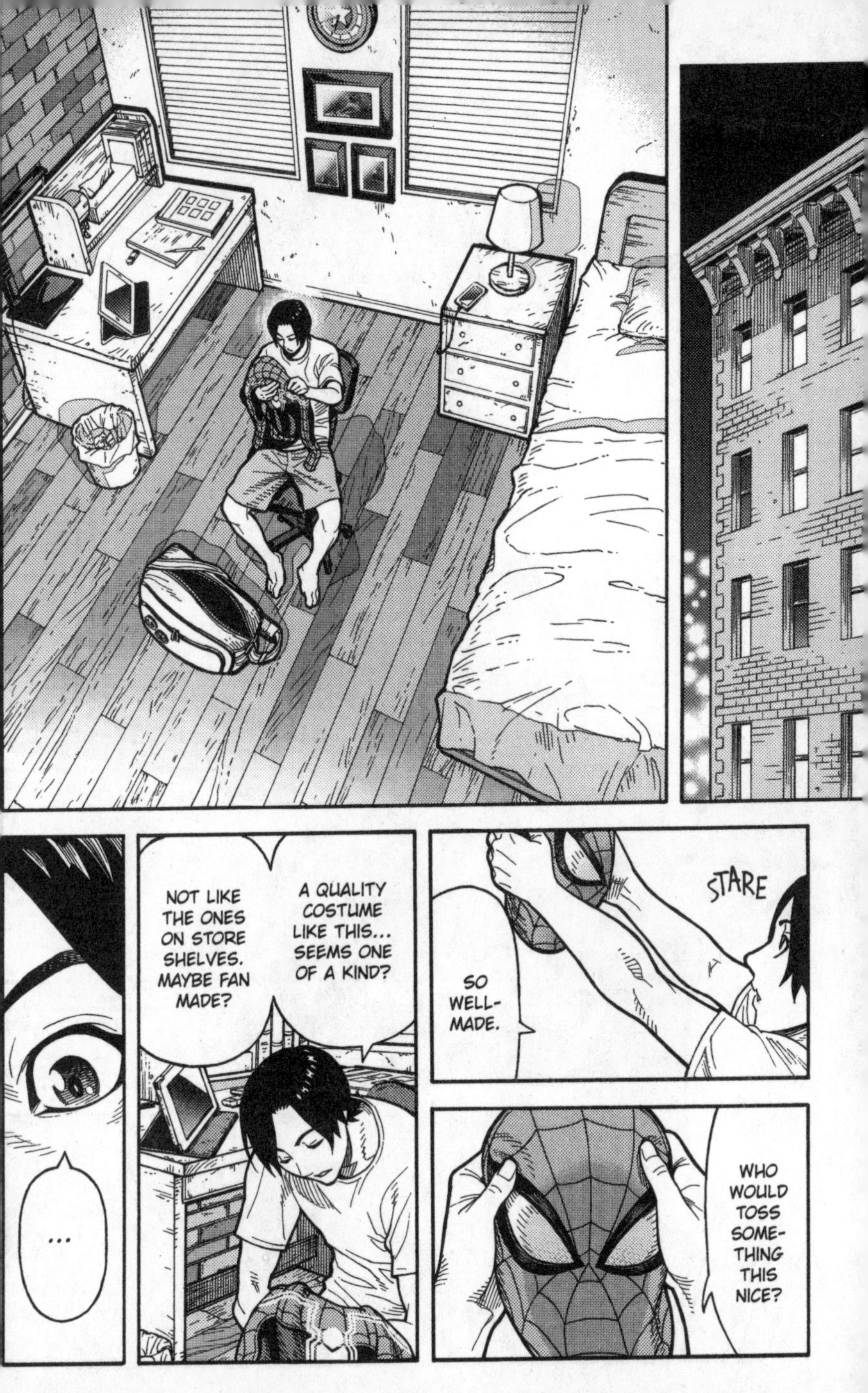
STARE
SO WELL-MADE.
WHO WOULD TOSS SOMETHING THIS NICE?
A QUALITY COSTUME LIKE THIS... SEEMS ONE OF A KIND?
NOT LIKE THE ONES ON STORE SHELVES. MAYBE FAN MADE?
...

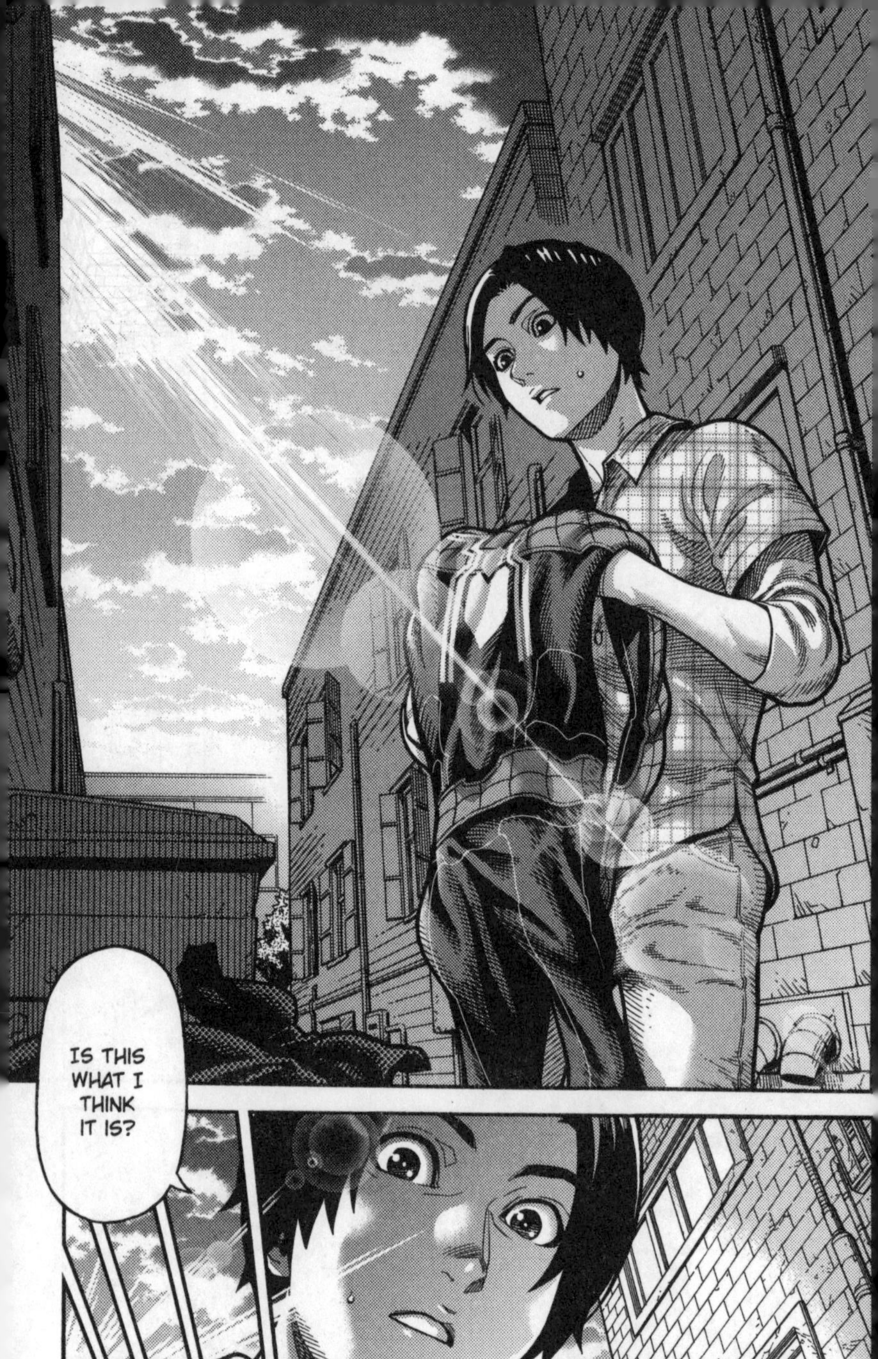
IS THIS WHAT I THINK IT IS?

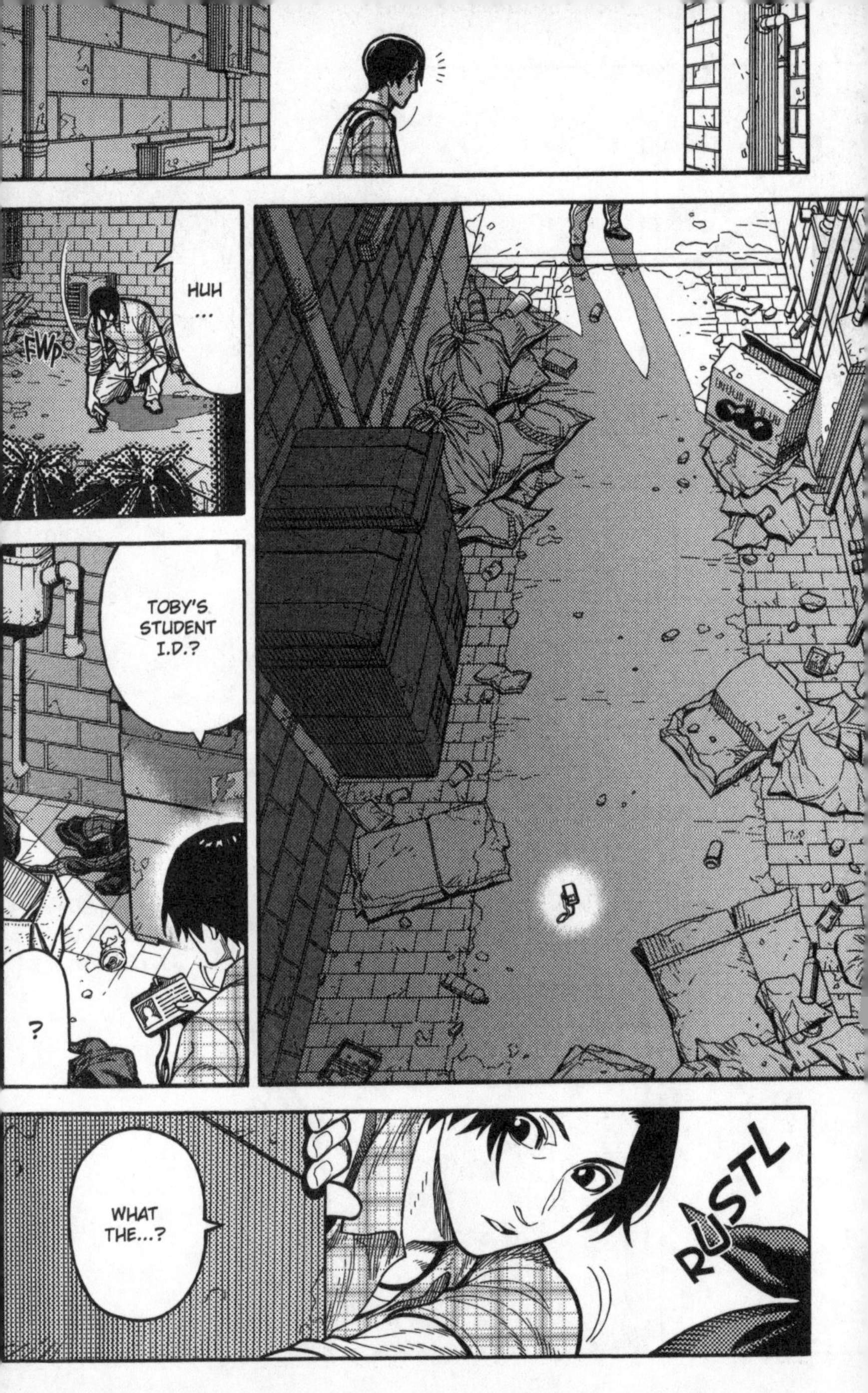

HUH ...
FWP
TOBY'S STUDENT I.D.?
?
RUSTL
WHAT THE...?

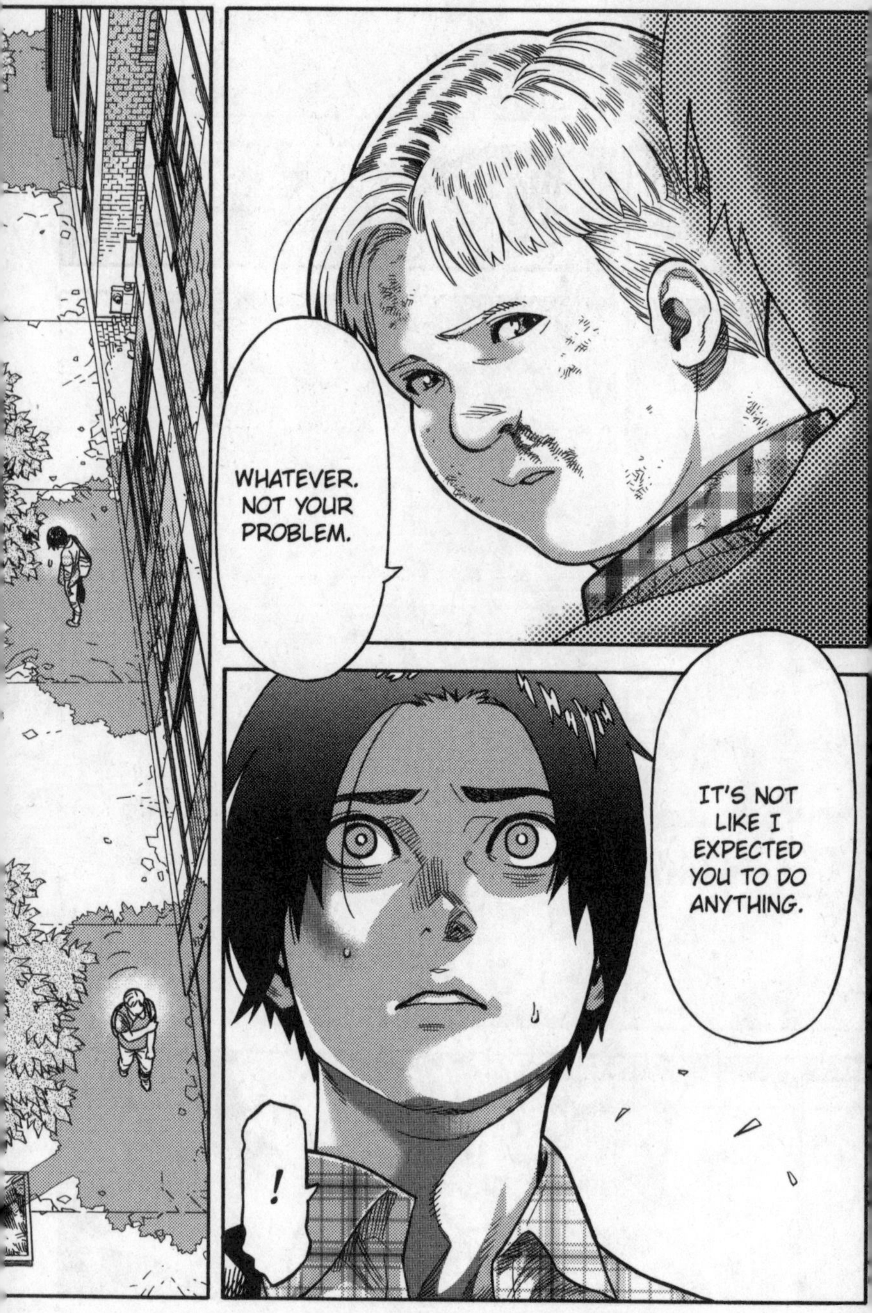
WHATEVER. NOT YOUR PROBLEM.
IT'S NOT LIKE I EXPECTED YOU TO DO ANYTHING.
!

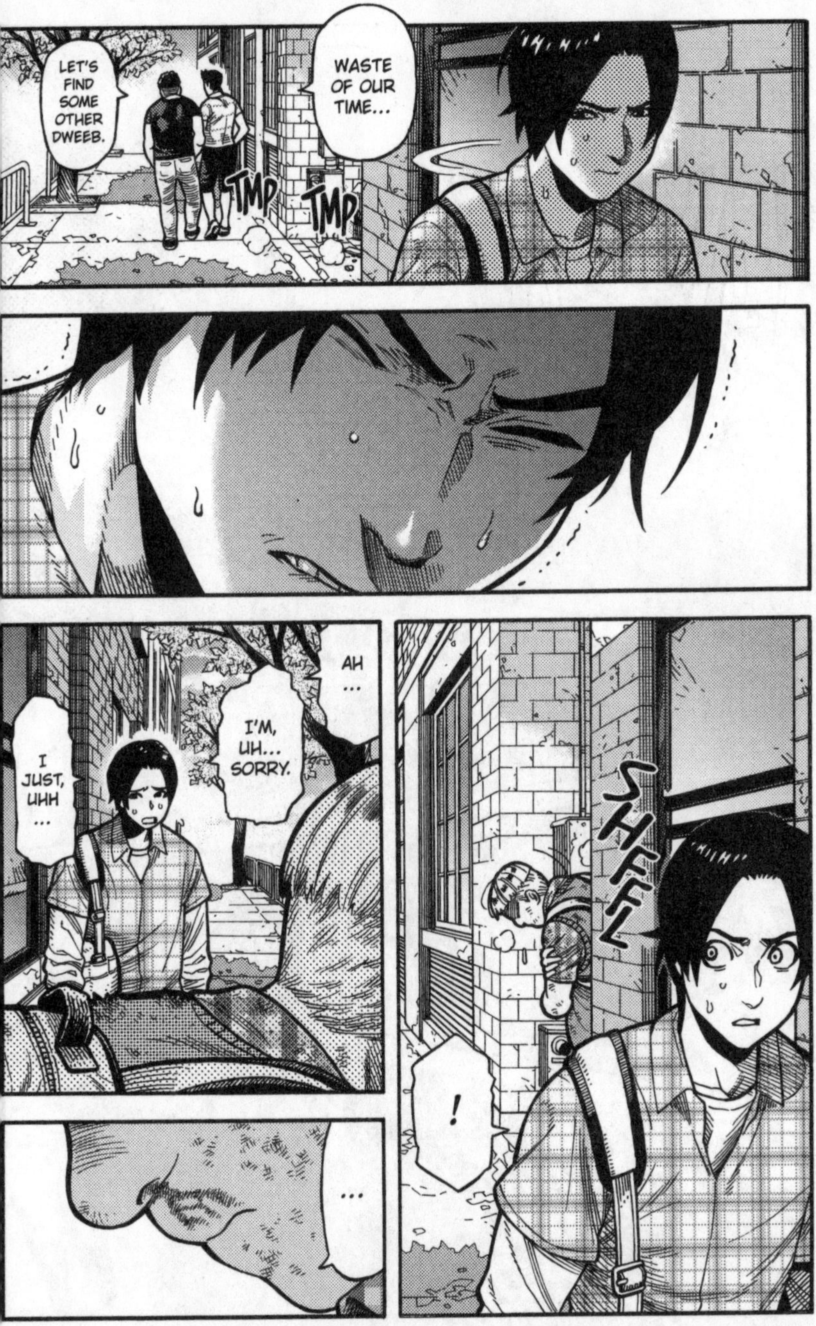
WASTE OF OUR TIME...
LET'S FIND SOME OTHER DWEEB.
TMP
TMP
SHFFL
!
AH ...
I'M, UH... SORRY.
I JUST, UHH ...
...

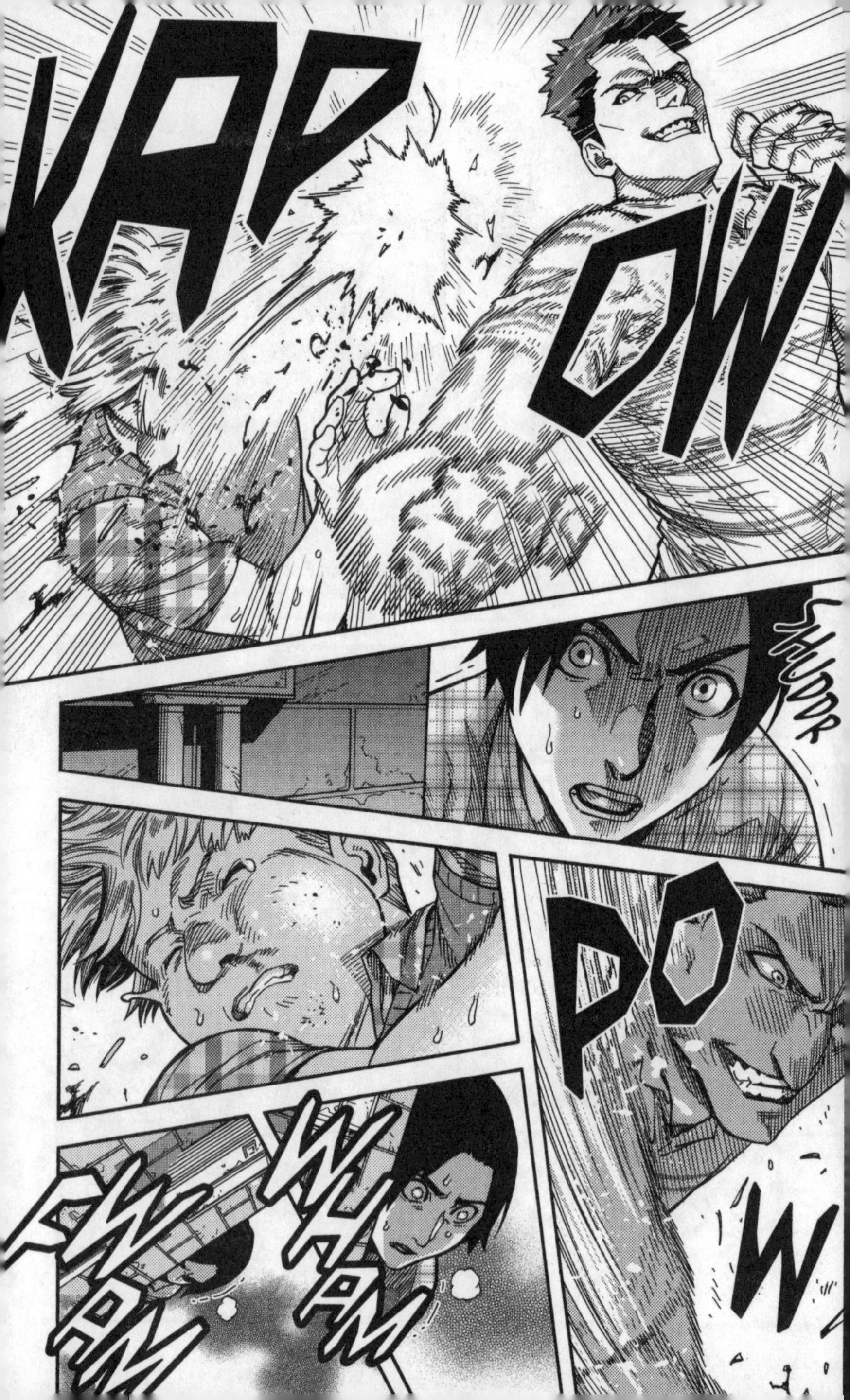
KAPOW
SHUDDR
POW
WHAM
WHAM

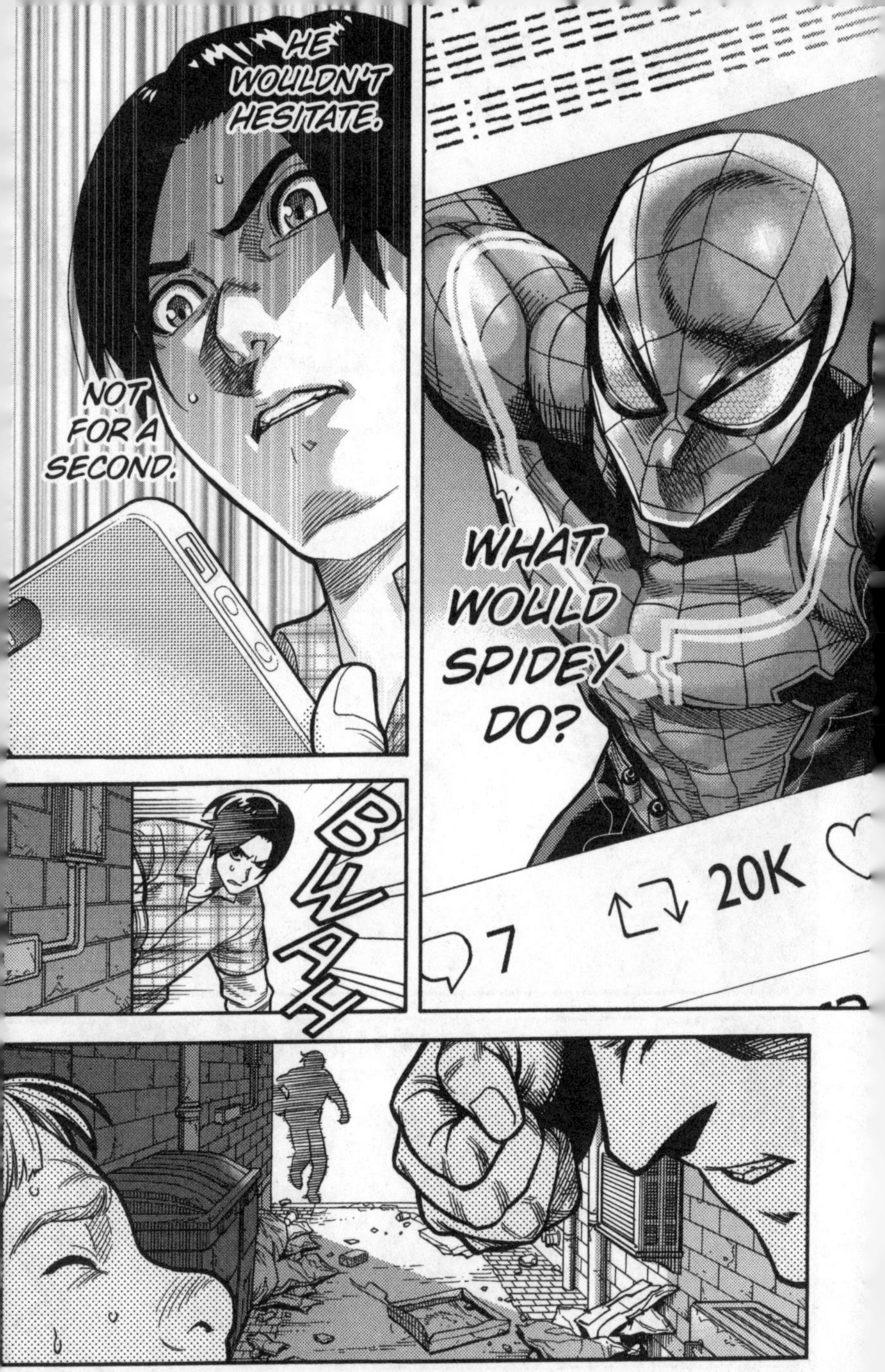
WHAT WOULD SPIDEY DO?
20K
7
HE WOULDN'T HESITATE.
NOT FOR A SECOND.
BWAH

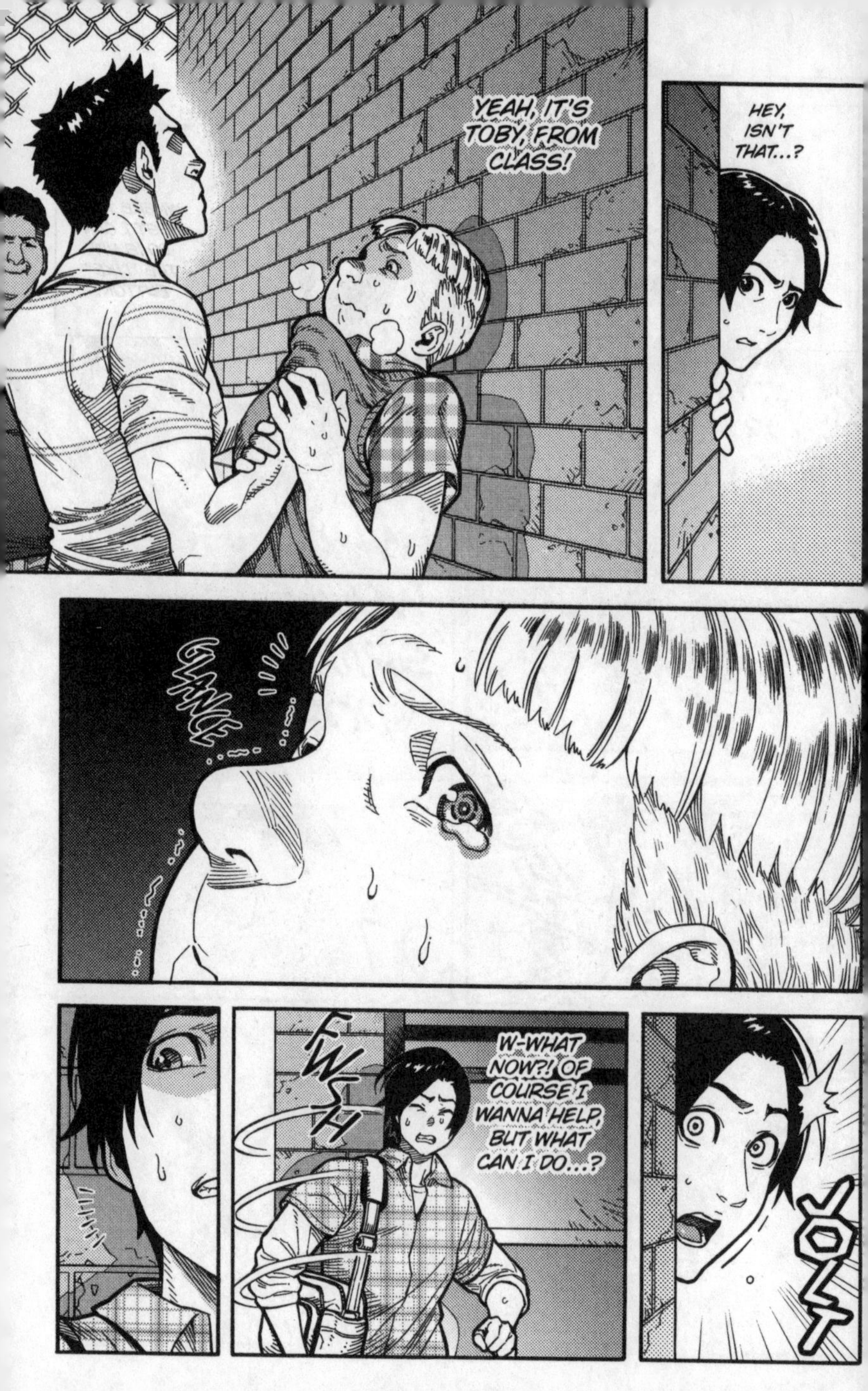
HEY, ISN'T THAT...?
YEAH, IT'S TOBY, FROM CLASS!
GLANCE
JOLT
W-WHAT NOW?! OF COURSE I WANNA HELP, BUT WHAT CAN I DO...?
FWSH

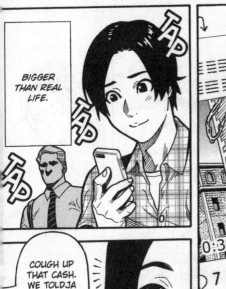

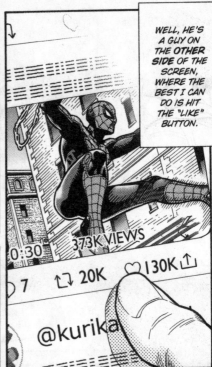

WELL, HE'S A GUY ON THE OTHER SIDE OF THE SCREEN, WHERE THE BEST I CAN DO IS HIT THE "LIKE" BUTTON.
373K VIEWS
0:30
130K
20K
7
@kurika
BIGGER THAN REAL LIFE.
TAP
TAP
TAP
COUGH UP THAT CASH. WE TOLDJA TO HAVE IT FOR US TODAY, YEAH?
!

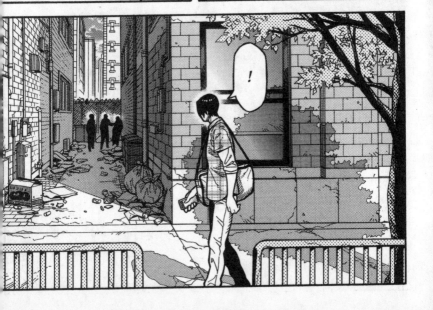

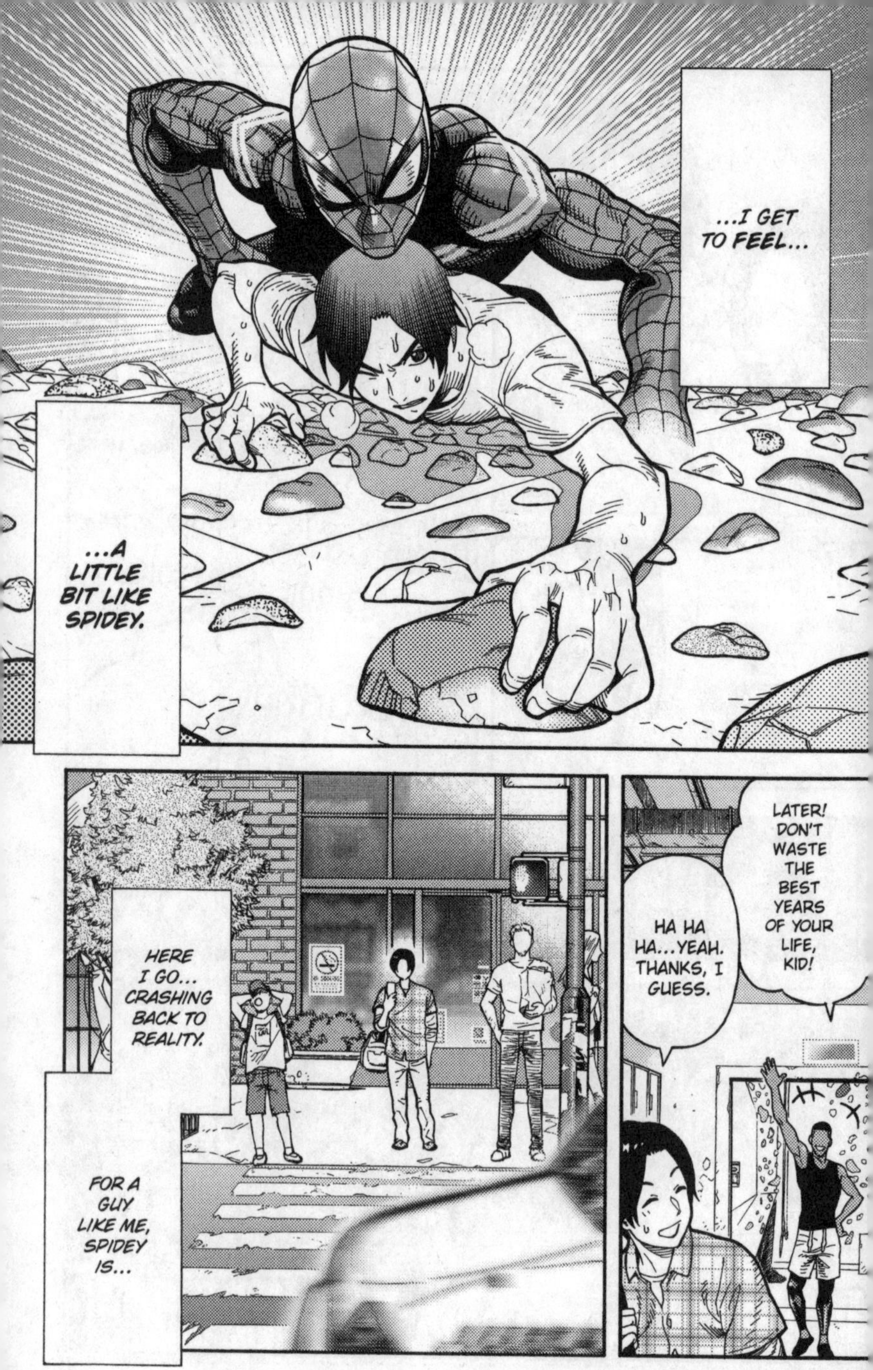
...I GET TO FEEL...
...A LITTLE BIT LIKE SPIDEY.
LATER! DON'T WASTE THE BEST YEARS OF YOUR LIFE, KID!
HA HA HA...YEAH. THANKS, I GUESS.
HERE I GO... CRASHING BACK TO REALITY.
FOR A GUY LIKE ME, SPIDEY IS...

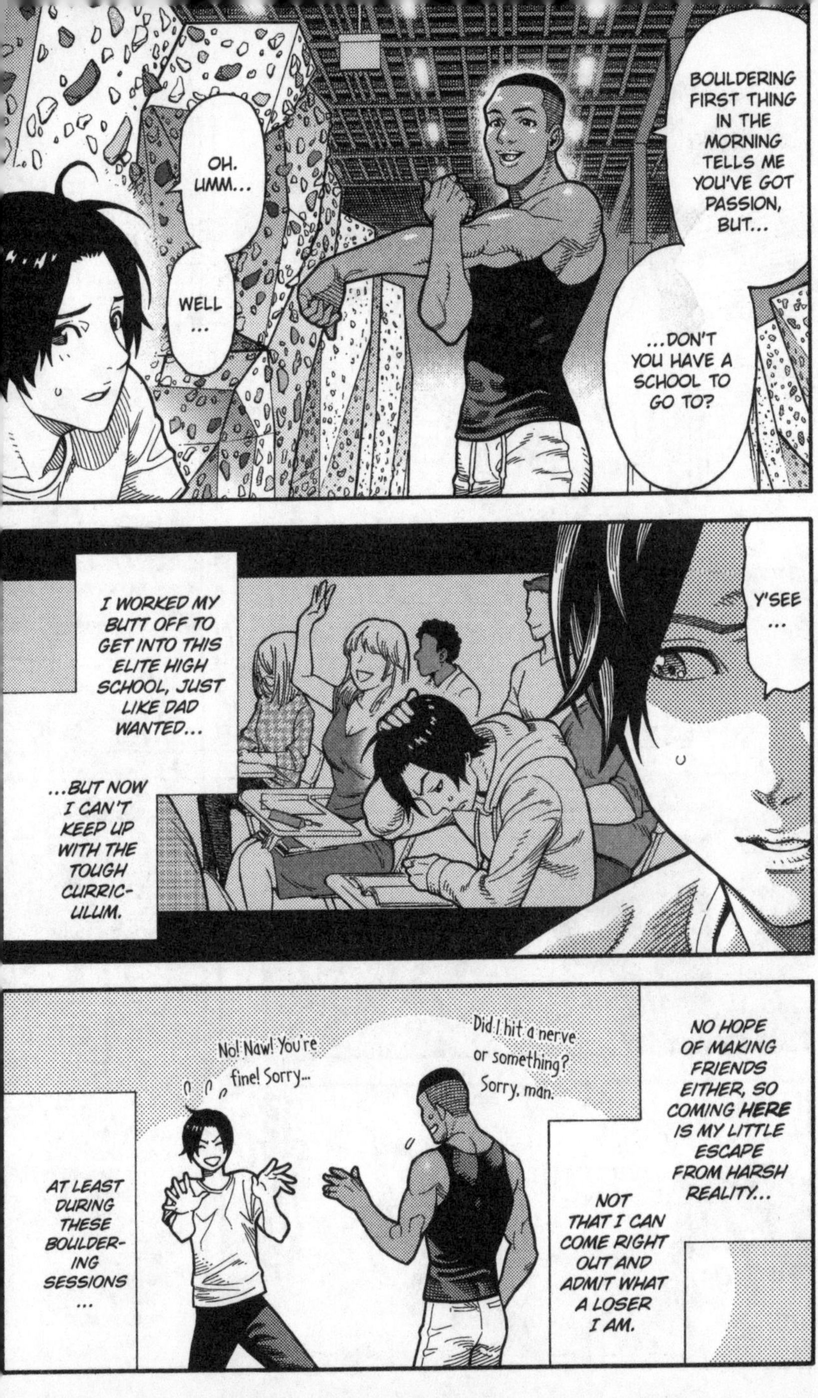
BOULDERING FIRST THING IN THE MORNING TELLS ME YOU'VE GOT PASSION, BUT...
...DON'T YOU HAVE A SCHOOL TO GO TO?
OH. UMM...
WELL...
Y'SEE...
I WORKED MY BUTT OFF TO GET INTO THIS ELITE HIGH SCHOOL, JUST LIKE DAD WANTED...
...BUT NOW I CAN'T KEEP UP WITH THE TOUGH CURRIC-ULUM.
NO HOPE OF MAKING FRIENDS EITHER, SO COMING HERE IS MY LITTLE ESCAPE FROM HARSH REALITY...
NOT THAT I CAN COME RIGHT OUT AND ADMIT WHAT A LOSER I AM.
Did I hit a nerve or something? Sorry, man.
No! Naw! You're fine! Sorry...
AT LEAST DURING THESE BOULDER-ING SESSIONS...

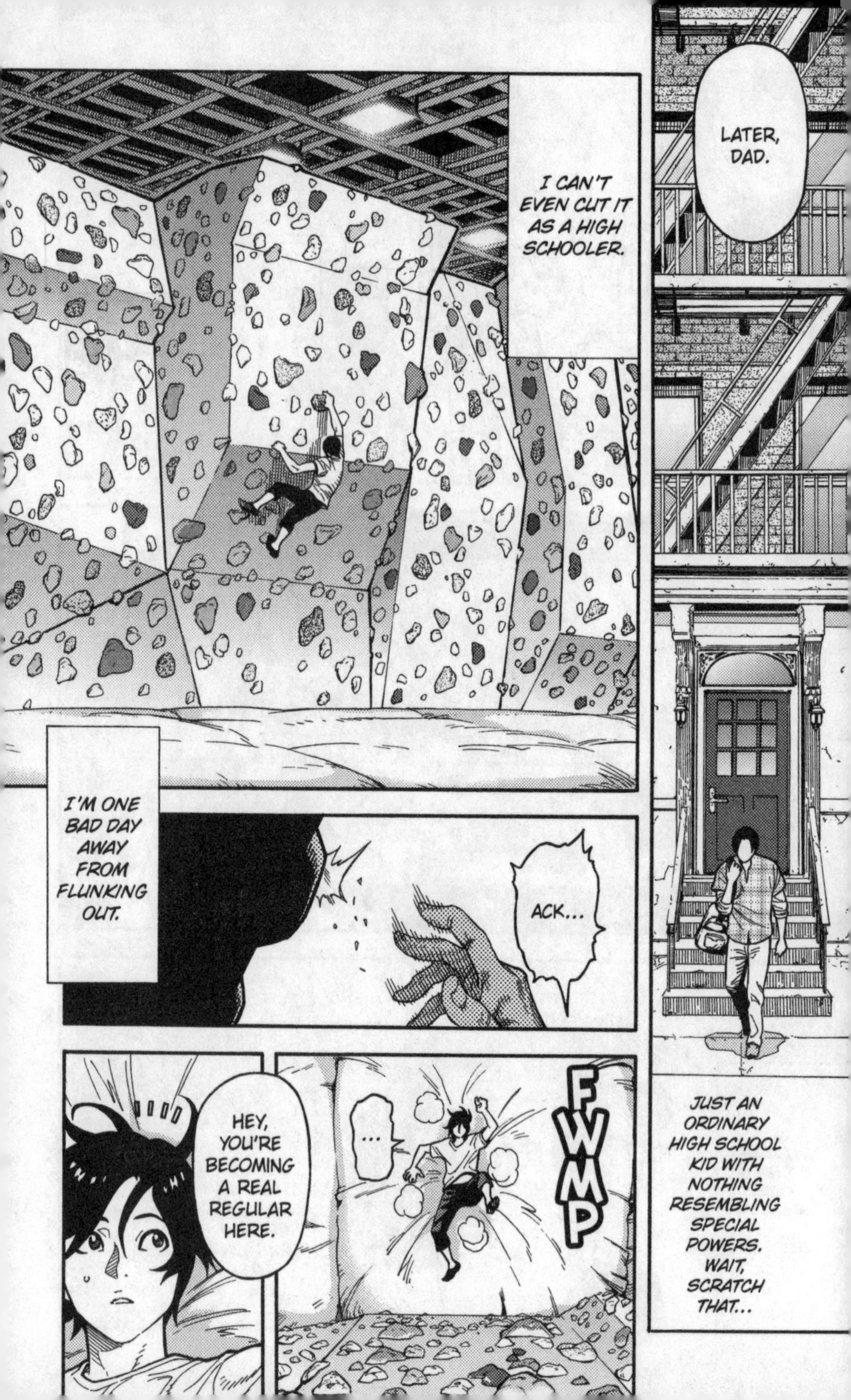
LATER, DAD.
JUST AN ORDINARY HIGH SCHOOL KID WITH NOTHING RESEMBLING SPECIAL POWERS. WAIT, SCRATCH THAT...
I CAN'T EVEN CUT IT AS A HIGH SCHOOLER.
I'M ONE BAD DAY AWAY FROM FLUNKING OUT.
ACK...
FWMP
...
HEY, YOU'RE BECOMING A REAL REGULAR HERE.

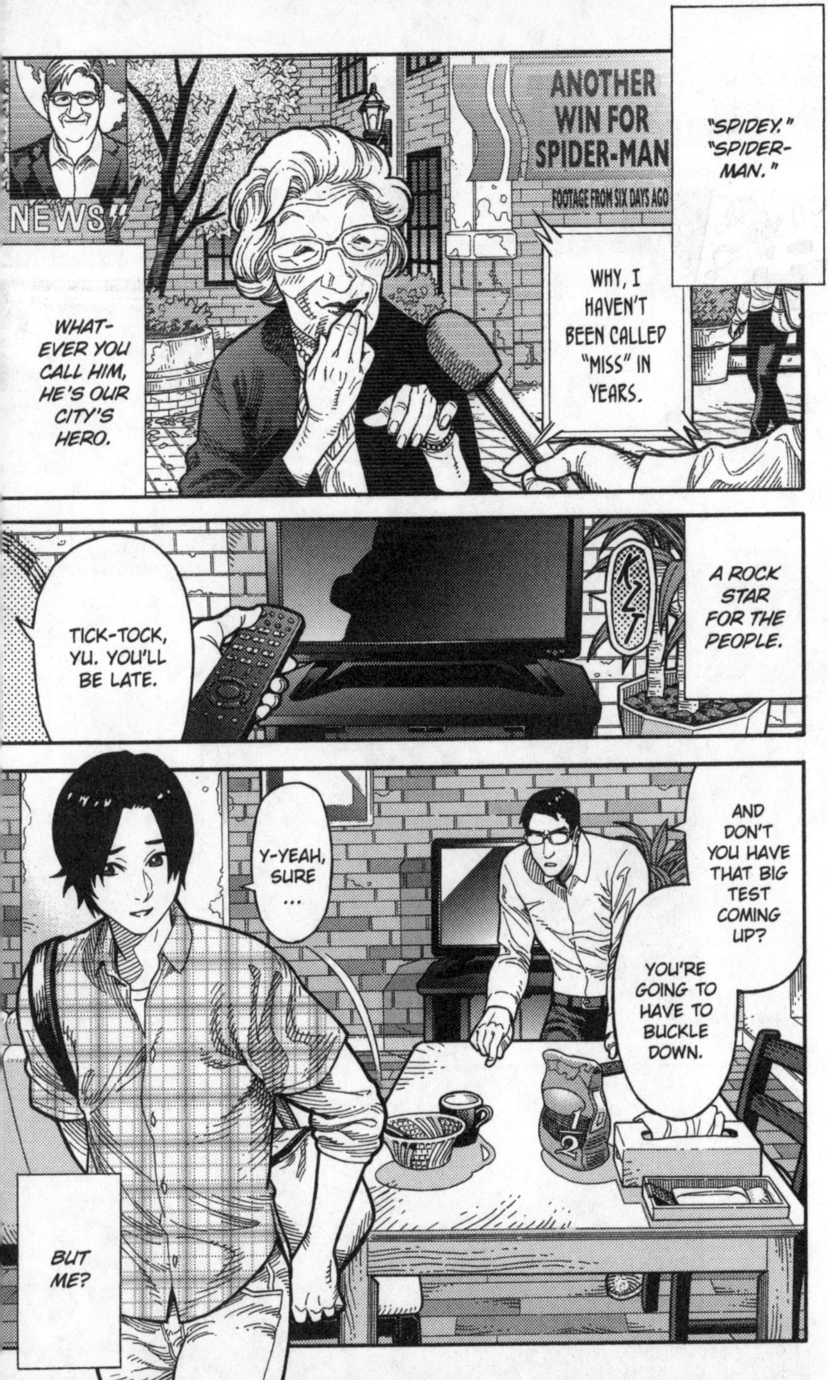
"SPIDEY." "SPIDER-MAN."
ANOTHER WIN FOR SPIDER-MAN
FOOTAGE FROM SIX DAYS AGO
WHY, I HAVEN'T BEEN CALLED "MISS" IN YEARS.
NEWS
WHATEVER YOU CALL HIM, HE'S OUR CITY'S HERO.
A ROCK STAR FOR THE PEOPLE.
KZT
TICK-TOCK, YU. YOU'LL BE LATE.
AND DON'T YOU HAVE THAT BIG TEST COMING UP?
YOU'RE GOING TO HAVE TO BUCKLE DOWN.
Y-YEAH, SURE ...
BUT ME?

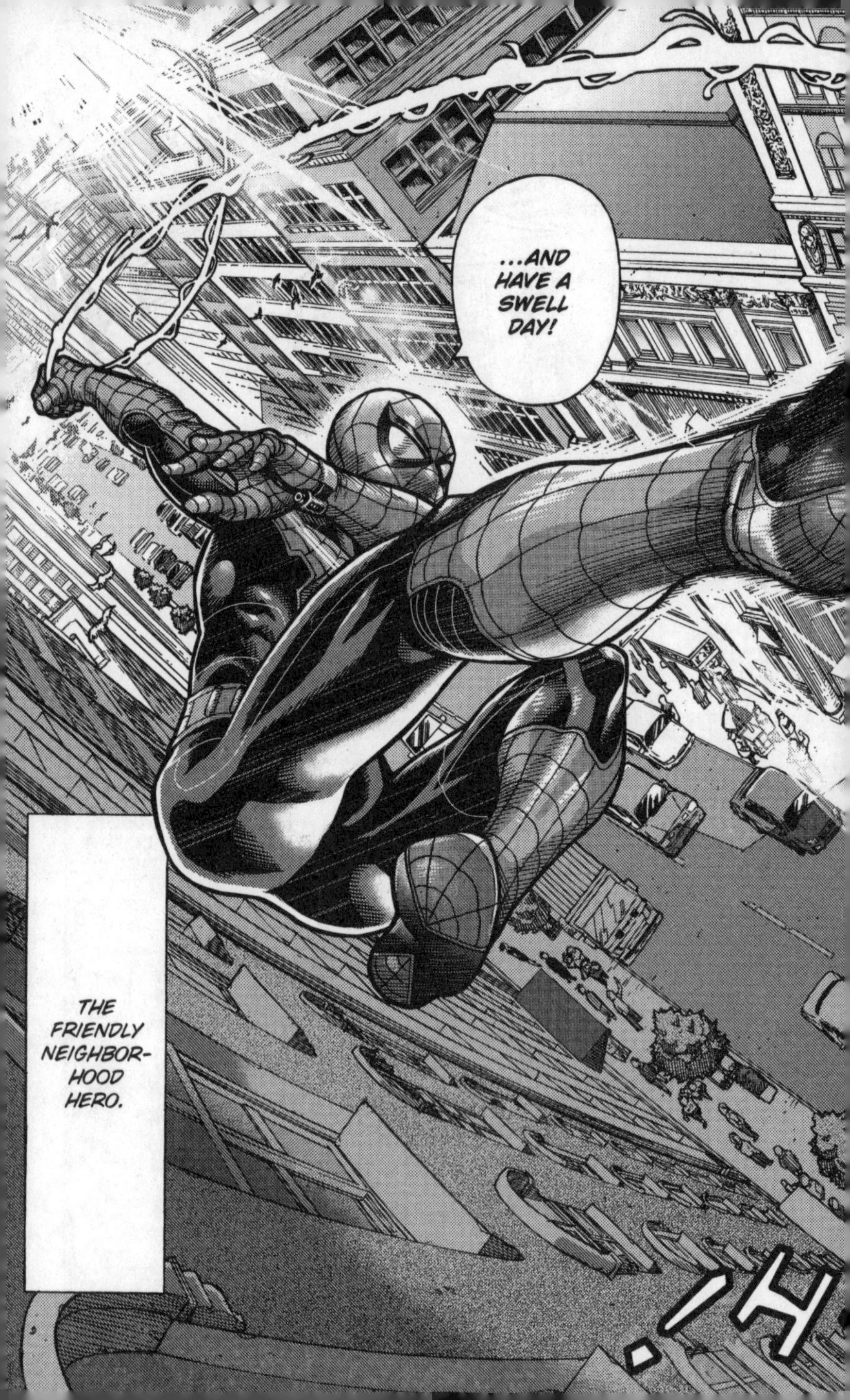
...AND HAVE A SWELL DAY!
THE FRIENDLY NEIGHBOR-HOOD HERO.

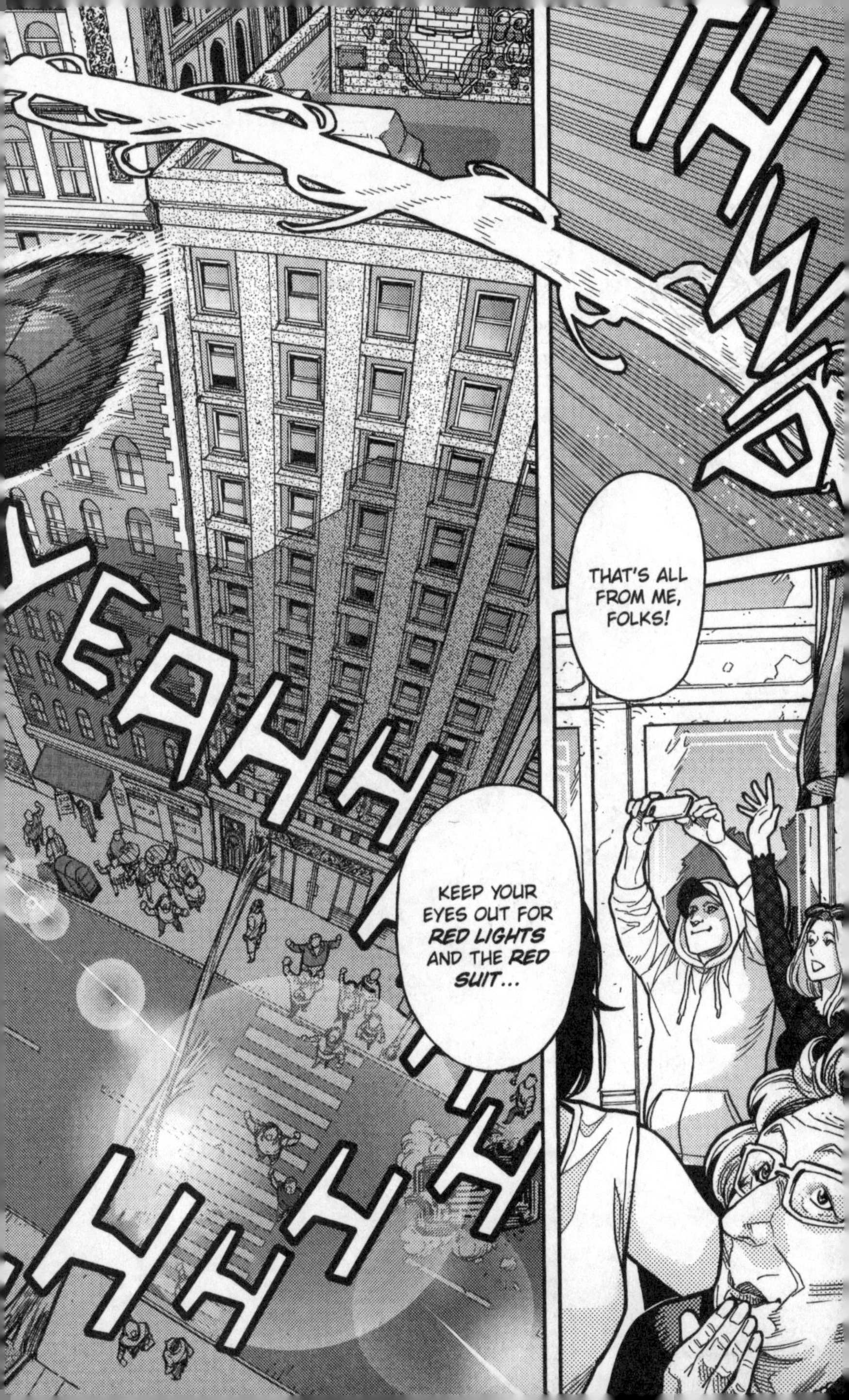
THWIP
THAT'S ALL FROM ME, FOLKS!
KEEP YOUR EYES OUT FOR *RED LIGHTS* AND THE *RED SUIT*...
YEAHHHHHHHHHH

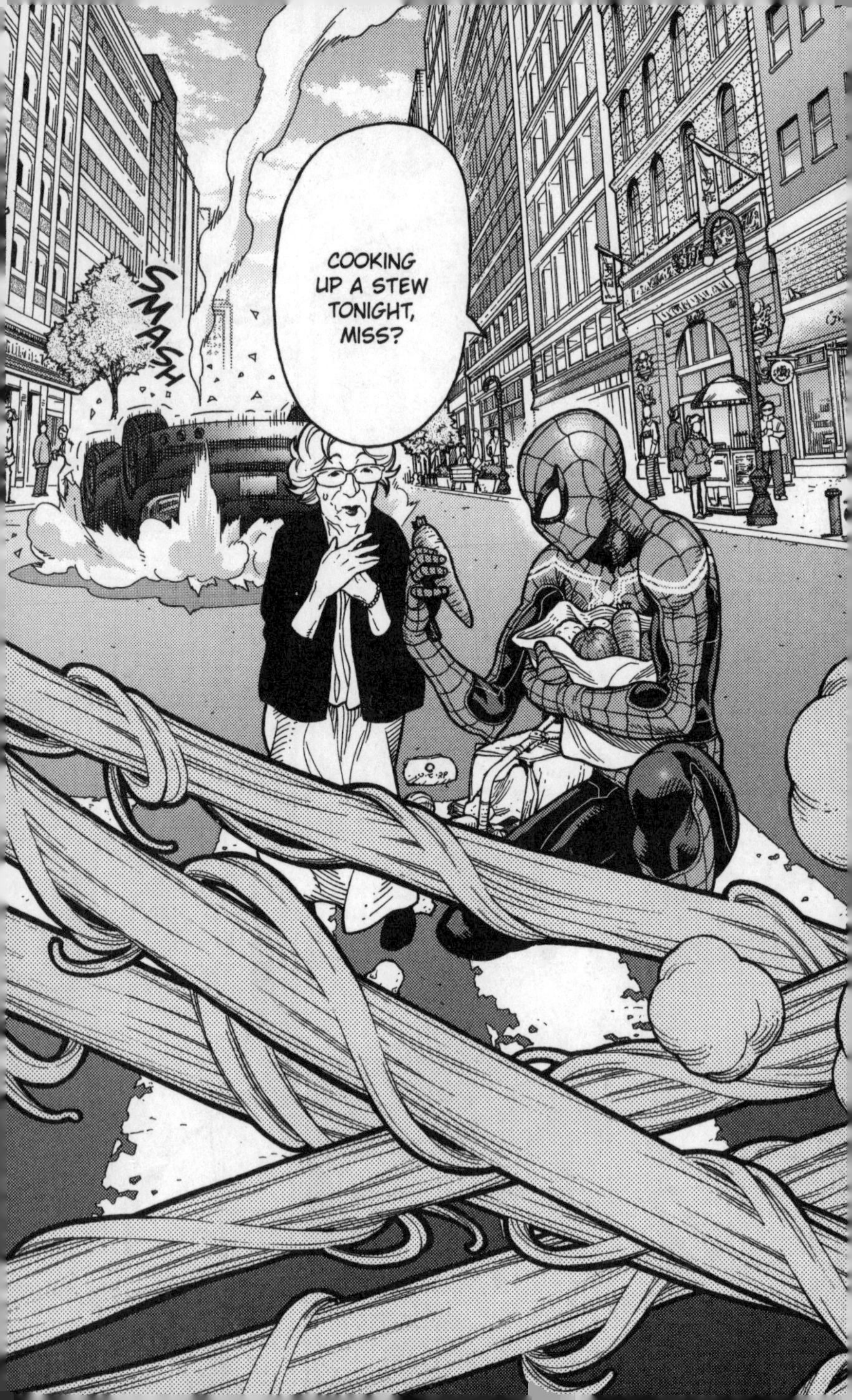
COOKING UP A STEW TONIGHT, MISS?
SMASH

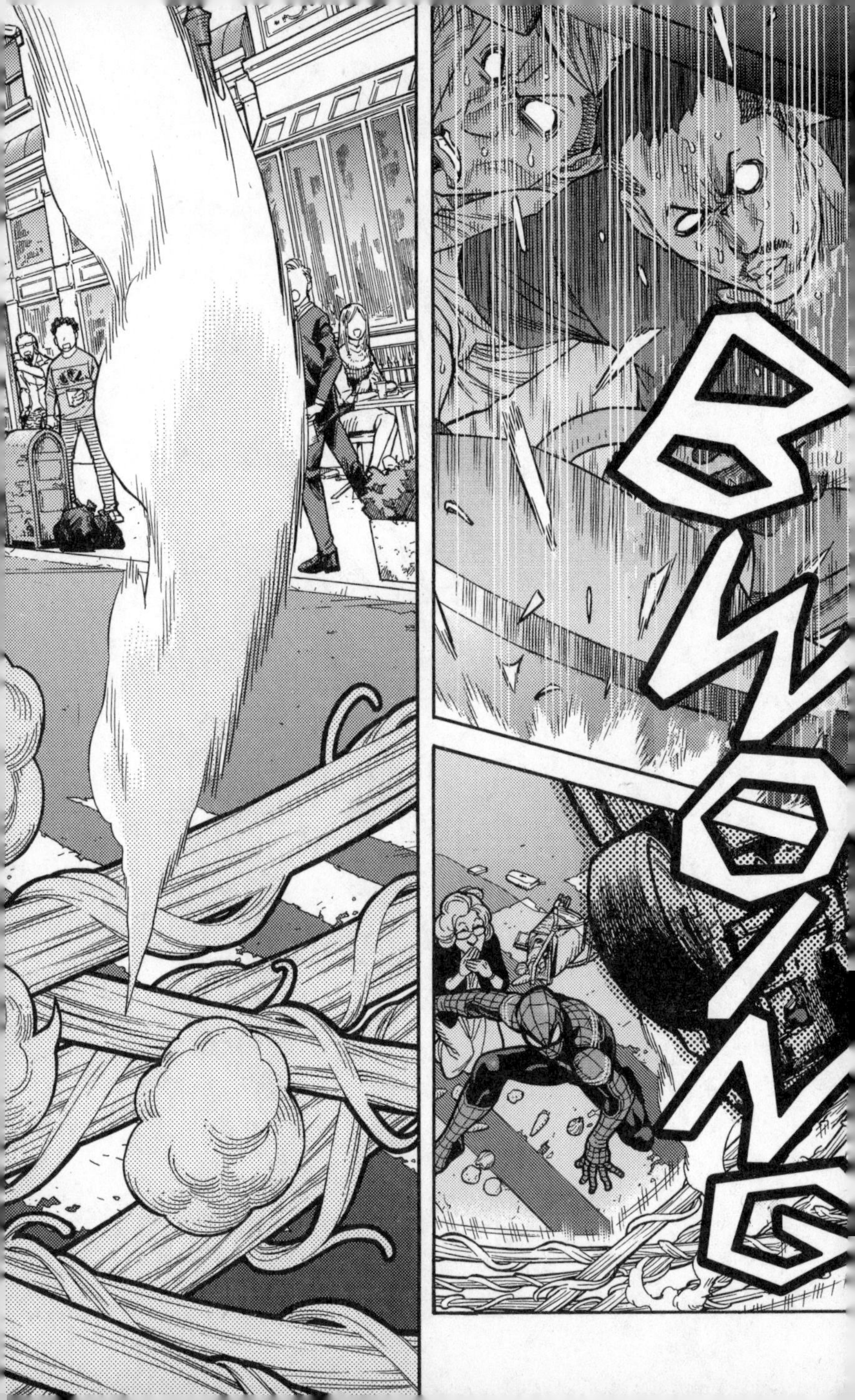
BWOING

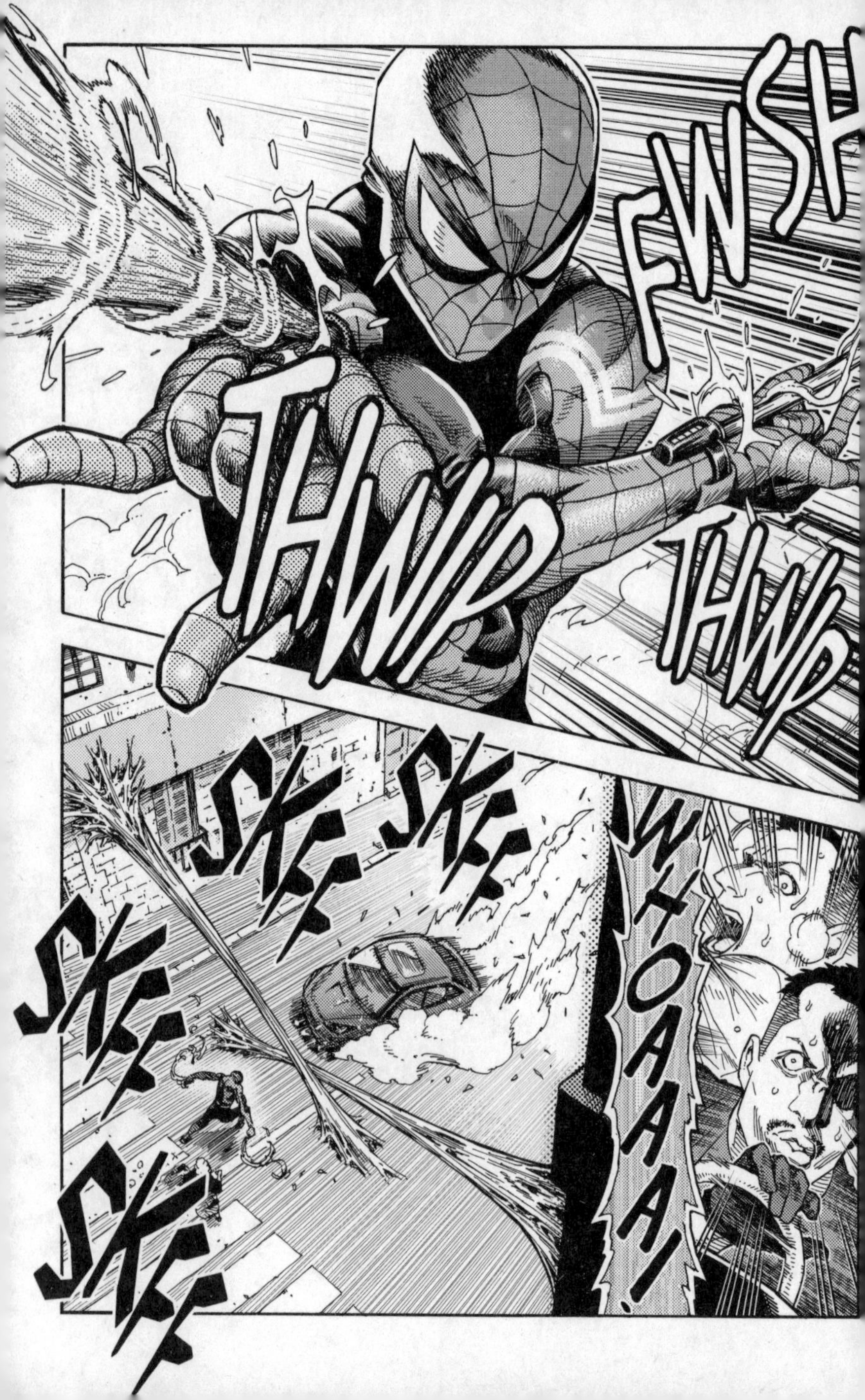
FWSH
THWIP
THWIP
WHOAAAA!
SKEE SKEE
SKEE
SKEE

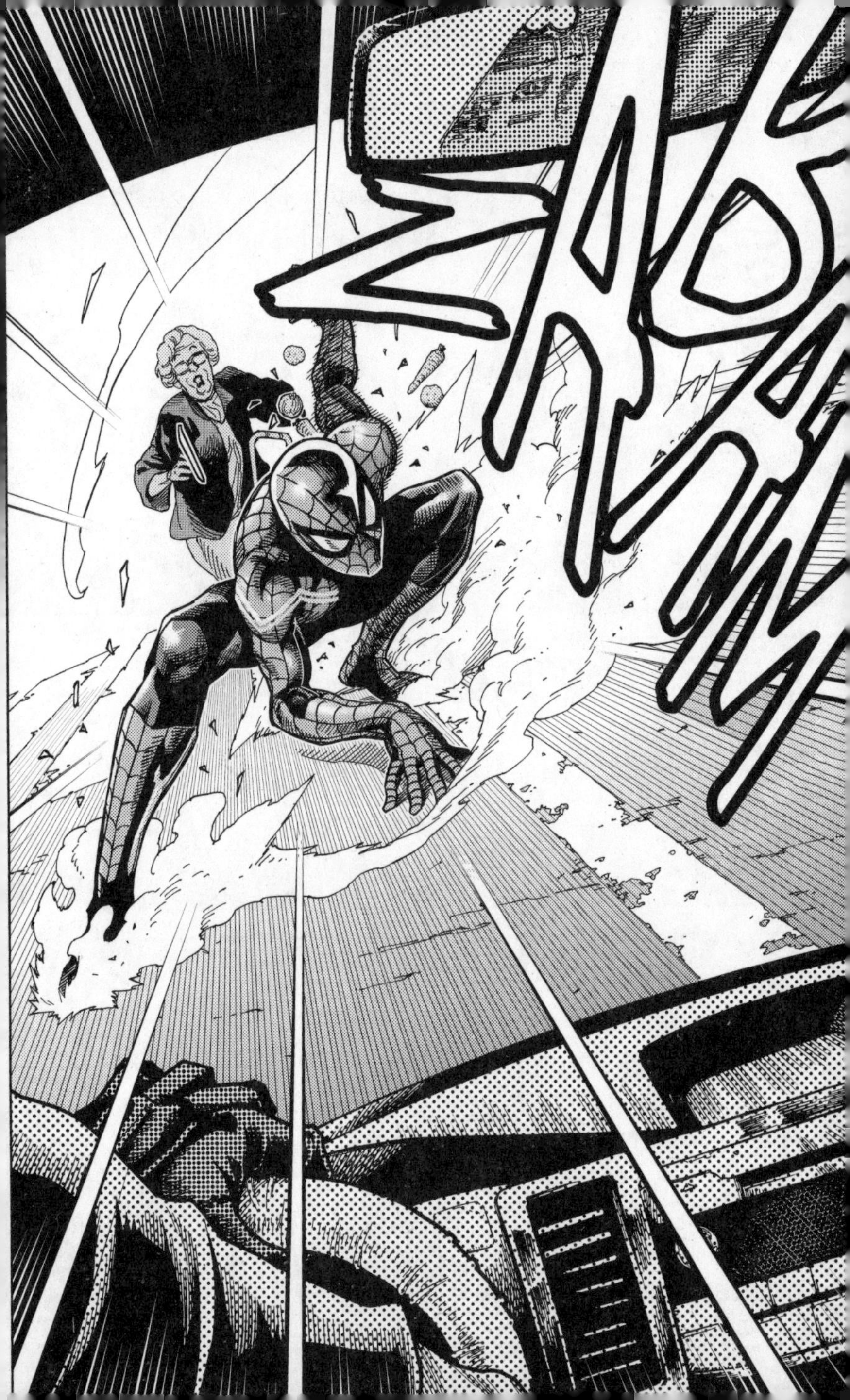

#1 FRIENDLY NEIGHBORHOOD HERO

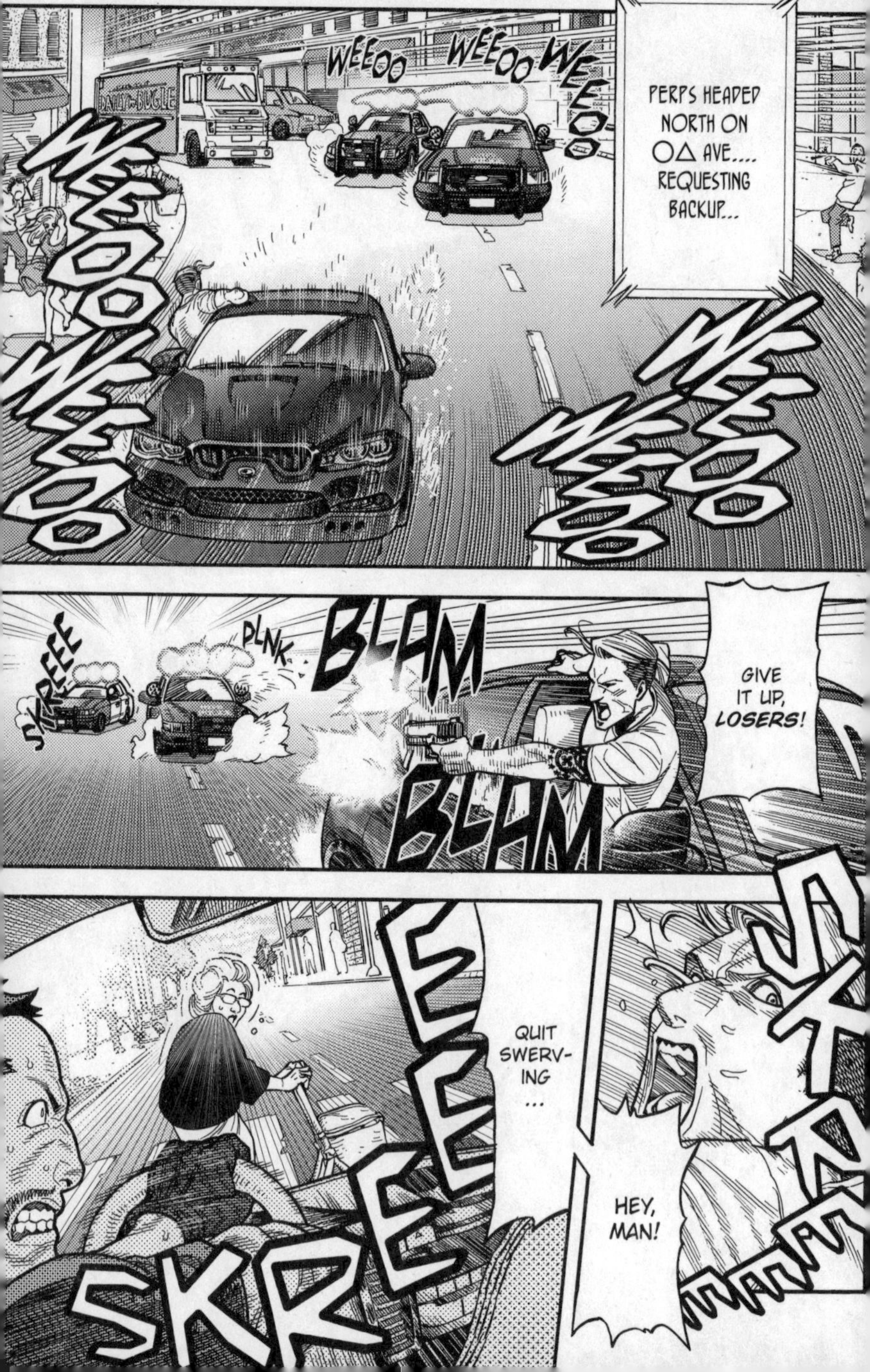

PERPS HEADED NORTH ON ○△ AVE.... REQUESTING BACKUP...
WEEOO WEEOO WEEOO
DAILY BUGLE
WEEOO WEEOO
WEEOO WEEOO
GIVE IT UP, LOSERS!
BLAM
BLAM
PLNK
SKREEE
HEY, MAN!
QUIT SWERV-ING...
SKREEE

MARVEL
SPIDER-MAN

FAKE RED

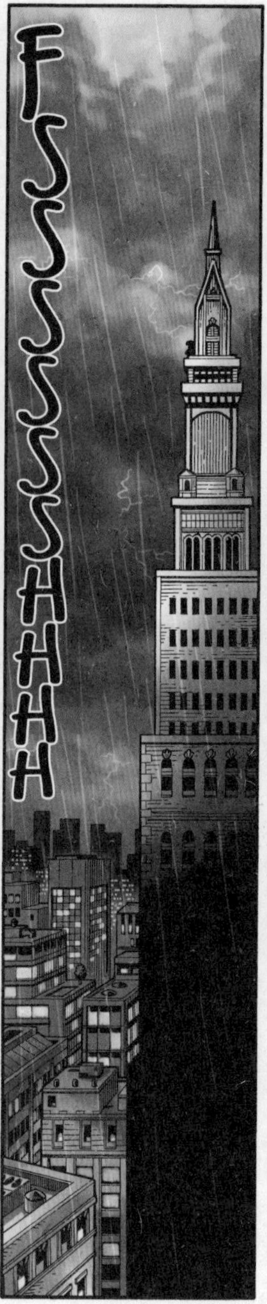
FSSSSSSHHHH
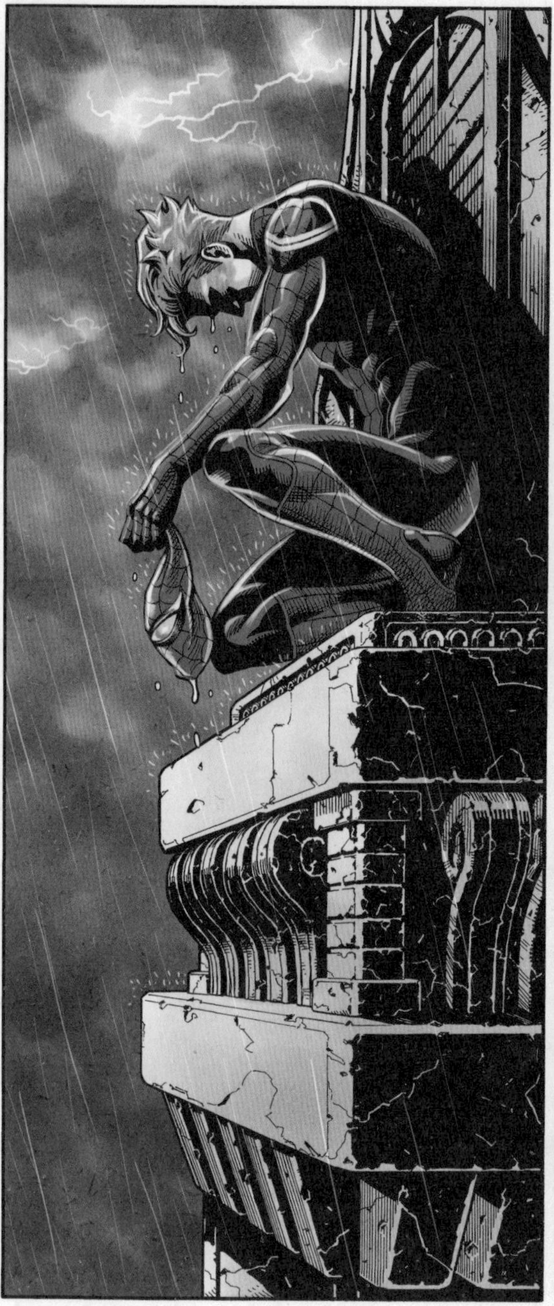

SPIDER-MAN FAKE RED

CONTENTS

SPIDER-MAN FAKE RED

STORY & ART BY
YUSUKE OSAWA

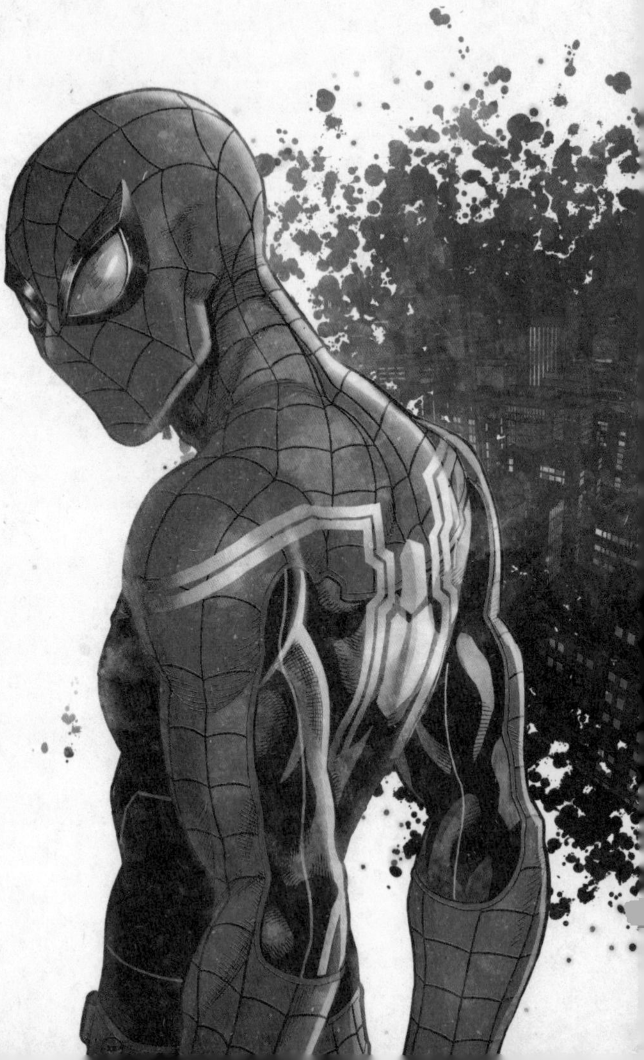